Lecture Notes in Computer Science 12891

More information about this subseries at http://www.springer.com/series/7407

Igor Farkaš · Paolo Masulli ·
Sebastian Otte · Stefan Wermter (Eds.)

Artificial Neural Networks and Machine Learning – ICANN 2021

30th International Conference on Artificial Neural Networks
Bratislava, Slovakia, September 14–17, 2021
Proceedings, Part I

Springer

Editors
Igor Farkaš ⓘⅅ
Comenius University in Bratislava
Bratislava, Slovakia

Paolo Masulli ⓘⅅ
iMotions A/S
Copenhagen, Denmark

Sebastian Otte ⓘⅅ
University of Tübingen
Tübingen, Baden-Württemberg, Germany

Stefan Wermter ⓘⅅ
Universität Hamburg
Hamburg, Germany

ISSN 0302-9743   ISSN 1611-3349 (electronic)
Lecture Notes in Computer Science
ISBN 978-3-030-86361-6   ISBN 978-3-030-86362-3 (eBook)
https://doi.org/10.1007/978-3-030-86362-3

LNCS Sublibrary: SL1 – Theoretical Computer Science and General Issues

This Springer imprint is published by the registered company Springer Nature Switzerland AG
The registered company address is: Gewerbestrasse 11, 6330 Cham, Switzerland

Preface

Research on artificial neural networks has progressed over decades, in recent years being fueled especially by deep learning that has proven, albeit data-greedy, efficient in solving various, mostly supervised, tasks. Applications of artificial neural networks, especially related to artificial intelligence, affect our lives, providing new horizons. Examples range from autonomous car driving, virtual assistants, and decision support systems to healthcare data analytics, financial forecasting, and smart devices in our homes, just to name a few. These developments, however, also provide challenges, which were not imaginable previously, e.g., verification of raw data, explaining the contents of neural networks, and adversarial machine learning.

The International Conference on Artificial Neural Networks (ICANN) is the annual flagship conference of the European Neural Network Society (ENNS). Last year, due to the COVID-19 pandemic, we decided not to hold the conference but to prepare the ICANN proceedings in written form. This year, due to the still unresolved pandemic, the Organizing Committee, together with the Executive Committee of ENNS decided to organize ICANN 2021 online, since we felt the urge to allow research presentations and live discussions, following the now available alternatives of online conference organization. So for the first time, ENNS and the Organizing Committee prepared ICANN as an online event with all its challenges and sometimes unforeseeable events!

Following a long-standing successful collaboration, the proceedings of ICANN are published as volumes within the Lecture Notes in Computer Science Springer series. The response to this year's call for papers resulted, unexpectedly, in a record number of 557 article submissions (a 46% rise compared to previous year), of which almost all were full papers. The paper selection and review process that followed was decided during the online meeting of the Bratislava organizing team and the ENNS Executive Committee. The 40 Program Committee (PC) members agreed to check the submissions for the formal requirements and 64 papers were excluded from the subsequent reviews. The majority of the PC members have doctoral degrees (80%) and 75% of them are also professors. We also took advantage of filled-in online questionnaires providing the reviewers' areas of expertise. The reviewers were assigned one to four papers, and the papers with undecided scores also received reports from PC members which helped in making a final decision.

In total, 265 articles were accepted for the proceedings and the authors were requested to submit final versions. The acceptance rate was hence about 47% when calculated from all initial submissions. A list of PC members and reviewers who agreed to publish their names is included in the proceedings. With these procedures we tried to keep the quality of the proceedings high while still having a critical mass of contributions reflecting the progress of the field. Overall we hope that these proceedings will contribute to the dissemination of new results by the neural network community during these challenging times and we hope that we can have a physical ICANN in 2022.

Finally, we very much thank the Program Committee and the reviewers for their invaluable work.

September 2021

Igor Farkaš
Paolo Masulli
Sebastian Otte
Stefan Wermter

Organization

Organizing Committee

Cabessa Jérémie	Université Paris 2 Panthéon-Assas, France
Kerzel Matthias	University of Hamburg, Germany
Lintas Alessandra	University of Lausanne, Switzerland
Malinovská Kristína	Comenius University in Bratislava, Slovakia
Masulli Paolo	iMotions A/S, Copenhagen, Denmark
Otte Sebastian	University of Tübingen, Germany
Wedeman Roseli	Universidade do Estado do Rio de Janeiro, Brazil

Program Committee Chairs

Igor Farkaš	Comenius University in Bratislava, Slovakia
Paolo Masulli	iMotions A/S, Denmark
Sebastian Otte	University of Tübingen, Germany
Stefan Wermter	University of Hamburg, Germany

Program Committee

Andrejková Gabriela	Pavol Jozef Šafárik University in Košice, Slovakia
Atencia Miguel	Universidad de Malaga, Spain
Bodapati Jyostna Devi	Indian Institute of Technology, Madras, India
Bougie Nicolas	Sokendai/National Institute of Informatics, Japan
Boža Vladimír	Comenius University in Bratislava, Slovakia
Cabessa Jérémie	Université Paris 2 Panthéon-Assas, France
Di Nuovo Alessandro	Sheffield Hallam University, UK
Duch Włodzisław	Nicolaus Copernicus University, Poland
Eppe Manfred	Universität Hamburg, Germany
Fang Yuchun	Shanghai University, China
Garcke Jochen	Universität Bonn, Germany
Gregor Michal	University of Žilina, Slovakia
Guckert Michael	Technische Hochschule Mittelhessen, Germany
Guillén Alberto	University of Granada, Spain
Heinrich Stefan	University of Tokyo, Japan
Hinaut Xavier	Inria, France
Humaidan Dania	University of Tübingen, Germany
Jolivet Renaud	University of Geneva, Switzerland
Koprinkova-Hristova Petia	Bulgarian Academy of Sciences, Bulgaria
Lintas Alessandra	University of Lausanne, Switzerland
Lü Shuai	Jilin University, China
Micheli Alessio	Università di Pisa, Italy

Oravec Miloš	Slovak University of Technology in Bratislava, Slovakia
Otte Sebastian	University of Tübingen, Germany
Peltonen Jaakko	Tampere University, Finland
Piuri Vincenzo	University of Milan, Italy
Pons Rivero Antonio Javier	Universitat Politècnica de Catalunya, Barcelona, Spain
Schmidt Jochen	TH Rosenheim, Germany
Schockaert Cedric	Paul Wurth S.A., Luxembourg
Schwenker Friedhelm	University of Ulm, Germany
Takáč Martin	Comenius University in Bratislava, Slovakia
Tartaglione Enzo	Università degli Studi di Torino, Italy
Tetko Igor	Helmholtz Zentrum München, Germany
Triesch Jochen	Frankfurt Institute for Advanced Studies, Germany
Vavrečka Michal	Czech Technical University in Prague, Czech Republic
Verma Sagar	CentraleSupélec, Université Paris-Saclay, France
Vigário Ricardo	Nova School of Science and Technology, Portugal
Wedemann Roseli	Universidade do Estado do Rio de Janeiro, Brazil
Wennekers Thomas	Plymouth University, UK

Reviewers

Abawi Fares	University of Hamburg, Germany
Aganian Dustin	Technical University Ilmenau, Germany
Ahrens Kyra	University of Hamburg, Germany
Alexandre Frederic	Inria Bordeaux, France
Alexandre Luís	University of Beira Interior, Portugal
Ali Hazrat	Umeå University, Sweden
Alkhamaiseh Koloud	Western Michigan University, USA
Amaba Takafumi	Fukuoka University, Japan
Ambita Ara Abigail	University of the Philippines Diliman, Philippines
Ameur Hanen	University of Sfax, Tunisia
Amigo Galán Glauco A.	Baylor University, USA
An Shuqi	Chongqing University, China
Aouiti Chaouki	Université de Carthage, Tunisia
Arany Adam	Katholieke Universiteit Leuven, Belgium
Arnold Joshua	University of Queensland, Australia
Artelt André	Bielefeld University, Germany
Auge Daniel	Technical University of Munich, Germany
Bac Le Hoai	University of Science, Vietnam
Bacaicoa-Barber Daniel	University Carlos III of Madrid, Spain
Bai Xinyi	National University of Defense Technology, China
Banka Asif	Islamic University of Science & Technology, India
Basalla Marcus	University of Liechtenstein, Liechtenstein
Basterrech Sebastian	Technical University of Ostrava, Czech Republic
Bauckhage Christian	Fraunhofer IAIS, Germany
Bayer Markus	Technical University of Darmstadt, Germany

Bečková Iveta	Comenius University in Bratislava, Slovakia
Benalcázar Marco	Escuela Politécnica Nacional, Ecuador
Bennis Achraf	Institut de Recherche en Informatique de Toulouse, France
Berlemont Samuel	Orange Labs, Grenoble, France
Bermeitinger Bernhard	Universität St. Gallen, Switzerland
Bhoi Suman	National University of Singapore, Singapore
Biesner David	Fraunhofer IAIS, Germany
Bilbrey Jenna	Pacific Northwest National Lab, USA
Blasingame Zander	Clarkson University, USA
Bochkarev Vladimir	Kazan Federal University, Russia
Bohte Sander	Universiteit van Amsterdam, The Netherlands
Bouchachia Abdelhamid	Bournemouth University, UK
Bourguin Grégory	Université du Littoral Côte d'Opale, France
Breckon Toby	Durham University, UK
Buhl Fred	University of Florida, USA
Butz Martin V.	University of Tübingen, Germany
Caillon Paul	Université de Lorraine, Nancy, France
Camacho Hugo C. E.	Universidad Autónoma de Tamaulipas, Mexico
Camurri Antonio	Università di Genova, Italy
Cao Hexin	OneConnect Financial Technology, China
Cao Tianyang	Peking University, China
Cao Zhijie	Shanghai Jiao Tong University, China
Carneiro Hugo	Universität Hamburg, Germany
Chadha Gavneet Singh	South Westphalia University of Applied Sciences, Germany
Chakraborty Saikat	C. V. Raman Global University, India
Chang Hao-Yuan	University of California, Los Angeles, USA
Chang Haodong	University of Technology Sydney, Australia
Chen Cheng	Tsinghua University, China
Chen Haopeng	Shanghai Jiao Tong University, China
Chen Junliang	Shenzhen University, China
Chen Tianyu	Northwest Normal University, China
Chen Wenjie	Communication University of China, China
Cheng Zhanglin	Chinese Academy of Sciences, China
Chenu Alexandre	Sorbonne Université, France
Choi Heeyoul	Handong Global University, South Korea
Christa Sharon	RV Institute of Technology and Management, India
Cîtea Ingrid	Bitdefender Central, Romania
Colliri Tiago	Universidade de São Paulo, Brazil
Cong Cong	Chinese Academy of Sciences, China
Coroiu Adriana Mihaela	Babes-Bolyai University, Romania
Cortez Paulo	University of Minho, Portugal
Cuayáhuitl Heriberto	University of Lincoln, UK
Cui Xiaohui	Wuhan University, China
Cutsuridis Vassilis	University of Lincoln, UK

Cvejoski Kostadin	Fraunhofer IAIS, Germany
D'Souza Meenakshi	International Institute of Information Technology, Bangalore, India
Dai Feifei	Chinese Academy of Sciences, China
Dai Peilun	Boston University, USA
Dai Ruiqi	INSA Lyon, France
Dang Kai	Nankai University, China
Dang Xuan	Tsinghua University, China
Dash Tirtharaj	Birla Institute of Technology and Science, Pilani, India
Davalas Charalampos	Harokopio University of Athens, Greece
De Brouwer Edward	Katholieke Universiteit Leuven, Belgium
Deng Minghua	Peking University, China
Devamane Shridhar	KLE Institute of Technology, Hubballi, India
Di Caterina Gaetano	University of Strathclyde, UK
Di Sarli Daniele	Università di Pisa, Italy
Ding Juncheng	University of North Texas, USA
Ding Zhaoyun	National University of Defense Technology, China
Dold Dominik	Siemens, Munich, Germany
Dong Zihao	Jinan University, China
Du Songlin	Southeast University, China
Edwards Joshua	University of North Carolina Wilmington, USA
Eguchi Shu	Fukuoka University, Japan
Eisenbach Markus	Ilmenau University of Technology, Germany
Erlhagen Wolfram	University of Minho, Portugal
Fang Tiyu	University of Jinan, China
Feldager Cilie	Technical University of Denmark, Denmark
Ferianc Martin	University College London, UK
Ferreira Flora	University of Minho, Portugal
Fevens Thomas	Concordia University, Canada
Friedjungová Magda	Czech Technical University in Prague, Czech Republic
Fu Xianghua	Shenzhen University, China
Fuhl Wolfgang	Universität Tübingen, Germany
Gamage Vihanga	Technological University Dublin, Ireland
Ganguly Udayan	Indian Institute of Technology, Bombay, India
Gao Ruijun	Tianjin University, China
Gao Yapeng	University of Tübingen, Germany
Gao Yue	Beijing University of Posts and Telecommunications, China
Gao Zikai	National University of Defense Technology, China
Gault Richard	Queen's University Belfast, UK
Ge Liang	Chongqing University, China
Geissler Dominik	Relayr GmbH, Munich, Germany
Gepperth Alexander	ENSTA ParisTech, France
Gerum Christoph	University of Tübingen, Germany
Giancaterino Claudio G.	Catholic University of Milan, Italy
Giese Martin	University Clinic Tübingen, Germany

Gikunda Patrick	Dedan Kimathi University of Technology, Kenya
Goel Anmol	Guru Gobind Singh Indraprastha University, India
Göpfert Christina	Bielefeld University, Germany
Göpfert Jan Philip	Bielefeld University, Germany
Goyal Nidhi	Indraprastha Institute of Information Technology, India
Grangetto Marco	Università di Torino, Italy
Grüning Philipp	University of Lübeck, Germany
Gu Xiaoyan	Chinese Academy of Sciences, Beijing, China
Guo Hongcun	China Three Gorges University, China
Guo Ling	Northwest University, China
Guo Qing	Nanyang Technological University, Singapore
Guo Song	Xi'an University of Architecture and Technology, China
Gupta Sohan	Global Institute of Technology, Jaipur, India
Hakenes Simon	Ruhr-Universität Bochum, Germany
Han Fuchang	Central South University, China
Han Yi	University of Melbourne, Australia
Hansen Lars Kai	Technical University of Denmark, Denmark
Haque Ayaan	Saratoga High School, USA
Hassen Alan Kai	Leiden University, The Netherlands
Hauberg Søren	Technical University of Denmark, Denmark
He Tieke	Nanjing University, China
He Wei	Nanyang Technological University, Singapore
He Ziwen	Chinese Academy of Sciences, China
Heese Raoul	Fraunhofer ITWM, Germany
Herman Pawel	KTH Royal Institute of Technology, Sweden
Holas Juraj	Comenius University in Bratislava, Slovakia
Horio Yoshihiko	Tohoku University, Japan
Hou Hongxu	Inner Mongolia University, China
Hu Ming-Fei	China University of Petroleum, China
Hu Ting	Hasso Plattner Institute, Germany
Hu Wenxin	East China Normal University, China
Hu Yanqing	Sichuan University, China
Huang Chenglong	National University of Defense Technology, China
Huang Chengqiang	Huawei Technology, Ltd., China
Huang Jun	Chinese Academy of Sciences, Shanghai, China
Huang Ruoran	Chinese Academy of Sciences, China
Huang Wuliang	Chinese Academy of Sciences, Beijing, China
Huang Zhongzhan	Tsinghua University, China
Iannella Nicolangelo	University of Oslo, Norway
Ienco Dino	INRAE, France
Illium Steffen	Ludwig-Maximilians-Universität München, Germany
Iyer Naresh	GE Research, USA
Jalalvand Azarakhsh	Ghent University, Belgium
Japa Sai Sharath	Southern Illinois University, USA
Javaid Muhammad Usama	Eura Nova, Belgium

Jia Qiaomei	Northwest University, China
Jia Xiaoning	Inner Mongolia University, China
Jin Peiquan	University of Science and Technology of China, China
Jirak Doreen	Istituto Italiano di Tecnologia, Italy
Jodelet Quentin	Tokyo Institute of Technology, Japan
Kai Tang	Toshiba, China
Karam Ralph	Université Franche-Comté, France
Karlbauer Matthias	University of Tübingen, Germany
Kaufhold Marc-André	Technical University of Darmstadt, Germany
Kerzel Matthias	University of Hamburg, Germany
Keurulainen Antti	Bitville Oy, Finland
Kitamura Takuya	National Institute of Technology, Japan
Kocur Viktor	Comenius University in Bratislava, Slovakia
Koike Atsushi	National Institute of Technology, Japan
Kotropoulos Constantine	Aristotle University of Thessaloniki, Greece
Kovalenko Alexander	Czech Technical University, Czech Republic
Krzyzak Adam	Concordia University, Canada
Kurikawa Tomoki	Kansai Medical University, Japan
Kurpiewski Evan	University of North Carolina Wilmington, USA
Kurt Mehmet Necip	Columbia University, USA
Kushwaha Sumit	Kamla Nehru Institute of Technology, India
Lai Zhiping	Fudan University, China
Lang Jana	Hertie Institute for Clinical Brain Research, Germany
Le Hieu	Boston University, USA
Le Ngoc	Hanoi University of Science and Technology, Vietnam
Le Thanh	University of Science, Hochiminh City, Vietnam
Lee Jinho	Yonsei University, South Korea
Lefebvre Grégoire	Orange Labs, France
Lehmann Daniel	University of Greifswald, Germany
Lei Fang	University of Lincoln, UK
Léonardon Mathieu	IMT Atlantique, France
Lewandowski Arnaud	Université du Littoral Côte d'Opale, Calais, France
Li Caiyuan	Shanghai Jiao Tong University, China
Li Chuang	Xi'an Jiaotong University, China
Li Ming-Fan	Ping An Life Insurance of China, Ltd., China
Li Qing	The Hong Kong Polytechnic University, China
Li Tao	Peking University, China
Li Xinyi	Southwest University, China
Li Xiumei	Hangzhou Normal University, China
Li Yanqi	University of Jinan, China
Li Yuan	Defence Innovation Institute, China
Li Zhixin	Guangxi Normal University, China
Lian Yahong	Dalian University of Technology, China
Liang Nie	Southwest University of Science and Technology, China
Liang Qi	Chinese Academy of Sciences, Beijing, China

Liang Senwei	Purdue University, USA
Liang Yuxin	Northwest University, China
Lim Nengli	Singapore University of Technology and Design, Singapore
Liu Gongshen	Shanghai Jiao Tong University, China
Liu Haolin	Chinese Academy of Sciences, China
Liu Jian-Wei	China University of Petroleum, China
Liu Juan	Wuhan University, China
Liu Junxiu	Guangxi Normal University, China
Liu Qi	Chongqing University, China
Liu Shuang	Huazhong University of Science and Technology, China
Liu Shuting	University of Shanghai for Science and Technology, China
Liu Weifeng	China University of Petroleum, China
Liu Yan	University of Shanghai for Science and Technology, China
Liu Yang	Fudan University, China
Liu Yi-Ling	Imperial College London, UK
Liu Zhu	University of Electronic Science and Technology of China, China
Long Zi	Shenzhen Technology University, China
Lopes Vasco	Universidade da Beira Interior, Portugal
Lu Siwei	Guangdong University of Technology, China
Lu Weizeng	Shenzhen University, China
Lukyanova Olga	Russian Academy of Sciences, Russia
Luo Lei	Kansas State University, USA
Luo Xiao	Peking University, China
Luo Yihao	Huazhong University of Science and Technology, China
Ma Chao	Wuhan University, China
Ma Zeyu	Harbin Institute of Technology, China
Malialis Kleanthis	University of Cyprus, Cyprus
Manoonpong Poramate	Vidyasirimedhi Institute of Science and Technology, Thailand
Martinez Rego David	Data Spartan Ltd., UK
Matsumura Tadayuki	Hitachi, Ltd., Tokyo, Japan
Mekki Asma	Université de Sfax, Tunisia
Merkel Cory	Rochester Institute of Technology, USA
Mirus Florian	Intel Labs, Germany
Mizuno Hideyuki	Suwa University of Science, Japan
Moh Teng-Sheng	San Jose State University, USA
Mohammed Elmahdi K.	Kasdi Merbah university, Algeria
Monshi Maram	University of Sydney, Australia
Moreno Felipe	Universidad Católica San Pablo, Peru
Morra Lia	Politecnico di Torino, Italy

Morzy Mikołaj	Poznań University of Technology, Poland
Mouček Roman	University of West Bohemia, Czech Republic
Moukafih Youness	International University of Rabat, Morocco
Mouysset Sandrine	University of Toulouse, France
Müller Robert	Ludwig-Maximilians-Universität München, Germany
Mutschler Maximus	University of Tübingen, Germany
Najari Naji	Orange Labs, France
Nanda Abhilasha	Vellore Institute of Technology, India
Nguyen Thi Nguyet Que	Technological University Dublin, Ireland
Nikitin Oleg	Russian Academy of Sciences, Russia
Njah Hasna	University of Sfax, Tunisia
Nyabuga Douglas	Donghua University, China
Obafemi-Ajayi Tayo	Missouri State University, USA
Ojha Varun	University of Reading, UK
Oldenhof Martijn	Katholieke Universiteit Leuven, Belgium
Oneto Luca	Università di Genova, Italy
Oota Subba Reddy	Inria, Bordeaux, France
Oprea Mihaela	Petroleum-Gas University of Ploiesti, Romania
Osorio John	Barcelona Supercomputing Center, Spain
Ouni Achref	Institut Pascal UCA, France
Pan Yongping	Sun Yat-sen University, China
Park Hyeyoung	Kyungpook National University, South Korea
Pateux Stéphane	Orange Labs, France
Pecháč Matej	Comenius University in Bratislava, Slovakia
Pecyna Leszek	University of Liverpool, UK
Peng Xuyang	China University of Petroleum, China
Pham Viet	Toshiba, Japan
Pietroń Marcin	AGH University of Science and Technology, Poland
Pócoš Štefan	Comenius University in Bratislava, Slovakia
Posocco Nicolas	Eura Nova, Belgium
Prasojo Radityo Eko	Universitas Indonesia, Indonesia
Preuss Mike	Universiteit Leiden, The Netherlands
Qiao Peng	National University of Defense Technology, China
Qiu Shoumeng	Shanghai Institute of Microsystem and Information Technology, China
Quan Hongyan	East China Normal University, China
Rafiee Laya	Concordia University, Canada
Rangarajan Anand	University of Florida, USA
Ravichandran Naresh Balaji	KTH Royal Institute of Technology, Sweden
Renzulli Riccardo	University of Turin, Italy
Richter Mats	Universität Osnabrück, Germany
Robine Jan	Heinrich Heine University Düsseldorf, Germany
Rocha Gil	University of Porto, Portugal
Rodriguez-Sanchez Antonio	Universität Innsbruck, Austria
Rosipal Roman	Slovak Academy of Sciences, Slovakia

Rusiecki Andrzej	Wroclaw University of Science and Technology, Poland
Salomon Michel	Université Bourgogne Franche-Comté, France
Sarishvili Alex	Fraunhofer ITWM, Germany
Sasi Swapna	Birla Institute of Technology and Science, India
Sataer Yikemaiti	Southeast University, China
Schaaf Nina	Fraunhofer IPA, Germany
Schak Monika	University of Applied Sciences, Fulda, Germany
Schilling Malte	Bielefeld University, Germany
Schmid Kyrill	Ludwig-Maximilians-Universität München, Germany
Schneider Johannes	University of Liechtenstein, Liechtenstein
Schwab Malgorzata	University of Colorado at Denver, USA
Sedlmeier Andreas	Ludwig-Maximilians-Universität München, Germany
Sendera Marcin	Jagiellonian University, Poland
Shahriyar Rifat	Bangladesh University of Engineering and Technology, Bangladesh
Shang Cheng	Fudan University, China
Shao Jie	University of Electronic Science and Technology of China, China
Shao Yang	Hitachi Ltd., Japan
Shehu Amarda	George Mason University, USA
Shen Linlin	Shenzhen University, China
Shenfield Alex	Sheffield Hallam University, UK
Shi Ying	Chongqing University, China
Shrestha Roman	Intelligent Voice Ltd., UK
Sifa Rafet	Fraunhofer IAIS, Germany
Sinha Aman	CNRS and University of Lorraine, France
Soltani Zarrin Pouya	Institute for High Performance Microelectronics, Germany
Song Xiaozhuang	Southern University of Science and Technology, China
Song Yuheng	Shanghai Jiao Tong University, China
Song Ziyue	Shanghai Jiao Tong University, China
Sowinski-Mydlarz Viktor	London Metropolitan University, UK
Steiner Peter	Technische Universität Dresden, Germany
Stettler Michael	University of Tübingen, Germany
Stoean Ruxandra	University of Craiova, Romania
Su Di	Beijing Institute of Technology, China
Suarez Oscar J.	Instituto Politécnico Nacional, México
Sublime Jérémie	Institut supérieur d'électronique de Paris, France
Sudharsan Bharath	National University of Ireland, Galway, Ireland
Sugawara Toshiharu	Waseda University, Japan
Sui Yongduo	University of Science and Technology of China, China
Sui Zhentao	Soochow University, China
Swiderska-Chadaj Zaneta	Warsaw University of Technology, Poland
Szandała Tomasz	Wroclaw University of Science and Technology, Poland

Šejnová Gabriela	Czech Technical University in Prague, Czech Republic
Tang Chenwei	Sichuan University, China
Tang Jialiang	Southwest University of Science and Technology, China
Taubert Nick	University Clinic Tübingen, Germany
Tek Faik Boray	Isik University, Turkey
Tessier Hugo	Stellantis, France
Tian Zhihong	Guangzhou University, China
Tianze Zhou	Beijing Institute of Technology, China
Tihon Simon	Eura Nova, Belgium
Tingwen Liu	Chinese Academy of Sciences, China
Tong Hao	Southern University of Science and Technology, China
Torres-Moreno Juan-Manuel	Université d'Avignon, France
Towobola Oluyemisi Folake	Obafemi Awolowo University, Nigeria
Trinh Anh Duong	Technological University Dublin, Ireland
Tuna Matúš	Comenius University in Bratislava, Slovakia
Uelwer Tobias	Heinrich Heine University Düsseldorf, Germany
Van Rullen Rufin	CNRS, Toulouse, France
Varlamis Iraklis	Harokopio University of Athens, Greece
Vašata Daniel	Czech Technical University in Prague, Czech Republic
Vásconez Juan	Escuela Politécnica Nacional, Ecuador
Vatai Emil	RIKEN, Japan
Viéville Thierry	Inria, Antibes, France
Wagner Stefan	Heinrich Heine University Düsseldorf, Germany
Wan Kejia	Defence Innovation Institute, China
Wang Huiling	Tampere University, Finland
Wang Jiaan	Soochow University, China
Wang Jinling	Ulster University, UK
Wang Junli	Tongji University, China
Wang Qian	Durham University, UK
Wang Xing	Ningxia University, China
Wang Yongguang	Beihang University, China
Wang Ziming	Shanghai Jiao Tong University, China
Wanigasekara Chathura	University of Auckland, New Zealand
Watson Patrick	Minerva KGI, USA
Wei Baole	Chinese Academy of Sciences, China
Wei Feng	York University, Canada
Wenninger Marc	Rosenheim Technical University of Applied Sciences, Germany
Wieczorek Tadeusz	Silesian University of Technology, Poland
Wiles Janet	University of Queensland, Australia
Windheuser Christoph	ThoughtWorks Inc., Germany
Wolter Moritz	Rheinische Friedrich-Wilhelms-Universität Bonn, Germany

Wu Ancheng   Pingan Insurance, China
Wu Dayan   Chinese Academy of Sciences, China
Wu Jingzheng   Chinese Academy of Sciences, China
Wu Nier   Inner Mongolia University, China
Wu Song   Southwest University, China
Xie Yuanlun   University of Electronic Science and Technology
                            of China, China
Xu Dongsheng   National University of Defense Technology, China
Xu Jianhua   Nanjing Normal University, China
Xu Peng   Technical University of Munich, Germany
Yaguchi Takaharu   Kobe University, Japan
Yamamoto Hideaki   Tohoku University, Japan
Yang Gang   Renmin University of China, China
Yang Haizhao   Purdue University, USA
Yang Jing   Guangxi Normal University, China
Yang Jing   Hefei University of Technology, China
Yang Liu   Tianjin University, China
Yang Sidi   Concordia University, Canada
Yang Sun   Soochow University, China
Yang Wanli   Harbin Institute of Technology, China
Yang XiaoChen   Tianjin University of Technology, China
Yang Xuan   Shenzhen University, China
Yang Zhao   Leiden University, The Netherlands
Yang Zhengfeng   East China Normal University, China
Yang Zhiguang   Chinese Academy of Sciences, China
Yao Zhenjie   Chinese Academy of Sciences, China
Ye Kai   Wuhan University, China
Yin Bojian   Centrum Wiskunde & Informatica, The Netherlands
Yu James   Southern University of Science and Technology, China
Yu Wenxin   Southwest University of Science and Technology,
                            China
Yu Yipeng   Tencent, China
Yu Yue   BNU-HKBU United International College, China
Yuan Limengzi   Tianjin University, China
Yuchen Ge   Hefei University of Technology, China
Yuhang Guo   Peking University, China
Yury Tsoy   Solidware, South Korea
Zeng Jia   Jilin University, China
Zeng Jiayuan   University of Shanghai for Science and Technology,
                            China
Zhang Dongyang   University of Electronic Science and Technology
                            of China, China
Zhang Jiacheng   Beijing University of Posts and Telecommunications,
                            China
Zhang Jie   Nanjing University, China
Zhang Kai   Chinese Academy of Sciences, China

Zhang Kaifeng	Independent Researcher, China
Zhang Kun	Chinese Academy of Sciences, China
Zhang Luning	China University of Petroleum, China
Zhang Panpan	Chinese Academy of Sciences, China
Zhang Peng	Chinese Academy of Sciences, China
Zhang Wenbin	Carnegie Mellon University, USA
Zhang Xiang	National University of Defense Technology, China
Zhang Xuewen	Southwest University of Science and Technology, China
Zhang Yicheng	University of Lincoln, UK
Zhang Yingjie	Hunan University, China
Zhang Yunchen	University of Electronic Science and Technology of China, China
Zhang Zhiqiang	Southwest University of Science and Technology, China
Zhao Liang	University of São Paulo, Brazil
Zhao Liang	Dalian University of Technology, China
Zhao Qingchao	Harbin Engineering University, China
Zhao Ying	University of Shanghai for Science and Technology, China
Zhao Yuekai	National University of Defense Technology, China
Zheng Yuchen	Kyushu University, Japan
Zhong Junpei	Plymouth University, UK
Zhou Shiyang	Defense Innovation Institute, China
Zhou Xiaomao	Harbin Engineering University, China
Zhou Yucan	Chinese Academy of Sciences, China
Zhu Haijiang	Beijing University of Chemical Technology, China
Zhu Mengting	National University of Defense Technology, China
Zhu Shaolin	Zhengzhou University of Light Industry, China
Zhu Shuying	The University of Hong Kong, China
Zugarini Andrea	University of Florence, Italy

Contents – Part I

Attention and Transformers I

Attention and Transformers II

Audio and Multimodal Applications

Bioinformatics and Biosignal Analysis

Capsule Networks

Cognitive Models

Adversarial Machine Learning

An Improved (Adversarial) Reprogramming Technique for Neural Networks

Eliska Kloberdanz$^{(\boxtimes)}$ [iD], Jin Tian, and Wei Le

Department of Computer Science, Iowa State University, Ames, IA 50011, USA
{eklober,jtian,weile}@iastate.edu

Abstract. Neural networks can be repurposed via adversarial reprogramming to perform new tasks, which are different from the tasks they were originally trained for. In this paper, we introduce new and improved reprogramming technique that, compared to prior works, achieves better accuracy, scalability, and can be successfully applied to more complex tasks. While prior literature focuses on potential malicious uses of reprogramming, we argue that reprogramming can be viewed as an efficient training method. Our reprogramming method allows for re-using existing pre-trained models and easily reprogramming them to perform new tasks. This technique requires a lot less effort and hyperparameter tuning compared training new models from scratch. Therefore, we believe that our improved and scalable reprogramming method has potential to become a new method for creating neural network models.

Keywords: Adversarial machine learning · Efficient deep learning · Reprogramming

1 Introduction

Reprogramming of neural networks was first introduced in [3] as a new form of adversarial attack that allows to "...reprogram the target model to perform a task chosen by the attacker - without the attacker needing to specify or compute desired output for each test-time input" [3].

We successfully replicated the results in Elsayed et al. [3]; however, when we applied their method to more complex tasks it did not perform well. In this paper we present new and improved reprogramming methodology, which we successfully applied to complex classification tasks. The reprogramming technique in [3] relies on hardcoding an arbitrary mapping between labels of the original and new tasks, and learning an adversarial program P. The program P is applied as a universal additive contribution to all examples from the new task domain regardless of their label to create $X' = X + P$. Our improved technique is instead based on transforming input X to conform to the dimensions that the target model accepts: $X' = f(X)$, and learning a new prediction layer. In particular, our reprogramming method reuses model hyperparameters of the original

© Springer Nature Switzerland AG 2021
I. Farkaš et al. (Eds.): ICANN 2021, LNCS 12891, pp. 3–15, 2021.
https://doi.org/10.1007/978-3-030-86362-3_1

model (i.e., the target model) for layers 1 through $L-1$, where L is the total number of layers. We then create a new L^{th} layer with number of neurons equal to number of labels the new task has and learn its parameters, which can be formulated as $\hat{\theta} = \arg\min_\theta (-logP(y|h))$, where h are the values of hidden units from the penultimate layer of the target model.

Using our methodology, we successfully reprogrammed several ImageNet models to perform classification on Caltech 101 and reduced Caltech 256 datasets. Moreover, we demonstrate that creating a new model using our reprogramming technique yields accurate results while requiring a lot less effort in terms of training time and tuning compared to training a new model from scratch. Therefore, we argue that reprogramming does not need to be adversarial, instead we view it as a new machine learning technique.

1.1   Contributions

Our main contributions are two-fold.

- We demonstrate the shortcomings of the methodology for reprogramming introduced in prior literature with various experiments to show that it does not scale to complex tasks. We hope that this finding will be helpful to other researchers.
- We develop a new methodology for reprogramming that addresses the limitations of the prior methodology. Our technique, compared to prior works, yields more accurate results, is scalable, and can be applied to complex tasks. We also show that our reprogramming method can be used to efficiently create new models. Creating new models using our reprogramming methodology requires significantly less effort in terms of training time and hyperparameter tuning compared to training models from scratch.

2   Background and Related Work

Adversarial reprogramming is a new research area of adversarial machine learning, which studies security vulnerabilities of machine learning models. It is a new type of attack first introduced in [3], which involves *reprogramming* an existing machine learning model to perform a different task. The adversarial reprogramming literature is very limited - to our best knowledge there are only three works that studied adversarial reprogramming: [3,14,23]. Elsayed et al. [3] successfully conducted white-box adversarial reprogramming on neural net models for image classification. Neekhara et al. [14] demonstrated that reprogramming also works on text classification neural networks by performing a white-box attack and also a black-box attack. And [23] claim to have developed a defense against reprogramming attacks.

A related area to reprogramming is transfer learning [12,17]. Transfer learning allows for reusing trained models. The idea behind transfer learning is that knowledge gained during learning one task is useful and can be applied to another task. Reprogramming and transfer learning share the same goal of repurposing a trained model to perform a new task; however, "transfer learning is very different from the adversarial reprogramming task in that it allows model parameters to be changed for the new task" [3].

2.1   The Rise of Adversarial Machine Learning

Traditionally, it has been assumed that the environment during training and evaluation of machine learning models is benign. Until the year 2014 the focus of machine learning research has been on accuracy. However, after [21] have shown that neural nets with human level accuracy can have 100% error rate on adversarial examples, robustness of machine learning models and protecting against adversarial attacks became an active research area. Goodfellow et al. [8] define adversarial examples as inputs to machine learning models that an attacker has intentionally designed to cause the model to make a mistake.

Adversarial examples are not created by adding random noise to legitimate inputs, instead they are carefully computed perturbations that possess the property of transferability. Adversarial examples crafted for a particular model *transfer* to other models, which means that the same adversarial examples can be applied to different models to cause mistakes [21]. In particular, adversarial examples generated against a neural network can fool other neural networks with the same architecture, but trained on different datasets [21]. It has also been shown that adversarial examples can also fool neural networks with different architectures and even models trained with different machine learning algorithms [15]. Therefore, adversarial examples must exploit some systematic issue or property of neural nets.

There are several hypotheses attempting to explain the existence of adversarial examples and adversarial vulnerability of machine learning models. According to [9] the reason is excessive linearity of neural net models. However, it is not only neural nets that are susceptible to attacks, so further aspects may play a role. Other works [5,7,11,19] argue that high dimensionality of the input space that prevents a classifier from learning a robust model that would be resilient to adversarial examples. On the other hand, [18] argued that adversarial examples arise due to insufficient information about the true data distribution. Tanay et al. [22] propose that overfitting causes adversarial examples, while [4] and [6] maintain that a classifier's robustness to noise determines the extent of its adversarial vulnerability. Shamir et al. [20] suggests that the piecewise-linear geometric structure of decision boundaries leads to adversarial perturbations. And [1,13] argue that computational constraints or model complexity cause the model to learn non-robust features, which means that the resulting model may be accurate on benign test data, but highly vulnerable to adversarial inputs. Finally, [10] claim that adversarial examples can be attributed to the presence of non-robust features. They define non-robust features as "highly predictive, yet brittle" features, which are well-generalizing on benign data, but vulnerable to adversarial perturbations. They present accuracy and robustness as almost a trade-off and claim that "robustness can be at odds with accuracy". Hence, the reasons for the existence of adversarial examples is still not fully understood.

Attacks can be either untargeted or targeted depending on the goal of the attacker – an attacker may design adversarial examples that cause the model to output any incorrect label, or a specific incorrect label. Formally, given a target model that takes x as input and outputs y, and a perturbation η, an adversarial example for an untargeted attack can be formulated as:

$$x' = x + \eta, f(x) = y, x \in X \ s.t. \ f(x') \neq y \tag{1}$$

Adversarial example for a targeted attack can be expressed as:

$$x' = x + \eta, f(x) = y, x \in X \ s.t. \ f(x') = y' \tag{2}$$

One important factor that determines the attack methods is the amount of knowledge that an attacker has about the target model. In a white-box scenario the attacker has access to the model architecture and parameters, whereas in a black-box scenario this information in not available and the attacker can only query the target model for labels.

There are several white-box scenario techniques for crafting adversarial examples. Some of the common ones are: Fast Gradient Sign Method (FGMS) [9], Limited memory Broyden-Fletcher-Goldfarb-Shanno (L-BFGS) algorithm [21], Jacobian-based Saliency Map Attack (JSMA) [16], and Carlini & Wagner (C&W) attack developed by [2]. The FGMS method is one of the most popular technique for its low computational cost. It fixes the size of perturbation and maximizes loss as follows:

$$\eta = \arg\max_\eta \ J(x + \eta, y) \ s.t. \ ||\eta||_\infty \leq \epsilon$$
$$\eta = \arg\max_\eta \ J(x, y) + \eta^T \nabla_x J(x, y) \ s.t. \ ||\eta||_\infty \leq \epsilon \tag{3}$$
$$\eta = \epsilon \times sgn(\nabla_x J(x, y))$$

where η is the perturbation, ϵ is the perturbation magnitude parameter, $\nabla_x J(x, y)$ is the loss function gradient, and sgn is the sign function.

There are three types of methods that can be deployed to conduct a black-box attack: (1) training a substitute model and leveraging white-box techniques for crafting adversarial examples, (2) estimating gradients using zeroth order approximation, or (3) GenAttack, a gradient-free optimization technique that uses genetic algorithms for synthesising adversarial examples.

2.2   Adversarial Reprogramming

Adversarial reprogramming is a type of attack introduced in [3], which reprograms a target model to perform a task chosen by the attacker. There are two primary differences between prior adversarial attacks and reprogramming in terms of their goals and methodology. First, the goal of reprogramming is to reprogram a target model to perform a different task, while the goal of adversarial examples is to degrade performance of the model. Second, reprogramming is achieved by finding a single adversarial perturbation, an adversarial program that can be added to all inputs without the need for crafting many different adversarial examples and computing their outputs.

Reprogramming does not require modifications to the target network architecture or parameters. Instead, only two reprogramming functions must be learned to map the inputs and outputs between the domains of the new and original task. The motivation of reprogramming is to reprogram an existing model in a computationally efficient way to perform a new task. Computational efficiency is key – if the desired results were achievable using a computationally inexpensive classifier created from scratch specifically for that task, this would defeat the purpose of reprogramming [14]. It has been shown that adversarial reprogramming is significantly less effective on randomly initialized untrained networks [3,14], which is evidence that reprogramming works.

Motivations for Reprogramming. There is a concern that reprogramming could be used for malicious purposes such as theft of computational resources through attacks on cloud-hosted machine learning models, which could be maliciously re-purposed by an attacker to, for example, create spam accounts. Such an attack should be a great concern to cloud providers offering machine learning APIs such as Google or Amazon. Nevertheless, despite the fact that the current literature on adversarial reprogramming focused on the security concerns created by adversarial reprogramming, we would like to argue that reprogramming does not need to be adversarial. Reprogramming has a great potential for developing high quality models at a significantly reduced computational cost.

Reprogramming Method. Adversarial reprogramming and its methods were first introduced in [3] and later used by [14]. Elsayed et al. [3] assume a white-box scenario and their reprogramming method is based on crafting an adversarial program, which they formulate as an additive contribution to network input. The adversarial program can be viewed as a "universal" adversarial perturbation that can be applied to all inputs, whose parameters are learned through backpropagation. The goal is to repurpose an existing trained target model with inputs x and outputs $f(x)$ as seen in Fig. 1 for a new task with inputs x' and outputs $g(x')$ as illustrated in Fig. 2.

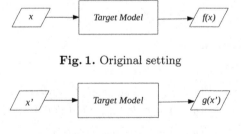

Fig. 1. Original setting

Fig. 2. New setting

Adversarial Program Crafting. In this section we describe the adversarial program crafting methodology from [3] with additional details and explanations. Let $x \in \mathbb{R}^{n \times n \times h}$ be an input image for the original task, where n is the image width and height, and h is the number of channels. Note that grayscale images have one channel and color images have three channels. Let $f(x)$ be an output of the original task. The new task sample input is defined as $x' \in \mathbb{R}^{k \times k \times h}$, where $k < n$. The output of the new task is represented as $g(x')$. In order to feed the new inputs into the original target model and receive outputs that are of the new task's domain as illustrated in Fig. 3, two mapping functions are required h_f and h_g. The function h_f maps x' into the domain of x, i.e., $h_f(x', \theta) = x$. And h_g maps $f(x)$ to $g(x')$, i.e., $h_g(f(x), \theta) = g(x')$.

Fig. 3. Reprogramming goal

The goal is to learn θ such that $h_g(f(h_f(x'))) = g(x')$. Prior to learning θ the label mapping function h_g is defined as a hard-coded one-to-one mapping function that can convert $f(x)$ to $g(x')$. Let P be the adversarial program, which is applied to all image inputs **x'** be defined as:

$$P = \tanh(\theta \odot M) \tag{4}$$

where tanh scales the adversarial program to in range of $(-1, 1)$, $\theta \in \mathbb{R}^{n \times n \times h}$ are the parameters of P, and M is a $n \times n \times h$ masking matrix $\in 0, 1$. Let x_{adv} be the image input after conversion of x' into the domain of x:

$$x_{adv} = h_f(x', \theta) \tag{5}$$

The adversarial program P is an additive variable applied to every input x':

$$x_{adv} = \mathbf{x'} + P \tag{6}$$

Let y_{adv} be the label of x_{adv}. The goal is:

$$max \; P(h_g(y_{adv})|x_{adv}) \tag{7}$$

which can be derived as follows:

$$\begin{aligned}
P(y'|x') &= P(g(x')|x') \\
P(y'|x') &= P(h_g(g(x'))|h_f(x', \theta)) \\
P(y'|x') &= P(h_g(y_{adv})|h_f(x', \theta)) \\
P(y'|x') &= P(h_g(y_{adv})|x_{adv}))
\end{aligned} \tag{8}$$

The probability $P(h_g(y_{adv})|x_{adv})$ can be maximized by solving the following optimization problem:

$$\theta^* = \arg\max_{\theta \in \mathbb{R}^{n \times n \times h}} (P(h_g(y_{adv})|h_f(x', \theta)))$$
$$\theta^* = \arg\min_\theta (-P(h_g(y_{adv})|h_f(x', \theta)))$$
$$\theta^* = \arg\min_\theta (-log P(h_g(y_{adv})|h_f(x', \theta)))$$
$$\theta^* = \arg\min_\theta (-log P(h_g(y_{adv})|h_f(x', \theta) + \lambda||\theta||_2^2))$$

(9)

where λ is a coefficient that serves as a regularization hyperparameter, which is multiplied by $L2$ norm squared of θ. Therefore, the adversarial program can crafted by solving the optimization problem $\arg\min_\theta (-log P(h_g(y_{adv})| h_f(x', \theta) + \lambda||\theta||_2^2)$.

3 Experiments with Prior Reprogramming Method

In this section we examine the reprogramming method introduced in [3] in more detail. First, we apply the method in new scenarios to test if this method also works for datasets other than the ones tested in [3]. Second, we attempt tweaking this method in various ways to investigate whether the shortcomings of this method discovered in the first set of experiments can be addressed with small changes to the method.

3.1 Experiment 1: Prior Reprogramming Method

We applied the reprogramming method introduced in [3] to various datasets and scenarios that have not been explored in other papers, and found that this method does not work reliably. It is not scaleable and cannot be applied to more complex tasks as evidenced in Table 1. Elsayed et al. [3] successfully reprogrammed six different models trained on ImageNet to perform three relatively simple tasks: counting number of squares in an image, MNIST and CIFAR. However, when the target model is trained on simpler datasets, the accuracy of the reprogrammed model on the new tasks is equivalent to random guessing. In addition to that, reprogramming Imagenet models using this technique to perform more complex tasks such as CIFAR 100 or Caltech 101 does not work well. Moreover, these operations are quite computationally expensive and therefore, not practical - using Nvidia GPU GeForce GTX 1080 it took approximately 12 h to reprogram a ResNet50V2 Imagenet model to perform MNIST. Based on the results there seems to be a relationship between the reprogramming performance and the nature of the new task - as the input dimension and number of categories get larger, reprogramming becomes less accurate and more computationally expensive.

Table 1. Reprogramming experiments with Elsayed et al. [3] methodology

Original task	New task	Train accuracy	Test accuracy
Imagenet[a]	MNIST	93.69%	94.36%
Imagenet	CIFAR 101	1.16%	1.21%
Imagenet	Caltech 101	0.40%	0.30%
Caltech 101[b]	MNIST	9.87%	9.61%
CIFAR 10[c]	MNIST	9.03%	8.92%
CIFAR 10	FASHION MNIST	14.32%	14.25%
CIFAR 10	MNIST 0 s and 1 s	53.17%	53.24%
MNIST FASHION[d]	MNIST	12.08%	12.30%
MNIST FASHION	MNIST 0 s and 1 s	42.82%	43.83%
MNIST[e]	MNIST FASHION	14.66%	14.94%

[a] Pretrained ResNet50V2 model
[b] Train accuracy: 99.58%, Test accuracy: 74.37%
[c] Train accuracy: 92.12%, Test accuracy: 80.18%
[d] Train accuracy: 99.99%, Test accuracy: 89.40%
[e] Train accuracy: 100.00%, Test accuracy: 99.25%

3.2 Experiment 2: Tweaking Prior Reprogramming Method

After concluding that the reprogramming method introduced in [3] does not work reliably on all datasets we attempted tweaking their methodology in different ways, but none of them yielded better results. First, we experimented with learning the label mapping function as opposed to hardcoding it. Second, we tried resizing the new task input image to smaller dimensions to achieve a higher ratio between the original and new input dimensions. In particular, we took a model pre-trained on MNIST FASHION with input dimension $28 \times 28 \times 1$ and reprogrammed it to classify resized handwritten 1 s and 0 s digits with input dimension $4 \times 4 \times 1$. Third, we investigated if changing the area of the image that is being trained makes a difference. The method in [3] trains the adversarial program only on the part of the image, where the new and original image don't overlap. We tried training the entire area; however, this also did not yield better results. Finally, we attempted changing the operations used to apply the adversarial program to the the new task input image. Specifically, we experimented with multiplying and subtracting the program from the input image as opposed to adding it as in [3].

4 Proposed Methodology

Our proposed methodology, like the one in [3], assumes access to target model parameters and architecture. The objective is to learn input and output reprogramming functions that allow for re-using a trained model without changing its parameters to create a new model that performs a new task. Prior works focused on crafting an adversarial program that served as additive contribution to inputs while hardcoding an arbitrary mapping between the original and new labels. This can be expressed as:

$$x + P, \tag{10}$$

where x is the new task inputs and P is the adversarial program.

Our improved technique does not rely on simple constant additive contribution to inputs and arbitrarily hardcoding label mappings, instead it is based on learning two programs. These programs can be viewed as functions - one applied to inputs and one to outputs. The first program applied to the new task inputs x can be viewed as a conversion or input adjustment function that outputs x', an adjusted input that can be passed into the target model, i.e.,

$$x' = f(x) \tag{11}$$

The purpose of function f is to resize the input image such that its dimensions match the ones that the target model accepts. The second program applied to the target model outputs and is represented as a new dense layer containing a number of neurons equal to number of new task labels and a softmax activation function.

The softmax function takes an input vector of k real numbers and outputs k probabilities that sum up to 1, where k is the total number of labels. This can be expressed as:

$$softmax(\mathbf{z})_i = exp(z_i)/\sum_j exp(z_j), \tag{12}$$

where z_i is the unnormalized log probability that $\mathbf{x}$ belongs to class i:

$$z_i = log\tilde{P}(y = i|\mathbf{x}) \tag{13}$$

The original target model parameters are not changed, only the last dense layer that outputs probabilities is removed. Therefore, the second program can be expressed as a function g:

$$y' = g(NN'(x')), \tag{14}$$

where y' is the new task label and NN' is the original model with the last layer removed.

The goal of a neural is to approximate some function f^*. In case of classification, f^* is a mapping function $f^*(x) = y$ that maps input $\mathbf{x}$ to class y. The objective is to find function f that approximates the true function f^*. Therefore, finding the mapping can be expressed as $y = f(\mathbf{x}, \theta)$. The parameter θ represents the neural network's weights and biases that and the goal is to learn θ, which results in the best approximation of f^*.

Deep neural network is a chain of functions, where each function represents one layer:

$$f(\mathbf{x}) = f^{(L)}(f^{(L-1)}...(f^{(1)}(\mathbf{x}))) \tag{15}$$

Training a neural network from scratch requires learning weights and biases for all functions $f^{(1)},..., f^{(L)}$. However, our reprogramming method allows us to re-use θ from a previously trained target model for layers $1,...,L-1$ and learn the parameters of the last layer only, which can be formulated as:

$$y = f^{(L)}(h; \theta), \tag{16}$$

where h are the values of hidden units from the penultimate layer.

Therefore, our goal is to maximize probability $P(y|f^{(l)}(f^{(l-1)}))$, which can be set up as an optimization problem:

$$\hat{\theta} = \arg \min_\theta \left(-log P(y|h) \right) \tag{17}$$

5   Results of Proposed Methodology

To demonstrate effectiveness and superiority of our reprogramming method, we conducted experiments on eight different architectures trained on ImageNet, which served as target models and were reprogrammed to perform new tasks: Caltech 101 and Caltech 256 - reduced image classification. The reduced version of the Caltech 256 dataset was created by randomly selecting 20 images from each class from the original Caltech 256 dataset. As a result, Caltech 256 - reduced contains 83% fewer labeled examples. The purpose of the reduced dataset is to test the effectiveness of the proposed reprogramming technique on a non-trivial task with a small dataset. As evidenced in Table 2, our reprogramming method yields higher accuracy than prior works even on more complex tasks. We also trained models on Caltech 101 and Caltech 256 - reduced datasets from scratch and compared them to models created using our proposed reprogramming methodology while holding hyperparameters and number of training epochs constant for a fair comparison. As shown in Table 2, the models created by reprogramming achieve much higher accuracy than models trained from scratch. It is possible to create models from scratch with much higher accuracy than the one we report; however, this requires increased training time and careful hyperparamenter tuning. The purpose of comparing reprogrammed models and models trained from scratch is to compare the two techniques in terms of the effort spent to create them.

Most models created with reprogramming performed very well - the average testing accuracy on Caltech 101 was 82.07% with the best testing accuracy of 89.81% achieved by reprogramming ResNet152V2. This is a significantly better result compared to the model created from scratch using the same hyperparameters, which achieved only 38.95% testing accuracy on Caltech 101. It is interesting that reprogrammed VGG16 performed slightly better than reprogrammed VGG19. VGG16 contains 16 layers while VGG 19 consists of 19 layers and therefore more parameters. The training accuracy for the two models is almost identical, but the testing accuracy is approximately 2.5% lower for VGG19 compared to VGG16. It seems that increased model complexity caused the model to slightly overfit. The Caltech 256 - reduced models also performed significantly better than the model made from scratch and trained with the same hyperparameters. The average testing accuracy of the models made using reprogramming was 55.95% with the best one of 69.65% created through reprogramming ResNet152V2, whereas the testing accuracy of the model made from scratch was only 3.63%. While an average testing accuracy of 55.95% is not very high, it should be noted that the training dataset had a very limited number of examples and that the testing accuracy of the model created from scratch using the same hyperparameters was a mere 3.63%. Additionally, it can be observed that there is a gap between training and testing accuracy of the Caltech 256 - reduced models. The most likely reason for this is overfitting, because the training set is small and the model complexity is high.

Overall, these results demonstrate that: (1) our reprogramming method is superior to the prior method, and (2) that our reprogramming method can be used to quickly create new accurate models without requiring much training time and hyperparameter tuning.

Table 2. Reprogramming experiments with proposed methodology

Original task	New task			
Imagenet	Caltech 101		Reduced Caltech 256	
Architecture	Train accuracy	Test accuracy	Train accuracy	Test accuracy
ResNet50V2	98.16%	88.73%	98.39%	66.93%
ResNet101V2	98.48%	89.48%	98.36%	70.04%
ResNet152V2	98.14%	89.81%	97.75%	69.65%
MobileNet	96.94%	83.05%	95.89%	53.96%
NASNetMobile	93.19%	82.73%	92.19%	67.06%
MobileNetV2	93.47%	83.05%	91.58%	60.05%
VGG16	80.79%	71.14%	54.10%	29.96%
VGG19	80.44%	68.56%	55.02%	29.96%
From scratch	85.16%	38.95%	27.47%	3.63%

6   Conclusion

The focus of this paper is reprogramming of neural networks, which involves re-purposing a target model to perform a new task without changing its parameters. We propose a new reprogramming methodology that improves upon [3], who first introduced reprogramming as an adversarial machine learning attack. We demonstrate that our method, compared to prior works, yields more accurate results, is more scalable, and can be applied to complex tasks. Furthermore, we argue that while reprogramming can be misused maliciously, it can also be viewed as an efficient learning technique.

References

1. Bubeck, S., Price, E., Razenshteyn, I.: Adversarial examples from computational constraints. In: ICML (2019)
2. Carlini, N., Wagner, D.: Towards evaluating the robustness of neural networks. In: 2017 IEEE Symposium on Security and Privacy, pp. 39–57 (2016)
3. Elsayed, G., Goodfellow, I., Sohl-Dickstein, J.: Adversarial reprogramming of neural networks. In: ICLR (2019)
4. Fawzi, A., Moosavi-Dezfooli, S,. Frossard, P.: Robustness of classifiers: from adversarial to random noise. In: NIPS (2016)
5. Fawzi, A., Fawzi, H., Fawzi, O.: Adversarial vulnerability for any classifier. In: NeurIPS (2018)
6. Ford, N., Gilmer, J., Carlini, N., Cubuk, E.: Adversarial examples are a natural consequence of test error in noise. In: Proceedings of the 36th International Conference on Machine Learning (2019)
7. Gilmer, J., et al.: Adversarial Spheres. In: ICLR (2018)
8. Goodfellow, I., McDaniel, P., Papernot, N.: Making machine learning robust against adversarial inputs. Commun. ACM **61**, 56–66 (2018)
9. Goodfellow, I., Shlens, J., Szegedy, Ch.: Explaining and Harnessing Adversarial Examples. In: ICLR (2014)
10. Ilyas, A., Santurkar, S., Tsipras, D., Engstrom, L., Tran, B., Madry, A.: Adversarial examples are not bugs. They are features, In: NeurIPS (2019)
11. Mahloujifar, S. Diochnos, D., Mahmoody, M.: The curse of concentration in robust learning: evasion and poisoning attacks from concentration of measure. In: AAAI (2019)
12. Mesnil, G., et al.: Unsupervised and transfer learning challenge: a deep learning approach. In: Proceedings of ICML Workshop on Unsupervised and Transfer Learning (PMLR), vol. 27, pp. 97–110 (2012)
13. Nakkiran, P.: Adversarial robustness may be at odds with simplicity. In: ICLR (2019)
14. Neekhara, P., Hussain, S., Dubnov, S., Koushanfar, F.: Adversarial reprogramming of text classification neural networks. In: Proceedings of the 2019 Conference on Empirical Methods in Natural Language Processing and the 9th International Joint Conference on Natural Language Processing (EMNLP-IJCNLP) (2019)
15. Papernot, N., McDaniel, P., Goodfellow, I., Jha, S., Celik, Z., Swami, A.: Practical black-box attacks against machine learning. In: ASIA CCS (2016)
16. Papernot, N., McDaniel, P., Jha, S., Fredrikson, M., Celik, Z., Swami, A.: The limitations of deep learning in adversarial settings. IEEE European Symposium on Security and Privacy (EuroS&P), pp. 371–387 (2015)
17. Raina, R., Battle, A., Lee, H., Packer, B., Ng, A.: Self-taught learning: transfer learning from unlabeled data. In: ICML (2007)
18. Schmidt, L., Santurkar, S., Tsipras, D., Talwar, K., Madry A.: Adversarially robust generalization requires more data. In: NeurIPS (2018)
19. Shafahi, A., Huang, W., Studer, Ch., Feizi, S., Goldstein, T.: Are adversarial examples inevitable? In: ICLR (2019)
20. Shamir, A., Safran, I., Ronen, E., Dunkelman, O.: A simple explanation for the existence of adversarial examples with small hamming distance. ArXiv, arXiv:1901.10861 (2019)
21. Szegedy, Ch., et al .: Intriguing properties of neural networks. In: 2nd International Conference on Learning Representations (2014)

22. Tanay, T., Griffin, L.D.: A boundary tilting persepective on the phenomenon of adversarial examples. ArXiv, arXiv:1608.07690 (2016)
23. Wang, X., et al.: Protecting neural networks with hierarchical random switching: towards better robustness-accuracy trade-off for stochastic defenses. In: IJCAI (2019)

Adversarial Robustness in Deep Learning: Attacks on Fragile Neurons

Chandresh Pravin[1]([✉])(iD), Ivan Martino[2](iD), Giuseppe Nicosia[3,4](iD), and Varun Ojha[1](iD)

[1] University of Reading, Reading, UK
`{kp826252,v.k.ojha}@reading.ac.uk`
[2] KTH Royal Institute of Technology, Stockholm, Sweden
`imartino@kth.se`
[3] University of Catania, Catania, Italy
[4] University of Cambridge, Cambridge, UK
`giuseppe.nicosia@unict.it, gn263@cam.ac.uk`

Abstract. We identify fragile and robust neurons of deep learning architectures using nodal dropouts of the first convolutional layer. Using an adversarial targeting algorithm, we correlate these neurons with the distribution of adversarial attacks on the network. Adversarial robustness of neural networks has gained significant attention in recent times and highlights an intrinsic weaknesses of deep learning networks against carefully constructed distortion applied to input images. In this paper, we evaluate the robustness of state-of-the-art image classification models trained on the MNIST and CIFAR10 datasets against the fast gradient sign method attack, a simple yet effective method of deceiving neural networks. Our method identifies the specific neurons of a network that are most affected by the adversarial attack being applied. We, therefore, propose to make fragile neurons more robust against these attacks by compressing features within robust neurons and amplifying the fragile neurons proportionally.

Keywords: Deep learning · Fragile neurons · Data perturbation · Adversarial targeting · Robustness analysis · Adversarial robustness

1 Introduction

Deep neural networks (DNNs) have been widely adapted to various tasks and domains, achieving significant performances in both the real world and in numerous research environments [11]. Previously considered state-of-the-art DNNs have been subjected to a plethora of tests and experiments in an attempt to better understand the underlying mechanics of how and what exactly these learning models actually learn [13]. In doing so, we now better recognise the strengths and more importantly the weaknesses of DNNs and have subsequently developed better networks building on from previous architectures [15].

Adversarial attacks are one the most used methods to evaluate the robustness of DNNs. Such methods introduce a small carefully crafted distortion to the

© Springer Nature Switzerland AG 2021
I. Farkaš et al. (Eds.): ICANN 2021, LNCS 12891, pp. 16–28, 2021.
https://doi.org/10.1007/978-3-030-86362-3_2

input of the network in an attempt to deceive the network into misclassifying the input with a high level of confidence [9,18]. The small distortions to the input, termed *adversarial perturbations*, are hardly perceptible to humans, even when the perturbation is amplified by several orders of magnitude [18]. This ability to fool DNNs with hardly perceptible changes in the input highlights an intrinsic difference between artificial intelligence and true intelligence.

There are many ways in which an adversarial perturbation can be crafted, utilising various tools and assumptions on the target model and dataset. Existing adversarial attacks, and methods for designing such distortions, can be broadly categorised into white-box and black-box attacks. The distinction between the two different types of attacks being the information that the adversary has on the model and its parameters. With the white-box attacks, the adversary is assumed to have complete access to the target model in question, including model parameters and architecture [4]. Conversely, the black-box attack is a type of perturbation designed by an adversary with no information to the model's parameters or architecture [14]. In this paper, we focus our efforts at evaluating the robustness [17] of ResNet-18, ResNet-50 and ResNet-101 networks against a simple yet effective white-box adversarial attack, the fast gradient sign method (FGSM) attack [9]. We apply the FGSM perturbations on the MNIST and CIFAR10 datasets for the mentioned models and present a correlative relationship between the distribution of neurons with high influence and targeting by an adversary. We also evaluate a method in minimising the effects of such distortions.

With the numerous adversarial attacks formed against DNNs, there have been equally as many defences proposed in literature [14]. The ability of a defence model to remain unbeaten by an ever-growing selection of adversarial attacks has proven to be difficult [14,20]. Adversarial defences, much like adversarial attacks, can be divided into different categories: (i) defences focusing on gradient masking/obfuscation, whereby the network weight gradients used by adversaries to form attacks are disguised; (ii) robust optimization [19], where the network structure/parameters are altered to increase adversarial defences; and (iii) adversarial example detection, where the goal is to detect an adversarial input and process this entity differently to ordinary inputs [15].

The goal of all adversaries is to deceive the network into predicting, classifying, or recognising an input as a different class to its true self. When the adversary has knowledge of the information held by the network, as is the case for white-box attacks, it utilises this to craft a perturbation that will exploit weaknesses within the network's representations of the data [14]. In this paper, we propose viewing an adversarial attack as an exploitative method that targets specific neurons within a given layer. We also draw a relationship between the adversaries' target neurons and neurons that show to have higher influence on the model's unperturbed performance.

We assume that, for a given layer, information about the input learned by the layer through back propagation is distributed unevenly amongst individual neurons. We propose using *nodal dropout* to find redundant nodes within a given layer of a network [12]. Thus, also finding *fragile neurons* that carry more information about the input [7]. We identify *null neurons* that once removed do not significantly affect the overall model performance and thus considered to carry less information about the dataset. We examine how the FGSM attack affects different models (ResNet-18, ResNet-50 and ResNet-101) at different stages (epochs) in learning, whilst also comparing how increasing the network architecture affects the effectiveness of the formed attack. Therefore, we propose to make fragile neurons more robust against these attacks by compressing robust neurons and amplifying the fragile neurons proportionally.

Furthermore, the FGSM attack utilises a given network's learned representations in the form of its layer weights to calculate an effective adversarial example. The adversarial examples can be used as a method of evaluating the robustness [16] of the model's composite representations. We aim to identify the fragile and robust neurons within specific parts of the network, and post-process them separately to investigate how they affect the overall model's robustness against an adversarial attack.

2   Related Work

Robustness analysis evaluates the defence of DNNs against malicious distortion of its input [1,9,20]. There are different types of attacks available for a potential adversary, each with their own strengths and limitations. Szegdey et al. [18] initially proposed adversarial examples for DNNs using the *Limited-memory Broyden-Fletcher-Goldfarb-Shanno* (L-BFGS) algorithm, an expensive linear search method for adversarial examples. Thereafter, the FGSM attack proposed by Goodfellow et al. [9] has become one of the benchmarks for adversarial attacks due to its computational process being less resource intensive when compared to other attacks. The FGSM attack performs a pixel-wise one step gradient update along the gradient sign direction of increasing loss. There are several other attack methods available in the literature. However, in this study, we focus specifically on the FGSM adversarial attack due to its one-step gradient calculation and effective performance against state-of-the-art DNN models.

In terms of defences against adversarial attacks, there are an equal number of approaches proposed in literature. For every newly developed adversarial attack, soon there have been suitable defences proposed by researchers [20]. One method of defending a DNN model is by masking the network's parameters, therefore making it more difficult for an adversary to exploit the network's learned information to generate adversarial examples. However, this method has shown to be ineffective against many types of attacks and there exist techniques to circumvent such defensive measures [15]. Some studies show that adversarial examples are drawn from a different distribution to the regular dataset [10]. Therefore, one method to defend against the effects of such adversarial examples is to identify them and deal with the perturbed inputs to the model separately [15]. These methods are also subjected to exploitation by techniques that can bypass the adversarial examples detection, making such defence methods weaker to some types of attacks [3].

In this paper we try to find a relationship between highly influential neurons and the likelihood of being targeted by an adversary, and accordingly, propose a method of regularising the specific neurons during post-training. As we, the observer, propagate through the network we notice that the deconstructed, abstract characteristics of the data begin to take a shape of salient features, which are then assigned semantic meaning in the form of target labels [21]. Literature on leveraging the information content of a DNN has been used for various applications, we direct the reader to Golatkar et al. [8] and their method of selective forgetting, in which they propose a framework for erasing the information about a particular subset of data from the model's learned weights. We take inspiration from this framework and propose that adversarial robustness is hinged on the distribution of *influential* and *uninfluential* neurons, referred to as sets S and S' respectively within the context of this study.

We are motivated by the works of Li and Chen [12] along with related literature in reducing network complexity by using techniques such as nodal pruning. We leverage the idea that there exist neurons within a network that can be classified as redundant, or uninfluential to the overall model performance. Removing redundant neurons in some cases also shows to improve robustness against attacks [5]. Conversely, we also consider the works of [7] that prove the existence of multi-model neurons within networks; multi-modal neurons being representations that hold a higher degree of influence in the network's understanding of the data. We investigate the correlation between representations that show a higher influence and the highest average concentration of an adversarial attack to these features. In consequence, we draw attention to the nature of adversarial attacks and how such perturbations target the model's learned knowledge specifically.

3   Adversarial Attack and Defense Formulations

We consider an image classifier model f_θ with L layers, and trainable parameters θ that accepts an input image x and its associated true class label y. The model returns $\hat{y}$ as its prediction for input x. The goal of the model is to reduce loss function $\mathcal{L}(f_\theta, x, y)$. The image $x' = x + \delta_\epsilon$ is an adversarial example produced by a distortion δ_ϵ added to image x, where ϵ is the perturbation magnitude.

Our objective is to minimise the difference in predictions values $\hat{y}$ obtained for unperturbed input x and perturbed input x'. We examine the model's learnable parameters $\theta_L \in \theta$ of layer L at various stages of the model's training. It should be noted that while assessing the significance of the neurons, we remove one-neuron at a time from θ_L. We, therefore, identified two sets of neurons indices, S and S' respectively representing (i) neuron indices within the layer L showing a higher influence on the overall model performance, and (ii) neurons indices with lower overall influence on model performance. In our work, we are concerned with removing one-neuron at a time, removing multiple neurons from the model f_θ would warrant an alternative method. We also assessed neurons of the first layer of the network because of its high importance and influence on features learned by subsequent layer in a network [5].

3.1   Attack Formulation

We formulated attack in this work using FGSM method. This method leverages a network's learned representations in the form of layer weights θ_L to construct an efficient and effective adversarial perturbation x'. The FGSM attack is a perturbation for an input x computed as:

$$\delta_\epsilon = \epsilon \; sign(\nabla_x \mathcal{L}(x, y, \theta)), \tag{1}$$

where ∇_x is the required gradients calculated using backpropagation. The adversarial example therefore is $x' = x + \delta_\epsilon$ [1,9].

We find that for a 100 epoch pre-trained ResNet-50 model on the CIFAR10 dataset, a baseline model accuracy of 75.87% on unperturbed input x is found. The same model applied to the CIFAR10 dataset with an FGSM attack, using a perturbation magnitude of $\epsilon = 0.01$, results in an accuracy of 58.88%. If we consider the same ResNet-50 architecture trained equally for 100 epochs, with the input dimensions adjusted to comply with the MNIST dataset, the baseline model accuracy on unperturbed MNIST dataset is 99.42%. While the model accuracy is found to be 79.4% when perturbed with an $\epsilon = 0.34$ attack. These are examples of the FGSM attack performance against CIFAR10 and MNIST datasets on the ResNet-50 DNN model.

If we consider a metric to assess the complexity of a given dataset, such as the cumulative spectral gradient (CSG) method [2], we notice that the CSG complexity measure for the for the CIFAR10 dataset is 1.00 and MNIST dataset is 0.11. As we may expect, the FGSM attack is more effective on more complex data (e.g., CIFAR10) compared to less complex data (e.g., MNIST). This can be realised from the perturbation magnitude ϵ required for the model performance to decrease proportionally. For example, to decrease performance by approximately 20%, a lower value of ϵ (small perturbation) is required for CIFAR10 and a higher value of ϵ (large perturbation) is required for MNIST.

3.2   Defence Formulation

To better understand how to form a suitable defence against an adversarial attack, we may consider how an adversary can form an effective attack. With the FGSM attack, a single step in the parameter space is taken in the direction of increasing loss. The perturbation is calculated using the network's weights to perturb the input data features in the direction of an incorrect class. Then it is natural to consider that this informed way of creating adversarial perturbations may, even with relatively low magnitudes, affect the neurons that are more influential to the model's performance (e.g., set of highly influencing neurons S).

We aim to show this effect of adversarial perturbations experimentally by comparing the output of the layer-wise convolution for original input x and perturbed input x' computed using pre-trained parameters θ. We expect the original model prediction $f(x, y, \theta)$ and the model prediction on perturbed input $f(x', y, \theta)$ to be not equal. In our defence formulation, we aim to modify the model's layer parameters θ_L as θ'_L such that a potential adversary is forced to distribute the attack strength throughout the layer. We propose that this will make the model's layer θ'_L more robust against an adversarial attack.

3.3   Fragile and Null Kernels Identification

We identified fragile neurons (kernels) S and null neurons (kernels) S' by dropping the kernels out systematically one-by-one and measuring the variance in model performance. Figure 1 show model's performance for each kernel along the x-axis being dropped. The indices of fragile kernels S are indicated with blue circled symbols and are below the mean performance line indicated in red, which is computed over each kernel's effect on the model's accuracy. The dropping of these fragile kernels has a higher influence on the model's performance when compared to the dropping of the null kernels indicted with black star symbol shown above mean performance line.

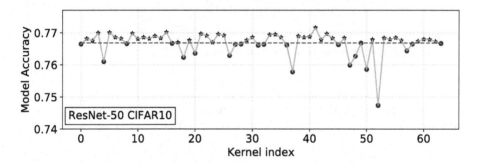

Fig. 1. Evaluated ResNet-50 model trained for 10 epochs. Fragile kernels S shown in blue below mean performance line in red and null kernels S' are shown in black star above mean line in red. (Color figure online)

4   Adversarial Targeting Algorithm

We assuming that the parameters $\theta_{L,S'}$ of null kernels S' in layer L, carry within them some noise that render the overall influence of these kernels on the model performance to be lower than the fragile kernel S, we propose to filter parameters $\theta_{L,S'}$ to remove noise. We assume the distribution of the noise in matrix $K_{L,\bar{s}}$ to be Gaussian noise. For this, we can use the works of Gavish and Donoho [6] to recover a lower rank matrix from noisy data and retaining only the most important features. The filtering of $\theta_{L,S'}$ produces the modified parameters $\theta'_{L,S'}$. The filtered parameters relating to null kernels $\theta'_{L,S'}$, are said to be more robust if the probability of predicting the true class using modified model parameters θ' is higher than θ as per:

$$P(\hat{y} = y | x', \theta') > P(\hat{y} = y | x', \theta). \tag{2}$$

We compose a matrix $K_{L,S'}$ by stacking flattened null kernel parameters $\theta'_{L,S'}$ and compress $K_{L,S'}$ to remove noise or redundant information, thus increasing the influence of these null kernels S' on the model's overall performance. While filtering the null kernels S', we proportionally amplify fragile kernel S. This is to maintain relative magnitude of the local features within the network and propagate the essential representations to deeper layers of the network better.

4.1   Filtering of Null Kernels S'

We decompose the null kernel's matrix $K_{L,S'}$ using singular value decomposition (SVD) and reduce the complexity of the representations by clamping all values below a filtering threshold τ. We apply this method only to the first convolutional layer because of its susceptibility to any distortions having a higher influence on the network's performance [5]. We use SVD to decompose our null kernel matrix $K_{L,\bar{s}}$ into its respective eigenvalues Σ and eigenvectors matrices U and V as:

$$K_{L,S'} = U\Sigma V^T. \tag{3}$$

We then compute a truncated matrix of singular values $\widetilde{\Sigma}$ by clamping all singular values to be at most equal to threshold value τ as per:

$$\tilde{\sigma}_i = \arg\min(\sigma, \tau), \tag{4}$$

where σ is the diagonal of Σ and $\tilde{\sigma}_i$ is the row upto which the matrix σ is truncated. The thresholding value τ for m-by-n matrix is given as:

$$\tau = \lambda(\beta) \cdot \sqrt{n}\varepsilon, \tag{5}$$

where $\beta = m/n$, ε is the noise level within the matrix, and the term $\lambda(\beta)$ is expressed as [6]:

$$\lambda(\beta) = \sqrt{2(\beta+1) + \frac{c_1\beta}{(\beta+1) + \sqrt{\beta^2 + c_2\beta + 1}}}, \tag{6}$$

where constants c_1 and c_2 respectively are 8 and 14.

We then find the noise level value ε in (5) experimentally through a systematic search method using a sample set of the parameters. As the final filtering step, we reconstruct the filtered weight matrix $\widetilde{K}_{L,\bar{s}}$ by using the clamped singular values and corresponding eigenvectors as:

$$\widetilde{K}_{L,\bar{s}} = U\widetilde{\Sigma}V^T. \tag{7}$$

4.2   Amplification of Fragile Kernels S

The amplification of fragile kernels parameters matrix $K_{L,S}$ by a scaling factor of α computed using (3) and (7) as per:

$$\widetilde{K}_{L,S} = \alpha K_{L,S}, \tag{8}$$

where scaling factor of α is

$$\alpha = 1 + ||K_{L,\bar{S}} - \widetilde{K}_{L,\bar{S}}||_2. \tag{9}$$

The aim of this process is to amplify the features within fragile kernels S, such that a greater magnitude of adversarial perturbation is required to vary such kernels.

4.3   Adversarial Targeting of Fragile and Null Kernels

We assess the robustness of the fragile kernels S and null kernels S' by our robustness targeting algorithm shown in Algorithm 1. The FSGM attack for varied range of perturbations ϵ is used to compute the evaluated first convolutional layer's outputs $\hat{y}_x$ and $\hat{y}_{x'}$. The mean difference between each kernel in the output of $\hat{y}_x$ and $\hat{y}_{x'}$ are calculated and compared to see which is highest, indicating a greater average concentration of the attack.

Algorithm 1. Adversarial targeting

1: Initialise $f() \to f_L()$ $\triangleright$ $f_L()$ is the L-th layer of full network $f()$
2: Compute indices of fragile kernels S and null kernels S' as per Sect. 3.3
3: $S_{attack} = \{\}$ $\triangleright$ an empty list to store examples that attacks S
4: **for** perturbation $\epsilon \in \mathbb{R}$ **do** $\triangleright$ where ϵ is perturbation magnitude
5:      $attack = \mathrm{FGSM}(f_L, \epsilon)$
6:      $S_{count} = 0$
7:      **for** (x, y) in (X_{test}, Y_{test}) **do**
8:          $x' = attack(x, y)$ $\triangleright$ create an adversarial example x' for input x and level y
9:          $\hat{y}_x = f_L(x)$ $\triangleright$ output of L-th layer on unperturbed input x
10:         $\hat{y}_{x'} = f_L(x')$ $\triangleright$ output of L-th layer on perturbed input x'
11:         $\mathbf{d} = ||\hat{y}_x - \hat{y}_{x'}||_2$ $\triangleright$ Euclidean distance $\mathbf{d} = (d_1, \ldots, d_k)$ between $\hat{y}_x$ and $\hat{y}_{x'}$
12:         $S_f = (\sum_j^{|S|} d_{j,S})/|S|$ $\triangleright$ Average of distances $d_{j,S}$ of all S select from $\mathbf{d}$
13:         $S_n = (\sum_j^{|S'|} d_{j,S'})/|S'|$ $\triangleright$ Average of distances $d_{j,S'}$ of all S' select from $\mathbf{d}$
14:         **if** $S_f > S_n$ **then**
15:            $S_{count} = S_{count} + 1$ $\triangleright$ increase counter of attacks for fragile kernels
16:         **end if**
17:      **end for**
18:      $S_{attack} \leftarrow S_{count}$ $\triangleright$ add S_{count} to the list S_{attack}
19: **end for**

---

5   Results and Discussion

In first series of experiments, we use the two sets S and S' obtained as per Fig. 1 on the ResNet-50 model and apply them to Algorithm 1 using the CIFAR10 dataset, resulting in Fig. 2 and the MNIST dataset, resulting in Fig. 3:

For Fig. 2, we measure the robustness of ResNet-50 models and compare the percentage of examples attacking fragile kernels S and the model accuracy against FGSM attack. In Fig. 2 (*Left*), we notice that as the number of training epochs increases, the model's accuracy also increases for both the unperturbed ($\epsilon = 0$) and perturbed ($\epsilon > 0$) examples. In Fig. 2 (*Right*), using the results from the adversarial targeting Algorithm 1, we also notice that the percentage of examples attacking fragile kernels S is higher for highly perturbed examples. However, for smaller perturbation magnitudes, 100 epoch model is more robust. This suggests that as the model becomes more robust (from epoch 10 to 100), the percentage of examples attacking fragile kernels S and null kernels S' tends to distribute equally.

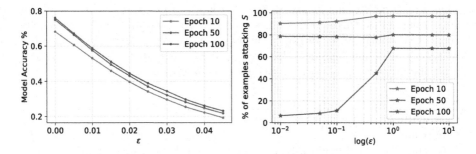

Fig. 2. *Left:* ResNet-50 model trained on the CIFAR10 dataset for epochs 10, 50 and 100 against the FGSM attack, with ϵ increasing linearly, marked by dots. *Right:* ResNet-50 model trained on the CIFAR10 dataset for epochs 10, 50 and 100 against the FGSM attack, with attack magnitude increasing logarithmically, marked by star symbols. Epoch 10, 50, 100 respectively indicated in colors grey, green, violet. (Color figure online)

After applying our framework proposed in Sects. 4.1 and 4.2 using ε value of 0.015 to the first convolutional layer θ_L, resulting in filtered layer parameters θ'_L, we observe the difference in attack distribution between original model and modified model using Algorithm 1.

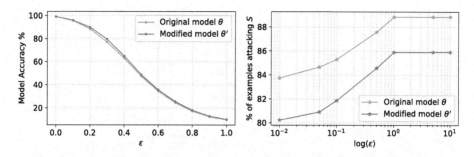

Fig. 3. Concentration of the adversarial attack on fragile kernels S for both the original model with parameters θ_L and the modified model, with θ'_L in a ResNet-50 model trained on the MNIST dataset for 10 epochs, using the methods proposed in Sects. 4.1 and 4.2.

We apply the parameter filtering framework to a ResNet-50 model trained on the MNIST for 10 epochs. The results of which is shown in Fig. 3. In this experiment, although the number of fragile kernels S are 37% of the total kernels within the layer, these kernels show a larger average distance between the outputs of the original layer θ_L and modified layer θ'_L for almost 89% of the tested input examples on original model. Furthermore, as the attack strength is increased by increasing ϵ, the average magnitude of the attack on kernels S also increased. However, our method of filtering parameters θ'_L kept the percentage of tested examples attacking fragile kernels S lower than the original model.

We observe from Fig. 4 how the influence of kernels in the first convolutional layer varies during the training process while we systematically drop and assess the kernels. In Fig. 4, red circles are the kernels that carry a higher influence through all stages of model training. We notice that as we change the model from ResNet-18 to ResNet-50 and ResNet-101, the number of influential fragile kernels increases on the CIFAR10 dataset. This is as we may expect, model architectures with greater complexities are able to learn the important features from the dataset faster than shallower model architectures. We notice from Fig. 4, that the average model performance of the kernels in θ_L increases to a limit for models trained on the CIFAR10 dataset and shows to increase and then decrease for the models trained on the MNIST dataset. This characteristic invites a separate set of experiments to better understand how model overfitting affects nodal dropouts.

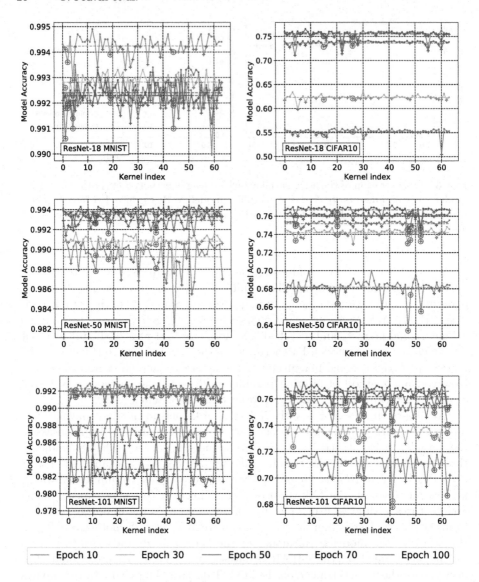

Fig. 4. Variance of model performance to individual kernels being dropped out within the first convolutional layer. Red circles indicate fragile kernels that remain fragile throughout the all training epochs, whereas red crosses indicate kernels that are observed as fragile for the specific training epoch length. (Color figure online)

6   Conclusion

In this study we show how an FGSM attack targets specific neurons within the first convolutional layer of ResNet-18, ResNet-50 and ResNet-101 models trained on both the CIFAR10 and NNIST datasets. To prove this property, we first identify fragile kernels S and null kernels S' sets within the evaluated layer using an iterative dropout method and measuring the variance in model performance. We use the kernel indices of S and S' to evaluate the highest average distance between the outputs of the layer using the original input x and perturbed example x'. In doing so, we find that for a ResNet-50 model trained on the CIFAR10 dataset for 50 epochs, the number of fragile kernels S account to 37% of the total number of kernels in the layer yet show to have a higher average difference for approximately 89% of the examples evaluated.

We also show how the robustness against the FGSM attack, and the targeting of fragile kernels S varies as the model is trained, thus showing a correlation between a model becoming more robust and the targeting of fragile kernels. Furthermore, we propose a layer parameter filtering algorithm that improves robustness in a model by removing information from null kernels S' and amplifying the information in S. This simple method, despite only being applied to the first convolutional layer, improves the robustness of a model with less training. It should be noted that, although our study focuses on the first convolutional layer only due to the layer being highly influence over the model's performance, other layers can also be evaluated using this proposed framework.

Acknowledgments. This work was supported by the EPSRC DTP matching funding from the University of Reading, UK and Kosnic Lighting Ltd. UK

References

1. Akhtar, N., Mian, A.: Threat of adversarial attacks on deep learning in computer vision: a survey. IEEE Access **6**, 14410–14430 (2018)
2. Branchaud-Charron, F., Achkar, A., Jodoin, P.M.: Spectral metric for dataset complexity assessment. In: IEEE CVPR (2019)
3. Carlini, N., Wagner, D.: Adversarial examples are not easily detected: bypassing ten detection methods. In: Proceedings of the 10th ACM Workshop Artificial Intelligence and Security, pp. 3–14 (2017)
4. Carlini, N., Wagner, D.: MagNet and "efficient defenses against adversarial attacks" are not robust to adversarial examples (2017). arXiv:1711.08478
5. Cheney, N., Schrimpf, M., Kreiman, G.: On the robustness of convolutional neural networks to internal architecture and weight perturbations (2017). arXiv:1703.08245
6. Gavish, M., Donoho, D.L.: The optimal hard threshold for singular values is $4/\sqrt{3}$. IEEE Trans. Inf. Theory **60**(8), 5040–5053 (2014)
7. Goh, G., et al.: Multimodal neurons in artificial neural networks. Distill **6**(3) (2021)
8. Golatkar, A., Achille, A., Soatto, S.: Eternal sunshine of the spotless net: selective forgetting in deep networks. In: IEEE CVPR, pp. 9304–9312 (2020)
9. Goodfellow, I.J., Shlens, J., Szegedy, C.: Explaining and harnessing adversarial examples. In: ICLR (2015)
10. Grosse, K., Manoharan, P., Papernot, N., Backes, M., McDaniel, P.: On the (statistical) detection of adversarial examples (2017). arXiv:1702.06280
11. LeCun, Y., Bengio, Y., Hinton, G.: Deep learning. Nature **521**(7553), 436–444 (2015)

12. Li, B., Chen, C.: First-order sensitivity analysis for hidden neuron selection in layer-wise training of networks. Neural Process. Lett. **48**(2), 1105–1121 (2018)
13. Papernot, N., et al.: The limitations of deep learning in adversarial settings. In: IEEE European Symposium on Security and Privacy, pp. 372–387 (2016)
14. Ren, K., Zheng, T., Qin, Z., Liu, X.: Adversarial attacks and defenses in deep learning. Engineering **6**(3), 346–360 (2020)
15. Silva, S.H., Najafirad, P.: Opportunities and challenges in deep learning adversarial robustness: a survey (2020). arXiv:2007.00753
16. Stracquadanio, G., Ferla, A.L., Felice, M.D., Nicosia, G.: Design of robust space trajectories. In: Bramer, M., Petridis, M., Nolle, L. (eds.) Research and Development in Intelligent Systems XXVIII. SGAI 2011, pp. 341–354. Springer, London (2011). https://doi.org/10.1007/978-1-4471-2318-7_26
17. Stracquadanio, G., Nicosia, G.: Computational energy-based redesign of robust proteins. Comput. Chem. Eng. **35**(3), 464–473 (2011)
18. Szegedy, C., Zaremba, W., Sutskever, I., Bruna, J., Erhan, D., Goodfellow, I., Fergus, R.: Intriguing properties of neural networks. In: ICLR (2014)
19. Umeton, R., Stracquadanio, G., Sorathiya, A., Liò, P., Papini, A., Nicosia, G.: Design of robust metabolic pathways. In: Stok, L., et al. (eds.) Proceedings of the 48th Design Automation Conference, DAC 2011, San Diego, California, USA, June 5–10, pp. 747–752. ACM (2011)
20. Yuan, X., He, P., Zhu, Q., Li, X.: Adversarial examples: attacks and defenses for deep learning. IEEE Trans. Neural Netw. Learn. Syst. **30**(9), 2805–2824 (2019)
21. Zhou, B., Bau, D., Oliva, A., Torralba, A.: Interpreting deep visual representations via network dissection. IEEE Transactions on Pattern Analysis and Machine Intelligence (2018)

How to Compare Adversarial Robustness of Classifiers from a Global Perspective

Niklas Risse[ID], Christina Göpfert[(✉)][ID], and Jan Philip Göpfert[ID]

Bielefeld University, Bielefeld, Germany
`cgoepfert@techfak.uni-bielefeld.de`

Abstract. Adversarial robustness of machine learning models has attracted considerable attention over recent years. Adversarial attacks undermine the reliability of and trust in machine learning models, but the construction of more robust models hinges on a rigorous understanding of adversarial robustness as a property of a given model. Point-wise measures for specific threat models are currently the most popular tool for comparing the robustness of classifiers and are used in most recent publications on adversarial robustness. In this work, we use robustness curves to show that point-wise measures fail to capture important global properties that are essential to reliably compare the robustness of different classifiers. We introduce new ways in which robustness curves can be used to systematically uncover these properties and provide concrete recommendations for researchers and practitioners when assessing and comparing the robustness of trained models. Furthermore, we characterize scale as a way to distinguish small and large perturbations, and relate it to inherent properties of data sets, demonstrating that robustness thresholds must be chosen accordingly. We hope that our work contributes to a shift of focus away from point-wise measures of robustness and towards a discussion of the question what kind of robustness could and should reasonably be expected. We release code to reproduce all experiments presented in this paper, which includes a Python module to calculate robustness curves for arbitrary data sets and classifiers, supporting a number of frameworks, including TensorFlow, PyTorch and JAX.

Keywords: Adversarial robustness · Deep learning

1 Introduction

Despite their astonishing success in a wide range of classification tasks, deep neural networks can be lead to incorrectly classify inputs altered with specially crafted adversarial perturbations [11,34]. These perturbations can be so small that they remain almost imperceptible to human observers [13]. Adversarial

---

N. Risse, C. Göpfert and J. P. Göpfert—Equal contribution.

I. Farkaš et al. (Eds.): ICANN 2021, LNCS 12891, pp. 29–41, 2021.
https://doi.org/10.1007/978-3-030-86362-3_3

robustness describes a model's ability to behave correctly under such small perturbations crafted with the intent to mislead the model. The study of adversarial robustness – with its definitions, their implications, attacks, and defenses – has attracted considerable research interest. This is due to both the practical importance of trustworthy models as well as the intellectual interest in the differences between decisions of machine learning models and our human perception. A crucial starting point for any such analysis is the definition of what exactly a small input perturbation is – requiring (a) the choice of a *distance function* to measure perturbation size, and (b) the choice of a particular *scale* to distinguish small and large perturbations. Together, these two choices determine a *threat model* that defines exactly under which perturbations a model is required to be robust.

The most popular choice of distance function is the class of distances induced by ℓ_p norms [5,11,34], in particular ℓ_1, ℓ_2 and ℓ_∞, although other choices such as Wasserstein distance have been explored as well [39]. Regarding scale, the current default is to pick some perturbation threshold ε without providing concrete reasons for the exact choice. Analysis then focuses on the *robust error* of the model, the proportion of test inputs for which the model behaves incorrectly under some perturbation up to size ε. This means that the scale is defined as a binary distinction between small and large perturbations based on the perturbation threshold. A set of canonical thresholds have emerged in the literature. For example, in the publications referenced in this section, the MNIST data set is typically evaluated at a perturbation threshold $\varepsilon \in \{0.1, 0.3\}$ for the ℓ_∞ norm, while CIFAR-10 is evaluated at $\varepsilon \in \{2/255, 4/255, 8/255\}$, stemming from the three 8-bit color channels used to represent images.

Based on these established threat models, researchers have developed specialized methods to minimize the robust error during training, which results in more robust models. Popular approaches include specific data augmentation, sometimes used under the umbrella term adversarial training [7,14,16,23], training under regularization that encourages large margins and smooth decision boundaries in the learned model [9,10,15,37], and post-hoc processing or randomized smoothing of predictions in a learned model [8,19].

In order to show the superiority of a new method, robust accuracies of differently trained models are typically compared for a handful of threat models and data sets, eg., $\ell_\infty(\varepsilon = 0.1)$ and $\ell_2(\varepsilon = 0.3)$ for MNIST. Out of 22 publications on adversarial robustness published at NeurIPS 2019, ICLR 2020, and ICML 2020, 12 publications contain results for only a single perturbation threshold. In five publications, robust errors are calculated for at least two different perturbation thresholds, but still, only an arbitrary number of thresholds is considered. Only in five out of the total 22 publications do we find extensive considerations of different perturbation thresholds and the respective robust errors. Out of these five, three are analyses of randomized smoothing, which naturally gives rise to certification radii [7,21,28]. [27] follow a learning-theoretical motivation, which results in an error bound as a function of the perturbation threshold. Only [25]

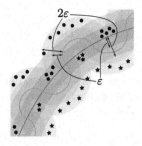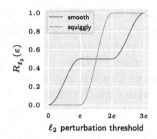

Fig. 1. Excerpt of a toy data set with two decision boundaries (left) and respective robustness curves (right). The data is separated perfectly by one smooth boundary (blue robustness curve), and one squiggly boundary (orange robustness curve). We indicate margins around the boundaries at distances ε and 2ε. Selecting a single perturbation threshold is not sufficient to decide which classifier is more robust. (Color figure online)

do not rely on randomization and still provide a complete, empirical analysis of robust error for varying perturbation thresholds.[1]

Our Contributions: In this work, we demonstrate that point-wise measures of ℓ_p robustness are not sufficient to reliably and meaningfully compare the robustness of different classifiers. We show that, both in theory and practice, results of model comparisons based on point-wise measures may fail to generalize to threat models with even slightly larger or smaller ε. Furthermore, we show that point-wise measures are insufficient to meaningfully compare the efficacy of different defense techniques when distance functions are varied. Finally, we analyze how scale depends on the underlying data space, choice of distance function, and distribution. Based on our findings we suggest that robustness curves, which represent the robust error for all perturbation thresholds, should become the standard tool when comparing adversarial robustness of classifiers, and that the perturbation threshold of threat models should be selected carefully in order to be meaningful, considering inherent characteristics of the data set. We release code to reproduce all experiments presented in this paper[2], which includes a Python module with an easily accessible interface (similar to Foolbox [30]) to calculate robustness curves for arbitrary data sets and classifiers. The module supports classifiers written in most of the popular machine learning frameworks, such as TensorFlow, PyTorch and JAX.

2   Methods

An adversarial perturbation for a classifier f and input-output pair (x, y) is a small perturbation δ with $f(x + \delta) \neq y$. Because the perturbation δ is small, it

---

[1] *Single thresholds:* [1,4,10,26,29,31–33,35,36,41,42], *multiple thresholds:* [3,16,20, 24,38], *full analysis:* [7,21,25,27,28].

[2] The full code is available at www.github.com/niklasrisse/how-to-compare-adversari al-robustness-of-classifiers-from-a-global-perspective.

is assumed that the label y would still be the correct prediction for $x + \delta$. The resulting point $x + \delta$ is called an *adversarial example*. The points vulnerable to adversarial perturbations are the points that are either already misclassified when unperturbed, or those that lie close to a decision boundary.

One tool to visualize and study the robustness behavior of a classifier are *robustness curves*, which represent the distribution of shortest distances between a set of points and the decision boundaries of a classifier:

Definition 1. *Given an input space $\mathcal{X}$ and label set $\mathcal{Y}$, distance function d on $\mathcal{X} \times \mathcal{X}$, and classifier $f : \mathcal{X} \to \mathcal{Y}$. Let data points $(x, y) \overset{i.i.d.}{\sim} P$. Then the d-robustness curve for f is the graph of the function*

$$R_d^f(\varepsilon) := P_{(x,y)} \left(\exists\, x' : d(x, x') \leq \varepsilon \wedge f(x') \neq y \right)$$

A model's robustness curve shows how data points are distributed in relation to the decision boundaries of the model, essentially visualizing simultaneously an extremely large number of point-wise measures. This allows us to take a step back from robustness regarding a specific perturbation threshold which in turn makes it easier to compare global robustness for different classifiers, distributions and distance functions. To see why this is relevant, consider Fig. 1, which shows toy data along with two possible classifiers that perfectly separate the data. For a perturbation threshold of ε, the blue classifier has robust error 0.5, while the orange classifier is perfectly robust. However, for a perturbation threshold of 2ε, the orange classifier has robust error 1, while the blue classifier remains at 0.5. By freely choosing a single perturbation threshold for comparison, it is therefore possible to make either classifier appear to be much better than the other, and no single threshold can capture the full picture. In fact, as the following Theorem shows, for any two disjoint sets of perturbation thresholds, it is possible to construct a data distribution and two classifiers f, f', such that the robust error of f is lower than that of f' for all perturbation thresholds in the first set, and that of f' is lower than that of f for all perturbation thresholds in the second set. This shows that even computing multiple point-wise measures to compare two models may give misleading results.

Theorem 1. *Let $T_1, T_2 \subset \mathbb{R}^{>0}$ be two disjoint finite sets. Then there exists a distribution P on $\mathbb{R} \times \{0, 1\}$ and two classifiers $c_1, c_2 : \mathbb{R} \to \{0, 1\}$ such that $R_{|\cdot|}^{c_1}(t) < R_{|\cdot|}^{c_2}(t)$ for all $t \in T_1$ and $R_{|\cdot|}^{c_1}(t) > R_{|\cdot|}^{c_2}(t)$ for all $t \in T_2$.*

Proof. Without loss of generality, assume that $T_1 = \{t_1, \ldots, t_n\}$ and $T_2 = \{t'_1, \ldots, t'_n\}$ with $t_i < t'_i < t_{i+1}$ for $i \in \{1, \ldots, n\}$. We will construct c_1, c_2 such that the robustness curves $R_{|\cdot|}^{c_1}(\cdot), R_{|\cdot|}^{c_2}(\cdot)$ intersect at exactly the points $(t_i + t'_i)/2$ and $(t_i + t'_{i+1})/2$ on the interval $(t_1, t'_n]$. Let $d = t'_n$ and

$$P\left(-d - \frac{t_i + t'_{i+1}}{2}, 0\right) = P\left(d + \frac{t_i + t'_i}{2}, 1\right) = \frac{2}{4n+1}, P\left(-d - \frac{t_1}{2}, 0\right) = \frac{1}{4n+1}$$

Let $c_1(x) = \mathbb{1}_{x \geq -d}$ and $c_2(x) = \mathbb{1}_{x \geq d}$. Both classifiers have perfect accuracy on P, meaning that $R_{|\cdot|}^{c_i}(0) = 0$. The closest point to the decision boundary of c_1

is $-d - \frac{t_1}{2}$ with weight $\frac{1}{4n+1}$, so $R^{c_1}_{|\cdot|}(\frac{t_1}{2}) = \frac{1}{4n+1}$. The second-closest point is $-d - \frac{t_1+t'_2}{2}$ with weight $\frac{2}{4n+1}$, so $R^{c_1}_{|\cdot|}(\frac{t_1+t'_2}{2}) = \frac{3}{4n+1}$, and so on. Meanwhile, the closest point to the decision boundary of c_2 is $d + \frac{t_1+t'_1}{2}$, so $R^{c_2}_{|\cdot|}(\frac{t_1+t'_1}{2}) = \frac{2}{4n+1}$, the second-closest point is $d\frac{t_2+t'_2}{2}$, so $R^{c_2}_{|\cdot|}(\frac{t_2+t'_2}{2}) = \frac{4}{4n+1}$, and so on.

3   The Weaknesses of Point-Wise Measures

In the following, we empirically evaluate the robustness of a number of recently published models, and demonstrate that the weaknesses of point-wise measures described above are not limited to toy examples, but occur for real-world data and models. We evaluate and compare the robustness of models obtained using the following training methods:

1. Standard training (ST), i.e., training without specific robustness considerations.
2. Adversarial training (AT) [23].
3. Training with robust loss (KW) [37].
4. Maximum margin regularization for a single ℓ_p norm together with adversarial training (MMR + AT) [9].
5. Maximum margin regularization simultaneously for ℓ_∞ and ℓ_1 margins (MMR-UNIV) [10].

Together with each training method, we state the threat model the trained model is optimized to defend against, eg., $\ell_\infty(\varepsilon = 0.1)$ for perturbations in ℓ_∞ norm with perturbation threshold $\varepsilon = 0.1$, if any. The trained models are those made publicly available by [9][3] and [10][4]. The network architecture is a convolutional network with two convolutional layers, two fully connected layers and ReLU activation functions. The evaluation is based on six real-world datasets: MNIST, Fashion-MNIST (FMNIST) [40], German Traffic Signs (GTS) [17], CIFAR-10 [18], Tiny-Imagenet-200 (TINY-IMG) [22], and Human Activity Recognition (HAR) [2]. Models are generally trained on the full training set for the corresponding data set, and robustness curves evaluated on the full test set, unless stated otherwise.

   For complex models, calculating the exact distance of a point to the closest decision boundary, and thus estimating the true robustness curve, is computationally very intensive, if not intractable. Therefore we bound the true robustness curve from below using strong adversarial attacks, which is consistent with the literature on empirical evaluation of adversarial robustness and also applicable to many different types of classifiers. We base our selection of attacks on the recommendations by [5]. Specifically, we use the ℓ_2-attack proposed by [6] for ℓ_2 robustness curves and PGD [23] for ℓ_∞ robustness curves. For both attacks, we use the implementations of Foolbox [30]. In the following, "robustness curve" refers to this empirical approximation of the true robustness curve.

---

[3] The models trained with ST, KW, AT and MMR + AT are avaible at www.github.com/max-andr/provable-robustness-max-linear-regions.

[4] The models trained with MMR-UNIV are avaible at www.github.com/fra31/mmr-universal.

Table 1. Three point-wise measures for different threat models. All threat models use the ℓ_∞ distance function, but differ in choice of perturbation threshold (denoted by ε). Each row contains the robust test errors for one point-wise measure. Each column contains the robust test errors for one model, trained with a specific training method (marked by column title). The lower the number, the better the robustness for the specific threat model. Each point-wise measure results in a different relative ordering of the classifiers based on the errors. The order is visualized by different tones of gray in the background of the cells.

ε	ST	AT	KW	MMR + AT	MMR–UNIV
1/255	0.60	0.38	0.43	0.42	0.54
4/255	0.99	0.68	0.57	0.63	0.74
8/255	1.00	0.92	0.73	0.84	0.91

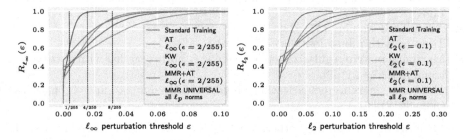

Fig. 2. ℓ_∞ robustness curves (left plot) and ℓ_2 robustness curves (right plot) resulting from different training methods (indicated by label), optimized for different threat models (indicated by label). The dashed vertical lines visualize the three point-wise measures from Table 1.

Point-wise measures are used to quantify robustness of classifiers by measuring the robust test error for a specific distance function and a perturbation threshold (eg., $\ell_\infty(\varepsilon = 4/255)$). In Table 1 we show three point-wise measures to compare the robustness of five different classifiers on CIFAR-10. If we compare the robustness of the four robust training methods (latter four columns of the table) based on the first point-wise threat model $\ell_\infty(\varepsilon = 1/255)$ (first row of the table), we can see that the classifier trained with AT is the most robust, followed by MMR + AT, followed by KW, and MMR–UNIV results in the least robust classifier. However, if we increase the ε of our threat model to $\varepsilon = 4/255$ (second row of the table), KW is more robust than AT. For a even larger ε (third row of the table), we would conclude that MMR–UNIV is preferable over AT, and that AT results in the least robust classifier. All three statements are true for the particular perturbation threshold (ε), and the magnitude of all perturbation thresholds is reasonable: publications on adversarial robustness typically evaluate CIFAR-10 on perturbation thresholds $\leq 10/255$ for ℓ_∞ perturbations. Meaningful conclusions

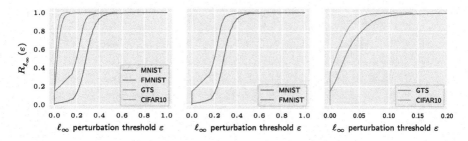

Fig. 3. ℓ_∞ robustness curves for multiple data sets. Each curve is calculated for a different model and a different test data set. The data sets are indicated by the labels. The models are trained with `MMR + AT`, Threat Models: `MNIST`: $\ell_\infty(\varepsilon = 0.1)$, `FMNIST`: $\ell_\infty(\varepsilon = 0.1)$, `GTS`: $\ell_\infty(\varepsilon = 4/255)$, `CIFAR-10`: $\ell_\infty(\varepsilon = 2/255)$. The curves for `MNIST` and `FMNIST` both show a change in slope, which can not be captured with point-wise measures and could be a sign of overfitting to the specific threat models for which the classifiers were optimized for.

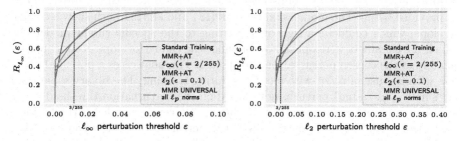

Fig. 4. ℓ_∞ robustness curves (left plot) and ℓ_2 robustness curves (right plot) resulting from different training methods (indicated by color and label), optimized for different threat models (indicated by label) on `CIFAR-10`.

on the robustness of the classifiers relative to each other can not be made without taking all possible ε into account.

A Global Perspective: Figure 2 shows the robustness of different classifiers for the ℓ_∞ (right plot) and ℓ_2 (left plot) distance functions from a global perspective using robustness curves. The plot reveals why the three point-wise measures (marked by vertical black dashed lines in the left plot) lead to different results in the relative ranking of robustness of the classifiers. Both for the classifiers trained to be robust against attacks in ℓ_∞ distance (left plot) and ℓ_2 distance (right plot), we can observe multiple intersections of robustness curves, corresponding to changes in the relative ranking of the robustness of the compared classifiers. Robustness curves, as opposed to point-wise measures, allow us to reliably compare the robustness of classifiers because they clearly show for which perturbation ranges robustness holds, and are not biased by an arbitrarily chosen perturbation threshold.

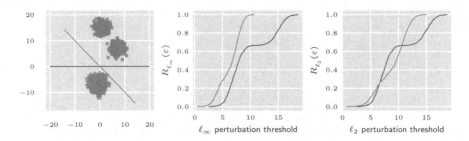

Fig. 5. Example of a data distribution and two linear classifiers such that the ℓ_2 robustness curves intersect, but not the ℓ_∞ robustness curves. (Color figure online)

Overfitting to Specific Perturbation Thresholds: In addition to the problem of robustness curve intersection, relying on point-wise robustness measures to evaluate adversarial robustness is prone to overfitting when designing training procedures. Figure 3 shows ℓ_∞ robustness curves for MMR + AT with ℓ_∞ threat model as provided by [9]. The models trained on MNIST and FMNIST both show a change in slope, which could be a sign of overfitting to the specific threat models for which the classifiers were optimized for, since the change of slope occurs approximately at the chosen perturbation threshold ε. This showcases a potential problem with the use of point-wise measures during training. The binary separation of "small" and "large" perturbations based on the perturbation threshold is not sufficient to capture the intricacies of human perception under perturbations, but a simplification based on the idea that perturbations below the perturbation threshold should almost certainly not lead to a change in classification. If a training procedure moves decision boundaries so that data points lie just beyond this threshold, it may achieve a low robust error, without furthering the actual goals of adversarial robustness research. Using robustness curves for evaluation cannot prevent this effect, but can be used to detect it.

Transfer of Robustness Across Distance Functions: In Fig. 4 we compare the robustness of different models for the ℓ_∞ (left plot) and ℓ_2 (right plot) distance functions. The difference to Fig. 2 is that the models (indicated by colour) are the same models in the left plot and in the right plot. We find that for MMR + AT, the ℓ_∞ threat model leads to better robustness than the ℓ_2 threat model *both* for ℓ_∞ *and* ℓ_2 robustness curves. In fact, MMR + AT with the ℓ_∞ threat model even leads to better ℓ_∞ and ℓ_2 robustness curves than MMR–UNIV, which is specifically designed to improve robustness for all ℓ_p norms. Overall, the plots are visually similar. However, since both plots contain multiple robustness curve intersections, the ranking of methods remains sensitive to the choice of perturbation threshold. For example, a perturbation threshold of $\varepsilon = 3/255$ (vertical black dashed line) for the ℓ_∞ distance function (left subplot) shows that the classifier trained with MMR + AT $(\ell_2(\varepsilon = 0.1))$ is approximately as robust as the classifier trained with MMR–UNIV. The same perturbation threshold for the ℓ_2 distance function (right subplot) shows that the classifier trained with MMR + AT is more robust than the classifier trained with MMR–UNIV for ℓ_2 threat models. Using typical perturbation

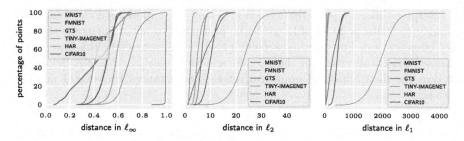

Fig. 6. Empirical inter-class distance distributions, measured in ℓ_∞, ℓ_2, and ℓ_1 norm.

thresholds from the literature for each distance function does not alleviate this issue: At perturbation threshold $\varepsilon = 2/255$ for ℓ_∞ distance, the classifier trained with MMR + AT ($\ell_2(\varepsilon = 0.1)$) is more robust than the one trained with MMR-UNIV, while at perturbation threshold $\varepsilon = 0.1$ for ℓ_2 distance, the opposite is true. This shows that even when robustness curves across various distance functions are qualitatively similar, this may be obscured by the choice of threat model(s) to compare on (Fig. 6).

For linear classifiers, the *shape* of ℓ_p robustness curves is the same for all p [12]. However, even for linear classifiers, robustness curve *intersections* do not transfer between distances induced by different ℓ_p norms. That is, for two linear classifiers, there may exist p, p' such that the robustness curves for the ℓ_p distance intersect, but not the robustness curves for the $\ell_{p'}$ distance.

Example: To see that robustness curve intersections do not transfer between different ℓ_p norms, consider the example in Fig. 5. The blue and orange linear classifiers both perfectly separate the displayed data. The ℓ_∞ robustness curves of the classifiers do not intersect, meaning that the robust error of the blue classifier is always better than that of the orange classifier. In ℓ_2 distance, the robustness curves intersect, so that there is a range of perturbation sizes where the orange classifier has better robust error than the blue classifier.

3.1   On the Relationship Between Scale and Data

As the previous sections show, robustness curves can be used to reveal properties of robust models that may be obscured by point-wise measures. However, some concept of scale, that is, some way to judge whether a perturbation is small or large, remains necessary. *Especially* when robustness curves intersect, it is crucial to be able to judge how critical it is for a model to be stable under the given perturbations. For many pairs of distance function and data set, canonical perturbation thresholds have emerged in the literature, but to the best of our knowledge, no reasons for these choices are given.

Since the assumption behind adversarial examples is that small perturbations should not affect classification behavior, the question of scale cannot be answered independently of the data distribution. In order to understand how to interpret different perturbation sizes, it can be helpful to understand how strongly the data point would need to be perturbed to *actually* change the *correct* classification. For each data point (x, y), we approximate this *inter-class distance* empirically over the data set S by $\min_{(x',y')\in S:y'\neq y} d(x, x')$. Below, we analyze the distribution of empirical inter-class distances for several popular data sets.

Table 2. Smallest and largest inter-class distances for subsets of several data sets, measured in l_∞, l_2, and l_1 norm, together with basic contextual information about the data sets. All data has been normalized to lie within the interval $[0, 1]$, and duplicates and corrupted data points (samples in TINY-IMG containing NaN elements) have been removed. Apart from HAR, all data sets contain images – the dimensionality reported specifies their sizes and number of channels.

| | | | | Inter-class distance | | | | | |
| | | | | Smallest | | | Largest | | |
Dataset	Samples	Classes	Dimensionality	l_∞	l_2	l_1	l_∞	l_2	l_1
MNIST	10 000	10	$28 \times 28 \times 1$	0.88	3.03	19.16	1.00	10.18	132.38
TINY-IMG	98 139	200	$64 \times 64 \times 3$	0.27	5.24	369.29	0.71	47.49	4184.37
FMNIST	10 000	10	$28 \times 28 \times 1$	0.36	2.00	24.87	1.00	10.70	194.29
GTS	10 000	43	$32 \times 32 \times 3$	0.07	0.90	31.46	0.62	19.54	833.22
CIFAR-10	10 000	10	$32 \times 32 \times 3$	0.27	3.61	130.77	0.70	18.57	831.44
HAR	2947	6	561	0.26	1.26	12.95	0.87	4.29	73.19

In Table 2, we summarize the smallest and largest inter-class distances in different norms together with additional information about the size, number of classes, and dimensionality of the all the data sets we consider in this work. Compare, for example, MNIST and GTS: While it appears reasonable to expect ℓ_∞ robustness of 0.3 for MNIST, the same threshold for GTS is not possible. Relating Table 2 and Fig. 3, we find entirely plausible the strong robustness results for MNIST, and the small perturbation threshold for GTS. Based on inter-class distances we also expect less ℓ_∞ robustness for CIFAR-10 than for FMNIST, but not as seen in Fig. 3. In any case, it is safe to say that, when judging the robustness of a model by a certain threshold, that number must be set with respect to the distribution the model operates on. Overall, the strong dependence of robustness curves on the data set and the chosen norm, emphasizes the necessity of informed and conscious decisions regarding robustness thresholds. We provide an easily accessible reference in the form of Table 2, that should prove useful while judging scales in a threat model.

4 Discussion

We have demonstrated that comparisons of robustness of different classifiers using point-wise measures can be heavily biased by the choice of perturbation threshold and distance function of the threat model, and that conclusions about rankings of classifiers with regards to their robustness based on point-wise measures therefore only provide a narrow view of the actual robustness behavior of the classifiers. Further, we have demonstrated different ways of using robustness curves to overcome the shortcomings of point-wise measures, and therefore recommend using them as the standard tool for comparing the robustness of classifiers. Finally, we have demonstrated how suitable perturbation thresholds necessarily depend on the data they pertain to. It is our hope that practitioners and researchers alike will use the methodology proposed and the code provided in this work, especially when developing and comparing adversarial defenses, and carefully motivate any concrete threat models they might choose, taking into account all available context.

References

1. Alayrac, J.-B., Uesato, J., Huang, P.-S., Fawzi, A., Stanforth, R., Kohli, P.: Are labels required for improving adversarial robustness? In: NeurIPS (2019)
2. Anguita, D., Ghio, A., Oneto, L., Parra, X., Reyes-Ortiz, J.: A public domain dataset for human activity recognition using smartphones. In: ESANN (2013)
3. Boopathy, A., et al.: Proper network interpretability helps adversarial robustness in classification. In: ICML (2020)
4. Brendel, W., Rauber, J., Kümmerer, M., Ustyuzhaninov, I., Bethge, M.: Accurate, reliable and fast robustness evaluation. In: NeurIPS (2019)
5. Carlini, N., et al.: On evaluating adversarial robustness (2019). arXiv: 1902.06705
6. Carlini, N., Wagner, D.A.: Towards evaluating the robustness of neural networks. In: 2017 IEEE Symposium on Security and Privacy (SP) (2017)
7. Carmon, Y., Raghunathan, A., Schmidt, L., Liang, P., Duchi, J.C.: Unlabeled data improves adversarial robustness. In: NeurIPS (2019)
8. Cohen, J., Rosenfeld, E., Kolter, Z.: Certified adversarial robustness via randomized smoothing. In: ICML (2019)
9. Croce, F., Andriushchenko, M., Hein, M.: Provable robustness of ReLU networks via maximization of linear regions. In: PMLR (2019)
10. Croce, F., Hein, M.: Provable robustness against all adversarial l_p-perturbations for p ≥ 1. In: International Conference on Learning Representations (2020)
11. Goodfellow, I.J., Shlens, J., Szegedy, C.: Explaining and harnessing adversarial examples. In: 3rd International Conference on Learning Representations (2015)
12. Göpfert, C., Göpfert, J.P., Hammer, B.: Adversarial robustness curves. In: Machine Learning and Knowledge Discovery in Databases (2020)
13. Göpfert, J.P., Artelt, A., Wersing, H., Hammer, B.: Adversarial attacks hidden in plain sight. In: Symposium on Intelligent Data Analysis (2020)
14. Guo, C., Rana, M., Cisse, M., van der Maaten, L.: Countering adversarial images using input transformations (2017). arXiv: 1711.00117
15. Hein, M., Andriushchenko, M.: Formal guarantees on the robustness of a classifier against adversarial manipulation (2017). arXiv: 1705.08475

16. Hendrycks, D., Mazeika, M., Kadavath, S., Song, D.: Using self-supervised learning can improve model robustness and uncertainty. In: NeurIPS (2019)
17. Houben, S., Stallkamp, J., Salmen, J., Schlipsing, M., Igel, C.: Detection of traffic signs in real-world images: the german traffic sign detection benchmark. In: IJCNN (2013)
18. Krizhevsky, A.: Learning multiple layers of features from tiny images. Technical report (2009)
19. Lecuyer, M., Atlidakis, V., Geambasu, R., Hsu, D., Jana, S.: Certified robustness to adversarial examples with differential privacy. In: 2019 IEEE Symposium on Security and Privacy (SP) (2019)
20. Lee, G.-H., Yuan, Y., Chang, S., Jaakkola, T.: Tight certificates of adversarial robustness for randomly smoothed classifiers. In: NeurIPS (2019)
21. Li, B., Chen, C., Wang, W., Carin, L.: Certified adversarial robustness with additive noise. In: NeurIPS (2019)
22. Li, F.-F., Karpathy, A., Johnson, J.: CS231n: convolutional neural networks for visual recognition (2016). http://cs231n.stanford.edu/2016/project.html. Accessed 28 Mar 2020
23. Madry, A., Makelov, A., Schmidt, L., Tsipras, D., Vladu, A.: Towards deep learning models resistant to adversarial attacks. In: ICLR (2018)
24. Mahloujifar, S., Zhang, X., Mahmoody, M., Evans, D.: Empirically measuring concentration: fundamental limits on intrinsic robustness. In: NeurIPS (2019)
25. Maini, P., Wong, E., Kolter, Z.: Adversarial robustness against the union of multiple threat models. In: ICML (2020)
26. Mao, C., Zhong, Z., Yang, J., Vondrick, C., Ray, B.: Metric learning for adversarial robustness. In: NeurIPS (2019)
27. Najafi, A., Maeda, S.-I., Koyama, M., Miyato, T.: Robustness to adversarial perturbations in learning from incomplete data. In: NeurIPS (2019)
28. Pinot, R., et al.: Theoretical evidence for adversarial robustness through randomization. In: NeurIPS (2019)
29. Qin, C., et al.: Adversarial robustness through local linearization. In: NeurIPS (2019)
30. Rauber, J., Brendel, W., Bethge, M.: Foolbox: a Python toolbox to benchmark the robustness of machine learning models (2017). arXiv: 1707.04131
31. Rice, L., Wong, E., Kolter, Z.: Overfitting in adversarially robust deep learning. In: ICML (2020)
32. Singla, S., Feizi, S.: Second-order provable defenses against adversarial attacks. In: ICML (2020)
33. Song, C., He, K., Lin, J., Wang, L., Hopcroft, J.E.: Robust local features for improving the generalization of adversarial training. In: ICLR (2020)
34. Szegedy, C., et al.: Intriguing properties of neural networks (2014). arXiv: 1312.6199
35. Tramer, F., Boneh, D.: Adversarial training and robustness for multiple perturbations. In: NeurIPS (2019)
36. Wang, Y., Zou, D., Yi, J., Bailey, J., Ma, X., Gu, Q.: Improving adversarial robustness requires revisiting misclassified examples. In: ICLR (2020)
37. Wong, E., Kolter, Z.: Provable defenses against adversarial examples via the convex outer adversarial polytope. In: ICML (2018)
38. Wong, E., Rice, L., Kolter, J.Z.: Fast is better than free: revisiting adversarial training. In: ICLR (2020)
39. Wong, E., Schmidt, F.R., Kolter, J.Z.: Wasserstein adversarial examples via projected Sinkhorn iterations. In: ICML (2019)

40. Xiao, H., Rasul, K., Vollgraf, R.: Fashion-MNIST: a novel image dataset for bench-marking machine learning algorithms (2017). arXiv: 1708.07747
41. Xie, C., Yuille, A.: Intriguing properties of adversarial training at scale. In: ICLR (2020)
42. Zhang, J., et al.: Attacks which do not kill training make adversarial learning stronger. In: ICML (2020)

Multiple-Model Based Defense for Deep Reinforcement Learning Against Adversarial Attack

Patrick P. K. Chan[1](✉), Yaxuan Wang[1], Natasha Kees[1], and Daniel S. Yeung[2]

[1] School of Computer Science and Engineering,
South China University of Technology, Guangzhou, China
patrickchan@scut.edu.cn
[2] IEEE SMC Society, Guangzhou, Hongkong

Abstract. Deep Reinforcement Learning models inherit not only generalization abilities but also vulnerabilities under adversarial attacks from Deep Neural Networks. The recent external model based defense method for Reinforcement Learning (RL) detects and corrects the action relying on only the observation prediction method. The observation prediction method may not perform well in complicated applications because of the knowledge of environment, which will downgrade the defense efficacy. This study proposes a multiple-model based defense method for RL which considers detection and correction tasks separately. Since the problem is broken down into two tasks, their complexity and difficulty is also lower, *i.e.,* a better performance is expected. We propose a Correlation Feature Map to extract the observation consistency in the temporal sequence which is destroyed by adversarial noise to separate clean and attacked states. Our correction only deal with the states classified as contaminated and maps them to proper actions. The performance of our proposed method is evaluated and compared to the state of the art method experimentally in various settings. The results confirm the superiority of our methods in terms of robustness and time.

Keywords: Adversarial learning · Reinforcement learning · Robustness

1 Introduction

Deep Neural Networks (DNNs) have been rapidly developed because of the excellent performance. However, many studies [5,16] show that DNNs are vulnerable in an adversarial environment in which an adversary may craft a sample in order to mislead a target system. Since Deep Reinforcement Learning (DRL) methods inherit the capabilities of DNNs, they have many landmark achievements

Supported by the Natural Science Foundation of Guangdong Province, China (No. 2018A030313203).

© Springer Nature Switzerland AG 2021
I. Farkaš et al. (Eds.): ICANN 2021, LNCS 12891, pp. 42–53, 2021.
https://doi.org/10.1007/978-3-030-86362-3_4

recently in various applications [11,12,15]. However, the vulnerability to adversarial samples of DNNs is also inherited by the DRL methods [3,7,9]. Recently, most of the discussions on adversarial attacks are in the framework of Supervised Learning which assumes samples are independent and identically distributed. However, this assumption does not apply to RL in which the consecutive states are closely related since they may share the same observations. As the setting of RL is different from Supervised Learning, the security of RL should be investigated separately. However, few studies focus on defense methods for RL. The influence of adversarial attacks is reduced by considering adversarial samples in training [8,14] using a robust loss function [4] or specially designed model structure [1,6], and using external models [10].

The defense methods using external models are focused in this study due to flexiblilty. To the best of our knowledge, there is only one defense method [10] in this type of defense. Both contamination detection and action correction of this method rely on an observation prediction model. We categorize this method as a single-model based defense method since both detection and correction only rely on one model, as shown in Fig. 1(a). The detection task is a simple comparison between the obtained state and corrected state, as shown in the green block. However, predicting an observation accurately in RL is difficult since comprehensive understanding of an environment is required. Unaccurate prediction will cause both incorrect detection and correction, *i.e.,* the mistakes will cumulate.

Our study devises a multiple-model based defense method for RL, shown in Fig. 1(b), which considers detection and correction tasks separately. Compared with a single-model based method, our multiple-model based method avoids the cumulation of mistakes in detection and correction tasks. In our detection model, a feature map named Correlation Feature Map (CFM) is proposed to extract the consistency of observations in the temporal sequence in a state in our detection method. The observation continuity is usually ignored when crafting an adversarial sample in recent attack methods as each state is modified independently. Therefore, the different patterns of observation continuity in clean and contaminated states are expected. Moreover, a correction method is devised in order to reduce the influence of the adversarial states. Since making a correct decision is the main objective, recovering an observation is difficult and unnecessary.

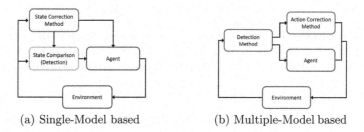

(a) Single-Model based   (b) Multiple-Model based

Fig. 1. Block diagrams of the Single-Model and Multiple-Model based Defense Method. (Color figure online)

Therefore, our method maps an attacked state to a correct decision directly. Simplicity is another advantage of our multiple-model based method compared to the single-model based one. As both detection and correction tasks are simpler than the observation prediction, a simpler model structure can be used. Not only a shorter training time but also a faster decision time is expected. Our proposed method is evaluated and compared experimentally with the state-of-the-art defense methods in three Atari games. Experimental results confirm the effectiveness of our proposed method in terms of robustness and speed, compared with the state-of-the-art defense methods.

The main contributions of this work are summarized as follows:

– A multiple-model based defense method combining detection and correction tasks against adversarial attacks in RL is proposed. It utilizes the accurate contamination detection to enhance the overall performance.
– The continuity of temporal observation sequence is captured by the proposed Correlation Feature Map in our detection model.
– A simple action correction method is proposed to reduce the impact of adversarial samples.
– Experimental results confirm the effectiveness of our method, compared with state-of-the-art methods.

2   Related Work

Adversarial Attack: Adversarial attack, sometimes called evasion attack [16], aims to reduce the performance of a model by manipulating samples in inference. Many studies prove that DNNs are sensitive to adversarial attacks [2,5,13,16]. In such attacks, it is assumed that samples in inference can be manipulated by a small change. Adversarial attacks against DRL mainly follow the idea of attacks in the Supervised Learning, $i.e.$, each sample is attacked independently. To be specific, an adversarial state $\tilde{s}$ is generated by an attack method A adding adversarial perturbation η to clean state s, $i.e.$, $\tilde{s} = A_\theta(s) = s + \eta$, where θ denotes the parameters of A. Fast Gradient Sign Method ($FGSM$) [5] is a common and famous $one\text{-}time\ attack$ due to its low time complexity. The adversarial perturbation is calculated by the gradient of the model function:

$$\eta = \epsilon * sign(\nabla_s J(\theta, s, a)) \tag{1}$$

where $J(\theta, s, a)$ denotes the cross-entropy loss, and ϵ controls the upper limit of the perturbation. Carlini & Wagner L2 ($CWL2$) [2], which optimizes a near-optimal adversarial state in terms of minimal adversarial perturbation:

$$minimize \quad \|\eta\|_2^2 + c * max(max\{\pi(s + \eta)_i : i \neq t\} - \pi(s + \eta)_t, -\kappa) \tag{2}$$

where $\pi()_i$ is the i-th output of the target RL policies π, κ controls the attack confidence.

Adversarial Defense: Some defense methods have been proposed in order to reduce the influence of adversarial attacks to RL models and can be divided into three categories: data modification, model modification and external models. Flexibility is a concern for both data and model modification methods, since retraining of the target model is required. The new models may perform worse than the original ones, especially when the attack is absent, *i.e.*, the general performance may be sacrificed for the robustness. As a result, our study focuses on the third type of defense methods which rely on external models. The only existing method using external models in RL Foresight [10] predicts the current observation x according to multiple historical observations and the last action by an action-conditioned observation prediction model. An observation considered contaminated based on whether or not it has a large difference from the predicted observation. The contaminated observation is then replaced by its predicted one for decision.

3   Analysis on Single-Model and Multiple-Model Based Defense

The performance analysis on single-model and multiple-model based defense is given in this section. We argue that a multiple-model based defense which contains the detection and correction models separately is able to achieve better performance. Let $p_{s,cor}$ be the accuracy of the only model used in a single-model based defense method, which quantifies the probability of corrected and original actions being the same. The defense accuracy of a single-model based method ACC_s is calculated as:

$$ACC_s = p_{s,cor} \tag{3}$$

On the other hand, let p_{det} and $p_{m,cor}$ be the detection and correction accuracy respectively for a multiple-model based defense method. Let α be the attack ratio defined as the probability of attack, *i.e.*, $\alpha \in [0,1]$. The detection model first determines whether a state is contaminated, and then the correction model corrects the contaminated states. The overall defense accuracy of the multiple model ACC_m is defined as:

$$ACC_m = (1 - \alpha) * p_{det} + \alpha * p_{det} * p_{m,cor} \tag{4}$$

We assume $p_{cor} = p_{s,cor} = p_{m,cor}$ for discussion since their corresponding tasks both aim at correcting actions. In other words, the model used in a single-model based method can be used in the correction task of multiple-model based defense. By considering Eq. (3) and (4), the following statement can be obtained:

$$p_{cor} \leq \frac{(1 - \alpha) * p_{det}}{1 - \alpha * p_{det}} \quad if \ and \ only \ if \quad ACC_m \geq ACC_s \tag{5}$$

Lines in Fig. 2 represents $ACC_m = ACC_s$ (*i.e.*, $p_{cor} = \frac{((1-\alpha)*p_{det})}{(1-\alpha*p_{det})}$) with $\alpha \in \{0, 0.01, 0.25, 0.5, 0.75, 0.99, 1\}$. Since the detection task is generally simpler than the correction task, it is reasonable to ignore the grey-triangle region ($p_{cor} \geq p_{det}$). By considering the triangle area under the diagonal, the area below and

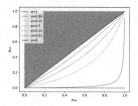

Fig. 2. Values of p_{cor} and p_{det} when $ACC_s = ACC_m$ with different α.

above the line $ACC_m = ACC_s$ are denoted by A_b and A_a respectively. A_b contains (p_{det}, p_{cor}) pairs which cause $ACC_m > ACC_s$, while A_a contains the ones which cause $ACC_m > ACC_s$. The size of A_b is much larger than A_a when $alpha$ tends to 0. This means that even slight improvement of p_{det} from p_{cor} will cause $ACC_m > ACC_s$. A_b/A_a decreases with the increase of α. When α tends to 1, A_b tends to 0. This analysis indicates that multiple-model based defense is more suitable to deal with attacks with smaller attack ratio compared with the single one. Moreover, the multiple-model based method prefers the situation in which the detection accuracy is much larger than the correction accuracy.

By considering the the partial derivative of ACC_m with respect to p_{det} and p_{cor}, p_{det} plays a more important role than p_{cor} in the performance of a multiple-method based model when α is smaller:

$$if \; \Delta p \leq \frac{1}{\alpha} - 1, \quad then \; \frac{\partial ACC_m}{\partial p_{det}} \geq \frac{\partial ACC_m}{\partial p_{cor}} \tag{6}$$

where $\Delta p = p_{det} - p_{cor}$. When α is smaller, $1/\alpha - 1$ is larger. It implies the chance of satisfying that the hypothesis (*i.e.*, $1/\alpha - 1 \geq \Delta p$) is higher. As a result, when the attack rate is smaller, p_{det} plays a more important role in the multiple-method based model than p_{cor}, and vice versa. As attacked states are the minority in reality, the detection performance is more important in a defense method. Therefore, the main contribution of our proposed defense method focuses on the detection method, which is discussed in next section.

4   Proposed Approach

The defense methods using external models are investigated in our study since they can be applied to any RL model without retraining. As discussed in the previous session, a multiple-model based defense method is more efficient than a single-method based one. A multiple-model based defense, including the detection and action correction models are proposed for RL. Our proposed method detects a contaminated state according to the correlation between observations in a state since the continuity of consecutive observations in a state is destroyed by the adversarial perturbation. The continuity of consecutive observations in a state is extracted by the proposed Correlation Feature Map (CFM). The decision on a clean state is then made by the original RL model, while a contaminated state is handled by our correction model.

4.1 Detection Model

A state containing a number of consecutive observations captures the responses of the environment in a sequence of time. However, most adversarial attack methods do not consider time continuity when crafting adversarial samples. As a result, the original distribution of observations in an adversarial state is disturbed, *i.e.*, the observations in adversarial states follow different distributions with ones in clean states.

Our detection method aims to capture the difference of observation distributions between adversarial and clean states. A state s_t at time t is defined as the stack of N consecutive observations in RL, *i.e.*, $s_t = \phi(x_{t-(N-1)}, ..., x_{t-1}, x_t)$, where $\phi()$ denotes a stacking function. The feature map of each observation of a state is first extracted independently based on the target DRL model. To extract the information from x_i, a state s_t^i is generated by setting all values in s_t to zero except the ones in x_i:

$$s_t^i = \phi(O, ..., O, x_i, O..., O) \tag{7}$$

where O is a zero matrix with the size of an observation. The feature map defined as the output of the m-th layer of the DRL model is then extracted for s_t^i. This setting preserves the information in x_i while ignoring the other observations. We propose the Correlation Feature Map (CFM) defined as the stack of the feature maps of all s_t^i in s_t, shown in Eq. (8). Figure 3 shows the CFM generation.

$$\text{CFM}(s_t) = \phi(f_m(s_t^{t-(N-1)}), ..., f_m(s_t^{t-1}), f_m(s_t^t))) \tag{8}$$

where $f_m()$ is defined as the feature map extracting function of the m-th layer of the target RL model. The last convolutional layer is chosen as f_m in this study since it preserves spatial information and contains more abstract features compared to other layers.

Finally, a detection model g_{det} is trained to distinguish clean states from adversarial ones based on their CFM difference. A dataset $\mathcal{D}$ containing clean states s and adversarial states $\tilde{s}$ is generated in advance. The clean states s are collected randomly from the interaction between the target RL model and environment. For each clean state s, corresponding adversarial state $\tilde{s}$ is crafted according to an attack method with particular parameters. A simple network

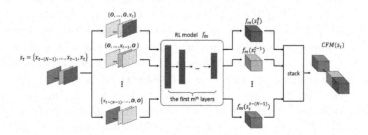

Fig. 3. Generation of Correlation Feature Map function (CFM)

structure of g_{det} should be used since the CFM are already extracted by the RL model. The structure consisting of two convolutional layers and four fully-connected layers is used in this study. All the convolutional layers have 512 channels with kernel size 3 * 3 and stride 1, while the sizes of fully-connected layers are 1024, 128, 16 and 1. The batch normalization is implemented after the first convolutional layer. The loss function is

$$L_{det} = -\log(h(\text{CFM}(\tilde{s}))) - \log(1 - h(\text{CFM}(s))) \tag{9}$$

where $h(a) = 1/[1 + exp(-g_{det}(a))]$. When detecting a new state s, its CFM is input to the detection model, *i.e.*, $g_{det}(\text{CFM}(s))$. If the output is larger than 0, s is classified as an attacked state; otherwise, it is clean.

4.2   Correction Model

This section devises an action correction model $\pi_{cor} : s \rightarrow a$ mapping an adversarial state $\tilde{s}$ to the decision made by the target model π on s, *i.e.*, $\pi_{cor}(\tilde{s}) = \pi(s)$. The model only handles the states classified as contaminated, which makes the correction task simpler since the characteristics of clean and contaminated states are different. The corrected action is then used to interact with the environment. Our correction model is trained by minimizing the following regression loss using s and $\tilde{s}$ in $\mathcal{D}$:

$$L_{cor} = \|\pi_{\text{cor}}(\tilde{s}) - \pi(s)\|_2 \tag{10}$$

The learning of π_{cor} is guided by the output of π on s. The structure of π_{cor} is set as the same as π since their tasks are similar. In order to take advantage of the feature extraction ability of π, its parameters are applied to initialize π_{cor}.

5   Experiment

5.1   Experimental Setting

Three Atari games (Freeway, MsPacman and Seaquest) are considered. DQN is used as the target agent, and all the settings follow [12]. The program codes will be available when the paper is accepted. Two popular adversarial attack methods, *FGSM* and *CWL2*, are used. Different attack parameters are considered, *i.e.*, $\epsilon = \{1, 2, ..., 10\}$ for *FGSM* and $\kappa = \{0, 1, ..., 10\}$ for *CWL2*. *Baseline* which contains only DQN but no defense method is considered for comparison. *Ours_A* represents our model trained with D contaminated by attack method A, *i.e.*, *Ours_FGSM* and *Ours_CWL2*. In D, 10,000 clean states are collected, and corresponding adversarial states generated with random attack parameters from the range mentioned above. The attack ratio α is 0.5. Our detection and correction models are trained for 50 and 200 epochs respectively. *Foresight* [10], *AT* [8], and *Noisy* [1] are used for comparison. All the settings follow the original papers.

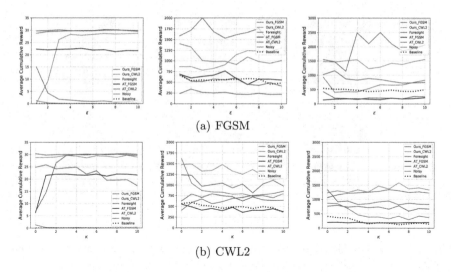

(a) FGSM

(b) CWL2

Fig. 4. Average cumulative reward of *baseline* and the defense methods. From left to right: Freeway, MsPacman, and Seaquest

5.2 Defense Performance

The performance of our proposed defense method and the other three methods are discussed in this section. Figure 4 shows the average cumulative reward of defense methods under *FGSM* and *CWL2* attacks with different parameters. When the attack methods in training and inference are the same, our methods perform significantly better than other all methods, except *Foresight* in Freeway. Our methods perform slightly worse than *Foresight* in Freeway. *Foresight* has excellent performance in Freeway but not in MsPacman and Seaquest, because the environment of Freeway is the simplest. Even when the attack methods used in training and inference are different, the performance of our methods is still satisfying. These results confirm the efficacy of our defense method against adversarial attacks. Although the knowledge on the attack strategy may be inaccurate, its performance is still consistently reasonable.

5.3 Transferability on Attack Parameters

This section discusses the transferability of our defense method across attack parameters used in the training and inference phases. Three levels of attack parameters are defined for each attack method according to the intensity: low, middle and high, which are $\epsilon \in [1, 3], [4, 6], [8, 10]$ for *FGSM*, and $\kappa \in [0, 2]$, $[4, 6]$, $[8, 10]$ for *CWL2*. Figure 5 shows the performance of our model training with one attack level under different levels. Better defense performance yields a higher average cumulative reward, which is illustrated by a darker color. The cells in the diagonal, representing that same parameter settings are used in both training and inference, achieve the largest rewards. Our method has the best

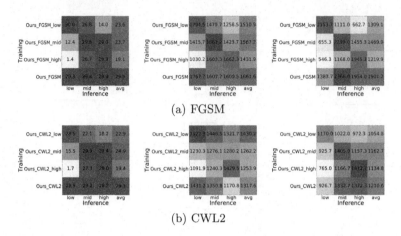

Fig. 5. Average cumulative reward of our method with different level of attack parameter. From left to right: Freeway, MsPacman, and Seaquest

performance when the full knowledge on the attack is obtained. On the other hand, more different attack settings used in training and inference reduces the efficacy of our method more significantly. For example, the reward achieved by the model using HIGH is lower than the ones using MID and LOW when the attack is using LOW in inference. When the real attack parameters are unknown, using weaker attack parameters is preferable. Regarding to the models trained with MID, its performance under HIGH is better than the one under LOW.

5.4   Performance on Detection Task

The detection performance of our method is discussed and compared with *Foresight* in this section. For each attack method, a test set consists of 10,000 clean states and 10,000 adversarial states. The experimental results are shown in Table 1. The largest accuracy in a column is bolded. Our method achieves excellent performance in detection compared with *Foresight*. Accuracy of our detection model is larger than *Foresight* in all cases no matter which attack method is used in training, except Freeway under *FGSM*. Accuracy of our method using the same attack method in training and inference is higher than 95% in all settings, while it is higher than 83% when the attack methods are different. The performance of our method drops when different attack methods are used in training and inference. Accuracy of *Ours_CWL2* is higher than *Ours_FGSM* under both attack methods. One possible explanation is adversarial samples generated by *CWL2* are more various than *FGSM*. On the other hand, the observation prediction in *Foresight* is inaccurate when the applications are complicated, *e.g.*, MsPacman and Seaquest.

Table 1. Detection accuracy (%).

(a) FGSM

	Freeway	MsPacman	Seaquest
Foresight	**99.99**	53.27	59.82
Ours_FGSM	99.77	**99.33**	**99.11**
Ours_CWL2	87.95	92.01	92.22

(b) CWL2

	Freeway	MsPacman	Seaquest
Foresight	95.18	66.56	72.63
Ours_FGSM	95.55	85.28	83.80
Ours_CWL2	**95.63**	**98.04**	**96.23**

Table 2. Correction accuracy on adversarial samples (%).

(a) FGSM

	Freeway	MsPacman	Seaquest
Foresight	**91.16**	**45.28**	29.61
Ours_FGSM	90.61	43.47	**30.79**
Ours_CWL2	67.21	38.11	15.57

(b) CWL2

	Freeway	MsPacman	Seaquest
Foresight	**89.74**	41.79	22.27
Ours_FGSM	44.27	37.45	14.31
Ours_CWL2	88.46	**47.46**	**22.92**

5.5 Performance on Correction Task

The performance on adversarial samples of the correction task is shown in Table 2. Our method and *Foresight* are evaluated by the probability of actions in clean states and corrected actions being the same. Since our correction model only deals with attacked states, only accuracy on adversarial samples is considered. Also, the results show that *Foresight* has similar accuracy on clean and adversarial samples. Our correction model performs similarly with *Foresight* when the same attack methods are considered in training and inference, *i.e.,* the accuracy difference is less than 5% in most cases. Although the accuracy of our correction is lower than *Foresight* when using different attack methods in training and inference, the overall performance of our defense method is still higher due to our better detection performance. This confirms the superiority of the multiple-model based defense compared with the single one, which is consistent with the analysis in Sect. 3. Also, similar to the results found in last discussion, the correction performance of *Foresight* highly relies on the complexity of the environment.

5.6 Influence of Attack Ratios

This section investigates the influence of the attack ratio α on the performance of our method and *Foresight*. Figure 6 show the average cumulative reward under *FGSM* with $\epsilon = 5$ when $\alpha = \{0.1, 0.2, ..., 0.9\}$ respectively. It shows in general, a larger α causes a smaller average cumulative reward. The reward decreases faster when attack methods in training and inference are different for our method. From the results shown in Table 1, the detection accuracy of our method when using different attack methods in training and inference is close to the one using the same attack methods. However, the correction accuracy of these two situations are much different, shown in Table 2. On the other hand, the performance of

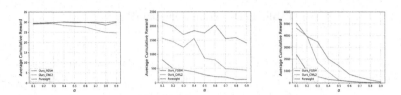

Fig. 6. Average cumulative reward with different levels of attack ratio α.

Foresight is more stable than our methods since its performance on both clean and contaminated states is similar. Moreover, the advantages of our method using different attack methods reduce compared to *Foresight* with the increase of α. This confirms the discussion in Sect. 3.

5.7 Time Complexity

The average training times in MsPacman are 7.8, 17.9, 18.5 and 53.0 h for our method, *Foresight*, *AT* and *Noisy* respectively. It show that our method require the shortest training time, *i.e.*, average 7.8 h although our model contains the RL agent, detection and correction models. This may be because our detection and correction models have relatively simple structures. *Noisy* needs the longest training time since the revised RL model is more complicated than the original one. The training time of *AT* and *Foresight* are more than double of our method because of retraining. On the other hand, the average inference times are 10.2, 16.2, 0.7 and 0.7 ms respectively. The inference time of *AT* and *Noisy* is the shortest among all methods since they do not rely on an external model. Our time is shorter than *Foresight* because of the simpler network structure.

6   Conclusion

The robustness of single-model based methods, *e.g.*, Foresight, relies on the accuracy of the state correction process, which is usually a difficult task since comprehensive understanding of the environment is required. Therefore, single-model based methods may not be suitable for complicated applications. A multiple-model based defense method containing the detection and correction tasks is proposed in this study. Since the complexity of these tasks is lower, a simpler model can be used and also better performance is expected. Our method distinguishes attacked states from clean states by using the proposed Correlation Feature Map (CFM) which captures the observation consistence in the temporal sequence of a state. The decision on an attacked state is made by our action correction method mapping an attacked state to its original action. All the experimental results illustrate that our proposed defense method achieves excellent performance and outperforms the other methods in terms of robustness and running time. This study provides a foundation for developing secure RL systems.

References

1. Behzadan, V., Munir, A.: Mitigation of policy manipulation attacks on deep q-networks with parameter-space noise. In: Computer Safety, Reliability, and Security - SAFECOMP 2018 Workshops, vol. 11094, pp. 406–417 (2018)
2. Carlini, N., Wagner, D.A.: Towards evaluating the robustness of neural networks (2017)
3. Chan, P.P., Wang, Y., Yeung, D.S.: Adversarial attack against deep reinforcement learning with static reward impact map. In: Proceedings of the 15th ACM Asia Conference on Computer and Communications Security, pp. 334–343 (2020)
4. Gallego, V., Naveiro, R., Insua, D.R.: Reinforcement learning under threats. In: Proceedings of the 33rd AAAI Conference on Artificial Intelligence, pp. 9939–9940 (2019)
5. Goodfellow, I.J., Shlens, J., Szegedy, C.: Explaining and harnessing adversarial examples. In: Proceedings of the 3rd International Conference on Learning Representations (2015)
6. Havens, A.J., Jiang, Z., Sarkar, S.: Online robust policy learning in the presence of unknown adversaries. In: Proceedings of the 2018 Annual Conference on Neural Information Processing Systems, pp. 9938–9948 (2018)
7. Huang, S., Papernot, N., Goodfellow, I., Duan, Y., Abbeel, P.: Adversarial attacks on neural network policies. arXiv preprint arXiv:1702.02284 (2017)
8. Kos, J., Song, D.: Delving into adversarial attacks on deep policies. In: Proceedings of the 5th International Conference on Learning Representations (2017)
9. Lin, Y.C., Hong, Z.W., Liao, Y.H., Shih, M.L., Liu, M.Y., Sun, M.: Tactics of adversarial attack on deep reinforcement learning agents. arXiv preprint arXiv:1703.06748 (2017)
10. Lin, Y.C., Liu, M.Y., Sun, M., Huang, J.B.: Detecting adversarial attacks on neural network policies with visual foresight. arXiv preprint arXiv:1710.00814 (2017)
11. Mnih, V., et al.: Asynchronous methods for deep reinforcement learning. In: International Conference on Machine Learning, pp. 1928–1937 (2016)
12. Mnih, V., et al.: Human-level control through deep reinforcement learning. Nature **518**(7540), 529–533 (2015)
13. Moosavi-Dezfooli, S., Fawzi, A., Frossard, P.: DeepFool: a simple and accurate method to fool deep neural networks. In: Proceedings of the 2016 IEEE Conference on Computer Vision and Pattern Recognition, pp. 2574–2582 (2016)
14. Pattanaik, A., Tang, Z., Liu, S., Bommannan, G., Chowdhary, G.: Robust deep reinforcement learning with adversarial attacks. In: Proceedings of the 17th International Conference on Autonomous Agents and MultiAgent Systems, pp. 2040–2042 (2018)
15. Silver, D., et al.: Mastering the game of go with deep neural networks and tree search. Nature **529**(7587), 484–489 (2016)
16. Szegedy, C., et al.: Intriguing properties of neural networks. arXiv preprint arXiv:1312.6199 (2013)

Neural Paraphrase Generation with Multi-domain Corpus

Lin Qiao$^{(\boxtimes)}$, Yida Li, and ChenLi Zhong

Peking University, Beijing, China
1801210620@pku.edu.cn

Abstract. Automatic paraphrase generation is an important task for natural language processing. However, progress in paraphrase generation has been hindered for a long time by the lack of large monolingual parallel corpora. We can alleviate the data shortage by effectively using multi-domain corpus. In this paper, we propose a novel model to exploit information from other source domains (out-of-domains) which benefits our target domain (in-domain). In our method, we maintain a private encoder and a private decoder for each domain which are used to model domain-specific information. In the meantime, we introduce a shared encoder and a shared decoder shared by all domains which only contain domain-independent information. Besides, we add a domain discriminator to the shared encoder to reinforce the ability to capture common features of shared encoder by adversarial training. Experimental results show that our method not only perform well in traditional domain adaptation tasks but also improve performance in all domains together. Moreover, we show that the shared layer learned by our proposed model can be regarded as an off-the-shelf layer and can be easily adapted to new domains.

Keywords: Paraphrase generation · Adversarial training

1 Introduction

Paraphrases refer to texts that convey the same meaning but with different expressions. Paraphrase generation is very important in many Natural Language Processing (NLP) applications such as information retrieval, information extraction, question answering, summarization and data augmentation. Deep learning theory formulate paraphrase generation as a Seq2Seq task and achieve better performance than traditional symbolic approaches. [4,6,10] apply deep learning theory to paraphrase generation task and made great progress. However, they all have the limitation that must rely on large-scale monolingual parallel data in a specific domain. The performances of their models will greatly degrade when there is no enough data in target domain, which greatly reduces the generalization ability of their models. Suppose we want to generate paraphrase in a target domain (such as novel domain). However, we often find that there is very little supervised data in our target novel domain due to the difficulty of obtaining parallel paraphrase. But we maybe have some sufficient data in some other domains

© Springer Nature Switzerland AG 2021
I. Farkaš et al. (Eds.): ICANN 2021, LNCS 12891, pp. 54–66, 2021.
https://doi.org/10.1007/978-3-030-86362-3_5

(such as news, or some public benchmark datasets). If we directly train the model with other domains data, the performance of model in the target domain will be poor. So we need to find a way to efficiently use datasets in other domains. Unsupervised paraphrase generation methods can solve the lack of parallel data problem to some extent, but [11] conclude that access to parallel data is still advantageous for paraphrase generation compared with unsupervised method. So it is of significant importance to explore paraphrase generation methods with multi-domain parallel corpus.

To this end, in this paper we propose a novel neural network model to generate paraphrases with multi-domain data. We employ a shared encoder and decoder among all the domains as well as a private encoder and decoder for each domain separately. The private encoder-decoder has direct influence to the generation and shared encoder-decoder serves as a supplement. This architecture is based on the consideration that out-of-domain data still embodies useful common knowledge shared between all the domains and incorporating this kind of information can help to generate target domain paraphrases. Inspired by [3] theory, which suggests that effective domain transfer must be made based on features that cannot discriminate between the in-domain and out-of-domains. So we attach a domain discriminator to the shared encoder and implement adversarial training between shared encoder and domain discriminator. Adversarial training force the shared encoder only to capture the domain invariant characteristic of the input sentences, which is useful for our target domain. Under the framework of our method, the paraphrase generation of each domain is predicted on the output of both the shared decoder and its corresponding private decoder. Experiments prove that our method consistently outperform all the baselines whether there are sufficient in-domain training data or not. Besides, we demonstrate that the well-trained shared encoder-decoder can generate domain-invariant representations, which can be considered as off-the-shelf knowledge and then used for unseen new domains.

2 Related Work

The task of multi-domain paraphrase generation aims to improve the result for each domain. Our work is most relevant to paraphrase generation and multi-task learning, which use some method to generate paraphrase and introduce other domain's information to help each domain's inner generation process.

Recent years, the application of deep learning models to paraphrase generation has been explored rigorously. [10] is one of the first major works that used deep architecture for paraphrase generation and introduce the residual recurrent neural networks. [4] use variational autoencoder (VAE) to generate multiple paraphrases for a given sentence, [6] learn word level and phrase level paraphrased pairs to generate paraphrases.

To make use of other domain parallel data, [14] select sentence pairs from the out-of-domain data set according to their similarity to the in-domain data and then add them to the in-domain training data. [15] combine the in-domain and out-of-domain data together as the training data but apply instance weighting to get a weight for each sentence pair in the out-of-domain data which is used in the parameter updating during back propagation.

3   Methodology

Before introducing our full method, we will first briefly describe our single encoder-decoder model with attention, which is a basic component of our full model.

3.1   Basic Encoder-Decoder Model

A neural approach to sequence to sequence modeling proposed by [13] is a model with two parts, where an input sequence is first encoded into some low dimensional representation that is later used to reproduce the sequence back to a high dimensional target sequence (i.e. decoding). Most of the deep learning models for NLP use Recurrent Neural Networks (RNNs). RNNs differ from normal perceptrons as they allow gradient propagation in time to model sequential data with variable-length input and output [12]. To avoid vanishing gradient problem for RNN, we use LSTM [5] as our basic architecture of encoder and decoder.

The Encoder uses LSTM to go through input words bidirectionally to get two hidden states $\overrightarrow{\mathbf{h}}_i$, $\overleftarrow{\mathbf{h}}_i$ for input word x_i, which are then concatenated to produce the final hidden states $\mathbf{h}_i = \left[\overrightarrow{\mathbf{h}}_i; \overleftarrow{\mathbf{h}}_i\right]$ for x_i.

The Attention Mechanism aims to extract weight distribution of each word in the input sentences, rather regarding them as the same. This allows the model to focus on parts of the input before producing each output token. First it evaluates the correlation between the previous decoder hidden state $\mathbf{s}_{i-1}$ and each source hidden state $\mathbf{h}_j$ by

$$e_{ij} = \mathbf{v}_\alpha^T \tanh\left(\mathbf{W}_\alpha \mathbf{s}_{i-1} + \mathbf{U}_\alpha \mathbf{h}_j\right)$$

Next, it calculates α_{ij} which is the correlation degree to each target hidden state h_j and then gets the attention c_j. The formulation is as follows

$$\alpha_{ij} = \frac{\exp\left(e_{ij}\right)}{\sum_{i'=1}^{l_s} \exp\left(e_{i'j}\right)}; \quad \mathbf{c}_j = \sum_{i=1}^{l_s} \alpha_{ij}\mathbf{h}_i$$

The Decoder also employs a LSTM to get the hidden state s_j for the target word y_j as

$$\mathbf{s}_j = g\left(y_{j-1}, \mathbf{s}_{j-1}, \mathbf{c}_j\right)$$

Then the probability of the target word y_j is defined as follows

$$p\left(y_j \mid \mathbf{s}_j, y_{j-1}, \mathbf{c}_j\right) \propto \exp\left(\mathbf{E}y_j^\top \mathbf{W}_o \mathbf{t}_j\right)$$

where t_j is computed by

$$\mathbf{t}_j = \mathbf{U}_o \mathbf{s}_{j-1} + \mathbf{V}_o \mathbf{E} y_{j-1} + \mathbf{C}_o \mathbf{c}_j$$

$\mathbf{U}_o$ $\mathbf{V}_o$ $\mathbf{C}_o$ are trainable parameters and $\mathbf{E}y_j$ is the embedding of y_j.

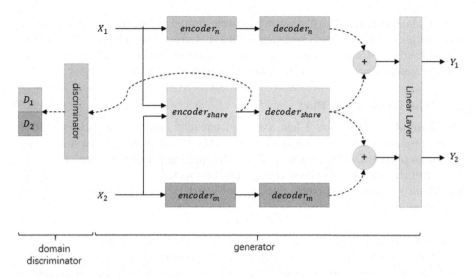

Fig. 1. The architecture of the full model. X_1, X_2 represent the input of the two domains, and Y_1, Y_2 represent the outputs. The output of shared encoder connects to a domain discriminator with a gradient reversal layer.

3.2 Full Model Architecture

Assume that $\mathcal{D}_1$ and $\mathcal{D}_2$ represent training datasets of two domains respectively,

$$\left\{\left(\mathbf{x}^k, \mathbf{y}^{*k}\right)\right\}_{k=1}^{N_1} \sim \mathcal{D}_1 \qquad\qquad \left\{\left(\mathbf{x}^k, \mathbf{y}^{*k}\right)\right\}_{k=1}^{N_2} \sim \mathcal{D}_2$$

where N_1, N_2 are the numbers of training data of the two domains, $\left(\mathbf{x}^k, \mathbf{y}^{*k}\right)$ is kth paraphrase pair. The main idea of our method is to extract domain invariant information from other domain data to improve target domain text generation. To this end, we employ a shared encoder-decoder model shared by both of the domains, and a private encoder-decoder for each domain. The main architecture is given in Fig. 1. In this paper, we use two private encoder-decoder models and one shared encoder-decode model. Encoder-decoder model has been described in the above section.

The working scenario of our method is as follows. A source sentence is input into the shared encoder and the private encoder of the corresponding domain simultaneously. Then the output of the shared encoder is fed into the shared decoder and the output of the private encoder into its corresponding private decoder. Finally, the shared decoder and the private decoder collaborate to generate the current target word with a gate to decide the contribution ratio.

In addition, to make the shared encoder only encodes domain invariant information, our method also introduce a discriminator to distinguish the domain of the input sentence based on the output of the shared encoder. When the discriminator cannot predict the domain of the input sentence, we can think the knowledge encoded in the shared encoder is domain invariant. This is achieved with a gradient reversal layer (GRL) so that the gradients are reversed during back-propagation.

The discriminator learns to distinguish between domains, but the encoder is forced to compute domain-invariant representations that are not useful to the discriminator, preventing it from making an accurate prediction. In this way, the adversarial training is performed between the generation part and the discriminator.

3.3 The Generation Part

The Encoder. Our model has a shared encoder and two private encoders, where the shared encoder accepts input from the two domains. Given a sentence of domain $\mathbf{p}$ ($\mathbf{p} \in \mathcal{D}_1, \mathcal{D}_2$), the shared encoder and the private encoder of domain $\mathbf{p}$ will roll the sentence as the encoder shown in Sect. 2.2 and the outputs of the shared encoder and the private encoder for word x_j are represented as $\mathbf{h}_j^c$ and $\mathbf{h}_j^p$ respectively.

The Attention Layer. As the output of the shared encoder is only fed to the shared decoder and the output of the private encoder of domain $\mathbf{p}$ only flows to the private decoder of domain $\mathbf{p}$, we only need to calculate the attention of the shared decoder over the shared encoder and the attention of the private decoder of domain $\mathbf{p}$ over the private encoder of domain $\mathbf{p}$. We calculate these two attentions as in Sect. 2.2 and denote them as $\mathbf{c}_j^c$ and $\mathbf{c}_j^p$ for the shared decoder and the private decoder, respectively

The Decoder. We also maintain a shared decoder and two private decoders corresponding to the two private encoders. For a sentence of domain $\mathbf{p}$ ($\mathbf{p} \in \mathcal{D}_1, \mathcal{D}_2$), the shared decoder and the private decoder of domain $\mathbf{p}$ produce the hidden states $\mathbf{s}_j^c$ and $\mathbf{t}_j^c$ for the shared decoder, and $\mathbf{s}_j^p$ and $\mathbf{t}_j^p$ for the private decoder. To predict the target word y_j, $\mathbf{t}_j^c$ and $\mathbf{t}_j^p$ are weighted added to get $\mathbf{t}_j$ as

$$z_j = \sigma \left(\mathbf{W}_z \mathbf{t}_j^c + \mathbf{U}_z \mathbf{t}_j^p \right)$$
$$\mathbf{t}_j = z_j \cdot \mathbf{t}_j^c + (1 - z_j) \cdot \mathbf{t}_j^p$$

Where $\sigma(\cdot)$ is the sigmoid function and $\mathbf{W}_z$ and $\mathbf{U}_z$ are learned parameters shared by the two private decoders. Finally the probability of the target word y_j is computed with

$$P(y_j \mid \dots) \propto \exp \left(y_j^\top \mathbf{W}_o \mathbf{t}_j \right)$$

3.4 Domain Discriminator

The domain discriminator serves as a text classification neural network. The discriminator uses encoded representation from the shared encoder of input sentence to predict the correct domain. When a well trained discriminator cannot classify the domain properly, we can think the knowledge in the shared encoder is domain invariant [3]. The output of domain discriminator can be described as:

$$d = \mathrm{softmax} \left(\mathbf{W} \mathbf{h}^k + \mathbf{b} \right)$$

where d is prediction probabilities of the kth sentence, $\mathbf{h}^k$ is the output of shared encoder, $\mathbf{W}$ is the weight which needs to be learned, and $\mathbf{b}$ is a bias term.

Gradient Reversal Layer. We introduce a special gradient reversal layer (GRL) between the shared encoder and the domain discriminator. The gradient reversal layer has no parameters associated with it. During forward propagation, the GRL has no influence to the model, while during back propagation training, it multiplies a certain negative constant *i.e*, multiplies it by -1, to the gradients back propagated from the discriminator to the shared encoder. In this way, GRL forces shared encoder to encode domain-independent representations.

3.5   Objective Function

Our final loss considers the text generation loss and the domain prediction loss. For the generation loss, we employ cross entropy to maximize the generation probability of the ground truth, so we have this loss as follows and the training objective is to minimize the loss.

$$\mathcal{L}_{\text{GEN}} = - \sum_{k=1}^{N_1+N_2} \sum_{j=1}^{L^k} \log p \left(y_j^{*k} | y_1^{*k}, \dots, y_{i-1}^{*k}, X \right)$$

where N_1 and N_2 are the numbers of training sentences in each of the two domains. L^k is the length of the k-th ground, and $p \left(y_j^{*k} | y_1^{*k}, \dots, y_{i-1}^{*k}, X \right)$ is the predicted probability of the j-th word for the k-th ground truth sentence given the input sentence X and previous ground truth target words $y_1^{*k}, \dots, y_{i-1}^{*k}$.

For the domain prediction loss, it is a n-class classification task, and n represent number of domains. In this paper n $= 2$. We also use cross-entropy to minimize the following loss

$$\mathcal{L}_{\mathfrak{D}} = - \sum_{k=1}^{N_1 + N_2} \log p \left(d^{*k} \right)$$

where d^{*k} is the ground truth domain label of the k-th input sequence. Adversarial learning is applied between the generation part and the discriminator by minimize $\mathcal{L}_{\mathfrak{D}}$.

Then the final loss is defined as

$$\mathcal{L} = \mathcal{L}_{\textbf{GEN}} + \lambda \mathcal{L}_{\mathfrak{D}}$$

where λ is a hyper-parameter to balance the effects of the two parts of loss. In order to choose the best λ, we select in the range of 0.1 to 1.5 with an interval of 0.1, taking the BLEU in test set as the evaluation metric, and selecting the best λ as 0.5.

At the beginning of the training, we just use the $\mathcal{L}_{\text{GEN}}$ to train the generation part on the combined data, including the shared encoder-decoder and the private encoder-decoders. Then we use $\mathcal{L}_{\text{D}}$ to only train the domain discriminator until the precision of the discriminator reach 90% while the parameters of the shared encoder keep fixed. In this way, we get an initially well-performed generator and well-performed discriminator. Finally, we train the whole model with the complete loss $\mathcal{L}$ with all the parameters updated. In the training process, the sentences in each batch is sampled from the two domains data at the same rate. During testing, we just use the shared encoder-decoder and the private target domain encoder-decoder to generate paraphrase.

4   Experiment

4.1   Datasets

We use two benchmark datasets, namely the MSCOCO and Quora datasets. And we also use WikiAnswers dataset to test the generalization ability of our model. **MSCOCO** is a large-scale image captioning dataset and we use different descriptions for a image as paraphrase. 20K instances are randomly selected from the data for testing, 10K instances for validation and remaining data over 320K instances for training. **Quora** dataset consists of over 400K potential question duplicate pairs. We use true examples of duplicate pairs as paraphrase generation dataset. There are a total of 155K paraphrase pairs. We spilit Quora to 145K training dataset, 5K validation dataset and 4K testing dataset. **WikiAnswers** [2] is a large question paraphrase corpus created by crawling the WikiAnswers website. Although WikiAnswer is also a question paraphrase corpus, it is quite different from Quora according to word distribution. We only use this dataset in our **Generalization Ability** experiment. We only pick 20K sentences pairs for training and 5K pairs for testing.

4.2   Evaluation Metric

To comprehensively evaluate the paraphrases, we rely on a combination of both automatic evaluation and human evaluation.

Automatic Evaluation. We use the well-known evaluation metrics for comparing parallel corpora: **BLEU** [9] and **METEOR** [7]. Previous work has shown that these metrics can perform well for paraphrase detection [8] and correlate well with human judgments in paraphrase generation [16]. BLEU considers exact matching between reference paraphrases and system generated paraphrases by considering ngram overlaps. METEOR uses stemming and synonymy in Word-Net to improve and smoothen this measure.

Human Evaluation. We also conduct human evaluation to evaluate the generated paraphrases more accurately. We randomly select 300 generated sentences and ask three human annotators to evaluate the generated paraphrases from two perspectives: semantic similarity with the original sentence (**Relevance**) and **Fluency**. Each aspect was scored from 1 to 5. We average the three scores from the three annotators as the final score.

4.3   Implementation Details

In our setup, we do not use any external word embeddings and we train these as part of the model-training. The all domains embedding sizes were set to 256 and the size of the hidden units in the shared encoder-decoder RNNs was also set to 256. All the parameters were initialized by using uniform distribution over $[0.1, 0.1]$. The mini-batched Adam algorithm is used to optimize the objective function. The batch size and base learning rates are set to 32 and 0.001, respectively.

We conducted three experiments based on different settings.

1. Domain Mixing: In this setting we aim to train a paraphrase generation model on two-domain data to improve test-time performance in each constituent domain. Supposed both domain contains a sufficient amount of data.

2. Domain Adaptation: Traditional domain adaptation task supposed that we have small quantity of target domain training data but a large amount of source domain data. Source domain and target domain data belong to the same task, but have different distribution. Practical applications often face this kind of situation. We implement this experiment by restricting the amount of in-domain's training data to **20K** and we only care about in-domain performances. Note that in the **Domain Mixing** experiment, we use all the data in both of the two domains.

3. Generalization Ability: In this setting, we use Quora and MSCOCO to pre-train our full model and then use the WikiAnswer to test the generalization ability of our shared encoder-decoder model.

4.4   Baselines

For the first two experiments, we compared our method with following models. Note that since our main purpose is to demonstrate the domain mixing ability of our model, we do not compared with some previous SOTA paraphrase generation models considering the model complexity and training speed.

- **Seq2Seq-Single: Seq2Seq** represents the basic encoder-decoder model described in our Methodology part. It is a component of our full model. **Single** means only use in-domain training data.
- **Seq2Seq-Mix** represents using all the two domains training data together on the **Seq2Seq** model, **Mix** means use two domain's mix data for training.
- **Without Discriminator** represents our proposed model but remove the discriminator part.

For the **Generalization Ability** experiment, we compared our method with following models:

- **Only Wiki** means only use 20K WikiAnswer data to train on the single encoder-decoder model.

- **Generalization** means use MSCOCO and Quora to pre-train our proposed model, and then use the shared encoder-decoder to generate WikiAnswer test set paraphrase. Note that in this setting we do not use any WikiAnswer data during training.
- **Fine-tune** means that after pre-train our model with MSCOCO and Quora, using WikiAnswer training data to fine-tune the shared encoder-decoder model. Then use it to generate paraphrase.

Table 1. Domain mixing results on MSCOCO and Quora dataset. Higher BLEU and METEOR score is better

Model	MSCOCO		Quora	
	BLEU	METEOR	BLEU	METEOR
Beam size = 1				
Seq2Seq-Single	24.56	23.54	25.25	29.86
Seq2Seq-Mix	25.43	24.14	25.48	30.03
Without Discriminator	25.79	22.99	25.97	29.16
Our method	**26.87**	**24.29**	**26.47**	**30.13**
Beam size = 10				
Seq2Seq-Single	26.03	24.13	26.58	30.25
Seq2Seq-Mix	27.65	24.75	27.22	30.70
Without Discriminator	27.93	25.17	27.06	31.53
Our method	**29.72**	**27.45**	**28.64**	**31.92**

Table 2. Domain adaptation results on MSCOCO and Quora dataset. Numbers in the table represents BLEU scores for greedy search. Higher BLEU score is better

Model	MSCOCO	Quora
Seq2Seq-Single	20.17	20.10
Seq2Seq-Mix	21.81	17.31
Without Discriminator	19.26	19.51
Our method	**21.96**	**20.90**

5   Results and Analysis

For **Domain Mixing** experiments, results are shown in Table 1. For **Domain Adaptation** experiment, automatic results are shown in Table 2 and human evaluation results of Quora shown in Table 3. For MSCOCO, the comparison between two models is significant at 95% CI, if the difference in their score is more than 0.2 in BLEU and 0.1 in METEOR. For Quora, the comparison between two models is significant at 95% CI, if the difference in their score is more than 0.2 in BLEU and 0.1 in METEOR. We can draw the following observations:

1. From Table 1, we demonstrate that our model consistently outperforms all
   the contrast models for both greedy search (beam size = 1) and beam search
   (beam size = 10) in the two datasets. Similar conclusion can be drawn from
   Table 2 Domain Adaptation results. Table 3 shows our method also outperforms the baselines from relevance and fluency perspective. These results
   conclude that our method successfully extract useful information from other
   domains which benefit to our target domain.
2. **Seq2Seq-Mix** outperforms **Seq2Seq-Single** in both of the two dataset at
   the **Domain Mixing** experiment, similar result can be seen in the MSCOCO
   dataset at the **Domain Adaptation** experiment. According to the theory
   proposed by [1], this result may be that the divergence between two domains
   is not significant enough, so the merging operation dosen't "contaminate"
   in-domain representation too much and also provided extra training data.
   We can see that this improvement is more obvious in MSCOCO. However,
   in the Quora at **Domain Adaptation** experiment, **Seq2Seq-Mix** BLEU
   scores drop compared with **Seq2Seq-Single**, this could because the model
   tend to fit MSCOCO feature as the amount of MSCOCO data is much more
   than Quora and Quora seems to be more sensitive and susceptible to other
   domains features.

Table 3. Human evaluation on the Quora dataset for domain adaptation experiments.

Model	Relevance	Fluency
Seq2Seq-Single	3.21	3.60
Seq2Seq-Mix	2.92	2.87
Without Discriminator	3.43	3.24
Our method	**3.66**	**3.75**

Table 4. Generalization Ability results. Numbers in the table represents BLEU
scores for greedy search. Higher BLEU score is better

Model	BLEU
Only Wiki	16.03
Generalization	19.35
Fine-tune	**21.44**

3. We can find our method outperforms **Without Discriminator** in all settings, which demonstrate the impact of domain discriminator in our full
   model. We can also find that our main architecture without discriminator
   cannot substantially improve generation performance. So simply divided the
   representation into common and private is not enough, our model may suffer
   a loss of information during the divided and merge process.

4. For **Generalization Ability** experiment, results are shown in Table 4. We can find that only using 20K WikiAnswer training data gets a poor 16.03 BLEU score. With the help of pre-train shared encoder-decoder, **Generalization** model can get substantial improvement compared with **Only Wiki** even without any WikiAnswer training data. We get further improvement when using 20K WikiAnswer to **Fine-Tune** on the shared encoder-decoder. These results demonstrate the domain generalization ability to unknown new domain of our well-trained shared encoder-decoder.

5.1 Case Study

Table 5 gives some examples of generated paraphrases by some contrast model and our proposed model. We can read from Table 5 that paraphrases generated by our system are not only well-formed and grammatically correct for the most part, but also brings more semantically sensible variant which does not appear in the target sentences compared with baseline. This could be because of the training data come from multi-source domains and bring more diversity to our model. These improvements can't reflect from the BLEU or METEOR score, still, our method outperforms all the baselines in BLEU and METEOR metrics.

Table 5. Example generated paraphrases

Source sentence	Proposed model	Seq2Seq-Single	Target sentence
How did Germany defeat France so quickly in 1940	How did Germany conquer France (in May 1940) in 1940	How did Germany win in May France in 1940 who were able to win	Why was France defeated so quickly during WW2
some sheep eating grass in the field	a herd of sheep grazing on a lush green field	a herd of sheep eating grass on a field	a bunch of sheep are standing in a field
what would hillary clinton do now that the election is over	what would hillary clinton do now that presidential election is going to the end	what would hillary clinton do now that the election is better	what role can hillary clinton play now that her presidential hopes are extinguished
how can we improve india's current education system	how can we change india's education system	how can india's education system be fixed	how can india's education system be fixed

For example, for the source sentence *How did Germany defeat France so quickly in 1940*, our method paraphrases *defeat* to *conquer*, which does not appear in the target sentences but semantically sensible while other baselines model just simply copies the word *defeat*. Surprisingly, due to the knowledge from mixing other domains, our proposed model 'remember' the exact month when German defeat France in the second world war. Similarity, for the input sentence *some sheep eating grass in the field*, our method retell *eating grass* to *grazing on*, this is a very idiomatic expression but fail to appear in the target sentence either. We use red color to denote these paraphrasing.

6   Conclusion and Future Work

In this paper, we present an effective method to make use of multi-domain data to help improve paraphrase generation performances. The key idea is to divide the knowledge into domain invariant and domain specific by employing a shared encoder-decode and private encoder-decoders for each domain to process knowledge of the corresponding domain. In addition, a discriminator is added to the shared encoder and apply adversarial learning to make sure the shared encoder can learn domain invariant knowledge by a gradient reversal layer. Experiments show that our method outperform all the baselines in different experiments settings. Moreover, we demonstrate that a well-trained shared encoder-decoder can be regarded as a off-the-shelf model and easily transfer to new domains. Our model can be easily adapted to multi-domain by concatenating more private encoder-decoder. In future work, we aim to use some other models to replace current Seq2Seq architecture (such as Transformer).

References

1. Britz, D., Le, Q., Pryzant, R.: Effective domain mixing for neural machine translation. In: Proceedings of the Second Conference on Machine Translation, pp. 118–126. Association for Computational Linguistics, Copenhagen, September 2017. https://doi.org/10.18653/v1/W17-4712. https://www.aclweb.org/anthology/W17-4712
2. Fader, A., Zettlemoyer, L., Etzioni, O.: Paraphrase-driven learning for open question answering, vol. 1, pp. 1608–1618 (2013)
3. Ganin, Y., et al.: Domain-adversarial training of neural networks. J. Mach. Learn. Res. **17**(1), 2096–2030 (2015)
4. Gupta, A., Agarwal, A., Singh, P., Rai, P.: A deep generative framework for paraphrase generation (2017)
5. Hochreiter, S., Schmidhuber, J.: Long short-term memory. Neural Comput. **9**(8), 1735–1780 (1997)
6. Huang, S., Yu, W., Wei, F., Ming, Z.: Dictionary-guided editing networks for paraphrase generation (2018)
7. Lavie, A., Agarwal, A.: METEOR: an automatic metric for MT evaluation with high levels of correlation with human judgments (2007)
8. Madnani, N., Tetreault, J., Chodorow, M.: Re-examining machine translation metrics for paraphrase identification. In: Conference of the North American Chapter of the Association for Computational Linguistics: Human Language Technologies (2012)
9. Papineni, K., Roukos, S., Ward, T., Zhu, W.J.: BLEU: a method for automatic evaluation of machine translation. In: Proceedings of Meeting of the Association for Computational Linguistics (2002)
10. Prakash, A., et al.: Neural paraphrase generation with stacked residual LSTM networks (2016)
11. Roy, A., Grangier, D.: Unsupervised paraphrasing without translation (2019)
12. Sutskever, I., Martens, J., Hinton, G.E.: Generating text with recurrent neural networks. In: International Conference on Machine Learning (2016)

13. Sutskever, I., Vinyals, O., Le, Q.V.: Sequence to sequence learning with neural networks (2014)
14. Wang, R., Finch, A., Utiyama, M., Sumita, E.: Sentence embedding for neural machine translation domain adaptation. In: Proceedings of the 55th Annual Meeting of the Association for Computational Linguistics (Volume 2: Short Papers), pp. 560–566. Association for Computational Linguistics, Vancouver, July 2017. https://doi.org/10.18653/v1/P17-2089. https://www.aclweb.org/anthology/P17-2089
15. Wang, R., Utiyama, M., Liu, L., Chen, K., Sumita, E.: Instance weighting for neural machine translation domain adaptation. In: Proceedings of the 2017 Conference on Empirical Methods in Natural Language Processing, pp. 1482–1488. Association for Computational Linguistics, Copenhagen, September 2017. https://doi.org/10.18653/v1/D17-1155. https://www.aclweb.org/anthology/D17-1155
16. Wubben, S., Van Den Bosch, A., Krahmer, E.: Paraphrase generation as monolingual translation: data and evaluation. In: International Natural Language Generation Conference (2010)

Leveraging Adversarial Training to Facilitate Grammatical Error Correction

Kai Dang, Jiaying Xie, and Jie Liu[✉]

College of Artificial Intelligence, Nankai University, Tianjin, China
{dangkai,ying}@mail.nankai.edu.cn, jliu@nankai.edu.cn

Abstract. Grammatical error correction (GEC) task aims to detect and correct grammatical errors in sentences. Recently, the pre-trained language model has provided a strong baseline for GEC and achieved excellent results by fine-tuning on a small amount of annotated data. However, due to the lack of large-scale erroneous-corrected parallel datasets, these models tend to suffer from the problem of overfitting. Previous researchers have proposed a variety of data augmentation methods to generate more training data and enlarge the dataset, but these methods either rely on rules to generate grammatical errors and are not automated, or produce errors that do not match human writing errors. The pre-trained model only improves significantly after task-specific data fine-tuning; otherwise, the highly noisy data can impair the performance of the pre-trained model. To address this issue, we propose a method to enhance the robustness of the model based on adversarial training. This approach constructs the adversarial samples and treats them as the augmented data. Unlike previous methods that introduce token-level noise, our method introduces embedding-level noise and can obtain extra samples that are close to human writing errors. Besides, we employ the adversarial consistency constraint to reduce the gap between the adversarial sample and the original sample. The experimental results demonstrate that our method can further boost the performance of the pre-trained model on GEC task.

Keywords: Grammatical error correction · Adversarial training · Consistency constraint

1 Introduction

Grammatical error correction (GEC) task is a promising natural language processing (NLP) application, whose goal is to detect and correct grammatical errors in sentences. Previous researchers regarded the erroneous sentence as the source sentence and the correct sentence as the target sentence, thus converting GEC task as a translation task from the erroneous sentence to the correct sentence [36]. They applied statistical machine translation (SMT) and neural machine translation (NMT) models to GEC task and produced remarkable results [5,13].

© Springer Nature Switzerland AG 2021
I. Farkaš et al. (Eds.): ICANN 2021, LNCS 12891, pp. 67–78, 2021.
https://doi.org/10.1007/978-3-030-86362-3_6

Table 1. Different data augmentation methods examples.

Method	Example
Clean	Safety is one of the crucial problems that many countries and companies are concerned about
Random noise	Safety is ~~one of~~ the crucial problems that many [mask] and companies are on concerned about
Back translation	Safety is one of the crucial problems which many country and company are concerned about
Adversarial training	Safety is one of the crucial problems that many countries and company are concerned on

Recently, the pre-trained language model provides a stronger baseline for GEC task [16]. By fine-tuning on a small number of annotated data, the pre-trained language model can reach an excellent performance.

However, GEC often faces the problem of lacking a large-scale parallel annotated dataset, making the model prone to over-fitting and poor generalization [14]. To address this problem, researchers have proposed a variety of data augmentation methods for GEC task, such as synthesizing data [12], random noise injection [37,38] and back translation [17]. These methods are able to generate a large amount of pseudo-data and enlarge the GEC dataset so that they facilitate the development of GEC. Nevertheless, these methods either require the use of prior knowledge like grammatical rules to yield grammatical errors, which are not automated enough [33], or create errors that do not match human writing errors, which may impair the performance of the model. As shown in Table 1, random noise severely impairs the sentences, so the model does not learn to correct errors well. Back translation tends to generate common errors, which is not conducive to the model solving rare errors. Furthermore, through preliminary experiments, we found that previous data augmentation methods applied to this stage can seriously damage the performance of the model. The reason for this phenomenon is that the previous approach introduced token-level noise, which reduced the quality of the dataset. Especially in the fine-tuning phase, only task-specific high-quality annotated data can improve the performance of the pre-trained model. Therefore, the previous methods are not suitable for the fine-tuning phase of pre-trained models.

To address this issue, inspired by adversarial training [11,22,25], we propose a new approach to enhance the robustness of GEC system. The concrete way is to construct adversarial samples with adversarial training and treat them as augmented data for training the model. The adversarial samples introduce perturbations in the word embedding space, which can be regarded as embedding-level noise. Unlike the previous token-level noise, the adversarial sample introduces lower noise, which makes the gap between the augmented sample and the original sample not too large. Besides that, we employ the adversarial consistency constraint, which constrains the adversarial sample to produce a similar probability distribution to the original sample. This regularization term also helps to avoid model overfitting. In this approach, our GEC system is more robust and has better generalization capability. To verify the effectiveness of our method, we conduct expensive experiments base on BART [18] model, which is a pre-trained encoder-decoder model and can provide high performance in GEC. The experimental results indicate that our approach can further boost the performance of the pre-trained model on GEC task. The contributions of our paper are as follows:

- We demonstrate the importance of high-quality annotated data in the fine-tuning stage and data augmentation can further improve the performance of the pre-trained model on GEC task.
- We propose a simple and effective method to enhance the robustness of GEC systems, i.e., constructing the adversarial samples by adversarial training and treating them as augmented data to train the model. To the best of our knowledge, this is the first work to introduce adversarial training into GEC task.
- We conduct extensive experiments on GEC datasets. The experimental results demonstrate that our approach can boost the performance of the pre-trained model on GEC task.

2 Related Work

2.1 Grammatical Error Correction

The early GEC systems are based on rules, relying on the parser and linguistic characteristics to detect and correct the errors [26]. However, designing rules and resolving conflicts between rules are complex and require a great magnitude of labor. Later, the classifier-based methods are used to solve type-specific errors, such as preposition errors and article errors [8]. Subsequently, the researchers converted GEC task into a machine translation task and applied statistical machine translation models [13].

Currently, neural networks based methods have become the mainstream approach for GEC. Chollampatt et al. [5] first applied neural machine translation (NMT) models to GEC task. Chollampatt and Ng [4] used a multilayer convolutional encoder-decoder neural network, which outperformed prior systems on this task. Recently, a novel edit-based approach has been proposed for GEC task. Relying on pre-trained language models, Awasthi et al. [1], Malmi et al. [23] and Omelianchuk et al. [27] designed different edit mode and achieved significant advances in speed and accuracy by predicting editing operations.

To improve the generalization of the model, researchers proposed various data augmentation methods. Zhao et al. [37] introduced the pretraining stage to GEC task and demonstrated the importance of pretraining. Kiyono et al. [17] borrowed the idea of back translation and trained an extra model to generate more corpus. Ge et al. [10] came up with round-trip translation, which iteratively corrected the sentences. Zhao and Wang [38] utilized a dynamic masking approach that enabled exponentially expanding the amount of data. These methods make the model more generalizable and greatly boost the performance of GEC.

2.2   Adversarial Training

PGD-based adversarial training method [11] has been proven effective in numerous tasks. It constructs adversarial samples according to the gradient and trains a more robust model [22]. Researchers applied it to NLP tasks and noticed it was effective in enhancing the generalization of the model [25]. Sato et al. [28] used adversarial training as a regularization technique and improved the performance of machine translation. Zhu et al. [39] suggested the FreeLB method, which gained enhancements in many NLU tasks. Wang et al. [31] presented an adversarial MLE training strategy for a language modeling task, improving the generalizability of the model without increasing the parameters and computational cost. Liu et al. [20] combined adversarial training with pre-training and found adversarial pretraining could improve both generalization and robustness. In parallel to our work, [32] proposed a data argumentation method for GEC task by constructing adversarial samples and emphasized the importance of high-quality samples, but it is still essentially word-level noise. We apply adversarial training to GEC task and introduce embedding level noise during training. These adversarial samples can be considered as enlarged data, so this is an implicit method of data augmentation.

3   Approach

3.1   Standard Method

We denote that the input sentence as $X = \{x_1, x_2, ..., x_m\}$, and the corresponding output sentence as $Y = \{y_1, y_2, ..., y_n\}$, where x_i denotes the i-th token in the input sentence, y_j denotes the j-th token in the output sentence, m and n are the lengths of input and output sentences, respectively. A sequence-to-sequence (Seq2Seq) model is often used in GEC task to produce the following conditional probabilities:

$$P(Y|X) = \prod_{t=1}^{n+1} p(y_t|X, y_{<t}) \tag{1}$$

where y_0 and y_{n+1} denote the beginning token and the end token of the sentence, respectively. And $y_{<t} = \{y_0, y_1, ..., y_{t-1}\}$ denotes the previous output.

Suppose $E \in \mathbb{R}^{D \times |V|}$ is the encoder and decoder embedding matrix, where D is the dimension of the embedding vectors and $|V|$ is the vocabulary size. Normally, an encoder and a decoder are used to produce $p(y_t|X, y_{<t})$ as follows:

$$e_i = Ex_i, \quad f_j = Ey_j$$
$$h_1, h_2, ..., h_m = Enc(e_1, e_2, ..., e_m) \tag{2}$$
$$p(y_t|X, y_{<t}) = Dec(f_1, ..., f_{t-1}, h_1, ..., h_m)$$

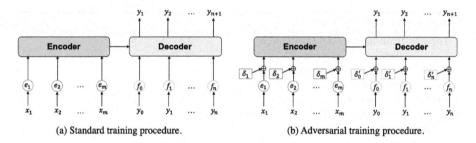

(a) Standard training procedure.   (b) Adversarial training procedure.

Fig. 1. Illustrations of standard training method (a) and adversarial training method (b). Adversarial training adds perturbations to the word embedding of the input at the encoder and decoder sides.

where $Enc(\cdot)$ and $Dec(\cdot)$ indicates the abstract functions for encoding and decoding procedures, respectively.

Finally, the model is usually optimized by using maximum likelihood estimation (MLE), which is equivalent to minimizing the negative log-likelihood (NLL) loss:

$$\ell_{nll} = -\sum_{t=1}^{n+1} \log p(y_t|X, y_{<t}; \theta) \tag{3}$$

3.2 Adversarial Training (AdvT)

In adversarial training, subtle perturbations δ are added to the word embedding space to noise the input. For a Seq2Seq model, as shown in the Fig. 1, the input includes both the encoder side and the decoder side, so we add perturbations δ and δ' to these two sides respectively. Suppose that $\delta_i \in \mathbb{R}^D$ and $\delta'_j \in \mathbb{R}^D$ are perturbation vectors for the i-th token in X and the j-th token in Y. The perturbed word embedding e'_i and f'_j are computed as follows:

$$e'_i = e_i + \delta_i, \quad f'_j = f_j + \delta'_j \tag{4}$$

Therefore, the optimization objective of the model becomes:

$$\ell_{adv} = -\sum_{t=1}^{n+1} \log p(y_t|X, y_{<t}; \theta, \delta, \delta') \tag{5}$$

In order to obtain the meanful perturbation vectors, previous work argued that meaningful perturbations should be those that are not conducive to model optimization, i.e., maximizing losses:

$$\delta, \delta' = \underset{\|\delta\|\leq\epsilon, \|\delta'\|\leq\epsilon}{\arg\max} \ \ell_{adv} \tag{6}$$

Algorithm 1: Algorithm(AdvT + AdvC)

Input: Training dataset $D = \{(X, Y)\}$,
         Number of iterations T,
         Number of adversarial samples K,
         Adversarial step η

1 Initialize the model parameters θ
2 **for** $t = 1, ..., T$ **do**
3   **for** $(x, y) \in D$ **do**
4   compute ℓ_{nll} according to Eq 3
5      $\mathcal{L} \leftarrow \ell_{nll}$
6   **for** $k = 1, ..., K$ **do**
7        $g \leftarrow \nabla_e \ell_{adv}, \quad g' \leftarrow \nabla_f \ell_{adv}$
8        $\delta \leftarrow \eta \cdot g/\|g\|_2,$
          $\delta' \leftarrow \eta \cdot g'/\|g'\|_2$
9   compute ℓ_{adv} according to Eq 5
10   compute ℓ_{kl} according to Eq 8
11       $\mathcal{L} \leftarrow \mathcal{L} + \ell_{adv} + \ell_{kl}$
12   **end for**
13   Calculate the gradient based on $\mathcal{L}$ and update the parameter θ
14   **end for**
15 **end for**

For a neural network model, estimating the exact values of δ and δ' is not feasible, thus Goodfellow et al. [11] proposed the approximation method by linearizing ℓ_{adv} around the input:

$$\begin{aligned}
\delta_i &= \eta \cdot g_i/\|g_i\|_2, \quad g_i = \nabla_{e_i} \ell_{adv} \\
\delta'_j &= \eta \cdot g'_j/\|g'_j\|_2, \quad g'_j = \nabla_{f_j} \ell_{adv}
\end{aligned} \tag{7}$$

3.3 Adversarial Consistency (AdvC)

The adversarial samples can be considered as noisy results of the original sample, and they are both different states of the same sample. Therefore, the probability distributions produced by the original sample and adversarial sample should be similar. We use Kullback-Leibler (KL) divergence as an additional constraint to ensure that these two probability distributions are close.

$$\ell_{kl} = KL(p(\cdot|X, y_{<t}; \theta) \| p(\cdot|X, y_{<t}; \theta, \delta, \delta')) \tag{8}$$

where $KL(\cdot\|\cdot)$ denotes the KL divergence.

In summary, Algorithm 1 shows the details of our approach. Lines 6–12 show that we could generate K adversarial samples for training. However, as the number of adversarial samples K increases, the consuming time increases linearly. Hence, in the subsequent experiments, we set $K = 1$.

Table 2. Dataset statistics for GEC.

Split	Dataset	#sents	#tokens	Scorer
Train	NUCLE	57k	1.16M	–
	FCE-train	28k	455k	–
	Lang-8	1.04M	11.86M	–
	W& I+LOCNESS	34.3k	628.7k	–
Valid	BEA-valid	4.3k	87k	–
Test	CoNLL-2014	1.3k	36.4k	M^2 scorer
	FCE-test	2.4k	42k	M^2 scorer
	BEA-test	4.4k	85.6k	ERRANT

4   Experiments

4.1   Datasets

Following the BEA 2019 shared task setting [2], we train our GEC models on NUCLE [7], FCE-train [35], Lang-8 Corpus [30], and W&I+LOCNESS [34] datasets. We use W&I-dev as the development dataset. We select the model checkpoint that performs best on the validation set for evaluation. In the evaluation phase, we evaluate our model on CoNLL2014 test set, FCE test set, and BEA 2019 test set, respectively. Table 2 shows the statistics of all datasets used in the experiments. During the pre-processing phase, hunspell[1] is used to correct spelling errors in all datasets. Byte pair encoding (BPE) [29] is applied to tokenize all the sentences.

4.2   Evaluation Metrics

For CoNLL-2014 test set and FCE-test, we report the scores measured by the M^2 scorer[2] [6]. For BEA-test, we use the ERRANT[3] [3,9] scores for evaluation. All our results are the average of five distinct trials using different random seeds.

4.3   Experimental Setting

We employ BART-large [18] model implemented by fairseq[4] toolkit as our base model and fine-tune it on the GEC data. We use AdamW [21] for the optimizer and the learning rate increases linearly from zero to 3×10^{-5} and then decays linearly to zero. The warmup steps is 500 and the total update steps is 10,000. The batch size is set to 2,000 tokens and the accumulation steps is set to 4. We set $\eta = 10^{-2}$ and $K = 1$ for training efficiency (i.e., generate one adversarial sample).

---

[1] https://github.com/hunspell/hunspell.
[2] https://github.com/nusnlp/m2scorer.
[3] https://github.com/chrisjbryant/errant.
[4] https://github.com/pytorch/fairseq.

Table 3. Comparison with existing models. A **bold** value denotes the best result within the column. A <u>underline</u> value denotes the second-best result within the column.

Model	CoNLL-2014			BEA-2019			FCE		
	P	R	$F_{0.5}$	P	R	$F_{0.5}$	P	R	$F_{0.5}$
Mita et al. [24]	63.8	**52.4**	61.1	59.9	**66.9**	61.2	–	–	–
Kiyono et al. [17]	67.9	44.1	61.3	65.5	59.4	64.2	–	–	–
Omelianchuk et al. [27]	**77.5**	40.1	**65.3**	**79.2**	53.9	**72.4**	–	–	–
Lichtarge et al. [19]	69.4	43.9	62.1	67.6	<u>62.5</u>	66.5	–	–	–
Kaneko et al. [15]	69.2	45.6	62.6	67.1	60.1	65.6	59.8	**46.9**	56.7
BART	69.4	<u>46.1</u>	63.0	66.6	59.5	65.0	69.4	<u>40.7</u>	60.8
BART+AdvT	70.3	45.9	63.5	71.1	57.9	68.0	<u>70.7</u>	40.5	<u>61.5</u>
BART+ AdvT+AdvC	<u>71.3</u>	44.7	63.7	<u>71.4</u>	58.9	<u>68.5</u>	**71.1**	40.5	**61.8**

In the inference phase, we use greedy decoding to generate, i.e., the beam size is 1. It is worth noting that, except for spelling correction, our system does not use additional corpus and no pre-processing and post-processing operations, such as ensembling models and re-ranking outputs, which are commonly used in GEC tasks.

4.4 Results

We compare our model with several well-known GEC systems, as shown in Table 3. In order to make a fair comparison, we choose single models of the same scale as baselines. Mita et al. [24] proposed a self-refinement strategy to remove inappropriate corrections in the dataset. Kiyono et al. [17] used a seed corpus and back translation to generate pseudo-data for GEC and applied it for training. Omelianchuk et al. [27] employed a GEC sequence tagger and achieved good results after pre-training and two-stage fine-tuning. Kaneko et al. [15] integrates mask language model into encoder-decoder architecture to improve the performance of the model.

The experimental results show that except for Omelianchuk et al. [27], which utilized an annotation dataset, our approach outperforms other existing GEC systems. Our enhancements come from two aspects. On the one hand, BART provides a strong baseline for GEC which can surpass most existing models by fine-tuning on a small amount of data. This indicates that pre-training is crucial for GEC task and it can significantly improve the performance of GEC system. On the other hand, our approach can effectively prevent pre-trained model overfitting and further boost the performance of the pre-trained model.

4.5 Effect of Adversarial Training

From Table 3, we can see that after introducing adversarial training, the model gains improvement on all benchmarks. Especially on the BEA-2019 dataset,

Table 4. Perturbation position analysis experimental results.

Perturbation position	CoNLL-2014			BEA-2019		
	P	R	F0.5	P	R	F0.5
No perturbation	69.39	46.12	63.03	66.57	59.50	65.02
Encoder-only	70.96	45.16	63.68	71.00	57.87	67.92
Decoder-only	70.45	45.06	63.31	70.64	57.92	67.67
Encoder-decoder	70.80	45.24	63.61	71.06	57.85	67.96

adversarial training brings a 3% improvement to the BART model. This is because the adversarial samples produced by adversarial training can be regarded as augmented data, which can help to avoid the model from overfitting. Previous data augmentation methods generate token-level noise, which is higher than the adversarial sample. When the noise does not match human writing errors, the augmented samples may damage GEC model. In contrast, the embedding-level noise is much lower and more targeted, and it can be considered as a general data augmentation method. Besides, we can observe that the noise makes slightly decreases the recall of the model but can enhance the precision of the model, which is crucial for GEC task.

4.6   Effect of Perturbation Position

Furthermore, to verify the role of the perturbation position, we conduct experiments on CoNLL-2014 and BEA-2019 by adding perturbations at different positions, adding perturbations to the encoder side (encoder-only), adding perturbations to the decoder side (decoder-only), and adding perturbations to both sides (encoder-decoder). The experimental results, as shown in Table 4, indicate that the perturbation is capable of improving the performance of the model regardless of the perturbation position. Moreover, the perturbation on the encoder side is more effective than that on the decoder side, because it is equivalent to constructing additional data. Perturbation on the decoder side can also bring enhancement, and we speculate that introducing noise to the decoder can alleviate the problem of exposure bias during decoding, which consequently enhances the robustness of the decoder.

4.7   Effect of Adversarial Consistency

The experimental results show that adversarial consistency is an effective regularization method. It achieves +0.2%, +0.5%, and +0.3% improvement over no AdvC on the three test sets, respectively. Due to the introduction of noise, the optimization direction of the model is biased. The adversarial consistent loss minimizes the difference between the output probability distribution of the adversarial sample and the original sample, which prevents the model from deviating from the optimization direction of the original sample. As well, this can be considered as a smoothing term, which makes the optimization process smoother and the model gradually converges to the optimal value.

5   Conclusion

In this paper, we proposed a simple and effective method for the GEC task, i.e., improving the robustness and generalization of GEC model by adversarial training. The experimental results demonstrate the effectiveness of the method, and we analyzed the reasons for this in detail. We viewed the adversarial samples as a kind of high-quality augmented data that can prevent the overfitting of the model. We believe that this approach can be used as a fundamental technique to improve the performance of GEC systems.

Acknowledgments. This research is supported by the National Natural Science Foundation of China under the grant [No. 61976119] and the Natural Science Foundation of Tianjin under the grant [No. 18ZXZNGX00310].

References

1. Awasthi, A., Sarawagi, S., Goyal, R., Ghosh, S., Piratla, V.: Parallel iterative edit models for local sequence transduction. Association for Computational Linguistics (2019). https://doi.org/10.18653/v1/D19-1435
2. Bryant, C., Felice, M., Andersen, Ø.E., Briscoe, T.: The BEA-2019 shared task on grammatical error correction, pp. 52–75. Association for Computational Linguistics (2019). https://doi.org/10.18653/v1/w19-4406
3. Bryant, C., Felice, M., Briscoe, T.: Automatic annotation and evaluation of error types for grammatical error correction. In: Barzilay, R., Kan, M. (eds.) ACL 2017, pp. 793–805. Association for Computational Linguistics (2017)
4. Chollampatt, S., Ng, H.T.: A Multilayer Convolutional Encoder-decoder Neural Network for Grammatical Error Correction, pp. 5755–5762. AAAI Press (2018). https://www.aaai.org/ocs/index.php/AAAI/AAAI18/paper/view/17308
5. Chollampatt, S., Taghipour, K., Ng, H.T.: Neural Network Translation Models for Grammatical Error Correction, pp. 2768–2774. IJCAI/AAAI Press (2016). http://www.ijcai.org/Abstract/16/393
6. Dahlmeier, D., Ng, H.T.: Better evaluation for grammatical error correction. The Association for Computational Linguistics (2012). https://www.aclweb.org/anthology/N12-1067/
7. Dahlmeier, D., Ng, H.T., Wu, S.M.: Building a large annotated corpus of learner English: the NUS corpus of learner English, pp. 22–31. The Association for Computer Linguistics (2013). https://www.aclweb.org/anthology/W13-1703/
8. De Felice, R., Pulman, S.: A classifier-based approach to preposition and determiner error correction in L2 English. In: Proceedings of the 22nd International Conference on Computational Linguistics (COLING 2008), pp. 169–176 (2008)
9. Felice, M., Bryant, C., Briscoe, T.: Automatic extraction of learner errors in ESL sentences using linguistically enhanced alignments. In: Calzolari, N., Matsumoto, Y., Prasad, R. (eds.) COLING 2016. pp. 825–835. ACL (2016)

10. Ge, T., Wei, F., Zhou, M.: Fluency boost learning and inference for neural grammatical error correction, pp. 1055–1065. Association for Computational Linguistics (2018). https://www.aclweb.org/anthology/P18-1097/
11. Goodfellow, I.J., Shlens, J., Szegedy, C.: Explaining and harnessing adversarial examples (2015). http://arxiv.org/abs/1412.6572
12. Grundkiewicz, R., Junczys-Dowmunt, M., Heafield, K.: Neural grammatical error correction systems with unsupervised pre-training on synthetic data, pp. 252–263. Association for Computational Linguistics (2019). https://doi.org/10.18653/v1/w19-4427
13. Junczys-Dowmunt, M., Grundkiewicz, R.: Phrase-based machine translation is state-of-the-art for automatic grammatical error correction, pp. 1546–1556. The Association for Computational Linguistics (2016). https://doi.org/10.18653/v1/d16-1161
14. Junczys-Dowmunt, M., Grundkiewicz, R., Guha, S., Heafield, K.: Approaching neural grammatical error correction as a low-resource machine translation task, pp. 595–606. Association for Computational Linguistics (2018). https://doi.org/10.18653/v1/n18-1055
15. Kaneko, M., Mita, M., Kiyono, S., Suzuki, J., Inui, K.: Encoder-decoder models can benefit from pre-trained masked language models in grammatical error correction, pp. 4248–4254. Association for Computational Linguistics (2020). https://doi.org/10.18653/v1/2020.acl-main.391
16. Katsumata, S., Komachi, M.: Stronger baselines for grammatical error correction using a pretrained encoder-decoder model, pp. 827–832. Association for Computational Linguistics (2020). https://www.aclweb.org/anthology/2020.aacl-main.83/
17. Kiyono, S., Suzuki, J., Mita, M., Mizumoto, T., Inui, K.: An empirical study of incorporating pseudo data into grammatical error correction, pp. 1236–1242. Association for Computational Linguistics (2019). https://doi.org/10.18653/v1/D19-1119
18. Lewis, M., et al.: BART: denoising sequence-to-sequence pre-training for natural language generation, translation, and comprehension, pp. 7871–7880 (2020). https://doi.org/10.18653/v1/2020.acl-main.703
19. Lichtarge, J., Alberti, C., Kumar, S.: Data weighted training strategies for grammatical error correction. Trans. Assoc. Comput. Ling. **8**, 634–646 (2020). https://transacl.org/ojs/index.php/tacl/article/view/2047
20. Liu, X., et al.: Adversarial training for large neural language models. CoRR abs/2004.08994 (2020). https://arxiv.org/abs/2004.08994
21. Loshchilov, I., Hutter, F.: Fixing weight decay regularization in adam. CoRR abs/1711.05101 (2017). http://arxiv.org/abs/1711.05101
22. Madry, A., Makelov, A., Schmidt, L., Tsipras, D., Vladu, A.: Towards deep learning models resistant to adversarial attacks. OpenReview.net (2018). https://openreview.net/forum?id=rJzIBfZAb
23. Malmi, E., Krause, S., Rothe, S., Mirylenka, D., Severyn, A.: Encode, tag, realize: High-precision text editing, pp. 5053–5064. Association for Computational Linguistics (2019). https://doi.org/10.18653/v1/D19-1510
24. Mita, M., Kiyono, S., Kaneko, M., Suzuki, J., Inui, K.: A self-refinement strategy for noise reduction in grammatical error correction, pp. 267–280. Association for Computational Linguistics (2020). https://doi.org/10.18653/v1/2020.findings-emnlp.26
25. Miyato, T., Dai, A.M., Goodfellow, I.J.: Adversarial training methods for semi-supervised text classification. OpenReview.net (2017). https://openreview.net/forum?id=r1X3g2_xl

26. Naber, D., et al.: A rule-based style and grammar checker (2003)
27. Omelianchuk, K., Atrasevych, V., Chernodub, A.N., Skurzhanskyi, O.: Gector - grammatical error correction: tag, not rewrite, pp. 163–170. Association for Computational Linguistics (2020). https://doi.org/10.18653/v1/2020.bea-1.16
28. Sato, M., Suzuki, J., Kiyono, S.: Effective adversarial regularization for neural machine translation, pp. 204–210. Association for Computational Linguistics (2019). https://doi.org/10.18653/v1/p19-1020
29. Sennrich, R., Haddow, B., Birch, A.: Neural machine translation of rare words with subword units. In: ACL 2016. The Association for Computer Linguistics (2016)
30. Tajiri, T., Komachi, M., Matsumoto, Y.: Tense and aspect error correction for ESL learners using global context, pp. 198–202. The Association for Computer Linguistics (2012). https://www.aclweb.org/anthology/P12-2039/
31. Wang, D., Gong, C., Liu, Q.: Improving neural language modeling via adversarial training, vol. 97, pp. 6555–6565. PMLR (2019). http://proceedings.mlr.press/v97/wang19f.html
32. Wang, L., Zheng, X.: Improving grammatical error correction models with purpose-built adversarial examples. In: Webber, B., Cohn, T., He, Y., Liu, Y. (eds.) EMNLP 2020, pp. 2858–2869. Association for Computational Linguistics (2020)
33. Wang, Y., Wang, Y., Liu, J., Liu, Z.: A comprehensive survey of grammar error correction. arXiv preprint arXiv:2005.06600 (2020)
34. Yannakoudakis, H., Andersen, Ø.E., Geranpayeh, A., Briscoe, T., Nicholls, D.: Developing an automated writing placement system for ESL learners. Appl. Measur. Educ. **31**(3), 251–267 (2018)
35. Yannakoudakis, H., Briscoe, T., Medlock, B.: A new dataset and method for automatically grading ESOL texts, pp. 180–189. The Association for Computer Linguistics (2011). https://www.aclweb.org/anthology/P11-1019/
36. Yuan, Z., Briscoe, T.: Grammatical error correction using neural machine translation. The Association for Computational Linguistics (2016). https://doi.org/10.18653/v1/n16-1042
37. Zhao, W., Wang, L., Shen, K., Jia, R., Liu, J.: Improving grammatical error correction via pre-training a copy-augmented architecture with unlabeled data, pp. 156–165. Association for Computational Linguistics (2019). https://doi.org/10.18653/v1/n19-1014
38. Zhao, Z., Wang, H.: MaskGEC: improving neural grammatical error correction via dynamic masking, pp. 1226–1233. AAAI Press (2020). https://aaai.org/ojs/index.php/AAAI/article/view/5476
39. Zhu, C., Cheng, Y., Gan, Z., Sun, S., Goldstein, T., Liu, J.: FreeLB: enhanced adversarial training for natural language understanding. OpenReview.net (2020). https://openreview.net/forum?id=BygzbyHFvB

Statistical Certification of Acceptable Robustness for Neural Networks

Chengqiang Huang[1]([✉]), Zheng Hu[1], Xiaowei Huang[2], and Ke Pei[1]

[1] Huawei Technology Co. Ltd., Shenzhen, China
{huangchengqiang,hu.zheng,peike}@huawei.com
[2] University of Liverpool, Liverpool, UK
xiaowei.huang@liverpool.ac.uk

Abstract. Neural network robustness measurement is a critical step before deploying neural network applications. However, existing methods, such as neural network verification and validation, do not fully meet our criteria for robustness measurement. From the industrial point-of-view, this paper proposes to use statistical robustness certificates (SRC) for measuring the robustness of neural networks against random noises as well as semantic perturbations and tries to bridge between verification and validation methods through Hoeffding Inequality. Our experiments show that our method is accurate in comparing robustness of different neural networks and has polynomial time complexity which leads to 3x-30x boost in efficiency compared to related methods. Together with the intrinsic statistical guarantee, the issued certificates are considered practical in comparing the robustness of various commercial neural networks.

1 Introduction

With the proliferation of AI applications, the topic of AI robustness and safety have drawn significant attention in the past few years. Especially in safety-critical applications, the intrinsic robustness of the AI components, e.g., neural networks, is vital. To build certain confidence in the application of neural networks, researchers have defined neural network robustness and proposed many different approaches concerning robustness validation and verification. For many studies, measuring the (deterministic) robustness of a neural network for an input x is expressed as an optimisation problem:

$$\max \sigma_x \tag{1}$$

$$\text{s.t.} \quad \forall x' : L(x, x') \leq \sigma_x \Rightarrow x' \text{ is not adversarial} \tag{2}$$

to find the maximum perturbation σ_x within which no adversarial example is possible (equivalent to finding the minimum adversarial perturbation [5]). L here measures the "distance" between x and its perturbed version x'. However, in this work, we propose to consider its statistical version, i.e., a statistical robustness. Let $g(x)$ be a function such that, $g(x) = 1$ if x is an adversarial example, and

© Springer Nature Switzerland AG 2021
I. Farkaš et al. (Eds.): ICANN 2021, LNCS 12891, pp. 79–90, 2021.
https://doi.org/10.1007/978-3-030-86362-3_7

$g(x) = 0$ otherwise. Formally, the statistical robustness can also be expressible as an optimisation problem:

$$\max \sigma_x \tag{3}$$

$$\text{s.t.} \quad P[g(x') = 1 | L(x, x') \leq \sigma_x] \leq \epsilon \tag{4}$$

which requires an acceptable level of robustness, i.e., $1 - \epsilon$, when finding the maximum perturbation σ_x. As suggested in [25], even for safety critical systems, a certain degree of safety risk must be accepted. Furthermore, in ISO/IEC Guide 51: Safety Aspects, it states that "There can be no absolute safety: some risk will remain, defined in this Guide as residual risk. Therefore, a product, process or service can only be relatively safe." Practically, with a certain level of acceptable robustness (95% as in our experiments), we can have a much larger σ_x as opposed to those that can be computed with verification approaches for deterministic robustness – this leads to the possibility of conducting a practical evaluation of robustness.

With the new robustness definition, the key contribution of this paper is a general method for robustness measurement of neural network classifiers which features in the following three important aspects:

- Comparing to neural network verification methods, many of which are inefficient and produce inconsistent measurements, our method allows fair robustness comparison among various neural networks and, more importantly, nicely scales to large commercial neural networks.
- Comparing to adversarial attacks, our method is attack-independent and supplies statistical commitments of the theoretical guarantee of the model robustness.
- The method is generally applicable with different types of classification model and various types of natural data perturbation, e.g., random noise, image rotation and scaling, with different data space assumptions and distance metrics.

We discuss and measure the applicability of our method, and show that it is currently the most practical method which supports neural network measurement with theoretical guarantee and circumvents the processing of the details of neural networks, such as, different activation functions and layer types.

2   Relative Work

In 2013, Szegedy et al. [5] propose the first practical definition of model robustness, i.e., the average of the minimum adversarial perturbations of different samples. Since then, many methods for robustness estimation have been introduced. Essentially, there are two primary approaches to estimate the model robustness: 1) verification and 2) validation. The next two subsections will discuss related methods concerning these two approaches, especially for neural networks.

2.1   Neural Network Verification

In the research domain of neural network verification, researchers are looking for efficient and effective ways to identify the minimum perturbation of a data sample under which no perturbed data will be misclassified by the neural network. It has been a hot research topic for the past several years and many distinguished approaches have been proposed [6]. Roughly speaking, the methods for neural network verification could be divided into optimization-based methods, reachability-based methods as well as search-based methods.

Given a certain perturbation, reachability-based methods try to find the upper and lower probability bounds of the output labels or the probability difference between two labels (one of which is the true label). If the lower bound is below a threshold, it is suspected that the given perturbation is not robust enough and should be reduced accordingly. As the process of calculating the output bounds of non-linear activation functions in neurons often requires over-approximation for verification efficiency, the resulting perturbation is much smaller than the actual minimum perturbation. The methods proposed by ETH [10, 15] and IBM [9] follow this research line and easing the negative effects of over-approximation has become a primary research problem. For the other research direction, optimization-based methods transform the neural network verification problem into optimization problems, e.g., MILP, and use existing programming solvers to find the minimum perturbation without approximation. [8, 16, 17] are all optimization-based methods. Although most optimization-based methods are not only sound but also complete for neural network verification, they typically consume much more computation time compared to reachability-based methods. This is due to the limited capability of optimization solvers and also the enormous number of optimization constraints introduced by the non-linear activation functions of the neurons.

In this paper, we choose CNN-Cert [9] as one of the compared methods in our experiments. This is because CNN-Cert is a general method that supports verification for both convolution neural networks and fully connected neural networks, and works for various types of neurons. Due to its intrinsic symbolic propagation schema, CNN-Cert is more efficient compared to many other methods.

2.2   Neural Network Validation

For neural network validation, the fundamental ideas are to 1) find perturbations as small as possible to attack the target neural network and 2) thoroughly test the generalization capability of the target neural network. The former idea links to the broad research area of adversarial attacks of neural networks. It has been a fruitful research direction over the past 5 year. The latter idea is simply to test the neural network with specific samples for measuring the capability of the neural network in certain situations.

For adversarial attacks, Google Cleverhans [18], Bethgelab Foolbox [7], and Baidu Benchmark [19] are practical tools for generating adversarial examples and validating the effectiveness of the target neural network. Gradient-based attack,

Fig. 1. From left to right: a) original image; b) image attached by C&W; c) image with maximum acceptable Gaussian noise (44.7%) calculated by SRC ($\epsilon = 5\%$, $c = 1.2\%$).

score-based attack, decision-based attack, and transfer-based attack are four fundamental types of adversarial attacks. Some famous attacks are FGSM [14], C&W attack [4], and Local Search Attack [20]. The robustness of neural networks are considered as the average minimum perturbation to find adversarial examples. In addition to adversarial attacks, designed neural network testing is another road to validate the robustness of neural networks. [3] presents ImageNet-C and ImageNet-P as two benchmark datasets for the evaluation of model robustness against common corruptions and perturbations. It gives a purely testing-based robustness measurement metric for neural networks. Nevertheless, compared to verification/certification methods, such as CNN-Cert and ours, [3,7,18,19] provide no guarantee concerning the robustness of the neural networks. On the other hand, [2] uses the inverse of the KL divergence between the classification result of the original data and that of the perturbed data as the metric for neural network robustness measurement. It is to design a novel metric for the measurement. Our method shares the same spirit as [2] but further extends the theoretical aspects of the neural network robustness to build certain confidence of the robustness of the target neural network. Additionally, [1] proposes adversarial frequency and severity as two primary metrics to measure the robustness. However, we try to find the point-wise ϵs that produce similar adversarial frequency for different neural networks and use the adversarial severity as the metric for robustness measurement. Compared to [1], our method features in that it supports a theoretical statement concerning the robustness and can be applied to all classification models.

3   Robustness Definition

This paper focuses on the robustness measurement of neural networks against natural perturbations. To clarify the difference between natural perturbations and digital space adversarial attacks, Fig. 1 illustrates an image with its two perturbed versions: perturbed by C&W attack and by maximum acceptable Gaussian noise (44.7%) calculated by SRC (our method). Practical neural network robustness measurement at this stage shall care more about the images with Gaussian noise and other semantic changes rather than the ones perturbed by C&W and other digital attacks. Thereby, we define the robustness of classifiers as:

$$\mathcal{R} = \mathbb{E}_{x \in X}[\max \sigma_x], \tag{5}$$

$$\text{s.t.} \quad P[g(x') = 1 | L(x, x') \leq \sigma_x] \leq \epsilon \tag{6}$$

where x and X are an input sample and the corresponding dataset respectively; σ_x represents the acceptable perturbation bound of x; x' is a perturbed version of x and its distance to x is measured by L, i.e., $L(x, x')$; and ϵ is an acceptable probabilistic bound for the ratio of adversarial examples in a given region. It is noted that this definition is a generalized version of that in [5] and [7] (set $\epsilon = 0$ and finding the minimum adversarial perturbation is equivelant to finding the maximum perturbation under which no adversarial example can be found) but emphasizes the acceptance of limited adversarial examples.

4   Statistical Robustness Certificates for Neural Networks

In many applications, sound and complete neural network verification is not practical due to limited computation resources and time. Consequently, rather than proving that a neural network is perfectly robust against some small perturbations, it is preferred to find a large bound which provides statistical guarantee of the limited existence of adversarial examples. According to the discussion in the last section, we are prone to finding a bound that is able to state with high confidence, e.g., 99%, that the chance that a neural network performs unexpectedly is below an acceptable threshold, e.g., 5%. This statement is regarded as a statistical robustness certificate that helps build our confidence in utilizing the corresponding neural network, and it aligns well with the robustness definition in Eqs. (5) and (6).

4.1   Hoeffding Inequality

To help identify the bound $\max \sigma_x$ in Eq. (5), we have to figure out a way to get P in Eq. (6). Due to the reason that the target region $S = \{x' | L(x, x') \leq \sigma_x\}$ has infinite samples, we resort to statistical sampling methods for estimating P. Hoeffding Inequality [21, 22] is a mathematical tool that discusses the feasibility of estimating the probability of an event happening, e.g., a tossed coin got landing heads up, through sampling. Its mathematical formulation is as follows:

$$P[|\nu - \mu| > \epsilon] \leq 2e^{-2\epsilon^2 N}, \tag{7}$$

where ν denotes the empirical probability of event happening, μ the ground-truth probability of event happening, ϵ the error bound, N the number of events being tested, and $P[|\nu - \mu| > \epsilon]$ the probability of the event $|\nu - \mu| > \epsilon$ happening. To fit the context of statistical robustness certificates, ν and μ represent respectively the estimated and real probability of adversarial examples of a data instance x within a certain nearby area parametrized by σ_x, i.e.,

$$\mu = \mathbb{E}[g(x') | L(x, x') \leq \sigma_x] = P[g(x') = 1 | L(x, x') \leq \sigma_x]. \tag{8}$$

By sampling and testing the perturbed data around x, ν is thereby available by simply calculating the percentage of the perturbed inputs that are adversarial. Note that, by estimating Eq. (8) with the sampling method, we assume that all the samples are independent, and all the features of the samples are independent. Hoeffding Inequality tells us that ν approximates μ as close as possible when the sample size grows to infinite, i.e., $N \to \infty$. As we could tolerate certain difference between ν and μ, i.e., $\epsilon \neq 0$, the sample size N can be limited.

Now, imagine that a bound σ_x and an error bound, e.g., $\epsilon = 5\%$, are given in the first place. With certain selected number of samples, e.g., $N = 1024$, by Hoeffding Inequality we have $P[|\nu - \mu| > 5\%] \leq 1.2\%$. If no adversarial example is found, i.e., $\nu = 0$, it becomes $P[\mu > 5\%] \leq 1.2\%$. This means we have more than 98.8% confidence to believe that $\mu \leq 5\%$. In other words, it is believed that the proportion of the adversarial examples in the given region is less than 5%. Building upon this idea, the key of statistical robustness certification is to identify the maximum perturbation $\max \sigma_x$ such that it suffices $\nu = 0$, so that:

$$P[\mu > \epsilon] \leq 2e^{-2\epsilon^2 N}, \tag{9}$$

with chosen ϵ and N. This could be easily achieved through dichotomizing search and sampling. Concerning the sample size, it is worth noting that, Hoeffding Inequality [21] works whenever the underlying population size is infinite, i.e., there are infinite data samples in a region around x. Therefore, the increased dimensions of x, e.g., the increased resolution of input images, do not change its applicability and the required sample size N remains unchanged. In the scenario when the population size is limited, a smaller sample size may be sufficient [22].

4.2   Statistical Robustness Certification

Algorithm 1: Statistical Robustness Certification (SRC)

Input: target data point x; number of samples N; perturbation bounds $[\sigma_L, \sigma_U]$; lower bound decrease factor γ; distance measurement L.

Output: a maximum perturbation $\max \sigma_x$ that satisfies Eq. (9)

1 select a perturbation σ_x from range $[\sigma_L, \sigma_U]$;
2 **while** *ending condition is not satisfied* **do**
3   sample N data uniformly from the selected region parametrized by σ_x, i.e., $x' \sim \{x'|L(x, x') \leq \sigma_x\}$;
4   **if** *All x' have the same label as x* **then**
5          $\lfloor$ set $\sigma_L = \sigma_x$;
6   **else**
7          $\lfloor$ set $\sigma_U = \sigma_x$ and $\sigma_L = \gamma \sigma_L$;
8      $\lfloor$ set $\sigma_x = \frac{1}{2}(\sigma_L + \sigma_U)$;
9 return σ_x;

With a slight modification of the Hoeffding Inequality, we are able to construct a simple certification process for identifying the robustness of a target neural network in a data instance. The robustness is quantified as the maximum distance $\max \sigma_x$ within which all the sampled data instances have the same label as x, the target data instance. The detailed process is illustrated in Algorithm 1. It takes as input the target data x, the number of samples N, and the distance measurement L which could be based on L_1, L_2 or other semantic distances, e.g., rotation degree. The perturbation bounds $[\sigma_L, \sigma_U]$ are to make sure the selected distance σ_x is within a controllable range and the decrease factor γ is to help decrease the lower perturbation bound σ_L so as to find tighter σ_xs. In addition, the termination condition could be based on the number of iterations or the change of σ_x and etc. In each iteration of the algorithm, we randomly pick N data samples from the region controlled by x, σ_x, and L, i.e., $S = \{x'|L(x, x') \leq \sigma_x\}$. All the N data samples are tested for their labels. If all the labels are the same as that of x, it means we get $\nu = 0$ and the corresponding σ_x is a potential valid bound. We thereby set the lower bound, i.e., $\sigma_L = \sigma_x$, and look for larger potential valid bounds. If it is not the case, i.e., $\nu \neq 0$, we set a sound upper bound, i.e., $\sigma_U = \sigma_x$, and penalize the lower bound, i.e., $\sigma_L = \gamma \sigma_L$. The new bound to be tested is selected as the mean of the upper and lower bounds. To sum up with, given a neural network $\mathcal{N}$ and a data x, a distance $\sigma = \max \sigma_x$ could be identified through sampling data instances surrounding x according to L so that it is able to claim that the probability of $\mu > \epsilon$ is upper bounded by $2e^{-2\epsilon^2 N}$. We call this (ϵ, c)-robustness, where $c = 2e^{-2\epsilon^2 N}$. In other words, with Algorithm 1, a neural network obtains a certificate of its robustness. If (ϵ, c) is fixed for all neural networks, the different distance σs indicate their discrepancies in robustness, i.e., larger σ represents better robustness.

5   Experiments

To validate the effectiveness and efficiency of the proposed method, experiments are conducted using various datasets and neural networks. We provide the detailed setting in the next subsection and the results follow. Note that in all the experiments if without further clarification, L_∞-norm is utilized as the distance measurement. We pick $\epsilon = 5\%$ and $N = 1024$ for identifying $(5\%, 1.2\%)$-robustness of different models. And all the experiments are conducted in a desktop computer with $3.20\,\mathrm{GHz}$ Inter(R) Core(TM) i7-8700 CPU. And no GPU is used in all the experiments.

5.1   Datasets and Neural Nets

In our experiments, we choose image classification as the task and pick MNIST [26], CIFAR-10 [27], ImageNet-C [3] and ImageNet-P [3] as the datasets. MNIST dataset contains grayscale images, each of which has 28×28 pixels, while CIFAR-10 and ImageNet-C/P datasets contains RGB images. 10 images are randomly selected from the repository in each experiment. Note that ImageNet-C and

Table 1. Model information

	Layer setting		Size
MNIST 2-FCNN	[1024]	**alexnet**	243 MB
CIFAR 2-FCNN	[1024]	**mn25**	2 MB
MNIST CNN (DD/Adv)	[32, 32, 64, 64, 200, 200]	**mn100**	19 MB
CIFAR CNN (DD/Adv)	[64, 64, 128, 128, 256, 256]	**resnet50**	121 MB

Table 2. Comparison of method effectiveness for neural network robustness measurement (MNIST and CIFAR-10)

	Perturbation [0, 1]	2-FCNN	CNN	CNN DD	CNN Adv
MNIST	**SRC**	**0.36815**	**0.44700**	**0.45402**	**0.52097**
	C&W attack	0.07393	0.12958	0.13602	0.17146
	CNN-Cert	0.00917	0.00790	0.00848	0.00826
CIFAR-10	**SRC**	**0.10191**	**0.08232**	**0.07455**	**0.08469**
	C&W attack	0.00746	0.00839	0.00900	0.00710
	CNN-Cert	0.00180	0.00092*	0.00092*	0.00092*

* The result is not accurate due to early stop.

Table 3. Comparison of method efficiency for neural network robustness measurement (MNIST and CIFAR-10)

	Time (s)	2-FCNN	CNN	CNN DD	CNN Adv
MNIST	**SRC**	2.00	**15.9**	**16.06**	**15.96**
	C&W attack	32.25	78.62	78.61	77.12
	CNN-Cert	**0.77**	445.69	453.77	454.61
CIFAR-10	**SRC**	6.16	**56.19**	**54.30**	**55.65**
	C&W attack	59.77	161.08	168.47	159.63
	CNN-Cert	**2.27**	331.82*	327.18*	327.79*

* The result is not accurate due to early stop.

ImageNet-P are generated using ImageNet dataset with "corruptions" and "perturbations" respectively which are detailed in [3].

For neural networks used in the experiments, we have trained 4 neural networks: a 2-layer fully connected neural network (2-FCNN), a 7-layer convolution neural network (CNN), a 7-layer CNN trained with defensive distillation [23] (CNN DD), and an adversarial trained 7-layer CNN using adversarial examples found by C&W attack (CNN Adv). In addition, 4 well-known pre-trained neural networks [28] for ImageNet dataset are also introduced. They are alexnet, mobilenet_v1_025 (mn25), mobilenet_v1_100 (mn100), and resnet_v2_50(resnet50). Selected details of these models are shown in Table 1.

5.2 Accuracy and Efficiency

Accuracy. In Table 2, the effectiveness of SRC in MNIST and CIFAR-10 datasets are illustrated comparing with C&W attack [4] and CNN-Cert [9], which are two existing methods that could be applied for robustness measurement of neural networks. It is shown that CNN-Cert produces the lowest perturbation bounds. This is due to the fact that CNN-Cert over-approximates its output bounds during the certification process and as a result largely shrinks the perturbation bounds. Larger and deeper neural networks will make the situation worse and result with perturbation bounds of little use. For example, the perturbation bounds provided by CNN-Cert in Table 2 have values lower than 0.0018 which means averagely a 0.2% change of the pixels in an image could result in a different label. This is usually not acceptable in practice. What is worse is that the results produced by CNN-Cert are not comparable because the effect of over-approximation vary according to different settings of a model. Therefore, CNN-Cert and other methods that leverage over-approximation have limitation in the task of neural network robustness measurement. On the other hand, C&W attack provides larger bounds but it does not support any guarantee concerning the robustness of the neural networks. Moreover, the results given by C&W attack primarily reflect the security of neural networks against carefully crafted digital attacks rather than the robustness of neural networks against natural perturbations. SRC gives the largest perturbation bounds among the three methods and, in MNIST, it aligns well with C&W attack. This demonstrates its effectiveness. In CIFAR-10, SRC and C&W attack do not agree with each other. This could be due to the increased complexity of the images in CIFAR-10 and the essential difference of the security against manually crafted adversarial examples and the robustness against natural perturbations.

Figure 2 represents the effectiveness of four well-known neural networks over ImageNet-C dataset. In detail, 6 types of perturbation, i.e., snow, blur, brightness, and three types of noise, are considered here and each perturbation contains 250 images with 5 different degrees. For the validation results measured by testing different models with the perturbed dataset, the values are in percentage. For example, the accuracy of alexnet over perturbed dataset 'snow' is 16%. For 'PERTURBATION [0,1]', the values are produced by SRC. For 0.06891, it means averagely in alexnet one has to perturb the pixels in an image (each pixel is normalized to [0,1]) by 0.06891 to randomly produce an adversarial example with more than 5% chance. The top part of Fig. 2 vividly illustrates the robustness of each neural network. The left axis is in percentage representing the testing accuracy (coloured bars) of different models against different perturbations, while the right axis is in range [0, 1] indicating the model robustness (red line) calculated by SRC. It is obvious that the results of SRC align well with the validation results using ImageNet-C. This strongly supports the effectiveness of SRC.

Efficiency. From the perspective of efficiency, SRC also demonstrates its advantageous. In Table 3, it is apparent that SRC consumes the least time in larger scale neural networks, having a 3x-30x boosting in time saving compared to

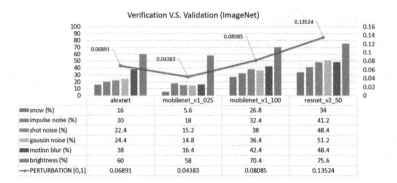

Fig. 2. Comparison of method effectiveness for neural network robustness measurement (ImageNet)

CNN-Cert and C&W attack. For small networks, i.e., 2-FCNN, CNN-Cert takes only 0.77 s and 2.27 s in MNIST and CIFAR-10 datasets respectively. This is because 2-FCNN has few neurons and layers so that CNN-Cert could solve the underlying matrix calculation and over-approximation efficiently, while SRC and C&W attack still have to go through many iterations to find a satisfactory result. In this study, we did not compare our method with optimization-based neural network verification method due to their low efficiency reported in [9].

5.3 Semantic Perturbations: Rotation, Scale, Shear, and Tilt

In the above experiments, SRC controls image perturbation according to individual pixels, i.e., focusing on the L_∞-norm of the image x. This is to measure the general robustness of a classifier. In practice, the concerns about specific risk scenarios, e.g., camera rotation, motivate the robustness measurement under specific types of perturbations. Image rotation, scaling, shear, and tilt are considered as four critical perturbations that intensely effect the performance of an image recognition system. The inability to work well with the perturbations will definitely undermine the trustworthiness of the system. To measure the robustness against specific perturbations, SRC can manipulate images according to the specific perturbation type. For example, if SRC is to measure the robustness of a neural network against image rotation, the perturbation bounds are picked as rotation bounds $[0°, 360°)$. The distance measurement L becomes the measurement of the rotated degree difference between the original and perturbed images. The N samples in each iteration of SRC are picked according to N randomly selected rotation degrees within the rotation bounds. In other words, as long as a semantic perturbation has a solid bound to pick samples from, SRC is applicable in measuring the robustness of neural networks against this perturbation. All the individual degrees are treat independently to meet the basic assumption of Hoeffding Inequality. Due to the intrinsic sampling procedure, the measurement process of SRC for semantic perturbations is much simpler than related formal

Table 4. Measure of model robustness against semantic perturbations (ImageNet)

	alexnet	mn25	mn100	resnet50
rotation (°)	48.71	16	63.96	**88.73**
upscale (%)	137	132	184	**249**
shear (factor)	19.67	16.70	**28.83**	27.29
tilt (factor)	24.94	18.18	29.38	**29.70**

verification methods, such as [24] which turns semantic perturbations into neural networks for verification.

In Table 4, the $(5\%, 1.2\%)$-robustness of different models are measured according to four semantic perturbations. In 10 randomly selected images, resnet_v2_50 maintains $(5\%, 1.2\%)$-robustness under average 88° rotation of the images. It can also averagely withstand 249% upscale and 29.7° tilt of the images. Other models do not show higher robustness in the three perturbations. It is only for shear that mobilenet_v1_100 model slightly outperforms resnet_v2_50. These results show that in average cases, resnet_v2_50 has better robustness compared with other three models. This result also aligns with the result in Fig. 2 indicating that SRC is useful in measuring model robustness against semantic perturbations.

6   Conclusion

In this paper, we propose a practical method SRC to efficiently measure the robustness of neural networks against natural perturbations which includes random noises and semantic perturbations. Through extensive experiments, it is shown that the method is effective and efficient, and most importantly it is applicable in comparing commercial neural networks such as alexnet and resnet with little resources. The distinct features of SRC make it a valid commercial tool for robustness measurement of neural networks.

References

1. Bastani, O., Ioannou, Y., Lampropoulos, L., Vytiniotis, D., Nori, A., Criminisi, A.: Measuring neural net robustness with constraints. In: Advances in Neural Information Processing Systems, pp. 2613–2621 (2016)
2. Yu, F., Qin, Z., Liu, C., Zhao, L., Wang, Y., Chen, X.: Interpreting and evaluating neural network robustness (2019). arXiv preprint arXiv:1905.04270
3. Hendrycks, D., Dietterich, T.: Benchmarking neural networks robustness to common corruptions and perturbations (2019). arXiv preprint arXiv:1903.12261
4. Carlini N., Wagner, D.: Towards evaluating the robustness of neural networks. In: IEEE Symposium on Security and Privacy, pp. 39–57 (2017)
5. Szegedy, C., et al.: Intriguing properties of neural networks (2013). arXiv preprint arXiv:1312.6199

6. Liu, C., Arnon, T., Lazarus, C., Barrett, C., Kochenderfer, M.J., Algorithms for verifying deep neural networks (2019). arXiv preprint arXiv:1903.06758

7. Rauber, J., Brendel, W., Bethge, M.: Foolbox: a python toolbox to benchmark the robustness of machine learning models (2017). arXiv preprint arXiv:1707.04131

8. Katz, G., Barrett, C., Dill, D.L., Julian, K., Kochenderfer, M.J.: Reluplex: an efficient SMT solver for verifying deep neural networks. In: International Conference on Computer Aided Verification, pp. 97–117 (2017)

9. Boopathy, A., Weng, T.W., Chen, P.Y., Liu, S., Daniel, L.: CNN-Cert: an efficient framework for certifying robustness of convolutional neural networks. Proc. AAAI Conf. Artif. Intell. **33**, 3240–3247 (2019)

10. Singh, G., Gehr, T., Püschel, M., Vechev, M.: An abstract domain for certifying neural networks. Proc. ACM Program. Lang. **3**, 1–30 (2019)

11. Krizhevsky, A., Sutskever, I., Hinton, G.E.: Imagenet classification with deep convolutional neural networks. In: Advances in Neural Information Processing Systems, pp. 1097–1105 (2012)

12. Howard, A.G., et al.: Mobilenets: efficient convolutional neural networks for mobile vision applications (2017). arXiv preprint arXiv:1704.04861

13. He, K., Zhang, X., Ren, S., Sun, J.: Deep residual learning for image recognition. In: Proceedings of the IEEE Conference on Computer Vision and Pattern Recognition, pp. 770–778 (2016)

14. Goodfellow, I.J., Shlens, J., Szegedy, C.: Explaining and harnessing adversarial examples (2014). arXiv preprint arXiv:1412.6572

15. Singh, G., Gehr, T., Mirman, M., Püschel, M., Vechev, M.: Fast and effective robustness certification. In: Advances in Neural Information Processing Systems, pp. 10802–10813 (2018)

16. Dutta, S., Jha, S., Sanakaranarayanan, S., Tiwari, A.: Output range analysis for deep neural networks (2017). arXiv preprint arXiv:1709.09130

17. Huang, X., Kwiatkowska, M., Wang, S., Wu, M.: Safety verification of deep neural networks. In: International Conference on Computer Aided Verification, pp. 3–29 (2017)

18. Papernot, N., et al.: Technical report on the cleverhans v2. 1.0 adversarial examples library (2016). arXiv preprint arXiv:1610.00768

19. Baidu (2019).https://github.com/advboxes/perceptron-benchmark

20. Narodytska, N., Kasiviswanathan, S.P.: Simple black-box adversarial perturbations for deep networks (2016). arXiv preprint arXiv:1612.06299

21. Hoeffding, W.: Probability inequalities for sums of bounded random variables. J. Am. Stat. Assoc. **58**, 13–30 (1963)

22. Serfling, R.: Probability inequalities for the sum in sampling without replacement. Ann. Stat. **38**, 39–48 (1973)

23. Papernot, N., McDaniel, P., Wu, X., Jha, S., Swami, A.: Distillation as a defense to adversarial perturbations against deep neural networks. In: IEEE Symposium on Security and Privacy, pp. 582–597 (2016)

24. Mohapatra, J., Chen, P.Y., Liu, S., Daniel, L.: Towards verifying robustness of neural networks against semantic perturbations (2019). arXiv preprint arXiv:1912.09533

25. FAA: System Safety Handbook, Washington, DC (2000)

26. https://github.com/MadryLab/mnist

27. https://github.com/MadryLab/cifar10

28. http://jaina.cs.ucdavis.edu/datasets/adv/imagenet/

Model Extraction and Adversarial Attacks on Neural Networks Using Switching Power Information

Tommy Li and Cory Merkel[✉]

Brain Lab, Rochester Institute of Technology, Rochester, NY 14623, USA
{txl2747,cemeec}@rit.edu
http://www.rit.edu/brainlab/

Abstract. Artificial neural networks (ANNs) have gained significant popularity in the last decade for solving narrow AI problems in domains such as healthcare, transportation, and defense. As ANNs become more ubiquitous, it is imperative to understand their associated safety, security, and privacy vulnerabilities. Recently, it has been shown that ANNs are susceptible to a number of adversarial evasion attacks - inputs that cause the ANN to make high-confidence misclassifications despite being almost indistinguishable from the data used to train and test the network. This work explores to what degree finding these examples may be aided by using side-channel information, specifically switching power consumption, of hardware implementations of ANNs. A black-box threat scenario is assumed, where an attacker has access to the ANN hardware's input, outputs, and topology, but the trained model parameters are unknown. Then, a surrogate model is trained to have similar functional (i.e. input-output mapping) and switching power characteristics as the oracle (black-box) model. Our results indicate that the inclusion of power consumption data increases the fidelity of the model extraction by up to 30% based on a mean square error comparison of the oracle and surrogate weights. However, transferability of adversarial examples from the surrogate to the oracle model was not significantly affected.

1 Introduction

Artificial neural networks (ANNs) have become increasingly popular in the past several years due to a convergence of better training algorithms, faster hardware, and the availability of large labeled datasets. However, as they become more ubiquitous, ANNs are facing mounting challenges related to their privacy, security, and safety. In large part, this is due to recent demonstrations that show ANNs such as deep convolutional neural networks (CNNs) can easily be fooled into providing high-confidence misclassifications through small, imperceptibly-perturbed versions of their inputs (a.k.a. adversarial examples) [13]. The study of these types of issues from a more general machine learning (ML) context (*adversarial machine learning or AML*) can be traced back to the mid-2000's

© Springer Nature Switzerland AG 2021
I. Farkaš et al. (Eds.): ICANN 2021, LNCS 12891, pp. 91–101, 2021.
https://doi.org/10.1007/978-3-030-86362-3_8

[5,10]. Today, AML research focus has been amplified by the popularity of deep learning, with over 3000 papers published on AML attacks, defenses, and theory since 2014 alone [4].

An important subset of AML research deals with so-called black-box attacks of ML models, where an attacker has no knowledge of the model parameters, but can query the model by controlling its inputs and observing its outputs (e.g. classification). Through this process, the attacker may be able to learn the model's behavior, or even its exact parameter values, which could hold private or proprietary information. Furthermore, if the behavior is extracted, then one may craft adversarial examples that cause the model to behave in an unintended way. In this work, we consider the case where attackers make use of not only model outputs, but also side-channel information, to perform black-box attacks. side-channel information can be described as unintended or non-primary sources of information about a computation that typically depend on low-level implementation details. Examples include power consumption, analyzing timing between inputs and outputs, observing emitted sound, and checking memory accesses [20]. In this work, we focus on power consumption as a source of side-channel information. A few existing works have explored the ability to extract information about black-box ANN models by measuring power consumption. Wei et al. utilized a hardware-based ANN's power to recover the inputs to the network [16]. Yoshida et al. mounted a model extraction attack on a small multilayer perceptron (MLP) model (20 model parameters) implemented on a field programmable gate array (FPGA) using correlation power analysis [19]. Hua et al. successfully performed a model extraction attack on a CNN by observing read and write memory accesses to extract layer parameters [7]. Batina et al. extracted all parameters of an MLP model using timing and power side-channel information [2]. The activation function was recovered using timing analysis, the weights were calculated using correlation power analysis, and the layer parameters were obtained using simple power analysis.

This work expands on these previous studies and provides the following novel contributions:

- A Siamese ANN-based methodology for extracting black-box ANN parameters using switching power consumption
- A study of the transferability of adversarial examples from the extracted model to the black-box model

The rest of this paper is organized as follows: Sect. 2 provides necessary background on AML. Section 3 details the simulation setup, including ANN parameters, power consumption model, and important metrics. Section 4 provides simulation results and analyses, and Sect. 5 concludes this work.

2   Background

AML concerns both the offensive and defensive measures associated with malperformance and/or privacy of ML. This paper focuses on offensive measures, or attacks, which can be placed into three categories [3,9,15]. 1.) Evasion attacks exploit the idea that most ML models such as ANNs learn small-margin decision boundaries. Legitimate inputs to the model are perturbed just enough to move them to a different decision region in the input space. 2.) Poisoning attacks typically use modified labeling or addition of training data to reduce the margins of decision boundaries or insert new boundaries that cause misclassifications and also make evasion attacks easier to perform. 3.) A third type of attack targets the privacy of ML models and/or training data. By querying models, these attacks can use statistical methods to infer private information about the parameters of the model or the training set itself. Of these types, evasion attacks are the most well-studied, especially in deep learning models. In the mid-2000's, evasion attacks were introduced as small perturbations to the content of emails, causing them to be misclassified by linear spam filters [5,10,11]. In 2014, Szegedy et al. [13] showed that imperceptible perturbations in the pixel space of images led to high-confidence misclassifications by CNNs. The goal of an evasion attack can be expressed as an optimization problem, where, for some model Π, a correctly-classified input $\mathbf{u}$, usually from the test or training set, is perturbed by $\mathbf{r}^*$ to maximize a loss function $\mathcal{L}$ and cause Π's classification of $\mathbf{u}' = \mathbf{u} + \mathbf{r}^*$ to be different from $\mathbf{u}$'s ground truth label:

$$\mathbf{r}^* = \underset{\mathbf{r} \in \mathcal{R},}{\arg\max} \quad \mathcal{L}_{\Pi}(\mathbf{u} + \mathbf{r}, l) \tag{1}$$
$$\text{s.t.} \quad l' \neq l$$

where l is $\mathbf{u}$'s ground truth label, l' is the model's label for $\mathbf{u}'$, and $\mathcal{R}$ is the set of set of allowed perturbations. $\mathbf{u}'$ is called an adversarial example. Often, the allowed set of perturbations takes the form of an ℓ^p-norm constraint: $\mathcal{R} = \{\mathbf{r} \in \mathbb{R}^N : ||\mathbf{r}||_p \leq D\}$ where N is the dimension of the input space. The ℓ^p-norm of $\mathbf{r}$ is usually bounded in a way that the difference between $\mathbf{u}$ and $\mathbf{u}'$ is difficult or impossible to perceive by a human. Attacks are usually performed using ℓ^p-norms with $p = 2$ or $p = \infty$. However, $p = 0$ and $p = 1$ are also common. $\mathcal{R}$ may also be formed using multiple ℓ^p-norms, box constraints (e.g. bounding all inputs between a minimum and maximum value), or by choosing $\mathbf{r}$ as some type of transformation that imposes a dependence between the elements of $\mathbf{r}$ (e.g. affine transformations such as rotation, scaling, etc.). A number of evasion attacks have been proposed based on (1), differing primarily in the way they define $\mathcal{R}$, how much information they assume is known about Π (white-box vs. black-box attacks), the way they approach the optimization procedure, and whether they are targeted (e.g. classifying a school bus image as an ostrich) or untargeted (e.g. classifying a school bus as anything other than a school bus).

This paper focuses on the untargeted fast gradient sign method (FGSM) evasion attack applied to ANN models. Introduced by Goodfellow et al. [6], FGSM can be written as

$$\mathbf{r}^* = \epsilon \times \text{sgn}\left(\nabla_{\mathbf{u}} \mathcal{L}_{\Pi}(\mathbf{u}, l)\right) \tag{2}$$

where $\text{sgn}(\cdot)$ is the sign function. This attack is easy to apply when full details of Π (i.e. structure and parameters) are known. However, a more realistic attack scenario is that limited information about Π is available to the attacker. In this case, Π is considered a black-box model, and attacking Π is called a black-box attack[1]. Specifically, in this work, we assume that the attacker does not know the weights and biases of the black-box ANN model, but does know the ANN topology, activation functions, etc. We believe that this is a likely scenario, since many applications employ well-known ANNs (e.g. CNNs such as ResNet-50, VGG-16, etc.) and then train them or fine tune them for their particular dataset. One of the popular methods for performing black-box attacks on ANNs is to estimate their behavior using a surrogate model $\hat{\Pi}$. Then, adversarial examples can easily be generated for the surrogate model since all of the model details are known (white-box attack). Finally, the adversarial examples generated against the surrogate model can be transferred to the black-box model. Note, in this context, the black-box model is often referred to as the oracle model. We can define the transferability as the probability that the oracle's label will be modified by the adversarial example given that the example also modified the surrogate's label and the original labels of both models matched the ground truth target label l_t:

$$Tr = \Pr\left(l' \neq l \middle| \hat{l}' \neq \hat{l} \wedge \hat{l} = l = l_t\right) \tag{3}$$

where l' and l are the oracle's label of the adversarial and original inputs and $\hat{l}'$ and $\hat{l}$ are the surrogate's label of the adversarial and original inputs. In general, the transferability depends on how well the oracle model is extracted and estimated by the surrogate. Interestingly, transferability does not necessarily depend on Π and $\hat{\Pi}$ having identical parameters, and extracting the model behavior is generally much easier than finding the exact parameter values [8,12,14]. Here, we adopt a query-based approach [12], where the surrogate model is trained on examples from the oracle's training set. The surrogate's target for each input is the label that the oracle assigns to it. The goal of this work is to determine if additional information (power consumption) from the query will lead to better transferability between the surrogate and the oracle with the same number of queries.

3   Simulation Setup

In this work, the oracle and surrogate models are MLPs with 784 inputs, a single 100-neuron hidden layer, and a 10-neuron softmax output layer, trained on the MNIST dataset [1]. The hidden neurons use a binary activation function:

$$b(s) = \begin{cases} 0 & s < 0 \\ 1 & s \geq 0 \end{cases} \tag{4}$$

Quantized activations, especially binary activations, are attractive from a hardware perspective, since they require fewer hardware resources (i.e. transistors)

---

[1] Note that sometimes gray-box is used to describe the situation where some, but not all details of Π are known, but here we use the term black-box to indicate imperfect knowledge of Π.

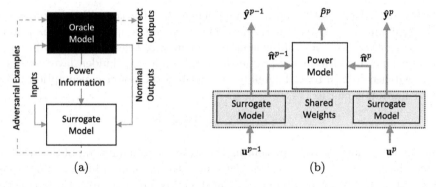

Fig. 1. Extraction of the oracle model using switching power information. (a) The surrogate model is trained using both the model outputs (i.e. classification label) and the oracle's switching power. (b) A Siamese network structure with shared weights is used to train the surrogate to match the oracle's classifications as well as its switching power.

and they often have a limited effect on the accuracy of an ANN [18]. One challenge of training ANNs with binary activations is that the gradient is undefined when the activation function input is 0. To overcome this challenge, we approximate the gradient as if b were a sigmoid function:

$$\frac{\partial b(s)}{\partial s} \approx \frac{\partial \sigma(2s)}{\partial s} = \sigma(2s)\left(1 - \sigma(2s)\right) \tag{5}$$

where $\sigma(\cdot)$ is the logistic sigmoid function. Here, we empirically found that scaling the sigmoid argument by 2 leads to better training results.

Both the oracle and surrogate models were implemented in tensorflow. The oracle model was trained on all 60,000 images of the MNIST training set and achieved an average test accuracy of $\approx$90%. The surrogate model was trained on different subsets of the MNIST training set, using the outputs of the trained oracle as the target labels. In addition, the relative switching power of the oracle model's hidden layer was simulated to use as an additional training target for the surrogate, as shown in Fig. 1(a). Here, we assume that the oracle model is implemented on digital hardware such as an FPGA, and that we can isolate the switching power of the hidden layer neurons from the rest of the power consumption profile. For a digital circuit, the switching power at a node can be written as

$$P_{switch} = \alpha C V_{dd}^2 f \tag{6}$$

where α is the probability that a circuit node changes from 0 to 1 within a clock period, C is the node's capacitance, V_{dd} is the supply voltage, and f is the clock frequency [17]. Since C, V_{dd}, and f are the same for the output of each hidden layer neuron, we can capture their relative power consumption by how often they switch from 0 to 1. However, note that an attacker would likely only have access to a total, aggregated power profile. Even if the hidden layer's switching power can be isolated from other power components, the attacker will only know the total switching power. Therefore, in essence, we can simplify our assumptions by stating that, for each subsequent pair of inputs, the attacker will be able to determine from the power profile the total number of hidden layer neurons that switched from 0 to 1. Therefore, we redefine the power consumption for a particular input pair as

$$P^p = (\pi^p - \pi^{p-1})(\pi^p)^\top \tag{7}$$

where π is a binary vector representing the state (neuron outputs) of the oracle's hidden layer. Note, that this is just the sum of the number of hidden nodes that switched from 0 to 1 when input $p-1$ switched to input p. Now, the surrogate can be trained using both the oracle outputs and power information, as shown in Fig. 1(b). Here, we adopt a Siamese network structure, where two surrogate models with shared weights are trained on two inputs that were subsequently used to query the oracle. The loss function for the surrogate can be written as

$$\mathcal{L} = \mathcal{L}_{CE}(\mathbf{y}^{p-1}, \hat{\mathbf{y}}^{p-1}) + \mathcal{L}_{CE}(\mathbf{y}^p, \hat{\mathbf{y}}^p) + \beta \left[P^p - \hat{P}^p \right]^2 \tag{8}$$

where $\mathcal{L}_{CE}$ is the cross entropy loss, $\beta \geq 0$ is the relative loss of the power consumption, and $\mathbf{y}$ and $\hat{\mathbf{y}}$ or the outputs of the oracle and surrogate models, respectively.

4 Results and Analysis

4.1 Model Estimation

In our first set of simulations, we analyzed the effect of including switching power consumption on the efficacy of query-based model estimation. The surrogate model was trained with different-sized subsets of the MNIST training data, raining from 1 to 60,000. The surrogate model was identically initialized for each training set size. After simulating each training set size, the weights between the oracle and the surrogate were compared using mean-squared error (MSE). The surrogate was trained on each of the training set sizes 50 times, and the results were averaged. A run consisted of the training of the oracle and each training set size for the surrogate. While the weights before the training of the surrogate were identically initialized during each run, they were not identically initialized between runs. Figure 2 shows the relationship between the number of training samples used to train the surrogate and the MSE of the weight matrices.

The MSEs between the various training sample numbers used to train the oracle grows linearly as the number of training examples increases. Initially, this may seem counter-intuitive. However, there are several valid solutions to the MNIST classification problem within the MLP's weight space. As a result, we can loosely think of the training process for both the oracle and surrogate models as two independent random walks starting at the same point. From this view, it is clear that their average distance and MSE will grow with more steps.

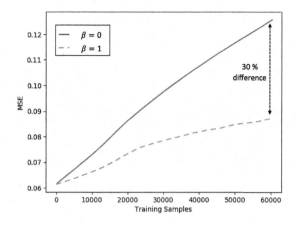

Fig. 2. MSE of the weights between the oracle and the surrogate models with $\beta = 0$ and $\beta = 1$.

We also observe that, with the introduction of power information, there is a decrease in MSE for the larger training set sizes - the MSE at 60,000 training samples decreased from 0.13 to about 0.087, or an overall decrease of 30%. The power information in the loss function likely constrained the weight updates at larger sample sizes.

4.2   Adversarial Transferability

Next, we studied FGSM attacks against the oracle and surrogate models. First, a white-box attack was performed on the trained oracle using the 10,000 test samples to obtain a set of adversarial images. A white-box attack was also performed on the trained surrogates, regardless of the number of training samples used to train it. Two relative accuracies were calculated - one for the white-box attack on the oracle, and a black-box attack on the oracle, where the adversarial images from the surrogate were used to attack the oracle. A relative accuracy is defined as the accuracy of the model on the adversarial examples divided by the accuracy of the model on the unperturbed images. This metric allows for the comparison of how strong the black-box attack is compared to the white-box attack.

Several values for the strength, ϵ, were used to test the effects of the scaling on the attack. Values used for ϵ ranged from 0 to 1. More ϵ values that were tested were between 0.1 and 1, as lower ϵ values did not add enough noise to the adversarial image to cause a large number of misclassifications. Figure 3 shows the average relative accuracy plot of the white-box attack on the oracle vs. the black-box attack on the oracle. Relative accuracy is defined as the accuracy of adversarial images divided by accuracy of unperturbed images. At lower ϵ values, the relative accuracies for both sets of attacks are very close to 1.0, as not much noise was added to the image. The first noticeable change in relative

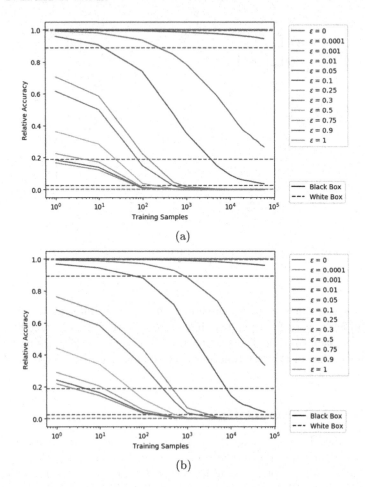

Fig. 3. White-box vs. black-box relative accuracies for (a) $\beta = 0$ and (b) $\beta = 1$.

accuracy occurs at $\epsilon = 0.01$. For all ϵ, the relative accuracy from the black-box attack asymptotically approaches the relative accuracy from the white-box attack. This is expected, as the differing weights between the oracle and surrogate would produce different gradients, and thus, different perturbations would be generated in the attack. For the attacks with the power information, the overall relative accuracy of the black-box attack was higher (such as 0.01 and 0.05), which implies the networks are more resistant to the adversarial examples. We believe that this is likely due to additional and unintended regularization of the surrogate model coming from the power loss.

The transferability of the attacks are presented in Fig. 4. At lower ϵ values, attacks are less likely to transfer, as the adversarial images are unlikely to cause either the oracle or surrogate to mispredict. As expected, more training samples result in higher transferability, as the functionality between the two networks is

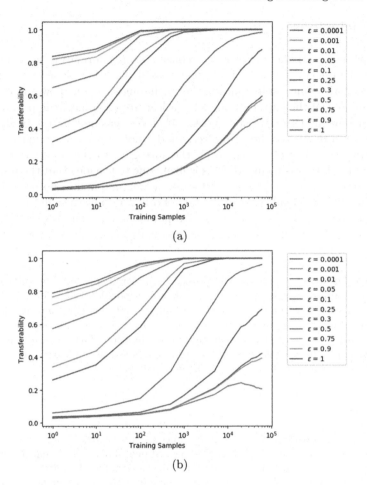

Fig. 4. Transferability of the FGSM attack for (a) $\beta = 0$ and (b) $\beta = 1$.

closer. As ϵ increases, surrogates trained on fewer training examples are more likely to have attacks transferred, as there was increased noise being added to the image. With power information, the overall transferability remained approximately the same and sometimes even decreased. One potential reason for this is that we observed the power component of the loss function often reached a local minimum. Since there are so many possible hidden layer switching behaviors that would lead to the same sum of total switches for two subsequent inputs, it is likely that the power loss landscape is highly non-convex. Further investigation into techniques to better optimize the power loss will be needed in order for this approach to improve transferability.

5   Conclusions

This work explored the use of power consumption information as a means to improve the query efficiency of surrogate-based black-box attacks on artificial neural networks. Our results indicate that including switching power information in the training of the surrogate model can lead to a significant improvement in the fidelity of model extraction (up to 30%) as measured by the MSE of the surrogate and oracle weights. However, we did not observe a significant change in the transferability of attacks from the surrogate to the oracle when power consumption data was included. This is likely due to the idea that the power loss is highly non-convex, and likely settles into a local minimum. Future directions for this work may include the exploration of other optimization techniques, such as genetic algorithms for minimizing the power loss, or smarter querying that allows more efficient integration of the power data into the surrogate training process.

Acknowledgments. This material is based on research sponsored by the Air Force Research Laboratory under agreement number FA8750-20-2-0503. The U.S. Government is authorized to reproduce and distribute reprints for Governmental purposes notwithstanding any copyright notation hereon. The views and conclusions contained herein are those of the authors and should not be interpreted as necessarily representing the official policies or endorsements, either expressed or implied, of the Air Force Research Laboratory or the U.S. Government.

References

1. The MNIST database. http://yann.lecun.com/exdb/mnist/
2. Batina, L., Bhasin, S., Jap, D., Picek, S.: CSI neural network: Using side-channels to recover your artificial neural network information, October 2018
3. Biggio, B., Roli, F.: Wild patterns: ten years after the rise of adversarial machine learning. Patt. Recogn. **84**, 317–331 (2018)
4. Carlini, N.: A complete list of all (arXiv) adversarial example papers. https://nicholas.carlini.com/writing/2019/all-adversarial-example-papers.html
5. Dalvi, N., Domingos, P., Sanghai, S., Verma, D.: Adversarial classification. In: Proceedings of the Tenth ACM SIGKDDI International Conference on Knowledge Discovery and Data mining, pp. 99–108 (2004)
6. Goodfellow, I., Shlens, J., Szegedy, C.: Explaining and harnessing adversarial examples (2015)
7. Hua, W., Zhang, Z., Suh, G.: Reverse engineering convolutional neural networks through side-channel information leaks, In: Proceedings of the 55th Annual Design Automation Conference, November 2018
8. Jagielski, M., Carlini, N., Bethelot, D., Kurakin, A., Papernot, N.: High accuracy and high fidelity extraction of neural networks (March 2020)
9. Joseph, A.D., Nelson, B., Rubinstein, B.I., Tygar, J.: Adversarial Machine Learning. Cambridge University Press, New York (2018)
10. Lowd, D., Meek, C.: Adversarial learning. In: Proceedings of the Eleventh ACM SIGKDD International Conference on Knowledge Discovery in Data Mining, pp. 641–647 (2005)

11. Lowd, D., Meek, C.: Good word attacks on statistical spam filters. In: CEAS, vol. 2005 (2005)
12. Papernot, N., McDaniel, P., Goodfellow, I., Somesh, J., Berkay Celik, Z., Swami, A.: Practical black-box attacks against machine learning, March 2017
13. Szegedy, C., et al.: Intriguing properties of neural networks (2013). arXiv preprint arXiv:1312.6199
14. Troung, J., Maini, P., Walls, R., Papernot, N.: Data-free model extraction, November 2020
15. Vorobeychik, Y., Kantarcioglu, M.: Adversarial machine learning. Synthesis. In: Lectures on Artificial Intelligence and Machine Learning, vol. 12, no. 3, 1–169 (2018)
16. Wei, L., Liu, Y., Luo, B., Xu, Q.: I know what you see: Power side-channel attack on convolutional neural network accelerators, March 2018
17. Weste, N., Harris, D.: CMOS VLSI Design: A Circuits and Systems Perspective. Addison-Wesley, Reading, MA (2005)
18. Yang, J., et al.: Quantization networks. In: Proceedings of the IEEE/CVF Conference on Computer Vision and Pattern Recognition, pp. 7308–7316 (2019)
19. Yoshida, K., Kubota, T., Shiozaki, M., Fujino, T.: Model-extraction attack against FPGA-DNN accelerator utilizing correlation electromagnetic analysis In: 2019 IEEE 27th Annual International Symposium on Field-Programmable Custom Computing Machines (FCCM) (2019)
20. Zhou, Y., Feng, D.: Side-channel attacks: ten years after its publication and the impacts on cryptographic module security testing (2005)

Anomaly Detection

CmaGraph: A TriBlocks Anomaly Detection Method in Dynamic Graph Using Evolutionary Community Representation Learning

Weiqin Lin[1], Xianyu Bao[2], and Mark Junjie Li[1(✉)]

[1] College of Computer Science and Software Engineering,
Shenzhen University, Shenzhen, China
`linweiqin2019@email.szu.edu.cn`, `jj.li@szu.edu.cn`
[2] Shenzhen Academy of Inspection and Quarantine, Shenzhen, China

Abstract. Anomaly detection for dynamic graphs, with graphs changing over time, is essential in many real-world applications. Existing works did not consider the accurate community structures in a dynamic graph. This paper introduces CmaGraph, a TriBlocks framework using an innovative deep metric learning block to measure the distances between vertices within and between communities from an evolution community detection block. A one-class anomaly detection block can capture the dynamic graph's anomalous edges after these two functional blocks. This method significantly enhances the capability to detect anomalous edges by reconstructing the distance between the evolutionary communities' vertices. We demonstrate the implications on three real-world datasets and compare them with the state-of-the-art method.

Keywords: Anomaly detection · Dynamic graph · Evolutionary community detection · Deep metric learning

1 Introduction

Anomaly detection in a dynamic graph has a wide range of applications, such as computer networks, economic systems, and social networks [16]. Many anomalies occur due to significant differences from the previous pattern [3]. For example, if a computer from a subnet suddenly sends many messages to other computers in another subnet that it has rarely sent before, the messages may be anomalous in a computer network. The dynamic graph represents a computer vertex with many edges connected to the surrounding vertices, resulting in a dense subgraph around the vertex or generating a community. These updated edges could be abnormal.

A crucial problem over anomaly detection in dynamic graphs is anomalous edge detection. Edges contain rich features about relationships and structures

Supported by the National key R&D project of China (No. 2018YFC1603601).

[17]. Therefore, finding anomalous edges can be used in security domain, such as an intrusion detection system, social network anomaly detection, and fault detection [3]. In this paper, we focus on anomalous edge detection in a dynamic graph.

Limited work has been done in community structures in dynamic graph anomaly detection [5]. Many of the existing anomaly detection methods for the dynamic graph used heuristic rules [1,5,15,15]. These methods heuristically defined the anomalies features in a dynamic graph and then used the defined features for anomaly detection. However, heuristic methods are challenging in adapting to complex and variable patterns of anomalies in large-scale dynamic graphs. With the popularity of deep learning, there have been many anomaly detection methods for a dynamic graph using deep learning technologies [21,22]. Compared with traditional heuristic rules, these methods can learn better features that can adapt to complex anomaly patterns. However, existing deep learning anomaly detection methods for dynamic graphs did not consider the dynamic graph's community structures.

The main difficulty in anomaly detection based on community structures is learning accurate community structures by using representation learning in a dynamic graph. First, attention or community-aware based representation learning method can transfer the dynamic graphs to feature space. Then using the above features for anomaly detection. Learning accurate features for anomaly detection will improve the performance of anomaly detection. Both the clique embedding of NetWalk [21] and anomalous score layer of AddGraph [22] are designed for anomaly detection, which all achieve good performance of anomaly detection. However, in community deep learning methods for dynamic graphs, existing works were aimed at the general domain and did not consider how to apply community structures to anomaly detection.

We propose a dynamic graph anomaly detection framework, CmaGraph, which detects a dynamic graph's evolution community structures and learns a community metric enhancement feature for subsequent anomaly detection. It significantly enhances the capability to detect anomalous edges by reconstructing the distances between vertices within and between communities. CmaGraph consists of three blocks, Evolution Community Detection Block (C-Block), Community Metric Enhancement Block (M-Block), and One Class Anomaly Detection Block (A-Block). Specifically, the contributions of CmaGraph are as follows:

- CmaGraph detects the evolutionary community structures of dynamic graph.
- CmaGraph uses deep metric learning to learn community metric enhancement feature for anomaly detection, which significantly enhances the capability to detect anomalous edges.
- We experiment on three real datasets to prove the effectiveness of CmaGraph.

The rest of this article is organized as follows. We first summarize the related work in Sect. 2. In Sect. 3, we propose the CmaGraph framework, including the formula of the method and the anomaly detection process. Then, in Sect. 4, we conduct experiments on three real datasets and show the performance of CmaGraph. Finally, we summarize this paper in the Sect. 5.

2   Related Work

Most of the existing methods were based on heuristic rules. GOutlier [1] designed a reservoir sampling method to maintain a structural summary of the dynamic graph and dynamically partitioned the graph to build a model of connection behavior. Then it defined the outliers by the model. CM-Sketch [15] used sketches to provide constant complexity of time and space, and extracted global and local structure feature to define outliers. StreamSpot [12] designed a similarity function of two graphs and used clustering algorithms to distinguish between normal and anomalous behaviors. GMicro [2] created hash-compressed micro-clusters from the graph stream by using hash-based edges, which can reduce the size of the representation. SpotLight [7] encoded the graph by randomly sample vertex sets and calculating the overlap between vertex sets and vertices of the current edge set. Finally, it used a clustering algorithm to find an anomalous graph. The above methods used heuristic rules to define the features of the dynamic graph. However, the anomalies patterns are variable and complex. Heuristic rules are challenging in adapting to complex anomalies patterns.

With the development of deep learning, some methods used graph embedding for anomaly detection. Most of existed works learned the static graph embedding at each timestamp through deep learning techniques [8,14,18]. The static graph embedding was extended to dynamic graph embedding by aggregation, sequence model, etc. [10,20]. However, in most cases, these dynamic graph embedding techniques were aimed at the general domain, and may not work well in anomaly detection. Therefore, there are some anomaly detection methods based on dynamic graph embedding recently. NetWalk [21] learned vertex embedding on a random walk sequence set by a custom autoencoder introduced clique embedding for anomaly detection. AddGraph [22] used Graph Convolutional Network [11] and Gated Recurrent Unit to capture the structural and temporal features of dynamic graph respectively, and introduced anomalous score layer for anomaly detection. These two methods were based on graph embedding for anomaly detection, which can learn better features, adapt to complex anomalies patterns, and have better performance than heuristic rules. However, in graph embedding methods for anomaly detection, existing methods did not consider the dynamic graph's community structures. We detect evolutionary community structures and reconstruct the distances between vertices within and between communities for anomaly detection.

3   Proposed Method

In this section, we formalize the problem and propose the framework of our method.

3.1   Problem Definition

A dynamic graph $\mathbb{G}$ where the element takes the form of $\mathcal{G}^t = (\mathcal{V}^t, \mathcal{E}^t)$ is a temporal graph. Here $\mathcal{G}^t$ is the graph in $\mathbb{G}$ at timestamp t, and $\mathbb{G} = \{\mathcal{G}^t\}_{t=1}^T$. With the update of the graph, the incoming edge set is denoted by E^t, and all vertices in E^t are denoted by set V^t. We set the entire vertex set $\mathcal{V}^t = \cup_{i=1}^t V^i$, the entire edge set $\mathcal{E}^t = \cup_{i=1}^t E^i$, $n = |\mathcal{V}^t|$, and $m^t = |E^t|$. At timestamp t, we use $\mathbf{A}^t \in \mathbb{R}^{n \times n}$ to represent the adjacency matrix of $\mathcal{G}^t$. We focus on undirected graph, so $\mathbf{A}^t$ is symmetrical. Given $\mathbb{G}$ and timestamp t, our goal is to find anomalous edges in E^t without labelled data. Specifically, this paper outputs anomalous score vectors $\{\mathbf{s}^t\}_{t=1}^T$ where $\mathbf{s}^t$ contains anomalous scores of all edges in E^t, and obtains anomalous edges by setting a threshold.

3.2   CmaGraph Framework

From a global perspective, the main idea of CmaGraph is to detect evolutionary community structures of $\mathbb{G}$ and enhance it for anomaly detection. Figure 1 shows the overview of CmaGraph. The details of each part of the overview are explained in the following.

Evolution Community Detection Block (C-Block). The goal of C-Block is to detect evolutionary community structures. We use adjacency matrices as the input of autoencoder to get vertex embedding and apply k-means to vertex embedding for community detection. Previous research proves that drastic variation in the network is not suitable in many real-life dynamic graph [19]. Therefore, inspired by [13] and [19], we introduce sparsity evolution autoencoder (SeAutoencoder), which can get the stable vertex embedding so that k-means can get stable community labels. It ensures that the changes of community structures cannot be changed drastically. Figure 2 shows the inputs and outputs of C-Block in a synthetic dynamic graph, which shows C-Block can get stable vertex embedding and community labels in dynamic graph.

Formally, at timestamp t, we receive the adjacency matrix $\mathbf{A}^t$ of $\mathcal{G}^t$ and set the hyper-parameter k which is the number of communities. We construct vertex embedding by a l_s layers SeAutoencoder which the forward propagation formula is given by

$$f_s^{l+1} = \sigma(f_s^l \mathbf{W}_s^l + \mathbf{b}_s^l) \tag{1}$$

where $l = 1, \ldots, l_s - 1$, $f_s^1 = \mathbf{A}^t$, $\mathbf{W}_s^l$ and $\mathbf{b}_s^l$ are the weight matrix and bias vector of the l-th layer of SeAutoencoder, and sigmoid function $\sigma(z) = \frac{1}{1+exp(z)}$. We set $\mathbf{H}^t = f_s^{\lceil \frac{l_s}{2} \rceil}$. We apply k-means with k communities to $\mathbf{H}^t$, so we can get a community label vector $\mathbf{c}^t$ that contains the community label of each vertex. Here, $\mathbf{H}^t \in \mathbb{R}^{n \times d}$, d is the dimension of vertex embedding, and $\mathbf{c}^t \in \mathbb{R}^n$. The reconstruction loss function of SeAutoencoder is

$$J_{AE} = \frac{1}{2} \left\| f_s^{l_s} - \mathbf{A}^t \right\|_F^2 \tag{2}$$

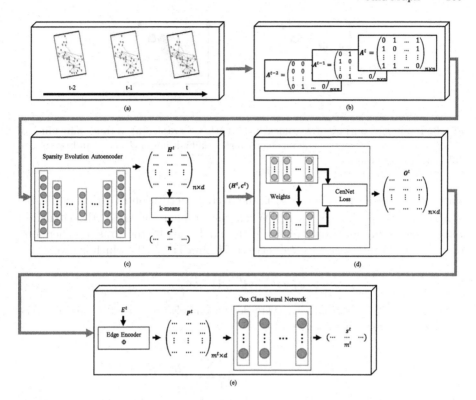

Fig. 1. The overview of CmaGraph. (a) dynamic graph, (b) adjacency matrices, (c) Evolution Community Detection Block, (d) Community Metric Enhancement Block, (e) One Class Anomaly Detection Block.

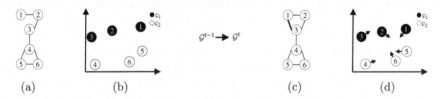

Fig. 2. Inputs and outputs of C-Block in a synthetic dynamic graph. (a) input graph $\mathcal{G}^{t-1}$, (b) output vertex embedding of $\mathcal{G}^{t-1}$, (c) input graph $\mathcal{G}^t$, (d) output vertex embedding of $\mathcal{G}^t$. c_1 and c_2 are two different communities. Arrows in (d) represent the direction of movement of vertex embedding compared to (c).

where $\|\cdot\|_F$ is frobenius norm. Since the adjacency matrices are sparse, we introduce a sparsity constraint. The penalty term of units of SeAutoencoder is defined by Kullback-Leibler divergence [13],

$$KL(\rho\|\hat{\rho}_j^l) = \rho log \frac{\rho}{\hat{\rho}_j^l} + (1-\rho)log \frac{1-\rho}{1-\hat{\rho}_j^l} \qquad (3)$$

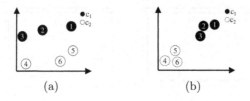

(a)   (b)

Fig. 3. Input and output of M-Block in a synthetic graph. (a) vertex embedding of $\mathcal{G}^{t-1}$, (b) community metric enhancement vertex embedding of $\mathcal{G}^{t-1}$. c_1 and c_2 are two different communities.

where ρ is sparsity parameter, $\hat{\rho}_j^l$ is the average activation of j-th units in the l-th layer, and $\hat{\rho}_j^l = \frac{1}{n}\sum_{i=1}^{n} f_{ij}^l$. When the graph is updated, the change of vertex embedding and community labels should not be too drastic. Therefore, we introduce a temporal loss J_T between $\mathbf{H}^t$ and $\mathbf{H}^{t-1}$ [19] which is given by

$$J_T = \frac{1}{2}\left\|\mathbf{H}^t - \mathbf{H}^{t-1}\right\|_F^2 \tag{4}$$

where $J_T = 0$ if $t = 1$. With l_s layers SeAutoencoder, we want to minimize the final loss function which is given by

$$J_{SeAutoencoder} = J_{AE} + \beta\sum_{l=1}^{l_s}\sum_{j} KL(\rho\|\hat{\rho}_j^l) + \lambda J_T \tag{5}$$

where β and λ control the weights of sparsity constraint and temporal loss respectively.

Community Metric Enhancement Block (M-Block). The goal of M-Block is to reconstruct the distances between the vertices, which makes the euclidean distance between vertices in the same community closer to each other, and the euclidean distance between vertices in different communities farther away from each other. As shown in Fig. 1d, vertex embedding and community label vector are the input of M-Block, and the output of M-Block is community metric enhancement vertex embedding. M-Block uses a community metric enhancement network (CenNet) which is a siamese network [6] for enhancement of vertex embedding, and siamese network is one of deep metric learning methods. It reconstructs the distances between the vertices within the evolutionary communities. As shown in Fig. 3, the enhancement vertex embedding is better than original vertex embedding because the euclidean distances between vertices are more indicative than before.

Formally, at timestamp t, we receive $\mathbf{H}^t$ and $\mathbf{c}^t$ from C-Block. We construct community metric enhancement vertex embedding $\mathbf{O}^t \in \mathbb{R}^{n \times d}$ by a l_c layers fully connected network CenNet with d units for each layer where forward propagation formula is given by

$$f_c^{l+1} = \sigma(f_c^l \mathbf{W}_c^l + \mathbf{b}_c^l) \tag{6}$$

Here $l = 1, \ldots, l_c - 1$, $f_c^1 = \mathbf{H}^t$, $\mathbf{W}_c^l$ and $\mathbf{b}_c^l$ are the weight matrix and bias vector of the l-th layer of CenNet respectively, and $\mathbf{O}^t = f_c^{l_c}$. The loss function of CenNet is contrastive loss which proposed by [6,9], and is given by

$$J_{CenNet} = \frac{1}{2n} \sum_{i=1}^{n} \sum_{j=1}^{n} (y_{ij} d_{ij}^2 + (1 - y_{ij}) max(b - d_{ij}, 0)^2) \tag{7}$$

where $d_{ij} = \|\mathbf{O}_{i\cdot}^t - \mathbf{O}_{j\cdot}^t\|_2$ represents the euclidean distance between sample i and j, $\mathbf{O}_{i\cdot}^t$ is the i-th row of matrix $\mathbf{O}^t$, $y_{ij} = 1$ if sample i and j are in the same community or $y_{ij} = 0$, and b is margin. Since n may be too large to make the calculation of (7) complicated, for a given sample i, instead of going through the whole dataset to get index j, we use negative sampling to get index j, which can reduce the complexity.

One Class Anomaly Detection Block (A-Block). Given E^t, the goal of A-Block is to obtain anomalous scores of all edges in E^t. As shown in Fig. 1e, A-Block applies an edge encoder to $\mathbf{O}^t$ for getting edge embedding. In A-Block, given each edge (u, v) in E^t and $\mathbf{O}^t$, the edge embedding of (u, v) is $exp(-(\mathbf{O}_{u\cdot}^t - \mathbf{O}_{v\cdot}^t)^2)$. It can make better use of the distance information of the embedding. Then A-Block inputs edge embedding into One Class Neural Network (OCNN) [4] which is an anomaly detection model.

Formally, at timestamp t, we receive $\mathbf{O}^t$ of M-Block and E^t. Edge encoder ϕ is an operator to compute edge embedding $\mathbf{P}^t \in \mathbb{R}^{m^t \times d}$ by using $\mathbf{O}^t$ and E^t. We introduce a l_a layers fully connected network OCNN with d hidden units for each hidden layer and its last layer have one unit that represents anomalous score. The forward propagation formula of OCNN is given by

$$f_a^{l+1} = \sigma(f_a^l \mathbf{W}_a^l + \mathbf{b}_a^l) \tag{8}$$

where $l = 1, \ldots, l_a - 2$. The last layer does not apply activation function which means $f_a^{l_a} = f_a^{l_a-1} \mathbf{W}_a^{l_a-1} + \mathbf{b}_a^{l_a-1}$. Here $f_a^1 = \mathbf{P}^t$, $\mathbf{W}_a^l$ and $\mathbf{b}_a^l$ are the weight matrix and bias vector of the l-th layer of OCNN, and anomalous score vector $\mathbf{s}^t = f_a^{l_a}$. The loss function of OCNN is proposed by [4] and is given by

$$J_{OCNN} = \frac{1}{2} \sum_{l=1}^{l_a-2} \|\mathbf{W}_a^l\|_F^2 + \frac{1}{2}\|\mathbf{W}_a^{l_a-1}\|_2^2 + \frac{1}{\nu} \times \frac{1}{m^t} \sum_{i=1}^{m^t} max(0, r - s_i^t) - r \tag{9}$$

where r is the bias of the hyper-plane. ν controls the number of data points that are allowed to cross the hyper-plane, and ν is equivalent to the percentage of anomalies [4]. Finally, we get $\mathbf{s}^t$ and we classify anomalous edges by setting threshold.

Dynamic Update. Formally, at timestamp t, we get the updated edge set Ω^t. We update the adjacency matrix $\mathbf{A}^t$ according to Ω^t, and we use $\mathbf{A}^t$ as the input of CmaGraph. Then we train the SeAutoencoder, CenNet, and OCNN with learning rate α and previous weights. Our framework is summarized in Algorithm 1.

Algorithm 1. CmaGraph

Input: Graph stream $\mathbb{G}$ which contains edge stream $\{E^i\}_{i=1}^t$, vertex set $\mathcal{V}^t$
Parameter: d, α, ρ, β, λ, k, b, ϕ, ν, r, l_s, l_c, and l_a
Output: anomalous score vector $\{\mathbf{s}^t\}_{t=1}^T$
1: Define the network structure of SeAutoencoder, CenNet, OCNN.
2: **for** t=1 to T **do**
3:     Update $\mathbf{A}^t$ according to E^t and $\mathcal{V}^t$
4:     Minimize $J_{SeAutoencoder}$ (5)
5:     $\mathbf{H}^t = f_s^{\lceil \frac{l_s}{2} \rceil}$
6:     Apply kmeans to $\mathbf{H}^t$ with hyper-parameter k to get community label $\mathbf{c}^t$
7:     Minimize J_{CenNet} (7) with the input $\mathbf{H}^t, \mathbf{c}^t$
8:     $\mathbf{O}^t = f_c^{l_c}$
9:     Minimize J_{OCNN} (9) with the input $\mathbf{O}^t, E^t$
10:    $\mathbf{s}^t = f_a^{l_a}$
11: **return** $\{\mathbf{s}^t\}_{t=1}^T$

---

4   Experiment

In this section, we show the setup of the experiment and the results compared with other methods.

4.1   Experiment Setup

Dataset. We evaluate the performance of CmaGraph on the datasets shown in Table 1. UCI Message is a directed graph which is based on an online community graph from the University of California where each vertex represents the user and each edge represents the interactions between users. Digg is based on reply graphs of the website *Digg*. Similar to the UCI Message, each vertex represents the user and each edge represents the reply between the users. DBLP-2010 is a collaboration network of authors from the computer science bibliography in 2010 where each vertex represents author and each edge represents collaboration between authors. Since the anomalous data is difficult to obtain, we use the method of [21] to inject anomalous edges into three datasets.

Table 1. Statistics of datasets

Dataset	#Node	#Edge	Max. Degree	Avg. Degree
UCI Message	1,899	13,838	255	14.57
Digg	30,360	85,155	283	5.61
DBLP-2010	300,647	807,700	238	5.37

Baseline. We compare CmaGraph with the following competing edge anomaly detection methods in dynamic graph.

- GOutlier [1]. It maintains summaries of a graph by designing a sampling method, defines the outliers of the dynamic graph, and outputs an anomalous score for a given edge.
- CM-Sketch [15]. It introduces a sketch-base method to approximate the global and local structural properties of graphs. These approximations are used to find outliers.
- NetWalk [21]. It uses a vertex reservoir strategy to maintain the summaries of dynamic graph, uses custom autoencoder to build vertex embedding, and uses stream k-means to detect anomalous edges.

Experimental Design. We evaluate CmaGraph in two settings: static and dynamic setting. In static setting, we see whether CmaGraph could effectively detect community structures and enhance it for anomaly detection without dynamic updates. In dynamic setting, we split the test set into multiple snapshots to see the performance of CmaGraph in dynamic updates. We use AUC as a metric to compare different methods.

4.2 Experimental Result

Static Setting. For static settings, we use 50% of the data as the normal edge and use them as the input of CmaGraph for training. We inject 1%, 5%, 10% anomalous edges into the remaining 50% of the data as the test set. The dimension d of vertex embedding is set to 64. For C-Block, the number of clusters k is set to 15, the sparsity parameter ρ is set to 0.1, the weight β of sparsity constraint is set to 0.1, the weight λ of temporal loss is set to 1, and the number of layer of C-Block l_s is set to 3. For M-Block, the parameter b is set to 1, and the number of layer of CenNet l_c is set to 2. For A-Block, ν and r are set to 0.05 and 1 respectively, the number of layer of OCNN l_a is set to 3, and the output dimension of OCNN is set to 1. For UCI, the learning rate α of the three networks is set to 0.0001, and $\alpha = 0.00001$ for DBLP-2010 and Digg.

Table 2. AUC results in static setting

Methods	UCI Messages			Digg			DBLP-2010		
	1%	5%	10%	1%	5%	10%	1%	5%	10%
GOutlier	0.7181	0.7053	0.6707	0.6963	0.6763	0.6353	0.7172	0.6891	0.6460
CM-Sketch	0.7270	0.7086	0.6861	0.6871	0.6581	0.6179	0.7097	0.6892	0.6332
Netwalk	0.7758	0.7647	0.7226	0.7563	0.7176	0.6837	0.7654	0.7388	0.6858
CmaGraph	**0.9520**	**0.9574**	**0.9523**	**0.9117**	**0.9124**	**0.9178**	**0.8131**	**0.8148**	**0.8157**

The results of CmaGraph and baselines are shown in Table 2. Because UCI and Digg are the same as those used by Netwalk, and DBLP-2010 is similar to DBLP dataset used by Netwalk, we use the results of baselines reported by Netwalk [21]. The results of CmaGraph are obtained by averaging 10 times and all variances are less than 0.001. CmaGraph surpasses all the other methods in all of the datasets. On UCI and Digg, CmaGraph has at least 0.1554 increment compared to the baselines. On DBLP-2010, it has at least 0.0477 increment compared to the baselines. Significant performance improvement is mainly due to CmaGraph can effectively detect community structures and enhance it for anomaly detection by using deep metric learning, and the learned features can adapt to complex anomalies patterns. It also demonstrates community structures can be effectively applied to graph anomaly detection by deep metric learning.

Dynamic Setting. For dynamic settings, we split test set into multiple snapshots. Averagely, we split 6, 7 and 10 snapshots for UCI, Digg and DBLP-2010 respectively. For each snapshot, we update CmaGraph according to Algorithm 1. The hyper parameters are the same as the static setting. Figure 4 reports the result of dynamic setting where the results of baselines are reported by NetWalk [21] and the results of CmaGraph are obtained by averaging 10 times and all variances are less than 0.001. We see that CmaGraph exceeds other baselines on all the datasets. On UCI, Digg and DBLP-2010, CmaGraph has at least 0.16, 0.08, 0.0045 increment compared to Netwalk respectively. The main reason that CmaGraph beats the baselines on all snapshots of all datasets is that CmaGraph can detect structural features of evolutionary communities and steadily enhance the features for anomaly detection. This also demonstrates that CmaGraph can learn the evolution community structures which can adapt to complex anomalous patterns.

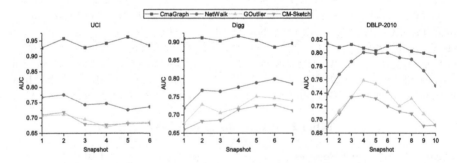

Fig. 4. AUC results in dynamic setting with 5% anomalies

Stability of CmaGraph over Different Percentages of Training Data. In this part, we test the performance of CmaGraph at different percentages of training data. In each percentage, with 5% anomalous edges and parameters in static setting, we run 20 times to get Fig. 5 on dataset Digg. We can see that the AUC of CmaGraph increases gradually with the increase of the percentage.

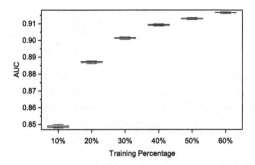

Fig. 5. Stability on Digg with different training percentages

From 10% to 20% training percentage, AUC increases the most. After 20% training percentage, the AUC grows steadily. In different training percentages, the standard deviations are between 0.0003 and 0.0008, which shows the stability of CmaGraph. Even we use 10% training percentage of Digg, CmaGraph also exceeds the best performance of baselines in static settings of 5% anomalous edges, which shows that CmaGraph can achieve good performance in the case of a small number of data.

5   Conclusion

In this paper, we propose the CmaGraph framework that can detect anomalous edges in a dynamic graph. CmaGraph uses three blocks to effectively detect evolutionary community structures and enhance it for anomaly detection. It significantly enhances the capability to detect anomalous edges by reconstructing the distances between the evolutionary communities' vertices. We conduct experiments based on three real-world datasets, and the results demonstrate the effectiveness and stability of CmaGraph, and CmaGraph has an outperformance than existing methods in dynamic graph anomaly detection.

References

1. Aggarwal, C.C., Zhao, Y., Philip, S.Y.: Outlier detection in graph streams. In: 2011 IEEE 27th International Conference on Data Engineering, pp. 399–409. IEEE (2011)
2. Aggarwal, C.C., Zhao, Y., Yu, P.S.: On clustering graph streams. In: Proceedings of the 2010 SIAM International Conference on Data Mining, pp. 478–489. SIAM (2010)
3. Chalapathy, R., Chawla, S.: Deep learning for anomaly detection: a survey (2019). arXiv preprint arXiv:1901.03407
4. Chalapathy, R., Menon, A.K., Chawla, S.: Anomaly detection using one-class neural networks((2018)). arXiv preprint arXiv:1802.06360
5. Chen, Z., Hendrix, W., Samatova, N.F.: Community-based anomaly detection in evolutionary networks. J. Intell. Inf. Sys. **39**(1), 59–85 (2012)

6. Chopra, S., Hadsell, R., LeCun, Y.: Learning a similarity metric discriminatively, with application to face verification. In: 2005 IEEE Computer Society Conference on Computer Vision and Pattern Recognition (CVPR'05), vol. 1, pp. 539–546. IEEE (2005)
7. Eswaran, D., Faloutsos, C., Guha, S., Mishra, N.: Spotlight: detecting anomalies in streaming graphs. In: Proceedings of the 24th ACM SIGKDD International Conference on Knowledge Discovery & Data Mining, pp. 1378–1386 (2018)
8. Grover, A., Leskovec, J.: node2vec: scalable feature learning for networks. In: Proceedings of the 22nd ACM SIGKDD International Conference on Knowledge Discovery and Data Mining, pp. 855–864 (2016)
9. Hadsell, R., Chopra, S., LeCun, Y.: Dimensionality reduction by learning an invariant mapping. In: 2006 IEEE Computer Society Conference on Computer Vision and Pattern Recognition (CVPR 2006). vol. 2, pp. 1735–1742. IEEE (2006)
10. Kazemi, S.M., et al.: Relational representation learning for dynamic (knowledge) graphs: a survey (2019). arXiv preprint arXiv:1905.11485
11. Kipf, T.N., Welling, M.: Semi-supervised classification with graph convolutional networks(2016). arXiv preprint arXiv:1609.02907
12. Manzoor, E., Milajerdi, S.M., Akoglu, L.: Fast memory-efficient anomaly detection in streaming heterogeneous graphs. In: Proceedings of the 22nd ACM SIGKDD International Conference on Knowledge Discovery and Data Mining, pp. 1035–1044 (2016)
13. Ng, A., et al.: Sparse autoencoder. CS294A Lect. Notes **72**(2011), 1–19 (2011)
14. Perozzi, B., Al-Rfou, R., Skiena, S.: Deepwalk: Online learning of social representations. In: Proceedings of the 20th ACM SIGKDD International Conference on Knowledge Discovery and Data Mining, pp. 701–710 (2014)
15. Ranshous, S., Harenberg, S., Sharma, K., Samatova, N.F.: A scalable approach for outlier detection in edge streams using sketch-based approximations. In: Proceedings of the 2016 SIAM International Conference on Data Mining, pp. 189–197. SIAM (2016)
16. Ranshous, S., Shen, S., Koutra, D., Harenberg, S., Faloutsos, C., Samatova, N.F.: Anomaly detection in dynamic networks: a survey. Wiley Interdiscipl. Rev. Comput. Stat. **7**(3), 223–247 (2015)
17. Rossetti, G., Cazabet, R.: Community discovery in dynamic networks: a survey. ACM Comput. Surv. (CSUR) **51**(2), 1–37 (2018)
18. Tang, J., Qu, M., Wang, M., Zhang, M., Yan, J., Mei, Q.: Line: Large-scale information network embedding. In: Proceedings of the 24th International Conference on World Wide Web, pp. 1067–1077 (2015)
19. Wang, Z., Wang, C., Gao, C., Li, X., Li, X.: An evolutionary autoencoder for dynamic community detection. Sci. China Inf. Sci. **63**(11), 1–16 (2020). https://doi.org/10.1007/s11432-020-2827-9
20. Yao, L., Wang, L., Pan, L., Yao, K.: Link prediction based on common-neighbors for dynamic social network. Procedia Comput. Sci. **83**, 82–89 (2016)
21. Yu, W., Cheng, W., Aggarwal, C.C., Zhang, K., Chen, H., Wang, W.: Netwalk: a flexible deep embedding approach for anomaly detection in dynamic networks. In: Proceedings of the 24th ACM SIGKDD International Conference on Knowledge Discovery & Data Mining, pp. 2672–2681 (2018)
22. Zheng, L., Li, Z., Li, J., Li, Z., Gao, J.: Addgraph: anomaly detection in dynamic graph using attention-based temporal GCN. In: IJCAI, pp. 4419–4425 (2019)

Falcon: Malware Detection and Categorization with Network Traffic Images

Peng Xu[1](✉), Claudia Eckert[1], and Apostolis Zarras[2]

[1] Technical University of Munich, Munich, Germany
peng@sec.in.tum.de
[2] Delft University of Technology, Delft, Netherlands

Abstract. Android is the most popular smartphone operating system. At the same time, miscreants have already created malicious apps to find new victims and infect them. Unfortunately, existing anti-malware procedures have become obsolete, and thus novel Android malware techniques are in high demand. In this paper, we present *Falcon*, an Android malware detection and categorization framework. More specifically, we treat the network traffic classification task as a 2D image sequence classification and handle each network packet as a 2D image. Furthermore, we use a bidirectional LSTM network to process the converted 2D images to obtain the network vectors. We then utilize those converted vectors to detect and categorize the malware. Our results reveal that Falcon could be an accurate and viable solution as we get 97.16% accuracy on average for the malware detection and 88.32% accuracy for the malware categorization.

Keywords: Malware detection · Malware categorization · Bi-directional LSTM · 2D image sequence classification

1 Introduction

As the most popular mobile operating system globally, Android has become the main target for many attackers who seek to exploit new victims. These adversaries leverage malicious apps to infect mobile devices to carry out miscreants' nefarious activities, such as sending spam emails, spreading new malware, generating revenue from online advertisements by performing click-frauds, or even tricking users into revealing personal and private data. On the other side, both industry and academia work on the domain of Android malware investigation, which includes malware detection and categorization in an attempt to mitigate the aforementioned phenomenon [7,10,14,18,20]. Many of the proposed approaches utilize the contextual information of Android applications (primarily Android APKs code). Chen et al. [8] propose a technique that examines Android malware based on its static behavior that involves the use of components, permissions, and sensitive *Application Programming Interface* (API) calls. Li et al. [14]

© Springer Nature Switzerland AG 2021
I. Farkaš et al. (Eds.): ICANN 2021, LNCS 12891, pp. 117–128, 2021.
https://doi.org/10.1007/978-3-030-86362-3_10

introduce a classifier based on the *Factorization Machine* (FM) architecture, in which they extract numerous Android app heuristics from both the manifest files and source code. However, both methods analyze the Android application statically without running the program. Gibert et al. [11] present a way to convert the executable files into a 2D image and achieve malware detection based on the 2D image classification.

Meanwhile, several works either utilize the Android dynamic features, which are generated by running the Android application in a sandbox [26,29] or capture the network traffic to detect legitimate and malicious behaviors [2,16,17,28,32]. The first approach is expensive because it monitors those running applications in different level calls (system-level, function-level, etc.) and performs several low-level operations during their running activities. In contrast, capturing network traffic to analyze the application's behavior is cheaper. However, most of the existing network traffic research is based on the manual indicated rules and builds rule-based classic machine learning classifiers (network port, deep packet inspection, statistical, and behavior-based features) to detect and categorize Android malware. Still, those methods face a new challenge which is how to pick up the appropriate features.

Representation learning [5], which can learn features from raw data automatically, has increasingly attracted researchers and engineers. It can solve the above challenge with the manual indicated methods. Wang et al. [28] present a representation learning method for malware traffic classification, which converts the raw network traffic/flow data to image and takes the converted images as the input. Then, it uses a *Convolutional Neural Network* (CNN) to extract features from the raw network traffic. However, converting the network flows to images, and pretrain the 2D-gray-image-sequence-based multi-class classification model, cannot classify those malware or benign samples based on each 2D gray image. Normally, each PCAP file includes hundreds or thousands of raw network packets and network flows. Therefore, the malware classification issue converts to a continuous 2D image classification task. In other words, that is a 2D image sequence classification or sequential image classification [4,15]. Most of the sequential image classification works combine *Recurrent Neural Networks* (RNNs) and CNNs, as they put the RNNs focus on the sequential task and the CNNs on the image features. Meanwhile, in the *Natural Language Processing* (NLP) field, in order to process the sequential issues with a pre-trained model, BERT [9], GPT (v2, v3) [6,23], and other transformers (e.g., ELMo [22], Transformer [27]) capture the sequence relationship by leveraging *Long Short Term Memory* (LSTM) or RNN networks.

In this paper, we present *Falcon*, a network-traffic-pattern-based malware detection and categorization framework. We operate *Falcon* as follows. First, we convert the network packets to 2D gray images and leverage CNNs to pretrain the classification network for the network traffic features. We then use a bi-directional LSTM network to process the continuous network traffic and perform malware classification similar to the 2D image sequence classification task. The results of our system are promising since *Falcon* exhibits 97.16% accuracy on average for the malware detection and 88.32% accuracy for the malware categorization.

In summary, we make the following main contributions:

- We introduce *Falcon*, a network-traffic-pattern-based Android malware detection and categorization framework.
- We design a bidirectional LSTM network to accomplish 2D gray image sequence classification, which takes the network packets (converted to 2D images) as input.
- We create a dataset, *AndroNetMnist*, which includes 3,255,391 2D gray images in five classes for network traffic classification.
- We evaluate the accuracy of our approach using real-world datasets.

2 Related Work

With the increasing popularity of Android smartphones in recent years, the topic of detecting Android malware and categorizing its families attracts several researchers' and engineers' attention. As with every malware detection system, Android malware detection can be classified into two types: the traditional feature-codes-based method and the machine/deep-learning-based methods. Regarding the conventional feature-codes-based approach, the detector checks the classic malicious behaviors. For machine/deep-learning-based methods, there are also multiple features based frameworks. Permission-based malware detection extract several types of permission features that are highly relevant to the manifest file and source code of each mobile application, including API calls and permissions [14, 21, 30].

Program-code-based malware detection methods extract features from the code itself. Technically those features include the API calls, N-gram, and control flow graph (CFG) based methods. API call based malware detection uses API calls to detect Android malware [1, 3, 14, 21, 30]. In general, this type of method first constructs two ranked lists of popular Android APIs. One is benign_API_list that contains the top popular APIs commonly used in benign apps, and the other malicious_API_list that contains the top popular APIs commonly used in malicious apps. N-gram-based Malware Detection is based on the n-gram opcode to detect Android malware [12, 18, 24]. Last but not least, Graph-based malware detection systems use graph structure to perform their detection [10, 19, 31].

Machine learning and deep learning techniques are heavily introduced into the network traffic analysis. Researchers use manual indicated features (e.g., port, deep packet inspection, statistical and behavior-based features) to recognize network traffic application patterns with traditional machine learning algorithms [2, 13, 17, 25, 28]. Finally, Gibert et al. [11] present a way to convert the executable files to 2D images and achieve malware detection based on the 2D image classification, which is different compared to the 2D image sequence classification problem.

3   System Design and Implementation

In our work, we consider that network packets are composed of many network flows. Those flows are counted as a binary representation and can be converted to 2D gray images. Therefore, we transform a malware detection and categorization problem into a continuous 2D image classification and categorization problem. For instance, randomly choosing one network packet from our dataset, it includes 3,329 network flows. *Falcon* converts those network flows to 3,329 2D gray images and then to 3,329 vectors to represent those network flows. Finally, we take those converted vectors into our classifier to accomplish the malware detection and categorization tasks.

3.1   Overview

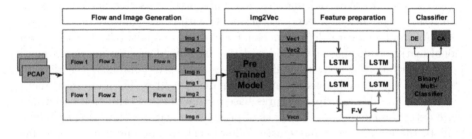

Fig. 1. The architecture of *Falcon*

The architecture of *Falcon* is presented in Fig. 1. Our malware detection and categorization framework includes a bi-directional LSTM to prepare the feature vectors (F-V block in Fig. 1) and a classifier to detect (DE block) and categorize (CA block) Android application. We input the *PCAP* files and convert each network flow contained in the PCAP file into a 2D image, and pre-train a model on 2D images with CNN network.[1] We use the pre-trained model to convert each 2D image to a vector and process the continuous network flows in a PCAP file as a 2D image sequence by a bi-directional LSTM network. We present this part in Sect. 3.2 in detail.

3.2   Features from Network Traffic

This section presents our method to convert network traffic to vectors based on image classification and transfer learning (see Fig. 2). To compare to other works in this field, we have two challenges. The first challenge (C1) is how to classify each network flow (several network packets) efficiently, and the second one (C2) is how to classify the whole network packets based on the split flows.

---

[1] https://wiki.wireshark.org/SampleCaptures.

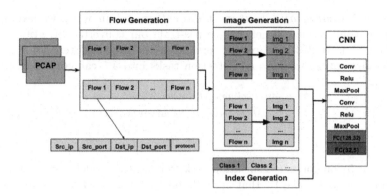

Fig. 2. Converting network traffic to vectors

Network Packets and Flows. For the network traffic analysis, there are three different granularity, raw packet level, flow level, and session level [28]. In our work, we take the network flow as our analysis target. All raw packets from the PCAP files are defined as a set $P = \{p^1, \cdots, p^{|P|}\}$, and every packet is defined as $p^i = (x^i, b^i, t^i)$, where $i = 1, 2, \cdots, |P|$ and x^i stands for a 5-tuple, which includes source IP, source port, destination IP, destination port, and the protocol types (e.g., TCP, UDP), where b^i and t^i stand for the packet's size and the starting time of the packet, respectively. Network flow groups several packets that have the same 5-tuple. In this way, we solve the challenge C1. Meanwhile, for the network flow level analysis, it is shown as the flow generation in Fig. 2. It is worth mentioning that we arrange all raw packets in the same network flow in time order.

Network Flows to Images. As we have previously mentioned, we split the network flow from the raw network packets. After getting network flow files, we convert them to 2D images like the image generation in Fig. 2. Here we utilize trimming and padding methods to normalize all network flows that have the same size. If the network flow's size is larger than 784 bytes, we trim it to 784 bytes. If those flow files' size is smaller than 784 bytes, we pad them by 0×00 to 784 bytes. Finally, we convert those trimmed and padded files to 2D gray images. Each byte of the original file represents a pixel, such as 0×80 is gray, and 0xff is white. We also generate the class label in this step, which stands for the different network traffic classes. We define five different labels in our work because we have four various malware families and one benign group. That is reasonable for our malware categorization task. We pre-train the model indirectly for our malware detection task based on the previous malware categorization. In total, for the malware categorization task, we label all samples with five classes (four malware classes and one benign class) and label all samples with two classes for the malware detection task (malware and benign).

Transfer Learning and Feature Generation. In our work, we leverage an 8-layer convolution neural network to pre-train our converted 2D gray images. Our model has 70,213 total parameters. After the previous step, we transform our malware categorization and detection tasks into a 5-category classification problem.

$$Y^1 = MaxPooling_{2*2}(Relu(conv2d_{3*3}(X_{28*28})))$$
$$Y^2 = MaxPooling_{2*2}(Relu(conv2d_{3*3}(Y^1)))$$
$$Y^3 = FC_{128,32}(Y^2)$$
$$Y = FC_{32,5}(Y^3)$$

$$(1)$$

We use our 5-categories classification task to train the model. After getting the pre-train model, we take Y^3 that has a 32-bit vector as our features for the next step. We use *sparse_categorical_crossentropy* loss and Adam optimizer and set the learning_rate as 0.001 and epoch as 50. We use one dropout layer between MaxPool2 and FC1, and we set the dropout rate as 0.5.

Continuous Network Traffic Processing. So far, we have converted the network flows to images and pre-train the 2D gray image-based multi-class classification model. However, we cannot classify those malware or benign samples based on each 2D gray image for our malware detection and categorization task. Typically, each PCAP file includes hundreds or thousands of raw network packets and network flows. Therefore, the malware classification issue converts to a continuous 2D image classification task. In other words, that is a 2D image sequence classification or sequential image classification [4,15]. Most sequential image classification works combine the RNN and CNN and put RNN focusing on the sequential task and CNN for the image features. Meanwhile, in the natural language processing (NLP) field, in order to process the sequential issues with the pre-trained model, BERT [9], GPT (v2, v3) [6,23] and other transformers (e.g., ELMo [22], Transformer [27]) are introduced into to capture the sequence relationship by leveraging the LSTM or RNN networks. Therefore, in our work, to capture the network traffic's continuous characteristics, we introduce a bidirectional LSTM network on top of the pre-trained 2D-image classification model, which helps to extract image features from the converted network flows. This method can solve the C2 effectively. Figure 3 presents our sequential image classification structure. The steps mentioned above prepare the image sequences and img2vec model, which replace each 2D gray image with a 32-bit vector. We take the 32-bit vectors from the second to last layer of the pre-trained CNNC model. We use a bidirectional LSTM network, and the input of LSTM has converted vectors with $(1, 32)$ shape. Both inputs for the forward and backward direction LSTM are the same. Furthermore, we concatenate the last hidden status $f_v, v \in N$ as our final output vectors, where N stands for the number of all PCAP files. After getting the f_v vectors for N PCAP files (N different Android samples), we use a full connection layer followed by a softmax layer to classify those raw network traffic into five different categories.

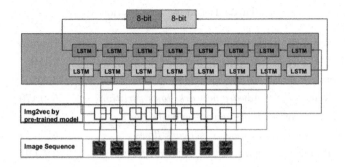

Fig. 3. 2D sequential image classification with bidirectional LSTM

3.3 Model Training and Prediction

After preparing the feature vectors by the bi-directional LSTM, we train and test our model by using the *sparse_categorical_crossentropy* loss function like Eq. 2.

$$Loss = -\sum_{N}^{i=1} y_{i_{label}} * log(y_{i_{pred}})$$

$$= -\sum_{N}^{i=1} y_{i_{label}} * log(< (< f_v, w_{i1} > +b_{i1}), w_{i2} > +b_{i2})$$

(2)

where $w_{i1}, w_{i2} \in R^p$ is the weight of the classifier and $b_{i1}, b_{i2} \in R^p$ is the offset from the origin of the vector space. In this setting, a converted vector f_v is classified into five categories.

4   Evaluation

4.1 Experimental Setup

We set up our experiments on our Euklid server, which runs on a Linux X86_64 platform and has 128 GB RAM and 16 GB GPU. Further, we trained our model with `Tensorflow 2.0.0-beta0`, `Keras 2.2.4`, and `Sklearn 0.20.0`. We also used the `SplitCap` tool to split the PCAP files.[2] Additionally, we used the `pillow 6.1.0` imaging library when we convert the network flows to images. Finally, we used other assistant libraries, such as `numpy 1.16.4` and `matplotlib 3.1.1`.

4.2 Dataset

For the train and evaluation dataset, we used the Android Malware CICMal2017 dataset [13, 25]. It includes 426 malware and 1700 benign samples and their corresponding network traffic raw files. Table 1 illustrates the number of various

---

[2] https://github.com/Master-13/SplitCap.

Table 1. Dataset explanation

Name	Description	Number
PCAP files	*All the raw network traffic files*	2,126
Network flows	*All network flows in Sect. 3.2*	3,255,391
Adware	*Adware network flows partition*	580,170
Ransomware	*Ransomware network flows*	382,279
Scareware	*Scareware network flows*	517,954
SMSmalware	*SMSmalware network flows*	245,691
Benign	*Network flows for benign applications*	1,529,297

categories in detail. For the network traffic, we extracted 3,255,391 network flows in total from 2,216 PCAP files. Here, to pre-train our 2D gray image classification task, we created our dataset, *AndroNetMnist*, which provides a benchmark to network traffic analysis with the convolution neural network. We split the dataset with 80% training and 20% testing in our experiment.

4.3   Results Comparison

This section compares our results with other related works, both from the program code and network traffic-based field. We reimplemented (Droidmat [30] and CICMal2017 [25]) and reproduced (Drebin [3][3], Adagio [10][4]) other related works and compared them with our framework. We should mention here that the results of those frameworks differ a little from the original works because of the different datasets.

For *Falcon*, after preparing the dataset as CSV files, we used the *Random Forest* (RF) classifier by default to perform our malware detection and malware categorization. Our RF is defined as 1,400 trees in the forest and 80 as the tree's maximum depth. We set min_samples_split as five and the number of features to consider when looking for the best split as sqrt. Table 2 illustrates the malware detection (binary classification) performance.

Table 2 shows that *Falcon*-CNN gets the best performance, which catches up to 98% accuracy. However, this experiment processes the malware classification on *AndroNetMnist* similar to the digital handwriting classification on the MNIST dataset, which indirectly did the classification. That means we firstly extract and convert all network flows to images and then classify all images that belong to one class. For example, for a PCAP file, we extracted and converted network flows to images and got 3,329 samples. The 98% accuracy means 98% of 3,329 samples are classified correctly. However, we cannot determine the whole network flows characteristics because most malicious behaviors are hidden in a few network flows by sophisticated attackers. Even if we get a high performance

---

[3] https://github.com/alisakhatipova/Drebin.
[4] https://github.com/hgascon/adagio.

Table 2. Malware detection comparison

Classifier	Accuracy	Precision	Recall	F1
Drebin [3]	96.58	95.37	97.85	96.59
Adagio [10]	89.32	91.27	95.28	93.23
Droidmat [30]	89.87	90.89	88.28	89.56
CICAndMal2017 [13]	87.52	87.14	87.73	87.18
Falcon-CNN	98.04	98.09	98.05	98.06
Falcon	97.16	97.13	97.16	97.09

of over 98%, we cannot infer that this malware detection system can accurately determine the malware's network traffic. Therefore, we introduced *Falcon*, which converts all 2D images to a 2D image sequence for each PCAP file. With this method, *Falcon* gets 95.39% accuracy. The results are illustrated in Table 2 in detail.

In our experiment, the malware categorization task is a multi-class classification issue. Similar to the malware detection (binary classification) task, *Falcon*-CNN on *AndroNetMnist* gets the best performance on the image classification task indirectly. Take the same example with malware detection above; 97.23 accuracy means that 97.23% of images from the same PCAP file are classified to Adware class. However, we cannot determinedly infer that this PCAP is Adware network traffic. Additionally, we compared our results only with CICAndMal2017 [13] because most Android malware detection works, such as Drebin, Adagio, and Droidmat did not consider the malware categorization problem. Although FM [14] considers the malware categorization task, it converts the multi-class task to binary-class (i.e., if one malware sample belongs to a specific malware family, then the label is 1; otherwise, that is 0). *Falcon* on the multiclass classification task gets better results than CICAndMal2017. The primary reason is that essential patterns for various malware families represent the manually indicated features by CICAndMal2017 that lose some information. Our method can catch up with better malware families' features by representation learning. Table 3 shows the performance results of malware categorization.

Table 3. Malware categorization comparison (the average is weighted)

Classifier	Accuracy	Precision	Recall	F1
CICAndMal2017 [13]	86.85	85.92	86.85	84.82
Falcon-CNN	97.23	97.28	97.23	97.24
Falcon	84.70	80.22	84.70	82.39

Last but not least, besides the Random Forest (RF) classifier, we also consider the other four classifiers by Sklearn implementation for malware detection and

Table 4. Various classifiers settings

Classifier	Settings
RF	*n_estimators = 1400, min_sample_split = 5, max_features = "sqrt", max_depth = 80*
AdaBoost	*All default values*
GradientBoost	*lr = 0.01, n_estimators = 1500, max_depth = 4, min_samples_split = 40, max_features = 4*
MLP	*sover = "sgd", alpha = 1e−5, hidden_layers_sizes = (400,400,200,100,10)*
DecisionTree	*min_samples_split = 10, max_features = "sqrt", max_depth = 20*

Table 5. *Falcon*'s performance with various classifiers

Classifier	Accuracy	Precision	Recall	F1
RF	97.16	97.13	97.16	97.09
AdaBoost	93.13	92.81	93.13	92.85
GradientBoost	96.88	96.83	96.88	96.80
MLP	91.01	90.48	91.01	90.02
DecisionTree	93.66	93.64	93.66	93.65

categorization. The classifiers are described in Table 4. Besides the settings in Table 4, we used all default parameters. Due to the limited space, we only present results in Table 5 for the malware detection (binary classification) task. Table 5 shows that the RF classifier gets the best performance and then is followed by the GradientBoost classifier. MLP gets the worst in our framework.

5   Limitations

In contrast with other machine and deep learning based works in the malware detection field, *Falcon* can catch up with the dynamic information of the Android application. Our work has more time consumption than port-matching or permission matching systems to contrast with other rule-based methods, such as port-based malware detection with network traffic and permission-based Android malicious program detection. On the other hand, in contrast to other Android malware detection works, the dataset, especially the dynamic network-traffic dataset, is too small. Although our evaluation demonstrates better performance than its precedent, we need to increase the number of samples in the future.

6   Conclusion

In this work, we present *Falcon*, a network-traffic-pattern-based malware detection and categorization framework. We use the transfer learning method to extract features from the network traffic with pre-trained models. We treat the network-traffic-based classification as a 2D gray image sequence classification task and use a bi-directional LSTM to process image sequences. For the 2D gray image, we use an 8-layer CNN to pre-train the gray images, which stand for the network flows.

Acknowledgments. This project has received funding from the European Union's Horizon 2020 research and innovation programme under grant agreements No. 883275 (HEIR) and No. 833115 (PREVISION).

References

1. Aafer, Y., Du, W., Yin, H.: DroidAPIMiner: mining API-level features for robust malware detection in android. In: International Conference on Security and Privacy in Communication Systems (2013)
2. Arora, A., Garg, S., Peddoju, S.K.: Malware detection using network traffic analysis in android based mobile devices. In: International Conference on Next Generation Mobile Apps, Services and Technologies (2014)
3. Arp, D., Spreitzenbarth, M., Hubner, M., Gascon, H., Rieck, K., Siemens, C.: DREBIN: effective and explainable detection of android malware in your pocket. In: Network & Distributed System Security Symposium (NDSS) (2014)
4. Bai, S., Kolter, J.Z., Koltun, V.: Trellis networks for sequence modeling. arXiv preprint arXiv:1810.06682 (2018)
5. Bengio, Y., Courville, A., Vincent, P.: Representation learning: a review and new perspectives. IEEE Trans. Pattern Anal. Mach. Intell. **35**(8), 1798–1828 (2013)
6. Budzianowski, P., Vulić, I.: Hello, it's GPT-2-how can i help you? Towards the use of pretrained language models for task-oriented dialogue systems. arXiv preprint arXiv:1907.05774 (2019)
7. Canfora, G., De Lorenzo, A., Medvet, E., Mercaldo, F., Visaggio, C.A.: Effectiveness of opcode ngrams for detection of multi family android malware. In: International Conference on Availability, Reliability and Security (2015)
8. Chen, C., Liu, Y., Shen, B., Cheng, J.J.: Android malware detection based on static behavior feature analysis. J. Comput. **29**(6), 243–253 (2018)
9. Devlin, J., Chang, M.W., Lee, K., Toutanova, K.: BERT: pre-training of deep bidirectional transformers for language understanding. arXiv preprint arXiv:1810.04805 (2018)
10. Gascon, H., Yamaguchi, F., Arp, D., Rieck, K.: Structural detection of android malware using embedded call graphs. In: ACM Workshop on Artificial Intelligence and Security (2013)
11. Gibert, D., Mateu, C., Planes, J., Vicens, R.: Using convolutional neural networks for classification of malware represented as images. J. Comput. Virol. Hack. Tech. **15**(1), 15–28 (2019)
12. Kang, B., Yerima, S.Y., Sezer, S., McLaughlin, K.: N-Gram opcode analysis for android malware detection. arXiv preprint arXiv:1612.01445 (2016)
13. Lashkari, A.H., Kadir, A.F.A., Taheri, L., Ghorbani, A.A.: Toward developing a systematic approach to generate benchmark android malware datasets and classification. In: International Carnahan Conference on Security Technology (2018)
14. Li, C., Zhu, R., Niu, D., Mills, K., Zhang, H., Kinawi, H.: Android malware detection based on factorization machine. arXiv preprint arXiv:1805.11843 (2018)

15. Li, S., Li, W., Cook, C., Zhu, C., Gao, Y.: Independently recurrent neural network (INDRNN): building a longer and deeper RNN. In: IEEE Conference on Computer Vision and Pattern Recognition (2018)
16. Malik, J., Kaushal, R.: CREDROID: android malware detection by network traffic analysis. In: ACM Workshop on Privacy-Aware Mobile Computing (2016)
17. Marín, G., Casas, P., Capdehourat, G.: DeepMAL-deep learning models for malware traffic detection and classification. arXiv:2003.04079 (2020)
18. McLaughlin, N., et al.: Deep android malware detection. In: ACM Conference on Data and Application Security and Privacy (2017)
19. Narayanan, A., Soh, C., Chen, L., Liu, Y., Wang, L.: Apk2vec: semi-supervised multi-view representation learning for profiling android applications. In: 2018 IEEE International Conference on Data Mining (ICDM) (2018)
20. Onwuzurike, L., Mariconti, E., Andriotis, P., Cristofaro, E.D., Ross, G., Stringhini, G.: MaMaDroid: detecting android malware by building Markov chains of behavioral models (extended version). ACM Trans. Privacy Secur. (TOPS) **22**(2), 1–34 (2019)
21. Peiravian, N., Zhu, X.: Machine learning for android malware detection using permission and API calls. In: IEEE International Conference on Tools with Artificial Intelligence (2013)
22. Peters, M.E., et al.: Deep contextualized word representations. arXiv preprint arXiv:1802.05365 (2018)
23. Radford, A., Narasimhan, K., Salimans, T., Sutskever, I.: Improving Language understanding with unsupervised learning. Technical report. OpenAI (2018)
24. Raff, E., Barker, J., Sylvester, J., Brandon, R., Catanzaro, B., Nicholas, C.: Malware detection by eating a whole exe. arXiv preprint arXiv:1710.09435 (2017)
25. Taheri, L., Kadir, A.F.A., Lashkari, A.H.: Extensible android malware detection and family classification using network-flows and API-calls. In: 2019 International Carnahan Conference on Security Technology (ICCST) (2019)
26. Tam, K., Khan, S.J., Fattori, A., Cavallaro, L.: CopperDroid: automatic reconstruction of android malware behaviors. In: Network & Distributed System Security Symposium (NDSS) (2015)
27. Vaswani, A., et al.: Attention is all you need. In: Advances in Neural Information Processing Systems (2017)
28. Wang, W., Zhu, M., Zeng, X., Ye, X., Sheng, Y.: Malware traffic classification using convolutional neural network for representation learning. In: 2017 International Conference on Information Networking (ICOIN) (2017)
29. Wong, M.Y., Lie, D.: IntelliDroid: a targeted input generator for the dynamic analysis of android malware. In: Network & Distributed System Security Symposium (NDSS) (2016)
30. Wu, D.J., Mao, C.H., Wei, T.E., Lee, H.M., Wu, K.P.: DroidMat: android malware detection through manifest and API calls tracing. In: Asia Joint Conference on Information Security (2012)
31. Xu, P., Eckert, C., Zarras, A.: Detecting and categorizing android malware with graph neural networks. In: Annual ACM Symposium on Applied Computing (SAC) (2021)
32. Zulkifli, A., Hamid, I.R.A., Shah, W.M., Abdullah, Z.: Android malware detection based on network traffic using decision tree algorithm. In: Ghazali, R., Deris, M.M., Nawi, N.M., Abawajy, J.H. (eds.) SCDM 2018. AISC, vol. 700, pp. 485–494. Springer, Cham (2018). https://doi.org/10.1007/978-3-319-72550-5_46

Attention-Based Bi-LSTM for Anomaly Detection on Time-Series Data

Sanket Mishra[1,2(✉)] , Varad Kshirsagar[1] , Rohit Dwivedula[1] ,
and Chittaranjan Hota[1]

[1] Department of Computer Science and Information Systems,
BITS Pilani - Hyderabad Campus, Hyderabad, Telangana, India
`sanket.mishra@vitap.ac.in`,
{`f20170141,f20170029,hota`}`@hyderabad.bits-pilani.ac.in`
[2] School of Computer Science and Engineering, Vellore Institute of Technology,
Amaravati, Andhra Pradesh, India

Abstract. Anomaly detection in time-series data is a significant research problem that has applications in multiple areas. Unsupervised anomaly detection is a fundamental aspect of developing intelligent automated systems. Existing work in this field has primarily focused on developing intelligent systems that use dimensionality reduction or regression-based approaches to annotate data based on a certain static threshold. Researchers in fields such as Natural Language Processing (NLP) and Computer Vision (CV) have realized considerable improvement by incorporating attention in prediction-related tasks. In this work, we propose an attention-based bi-directional long short term memory (Attention-Bi-LSTM) networks for anomaly detection on time-series data. It helps in assigning optimal weights to instances in sequential data. We evaluate the proposed approach on the entirety of the popularly used Numenta Anomaly Benchmark (NAB). Additionally, we also contribute by creating new baselines on the NAB with recent models such as REBM, DAGMM, LSTM-ED, and Donut, which have not been previously used on the NAB.

Keywords: Anomaly detection · Attention based neural networks · Univariate time-series

1 Introduction

Unsupervised anomaly detection is a dynamic field of research with a myriad of applications, including climate monitoring, image, and video processing tasks, and many other applications in fraud detection, public health, and industrial and sensor monitoring [7].

The advent of inexpensive computing devices flooding the markets, in conjunction with ever-expanding reliable internet access, has led to an explosion in "smart" devices, often dubbed as the *Internet of Things* (IoT). This unprecedented level of connectedness and distributed computing power at scale enables

© Springer Nature Switzerland AG 2021
I. Farkaš et al. (Eds.): ICANN 2021, LNCS 12891, pp. 129–140, 2021.
https://doi.org/10.1007/978-3-030-86362-3_11

the creation of real-time data streams from a wide range of sensors. Such systems are employed in a wide range of scenarios, ranging from agriculture [25] to manufacturing, business analytics, and monitoring in almost any enterprise [15]. Abnormal behavior in any of these cases might indicate a fault in the sensors or some abnormal activity in the region where the sensors are placed. There is a need for automated models to detect anomalous points in streaming data to ensure necessary interventions can occur.

In this paper, we use the Numenta Anomaly Benchmark (NAB) [14] to test and validate our model. The NAB is a benchmark dataset consisting of seven real-world and diverse univariate streams of data. We present an attention-based bi-directional LSTM for anomaly detection on time-series. The proposed framework uses an unsupervised model to predict the values of incoming data points (forecasting). The difference between actual values and predicted values is called the *anomaly score*. This anomaly score is then sent into a thresholding mechanism which classifies points as anomalous or not. We outline the significant contribution of this work below:

- We have used a novel hybrid mechanism of allotting anomaly scores and using it as a feedback in the thresholding mechanism for identifying anomalies.
- A significant performance improvement on the widely used Numenta Anomaly Benchmark, compared to the existing state-of-the-art forecasting approaches such as DeepAnT [18] and FuseAD [19].
- The proposed approach is **not data intensive** as it uses a *windowing mechanism* estimated by the Least Spectral Square Analysis (LSSA) method.
- To the best of our knowledge, this is the first work that experiments with new baselines like REBM, Donut, & DAGMM, which haven't been applied on the NAB before but have shown promise in other anomaly detection applications.

2   Related Work

Anomaly detection is an active area of research with a wide variety of models being experimented with, including various statistical approaches, density, and distance-based approaches, and recently machine learning and deep learning models as well [6].

Researchers have used a wide variety of methods on the Numenta Anomaly Benchmark. DeepAnT [18] proposes a Convolutional Neural Network (CNN) architecture to predict the upcoming univariate values - the difference between predicted and actual values is the *anomaly score* of the point. DeepAnT uses a sliding window mechanism where a fixed number of points are passed as input to the model, which it uses to predict the next point's value. FuseAD [19] leverages the power of an ARIMA (Auto-Regressive Integrated Moving Average) model fused with a CNN-based deep learning model to predict incoming values. Numenta [14] and NumentaTM (NTM) [2] use a Hierarchical Temporal Memory (HTM) methodology to detect anomalies. Skyline [8], a widely used [1,11] real-time anomaly detection software developed by the e-commerce website Etsy, uses an ensemble of simpler models to detect anomalies, where each model *votes* on each point to decide whether to classify as an anomaly or not. Some approaches include deep learning models, such as *autoencoders* and *Long Short-Term Memory (LSTM)* networks. Attention mechanisms [3] have been used for a wide range of tasks on sequential data, in machine translation [23], computer vision [9] and natural language processing [10]. Pereira and Silveira [20] use an attention-based autoencoder for anomaly detection in smart grids while [26] uses an attention based model for detecting anomalies in HTTP traffic.

3 Proposed Model

This section discusses the various modules of the proposed framework that detects anomalies in time-series data. Figure 1 provides a broad overview of the framework along with its modules. The proposed framework consists of the following modules:

1. Optimum window size estimation
2. Forecasting model - attention based bi-directional LSTM
3. Thresholding mechanism.

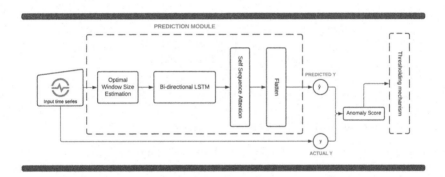

Fig. 1. Proposed framework

We first capture a section of the incoming time-series into a window size estimation module. This module approximates the periodicity of the time-series given by ω. We use this window size in the next step, for training the attention-based neural network. The neural network learns to predict the $(\omega + 1)^{th}$ point given ω consecutive points. To make predictions, we pass ω consecutive points as input to the neural network, which predicts the $(\omega + 1)^{th}$ point. The difference between the predicted value of the point and the actual value of that point is called the *anomaly score*. Higher absolute anomaly scores indicate that the point is likely to be an anomaly. The knowledge gained from anomaly scores helps in the thresholding mechanism then determines whether this point is anomalous or not.

3.1   Windowing Mechanism

This module of the framework estimates the periodicity of the incoming data stream. Accurate estimation is necessary to get better predictions. Finding an optimal window size is primarily experimental in many works [18,19]. Finding the ideal window size is a trade-off between capturing patterns and trends in data and increased susceptibility to noise due to redundant points (as the window size gets bigger). We use the Lomb-Scargle periodogram [16,22] as it detects weak periodicity in unevenly sampled data. The data we are dealing with has very weak periodicity as it is real-time streaming data. This motivated us to employ this method for window size estimation. The Lomb Scargle method is outlined as follows $P_X(f)$:

$$\frac{1}{2\sigma^2}\left\{\frac{\left[\sum\limits_{n=1}^{N}(x(t_n)-\bar{x})\cos(2\pi f(t_n-\tau))\right]^2}{\sum\limits_{n=1}^{N}\cos^2(2\pi f(t_n-\tau))}+\frac{\left[\sum\limits_{n=1}^{N}(x(t_n)-\bar{x})\sin(2\pi f(t_n-\tau))\right]^2}{\sum\limits_{n=1}^{N}\sin^2(2\pi f(t_n-\tau))}\right\}\tag{1}$$

where $\bar{x}$ and σ^2 are the mean and variance of data and the value of τ is defined as

$$\tan(4\pi f\tau)=\frac{\left(\sum\limits_{n=1}^{N}\sin(4\pi ft_n)\right)}{\left(\sum\limits_{n=1}^{N}\cos(4\pi ft_n)\right)}\tag{2}$$

3.2   Forecasting and Thresholding Models

The core part of our framework relies on a forecasting model - given ω consecutive points of the univariate stream, the forecasting model predicts the $(\omega+1)^{th}$ point. These predictions are then used in the next step to calculate the *anomaly scores*. CNN and LSTM based neural networks are highly effective for time-series related tasks [13,21]. Bi-directional LSTMs or Bi-LSTMs are neural networks in which the signal propagates both backward and forward on the input data. In this we work, we experiment with attention-based CNNs, LSTMs, and Bi-LSTMs as our forecasting models. We attempt to build and then train forecasting models using all three types of these models (CNN, LSTM, Bi-LSTM) and then select the best performing model to be our forecasting model. We measure these forecasting models' performance by their ability to predict the $(\omega+1)^{th}$ with minimal error.

Bi-directional LSTMs: Consider a time-series dataset D $= d^1, d^2, \ldots, d^n$ where each step $d^t \ \epsilon \ \mathbb{R}$. Each data point represents an n dimensional vector $d^1, d^2, \ldots, d^n$. We have used a windowing mechanism estimated using Least Spectral Square Analysis (LSSA) method to identify periodicity in time-series data.

The model predicts a sequence of length l, for d dimensions of $d^t \epsilon$ D for length $l < t \leq n - l$ is predicted 1 times. Then we compute an error vector $e^{(t)} = [e_{1l}^{(t)}, \ldots, e_{dl}^{(t)}]$, where $e_{mn}^{(t)}$ represents the difference between actual value and predicted value.

Attention Mechanism: For a certain query, the vector is represented by the attention mechanism that uses a parameterized computability function $f(x^t, q)$ that computes the dependencies between x^t and q^t, i.e., the attention of q to x^t. To transform the alignment score $a \in \mathbb{R}^n$ to a probability distribution $p(z|x, q)$, we employ a softmax function that normalizes over all the n tokens on q for a particular task, where z indicates the importance of specific tokens to q. Thus, the process can be summarized as follows:

$$a = [f(x^t, q)], \text{for } t = 1, \ldots, n, p(z|x, q) = softmax(a) \qquad (3)$$

The attention mechanism gives the weighted expectation of a sample taken based on its importance. The most commonly used attention mechanisms are additive attention and multiplicative attention. In this work, we use an extended version of additive attention known as *self-attention*, which substitutes the token embedding x_j in place of the vector representation, q. It utilizes latent correlation for exploiting local dependencies at different positions for various dependencies [29].

Thresholding Mechanism: We used a supervised thresholding mechanism to detect the optimal threshold for binarizing points as anomalous or not. We obtain the minimum and maximum values of the anomaly scores calculated on the training set and then consider each value from the minimum score to the maximum score with a small step and select the value returning the highest F-Score as the overall model threshold.

3.3   Implementation

We implement the CNN, LSTM, and Bi-LSTM attention-based neural network models in Python3 using the Tensorflow framework and the Keras-Self-Attention library [28][1]. The models were trained with a batch size of 32 using the Adaptive Moment Estimation (Adam) optimizer to minimize the mean square error (MSE). The input to neural networks is a one-dimensional vector of size (ω) where ω is the window size, and the output shape is that of one single value, i.e., size (1).

The CNN consists of a 1D-Convolution layer (16 units, filter size 2) followed by a 1D-MaxPooling layer. The MaxPooling layer's output is flattened to form a vector, which is connected to the output layer, which consists of one node. The CNN layers use the relu activation function, and the penultimate layer uses a dropout of 50%. In the LSTM, the input layer is connected to a layer of

---

[1] All code and models to reproduce the results of this paper are available in this Github repository: https://github.com/Varad2305/Time-Series-Anomaly-Detection.

LSTM nodes (10 units), which is then flattened. This flattened layer (with 50% dropout) is connected to the output layer. The Bi-LSTM is structured similarly, with Bi-LSTM units replacing LSTM units in the second layer. We use the tanh activation function for both LSTM and Bi-LSTM. The attention Bi-LSTM creates an attention layer over the Bi-LSTM units with a sigmoid activation unit. We arrive at these values of hyperparameters (number of units in each layer and batch size) on each of these models through the use of the Tree of Parzen Estimators (TPE) algorithm [5] from the *hyperopt* library [4], with mse (mean squared error) being used as the objective function.

We use standard evaluation metrics, F-score and AUC, for measuring performance of models. F-score is defined as the harmonic mean of precision and recall. Area under curve (AUC), which is the area under the Receiver Operator Characteristic curve, depicts to what degree a model can distinguish between classes. Since NAB consists of multiple datasets belonging to various domains, we average scores for each model on each domain, similar to how existing works on the NAB have evaluated performances [2,18].

4 Experimental Results and Analysis

In this section, we discuss the outcomes of the experiments performed with the proposed approach.

4.1 Dataset Description

The publicly released Numenta Anomaly Benchmark [14] comprises 58 time-series data streams, with each stream consisting of 1000 to 22000 data points, totalling to $356,551$ data points across all the files. The dataset contains data streams from many areas, such as road traffic, AWS (Amazon Web Service) server metrics, internet traffic data, tweets, and online advertisements. The data points are labelled as outliers or inliers, based on the ground truth cause of the anomaly, following the procedural guidelines explained in the white paper [14]. The files in the dataset primarily contain time-series data, while separate files are maintained for anomaly labels. We use the NAB dataset for assessing and comparing the performance of the proposed approach.

We use **Least Spectral Square Analysis** (LSSA) to estimate an optimal window size for training the deep learning model. The resulting periodogram for the realTweets dataset[2] is shown in Fig. 2.

One of the most commonly used approaches to detect periodicity in time-series data is the Fast Fourier Transform (FFT) which identifies periodicity by exploring high peaks in the Fourier transform of the given time-series data. The FFT method assumes the data to be evenly spaced. However, this assumption that FFT makes may or may not hold in real-world datasets, motivating our use of LSSA. LSSA makes no assumptions regarding the periodicity of the dataset but searches for the highest periodic component.

---

[2] Similar results are obtained for other datasets not depicted in this work. In this paper, visualizations are restricted to the realTweets and realTraffic datasets only.

4.2 Windowing Mechanism

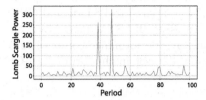 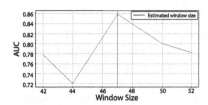

(a) Periodogram representing the spectral nature of data

(b) Variation of model performance with window size

Fig. 2. Windowing mechanism summarised (Color figure online)

Figure 2a exhibits the resultant periodogram after the application of the LSSA method, representing the inherent periodic nature of most real-world time-series datasets. The windowing algorithm is executed for each dataset, and unlike Deepant [18], or FuseAD [19], the window size in our proposed model varies for each dataset depending upon its underlying statistical properties. Figure 2b presents the variation in model performance as the window size changes - we notice that the window size predicted by LSSA (red line) corresponds to the maxima identified through experimentation with multiple window sizes.

4.3 Forecasting Model

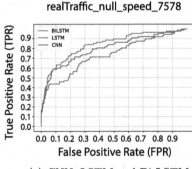

(a) CNN, LSTM and Bi-LSTM

(b) Bi-LSTM model with and without the use of self-attention

Fig. 3. Performance Comparisons based on (a) AUC and (b) F-scores on one file from realTraffic and realTweets dataset respectively

In this section, we describe the neural network models used for forecasting. We decide on using an attention-based bi-directional LSTM as our proposed model of choice after extensive experimentation. As discussed in Sect. 3.2 and 3.3, we experiment with CNNs, LSTMs and Bi-LSTMs for the forecasting models. Firstly, we perform experiments with CNNs, LSTMs, and Bi-LSTMs to compare their relative performance. Experiments with these models consistently depicted Bi-LSTM as having superior forecasting ability compared to LSTMs and CNNs for most of the data files, which is why we choose a Bi-LSTM model over the other models. Figure 3a depicts one representative performance comparison of these models on a data file from the *realTraffic* dataset in the form of a ROC curve.

Figure 3 depicts a similar comparison between the performance of a Bi-LSTM used with and without attention module. We notice that the usage of the attention boosts the performance of the Bi-LSTM. Based on these experiments and comparisons, we observe that attention-based bi-directional LSTM to have the best performance out of the experimented models.

4.4   The Baselines and Results

We divide this subsection into two further subsections. In the first subsection, we depict the performance on the Numenta Anomaly Benchmark (NAB) of our model against the reported performances of other state-of-the-art models identified in the literature review. In the second subsection, we experiment with general time-series anomaly detection methods[3] that have been used successfully for other anomaly detection tasks but have not been used for the NAB dataset. By reporting results for these models, we aim at comprehensively investigating the performance of our model against state-of-the-art approaches.

Table 1. Averaged F-score on NAB

Dataset	Our model	DeepAnT [18]	WG [18]	AdVec [12]	Skyline [8]	NTM [18]	Numenta [2]	KNNCAD [18]	HTMJava [18]
artificialWithNoAnomaly	0	0	0	0	0	0	0	0	0
artificialWithAnomaly	**0.402**	0.156	0.013	0.017	0.043	0.017	0.012	0.003	0.017
realAdExchange	**0.214**	0.132	0.026	0.018	0.005	0.035	0.040	0.024	0.034
realAWSCloudwatch	**0.269**	0.146	0.060	0.013	0.053	0.018	0.017	0.006	0.018
realKnownCause	**0.331**	0.200	0.006	0.017	0.008	0.012	0.015	0.008	0.013
realTraffic	**0.398**	0.223	0.045	0.020	0.091	0.036	0.033	0.013	0.032
realTweets	**0.165**	0.075	0.026	0.018	0.035	0.010	0.009	0.004	0.010

State-of-the-Art Performance on NAB: Tables 1 and 2 depict the average F-scores and the AUC scores of our model and results reported from literature compiled from [2,14,18,19]. In these tables, WG refers to the Windowed Gaussian method reported in [18], while AdVec refers to Twitter's open-source Anomaly Detection program [12]. We note that our proposed approach has the highest average F-score across all six datasets of the Numenta Anomaly Benchmark. The FuseAD [19] framework returns *only* anomaly scores, and not direct

---

[3] We use the four recent models from the KDD-OpenSource Repository DeepADoTS on Github - DAGMM (2018), Donut (2018) REBM (2016) and LSTMED (2016).

predictions of whether a point is an anomaly or not, meaning that comparisons in terms of F-score are not possible for this model. Therefore, we present a comparison of AUCs of these models as well, in Table 2. Even here, we note that our proposed approach outperforms all other approaches on all the datasets. The fact that the proposed model outperforms existing benchmarks for multiple different datasets attests to the proposed model's robustness and generalisability.

Figure 4 depicts a comparison of the proposed model against current benchmarks on the NAB. Each box in the boxplot corresponds to the results (average F-scores) obtained by the proposed model on each of the NAB datasets.

Table 2. Averaged AUC-score on NAB

Dataset	Our model	FuseAD [19]	DeepAnT [18]	WG [18]	AdVec [12]	Skyline [8]	Numenta [2]	HTMJava [18]
artificialWithNoAnomaly	0	0	0	0	0	0	0	0
artificialWithAnomaly	**0.678**	0.544	0.555	0.406	0.503	0.558	0.531	0.653
realAdExchange	**0.673**	0.588	0.563	0.538	0.504	0.534	0.576	0.568
realAWSCloudwatch	**0.640**	0.572	0.583	0.614	0.503	0.602	0.542	0.587
realKnownCause	**0.909**	0.587	0.601	0.572	0.504	0.610	0.590	0.584
realTraffic	**0.737**	0.619	0.637	0.553	0.505	0.556	0.679	0.691
realTweets	**0.729**	0.546	0.554	0.560	0.505	0.559	0.586	0.549

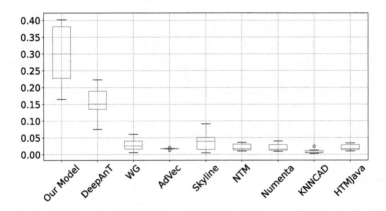

Fig. 4. Performance comparison of the proposed model based on F-Scores against current benchmarks on the NAB on all datasets

New Baselines: Table 3 depicts our proposed framework's performance against new baselines that we have created - DAGMM, REBM, Donut, and LSTMED. We notice that our proposed model outperforms all of these four new models on four of six datasets. For the *realAdExchange* dataset, we notice that DAGMM outperforms our proposed approach but underperforms compared to our proposed approach on all other datasets. Similarly, for the *realTweets* dataset, LSTMED performs better than the proposed approach, but in four other cases, the proposed approach works better.

Table 3. Performance comparison based on averaged F-score

Dataset	Our model	DAGMM [30]	REBM [27]	Donut [24]	LSTMED [17]
artificialWithNoAnomaly	0	0	0	0	0
artificialWithAnomaly	**0.402**	0.400	0.325	0.399	0.346
realAdExchange	0.214	**0.279**	0.167	0.173	0.222
realAWSCloudwatch	**0.269**	0.226	0.209	0.207	0.208
realKnownCause	**0.331**	0.326	0.155	0.197	0.326
realTraffic	**0.398**	0.327	0.288	0.315	0.365
realTweets	0.165	0.132	0.117	0.127	**0.182**

5   Conclusion

This paper presents an attention-based bi-directional LSTM framework for anomaly detection on univariate time-series data. We benchmark our proposed model against eleven different models on six datasets that are a part of the Numenta Anomaly Benchmark (NAB). We outperform the current state-of-the-art models, DeepAnT and FuseAD, on all six datasets. Additionally, we create new baselines on the NAB with the anomaly detection models DAGMM, REBM, LSTM-ED, and Donut, to facilitate better comparison of future research on the NAB against state-of-the-art methods that are being used for other time-series anomaly detection tasks today. Directions for future work could involve extending this model to support multivariate streams, applying this forecasting-thresholding-prediction anomaly on other anomaly benchmark datasets, or experimenting with other forms of attention or transformer models [23], that have seen success in NLP applications.

Acknowledgement. The authors would like to thank TCS R&D for funding this research through PhD fellowship to the first author.

References

1. Ahmad, S., Purdy, S.: Real-time anomaly detection for streaming analytics. arXiv preprint arXiv:1607.02480 (2016)
2. Ahmad, S., Lavin, A., Purdy, S., Agha, Z.: Unsupervised real-time anomaly detection for streaming data. Neurocomputing **262**, 134–147 (2017). https://doi.org/10.1016/j.neucom.2017.04.070. ISSN 0925–2312
3. Baziotis, C., Pelekis, N., Doulkeridis, C.: DataStories at SemEval-2017 task 4: deep LSTM with attention for message-level and topic-based sentiment analysis. In: Proceedings of the 11th International Workshop on Semantic Evaluation (SemEval 2017), Vancouver, Canada, August 2017, pp. 747–754. https://doi.org/10.18653/v1/S17-2126
4. Bergstra, J., Yamins, D., Cox, D.: Making a science of model search: hyperparameter optimization in hundreds of dimensions for vision architectures. In: International Conference on Machine Learning, pp. 115–123. PMLR (2013)

5. Bergstra, J., Bardenet, R., Bengio, Y., Kégl, B.: Algorithms for hyper-parameter optimization. In: 25th Annual Conference on Neural Information Processing Systems (NIPS 2011), vol. 24. Neural Information Processing Systems Foundation (2011)
6. Chalapathy, R., Chawla, S.: Deep learning for anomaly detection: a survey. arXiv preprint arXiv:1901.03407 (2019)
7. Chandola, V., Banerjee, A., Kumar, V.: Anomaly detection: a survey. ACM Comput. Surv. (CSUR) **41**(3), 1–58 (2009)
8. Etsy: etsy/skyline. https://github.com/etsy/skyline
9. Fukui, H., Hirakawa, T., Yamashita, T., Fujiyoshi, H.: Attention branch network: Learning of attention mechanism for visual explanation. CoRR, abs/1812.10025 (2018). http://arxiv.org/abs/1812.10025
10. Hu, D.: An introductory survey on attention mechanisms in NLP problems. In: Bi, Y., Bhatia, R., Kapoor, S. (eds.) SAI Intelligent Systems Conference. AISC, vol. 1037, pp. 432–448. Springer, Cham (2019). https://doi.org/10.1007/978-3-030-29516-5
11. Huang, C., Min, G., Wu, Y., Ying, Y., Pei, K., Xiang, Z.: Time series anomaly detection for trustworthy services in cloud computing systems. IEEE Trans. Big Data, 1 (2017). https://doi.org/10.1109/TBDATA.2017.2711039
12. Introducing practical and robust anomaly detection in a time series, January 2015. https://blog.twitter.com/engineering/en_us/a/2015/introducing-practical-and-robust-anomaly-detection-in-a-time-series.html
13. Karim, F., Majumdar, S., Darabi, H., Chen, S.: LSTM fully convolutional networks for time series classification. IEEE Access **6**, 1662–1669 (2017)
14. Lavin, A., Ahmad, S.: Evaluating real-time anomaly detection algorithms-the numenta anomaly benchmark. In: 2015 IEEE 14th International Conference on Machine Learning and Applications, pp. 38–44. IEEE (2015)
15. Lee, I., Lee, K.: The internet of things (IoT): applications, investments, and challenges for enterprises. Bus. Horiz. **58**(4), 431–440 (2015)
16. Lomb, N.R.: Least-squares frequency analysis of unequally spaced data. Astrophys. Space Sci. **39**(2), 447–462 (1976)
17. Malhotra, P., Ramakrishnan, A., Anand, G., Vig, L., Agarwal, P., Shroff, G.: LSTM-based encoder-decoder for multi-sensor anomaly detection, July 2016
18. Munir, M., Siddiqui, S.A., Dengel, A., Ahmed, S.: DeepAnT: a deep learning approach for unsupervised anomaly detection in time series. IEEE Access **7**, 1991–2005 (2019). https://doi.org/10.1109/ACCESS.2018.2886457
19. Munir, M., Siddiqui, S., Chattha, M., Dengel, A., Ahmed, S.: FuseAD: unsupervised anomaly detection in streaming sensors data by fusing statistical and deep learning models. Sensors **19**, 05 (2019). https://doi.org/10.3390/s19112451
20. Pereira, J., Silveira, M.: Unsupervised anomaly detection in energy time series data using variational recurrent autoencoders with attention. In: 2018 17th IEEE International Conference on Machine Learning and Applications (ICMLA), pp. 1275–1282 (2018). https://doi.org/10.1109/ICMLA.2018.00207
21. Sadouk, L.: CNN approaches for time series classification. In: Time Series Analysis-Data, Methods, and Applications, pp. 1–23. IntechOpen (2019)
22. Scargle, J.D.: Studies in astronomical time series analysis. II-statistical aspects of spectral analysis of unevenly spaced data. Astrophys. J. **263**, 835–853 (1982)
23. Vaswani, A., et al.: Attention is all you need (2017). https://arxiv.org/pdf/1706.03762.pdf

24. Xu, H., et al.: Unsupervised anomaly detection via variational auto-encoder for seasonal KPIs in web applications. In: Proceedings of the 2018 World Wide Web Conference, pp. 187–196 (2018)

25. Yoon, C., Huh, M., Kang, S.-G., Park, J., Lee, C.: Implement smart farm with IoT technology. In: 2018 20th International Conference on Advanced Communication Technology (ICACT), pp. 749–752. IEEE (2018)

26. Yu, Y., Liu, G., Yan, H., Li, H., Guan, H.: Attention-based BI-LSTM model for anomalous http traffic detection. In: 2018 15th International Conference on Service Systems and Service Management (ICSSSM), pp. 1–6 (2018). https://doi.org/10.1109/ICSSSM.2018.8465034

27. Zhai, S., Cheng, Y., Lu, W., Zhang, Z.: Deep structured energy based models for anomaly detection. arXiv preprint arXiv:1605.07717 (2016)

28. Zhao, H.G.: Keras-self-attention (2018). https://github.com/CyberZHG

29. Zheng, G., Mukherjee, S., Dong, X.L., Li, F.: OpenTag: open attribute value extraction from product profiles. In: Proceedings of the 24th ACM SIGKDD International Conference on Knowledge Discovery & Data Mining, KDD 2018, pp. 1049–1058. Association for Computing Machinery (2018). https://doi.org/10.1145/3219819.3219839. ISBN 9781450355520

30. Zong, B., et al.: Deep autoencoding gaussian mixture model for unsupervised anomaly detection. In: International Conference on Learning Representations (2018)

Semi-supervised Graph Edge Convolutional Network for Anomaly Detection

Zhicheng Lun[1,2], Xiaoyan Gu[1(✉)], Haihui Fan[1], Bo Li[1], and Weiping Wang[1]

[1] Institute of Information Engineering, Chinese Academy of Sciences, Beijing, China
{lunzhicheng,guxiaoyan,fanhaihui,libo,wangweiping}@iie.ac.cn
[2] School of Cyber Security, University of Chinese Academy of Sciences, Beijing, China

Abstract. In recent years, with deep learning development, graph-based deep anomaly detection has attracted more and more researchers' attention due to graph data's strong expression ability. However, at present, graph-based methods mainly focus on node-level anomaly detection, while edge-level anomaly detection is relatively minor. Anomaly detection at the edge level can distinguish the specific edges connected to nodes as detection objects, so its resolution granularity is more detailed than that of the node-based method. Second, the rules of anomalies are challenging to learn. At present, most of the algorithms adopt the unsupervised method to train the model. As a result, the detected result is likely to be noise data. In this paper, we propose a Graph Edge Anomaly Detection model based on a Semi-supervised auto-encoder (GEADS). In this model, we first adjust the traditional mini-batch training strategy to train the model on a large-scale graph. It improves the scalability of the model. Second, we design an edge convolutional neural network layer to realize the fusion of edge neighborhood information. We take the reconstruction error as the evaluation criterion after stacking multiple edge convolutional neural network layers that encode and decode the edges. Third, the few abnormal samples with known labels are utilized to guide the model's parameter optimization process. While ensuring the generalization ability of the model, it also improves the pertinence to specific anomalies. Finally, we show the effectiveness of the proposed algorithm through experiments on two real-world datasets.

Keywords: Anomaly detection · Neural networks · Semi-supervised learning · Deep auto-encoder

1 Introduction

Due to graph data's strong representation ability, data in many fields can be expressed in a graph, such as in social media networks [1], financial transaction networks [2], and computer networks [3]. Currently, these networks are rife

Supported by XDC02050200, Z191100007119003.

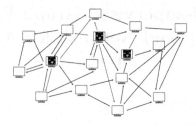

Fig. 1. Example computer network diagram. The node is the host, and the edge is the traffic between the hosts. The attack anomaly in the computer network is the anomaly of traffic, the anomaly of the edge.

with many kinds of anomalies. Anomaly refers to the patterns whose behavior is unexpected in a dataset [4]. These are intrinsically harmful to the network ecosystem. For example, the spread of rumors in social media may cause social shock and endanger public safety. Malicious users can obtain improper wealth through abnormal transactions and even harm the whole financial system. Effective and accurate detection of such anomalies plays a vital role in such systems. Anomaly detection technology has attracted wide attention in academia and industry, and many anomaly detection methods are introduced.

Traditional algorithms identify anomalies by distinguishing certain features such as distance and density [5–7]. However, the effect of the traditional method highly depends on feature engineering. Once the feature selection is not reasonable, the detection effect will not be ideal. The deep learning methods [8–13] can automatically learn the complex nonlinear features between data. In addition to attribute characteristics, complex interaction structure information also exists in the graph data, which is very important for recognizing abnormal data. Many graph-based deep learning methods [1,14] have been proposed for anomaly detection to fully use the interactive information.

However, there are still some shortcomings in the current graph-based methods. First, the current methods mainly focus on node-level anomaly detection. As shown in Fig. 1, we found that abnormalities sometimes occur at the edges. Besides, the degree of nodes in the graph is power-law distribution [15]. The number of edges attached to a node can be huge. Therefore, when we detect abnormal interaction behavior between entities, we find the anomaly's most direct evidence. Besides, when the node's anomaly does not reach a significant level, it will lead to the anomaly detection model's omission. Second, anomalies' rules are hard to learn because of the scarcity of abnormal samples and the variability of anomaly type. Most current algorithms adopt the unsupervised method to train the model to solve this problem. As a result, precious abnormal samples are not fully used, the pertinence of the model is poor, and the detected result is likely to be noise data.

In this paper, we propose a Graph Edge Anomaly Detection model based on a Semi-supervised auto-encoder (GEADS). First, we design the edge convolutional neural network layer. It realizes the edge neighborhood information fusion and improves the edge representation ability. Second, to solve the problem that the proportion of abnormal samples is too tiny in anomaly detection inspired by the auto-encoder [16], we construct an auto-encoder by using the overlapping method of multiple edge convolutional neural network layers. It completes the encoding and decoding of the edge, and we use the reconstruction error as the evaluation criterion of the anomaly. In addition, in the model training process, we use a few abnormal samples with known labels to guide the parameter optimization process and achieve semi-supervised learning. In this way, both the detection of abnormal edges and the application of a few abnormal samples are achieved. While ensuring the generalization ability of the model, it also improves the pertinence to specific anomalies. Finally, to solve the difficulty of training the model on large-scale data, we design a neighborhood sampling strategy specifically for the edge. The purpose is to make the space complexity in the process of model training controllable. The significant contributions of this work are as follows:

- The edge convolutional neural network layer is designed, and it fuses the edge neighborhood based on the structure information.
- An auto-encoder is constructed to measure edge anomaly through the reconstruction error, and the model parameters are learned through semi-supervised learning.
- A batch sampling strategy for edges is designed, and the sub-graph of each batch of data is determined by neighborhood sampling after batch.
- Experimental results on two real-world datasets show the we proposed method outperforms several state-of-the-art approaches.

2 Related Work

The traditional anomaly detection methods include the distance-based [5,6] method, density-based [7] method, etc. Deep learning has been developing in recent years. It is a subset of machine learning, which uses neural networks to learn data embedded in different layers to achieve excellent performance with a substantial degree of flexibility. The research shows that performing deep learning is better than the traditional method with increased data size. Deep learning algorithms are primarily divided into two stages. First, the neural network is used to learn the high-quality representation of data, and then the anomaly evaluation process is designed based on some assumptions, such as RandNet [16], REPEN [8], FSNET [11], DSVDD [9]. Besides representation learning, other methods use an end-to-end approach to learn the abnormal scores of data directly. For example, DevNet [10] proposes an end-to-end anomaly detection framework, which outputs an anomaly score directly after passing through a multi-layer neural network instead of being a feature representation.

In anomaly detection, the complex interaction between graph data is undoubtedly a piece of precious information. The proposal of graph convolutional neural network GCN [17] extends the convolution operation to graph structure data. As the graph convolutional neural network can comprehensively use

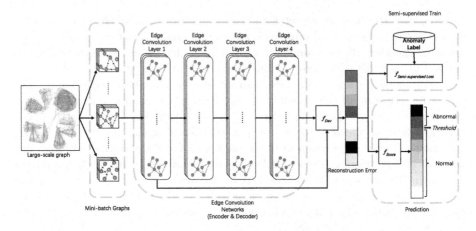

Fig. 2. The overall framework of our proposed graph edge anomaly detection based on a semi-supervised auto-encoder.

the attribute information and structural information, some GCN-based anomaly detection technologies have been proposed successively [14,18]. However, most of the algorithms based on GCN can only achieve node-level anomaly evaluation. In practice, the anomaly to be detected can be traced back to some specific abnormal behavior, represented as an edge between entities in the graph. For example, users spread rumors among each other, computers between the network attack traffic, etc. Therefore, compared with node-level anomaly detection, edge-level anomaly detection can provide more detailed detection granularity and more specific detection results. Some abnormal means some accidents such as network attack, so abnormal sample is precious. How to make full use of these precious abnormal samples is essential. Otherwise, the anomalies detected by the model may be noise data unrelated to the problem. Although there are some semi-supervised learning methods [19,20] that utilize abnormal samples, these methods are not suitable for the edges of the graph.

3   The Proposed Approch

In this paper, a semi-supervised learning algorithm for graph anomaly detection is designed by studying graph anomaly detection's essential techniques. It shows the overall technology roadmap in Fig. 2. Next, we will introduce three aspects of the model in detail.

3.1   Mini-Batch Training for Edges in Graphs

In deep learning, when the gradient descent algorithm is used to update the model's parameters, the efficiency will be very low or even unable to be trained if all the samples are processed. The common method is the mini-batch training

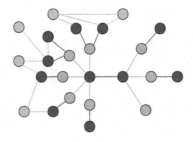

Fig. 3. The feature representation of an edge at the h-layer is only related to its h order subgraph. Red is the central region, blue is the first-order neighborhood, and purple is the second-order neighborhood. (Color figure online)

strategy. The practice shows that the mini-batch training strategy also introduces randomness into the model's training and avoids the local optimization problem. However, in graph-based algorithms, due to structural information's interdependence, the input data involved in each calculation cannot be determined by simple sample batch processing. Simultaneously, since the number of abnormal samples marked in the anomaly detection task is tiny, it is necessary to ensure that a few abnormal samples take part in the guidance in each optimization process of the model.

In this paper, we design a mini-batch model training strategy for the edge to solve the model's training problem on large-scale data. We can know from the edges' neighborhood information fusion process that the features of an edge in the $h + 1$-layer are only related to its neighborhood features in the h-layer. Therefore, it is only necessary to consider the h-order subgraph of an edge to create the h-layer characteristics of an edge, as shown in Fig. 3 for a specific example. We first separate the large-scale graph data into small batches to control the subgraph size. We then make each batch of samples as the center to sample the h-hop neighbor of the sample according to the number of layers h of the edge aggregation network. To control the subgraph scale, we fix the number of samples in each layer as S_i to limit the subgraph of order h to the factorial level. In addition, we ensure that each batch is semi-supervised by ensuring that there is a certain amount of abnormal data in each batch. It further improves the utilization of abnormal data in the model.

3.2 Edge Convolutional Layer

At present, the anomaly detection technology based on the deep neural network has realized the detection of abnormal nodes based on attribute information and structural information. However, in graph data, besides nodes, edges between nodes are another critical element. In practical applications, edges between nodes such as traffic between hosts in the computer network or messages sent between users in the social media network represent some specific association between entities. Edge-level anomaly detection can accurately locate

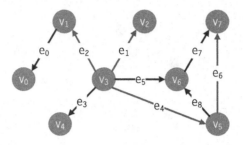

Fig. 4. An example of abnormal edges' correlation, where the red edges represent anomal, and the blue edges represent normal. For node V_3, the proportion of abnormal edges in the total number of edges is 0.6, which is significantly higher than that of other nodes. Also, in the neighboring nodes, the proportion of emitting abnormal edges is 0.2, which is significantly higher than that of other nodes.

the detected anomaly to a subset of the nodes' many edges. So the detection granularity provided by edge detection is more refined than that provided by node detection. Besides, for the edge in the graph, its abnormal situation often has a specific correlation. For example, in a social media network, if a user posts a message related to the plan of a terrorist attack, it is more likely that a user who is in close contact with the user will also post such a message rather than others. Therefore, the fusion of neighborhood information is essential to judge whether an edge is an anomaly. As shown in Fig. 4 is a specific example.

This paper's second major innovation is the strategy designing the edges' neighborhood information fusion. The goal is to realize the detection of abnormal edges in the graph and improve edge embedding's expression ability. The edge convolution layer adds the weighted attribute information of adjacent edges. One edge convolution layer can realize information aggregation of first-order adjacent edges. The h-order neighborhood information of the edge is gathered by stacking the multi-layer edge convolution network. In the process of multi-layer edge convolution, we adopt an automatic encoder to encode and decode the edge features. The edge features are first embedded into the low-dimensional space and then mapped back to the original dimensional space. Finally, the loss function is designed based on reconstruction error. We can express the formula of the edge convolutional neural network layer as:

$$H^{(l+1)} = \sigma[AD^{-1/2}(D^{-1/2})^T A^T H^{(l)} W^{(l)}], \tag{1}$$

where $A \in R^{N_e \times N_v}$ is the adjacency vertex matrix of the edge, and each row represents an edge. If edge i is connected to vertex j, the $a_{ij} = 1$ in the matrix A, otherwise $a_{ij} = 0$. $D \in R^{N_v \times N_v}$ is the diagonal matrix of vertex degrees, that is, $d_{ii} = \sum_j a_{ji}$, and $d_{ij} = 0$ if i not equal to j. $H^{(l)} \in R^{N_e \times d^{(l)}}$ is the representation matrix of edges in the l-th layer. $W^{(l)} \in R^{d^{(l)} \times d^{(l+1)}}$ is the parameter matrix at the l-th level. σ is the activation function.

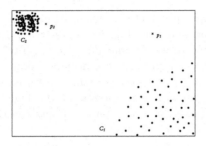

Fig. 5. An example of anomaly evaluation based on nearest-neighbor distance, when using an unsupervised algorithm, assumes that the data's characteristics can be represented eventually as the graph's data points, the abnormal data for p_1 and p_2. If the measurement method based on the nearest-neighbor distance is used to evaluate the degree of anomalies in the data, the nearest-neighbor distance of points in C_1 is between the nearest-neighbor distances of p_1 and p_2. So the algorithm cannot accurately distinguish points in p_1, p_2, and points in C_1.

3.3 Semi-supervised Learning Strategy Based on Auto-Encoder

As the high cost of collecting anomaly data, it is challenging to get large-scale labeled data to train the anomaly detection model. However, the purpose of the unsupervised algorithm is to find the data significantly different from most of the data, which will lead to the anomaly detected by the model is the data unrelated to the problem or noise, making the model less targeted. As shown in Fig. 5 is a specific example. The third research content of this paper is the semi-supervised model training strategy we designed. The purpose is to make full use of rare abnormal data to improve the model's pertinence while ensuring generalization.

In this paper, the earlier edge convolution neural network encodes the edge characteristics. We can obtain a high-quality low-dimensional representation of the edge. Then the encoded feature is decoded to map the edge feature vector back to the original dimensional space. Finally, based on the decoded output and original input features' reconstruction errors, the loss function guided by a few samples is designed. We argue that instances of data with significant reconstruction errors are more likely to be anomalies because their patterns differ significantly from most cases and cannot be accurately reconstructed from observed data. Through a literature review, the hypothesis has been validated by many unsupervised methods [16,21–23]. Based on this hypothesis, our loss function's optimization aim is to gradually reduce the reconstruction errors of unmarked data while the reconstruction errors of abnormal samples gradually increase. So far, we have completed the auto-encoder design based on the edge convolutional neural network and the model optimization process based on the small sample guide. We can express the loss function of a few samples guide designed by us as:

$$loss = \frac{\exp(\alpha \frac{1}{|E_{abnormal}|} \sum_{e \in E_{abnormal}} dev(x_e, \hat{x}_e))}{1 + \beta \frac{1}{|E_{non-abnormal}|} \sum_{e \in E_{non-abnormal}} dev(x_e, \hat{x}_e)}, \tag{2}$$

where α and β are super parameters, which are used to control the influence degree of abnormal data and non-abnormal data. $E_{abnormal}$ refers to the set of abnormal edges with known marks, and $E_{non-abnormal}$ refers to the set of other edges except $E_{abnormal}$. x_e represents the original input feature vector of edge e, and $\hat{x}_e$ represents the feature vector of edge e after encoded and decoded by the auto-encoder. The function dev represents the calculation of reconstruction error. The reconstruction error in this paper adopts the Euclidic distance, and we can express its specific formula as:

$$\mathrm{dev}(\mathrm{x}_a, x_b) = \sqrt{\sum_i (x_{ai} - x_{bi})^2}. \tag{3}$$

4   Experiments

4.1   Data Sets

According to this paper's research content, we select the dataset that can be represented as the graph structure and the edges in the graph have attributes. Such as network traffic datasets for intrusion detection. We can set the host or IP as nodes in the graph and treat traffic as edges. Similarly, for social public media datasets, such as Weibo, Twitter, and Facebook. We can set users as vertices and set communication or interactive posts between users as edges. There are two datasets applied in this experiment, namely UNSW-NB 15 [24] and Weibo [25].

The raw network packets of the UNSW-NB 15 dataset are created by the IXIA PerfectStorm tool in the Cyber Range Lab of the Australian Centre for Cyber Security (ACCS) for generating a hybrid of normal activities and attack behaviors. This dataset has nine families of attacks: Fuzzers, Analysis, Backdoors, DoS, Exploits, Generic, Reconnaissance, Shellcode, and Worms. The dataset contains 2,540,047 traffic, of which 174,348 are abnormal, accounting for 6.86% of the total traffic. Weibo dataset is collected from Sina Weibo, the most popular social media site in China, and is mainly used for rumor detection. As rumor is false information that mainly fast disseminated through interpersonal communication. Meanwhile, it is rare and significantly different from other massive data due to their particularity. So we consider that rumors are a kind of anomaly. The dataset contains a total of 3,805,656 microblogs. These microblogs come from 4,664 source posts, of which 2,351 were marked as abnormal, accounting for 0.06% of the total microblog posts. We show detailed statistics of the two datasets in Table 1.

4.2   Baselines Methods

We compare the proposed method with some state-of-the-art baselines, including:

Table 1. Detailed statistics of the two datasets

Statistic	UNSW-NB 15	Weibo
Time length	649 h	2,461 h
# nodes	49	2,746,818
# edges	2,540,047	3,805,656
# features	87	5000
# anomalies	174,348	2,351
Proportion of anomalies	6.86%	0.06%

- REPEN [8]: A model of deep anomaly detection with limited labeled data. By unifying representation learning and anomaly detection, the model learns customized low-dimensional representations of ultrahigh-dimensional data for random distance-based detectors.
- FSNet [11]: A few-shot classifier. It can represent each class by the mean of its examples in a representation space learned by a neural network. The model performs well in the few-shot setting by using episodic training.
- DSVDD [9]: A feature learning method for anomaly detection. It inspires the method by kernel-based one-class classification and minimum volume estimation. By training a neural network while minimizing the volume of a hypersphere encloses the data's network representations, the model can extract the common factors of variation since the network must closely map the data points to the sphere's center.
- DevNet [10]: The framework fulfills end-to-end differentiable learning of anomaly scores by leveraging a few labeled anomalies with a prior. Instead of representation learning, the method leverage a few labeled anomalies and a prior probability to directly enforce statistically significant deviations of the anomaly scores of anomalies from that of normal data objects in the upper tail.
- Bi-GCN [1]: A bi-directional graph model. It leverages a GCN with a top-down directed graph of rumor spreading to learn the rumor propagation patterns and a GCN with an oppositely directed graph of rumor diffusion to capture the structures of rumor dispersion. It involves the information from the source post in each GCN layer to enhance the influences from the roots of rumors.

4.3 Overall Performance

In experiments, we evaluate the performance of our method GEADS by comparing it with the baselines above. We first present the results in Table 2.

Experimental results show that our method GEADS is better than other methods in three indexes, AUC-ROC, AUC-PR, and F1. Although the F1 score on UNSW-NB 15 dataset is not as good as that of DevNet, this method's feasibility and effectiveness in anomaly detection of graph data are proved. The model's

Table 2. AUC-ROC, AUC-PR and F1 performance of our method and five baseline methods.

Method	Weibo			UNSW-NB 15		
	AUC-ROC	AUC-PR	F1	AUC-ROC	AUC-PR	F1
REPEN [8]	0.791	0.795	0.712	0.878	0.116	0.104
FSNet [11]	0.819	0.782	0.754	0.928	0.573	0.427
DSVDD [9]	0.847	0.845	0.837	0.952	0.856	0.736
DevNet [10]	0.943	0.948	0.902	0.969	0.883	**0.875**
Bi-GCN [1]	0.960	0.962	0.961	0.921	0.472	0.423
GEADS	**0.980**	**0.986**	**0.963**	**0.981**	**0.897**	0.872

Table 3. The ROC-AUC index of the proposed method based on edge convolutional neural network compared with that of various point-based GCNs and unsupervised learning in two datasets.

Method	Weibo	UNSW-NB 15
DGCN	0.953	-
UDGCN	0.956	-
Bi-GCN	0.960	-
GEADS-semi	0.743	0.960
GEADS	**0.980**	**0.981**

excellent performance on two datasets from different application fields further highlights the superiority of our method GEADS, which can be well extended to different applications.

4.4 Ablation Study

To analyze the importance of the key components of our method GEADS. First, we compare the proposed method with D-GCN, UD-GCN, and Bi-GCN in *Weibo* dataset. Table 3 shows the experimental results. D-GCN, UD-GCN, and Bi-GCN represent directed GCN, undirected GCN, and Bi-Directional GCN, respectively. For the relationship between posts in *Weibo*, we can easily compose the graph with posts as the point and the relationship between posts and comments as the edge in the experiment. Compared to how we construct the graph in this paper, the GCN-based approach lacks the user's additional information. Experimental results show that our method is optimal, which further shows the edge convolutional neural network's importance. However, in the network traffic dataset *UNSW-NB15*, there is no convenient condition to construct such a graph as described above, so we only carry the experimental analysis out on the *Weibo* dataset here.

Then, to analyze the effectiveness of semi-supervised learning, we conduct a comparative experiment on two datasets. In semi-supervised learning, we use a few abnormal samples with known labels to guide the model, while the method of unsupervised learning has no guidance. It shows the experimental results in Table 3. The results show that a few abnormal samples taking part in the model's optimization can significantly improve performance. It indicates that although guidance without abnormal samples can achieve great results, if a few abnormal samples are added, the model will be more targeted, and the false positives and missed positives of the model can be effectively reduced to a certain extent.

5   Conclusion

In this paper, a novel Graph Edge Anomaly Detection algorithm based on a Semi-supervised auto-encoder (GEADS) is proposed. We design edge convolutional neural networks to realize edge neighborhood information fusion to realize edge-level anomaly detection in graph data and make full use of attribute information and structure information. A semi-supervised learning strategy based on an auto-encoder is adopted, anomaly samples are fully utilized to improve the model's specificity. Besides, a mini-batch training method is designed for the edges of graphs enables the model to be extended to large-scale graphs. The experimental results on two real-world datasets show that the proposed model is superior to most advanced methods.

References

1. Bian, T., Xiao, X., Xu, T., et al.: Rumor detection on social media with bi-directional graph convolutional networks. In: Proceedings of the AAAI Conference on Artificial Intelligence, pp. 549–556 (2020)
2. Behdad, M., Barone, L., Bennamoun, M., et al.: Nature-inspired techniques in the context of fraud detection. IEEE Trans. Syst. Man Cybern Part C (Applications and Reviews) **42**(6), 1273–1290 (2012)
3. Alpaydın, G.: An adaptive deep neural network for detection, recognition of objects with long range auto surveillance. In 2018 IEEE 12th International Conference on Semantic Computing (ICSC), pp. 316–317. IEEE (2018)
4. Chandola, V., Banerjee, A., Kumar, V.: Anomaly detection: a survey. ACM Comput. Surv. (CSUR) **41**(3), 1–58 (2009)
5. Angiulli, F., Pizzuti, C.: Fast outlier detection in high dimensional spaces. In: Elomaa, T., Mannila, H., Toivonen, H. (eds.) PKDD 2002. LNCS, vol. 2431, pp. 15–27. Springer, Heidelberg (2002). https://doi.org/10.1007/3-540-45681-3_2
6. Ramaswamy, S., Rastogi, R., Shim, K.: Efficient algorithms for mining outliers from large data sets. In: Proceedings of the 2000 ACM SIGMOD International Conference on Management of Data, pp. 427–438 (2000)
7. Breunig, M.M., Kriegel, H.P., Ng, R.T., et al.: LOF: identifying density-based local outliers. In: Proceedings of the 2000 ACM SIGMOD International Conference on Management of Data, pp. 93–104 (2000)
8. Pang, G., Cao, L., Chen, L., et al.: Learning representations of ultrahigh-dimensional data for random distance-based outlier detection. In: Proceedings of the 24th ACM SIGKDD International Conference on Knowledge Discovery & Data Mining, pp. 2041–2050 (2018)

9. Ruff, L., Vandermeulen, R., Goernitz, N., et al.: Deep one-class classification. In: International Conference on Machine Learning, pp. 4393–4402. PMLR (2018)

10. Pang, G., Shen, C., van den Hengel, A.: Deep anomaly detection with deviation networks. In: Proceedings of the 25th ACM SIGKDD International Conference on Knowledge Discovery & Data Mining, pp. 353–362 (2019)

11. Snell, J., Swersky, K., Zemel, R.S.: Prototypical networks for few-shot learning (2017). arXiv preprint arXiv:1703.05175

12. Cheng, Y., Liu, W., Duan, P., et al.: PyAnomaly: a Pytorch-based toolkit for video anomaly detection. In: Proceedings of the 28th ACM International Conference on Multimedia, pp. 4473–4476 (2020)

13. Wang, Q., Liu, X., Liu, W., et al.: MetaSearch: incremental product search via deep meta-learning. IEEE Trans. Image Process. **29**, 7549–7564 (2020)

14. Ding, K., Li, J., Bhanushali, R., et al.: Deep anomaly detection on attributed networks. In: Proceedings of the 2019 SIAM International Conference on Data Mining, pp. 594–602. Society for Industrial and Applied Mathematics (2019)

15. Wang, X.F., Chen, G.: Complex networks: small-world, scale-free and beyond. IEEE Circ. Syst. Mag. **3**(1), 6–20 (2003)

16. Chen, J., Sathe, S., Aggarwal, C., et al.: Outlier detection with autoencoder ensembles. In: Proceedings of the 2017 SIAM International Conference on Data Mining, pp. 90–98. Society for Industrial and Applied Mathematics (2017)

17. Kipf, T.N., Welling, M.: Semi-supervised classification with graph convolutional networks (2016). arXiv preprint arXiv:1609.02907

18. Li, A., Qin, Z., Liu, R., et al.: Spam review detection with graph convolutional networks. In: Proceedings of the 28th ACM International Conference on Information and Knowledge Management, pp. 2703–2711 (2019)

19. Nadeem, M., Marshall, O., Singh, S., et al.: Semi-Supervised Deep Neural Network for Network Intrusion Detection (2016)

20. Song, H., Jiang, Z., Men, A., et al.: A hybrid semi-supervised anomaly detection model for high-dimensional data. Comput. Intell. Neurosci. **2017**, 1–9 (2017)

21. Zhou, C., Paffenroth, R.C.: Anomaly detection with robust deep autoencoders. In: Proceedings of the 23rd ACM SIGKDD International Conference on Knowledge Discovery and Data Mining, pp. 665–674 (2017)

22. Schlegl, T., Seeböck, P., Waldstein, S.M., et al.: Unsupervised anomaly detection with generative adversarial networks to guide marker discovery. In: International Conference on Information Processing in Medical Imaging, pp. 146–157. Springer, Cham (2017)

23. Zenati, H., Romain, M., Foo, C.S., et al.: Adversarially learned anomaly detection. In: 2018 IEEE International Conference on Data Mining (ICDM), pp. 727–736. IEEE (2018)

24. Moustafa, N., Slay, J.: UNSW-NB15: a comprehensive data set for network intrusion detection systems (UNSW-NB15 network data set). In: 2015 Military Communications and Information Systems Conference (MilCIS), pp. 1–6. IEEE (2015)

25. Ma, J., Gao, W., Mitra, P., et al.: Detecting rumors from microblogs with recurrent neural networks. In: Proceedings of the Twenty-Fifth International Joint Conference on Artificial Intelligence (2016)

Feature Creation Towards the Detection of Non-control-Flow Hijacking Attacks

Zander Blasingame[1](✉) ⓘ, Chen Liu[1] ⓘ, and Xin Yao[2] ⓘ

[1] Clarkson University, Potsdam, NY 13699, USA
{zblasingame,cliu}@clarkson.edu
[2] Research Institute of Trustworthy Autonomous Systems, Southern University of Science and Technology, Shenzhen, Guangdong, China
xiny@sustc.edu.cn

Abstract. With malware attacks on the rise, approaches using low-level hardware information to detect these attacks have been gaining popularity recently. This is achieved by using hardware event counts as features to describe the behavior of the software program. Then a classifier, such as support vector machine (SVM) or neural network, can be used to detect the anomalous behavior caused by malware attacks. The collected datasets to describe the program behavior, however, are normally imbalanced, as it is much easier to gather regular program behavior than abnormal ones, which can lead to high false negative rates (FNR). In an effort to provide a remedy to this situation, we propose the usage of Genetic Programming (GP) to create new features to augment the original features in conjunction with the classifier. One key component that will affect the classifier performance is to construct the Hellinger distance as the fitness function. As a result, we perform design space exploration in estimating the Hellinger distance. The performance of different approaches is evaluated using seven real-world attacks that target three vulnerabilities in the OpenSSL library and two vulnerabilities in modern web-servers. Our experimental results show, by using the new features evolved with GP, we are able to reduce the FNR and improve the performance characteristics of the classifier.

Keywords: Feature construction · Anomaly detection · Hardware performance counters · Data-only attacks · Machine learning

1 Introduction

Malware is a common type of cybersecurity attacks. It often takes advantage of vulnerabilities that exist in programs. Of these, low-level memory corruption errors are very common and very dangerous [16]. Malicious agents exploit these memory errors so as to manipulate both control and non-control data structures within the program's memory to alter the program behavior. As a result, these attacks can be classified as *control-oriented attacks* or *non-control-flow hijacking attacks*, depending on what data structures are manipulated. Prior

© Springer Nature Switzerland AG 2021
I. Farkaš et al. (Eds.): ICANN 2021, LNCS 12891, pp. 153–164, 2021.
https://doi.org/10.1007/978-3-030-86362-3_13

work has shown that hardware-level information can be used to detect *control-oriented attacks* with high accuracy [1,12,18]. This is achieved by collecting hardware event counts such as number of instructions, cache misses and mispredicted branches, etc., during the execution of a software application, and use these hardware events as features to describe the behavior of the software program. Then a classifier, such as support vector machine (SVM) or neural network, can be used to detect the anomalous behavior caused by malware attacks. *Non-control-flow hijacking attacks*, however, maintain the control-flow of the victim application to follow a valid execution path, making them more difficult to detect [13]. Conversely, prior work [1,6–8,17] regarding *non-control-flow hijacking attacks* have suggested using non-hardware-based techniques such as manual code re-factoring with significant overhead.

In addition to its stealth nature, another reason why developing a highly accurate model for detecting a *non-control-flow hijacking attack* is challenging is due to limited hardware resources available when using hardware events as features. To further compound the difficulty of this problem, during the training process, the amount of behavior that is measured to be malicious is vastly smaller than the amount of behavior that is deemed normal. This large imbalance can lead to models with very high false negative rates (FNR), which is the error rate when malicious behavior is classified as normal system behavior. Considering a busy webserver that receives numerous requests and connections made every day in a real world scenario, even a 1% difference in FNR actually corresponds to a non-trivial amount of undetected malicious actions.

Due to these aforementioned difficulties, we propose to use Genetic Programming (GP) to construct new features to augment the original hardware-level features for the detection of *non-control-flow hijacking attacks* in order to achieve high detection accuracy. Under the constraints of highly imbalanced dataset, we use the Hellinger distance as a fitness function to evaluate the feature quality, which has been shown being skew insensitive in prior work under similar scenarios [2,5]. This paper is novel in terms of applying evolutionary computing techniques to hardware-level information for the purposes of anomaly detection for malware, which is a research territory has not been touched before. Especially, we contribute a novel study and estimation of the Hellinger distance in the context of using the Hellinger distance as a fitness function for the creation of new features.

2   Background

The performance of a classification algorithm is impacted by how well the dataset represents the underlying probability distributions and the degree of similarity between different classes [15]. Datasets with a large degree of similarity or highly imbalanced representation of each class creates difficult classification problems. To combat this, it is advantageous to create new features to maximize the degree of separability. This can be achieved by using Genetic Programming for creating functions to generate new features, i.e., the GP algorithm creates trees of deterministic n-ary operators and constants, which may evolve within each iteration [19]. Each tree is a representation of a program, i.e., a function, wherein the inputs to this program represent a subset of the original features and the output is a new feature built from a deterministic function of the inputs. The fitness function is a heuristic used to guide the evolution of the programs towards a more desirable program. As such the fitness function is chosen so that it maximizes the degree of separability between the two classes [19]. In the evolutionary algorithm the programs with the highest fitness are selected and reproduced, using crossover of nodes in the tree representations. Additionally, random mutations are introduced to the members of the population with high fitness, where a mutation is defined as a substitution of a random part of a program with another random part of program. In general each generation is more fit than its predecessors.

While a universal approximator, e.g., a deep neural network, could be used to solve this problem, the mechanisms behind the final model are often unintuitive, as the models tend to have many thousands of parameters if not more. Conversely, evolutionary approaches allow the model to be built with a limited number of parameters and greater flexibility in the types of deterministic operators used to construct the model. Common methods of assessing the quality of newly created features are Information Gain, Gini Index, and Chi-square [15]. Hart et al. [5] showed that the use of the Hellinger distance as the choice of fitness criterion performed well with imbalanced datasets. While the Hellinger distance has been shown to be a helpful fitness criterion, there has been little consensus and work on showing how to estimate the Hellinger distance in this context. Naturally, while the GP algorithm yields the feature creation function, it does not provide an estimation of the distribution function. However, the Hellinger distance relies on the knowledge of the distribution functions of both classes. This now necessitates a strategy for estimating the underlying probability distribution from the discrete samples. In this work we explore different possible implementations of the Hellinger distance that have tractable solutions. Primarily, we are trying to answer the following questions:

i) Over what values is the Hellinger distance evaluated?
ii) What role does normalization play in the feature creation process?
iii) Which distributions should the Hellinger distance be applied to?
iv) How should the distribution functions be estimated?

3 Dataset

There exists no standard dataset for the testing of security mechanisms in a consistent manner, which is one of the main difficulties with the evaluation of anomaly detection systems [11]. This difficulty is more apparent with the study of *non-control-flow hijacking attacks*, which are more difficult to deploy. Additionally, there exists no standard exploit benchmarks for evaluating *non-control-flow hijacking attacks* and very few working instances of these attacks exist publicly.

We used seven real-world exploits, four of these exploits target vulnerable web servers as described by Hu et al. [6], and the other three target different vulnerabilities in the OPENSSL library. Table 1 lists the vulnerabilities targeted in this study. Each of these exploits were manually recreated on real machines

Table 1. Vulnerabilities and exploits

Vulnerability	Type	Program	Exploit	Type
bugtraq ID: 41956	FS*	ORZHTTPD	ORZHTTPD_ROOTDIR	Data leak
			ORZHTTPD_LEAKADDR	Mem leak
CVE-2013-2028	SBO†	NGINX	NGINX_ROOTDIR	Data leak
			NGINX_KEYLEAK	Data leak
CVE-2014-3566	ED‡	OpenSSL	POODLE	Data leak
CVE-2015-0204	ED‡	OpenSSL	FREA	Data leak
CVE-2015-0400	ED‡	OpenSSL	LOGJAM	Data leak

(∗) Format string   (†) Stack buffer overflow   (‡) Encryption downgrade

hosting web servers. The experiments of the vulnerable ORZHTTPD and NGINX were conducted on a 32-bit system with an Intel Core i5 M540 (DualCore, HT, 2.53 GHz) processor with 4 GB of memory running Ubuntu 12.04 with version 3.2.0 of the Linux kernel. The experiments for the exploits targeting OpenSSL were conducted on a 64-bit system with an Intel Core i7 950 (QuadCore, HT, 3.06 GHz) processor with 8 GB of memory running Ubuntu 13.04 with version 3.8.0 of the Linux kernel.

Modern processors are equipped with Performance Monitoring Unit (PMU) that can track hardware-level events during the software program execution. We used a set of 12 hardware events as original features. They are the numbers of load instructions, store instructions, direct new calls, indirect near calls, near returns, mis-predicted branches, mis-predicted conditional branches, I-TLB misses, D-TLB misses, shared-TLB hits, I-cache misses and last-level cache misses. The choice of events is based on those reported in recent literature on using low-level hardware information to model the execution of software [12,13,18]. Hardware event counts are collected during the "point-of-attack", i.e., we read the hardware event count before we enter and after we exit the software function (procedure) where the vulnerability resides, the delta between these two readings forms the datasets we used in this study[1]. The same 12 hardware events were measured on both hardware platforms we used in experiments.

4   Methodology

We first employ the GP algorithm to find the m best performing individuals using the Hellinger distance as the fitness criterion. Thereafter, these new features are used to augment the dataset and sent to a detection algorithm, either a support vector machine (SVM) or a neural network (NN). We use the detection algorithm to differentiate the benign behavior of the program from the malicious behavior resulted from attacks.

---

[1] The datasets may be found at https://github.com/camel-clarkson/non-controlflow-hijacking-datasets.

4.1   Genetic Programming

The genetic program creates functions $f : \mathcal{X} \to \mathbb{R}$ whose purpose is to construct a new feature out of the original features, where $\mathcal{X}$ denotes the feature space. The objective of the GP is to find such a function that maximizes the distance between the two classes.

In our experiment, the genetic program is initialized using a ramped half and half scheme that uses sub-tree crossover and mutation to create the next generation of individuals. This is done with an initial population of 300 individuals. A number of tournaments with three individuals are conducted. Those with the highest fitness criterion are passed to the next generation. We apply crossover and mutation with a probability of 80% and 10%, respectively [5]. The expression generation scheme creates trees with a depth of one or two, and the maximum bloat depth varies between 6 and 17 [9]. The terminal nodes consist of the original 12 features with three additional constants, which are a fixed-point number, a floating-point number and -1. The function node set consists of the following operators: ADD, SUB, MUL, DIV, MAX, MIN, NEG, COS, SIN, LOG and ABS.

4.2   Fitness Function

Prior work has shown that the Hellinger metric is strongly skew insensitive, lending it useful as a fitness criterion for imbalanced datasets [2]. The fitness function is a functional F on the space of functions mapping $\mathcal{X} \to \mathbb{R}$. Let X, Y be random variables with X denoting the feature vector and Y denoting the label. Then the new features would be denoted as $f(X)$. Let $T_0, T_1 \subsetneq \mathcal{X}$ denote the two datasets of features for anomalous and normal samples, respectively. A natural choice for the fitness function would be a measure of distance between the transformed anomalous distribution and transformed normal distribution. Let ρ_i denote the density (or mass) function of the distribution $P(f(X)|Y = i)$. Often the data space $\mathcal{X}$ is discrete, as is the case in our application. Therefore $f(\mathcal{X}) \subsetneq \mathbb{R}$ is discrete as well. So, the Hellinger distance can be written as

$$F^2[f] = \frac{1}{2} \sum_{a \in f(\mathcal{X})} \left(\sqrt{\rho_1(a)} - \sqrt{\rho_0(a)} \right)^2 \tag{1}$$

as the expression for our fitness function. However, this form is not guaranteed to be tractable for all ρ_i induced by f.

This leads to our first question concerning implementation: *Over what values is the Hellinger distance evaluated?* The first option is to evaluate only over the samples we are given. Note, this approach can also be viewed as taking an expectation on $P(f(\mathcal{X}))$ rather than a sum over all the samples which form our dataset drawn from $P(f(\mathcal{X}))$, so Eq. (1) becomes

$$F^2[f] = \frac{1}{2} \mathbb{E}_{a \sim P(f(\mathcal{X}))} \left[\left(\sqrt{\rho_1(a)} - \sqrt{\rho_0(a)} \right)^2 \right] \tag{2}$$

The alternative option is to evaluate over a finite subset of $f(\mathcal{X})$. We use a uniformly discrete subset from $\min f(T_0 \cup T_1)$ to $\max f(T_0 \cup T_1)$.

The second question concerning implementation is: *Should f be applied purely to samples from original space or from a normalized space?* Often features are normalized to ensure that one does not dominate the others. Therefore, we test an approach using feature rescaling to map each feature onto $[-1, 1]$ before passing to the GP algorithm.

Intuitively, the fitness criterion would be the Hellinger distance between $P(f(X)|Y = 1)$ and $P(f(X)|Y = 0)$. However, prior work has suggested using another distance derived from the Hellinger distance by using the posterior distributions, but evaluating on $f(X)$ and not Y. This can be thought of as minimizing the overlap between two classifiers on the scoring space rather than two distributions on the scoring space. This discussion leads into our third question concerning implementation: *Which distributions should the Hellinger distance be applied to?* At the suggestion of Hart et al. [5], the implementation of the fitness criterion becomes:

$$F^2[f] = \sum_{a \in f(X)} \left(\sqrt{\frac{\rho_1(a) P(Y = 1)}{\rho(a)}} - \sqrt{\frac{\rho_0(a) P(Y = 0)}{\rho(a)}} \right)^2 \tag{3}$$

where ρ is the density of $P(f(X))$. Note, the normalization term $\frac{1}{2}$ is droped in favor of the unnormalized Hellinger distance, i.e., the fitness criterion now has a range of $[0, \sqrt{2}]$ rather than $[0, 1]$.

4.3   Density Estimation

The caveat with using the Hellinger distance is that we need ρ_i. However, we only have discrete samples $A_i = f(T_i)$. This leads to our fourth question concerning implementation: *How should the distribution functions be estimated?* One approach is to create a histogram of the observed data and normalizing it so that it becomes a probability mass function. The caveat is that often the samples, A_i, form a sparse covering of $f(\mathcal{X})$, and may lack information about the relative density. Therefore, we propose the usage of kernel density estimation (KDE) to model the densities ρ_i from the data A_i. KDE is a statistical model used to approximate a density function which has the following definition

$$\hat{\rho}_i(a) = \frac{1}{\beta_i |A_i|} \sum_{a' \in A_i} K \left(\frac{a - a'}{\beta_i} \right) \tag{4}$$

where $K : \mathbb{R} \to \mathbb{R}^+$ is the kernel and $\beta_i > 0$ is a smoothing parameter known as the bandwidth. We chose the Gaussian kernel and used Scott's rule to determine the bandwidth, which is given as $\beta_i = |A_i|^{-0.2} \sigma_i$, where σ_i is the standard deviation of the samples A_i [4]. As we consider the true densities ρ_i to be discrete mass functions, we account for this in the KDE estimation by normalizing $\hat{\rho}_i$ by

$\sum_{a' \in A_i} \hat{\rho}_i(a)$ so that the total mass is one. Let the normalized estimate of ρ_i be denoted as $\hat{p}_i$, the Hellinger distance becomes

$$F^2[f] = \sum_{a \in f(T'_0 \cup T'_1)} \left(\sqrt{\hat{p}_1(a)} - \sqrt{\hat{p}_0(a)} \right)^2 \tag{5}$$

where T'_0, T'_1 denote the normalized datasets.

4.4 Classifiers

We use three models to differentiate the benign behavior of the program from the malicious behavior created by the attacks, these are: a Support Vector Machine (SVM) with linear kernel, a SVM with radial basis function (RBF) kernel, and a Neural Network. Both SVMs are implemented with the scikit-learn package with the default parameters for their respective kernels. The neural network is implemented in TensorFlow with 4 fully connected layers, dropout, and leaky rectified linear unit; the neural network trained using softmax regression to minimize the cross entropy of the output with labelled data. Gradient descent is performed using the Adam optimization algorithm. Torres et al. [13,14] and Liu et al. [10] provided detailed studies on constructing classifiers using low-level hardware information to detect *Non-control-flow hijacking attack* using a variety of detection models, where they also used an SVM with RBF kernel as the baseline. Remark the focus of this work is on the usage of GP to generate new features to augment the original hardware-level features may be used with other classifiers.

5 Experimental Setup

The following procedure was used to construct the new features and datasets:

i) Run the GP algorithm with the different Hellinger distance implementations on the entire original dataset and select the top-4 performing individuals, i.e., the programs that construct the new features.
ii) Create 5 pairs of new training and testing sets from the original data using stratified k-fold cross-validation.
iii) The individuals created by the GP algorithm are used to construct new features. These new features are partitioned in accordance to the scheme from the previous step.

The data imbalance is preserved across all the datasets so that the constraint of the imbalanced dataset is preserved equally on all runs; the entire imbalanced dataset is provided to the GP algorithm. After creating the new datasets, the new features are evaluated using the three classifiers with k-fold cross-validation. The partitions for cross-validation is kept the same between each dataset so the partitions cannot bias the classifier performance. The genetic program is implemented using DEAP (Distributed Evolutionary Algorithms) in Python [3].

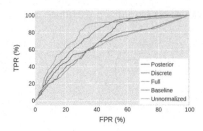
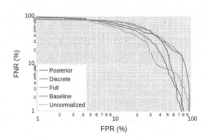

Fig. 1. Average ROC curve of classifiers using different Hellinger distance
estimates

Fig. 2. Average DET curve of classifiers using different Hellinger distance
estimates

Note, we collected the hardware event at run-time, however, at the current stage, the classifier is not operated in an online fashion yet, i.e., the classification is done off-line. On the other hand, our proposed approach will greatly pave the way towards online detection scheme.

Each genetic program was run with 20 generations using the Hall of Fame (HoF) algorithm to select the top 4 performing individuals through the entire execution of the algorithm. The GP was implemented using the parameters outlined in Sect. 4.1 and varied in accordance with different implementations of the Hellinger distance described in Sects. 4.2 and 4.3. Cross-validation was performed via the scikit-learn package using all three classifiers. After training the model on a particular dataset, it was evaluated via the detection accuracy metric.

6   Experimental Results

In this section we examine the performance of different implementations of the Hellinger distance as outlined in Sect. 4. For each of the Hellinger variants discussed in Sect. 4, only one component was changed from the implementation found in Eq. (5), which is treated as the baseline implementation labelled *baseline*. For example, the implementation that uses discrete estimation over KDE does not use the posterior probabilities, the samples are normalized, and it is evaluated strictly over samples in the dataset.

6.1   Hellinger Implementation Analysis

Figure 1 illustrates the average ROC curves for classifiers using only features generated by the GP algorithm with different Hellinger implementations. Each curve in the plot denotes the average ROC of all three classifier variants averaged overall all exploits; whereas, Fig. 2 illustrates the average Detection Error Tradeoff (DET) curves for classifiers for the same curves as in the ROC plot.

Table 2. Detection performance of different models using different GP approaches where EER denotes the Equal Error Rate and AUC denotes the AUC-ROC. Best performing approach is in bold.

Exploit	Model	Posterior		Discrete		Full		Baseline		Unnormalized	
		EER	AUC	EER	AUC	EER	AUC	EER	AUC	EER	AUC
FREAK	SVM linear	0.00	**100.00**	0.00	100.00	0.00	100.00	0.00	**100.00**	0.00	100.00
	SVM RBF	0.00	**100.00**	0.00	**100.00**	0.00	**100.00**	0.00	**100.00**	0.00	100.00
	NN	0.00	100.00	0.00	**100.00**	0.04	100.00	0.00	**100.00**	0.00	100.00
POODLE	SVM linear	2.97	98.74	6.71	96.07	2.89	98.91	2.67	**98.98**	6.62	96.06
	SVM RBF	1.94	99.04	3.06	98.45	1.97	99.06	2.01	99.02	1.61	**99.29**
	NN	2.35	99.38	4.09	98.59	2.56	99.37	2.40	99.29	2.41	**99.40**
NGINX_KEYLEAK	SVM linear	35.34	70.37	33.44	71.57	34.98	70.77	31.20	66.11	25.87	**84.16**
	SVM RBF	17.00	92.94	18.18	90.33	20.10	88.84	17.80	92.77	6.77	**96.81**
	NN	20.79	80.72	17.36	80.77	14.93	81.34	24.96	79.02	16.11	**95.31**
NGINX_ROOTDIR	SVM linear	16.97	**88.94**	11.77	81.07	12.62	78.28	17.42	86.06	16.16	77.70
	SVM RBF	16.48	88.75	17.49	80.28	14.81	82.90	16.33	88.40	13.10	**94.78**
	NN	16.42	88.16	12.30	79.64	12.39	77.38	17.04	84.06	14.71	**92.85**
LOGJAM	SVM linear	0.56	**99.96**	5.30	97.61	5.35	97.77	1.46	99.86	5.18	97.54
	SVM RBF	0.00	**100.00**	4.21	97.90	3.79	98.12	0.22	100.00	2.50	98.90
	NN	1.66	**99.82**	5.71	98.19	5.46	98.55	3.12	98.99	3.34	99.11
ORZHTTPD_ROOTDIR	SVM linear	18.04	**82.65**	21.13	79.96	16.84	82.14	18.44	81.45	13.96	80.90
	SVM RBF	19.74	81.20	17.92	81.65	20.23	82.19	18.07	83.07	15.17	**85.65**
	NN	10.70	73.91	15.06	74.45	16.17	69.40	16.40	69.91	10.96	**88.49**
ORZHTTPD_RESTORE	SVM linear	24.07	**80.89**	24.56	80.37	23.94	80.54	21.83	80.87	20.98	75.36
	SVM RBF	19.55	78.13	25.24	78.89	25.12	80.16	24.07	79.40	14.95	**92.34**
	NN	18.28	82.46	11.93	81.65	18.71	63.28	19.99	82.78	19.43	**84.93**

What we can see is the *unnormalized* approach has the best ROC curve overall, followed closely by the *posterior* approach. The other approaches have different regions in the ROC plot where they dominate the other approaches, but the performance hierarchy is less clear for the remaining approaches. Table 2 provides a focused view per exploit and per classifier using both the original and created features on two performance metrics: the Equal Error Rate (EER) and Area Under the Curve ROC (AUC-ROC). EER refers to the point when the false positive rate and false negative rate are equal, while AUC-ROC is the integral of the ROC curve. For each exploit and classifier, the Hellinger estimation that yielded the highest AUC-ROC is denoted in bold; if there is a tie all the entries are in bold.

Figure 1 shows that the Hellinger approach which evaluates over a uniform discrete subset of the feature space, labelled *full*, performs worse than the baseline approach. Additionally, when used to augment the original features, it does not generally provide as much improvement as other approaches as shown in Table 2. While only evaluating the Hellinger distance over the samples from the dataset could potentially cause the distance to deviate significantly from the true Hellinger distance, the pitfall of the *full* approach is that it necessitates perfect knowledge of the density functions; however, in practice this generally is not feasible and therefore it actually increases the error in estimation when evaluating on samples that lie outside the training data. Similarly, the *discrete* approach,

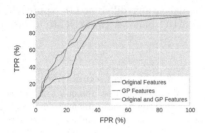
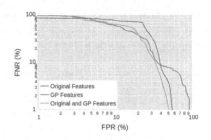

Fig. 3. Average ROC curve of classi-   Fig. 4. Average DET curve of classifiers using different features.   fiers using different features.

i.e., using a histogram to estimate density, is found to be lacking in performance capabilities both on its own and when used to augment the original features. This particular approach has the worst DET curve with high FNR rates until reaching an FPR of roughly 80%.

Examining Table 2 together with Figs. 1 and 2, it is clear that one Hellinger approach outperforms the others, i.e., the *unnormalized* approach. In addition to having a generally low EER across all exploits, this approach yields the best performing model consistently where its AUC-ROC readings have 14 instances of being the best performing approach. The performance of the *posterior* nearly outperforms the baseline in every run with a few exceptions. While the baseline approach is a more faithful implementation of the Hellinger distance, the *posterior* is, in reality, another statistical divergence that accounts for the class imbalances by using the class priors leading to better performance, at the relatively minor cost of losing the proven properties of the Hellinger distance. Interestingly, the *posterior* approach tends to outperform the *unnormalized* approach when used by the linear kernel SVM; whereas, the *unnormalized* approach performs better when used by the other models. Moreover, it is common for the AUC-ROC to vary little across classifiers for the *posterior* approach, implying that the additional information provided by this approach did not yield information usable by the more complicated NN and RBF kernel SVM. Conversely, those two models perform significantly better across the board when compared against the linear kernel SVM using the *unnormalized* features. The *unnormalized* approach allows the GP algorithm to exploit the latent meaning of the hardware-level features the differences in the range of the features can be important in creating new features.

6.2 Performance Improvement Analysis

Figure 3 shows the difference in performance in terms of the ROC, averaged over exploits, models, and using the *unnormalized* approach, when using the original features only, the GP created features, and the combination of the two; whereas, Fig. 4 shows the same curves but in a DET plot. Equation 6 is an example of a created feature from the NGNINX_KEYLEAK exploit.

$$F = \cos(\max(\text{LOAD}, -\text{CALL\_D} \cdot \text{CALL\_D})) \qquad (6)$$

This demonstrates the power of the proposed approach of using GP to generate new features. As we can see, this is a fairly complex new feature generated by the GP algorithm. First of all, no such hardware event exists at the hardware level. Secondly, this can also serve as a recommendation to computer architect engineers as a new hardware event for future microprocessors. Figures 3 and 4 illustrate the performance improvements gained by using GP features, where there is a significantly lower FNR for an FPR between roughly 5% and 45%. Moreover, when using both the original and GP features, the best performance characteristics of each are combined together resulting in superior performance. This greatly improves performance especially at lower FPR rates.

7   Conclusion

In this work, we presented a novel approach using genetic programming (GP) to create new optimal features to augment the original features from low-level hardware information towards the detection against *non-control-flow hijacking attacks*. With a neural network and SVMs acting as classifiers, our proposed approach is effective in improving the overall detection accuracy across all studied exploits. Importantly, we have performed in-depth study for estimating the Hellinger distance in the context of GP in order to generate optimal features. We thoroughly compared different facets concerning the estimation of the Hellinger distance in improving the classification accuracy and error rates. Our experimental results show that using a smooth estimator, like KDE, yields a superior fitness function than using a discrete estimator. Additionally, we show that it is not necessary to evaluate the Hellinger distance over the full support of the distribution functions to yield a usable fitness function. This allows the estimation of the Hellinger problem to become computationally feasible and efficient.

Acknowledgements. This work was partially supported by Shenzhen Science and Technology Program through the Research Institute of Trustworthy Autonomous Systems (RITAS).

References

1. Chen, S., Xu, J., Sezer, E.C., Gauriar, P., Iyer, R.K.: Non-control-data attacks are realistic threats. In: Proceedings of the 14th Conference on USENIX Security Symposium, SSYM 2005, vol. 14, p. 12 (2005)
2. Cieslak, D.A., Hoens, T.R., Chawla, N.V., Kegelmeyer, W.P.: Hellinger distance decision trees are robust and skew-insensitive. Data Min. Knowl. Disc. **24**(1), 136–158 (2012). https://doi.org/10.1007/s10618-011-0222-1
3. Fortin, F.A., De Rainville, F.M., Gardner, M.A., Parizeau, M., Gagné, C.: DEAP: evolutionary algorithms made easy. J. Mach. Learn. Res. **13**, 2171–2175 (2012)
4. Härdle, W., Müller, M., Sperlich, S., Werwatz, A.: Nonparametric and Semiparametric Models. Springer Series in Statistics, Springer, Heidelberg (2004). https://doi.org/10.1007/978-3-642-17146-8

5. Hart, E., Sim, K., Gardiner, B., Kamimura, K.: A hybrid method for feature construction and selection to improve wind-damage prediction in the forestry sector. In: GECCO 2017, vol. 8, pp. 1121–1128
6. Hu, H., Chua, Z.L., Adrian, S., Saxena, P., Liang, Z.: Automatic generation of data-oriented exploits. In: 24th USENIX Security Symposium, pp. 177–192 (2015)
7. Hu, H., Shinde, S., Adrian, S., Chua, Z.L., Saxena, P., Liang, Z.: Data-oriented programming: On the expressiveness of non-control data attacks. In: 2016 IEEE Symposium on Security and Privacy (SP), pp. 969–986 (2016)
8. Kittel, T., Vogl, S., Kirsch, J., Eckert, C.: Counteracting data-only malware with code pointer examination. In: Bos, H., Monrose, F., Blanc, G. (eds.) Research in Attacks, Intrusions, and Defenses. LNCS, vol. 7462, pp. 177–197. Springer, Heidelberg (2015). https://doi.org/10.1007/978-3-642-33338-5
9. Koza, J., Rice, J.: Genetic Programming: On the Programming of Computers by Means of Natural Selection. A Bradford Book, Bradford (1992)
10. Liu, C., Yang, Z., Blasingame, Z., Torres, G., Bruska, J.: Detecting data exploits using low-level hardware information: a short time series approach. In: Proceedings of the First Workshop on Radical and Experiential Security, pp. 41–47 (2018)
11. Sommer, R., Paxson, V.: Outside the closed world: on using machine learning for network intrusion detection. In: 2010 IEEE Symposium on Security and Privacy, pp. 305–316, May 2010. https://doi.org/10.1109/SP.2010.25
12. Tang, A., Sethumadhavan, S., Stolfo, S.J.: Unsupervised anomaly-based malware detection using hardware features. In: Stavrou, A., Bos, H., Portokalidis, G. (eds.) RAID 2014. LNCS, vol. 8688, pp. 109–129. Springer, Cham (2014). https://doi.org/10.1007/978-3-319-11379-1_6
13. Torres, G., Liu, C.: Can data-only exploits be detected at runtime using hardware events?: a case study of the heartbleed vulnerability. In: Proceedings of the Hardware and Architectural Support for Security and Privacy, pp. 2:1–2:7 (2016)
14. Torres, G., Yang, Z., Blasingame, Z., Bruska, J., Liu, C.: Detecting non-control-flow hijacking attacks using contextual execution information. In: Proceedings of the 8th International Workshop on Hardware and Architectural Support for Security and Privacy, HASP@ISCA 2019, 23 June 2019, pp. 1:1–1:8 (2019)
15. Tran, B., Xue, B., Zhang, M.: Genetic programming for feature construction and selection in classification on high-dimensional data. Memetic Comput. 8 (2015). https://doi.org/10.1007/s12293-015-0173-y
16. van der Veen, V., dutt Sharma, N., Cavallaro, L., Bos, H.: Memory errors: the past, the present, and the future. In: Proceedings of the 15th International Conference on Research in Attacks, Intrusions, and Defenses, pp. 86–106 (2012)
17. Vogl, S., Pfoh, J., Kittel, T., Eckert, C.: Persistent data-only malware: function hooks without code. In: Proceedings of the 21th Annual Network & Distributed System Security Symposium (NDSS), February 2014
18. Wang, X., Karri, R.: NumChecker: detecting kernel control-flow modifying rootkits by using hardware performance counters. In: 2013 50th ACM/EDAC/IEEE Design Automation Conference (DAC), pp. 1–7, May 2013
19. Xue, B., Zhang, M., Browne, W.N., Yao, X.: A survey on evolutionary computation approaches to feature selection. IEEE Trans. Evol. Comput. 20(4), 606–626 (2016). https://doi.org/10.1109/TEVC.2015.2504420

Attention and Transformers I

An Attention Module for Convolutional Neural Networks

Baozhou Zhu[1(✉)], Peter Hofstee[1,2], Jinho Lee[3], and Zaid Al-Ars[1]

[1] Delft University of Technology, Delft, The Netherlands
{b.zhu-1,z.al-ars}@tudelft.nl
[2] IBM Systems, Austin, TX, USA
[3] Yonsei University, Seoul, South Korea

Abstract. Attention mechanism has been regarded as an advanced technique to capture long-range feature interactions and to boost the representation capability for convolutional neural networks. However, we found two ignored problems in current attentional activations-based models: the approximation problem and the insufficient capacity problem of the attention maps. To solve the two problems together, we initially propose an attention module for convolutional neural networks by developing an AW-convolution, where the shape of attention maps matches that of the weights rather than the activations. Our proposed attention module is a complementary method to previous attention-based schemes, such as those that apply the attention mechanism to explore the relationship between channel-wise and spatial features. Experiments on several datasets for image classification and object detection tasks show the effectiveness of our proposed attention module. In particular, our proposed attention module achieves 1.00% Top-1 accuracy improvement on ImageNet classification over a ResNet101 baseline and 0.63 COCO-style Average Precision improvement on the COCO object detection on top of a Faster R-CNN baseline with the backbone of ResNet101-FPN. When integrating with the previous attentional activations-based models, our proposed attention module can further increase their Top-1 accuracy on ImageNet classification by up to 0.57% and COCO-style Average Precision on the COCO object detection by up to 0.45. Code and pre-trained models will be publicly available.

Keywords: Attention mechanism · Convolution · Representation

1 Introduction

Recent literature [6,12,31] have investigated the attention mechanism since it can improve not only the representation power but also the representation of interests. Convolutional neural networks can extract informative features by blending cross-channel and spatial information [9]. Attention modules [19,29] can learn "where" and "what" to attend in channel and space axes, respectively, by focusing on important features and suppressing unnecessary ones of the activations.

© Springer Nature Switzerland AG 2021
I. Farkaš et al. (Eds.): ICANN 2021, LNCS 12891, pp. 167–178, 2021.
https://doi.org/10.1007/978-3-030-86362-3_14

Dynamic Filter Networks [13,17] generate the filters conditioned on the input and show the flexibility power of such filters because of their adaptive nature, which has become popular in prediction [15] and Natural Language Processing [30]. Both Dynamic Filter Networks and attention-based models are adaptive based on the inputs, but there are significant differences between them. Attention-based models [9,29] produce attention maps using the attention mechanism to operate on the activations of convolution. On the contrary, Dynamic Filer Networks [22] generate input information-specific kernels, such as position-specific kernels [22] and few-shot learning setting-specific kernels [32], which work as the weights of convolution. Our proposed attention module leverages the attention mechanism to compute the attention maps for attending the activations of convolution, so it is clear to categorized the models applied with our proposed attention module as attention-based models instead of Dynamic Filter Networks.

In this paper, we analyze two ignored problems of the current attentional activations-based models: the approximation problem and the insufficient capacity problem of the attention maps. To address the two problems together, we originally propose an attention module by developing an AW-convolution, where the shape of the attention maps matches that of the weights instead of the activations. Besides, we present and refine the architecture of calculating attention maps A. Our proposed attention module is a complementary method to previous attention mechanism-based modules, such as Attention Augmented (AA) convolution [2], the SE [10] and CBAM [29] modules in the attentional activations-based models. Integrating with our proposed attention module, the accuracy of SE-Net, and CBAM-Net will be improved further.

We use image classification and object detection tasks to demonstrate the effectiveness of our proposed attention module. With negligible computational complexity increase, our proposed attention module can boost the image classification and object detection task performance, and it can achieve better accuracy when integrating with other attention-based models. In particular, our proposed attention module achieves 1.00% Top-1 accuracy improvement on ImageNet classification over a ResNet101 baseline and 0.63 COCO-style Average Precision improvement on the COCO object detection on top of a Faster R-CNN baseline with the backbone of ResNet101-FPN. When integrating with the previous attentional activations-based models, our proposed attention module can further increase their Top-1 accuracy on ImageNet classification by up to 0.57% and COCO-style Average Precision on the COCO object detection by up to 0.45.

2   Related Work

2.1   Network Engineering

Increasing the depth of convolutional neural networks has been regarded as an intuitive way to boost performance, which is the philosophy of VGGNet and ResNet [7]. In addition, since the skip connection from ResNet shows a strong ability to assist the gradient flow, WideResNet, PyramidNet, Inception-ResNet [23], and ResNeXt are ResNet-based versions proposed to explore further the

influence of the width, the increase of the width, the multi-scale and the cardinality of convolution, respectively. In terms of efficiency, DenseNet [11] reuses
the feature maps by concatenating the feature maps from different layers. In
particular, MobileNet [8] and ShuffleNet [20] series present the advantage of
depthwise convolution and the shuffle operation between various group convolutions, respectively. Another design approach uses automated neural architecture
search, which achieves state-of-the-art performance regarding both accuracy and
efficiency across a range of computer vision tasks [24].

2.2 Attention Mechanism

The attention mechanism plays an important role in the human vision perceptron since it can allocate the available resources to selectively focus on processing
the salient part instead of the whole scene [5]. Multiple attention mechanisms
are used to address a known weakness in convolution [3,4,10,14,19], by capturing long-range information interactions [1,26]. The Inception family of architectures [23], Multigrid Neural Architectures [14], and Octave Convolution [3]
aggregate the scale-space information, while Squeeze-and-Excitation Networks
[10] and Gather-Excite [9] adaptively recalibrate channel-wise response by modeling interdependency between channels. GALA [19], CBAM [29], and BAM [21]
refine the feature maps separately in the channel and spatial dimensions. Attention Modules [27] and self-attention [2,25] can be used to exploit global context
information. Precisely, non-local networks [28] deploy self-attention as a generalized global operator to capture the relationship between all pairwise convolutional feature maps interactions. Except for applying the attention mechanism
to computer vision tasks [16], it has been a widespread adoption to modeling
sequences in Natural Language Processing [30].

3   Proposed Attention Module

In this section, we analyze the two ignored problems in current attentional
activations-based models and develop an attention module that mainly refers
to the AW-convolution. Besides, we refine the branch of calculating the attention maps. Last but not least, we integrate our proposed attention module with
other attention-based models.

3.1 Motivation

First, we define basic notations in a traditional convolutional layer. In a traditional convolutional layer, the input activations, weights, and output activations are denoted as I, K, and O, respectively. For the input activations
$I \in R^{N \times C_1 \times H \times W}$, N, C_1, H, and W refer to the batch size, the number of
input channels, the height, and width of the input feature maps, respectively.
For the weights $K \in R^{C_2 \times C_1 \times h \times w}$, C_2, h and w refer to the number of output channels, the height and width of the weights, respectively. For the output

activations $O \in R^{N \times C_2 \times H \times W}$, it is computed as the convolution between the input activations I and the weights K. In particular, every individual value of the output activations $O_{[l,p,m,n]}$ is calculated as follows.

$$O_{[l,p,m,n]} = \text{Convolution}(I, K) = \sum_{o=1}^{C_1} \sum_{j=1}^{h-1} \sum_{k=1}^{w-1} I_{[l,o,m'+j,n'+k]} \times K_{[p,o,j,k]} \quad (1)$$

where $l = 0, ..., N - 1$, $m = 0, ..., H - 1$, $n = 0, ..., W - 1$, $o = 0, ..., C_1 - 1$, $p = 0, ..., C_2 - 1$, $m' = m - \frac{h-1}{2}$, $n' = n - \frac{w-1}{2}$.

To apply the attention mechanism on the input activations I, previous attentional activations-based models produce the channel attention maps $A_c \in R^{N \times C_1 \times 1 \times 1}$ and spatial attention maps $A_s \in R^{N \times 1 \times H \times W}$ separately. For example, applying the channel attention maps A_c on the input activations I is presented as $O = \text{Convolution}((I \odot A_c), K)$, where $\odot$ refers to the Hadamard product and broadcasting during element-wise multiplication is omitted.

Approximation Problem of the Attention Maps. To thoroughly attend the input activations I, we need to compute the attention maps $A_f \in R^{N \times C_1 \times H \times W}$ and apply it as $O = \text{Convolution}((I \odot A_f), K)$, which requires too much computational and parameter overhead. Thus, all the current attentional activations-based models produce the attention maps separately into the channel attention maps A_c and spatial attention maps A_s. We use A_c and A_s to approximate the four-dimensional attention map A_f, which leads to the approximation problem of attention maps.

Inspired by convolution, we adopt local connection and attention maps sharing to reduce the size of the attention maps. We compute the attention maps $A_a \in R^{N \times C_1 \times h \times w}$ as follows, where $\otimes$ is a special element-wise multiplication since it only works associated with convolution.

$$O_{[l,p,m,n]} = \text{Convolution}(I \otimes A_a, K)$$
$$= \sum_{o=1}^{C_1} \sum_{j=1}^{h-1} \sum_{k=1}^{w-1} (I_{[l,o,m'+j,n'+k]} \times A_{a[l,o,j,k]}) \times K_{[p,o,j,k]} \quad (2)$$

Insufficient Capacity Problem of the Attention Maps. To compute different channels of the output activations of the convolution, the input activations are constrained to be recalibrated by the same attention map, i.e., the four-dimensional attention map A_f, which indicates the insufficient capacity of the attention maps. As each channel of the feature maps is considered as a feature detector, different channels of the output activations of the convolution expect the input activations to be adapted by different attention maps.

Take two channels of output activations of a convolutional layer as an example, the two channels are responsible for recognizing rectangle shape and triangle shape, respectively. Thus, it is reasonable for the two channels to expect that there are different attention maps for attending the input activations of the

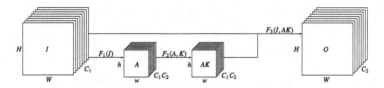

(a) The AW-convolution architecture.

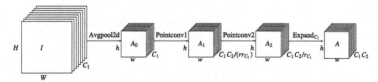

(b) The architecture of calculating attention maps A.

Fig. 1. The architecture of our proposed attention module.

convolution (i.e., the attention maps to compute the channel of recognizing the rectangle shape should be different from the attention maps to compute the channel of recognizing the triangle shape). To meet this expectation, we need to compute the five-dimensional attention map $A_{ic} \in R^{N \times C_2 \times C_1 \times 1 \times 1}$ and apply it on the input activations as follows.

$$
\begin{aligned}
O_{[l,p,m,n]} &= \text{Convolution}(I \odot A_{ic[l,p,:,:,:]}, K) \\
&= \sum_{o=1}^{C_1} \sum_{j=1}^{h-1} \sum_{k=1}^{w-1} (I_{[l,o,m'+j,n'+k]} \times A_{ic[l,p,o,0,0]}) \times K_{[p,o,j,k]}
\end{aligned}
\tag{3}
$$

To solve the approximation problem and the insufficient capacity problem of the attention maps together (i.e., combining the solution of Eq. 2 and the solution of Eq. 3), we introduce our proposed attention module by developing the AW-convolution. Specifically, we propose to compute the attention maps $A \in R^{N \times C_2 \times C_1 \times h \times w}$ and apply it as follows where the attention maps $A_{[l,:,:,:,:]}$ has the same shape as that of the weights instead of the input activations. In this paper, "Attentional weights" refers to the element-wise multiplication result between the attention maps and the weights. Similarly, "Attentional activations" refers to the element-wise multiplication result between the attention maps and the activations in previous attentional activations-based models. Thus, $I \otimes A$ and $A_{[l,:,:,:,:]} \odot K$ represent the attentional activations and attentional weights, respectively. To reduces half the number of element-wise multiplications, we calculate attentional weights instead of attentional activations as follows.

$$
\begin{aligned}
O_{[l,p,m,n]} &= \text{Convolution}(I \otimes A, K) \\
&= \sum_{o=1}^{C_1} \sum_{j=1}^{h-1} \sum_{k=1}^{w-1} I_{[l,o,m'+j,n'+k]} \times (A_{[l,p,o,j,k]} \times K_{[p,o,j,k]}) \\
&= \text{Convolution}(I, A_{[l,:,:,:,:]} \odot K) = \text{AW-Convolution}(I, A \odot K)
\end{aligned}
\tag{4}
$$

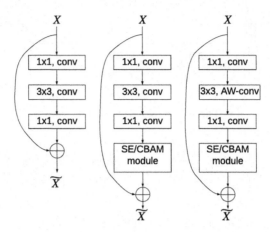

Fig. 2. The schema of bottlenecks when integrating with our proposed attention module. **Left:** bottleneck in ResNet. **Middle:** bottleneck in SE-ResNet/CBAM-ResNet. **Right:** bottleneck in AW-SE-ResNet/AW-CBAM-ResNet.

3.2 AW-Convolution in Proposed Attention Module

The AW-convolution in our proposed attention module is presented in Fig. 1a. In this figure, the attention maps A has five dimensions, which is computed from the input activations I as $A = F_1(I)$. F_1 is a function to calculate the attention maps A given the input activations I. Then, the attentional weights $AK \in R^{N \times C_2 \times C_1 \times h \times w}$ is calculated as $AK = F_2(A, K) = K + A \odot K$. F_2 is a function to calculate the attentional weights AK given the weights K and the attention maps A. Finally, the output activations O is calculated from the input activations I and the attentional weights AK as follows.

$$O_{[l,p,m,n]} = F_3(I, AK) = \text{AW-Convolution}(I, AK)$$
$$= \sum_{i=1}^{C_1} \sum_{j=1}^{h-1} \sum_{k=1}^{w-1} I_{[l,o,m'+j,n'+k]} \times AK_{[l,p,o,j,k]} = \text{Convolution}(I, AK_{[l,:,:,:,:]}) \quad (5)$$

where F_3 is a function to calculate the output activations O given the input activations I and the attentional weights AK. Compared with the traditional convolution, the attentional weights AK of the AW-convolution in our proposed attention module has five dimensions rather than four dimensions, which are different from each other for every individual sample of the input activations batch to convolute.

It is also worth explaining the definition of the function F_2. $AK = K + A \odot K$ instead of $AK = A \odot K$ is used to describe the function F_2 since it can be regarded as a residual design as follows.

$$O = F_3(I, AK) = \text{AW-Convolution}(I, F_2(A, K))$$
$$= \text{Convolution}(I, K) + \text{AW-Convolution}(I, A \odot K) \quad (6)$$

3.3 Calculating the Attention Maps A

As shown in Fig. 1b, the architecture to compute the attention maps A (i.e., the definition of the function F_1) is presented, which can be expressed as follows. Avgpool2d aggregates feature responses from the whole spatial extent and embeds them into A_0, and Pointconv1 and Pointconv2 followed by Relu redistribute the pooled information to capture the dynamic and no-linear dependencies between channels and spatial spaces.

$$
\begin{aligned}
A = F_1(I) &= \mathrm{Expand}_{C_1}(A_2) = \mathrm{Expand}_{C_1}(\mathrm{Pointconv2}(A_1)) \\
&= \mathrm{Expand}_{C_1}(\mathrm{Pointconv2}(\mathrm{Pointconv1}(A_0))) \\
&= \mathrm{Expand}_{C_1}(\mathrm{Pointconv2}(\mathrm{Pointconv1}(\mathrm{Avgpool2d}(I))))
\end{aligned}
\tag{7}
$$

where Pointconv1 and Pointconv2 are pointwise convolutions. We add Batch Normalization and Relu layers after Pointconv1, while adding Batch Normalization and Sigmoid layers after Pointconv2, and they are omitted here to provide a clear expression.

In Fig. 1b, Expand function along C_1 dimension, denoted as Expand_{C_1}, is used as an example, and Expand function can be also executed along N, C_2, h, and w dimensions in a similar way. Expand_{C_1} function is used to expand the tensor $A_2 \in R^{N \times (C_2 C_1/r_{C_1}) \times h \times w}$ into the attention maps $A \in R^{N \times C_2 \times C_1 \times h \times w}$ with the reduction ratio r_{C_1}, including necessary squeeze, reshape, and expand operations. Expand_{C_1} can be expressed as follows.

$$
\begin{aligned}
A = \mathrm{Expand}_{C_1}(A_2) &= A_2.\mathrm{reshape}(N, C_2, C_1/r_{C_1}, h, w).\mathrm{unsqueeze}(\mathrm{dim} = 3) \\
&.\mathrm{expand}(N, C_2, C_1/r_{C_1}, r_{C_1}, h, w).\mathrm{reshape}(N, C_2, C_1, h, w)
\end{aligned}
\tag{8}
$$

Calculating the five-dimension attention maps A is not an easy computational task without careful design. Thus, we analyze the additional computational complexity of an AW-convolution compared with a traditional convolution as a reference to refine this design. Considering the trade-off between computational complexity and accuracy, all the experiments in the remainder of this paper use the same settings for the architecture of calculating the attention maps A in our proposed attention module, including $r_{C1} = C_1$, $r_{C_2} = r_{hw} = 1$, $r = 16$, used in all the stages, and $AK = K + A \odot K$ as the definition for the function F_2.

3.4 Integrating with Other Attention-Based Modules

In this section, we show how to integrate our proposed attention module with the previous attention-based convolutional neural networks to demonstrate the complementary relationship between our proposed attention module and other attention-based modules. Since applying our proposed attention module is using the AW-convolution to replace the traditional convolution, we can easily integrate our proposed attention module with any convolutional neural networks consisting of traditional convolution, including all the recently developed attention-based models [2,10,19,21,29].

We choose the recent attentional activations-based models, i.e., SE-Net and CBAM-Net, as examples to show how to integrate our proposed attention module with other attention-based models. Here we use the popular ResNet [7] as the backbone to apply the attention mechanism. As shown in Fig. 2, the left side is the structure of a primary bottleneck in ResNet. The middle one is the structure of a bottleneck with SE/CBAM modules in SE-ResNet/CBAM-ResNet. Integrating the central bottleneck with our proposed attention module is completed by replacing its 3×3 convolution with a 3×3 AW-convolution, and its final structure in AW-SE-ResNet/AW-CBAM-ResNet is shown on the right side. In summary, our proposed attention module is a general module to be integrated seamlessly with any CNNs architectures, including previous attention-based CNNs.

4   Experimental Results

4.1   ImageNet Image Classification

According to the results shown in Table 1, our proposed attention module is complementary to other attentional activations-based models. AW-ResNet50 achieves a 1.18% Top-1 error reduction compared with the ResNet50 baseline. Integrating with our proposed attention module, SE-ResNet50 [10] can improve further by 0.42% Top-1 accuracy. The Top-1 accuracy of our AW-SE-ResNet101 is 1.60% and 0.57% higher than that of ResNet101 and SE-ResNet101, respectively. To integrate with CBAM-ResNet [29] more carefully, we define CBAM-ResNet (MaxPool) and CBAM-ResNet (Spatial) separately to reduce computational complexity. We do not use max-pooled features in CBAM-ResNet. The Top-1 accuracy of AW-CBAM-ResNet50 is better than AW-ResNet50 by 0.18% but worse than AW-SE-ResNet50. The number of additional parameters for our proposed attention module is 0.16 M, which is much smaller than 2.83 M (i.e., one-sixteenth) of SE and CBAM modules. Moreover, it takes only 0.01 GFLOPs to apply our proposed attention module on the ResNet50 model on ImageNet classification, which is comparable with 0.01 GFLOPs and 0.04 to adopt the SE and CBAM modules and is negligible in terms of FLOPs to implement the baseline model.

Resource-Constrained Architecture. To inspect the generalization of our proposed attention module in this resource-constrained scenario, we conduct the ImageNet classification with the MobileNet architecture [8]. We apply our proposed attention module to pointwise convolution instead of depthwise convolution in every two depthwise separable convolutions. When integrating with the CBAM models [29], we remove the max-pooled features and keep spatial attention maps. As shown in Table 1, AW-SE-MobileNet and AW-CBAM-MobileNet achieve 0.56% and 0.19% Top-1 accuracy improvements compared with SE-MobileNet [10] and CBAM-MobileNet, respectively. It is an impressive result that the Top-1 accuracy of AW-CBAM-MobileNet is 2.57% better than that of

Table 1. Comparisons of attention-based models on ImageNet classification. * refers to the baseline results from [29]. All the rest results are produced using the source code from [29].

Model	Top-1 error	Top-5 error	GFLOPs	Parameters (M)
ResNet50 [7] *	24.56%(+0.00%)	7.50%	3.86	25.56
AW-ResNet50	23.38%(+1.18%)	6.79%	3.87	25.72
SE-ResNet50 [10] *	23.14%(+1.42%)	6.70%	3.87	28.09
AW-SE-ResNet50	22.72%(+1.84%)	6.47%	3.88	28.25
AW-CBAM-ResNet50 (MaxPool)	22.82%(+1.74%)	6.41%	3.89	28.25
AW-CBAM-ResNet50 (Spatial)	23.20%(+1.36%)	6.58%	3.90	28.25
ResNet101 Baseline [7] *	23.38%(+0.00%)	6.88%	7.57	44.55
AW-ResNet101	22.38%(+1.00%)	6.21%	7.58	44.95
SE-ResNet101 [10] *	22.35%(+1.03%)	6.19%	7.58	49.33
AW-SE-ResNet101	21.78%(+1.60%)	5.74%	7.59	49.73
AW-CBAM-ResNet101 (MaxPool)	21.64%(+1.74%)	5.76%	7.60	49.73
AW-CBAM-ResNet101 (Spatial)	22.32%(+1.06%)	6.18%	7.61	49.73
MobileNet Baseline [8] *	31.39%(+0.00%)	11.51%	0.569	4.23
SE-MobileNet [10] *	29.97%(+1.42%)	10.63%	0.581	5.07
AW-SE-MobileNet	29.41%(+1.98%)	10.59%	0.623	5.52
CBAM-MobileNet [29]	29.01%(+2.38%)	9.99%	0.611	5.07
AW-CBAM-MobileNet (Spatial)	28.82%(+2.57%)	9.98%	0.652	5.52

the MobileNet baseline. For the MobileNet model, our proposed attention module increases the computation by 0.041 GFLOPs, while SE and CBAM modules need 0.012 and 0.041 GFLOPs, respectively. Also, the required parameters for our proposed attention module are 0.45 M, which is much less than 0.84 M for SE and CBAM modules.

4.2 Object Detection on COCO

To show the generalization of our proposed attention module, we apply it to object detection tasks. We evaluate our proposed attention module further on the COCO dataset, which contains $118K$ images (i.e., train2017) for training and $5K$ images (i.e., val2017) for validating. Here we intend to evaluate the benefits of applying our proposed attention module on the ResNet101-FPN backbone [18], where all the lateral and output convolutions of the FPN adopt our AW-convolution. The SE and CBAM modules are placed right before the lateral and output convolutions. As shown in Table 2, applying our proposed attention module on ResNet101-FPN boosts mAP@[0.5, 0.95] by 0.63 for the Faster R-CNN baseline. Integrating with attentional activations-based models, Faster R-CNNs with the backbones of ResNet101-AW-SE-FPN and ResNet101-AW-CBAM-FPN outperform Faster R-CNNs with the backbones of ResNet101-SE-FPN and ResNet101-CBAM-FPN by 0.34 and 0.45 on COCO's standard metric AP.

Table 2. Comparisons of attention-based Faster R-CNN on COCO. All the results are produced using Pytorch.

Backbone	Detector	mAP@[0.5, 0.95]	mAP@0.5	mAP@0.75
ResNet101-FPN [18]	Faster R-CNN	37.13(+0.00%)	58.28	40.29
ResNet101-AW-FPN	Faster R-CNN	37.76(+0.63%)	59.17	40.91
ResNet101-SE-FPN [10]	Faster R-CNN	38.11(+0.98%)	59.41	41.33
ResNet101-AW-SE-FPN	Faster R-CNN	38.45(+1.32%)	59.70	41.86
ResNet101-CBAM-FPN [29]	Faster R-CNN	37.74(+0.61%)	58.84	40.77
ResNet101-AW-CBAM-FPN	Faster R-CNN	38.19(+1.06%)	59.52	41.43

5   Conclusion

In this paper, we analyze the two ignored problems in attentional activations-based models: the approximation problem and the insufficient capacity problem of the attention maps. To address the two problems together, we propose an attention module by developing the AW-convolution, where the shape of the attention maps matches that of the weights rather than the activations, and integrate it with attention-based models as a complementary method to enlarge their attentional capability. We have implemented extensive experiments to demonstrate the effectiveness of our proposed attention module, both on image classification and object detection tasks.

Acknowledgment. This work was carried out on the Dutch national e-infrastructure with the support of SURF Cooperative.

References

1. Bello, I., et al.: Seq2Slate: re-ranking and slate optimization with RNNs. CoRR abs/1810.02019 (2018). http://arxiv.org/abs/1810.02019
2. Bello, I., Zoph, B., Vaswani, A., Shlens, J., Le, Q.V.: Attention augmented convolutional networks. In: The IEEE International Conference on Computer Vision (ICCV), October 2019
3. Chen, Y., et al.: Drop an octave: reducing spatial redundancy in convolutional neural networks with octave convolution. In: The IEEE International Conference on Computer Vision (ICCV), October 2019
4. Chen, Y., Kalantidis, Y., Li, J., Yan, S., Feng, J.: A 2-nets: double attention networks. In: Advances in Neural Information Processing Systems, pp. 352–361 (2018)
5. Corbetta, M., Shulman, G.L.: Control of goal-directed and stimulus-driven attention in the brain. Nat. Rev. Neurosci. **3**(3), 201 (2002)
6. Gregor, K., Danihelka, I., Graves, A., Rezende, D., Wierstra, D.: Draw: a recurrent neural network for image generation. In: International Conference on Machine Learning, pp. 1462–1471 (2015)
7. He, K., Zhang, X., Ren, S., Sun, J.: Deep residual learning for image recognition. In: Proceedings of the IEEE Conference on Computer Vision and Pattern Recognition, pp. 770–778 (2016)

8. Howard, A.G., et al.: MobileNets: efficient convolutional neural networks for mobile vision applications. CoRR abs/1704.04861 (2017). http://arxiv.org/abs/1704.04861

9. Hu, J., Shen, L., Albanie, S., Sun, G., Vedaldi, A.: Gather-excite: exploiting feature context in convolutional neural networks. In: Advances in Neural Information Processing Systems, pp. 9401–9411 (2018)

10. Hu, J., Shen, L., Sun, G.: Squeeze-and-excitation networks. In: Proceedings of the IEEE Conference on Computer Vision and Pattern Recognition, pp. 7132–7141 (2018)

11. Huang, G., Liu, Z., Van Der Maaten, L., Weinberger, K.Q.: Densely connected convolutional networks. In: Proceedings of the IEEE Conference on Computer Vision and Pattern Recognition, pp. 4700–4708 (2017)

12. Jaderberg, M., Simonyan, K., Zisserman, A., et al.: Spatial transformer networks. In: Advances in Neural Information Processing Systems, pp. 2017–2025 (2015)

13. Jia, X., De Brabandere, B., Tuytelaars, T., Gool, L.V.: Dynamic filter networks. In: Advances in Neural Information Processing Systems, pp. 667–675 (2016)

14. Ke, T.W., Maire, M., Yu, S.X.: Multigrid neural architectures. In: Proceedings of the IEEE Conference on Computer Vision and Pattern Recognition, pp. 6665–6673 (2017)

15. Klein, B., Wolf, L., Afek, Y.: A dynamic convolutional layer for short range weather prediction. In: Proceedings of the IEEE Conference on Computer Vision and Pattern Recognition, pp. 4840–4848 (2015)

16. Li, H., Liu, Y., Ouyang, W., Wang, X.: Zoom out-and-in network with map attention decision for region proposal and object detection. Int. J. Comput. Vision 127(3), 225–238 (2019)

17. Li, X., Wang, W., Hu, X., Yang, J.: Selective kernel networks. In: Proceedings of the IEEE Conference on Computer Vision and Pattern Recognition, pp. 510–519 (2019)

18. Lin, T.Y., Dollár, P., Girshick, R., He, K., Hariharan, B., Belongie, S.: Feature pyramid networks for object detection. In: Proceedings of the IEEE Conference on Computer Vision and Pattern Recognition, pp. 2117–2125 (2017)

19. Linsley, D., Shiebler, D., Eberhardt, S., Serre, T.: Learning what and where to attend with humans in the loop. In: International Conference on Learning Representations (2019). https://openreview.net/forum?id=BJgLg3R9KQ

20. Ma, N., Zhang, X., Zheng, H.-T., Sun, J.: ShuffleNet V2: practical guidelines for efficient CNN architecture design. In: Ferrari, V., Hebert, M., Sminchisescu, C., Weiss, Y. (eds.) Computer Vision – ECCV 2018. LNCS, vol. 11218, pp. 122–138. Springer, Cham (2018). https://doi.org/10.1007/978-3-030-01264-9_8

21. Park, J., Woo, S., Lee, J.Y., Kweon, I.S.: BAM: Bottleneck attention module. In: British Machine Vision Conference (BMVC). British Machine Vision Association (BMVA) (2018)

22. Su, H., Jampani, V., Sun, D., Gallo, O., Learned-Miller, E., Kautz, J.: Pixel-adaptive convolutional neural networks. In: Proceedings of the IEEE Conference on Computer Vision and Pattern Recognition, pp. 11166–11175 (2019)

23. Szegedy, C., Ioffe, S., Vanhoucke, V., Alemi, A.A.: Inception-v4, inception-ResNet and the impact of residual connections on learning. In: Thirty-First AAAI Conference on Artificial Intelligence (2017)

24. Tan, M., et al.: MNASNet: platform-aware neural architecture search for mobile. In: Proceedings of the IEEE Conference on Computer Vision and Pattern Recognition, pp. 2820–2828 (2019)

25. Vaswani, A., et al.: Attention is all you need. In: Advances in Neural Information Processing Systems, pp. 5998–6008 (2017)

26. Vinyals, O., Fortunato, M., Jaitly, N.: Pointer networks. In: Cortes, C., Lawrence, N.D., Lee, D.D., Sugiyama, M., Garnett, R. (eds.) Advances in Neural Information Processing Systems, vol. 28, pp. 2692–2700. Curran Associates, Inc. (2015). http://papers.nips.cc/paper/5866-pointer-networks.pdf

27. Wang, F., et al.: Residual attention network for image classification. In: Proceedings of the IEEE Conference on Computer Vision and Pattern Recognition, pp. 3156–3164 (2017)

28. Wang, X., Girshick, R., Gupta, A., He, K.: Non-local neural networks. In: Proceedings of the IEEE Conference on Computer Vision and Pattern Recognition, pp. 7794–7803 (2018)

29. Woo, S., Park, J., Lee, J.-Y., Kweon, I.S.: CBAM: convolutional block attention module. In: Ferrari, V., Hebert, M., Sminchisescu, C., Weiss, Y. (eds.) ECCV 2018. LNCS, vol. 11211, pp. 3–19. Springer, Cham (2018). https://doi.org/10.1007/978-3-030-01234-2_1

30. Wu, F., Fan, A., Baevski, A., Dauphin, Y., Auli, M.: Pay less attention with lightweight and dynamic convolutions. In: International Conference on Learning Representations (2019). https://openreview.net/forum?id=SkVhlh09tX

31. Xu, K., et al.: Show, attend and tell: neural image caption generation with visual attention. In: International Conference on Machine Learning, pp. 2048–2057 (2015)

32. Zhao, F., Zhao, J., Yan, S., Feng, J.: Dynamic Conditional Networks for Few-Shot Learning. In: Ferrari, V., Hebert, M., Sminchisescu, C., Weiss, Y. (eds.) ECCV 2018. LNCS, vol. 11219, pp. 20–36. Springer, Cham (2018). https://doi.org/10.1007/978-3-030-01267-0_2

Attention-Based 3D Neural Architectures for Predicting Cracks in Designs

Naresh Iyer[✉], Sathyanarayanan Raghavan, Yiming Zhang, Yang Jiao, and Dean Robinson

GE Research, Niskayuna, NY 12309, USA
iyerna@ge.com
https://www.ge.com/research

Abstract. The rapid and accurate prediction of residual stresses in metal additive manufacturing (3D printing) processes is crucial to ensuring defect-free fabrication of parts used in critical industrial applications. This paper presents promising outcomes from applying attention-based neural architectures for predicting such 3D stress phenomena accurately, efficiently, and reliably. This capability is critical to drastically reducing the design maturation time for additively manufactured parts. High fidelity, physics-based numerical models of the additive melting process exist that can simulate the thermal gradients and consequent stresses produced during manufacturing, which can then be used to synthesize a 3D crack index field for the entire part volume, capturing the likelihood that a region in a part will crack upon heat treatment. However, these models are expensive and time-consuming to run. In response, a Deep Convolutional Neural Network (DCNN) model is explored as a surrogate for the physics-based model, so that it can be used to time-efficiently estimate the crack index for a given part-design. This requires careful design of the training regime and dataset for a given design problem. Using the U-Net architecture as the baseline, we expand the standard 2D application of this architecture for segmentation to the estimation of the full 3D, continuous valued, stress field. We illustrate the primary challenge faced by the standard U-Net architecture with L2-loss arising from sparsity in critical values of the crack index and show how augmenting the architecture with attention mechanisms helps address the issue as well as improve the overall accuracy of estimation.

Keywords: Attention mechanism · 3D segmentation · Regression · Additive manufacturing · 3D printing · Generative design

1 Introduction

Laser Powder Bed Fusion (LPBF) of Ni-based Superalloys is a popular paradigm of additive manufacturing (AM) applied in the fabrication of turbomachinery components in aerospace and land-based turbines [1]. LBPF-AM involves the use of a focused beam to selectively melt powder in a layer-by-layer fashion [2]. Each

© Springer Nature Switzerland AG 2021
I. Farkaš et al. (Eds.): ICANN 2021, LNCS 12891, pp. 179–190, 2021.
https://doi.org/10.1007/978-3-030-86362-3_15

powder layer is a few tens of microns thick and after melting each layer, it is cooled to solidify the layer before sequentially depositing the next layer on top. Such rapid heating and cooling can induce high thermal stresses in the part resulting in the generation of significant thermal residual stresses. These residual stresses manifest in the form of part deformation or if significantly high, it can result in the part cracking at multiple locations [3]. A cracked part results in the need to refine the part-design and to repeat the print, leading to multiple iterations from design to full scale manufacture of the part. As a result, the overall design maturation time can span months to years, involving multiple hand-offs between design and manufacturing engineers. Moreover, as metal additive manufacturing evolves from manufacturing part prototypes to large scale, high volume industrial parts, its throughput is a critical factor for its adoption. Addressing this inefficiency and cost, due to cracking during manufacturing, requires understanding and modeling the phenomena that lead to the initiation of cracks. Several commercially available high fidelity, physics-based software tools can simulate the additive melting process, the resulting thermal gradients and consequent residual stresses during manufacturing. These stresses can then be used to synthesize a 3D crack index field for the entire part, capturing the likelihood of failure around specific locations in the part. However, high-fidelity simulation of the nonlinear, transient, multiphysics melting process is resource intensive and time consuming, often requiring several days to complete one simulation of a part even few inches tall. For example, the process simulation of a 7-inch tall part can take more than a week on a 24 core high performance processor with 256 GB of memory. This inhibits designers from iterating on the part design, and evaluating part designs in terms of their propensity to crack. In response, we explore the hypothesis of whether time-efficient and accurate surrogates can be designed, leveraging these expensive physics-based models, so that they can provide a reliable estimate of the crack index for a given candidate of the design problem.

2   Related Work

The application of 3D segmentation techniques using CNNs, while prevalent in medical imaging domain [10–15], is fairly new in the domain of additive manufacturing. Many of the workflows implement a 2D based inference followed by postprocessing to stitch the outcomes volumetrically. [19] provides a broad survey into the application of deep learning to AM. The work described in [16] is analogous to ours, where a 3D U-Net is applied for segmentation of 3D printed volumes to facilitate automated identification of defects in the part. Unlike our paper, this work targets the standard segmentation task, formulated as classification and does not need to target the voxel-level spatial resolution for regression that is critical for the problem targeted in our paper. Some other related efforts in the space of AM include [14,16] that make use of 2D inference of defects during AM, by analysis of 2D camera images during part printing. [17] deals with stress prediction for AM parts; while it employs high-fidelity physics-based simulation, and a deep learning based model as a surrogate, to estimate stress for varying geometries, it is largely focused on modeling 2D separation stress at the interface that occurs in bottom-up stereolithography printing. [18] makes use of finite element model and deep learning to estimate surface Von Mises stress distribution on aorta walls; however, it also abstracts the estimation problem into a 2D modeling problem by unrolling the aorta wall into a 2D surface, by applying a shape abstraction model. [20] presents the application of deep neural networks for predicting the 2D stress fields on cantilevered structures. To the best of our knowledge, our paper is the first body of work to look at the application of attention-based 3D architectures for a full end to end volumetric regression of 3D stress fields in AM.

3   Approach

This work leverages Deep Convolutional Neural Networks (DCNN) to construct high fidelity and time-efficient surrogates for the high fidelity physics-based models of residual stress. Using the U-Net architecture [4] as the baseline, we expand the standard application of this architecture for 2D segmentation to the estimation of the full 3D, continuous valued, stress field. We illustrate the primary challenge faced by the standard U-Net architecture with L2-loss arising from sparsity in critical values of the crack index - part regions with high values of the crack index are often in a much smaller minority of the overall volume of the dataset used to train the surrogate. As a result, using standard metrics of loss like L2-loss can lead to a surrogate that only learns to reliably predict in regions where the crack index values are from the likely values of the overall distribution, but ignore or poorly model the rarer high values of crack index, which are critical to the problem at hand. More recently, the idea of attention, inspired from cognitive attention as seen in humans, has been explored to address this problem, predominantly in the NLP community [6,7] with promising outcomes. We extend this idea to the crack index prediction problem and show how augmenting the architecture with attention mechanisms helps address the issue as well as improve the overall accuracy of estimation.

3.1   Design Problem Formulation

The design problem we focused on is represented by Fig. 1, which shows 2 instances of design candidates. The problem tackles design of a hole near a triangular notch at the bottom of the design coupon. This configuration and its variants represent a class of design problems that are relevant to features like cooling holes or weight reduction holes commonly used in industrial design components. The primary variant (parameter) in this configuration space, in our experiment, involves the shape and volume of the hole; it is known that there are variants of this configuration that can be printed reliably without the appearance of any cracks, and others which almost always lead to cracks after manufacture. The goal then is to understand the relationship between the hole shape, volume and the crack index distribution, so that designs that lead to high crack index

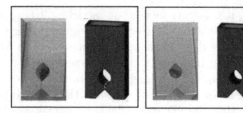

Fig. 1. Example coupons showing the design problem tackled in this paper. The second, blue volume in each subfigure shows the crack index distribution with red values indicating high propensity of cracking upon printing. The first design-instance clearly shows a high likelihood of cracking at the bottom wall of the hole (red values), while the second design-instance looks to have low crack index values. (Color figure online)

values can be avoided at the outset during the design phase. While approaches like transfer learning can facilitate extending the surrogate model generated for a given feature to other design problems that are only incrementally different, or to varying feature-sizes, for a drastically different design feature or geometry, a new surrogate might need to be created emulating the workflow presented in this paper. In that sense, the vision is for there to be a library of surrogates each of which would apply to a distinctly different feature and help optimize it for crack free manufacturing, within a class of design problems.

3.2 Training Data Generation

A parametric data generator was designed to invoke suitably diverse variants of the design problem, thereby enriching the training data for developing the surrogate model. A few examples of the samples, illustrated as 2D slices for clarity, are shown in Fig. 2 along with their corresponding crack index evaluations. The generator runs a set of topology optimization (TO) simulations across a broad range of boundary conditions, loading conditions, design constraints and combinations of those to create a series of topology optimized design variants. These 3D design variants, voxelised at an appropriate resolution, are the inputs for training the surrogate. Given that these design variants are targeted for additive manufacturing, additional constraints like presence of overhangs, enforcing the hole to remain open through the volume for each sample are also accounted for, by the design generator, to ensure that the candidates are feasible and can be reliably printed by an AM machine. The two baseline geometries that were shown in Fig. 1 were considered as seed designs for the design generation, since these two geometries represent samples that respectively have a low and a high propensity for cracking when printed. This is expected to bring valuable variability in the generated set of samples across the spectrum of the crack index. One way to explicitly introduce variation in the samples was to vary the direction and magnitude of the external loads applied to the coupon. To this end, a set of loading conditions were proposed featuring traction force applied directly on the surface of the design domain which is herein just the initial hole in the

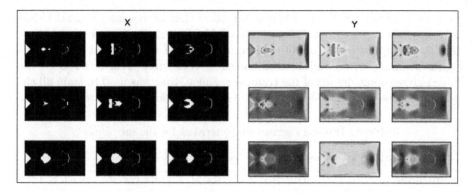

Fig. 2. Few examples of the 3D data used for training the surrogate - shown using 2D slices for clarity of depiction.

coupon. To introduce more variation, the inner surface of the initial hole was divided into four segments with the vertical and horizontal symmetrical planes of the hole as the cutting planes. Each of these four segments is subjected to an independently varying traction force. Each such design variant is evaluated using the physics-based additive simulation model to estimate the crack index. Using additive build simulation to estimate crack index values in 3D is computationally intensive (almost 18 h per design candidate), with complexity that increases exponentially with the number of voxels (i.e. resolution) used to mesh the geometry. In order to manage this complexity, the design evaluation was conducted at a lower resolution, which reduced the required computation time to a more feasible value of 4 h, followed by the application of trilinear interpolation to reconstruct the crack index at the desired high resolution. The output from this upsampling step was validated using a few samples which were evaluated at both resolutions; the interpolation outcomes successfully preserve the critical, spatial trends of the crack signal. A set of 116 distinct design samples were generated and evaluated as described above to generate the training data for the crack index surrogate.

3.3   3D U-Net for Crack Prediction

A 3D U-Net architecture inspired from [4] was implemented for dense, voxel-wise prediction of the 3D crack index from the 3D geometry. The choice of architecture for the surrogate was influenced by multiple factors: 1) the successes shown in literature in the application of the U-Net architecture to semantic segmentation, 2) the ability of the U-Net to perform equally well, if not better, with fewer parameters compared to a fully connected network, and 3) the ability of U-Nets to improve spatial localization. Whereas the standard invocation of U-Net for semantic segmentation addresses a classification problem (going from pixel intensities to categorical labels for each pixel), in our case we need to estimate a continuous number (i.e., crack index) for each voxel, which is a regression problem. In summary, the baseline architecture that we consider is a 3D U-Net for voxel-wise regression that makes use of *MaxPooling* for feature abstraction. The high computational cost of training a 3D U-Net is addressed by conducting the training on an Nvidia DGX machine configured with 8, P100 GPUs. Table 1 shows some details of the training regimen, that was used to train all the surrogates. The use of standard metrics of loss like L2-loss can lead to a surrogate

Table 1. Training regimen characteristics for the surrogates

Training parameter	Description
Architecture	3D U-Net, 3 × 3, ReLU, 1-32-64-128-256-128-64-32-1
Feature abstraction	Max pooling
Output layer activation	Linear
Loss function	L2/MSE
Target	Raw crack index values
Optimizer	ADAM, init-lr = 1e−4
Number of samples	116
Batch normalization	No
Dropout	No
Input sample	$100 \times 60 \times 178$ volume
Train/test split	100/16 samples
Batch size per GPU	8
#epochs	150, with early stopping check
Early stopping	val-loss, min-delta = 1e−9, patience = 5
Initialization	Glorot-uniform
Compute	Parallel 4-GPU

that only learns to reliably predict in regions where the crack index values belong to the likely values of the overall distribution, but ignore or poorly model the rarer high crack index values, which are critical to the problem at hand. Whereas approaches like Focal Loss [5] can be used to dynamically tweak the training to target harder-to-estimate values in the input data, our initial exploration did not show much promise in using Focal Loss to our problem. In response, we consider the application Attention mechanisms to the standard U-Net architecture to help better capture the critical crack index values in the part. The concept of Attention is well-suited to the crack index prediction problem because it helps to focus learning on areas of interest with high crack index that are often present only in small regions of the overall training data.

3.4   Attention Mechanisms for 3D U-Net

The idea of attention, inspired from cognitive attention as seen in humans, has been explored predominantly in the NLP community [6,7] with promising outcomes. An attention mechanism is formalized as a part of the learning architecture and it allows focusing on the most important parts of the input, while leaving out the irrelevant components, for a task at hand. In other words, attention is a mechanism by which task-relevant weights can be learned for different components of the inputs, thereby improving learning performance. In computer vision, tasks that involve object detection require reliable differentiation between foreground and background pixels. The attention module can learn to produce and present soft proposals for regions of interest, and further amplify the learning of objects within those regions of interest, while pixels outside those regions are largely rendered irrelevant to the learning. Specifically, as shown in Fig. 3, we looked at two alternate mechanisms of encoding attention, from literature, within the baseline U-Net architecture, by extending them to their 3D versions. One variant, as in Fig. 3(a), is inspired from [8] where the spatial attention map is computed on the bottleneck features that connects the encoder of the U-Net to the Decoder: it entails applying average-pooling and max-pooling operations on the bottleneck features, concatenating them and then using a single 7×7 Sigmoid-activated, convolution kernel to construct the spatial attention map. The features at the bottleneck are multiplied with this attention map, which acts as spatial weights to help focus on the regions most relevant for accurate estimation of the crack index, by emphasizing or suppressing the feature channels. The other one, as in Fig. 3(b), is inspired from [9] in which an additive attention gating mechanism is encoded allowing for attention-based coefficients to be learned specific to sub-regions in the image. The gating signal helps amplify critical, task-specific and spatial features in the input at multiple scales, that is already encoded in the skip connections in a U-Net. The attention gates further ensure that only salient features pass through the skip connections. Unlike classification models, the attention gating signal in these segmentation problems is not represented as a single, global vector for all image pixels, but as a grid signal that carries image spatial information. This enables amplify spatially relevant features in the encoder skip connections before it is merged with the decoder signal. As stated in [9], because the gating signal helps filter the neuron activations during the forward pass as well as during the backward pass, the gradients originating from background regions are down weighted during the backward pass, thus emphasizing the objects in the foreground.

4   Outcomes

While L2-loss is used for training the surrogate and for measuring its performance, its values are in the units of the quantity being measured, in this case the crack index. Hence, we make use of the normalized metric, *Mean Relative Error, MRE*, defined below, to report performance, since it captures the relative error rate in percent units when comparing deviation of predictions from ground truth, and thus expressed within a standard range (0–1).

$$MRE = \frac{1}{n} \sum_{j=1}^{n} \frac{|y_j - \hat{y_j}|}{\epsilon + max(|y_j|, |\hat{y_j}|)}$$

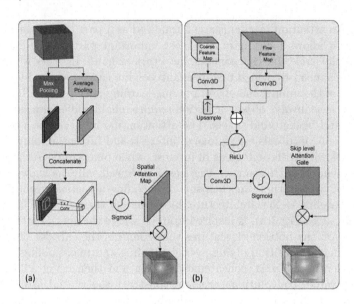

Fig. 3. The two attention mechanisms explored in this paper: (a) SA U-Net [8] and (b) AG U-Net [9]

This metric, defined below, also allows us the report performance of the model in terms of its mean voxelwise accuracy. Table 2 compares the relative performance of the 3 surrogates in terms of both MRE and Accuracy for each of the 3 surrogates. The metrics reflect the mean relative error (or accuracy) across all voxels

Table 2. Performance comparison

Surrogate description	%Mean relative error	%Accuracy
Standard 3D U-Net for regression	21.78	78.22
U-Net with spatial attention	20.25	79.75
U-Net with attention gates on skip	19.89	80.11

in the set of test samples. The numbers indicate that both U-Net architectures with attention mechanisms perform marginally better than the baseline U-Net. However, much like the L2-loss, the MRE can easily mislead true performance since being able to predict the sparsely occurring, high crack index values, is more critical than the average performance across all the voxels. The real benefit of using attention mechanisms is better illustrated from outcomes captured in Fig. 4, which shows the predictions of the 3 surrogates, viewed on the same samples visuo-spatially across the part slice. A careful inspection of each of the 3 samples (columns) shows how the attention-based architectures (rows (c) and (d)) tend to capture salient aspects (red dotted ellipses) of the crack index distribution as shown by the ground truth (row (a)) relatively better compared to the prediction by the baseline U-Net architecture (row (b)). Reliable estimation of the rare, but high values of the crack index are critical since these regions of the part are the one most prone to cracking, thus making the design candidate inferior or less-producible. One primary reason why the U-Net architecture is

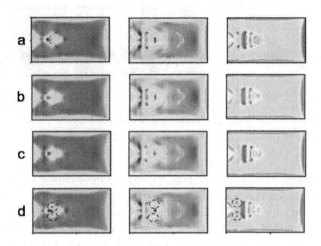

Fig. 4. Comparing surrogate predictions on 3 test samples: (a) shows ground-truth distribution of crack index on 2D slice, (b) shows predictions from baseline U-Net, (c) shows predictions from spatial attention U-Net architecture and (d) predictions from attention gated U-Net architecture. Red dashed ellipses show critical crack features that are picked up only by the attention-based model (Color figure online)

ideally suited for dense prediction tasks like segmentation task is its ability to extract and merge features at multiple scales. The introduction of attention gates on these skip connections helps further amplify task-specific features at these different scales, thus additionally improving the information capture from the multi-scale feature-maps towards estimation of the crack index.

4.1   Discussion

The sample design candidates illustrated in Fig. 2 show that design candidates have critical geometric features of varying shapes and size, which are dominant at different spatial scales, and therefore this is expected to be true of the crack index distribution as well. What attention coefficients enable is give higher weights to the estimation of crack index in regions where critical features of a design occur, which is precisely the challenge related to being able to estimate the critical crack index values accurately. This is seen more clearly by looking at the attention coefficients that are created during the prediction task. Figure 5 shows the attention coefficients generated at each of the 3 skip connections of the AG-UNet architecture (rows 2, 3, and 4) for 4 design candidates; the topmost

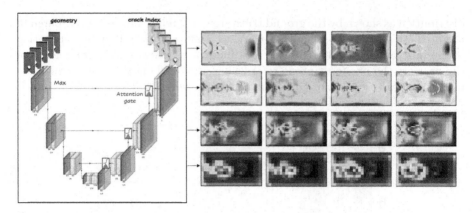

Fig. 5. Multi-scale features for the crack index captured by Attention coefficients in the skip connections [9]

row shows the actual crack index value. The figure shows more clearly how these coefficients weight all the feature maps, spatially, at each skip connection so as to emphasize portions of the feature-maps in regions of the part where dominant geometric features are visible at that scale. Finally, attention mechanisms can help regularize the learning process to construct the right semantic representation and put the network parameters to use in learning the right function that is also semantically aligned with the task at hand. More specifically, the presence of geometric features semantically signal the existence of interesting behaviour of the crack index near those features; attention mechanisms help reinforce the need for the network to learn those crack index values better.

5   Conclusions

The accurate, reliable and time-efficient prediction of crack likelihood of LPBF manufactured parts based on part geometry is critical to reducing design maturation cost, time and to the adoption of additive manufacturing in the industry. While high-fidelity physics based models exist that can accurately estimate crack-relevant stresses induced by the LPBF process, however, their runtime complexity and resource intensive framework creates a barrier in their application to the problem at hand. We demonstrated early, promising outcomes in creating accurate and time-efficient surrogates for such physics-based models by the application of deep convolutional neural network architectures. Crack index prediction is a regression problem in 3D, unlike semantic segmentation, and we show how the extension of the U-Net architecture to a 3D, dense prediction regression problem is highly effective. However, whereas the U-Net architecture has many characteristics that are critical to the crack index prediction problem, we show how an L2-Loss trained U-Net alone can miss accurate estimation of rare, but extreme values of the crack index. We experimented with 2 different attention mechanisms to address this issue and show that attention mechanisms can effectively help amplify task-specific features at different scales of the input already represented in the U-Net architecture within the skip connections. We extract and plot attention coefficients encoded in the skip connection of the AG-UNet architecture and show how attention coefficients encode higher feature-weights in regions where critical features of a design occur, which is precisely the challenge related to being able to estimate the critical crack index values accurately. We show that the attention mechanisms also marginally improve the prediction accuracy of the baseline U-Net architecture. Finally, in addition to the features themselves, attention mechanisms also help focus the overall network towards parsimonious learning of the right approximation function that is aligned with the underlying physics related to the phenomena being modeled. Our outcomes show that attention-based architectures can help usher in a new era of design that will target discovery of designs that are not only optimal to meet design requirements, but additionally conducive to being manufactured reliably, after their discovery. The next phase of the experiment will target the generation and use of a larger data set to further strengthen and generalize the findings of the work reported in this paper, based on statistical ablation studies.

Acknowledgments. The information, data, or work presented herein was funded in part by the Advanced Research Projects Agency-Energy (ARPA-E), U.S. Department of Energy, under Award Number DE-AR0001203. The views and opinions of authors expressed herein do not necessarily state or reflect those of the United States Government or any agency thereof.

References

1. DebRoy, T., et al.: Additive manufacturing of metallic components-process, structure and properties. Prog. Mater Sci. **92**, 112–224 (2018)
2. Frazier, W.E.: Metal additive manufacturing: a review. J. Mater. Eng. Perform. **23**(6), 1917–1928 (2014). https://doi.org/10.1007/s11665-014-0958-z
3. Khairallah, S.A., Anderson, A.T., Rubenchik, A., King, W.E.: Laser powder-bed fusion additive manufacturing: physics of complex melt flow and formation mechanisms of pores, spatter, and denudation zones. Acta Mater. **108**, 36–45 (2016)
4. Ronneberger, O., Fischer, P., Brox, T.: U-Net: convolutional networks for biomedical image segmentation. In: Navab, N., Hornegger, J., Wells, W.M., Frangi, A.F. (eds.) MICCAI 2015. LNCS, vol. 9351, pp. 234–241. Springer, Cham (2015). https://doi.org/10.1007/978-3-319-24574-4_28
5. Lin, T.Y., Goyal, P., Girshick, R., He, K., Dollár, P.: Focal loss for dense object detection. In: Proceedings of the IEEE International Conference on Computer Vision, pp. 2980–2988 (2017)
6. Bahdanau, D., Cho, K., Bengio, Y.: Neural machine translation by jointly learning to align and translate. arXiv preprint arXiv:1409.0473 (2014)
7. Vaswani, A., et al.: Attention is all you need. In: Advances in Neural Information Processing Systems, pp. 5998–6008 (2017)
8. Guo, C., Szemenyei, M., Yi, Y., Wang, W., Chen, B., Fan, C.: SA-UNet: spatial attention U-Net for retinal vessel segmentation. arXiv preprint arXiv:2004.03696 (2020)

9. Schlemper, J., et al.: Attention gated networks: learning to leverage salient regions in medical images. Med. Image Anal. **53**, 197–207 (2019)
10. Çiçek, Ö., Abdulkadir, A., Lienkamp, S.S., Brox, T., Ronneberger, O.: 3D U-Net: learning dense volumetric segmentation from sparse annotation. In: Ourselin, S., Joskowicz, L., Sabuncu, M.R., Unal, G., Wells, W. (eds.) MICCAI 2016. LNCS, vol. 9901, pp. 424–432. Springer, Cham (2016). https://doi.org/10.1007/978-3-319-46723-8_49
11. Milletari, F., Navab, N., Ahmadi, S.-A.: V-Net: fully convolutional neural networks for volumetric medical image segmentation. In: IEEE International Conference on 3D Vision, pp. 565–571 (2016)
12. Lee, K., Zung, J., Li, P., Jain, V., Seung, H.S.: Superhuman accuracy on the SNEMI3D connectomics challenge. arXiv preprint arXiv:1706.00120 (2017)
13. Yu, L., Yang, X., Chen, H., Qin, J., Heng, P.: Volumetric ConvNets with mixed residual connections for automated prostate segmentation from 3D MR images. In: AAAI Conference on Artificial Intelligence, pp. 66–72 (2017)
14. Zhou, X., et al.: Performance evaluation of 2D and 3D deep learning approaches for automatic segmentation of multiple organs on CT images. In: Medical Imaging: Computer-Aided Diagnosis, vol. 10575, p. 105752C (2018)
15. Ghavami, N., et al.: Automatic segmentation of prostate MRI using convolutional neural networks: investigating the impact of network architecture on the accuracy of volume measurement and MRI-ultrasound registration. Med. Image Anal. **58**, 101558 (2019)
16. Scime, L., Beuth, J.: A multi-scale convolutional neural network for autonomous anomaly detection and classification in a laser powder bed fusion additive manufacturing process. Addit. Manuf. **24**, 273–286 (2018)
17. Khadilkar, A., Wang, J., Rai, R.: Deep learning-based stress prediction for bottom-up SLA 3D printing process. Int. J. Adv. Manuf. Technol. **102**, 2555–2569 (2019). https://doi.org/10.1007/s00170-019-03363-4
18. Liang, L., Liu, M., Martin, C., Sun, W.: A deep learning approach to estimate stress distribution: a fast and accurate surrogate of finite-element analysis. J. Roy. Soc. Interface **15**(138), 20170844 (2018)
19. Qi, X., Chen, G., Li, Y., Cheng, X., Li, C.: Applying neural-network-based machine learning to additive manufacturing: current applications, challenges, and future perspectives. Engineering **5**(4), 721–729 (2019). ISSN: 2095-8099
20. Nie, Z., Jiang, H., Kara, L.B.: Stress field prediction in cantilevered structures using convolutional neural networks. ASME J. Comput. Inf. Sci. Eng. **20**(1), 011002 (2020)

Entity-Aware Biaffine Attention
for Constituent Parsing

Xinyi Bai[1], Nan Yin[1], Xiang Zhang[1,2(✉)], Xin Wang[1], and Zhigang Luo[1,3(✉)]

[1] College of Computer, National University of Defense Technology,
Changsha 410073, China
{baixinyi19,zhangxiang08,zgluo}@nudt.edu.cn

[2] Institute for Quantum and State Key Laboratory of High Performance Computing,
National University of Defense Technology, Changsha 410073, China

[3] Science and Technology on Parallel and Distributed Laboratory,
National University of Defense Technology, Changsha 410073, China

Abstract. Constituency parsing is the process of analyzing a sentence by breaking it down into sub-phrases also known as constituents. Although many deep neural models have achieved state-of-the-art results on this task, few consider entity-violating issue, i.e. an entity cannot form a complete sub-tree in the resultant constituent parsing tree. To attack this issue, this paper proposes an entity-aware biaffine attention model for constituent parsing. It leverages entity information for a potential phrase when conducting biaffine attention between the start and end words of the phrase. In the absence of the proper metric for comparison, the entity violating rate (EVR) as a new metric is introduced here to evaluate how many the final parsing trees suffer from entity violating issue. The lower the EVR, the better the model. This metric from a brand perspective helps us understand the potential of existing arts. Experiments on three publicly popular datasets including ONTONOTES, PTB and CTB show that our model achieves the lowest EVR while almost achieving the same performance in terms of the three conventional metrics, i.e., precision, recall, and F1-score. Moreover, extensive experiments of sentence sentiment analysis as a downstream application further exhibit the efficacy of our model and the validity of the proposed metric EVR.

Keywords: Constituent parsing · Entity information · Biaffine attention

1 Introduction

Constituent parsing is to construct the syntactic tree for a given sentence whose words constitute leaf nodes. In the syntactic tree, non-terminal nodes are called constituents. For intuition, Fig. 1(a) illustrates a constituent parsing tree of the phrase "vice-minister of the US Department of Defense Doetch". This tree serves as an important feature to represent a sentence, and has been applied in many

© Springer Nature Switzerland AG 2021
I. Farkaš et al. (Eds.): ICANN 2021, LNCS 12891, pp. 191–203, 2021.
https://doi.org/10.1007/978-3-030-86362-3_16

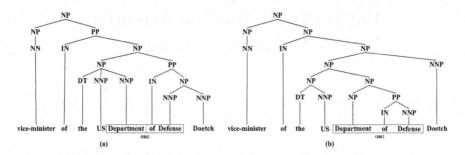

Fig. 1. Constituent parsing tree of phrase "vice-minister of the US Department of Defense Doetch". (a) The entity-violating case. (b) The entity consistent case.

high-level natural language tasks, such as sentiment analysis [9], relation extraction [8], natural language inference [2], and machine translation [14].

In this subject recent chart-based neural models have achieved state-of-the-art results by using advanced text encoders (i.e., BERT and XLNet) to represent all possible spans, where each span stands for a single word or several consecutive words from a sentence. Such models score each span, and then employs CKY algorithm to choose the resultant tree in terms of the highest score [10,11,15,17]. Despite their astonishing success in light of precision, recall and F1-score, few consider whether such arts also work well in the entity-violating issue: the entity span parsed by a neural model does not conform to the true phrasal one of human natural language. As in Fig. 1, "Department of Defense" as a true organization (ORG) entity should be in a complete sub-tree (b) but is parsed by previous neural models so that its words are distributed into two separate sub-trees (a).

Finkel et al. [5,6] firstly focus on this issue. They manually annotate the original dataset ONTONOTES [7] by adding entity nodes to the constituent parsing trees. This new dataset can greatly promote the model to output the consistent entity spans. Besides, other works [12,13] endeavor to explore the entity-related label as heuristic information, for instance, Chinese word '市' can be labeled with 'GPE-END'. Different from aforesaid works that absorb entity-related information, Yang et al. [20] considered utilizing the named entity recognition (NER) task to capture the entity information, and combining the PCFG algorithm for parsing, of which the parameter sharing enjoys the benefits of two tasks. However, since these entity-related parsing models either demand manual annotations or implicitly merge entity information into training process of constituent parsing, it may be underestimate the potential of the entity information.

To attack such problems above, we propose a biaffine attention based parsing model by integrating entity information into constituent parsing process without any manual annotations. Our model overall follows the basic biaffine attention model [23]. Similarly, each word is represented as two role vectors: start role vector and end role vector. Differently, we encode the entity information as the entity role vector and append it to the previous two role vectors. In this simple way, the proposed vector is more informative and reasonable than before.

By using the proposed entity-aware vector for each word, the basic biaffine attention model can boost potential score for each entity span. In our empirical studies, we find that although the entity information reinforces the ability of attention model to parse consistent phrasal span, it is lack of effective supervision and the entity information might be ignored in the learning process. To this end, we treat a simple NER task as the supervision similar to [22]. In our model, we add a binary NER model to share the same word embeddings with the primary parsing model. It helps our parsing model to capture informative entity structures. The overall model is light-weight, simple yet effective, free from large amounts of manual annotations, and even achieves the state-of-the-art performance on the benchmarks. To evaluate the entity-violating degree, we propose an very intuitive metric to calculate the ratio of the entity-violating spans to the entire samples.

In summary, this paper makes the following contributions.

1) We put forward an entity-aware biaffine attention model for constituent parsing, which encodes the entity information of a span as the attention input component.
2) To further exert the entity information in the attention model, we introduce an auxiliary bi-nary NER model in the whole parsing model, in order to make the parsing model aware of entity information.
3) Experiments on three datasets including ONTONOTES, PTB and CTB show that our strategy greatly promote the parsing performance, especially based on entity-violating metric. More importantly, the proposed model achieves the sound performance in terms of precision, recall and F1-score.
4) To make our model more convincing, we apply our parsing model for a typical downstream task—sentence classification [9]. Extensive results verify that our model performs best when comparing with several well-behaved parsing siblings.

2   Related Work

Constituent Parsing. Most constituent parsing models can be roughly classified into three types: transition-based, sequence-based and chart-based ones, according to which decoding algorithm they choose. For transition-based models, without no need of the decoder, they directly build the parsing trees through a sequence of 'shift' or 'reduce' actions, or other extended actions [1,3,21]. A recent representative model proposed by Yang and Deng starts with current partial parsing tree, then builds the corresponding graph and applies dynamic graph neural network to decide the next action [21]. This process will continuously iterate until the entire parsing tree is built successfully. Sequence-based approaches primarily convert a tree structure into a linear sequence form and generate a sequence of pertinent labels using seq2seq model [16,18,19]. Differently, chart-based methods firstly score all possible spans, then use CKY dynamic algorithm to decode out a highest scored tree [4,10,11,15,17,23]. In this regard, attention mechanism is introduced to represent a span by using self-attention [11], labeling attention [15] and n-gram attention [17] to complement those span boundary information. These models focus on how to construct a more powerful word representation for model inference. However, none of these models above consider entity-violating issue. Although these models take entity information into consideration [5,6,12,13,20], they are either suffer from massive manual labeling work [5,6,12,13] or cannot effectively convey entity information directly in parsing process [20]. To this end, we introduce an entity-aware parsing model which can apply entity information directly into inference process without extra labeling work.

3   Method

3.1   Parsing Model

This section explores the entity-aware biaffine attention model for constituent parsing, which follows the two-step parsing model [23]. The first step (span-parsing) decides whether a span is a node in the resultant constituent tree, and the second label-parsing model labels each node with POS tag. The two steps share the same contextual word embeddings.

Figure 2 shows the overall architecture of constituent parsing. For the given sentence, the first input embedding for each word (e.g. X_i) is the concatenation of word embedding, and its char-level feature gained through CharLSTM on each word. To obtain contextual information, we feed the embedding of each word into a 3-layer BiLSTM layer. The BiLSTM module outputs two hidden embeddings f and b for each word from forward and backward direction. Then for each word, e.g. $word_i$ we concatenate f_i and b_{i+1} to form its contextual representation h_i:

$$h_i = [f_i; \ b_{i+1}].\tag{1}$$

In biaffine model, the role of each word could be either the start of a span or the end of a span. After yielding the contextual representation h of each word, we implement four MLP (multi-layer perceptron) modules for each word, resulting in four vectors, v_{span_l}, v_{span_r}, v_{label_l} and v_{label_r} (collectively referred to as $v_{l,i}$, $v_{r,i}$ in Fig. 2). The first two participate the span-parsing model deciding whether a span exists or not while v_{label_l} and v_{label_r} are used to label the span with POS tag. The dimension size of v_{span_l} and v_{span_r} is 450, while that of v_{label_l} and v_{label_r} is 100.

Span Parsing. We construct an entity-aware biaffine attention model for constituent parsing. In our baseline biaffine model [23], $word_i$ always uses the same start vector $v_{span_{l,i}}$ when pairs with different end $word_j$ or $word_k$. We design a unique start and end vector for each $span_{(i,j)}$ based on start vector of $word_i$ i.e. $v_{span_{l,i}}$, end vector of $word_j$ i.e. $v_{span_{r,j}}$ and entity information of $span_{(i,j)}$. More specifically, for a given sentence with n words, we construct two $n*n$ embedding matrixes, embed-matrix-l: L and embed-matrix-r: R, which store the start and end vectors for all possible spans. For example, $L[i,j]$ and $R[i,j]$ are the start and end vectors applied in biaffine calculation of $span_{(i,j)}$. As a consequence, the issue left now is how to build L and R? For a given sentence with n words,

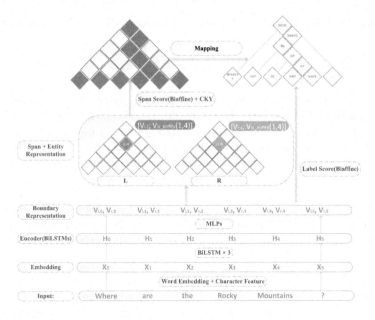

Fig. 2. The framework of entity-aware constituent parsing approach

the $n * n$ matrix S represent all possible spans. $S[i, j]$ means a span start from $word_i$ and end at $word_j$. It is obvious that these nodes in the Lower triangle of matrix S bear no meaning (we cannot build a span of words starts from the back and ends at the front), which will not be considered in practice. We traverse every node located in the upper triangle of S. For a certain node $S[i, j]$, we check whether $span_{(i,j)}$ is an entity, and embed entity information (i.e. 0 or 1) into a vector v_{is_entity} with length 50. Then we concatenate v_{is_entity} to $v_{span_{l,i}}$ and $v_{span_{r,j}}$, resulting in two vector $v_{l(i,j)}$ and $v_{r(i,j)}$ of length 500. Store $v_{l(i,j)}$ in L and $v_{r(i,j)}$ in R at position (i, j), respectively. When doing biaffine operation, we traverse the upper triangle of matrix S again, for every $node(i, j)$, and fetch the start vector $v_{l(i,j)}$ from L and end vector $v_{r(i,j)}$ from R at position (i, j). Then both $v_{l(i,j)}$ and $v_{r(i,j)}$ are fed to the following biaffine operation:

$$v_{l(i,j)}^T W v_{r(i,j)}, \tag{2}$$

where $v_{l(i,j)}$ and $v_{r(i,j)}$ are vectors with length $d = 500$, and W is the learning parameter with $d * d$. The result is a scalar indicating the potential score for $span_{(i,j)}$ being a node in the sentence's constituent parsing tree, and we mark it as $s(i, j)$.

For a sentence x, the score of a tree y is the sum score of all spans containing in the tree:

$$s(x, y) = \sum_{(i,j) \in y} s(i, j). \tag{3}$$

Under TreeCRF algorithm, the condition probability of the golden tree is:

$$p(\hat{y} \mid x) = \frac{e^{s(x,\hat{y})}}{Z(x) \equiv \sum_{y' \in \mathcal{T}(x)} e^{s(x,y')}}, \tag{4}$$

where $Z_{(x)}$ is the sum score for all possible trees, which can be calculated by inside algorithm. $\mathcal{T}(x)$ is a set including all possible trees for x.

Based on the scores of all spans calculated above, we use the CKY algorithm to decode the parse tree with the highest score:

$$\bar{y} = \arg\max_y s(x, y) = \arg\max_y p(y \mid x). \tag{5}$$

As illustrated above, we build unique start and end vectors for each span by adding their entity attribute embedding (whether it is an entity or not). Through this processing, parsing inference can then consider the entity information, which is entity-aware.

Label Parsing. After finishing the span parsing work, we obtain a constituent tree structure without labels. We feed $v_{label_{l,i}}$ and $v_{label_{r,j}}$ into the following biaffine attention operation to finish the labeling job for $span_{(i,j)}$:

$$v_{label_{l,i}}^T W v_{label_{r,j}}. \tag{6}$$

In this module, the corresponding parameter W is $c * d * d$, where c is the number of POS types and d is the length of $v_{label_{l,i}}$ and $v_{label_{r,j}}$. The result is a probability vector of length c.

3.2   Entity Compatible Split Method

Our model belongs to chart-based parsing model. It relies on CKY algorithm to decode. The result trees are binarized trees agreeing with CNF rule. However, little training data satisfies a binarized tree structure. It is common to use third-party tool (e.g. NLTK) to convert an original parsing tree into its binarized form with split choice right or left. As we observed, many entities satisfy a subtree structure in their original non-binarized parsing trees, violating after these trees binarized. One group of samples suffers from left binarized operation, while other samples suffering from right choice. The baseline biaffine attention model [23] uniformly chooses left split mechanism, which is not friendly to first group. In our model, we compare entity violating number of the two split choices for every single sample, and choose those results suffering from lower entity violating number.

3.3   NER Sub-task

Besides adding entity information in parsing process, to make our model more related with entity structure, we add a binary NER model that only judges whether a span is an entity or not. The NER model is also implemented with biaffine attention architecture, which shares the same contextual word embedding h with parsing model. Computing entity score of a certain $span_{(i,j)}$ is analogous to parsing model above. Two extra MLPs are applied to obtain entity span boundaries representation v_{entity_l} and v_{entity_r}, then follows the same biaffine process as Label parsing, $v_{entity_{l,i}}^T W v_{entity_{r,j}}$. W is a $2 * d' * d'$ tensor, 2 represents two types (a span is an entity or not). d' is the dimensions of $v_{entity_{l,i}}$, $v_{entity_{r,j}}$ and is set to 150 in this paper.

3.4   Training Loss

The losses for the whole model originate from three parts: Span parsing loss, Label parsing loss and NER loss:

$$Loss = Loss_{span} + Loss_{label} + Loss_{entity}. \tag{7}$$

The first item $Loss_{span}$ is to maximize the probability of the golden parsing tree and has the following form:

$$L_{span}(\boldsymbol{x}, \hat{\boldsymbol{y}}) = -s(\boldsymbol{x}, \hat{\boldsymbol{y}}) + \log Z(\boldsymbol{x}). \tag{8}$$

The latter two terms correspond to label parsing loss and NER loss, which belong to classification tasks and have the common cross entropy loss, i.e.,

$$p(i, j)_c = \frac{\exp\left(score(i, j)_c\right)}{\sum_{c'=1}^{C} \exp\left(score(i, j)_{c'}\right)}, \tag{9}$$

$$loss = - \sum_{(i,j)\in\hat{y}} \sum_{c'=1}^{C} y_{(i,j)_{c'}} \log p_{(i,j)_{c'}}, \tag{10}$$

where $p(i, j)_c$ is the probability of entity $span_{(i,j)}$ with label c in NER task, or the parse span probability with label c for label parsing task. $y(i, j)$ is a one-hot vector with golden label position setting 1 and the other positions setting 0. $\hat{y}$ here can be a golden parsing tree or a set containing all golden entity spans of sentence x.

4   Experiment

Dataset. We conduct experiments on PTB, CTB, and ONTONOTES. The first two datasets are popular benchmarks in constituent parsing tasks, while ONTONOTES contains both parsing and NER tags, which is rather suitable for discussing the entity-violating issue. Given that there is no NER tags in datasets PTB and CTB5.1, we use third party tool StanfordCoreNLP to obtain the entities on these two datasets. We follow the conventional train/dev/test data split approaches on the three datasets.

Metrics. The main idea of this paper is to alleviate the entity-violating issue in constituent parsing task. Besides the following frequently-used three metrics, i.e. precision, recall and F1-score, we introduce a new metric named entity-violating rate named EVR, which indicates how many samples suffer from entity violating problem. We calculate EVR as follows:

$$EVR = num_v/num_s, \tag{11}$$

where num_v is the number of entities conflicting with constituent trees, and num_s is the total number of samples.

Parameter Setting. To compare with baseline biaffine attention method and illustrate the effectiveness of our model in EVR aspect, we follow most of hyper-parameter values in [23]. The main parameters are shown in Table 1. We set all the dropout rate to 0.33, and the batch size to 1000, respectively. Our model is optimized by Adam, and the learning rate is 0.001 with decay rate 0.999 after every 100 steps.

Table 1. Hyper-parameter setting

$word_{embed}$	$feature_{embed}$	$BiLSTM_{hidden}$	$v_{span_{l/r}}$	$v_{label_{l/r}}$	v_{entity}	$v_{entity_{l/r}}$
300	100	400	450	100	50	150

Compared Models. We compare our model with 5 methods that have ranked among the best in constituent parsing. The abbreviation of model names are shown in Table 2. $B-biaffine$ [23] is the abbreviation of baseline biaffine model, it achieves constituent parsing through basic biaffine attention. $Benepar^{T5}$ [11] is proposed by Kitaev and Klein, it encodes spans with self-attention, using MLP to obtain the confidence score of a span to be a node in constituent tree. LAL^{XLNet} [15] is a model that represents spans with label attention and follows the same decoding framework as $Benepar^{T5}$ [11]. $SAPar^{Bert}$ [17] is also a chart-based model, it encodes spans by n-gram attention. $HPSG^{Bert}$ [24] adjusts the form of Head-Driven phrase structure grammar (HPSG) to satisfy both constituent parsing and dependency parsing, and fulfills a joint constituent and dependency parsing model sharing syntactic information of each task.

Given that $Benepar^{T5}$ [11], LAL^{XLNet} [15], $SAPar^{Bert}$ [17] and $HPSG^{Bert}$ [24] have not been trained on ONTONOTES dataset, we just run prediction on PTB and CTB for these four models. For $Benepar^{T5}$ [11], we run parsing operation based on the published benepar tool package. For LAL^{XLNet} [15], $SAPar^{Bert}$ [17] and $HPSG^{Bert}$ [24], we download their published pre-trained models on websites corresponding to PTB and CTB datasets.

Table 2. Results on ONTONOTES and PTB

	ONTONOTES				PTB			
	P	R	F1	EVR	P	R	F1	EVR
$Benepar^{T5}$ [11]	-	-	-	-	93.22	93.06	93.14	18.53
$SAPar^{Bert}$ [17]	-	-	-	-	95.64	95.64	95.64	17.73
LAL^{XLNet} [15]	-	-	-	-	94.43	94.34	94.39	18.70
$HPSG^{Bert}$ [24]	-	-	-	-	**95.69**	**95.69**	**95.69**	17.57
$B-biaffine$ [23]	91.44	91.42	91.43	2.64	93.79	93.85	93.82	17.60
$Ours^{GC}$	92.15	92.32	92.23	**[0.65]**	93.54	93.91	93.72	12.51
$Ours^{GB}$	95.36	95.02	95.18	1.10	94.91	94.54	94.72	**[10.29]**
$Ours^{B}$	**95.34**	**95.49**	**95.41**	0.98	94.55	94.45	94.50	12.12
$Ours^{right}$	92.13	92.40	92.26	1.10	93.95	93.84	93.89	17.58
$Ours^{noNER}$	92.03	92.19	92.11	1.21	93.36	93.45	93.40	12.96

Table 3. Results on CTB5.1

	CTB			
	P	R	F1	EVR
$SAPar^{Bert}$ [17]	**92.62**	**92.62**	**92.62**	16.51
$B-biaffine$ [23]	88.53	88.64	88.58	17.14
$Ours^{B}$	88.42	89.71	89.06	**[14.92]**
$Ours^{right}$	88.30	88.58	88.44	16.50
$Ours^{noNER}$	88.75	88.75	88.75	15.87

Results. The results of three conventional metrics precision, recall, F1-score and our introduced EVR are shown in Tables 2 and Table 3. In each experiment performance was averaged over seven runs. The superscripts of these compared models indicate the pre-trained embeddings, while in the lower part of our models, these superscripts bear the following meaning: $Ours^{GC}$ means that we use glove word embedding concatenating char-level features as initial input, which is also our kernel method mentioned above. $Ours^{GB}$ replaces char-level feature with Bert-feature, and $Ours^{B}$ initializes word embedding randomly (without glove), using Bert embedding as feature. $Ours^{right}$ is a variant based on $Ours^{GC}$, using right-choice binarized tree to compare with our proposed entity compatible split method. $Ours^{noNER}$ cuts off the NER model of $Ours^{GC}$.

Comparison with Other Methods: When comparing our proposed model with the other five baseline models, we can see that our proposed models outperform all the other models on metric EVR. The observations are detailed as follows: a) On ONTONOTES dataset, $Ours^{GC}$ reduces more than 75% of EVR when compared with $B-biaffine$, while maintaining a higher level of the other three metric (precision, recall, F1-score). b) On PTB dataset, $HPSG^{Bert}$ obtains the highest performance on F1-score with the pre-trained Bert embeddings and shared syntactic information between constituent and dependency parsing. However, these 5 models perform worse more than 5 points of EVR than our proposed models $Ours^{GC}$, $Ours^{GB}$. c) On CTB dataset, $Ours^B$ achieves lower F1-score than $SAPar^{Bert}$, may be due to the inappropriate way of Bert feature used in our model, however we still gain the best performance on EVR indicator. d) The EVR on ONTONOTES is much lower than that on PTB and CTB. Since ONTONOTES is a professional NER dataset with high quality NER labeled data while we apply the third-party tool on PTB and CTB to get NER labels, which has an unexpected result with noise.

Ablation Study: a) When comparing $Ours^{GC}$ with $Ours^{GB}$ across the three datasets, the latter improves performance on PTB and CTB datasets after using Bert features while $Ours^{GC}$ achieves the lowest violating rate on ONTONOTES. It indicates that our defined EVR is not that sensitive to these pre-trained embeddings. b) When the original binarized tree method is applied, $Ours^{right}$ suffers from higher EVR than $Ours^{GC}$ across all the three datasets, which proves the effectiveness of our proposed compatible split method. c) $Ours^{noNER}$ cuts off the NER sub-task module and performs worse than $Ours^{GC}$, which suggests that the NER sub-task helps our model to understand the added NER feature better.

Table 4. Comparison of downstream task performance

Parsing data	Accuracy
$SAPar^{Bert}$ [17]	95.4
$HPSG^{Bert}$ [24]	96.0
LAL^{XLNet} [15]	96.2
$Benepar^{T5}$ [11]	95.4
$B - biaffine$ [23]	95.0
Ours	**96.2**

Performance in Downstream Tasks. To make our method and the introduced EVR metric more convincing, we extend our parsing model to a downstream task: Sentiment Analysis. Kim et al. [9] introduced a Tree-LSTM framework for sentence sentiment classification based on constituent parsing tree. It implements bottom-up LSTM operation recursively and sends the root node embedding into a inference layer for classification results. We deploy the tree structure used in [9] with the counterparts from $Benepar^{T5}$ [11], LAL^{XLNet} [15], $SAPar^{Bert}$ [17], $HPSG^{Bert}$ [24] and $B - biaffine$ [23], and our proposed model, respectively, in order to compare the effectiveness of parsing tree generated by our model.

Tabel 4 depicts the results. Our model and LAL^{XLNet} [15] achieve the highest accuracy 96.2% on sentence classification on TREC. It implies that our entity-aware biaffine attention model is more in line with the language model.

Case Study. Figure 3 illustrates a case study performed by our proposed model (Fig. 3(a)) and the baseline biaffine attention model (Fig. 3(b)) for sentence "Where is John Wayne airport?". Our model treats the PERSON entity "John Wayne" as a complete constituent, while the baseline model splits it, and integrates the two words "Wayne" and "airport" into a sub-tree. The example indicates that our model can learn additional entity structure knowledge.

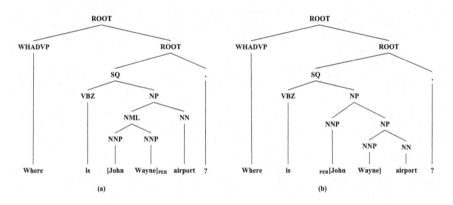

Fig. 3. Comparison of the parsing result for "Where is John Wayne airport?" between (a) our model and (b) $B - biaffine$ [23].

5   Conclusion

In this paper, we investigate entity-violating problem in constituent parsing tasks. To alleviate the violating issue, we construct an entity-aware parsing model based on biaffine attention method. We modify the basic biaffine model, making every biaffine operation correlated with its span's entity information, without extra manual annotations. Experimental results on ONTONOTES, PTB and CTB show that our proposed model achieves lowest EVR on the three datasets. The best performance of our parsing model on downstream task also demonstrates the superiority of our method.

References

1. Bowman, S.R., Gauthier, J., Rastogi, A., Gupta, R., Manning, C.D., Potts, C.: A fast unified model for parsing and sentence understanding. In: Proceedings of the ACL Conference (2016)

2. Chen, Q., Zhu, X., Ling, Z., Wei, S., Jiang, H., Inkpen, D.: Enhanced LSTM for natural language inference. In: Proceedings of the ACL Conference (2017)
3. Cheng, J., Lopez, A., Lapata, M.: A generative parser with a discriminative recognition algorithm. In: Proceedings of the ACL Conference (2017)
4. Collins, M.: Three generative, lexicalised models for statistical parsing. In: Proceedings of the ACL Conference (1997)
5. Finkel, J.R., Manning, C.D.: Joint parsing and named entity recognition. In: Proceedings of the ACL Conference, pp. 326–334 (2009)
6. Finkel, J.R., Manning, C.D.: Hierarchical joint learning: Improving joint parsing and named entity recognition with non-jointly labeled data. In: Proceedings of the ACL Conference, pp. 720–728 (2010)
7. Hovy, E., Marcus, M., Palmer, M., Ramshaw, L., Weischedel, R.: Ontonotes: the 90% solution. In: HLT-NAACL, pp. 57–60 (2006)
8. Jiang, M., Diesner, J.: A constituency parsing tree based method for relation extraction from abstracts of scholarly publications. In: Proceedings of the Thirteenth Workshop on Graph-Based Methods for Natural Language Processing. pp. 186–191 (2019)
9. Kim, T., Choi, J., Edmiston, D., Bae, S., Lee, S.g.: Dynamic compositionality in recursive neural networks with structure-aware tag representations. In: Proceedings of the AAAI Conference on Artificial Intelligence, pp. 6594–6601 (2019)
10. Kitaev, N., Cao, S., Klein, D.: Multilingual constituency parsing with self-attention and pre-training. In: Proceedings of the ACL Conference, pp. 3499–3505 (2019)
11. Kitaev, N., Klein, D.: Constituency parsing with a self-attentive encoder. In: Proceedings of the ACL Conference (2018)
12. Li, D., Zhang, X., Wu, X.: Improved Chinese parsing using named entity cue. In: Proceedings of the 13th International Conference on Parsing Technologies, pp. 45–53 (2013)
13. Li, D., Zhang, X., Wu, X.: Integrated Chinese segmentation, parsing and named entity recognition. Chin. J. Electr. **27**(4), 756–760 (2018)
14. Ma, C., Tamura, A., Utiyama, M., Zhao, T., Sumita, E.: Forest-based neural machine translation. In: Proceedings of the ACL Conference, pp. 1253–1263 (2018)
15. Mrini, K., Dernoncourt, F., Tran, Q., Bui, T., Chang, W., Nakashole, N.: Rethinking self-attention: towards interpretability in neural parsing. In: Proceedings of the EMNLP Conference, pp. 731–742 (2020)
16. Strzyz, M., Vilares, D., Gómez-Rodríguez, C.: Sequence labeling parsing by learning across representations. In: Proceedings of the ACL Conference, pp. 5350–5357 (2019)
17. Tian, Y., Song, Y., Xia, F., Zhang, T.: Improving constituency parsing with span attention. In: Proceedings of the EMNLP Conference (2020)
18. Vaswani, A., et al.: Attention is all you need. In: Advances in Neural Information Processing Systems, pp. 6000–6010 (2017)
19. Vinyals, O., Kaiser, L., Koo, T., Petrov, S., Sutskever, I., Hinton, G.: Grammar as a foreign language. In: Advances in Neural Information Processing Systems, pp. 2773–2781 (2014)
20. Wang, R., Xin, X., Chang, W., Ming, K., Li, B., Fan, X.: Chinese NER with height-limited constituent parsing. In: Proceedings of the AAAI Conference on Artificial Intelligence, vol. 33, pp. 7160–7167 (2019)
21. Yang, K., Deng, J.: Strongly incremental constituency parsing with graph neural networks. In: Neural Information Processing Systems (2020)
22. Yu, J., Bohnet, B., Poesio, M.: Named entity recognition as dependency parsing. In: Proceedings of the ACL Conference (2020)

23. Zhang, Y., Zhou, H., Li, Z.: Fast and accurate neural CRF constituency parsing. In: Proceedings of the Twenty-Ninth International Joint Conference on Artificial Intelligence (IJCAI 2020), pp. 4046–4053 (2020)
24. Zhou, J., Zhao, H.: Head-driven phrase structure grammar parsing on PENN treebank. In: Proceedings of the ACL Conference (2019)

Attention-Based Multi-view Feature Fusion for Cross-Domain Recommendation

Feifei Dai[1,2] , Xiaoyan Gu[1,2(✉)], Zhuo Wang[3], Bo Li[1], Mingda Qian[1,2], and Weiping Wang[1]

[1] Institute of Information Engineering, Chinese Academy of Sciences, Beijing, China
{daifeifei,guxiaoyan,libo,qianmingda,wangweiping}@iie.ac.cn
[2] School of Cyber Security, University of Chinese Academy of Sciences, Beijing, China
[3] Sangfor Inc., Shenzhen, China
wangzhuo@hit-cs.com

Abstract. Cross-domain recommendation can effectively alleviate the data sparsity problem in recommender systems. Existing methods for cross-domain recommendation can be roughly divided into two categories: specific-feature-based methods and sharing-feature-based methods. Specific-feature-based methods focus on learning users' and items' domain-specific features in each domain and transferring the same or similar features across domains for recommendation. Sharing-feature-based methods concentrate on obtaining latent transferable features cross domains and utilizing them for recommendation. However, both methods have defects: 1) specific-feature-based methods fail to capture latent transferable features cross domains, which greatly reduces the availability of source domain information; 2) sharing-feature-based methods ignore users' and items' domain-specific features so that the recommended items of different domains have high similarity. Since user preferences are distinct in different domains, the recommended items may be unsuitable for users. To overcome the above problems, we propose an **A**ttention-based **M**ulti-**V**iew **F**eature fusion model (**AMVF**). To improve the availability of source domain information and recommend suitable items, AMVF learns latent transferable features and domain-specific features simultaneously. Since various features make distinct contributions to recommendation, seamlessly fusing different features is a challenge. Therefore, an attention-based feature fusion algorithm is designed to learn different importance of various features. To demonstrate the effectiveness of AMVF, extensive experiments are conducted on two pairs cross-domain datasets. The results empirically verify the superior performance of AMVF.

Keywords: Cross-domain recommendation · Domain-specific feature · Latent transferable feature · Attention-based feature fusion

Supported by XDC02050200, Z191100007119003.

I. Farkaš et al. (Eds.): ICANN 2021, LNCS 12891, pp. 204–216, 2021.
https://doi.org/10.1007/978-3-030-86362-3_17

1   Introduction

In recent years, cross-domain recommendation has attracted great interest as they can solve the data sparsity problem in recommender systems [1–4]. The cross-domain recommendation aims to utilize the information of the source domain to enrich the target domain. Thus, the data sparsity problem in the target domain can be alleviated effectively.

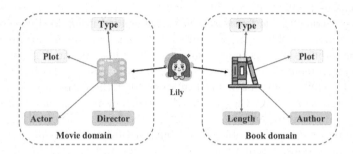

Fig. 1. An illustration of the movie's and book's features in the movie domain and book domains.

Existing methods for cross-domain recommendation can be roughly divided into two categories according to features' learning and utilization: specific-feature-based methods and sharing-feature-based methods. For specific-feature-based methods, they first obtain users' and items' domain-specific features in each domain. Thereafter, the same or similar features are transferred through common users across domains for recommendation [5–8]. As shown in Fig. 1, these methods first obtain the features of the movie that *Lily* has watched in the movie domain (i.e., the type, plot, actor, and director). Meanwhile, they learn books' features in the book domain (i.e., the type, plot, author, and length). Then, the same or similar features (i.e., the type and plot) are transferred by *Lily* from the movie domain to the book domain. Finally, the specific-feature-based methods recommend the book with the same/similar type/plot as the movie to *Lily*. For the sharing-feature-based methods, they directly learn users' and items' latent transferable feature cross domains and then utilize these features for recommendation [9,10]. For instance, in Fig. 1, if these methods learn that the movie *Lily* has watched involves mathematical knowledge, they will get the correlation between the movie and a mathematics book. Then, they treat the correlation as a latent transferable feature. According to the latent transferable feature, the sharing-feature-based methods recommend a mathematics book to *Lily*.

However, both specific-feature-based methods and sharing-feature-based methods have their own problems.

First, specific-feature-based methods are difficult to capture the latent transferable features cross domains. These methods focus on learning users' and items' domain-specific features in their respective domains. Without considering the relation between two domains, the specific-feature-based methods failed to capture users' and items' latent correlation cross domains. Therefore, the latent transferable features cross domains are difficult to capture, so that the utilization of source domain information is greatly reduced. As illustrated in Fig. 1, if *Lily* has watched a suspense movie that involves mathematical knowledge in the process of reasoning, she may read a mathematics book. However, the specific feature-based methods cannot obtain this latent transferable feature between the movie and the book. Second, sharing-feature-based methods ignore users' and items' domain-specific features. Since they attach great importance to users' and items' latent transferable features, the recommended items in diverse domains have high similarity. Thus, the recommended items may be unsuitable for users as user preferences are distinct in different domains. As Fig. 1 shows, if these methods recommend a mathematics book to *Lily* just as she has watched a movie that involves some mathematical knowledge, the book may be unsuitable for her. The reason is that they ignore the book's domain-specific features (i.e., the author and length), and *Lily* may dislike the book's author or length.

To address the above problems, we put forward the following ideas. First, the users' and items' latent transferable features and domain-specific features should be learned simultaneously. In this way, the latent transferable features and domain-specific features can work together in recommendation. Therefore, the utilization of source domain information can be improved, and the recommender system can recommend suitable items to users. Second, seamlessly fusing different features is a challenge as various features make distinct contributions to the recommendation. Different importance of latent transferable features and domain-specific features should be learned so that the features can be fully utilized for recommendation.

Motivated by the above ideas, we propose an **A**ttention-based Multi-**V**iew **F**eature fusion model for cross-domain recommendation (**AMVF**). Multi-view features include users' and items' latent transferable features and domain-specific features. Figure 2 shows the architecture of AMVF. First, heterogeneous graphs G_S, G_T, and G_{ST} are constructed to store the user-item historical interactions in domain S, domain T, and cross domain S and domain T, respectively. Then, AMVF learns users' and items' features from G_S, G_T, and G_{ST} simultaneously. The latent transferable features are fully captured from G_{ST}, and the domain-specific features are obtained from G_S and G_T. Therefore, the latent transferable features and domain-specific features work together to improve the performance of AMVF. Next, an attention-based feature fusion algorithm is designed to fuse different features seamlessly. Through considering different importance of various features, the features are fully utilized, and suitable items are recommended to users. Finally, user preferences in different domains are predicted, and the list of recommended items is given.

In summary, this paper makes the following contributions:

- To our best knowledge, this is the first work to learn and utilize both users' and items' domain-specific features and latent transferable features for cross-domain recommendation.

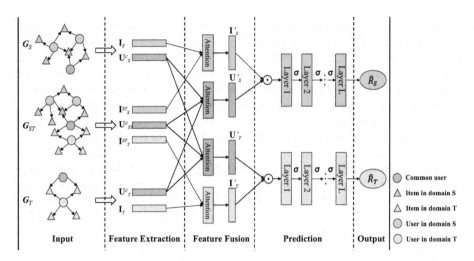

Fig. 2. The architecture of AMVF. Heterogeneous graphs G_S and G_T are used to learn users' and items' domain-specific features in each domain. Heterogeneous graph G_{ST} is used to capture users' and items' latent transferable features cross domain S and domain T.

- AMVF learns users' and items' domain-specific features and latent transferable features on three graphs simultaneously. Hence, these features work together to recommend suitable items to users.
- To fuse different features seamlessly, an attention-based feature fusion algorithm is designed to learn different importance of various features. Therefore, AMVF fully utilizes the features and its performance is improved.
- We conduct extensive experiments on two pairs cross-domain datasets. The results empirically verify the superior performance of AMVF.

2   Related Work

Along with the explosive growth of information, recommender systems have become an essential tool to help users find suitable items [11,12]. Among various recommender systems, collaborative filtering is an early popular and widely used method [13,14]. For instance, BPR [13] is a classic technology for collaborative filtering, which learns users' and items' features based on matrix factorization. NCF [14] is one representative neural network architecture to model users' and items' features by collaborative filtering. However, these methods are faced with the data sparsity problem.

To alleviate the data sparsity problem, several cross-domain recommendation methods have been proposed and achieved promising performance, such as NCF+ [14], CoNet [6], SCoNet [6], BiTGCF [8], and PPGN [9]. NCF+ [14] is a cross-domain recommendation model modified from NCF with conducting multi-task training and transferring users' features. CoNet [6] learns users' and items' features in each domain and transfers them cross domains based on the cross-stitch network. SCoNet [6] is a modified version of CoNet with sparsity-induced regularization. BiTGCF [8] initializes users' and items' features in each domain and considers users' domain-specific features and domain-sharing features when transferring. PPGN [9] fuses the historical interactions cross two domains into a graph and learns users' and items' latent transferable features from the graph.

However, these methods cannot learn and utilize both users' and items' domain-specific features and latent transferable features for cross-domain recommendation. Thus, the utilization of source domain information is greatly reduced, and the recommended items may be unsuitable for users. In this work, we propose an attention-based multi-view feature fusion model to solve the above problems. Since users' and items' domain-specific features and latent transferable features are learned simultaneously, the features work together to improve the performance of the recommender system. Moreover, an attention-based feature fusion algorithm is designed to learn the importance of various features. Thus, the features are seamlessly fused to recommend suitable items to users.

3 The Proposed Model: AMVF

3.1 Input

The inputs of AMVF comprise three parts: the user-item historical interactions of domain S (stored in graph $\boldsymbol{G}_S$); the user-item historical interactions of domain T (stored in graph $\boldsymbol{G}_T$); the total user-item historical interactions integrate from domain S and domain T (stored in graph $\boldsymbol{G}_{ST}$). Blue stands for items in domain S, orange stands for items in domain T, and green stands for common users. Note that common users exist in both domain S and domain T.

3.2 Feature Extraction

To fully capture users' and items' features, deep learning models are considered [15]. In this paper, Node2vec [16] is used to generate the feature matrices. Node2vec maps users and items to low-dimensional space features that maximizes the likelihood of preserving users' and items' neighborhoods in $\boldsymbol{G}_S$, $\boldsymbol{G}_T$, and $\boldsymbol{G}_{ST}$. The biased random walk procedure helps us capture users' and items' domain-specific features from $\boldsymbol{G}_S$ and $\boldsymbol{G}_T$, and their latent transferable features from $\boldsymbol{G}_{ST}$. We use $\boldsymbol{U}_S^c, \boldsymbol{U}_T^c, \boldsymbol{U}_{ST}^c \in \mathbb{R}^{m \times d}$ to represent common users' domain-specific features in domain S, domain T, and latent transferable features cross domain S and domain T. Meanwhile, $\boldsymbol{I}_S \in \mathbb{R}^{n \times d}$ and $\boldsymbol{I}_T \in \mathbb{R}^{o \times d}$ denote items' domain-specific features in domain S and domain T, respectively. Moreover, $\boldsymbol{I}_S^{ST} \in \mathbb{R}^{n \times d}$ and $\boldsymbol{I}_T^{ST} \in \mathbb{R}^{o \times d}$ stand for items' latent transferable features of domain S and domain T. m, n, o are the numbers of common users, items in domain S, and items in domain T. d is the dimension of the features.

3.3   Feature Fusion

To seamlessly fuse different features and make full use of them, an attention-based feature fusion algorithm is designed to learn the importance of various features. Since different features contribute differently to the cross-domain recommendation, lack of differentiating them can result in suboptimal suggestions. Therefore, we take advantage of the attention mechanism to discriminate the importance of these features. Features with large contribution are given high weights, while features with small contribution are given low weights.

We use $\boldsymbol{W}_S \in \mathbb{R}^{n \times d}$, $\mathbf{W}_S^S \in \mathbb{R}^{m \times d}$, and $\mathbf{W}_S^T \in \mathbb{R}^{m \times d}$ to denote the weight matrices for the attention network of items' domain-specific features in domain S, common users' domain-specific features in domain S and domain T, respectively. The fused features of common users $\mathbf{U}_S' \in \mathbb{R}^{m \times d}$ and items $\mathbf{I'}_S \in \mathbb{R}^{n \times d}$, used for the recommendation of domain S, are given as follows:

$$\mathbf{U}_S' = \mathbf{W}_S^S \odot \mathbf{U}_S^c + \mathbf{W}_S^T \odot \mathbf{U}_T^c + (1 - \mathbf{W}_S^S - \mathbf{W}_S^T) \odot \mathbf{U}_{ST}^c, \tag{1}$$

$$\mathbf{I}_S' = \mathbf{W}_S \odot \mathbf{I}_S + (1 - \mathbf{W}_S) \odot \mathbf{I}_S^{ST}, \tag{2}$$

where $\odot$ is the element-wise multiplication.

Similarly, the fused features of common users $\mathbf{U'}_T \in \mathbb{R}^{m \times d}$ and items $\mathbf{I'}_T \in \mathbb{R}^{o \times d}$, used for the recommendation of domain T, are given as follows:

$$\mathbf{U}_T' = \mathbf{W}_T^S \odot \mathbf{U}_S^c + \mathbf{W}_T^T \odot \mathbf{U}_T^c + (1 - \mathbf{W}_T^S - \mathbf{W}_T^T) \odot \mathbf{U}_{ST}^c, \tag{3}$$

$$\mathbf{I}_T' = \mathbf{W}_T \odot \mathbf{I}_T + (1 - \mathbf{W}_T) \odot \mathbf{I}_T^{ST}, \tag{4}$$

where $\mathbf{W}_T \in \mathbb{R}^{o \times d}$, $\mathbf{W}_T^S \in \mathbb{R}^{m \times d}$, and $\mathbf{W}_T^T \in \mathbb{R}^{m \times d}$ denote the weight matrices of items' domain-specific features in domain T, common users' domain-specific features in domain S and domain T, respectively.

3.4   Prediction

To predict users' preferences on non-interactive items, we apply the Multi-Layer Perceptron (MLP) to represent the relationship between users and items on domain S. First, we merge common users' fused features $\mathbf{U}_S'$ and items' fused features $\mathbf{I}_S'$ with the element-wise multiplication. Then, we place MLP above the element-wise multiplication. By specifying the non-linear activation function (Leaky_Relu), we allow the model to learn higher-order feature interactions in a non-linear way. The predicted score of domain S is obtained by:

$$R_S' = MLP(\mathbf{U}_S' \odot \mathbf{I}_S'). \tag{5}$$

The predicted score of domain T is obtained in the same way as R_S':

$$R_T' = MLP(\mathbf{U}_T' \odot \mathbf{I}_T'). \tag{6}$$

3.5   Output

To get the lists of items to be recommended to users in each domain, we rank the prediction scores into a descending ordered list. According to the list, we select the items with the top-K highest prediction scores as the recommendations for users. The lists of items to be recommended to users in domain S and domain T are defined as:

$$\hat{R}_S = topK(RankDes(R'_S)), \tag{7}$$

$$\hat{R}_T = topK(RankDes(R'_T)). \tag{8}$$

The complete AMVF framework is presented in Algorithm 1.

Algorithm 1. The AMVF framework.

Input: the user-item historical interactions of domain S, domain T, and the integration of domain S and domain T (stored in graph G_S, G_T, and G_{ST});

Output: the lists of items to be recommended to users in domain S ($\hat{R}_S$) and domain T ($\hat{R}_T$);

1: Learn items' domain-specific features $\mathbf{I}_S$ from G_S, $\mathbf{I}_T$ from G_T, and latent transferable features $\mathbf{I}_S^{ST}$ and $\mathbf{I}_T^{ST}$ from G_{ST}; learn users' domain-specific features $\mathbf{U}_S^c$ from G_S, $\mathbf{U}_T^c$ from G_T, and latent transferable features $\mathbf{U}_{ST}^c$ from G_{ST};

2: Obtain the fused features $\mathbf{U}'_S$, $\mathbf{I}'_S$, $\mathbf{U}'_T$, and $\mathbf{I}'_T$ based on (1), (2), (3), and (4);

3: Predict users' preferences on non-interactive items of domain S (R'_S) and domain T (R'_T) based on (5) and (6);

4: Get the recommendation lists $\hat{R}_S$ and $\hat{R}_T$ based on (7) and (8).

3.6   Optimization Strategy

The input of training instances in AMVF requires positive samples and negative samples, and the ratio between them is 1: η ($\eta > 1$). Following [9], to solve this sample imbalance problem, we apply a weighting strategy to the objective function. The overall objective to be optimized is defined as:

$$L_* = -\sum \alpha(R_* log R'_* + (1 - R_*)log(1 - R'_*)) + \lambda_* \sum |\Theta|, \tag{9}$$

$$\alpha = \begin{cases} \eta, & if R_{*(u,i)} = 1; \\ 1, & if R_{*(u,i)} = 0, \end{cases} \tag{10}$$

where $* \in \{S, T\}$, $R_* = \{R_{*(u,i)}\}^\tau$ denotes users' true preferences on items, τ is the number of the user-item pair that we need to predict, λ_* is the regularization coefficient, and α is the weight value determined by the labels of input set, which speeds up the training process.

4   Experiments

4.1   Datasets

To demonstrate the effectiveness of AMVF, we conduct extensive experiments on two pairs cross-domain datasets from Amazon-5cores[1] [17]. They are *CD* (named "CDs and Vinyl" in Amazon), *Music* (named "Digital Music" in Amazon), *Book* (named "Books" in Amazon), and *Movie* (named "Movies and TV" in Amazon), respectively. Moreover, each user or item of these datasets has at least five ratings. For these two couple datasets, we first transform them into implicit data, where each entry is marked as 0 or 1, indicating whether the user has rated the item. Then, we extract the common users in both domains for training and testing. Table 1 summarizes the detailed statistics of the two couple datasets.

Table 1. The detailed statistics of the two pairs cross-domain datasets. #Users, #Items, #Ratings, and #C.users denote the numbers of users, items, user-item ratings, and common users, respectively. The density of the after extracting datasets is calculated by #Ratings/(#C.users × #Items).

Datasets	Before extracting			After extracting			
	#Users	#Items	#Ratings	#C.users	#Items	#Ratings	Density
CD	75,258	64,443	1,097,592	5,331	55,848	376,347	0.126%
Music	5,541	3,568	64,706	5,331	3,563	63,303	0.333%
Book	603,668	367,982	8,898,041	37,388	269,301	1,254,288	0.012%
Movie	123,960	50,052	1,697,533	37,388	49,273	792,319	0.043%

4.2   Evaluation Measures

To evaluate the performance of AMVF and baselines, we adopt the ranking-based evaluation strategy, i.e., leave-one-out evaluation, which has been widely used in the top-K recommendation task [8,20,21]. Specifically, we take a random sample from each user's historical interactions as the test set, and the remaining are utilized for training. Following [9], we randomly sample 99 unobserved interactions for the test user and 4 unobserved interactions for the train user. AMVF predicts 100 records (99 negative samples and 1 positive sample) of the user and output top-K items. We use the commonly used Hit Ratio (HR), Mean Reciprocal Rank (MRR), and Normalized Discounted Cumulative Gain (NDCG) to evaluate the performance of all the models. For these measures, we truncate the ranked list at 10, i.e., $K = 10$.

---

[1] http://jmcauley.ucsd.edu/data/amazon/.

4.3 Baselines

We consider three categories of recommendation methods: the single-domain recommendation, which only uses a single dataset (i.e., BPR [13] and NCF [14]), specific-feature-based methods for cross-domain recommendation (i.e., NCF+ [14], CoNet [6], SCoNet [6], and BiTGCF [8]), and sharing-feature-based methods for cross-domain recommendation (i.e., PPGN [9]).

4.4 Implementation Details

We use Tensorflow to implement AMVF and deploy it on an Nvidia GeForce GPU with 11 GB memory. The dimensionality of users' and items' features is fixed to 128 for all datasets. The negative/positive sample ratio η is set as 4. The optimizer of AMVF is Adam [18, 19, 22]. We test the learning rate in {0.01, 0.001, 0.0001} and fine-tune it in a small step. The batch size is tuned among {512, 1024, 2048, 4096, 8192}. The scores of BPR, NCF, NCF+, CoNet, ScoNet, and PPGN are directly taken from [9]. The optimal hyper-parameter settings for BiTGCF are determined by either our experiments or the original papers.

Table 2. Performance comparison of two pairs cross-domain datasets. The best method appears in boldface. The best performing baseline appears underlined.

Methods	HR@10	MRR@10	NDCG@10	HR@10	MRR@10	NDCG@10
	CD			Music		
BPR [13]	0.5532	0.2742	0.3532	0.4742	0.1431	0.2045
NCF [14]	0.6421	0.3092	0.3933	0.5322	0.1549	0.2432
NCF+ [14]	0.6655	0.3593	0.4303	0.5991	0.2472	0.3297
CoNet [6]	0.7539	0.4735	0.5227	0.7179	0.3855	0.4436
SCoNet [6]	0.7547	0.4875	0.5291	0.7205	0.3878	0.4603
BiTGCF [8]	<u>0.8255</u>	<u>0.5458</u>	<u>0.6130</u>	0.7766	<u>0.4403</u>	<u>0.5204</u>
PPGN [9]	0.7839	0.5012	0.5697	<u>0.7874</u>	0.4388	0.5147
AMVF	**0.8411**	**0.5557**	**0.6223**	**0.8839**	**0.5601**	**0.6378**
Methods	HR@10	MRR@10	NDCG@10	HR@10	MRR@10	NDCG@10
	Book			Movie		
BPR [13]	0.3654	0.1543	0.2365	0.4538	0.2034	0.2654
NCF [14]	0.4300	0.2241	0.2725	0.5665	0.2775	0.3445
NCF+ [14]	0.4291	0.2249	0.2724	0.5605	0.2742	0.3416
CoNet [6]	0.5223	0.3273	0.3396	0.6460	0.3651	0.4060
SCoNet [6]	0.5141	0.3261	0.3370	0.6465	0.3829	0.4210
BiTGCF [8]	<u>0.6801</u>	<u>0.4151</u>	<u>0.4782</u>	**0.7561**	**0.4555**	**0.5274**
PPGN [9]	0.5770	0.3280	0.3574	0.6909	0.3869	0.4249
AMVF	**0.7337**	**0.4735**	**0.5353**	0.6817	0.3815	0.4527

Table 3. The ablation test on two pairs cross-domain datasets.

Methods	HR@10	MRR@10	NDCG@10	HR@10	MRR@10	NDCG@10
	CD			*Music*		
AMVF	**0.8411**	**0.5557**	**0.6223**	**0.8839**	**0.5601**	**0.6378**
AMVF-spec	0.8314	0.5456	0.6134	0.8732	0.5512	0.6285
AMVF-shar	0.8234	0.5318	0.6017	0.6557	0.3610	0.4304
AMVF-single	0.8202	0.5270	0.5972	0.6551	0.3602	0.4297
AMVF-add	0.8090	0.5118	0.5825	0.7706	0.4383	0.5174
Methods	HR@10	MRR@10	NDCG@10	HR@10	MRR@10	NDCG@10
	Book			*Movie*		
AMVF	**0.7337**	**0.4735**	**0.5353**	**0.6817**	**0.3815**	**0.4527**
AMVF-spec	0.7286	0.4699	0.5322	0.6774	0.3762	0.4473
AMVF-shar	0.7275	0.4662	0.5331	0.6452	0.3849	0.4464
AMVF-single	0.7263	0.4630	0.5325	0.6397	0.3805	0.4417
AMVF-add	0.7073	0.4404	0.5040	0.6339	0.3466	0.4143

4.5   Performance Comparison

The experimental results of AMVF and the baselines are reported in Table 2. From Table 2, we have the following observations:

– AMVF achieves the best performance in all cases except the movie dataset which demonstrates its effectiveness. Since learning both users' and items' domain-specific features and latent transferable features, AMVF improves the availability of source domain information and recommends suitable items to users. Moreover, the attention-based feature fusion algorithm fuses different features seamlessly and fully utilizes them by learning different importance of various features. Therefore, the performance of AMVF is improved.

– The performance improvement of AMVF is most obvious on the music dataset. The reason is that the common users are 96% of total users in this dataset, so AMVF captures more transferable features from the CD domain than other datasets. Therefore, the information of the CD domain is fully utilized to improve the performance of AMVF. On the contrary, AMVF performs worst on the movie dataset. This is because the common users are only 30% of the total users in the movie dataset. Hence, AMVF only captures limited transferable features from the book domain. Finally, the performance improvement of AMVF is unsatisfactory.

– Compared to the recommender systems in single domain, the systems cross domains perform better. Since the cross-domain recommendation can transform knowledge from source domain to target domain, the performance of the recommender system on target domain is improved effectively.

4.6   Ablation Study

To verify the impact of different features and the attention-based feature fusion algorithm on the performance of AMVF, we design four diverse baselines for experiments: a) AMVF-spec: AMVF only considers users' and items' latent transferable features; b) AMVF-shar: AMVF only considers users' and items' domain-specific features; c) AMVF-single: AMVF makes the recommendation in a single domain; d) AMVF-add: AMVF without the attention-based feature fusion algorithm, and the features are fused by simple addition.

Table 3 shows that AMVF's performance is most affected by the latent transferable features. Since latent transferable features are transferred easily cross domains, the source domain information is fully utilized to improve AMVF's performance in target domain. Meanwhile, the attention-based feature fusion algorithm also plays a crucial role. The reason is that discriminating the importance of different features helps AMVF make full use of the features. Moreover, users' and items' domain-specific features also contribute to helping AMVF recommend suitable items to users.

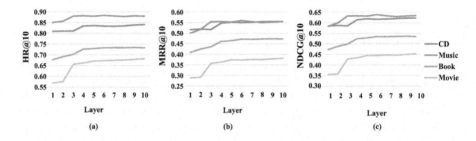

Fig. 3. Impact of MLP with different layers on two pairs cross-domain datasets.

4.7   Impact of MLP with Different Layers

We also verify the impact of MLP with different layers. The results are shown in Fig. 3. We can observe that the performance of AMVF is gradually improved when the layer of MLP increases from 1 to 5. Then, the performance of AMVF tends to be stable. The reason is that 5 layers are enough to capture the non-linearity interaction of higher-order features which is important in capturing helpful information for rating prediction.

5   Conclusion

In this paper, we propose an **A**ttention-based **M**ulti-**V**iew **F**eature fusion model for cross-domain recommendation (**AMVF**). To fully capture latent transferable features and take domain-specific features into account, AMVF learns these features on three graphs simultaneously. Since seamlessly fusing different features is a challenge, an attention-based feature fusion algorithm is designed to learn different importance of various features. In this way, AMVF can effectively fuse and fully utilize these features. Therefore, AMVF recommends suitable items to users. We conduct extensive experiments on four popular datasets, and the results empirically verify the superior performance of AMVF.

References

1. Pan, W., Xiang, E.W., Liu, N.N., Yang, Q.: Transfer learning in collaborative filtering for sparsity reduction. In: AAAI, Atlanta, pp. 230–235. ACM (2010)
2. Zhu, F., Wang, Y., Chen, C., Liu, G., Orgun, M., Wu, J.: A deep framework for cross-domain and cross-system recommendations. In: IJCAI, Stockholm, pp. 3711–3717. ACM (2018)
3. Yuan, F., Yao, L., Benatallah, B.: DARec: deep domain adaptation for cross-domain recommendation via transferring rating patterns. In: IJCAI, Macao, pp. 4227–4233. ACM (2019). https://doi.org/10.24963/ijcai.2019/587
4. Li, P., Tuzhilin, A.: DDTCDR: deep dual transfer cross domain recommendation. In: WSDM, Houston, pp. 331–339. ACM (2020). https://doi.org/10.1145/3336191.3371793
5. Man, T., Shen, H., Jin, X., Cheng, X.: Cross-domain recommendation: an embedding and mapping approach. In: IJCAI, Melbourne, pp. 2464–2470. ACM (2017). https://doi.org/10.24963/ijcai.2017/343
6. Hu, G., Zhang, Y., Yang, Q.: CoNet: collaborative cross networks for cross -domain recommendation. In: CIKM, Torino, pp. 667–676. ACM (2018). https://doi.org/10.1145/3269206.3271684
7. Zhu, F., Wang, Y., Chen, C., Liu, G., Zheng, X.: A graphical and attentional framework for dual-target cross-domain recommendation. In: IJCAI-PRICAI, Yokohama, pp. 3001–3008. ACM (2020). https://doi.org/10.24963/ijcai.2020/415
8. Liu, M., Li, J., Li, G., Pan, P.: Cross domain recommendation via bi-directional transfer graph collaborative filtering networks. In: CIKM, Virtual, pp. 885–894. ACM (2020). https://doi.org/10.1145/3340531.3412012
9. Zhao, C., Li, C., Fu, C.: Cross-domain recommendation via preference propagation GraphNet. In: CIKM, Beijing, pp. 2165–2168. ACM (2019). https://doi.org/10.1145/3357384.3358166
10. Singh, A.P., Gordon, G.J.: Relational learning via collective matrix factorization. In: SIGKDD, Las Vegas, pp. 650–658. ACM (2008). https://doi.org/10.1145/1401890.1401969
11. Zhang, X., Zhou, Q., He, T., Liang, B.: Con-CNAME: a contextual multi-armed bandit algorithm for personalized recommendations. In: Kůrková, V., Manolopoulos, Y., Hammer, B., Iliadis, L., Maglogiannis, I. (eds.) ICANN 2018. LNCS, vol. 11140, pp. 326–336. Springer, Cham (2018). https://doi.org/10.1007/978-3-030-01421-6_32
12. Florea, A.-C., Anvik, J., Andonie, R.: Parallel implementation of a bug report assignment recommender using deep learning. In: Lintas, A., Rovetta, S., Verschure, P.F.M.J., Villa, A.E.P. (eds.) ICANN 2017. LNCS, vol. 10614, pp. 64–71. Springer, Cham (2017). https://doi.org/10.1007/978-3-319-68612-7_8
13. Rendle, S., Freudenthaler, C., Gantner, Z., Schmidt-Thieme, L.: BPR: Bayesian personalized ranking from implicit feedback. In: UAI, Montreal, pp. 452–461 (2009)

14. He, X., Liao, L., Zhang, H., Nie, L., Chua, T.S.: Neural collaborative filtering. In: WWW, Perth, pp. 173–182. ACM (2017). https://doi.org/10.1145/3038912.3052569
15. Wang, Q., Liu, X., Liu, W., Liu, A., Liu, W., Mei, T.: MetaSearch: incremental product search via deep meta-learning. IEEE Trans. Image Process. **29**, 7549–7564 (2020). https://doi.org/10.1109/TIP.2020.3004249
16. Grover, A., Leskovec, J.: node2vec: scalable feature learning for networks. In: SIGKDD, San Francisco, pp. 855–864. ACM (2016). https://doi.org/10.1145/2939672.2939754
17. He, R., Mcauley, J.: Ups and downs: modeling the visual evolution of fashion trends with one-class collaborative filtering. In: WWW, Montreal, pp. 507–517. ACM (2016). https://doi.org/10.1145/2872427.2883037
18. Zhang, Z.: Improved Adam optimizer for deep neural networks. In: IWQoS, Banff, pp. 1–2. IEEE/ACM (2018). https://doi.org/10.1109/IWQoS.2018.8624183
19. Liu, W., Bao, Q., Sun, Y., Mei, T.: Recent advances in monocular 2D and 3D human pose estimation: a deep learning perspective. CoRR abs/2104.11536 (2021)
20. Lenz, D., Schulze, C., Guckert, M.: Real-time session-based recommendations using LSTM with neural embeddings. In: Kůrková, V., Manolopoulos, Y., Hammer, B., Iliadis, L., Maglogiannis, I. (eds.) ICANN 2018. LNCS, vol. 11140, pp. 337–348. Springer, Cham (2018). https://doi.org/10.1007/978-3-030-01421-6_33
21. Wang, J., Gao, N., Peng, J., Mo, J.: DCAR: deep collaborative autoencoder for recommendation with implicit feedback. In: Tetko, I.V., Kůrková, V., Karpov, P., Theis, F. (eds.) ICANN 2019. LNCS, vol. 11730, pp. 172–184. Springer, Cham (2019). https://doi.org/10.1007/978-3-030-30490-4_15
22. Liu, X., Liu, W., Zheng, J., Yan, C., Mei, T.: Beyond the parts: learning multi-view cross-part correlation for vehicle re-identification. In: MM, Seattle, pp. 907–915. ACM (2020). https://doi.org/10.1145/3394171.3413578

Say in Human-Like Way: Hierarchical Cross-modal Information Abstraction and Summarization for Controllable Captioning

Xiaoyi Wang and Jun Huang[(✉)]

Shanghai Advanced Research Institute, Chinese Academy of Sciences,
Shanghai, China
{wangxiaoyi2019,huangj}@sari.ac.cn

Abstract. Image captioning aims to generate proper textual sentences for an image. However, many existing captioning models explore information incompletely and generate coarse or even incorrect descriptions of region details. This paper proposes a controllable captioning approach called Say in Human-like Way (Shway), which exploits intra- and inter-modal information in vision and language hierarchically in a diamond shape with the control signal of image regions. Shway is divided into abstraction and summarization stages. It can adequately explore cross-modal information in the first stage and effectively summarize generated contexts with a novel fusion mechanism for making predictions in the second stage. Our experiments are conducted on COCO Entities and Flickr30k Entities. The results demonstrate that our proposed model achieves state-of-the-art performances compared with current methods in terms of controllable caption quality.

Keywords: Attention mechanism · Cross-modal information · Hierarchical LSTM · Image captioning

1 Introduction

Image captioning is an essential task in the interaction between computer vision and natural language. Moreover, it is also a fundamental step towards artificial intelligence as it combines image understanding and language generation. With the rapid development of deep learning, the encoder-decoder framework has been introduced to generate natural languages for images efficiently [2,16,17,28,32].

A modern solution is to utilize a convolutional neural network (CNN) as an encoder to extract the representation of images and a recurrent neural network (RNN) as a decoder to generate sentences for the images. However, despite encouraging success in image captioning, previous methods still suffer limitations such as generating coarse or even incorrect descriptions of region details,

This paper was supported by National Key R&D Program of China (2019YFC1521204).

© Springer Nature Switzerland AG 2021
I. Farkaš et al. (Eds.): ICANN 2021, LNCS 12891, pp. 217–228, 2021.
https://doi.org/10.1007/978-3-030-86362-3_18

reflecting that there is still room to explore and effectively utilize information adequately.

The attention mechanism has been proposed to trigger the interaction between visual content and natural sentence successfully [2,32]. However, intra-modal information of a single modality should also be exploited adequately to maintain the essential details. Meanwhile, unlike the Transformer-based method with a multi-head mechanism [26], many LSTM-based methods explore generated multi-modal representations from a single perspective. Limiting the width of exploiting intra- and inter-modal information may lead to inaccurate and coarse predictions.

In addition, most captioning models compress cross-modal representations into few context vectors to predict words [2,3,9,12,22,28]. Therefore, it is especially crucial to merge generated multi-modal representations into comprehensive, high-quality ones. However, many existing approaches directly input earlier cross-modal information into the last decoding unit and then predict words. The inadequate interaction between decoding units may limit the depth of multi-modal information mining. Also, the long chain of parameter optimization may overstress the last decoding unit and harm the deep network training procedure, resulting in performance degrading and generating inaccurate words.

When humans describe an image, we take visual contents from the visual system into the brain and combine them with existing semantic information. Then complex reasoning will be performed after extracting meaningful information. Finally, describing words for the image will be determined by summarizing all reasoned information. Inspired by the human captioning procedure and also to alleviate the problems mentioned above, we propose a hierarchical cross-modal information abstraction and summarization method called Say in Human-like Way (Shway), as is shown in the left part of Fig. 1. Taking visual contents with the control signal, Shway is built on a hierarchically recurrent architecture in a diamond shape, which increases the width and depth of the network to exploit intra- and inter-modal information from vision and language fully. The proposed model is divided into abstraction and summarization stages. In the abstraction stage, we design two branches with selective information input to emphasize language and vision separately. In the summarization stage, We introduce a novel fusion mechanism coupled with multi-LSTM to obtain comprehensive information from generated cross-modal representations for predicting words.

In summary, our main contributions are as follows:

- We propose a hierarchical controllable captioning method called Shway, which is in a diamond shape to exploit wider and deeper information for generating better descriptions.
- We model Shway from a cross-modal perspective to explore information adequately in vision and language. Specifically, two branches with selective information input are designed for two modalities severally.
- We introduce a novel fusion mechanism to couple with proposed architecture to utilize and merge information effectively for improving captioning performance.

2   Related Work

Image captioning has achieved significant improvements with the introduction of encoder-decoder framework in the recent years [2,3,28,32]. Mostly, a CNN is adopted as an encoder, e.g., ResNet-101 [12], and RNN or its variants are adopted as a decoder, e.g., GRU and LSTM.

Extensive works have been proposed on the RNN-based decoder in both network depth and width increments to exploit information fully. Attentive models are proposed to extract relevant auxiliary information from a grid of features or image regions at every step [2,32], or model a visual sentinel to adaptively guide the model in knowing when to look [16]. Then the two-layer LSTM structure is deployed for attention and language, respectively, and becomes popular [2,6,17]. To explore overall and salient information, Ge et al. [10] propose a bi-direction LSTM and cross-modal attention method. Moreover, three-layer LSTM structures are proposed to model a coarse-to-fine architecture or generate two words at one timestep [11,22].

From the point of depth increment of the network, a three-branch method taking the object, subject, and the union feature as inputs respectively is designed to model the relationship between the object and the subject [14]. Swell-and-Shrink [29] decomposes image captioning into dense captioning and text summarization tasks. Furthermore, basic operations, such as add, multiplication, and concatenation, are commonly used in existing models to fuse information. The Tree-LSTM unit is proposed to make connections between words in a sentence, which performs well on semantic relatedness prediction and sentiment classification tasks [25]. Early-fusion and late-fusion methods are proposed to merge the context of different units [33]. Also, the context gate projected from the main context is utilized by some approaches to merge contexts from different units [9,30,31].

In addition, controllable image captioning with designated control signals is proposed recently to make captioning more controllable, interpretable, and easier. Some captioning methods have conditioned the generation with a specific style or sentiment [8,18,19]. To generate more diverse or grained captioning, some methods are proposed with Part-of-Speech (POS) syntax, region control signals, and abstracted scene graph [5–7].

Our work is based on *Show, control and tell* [6], which is denoted as SCT for simply. SCT mainly introduces the region control signal into the captioning and builds the entities dataset where entity mentions in the caption are linked with one or more corresponding bounding boxes in the image. It forces the model to focus on different visual contents at different time steps by a Chunk-shifting gate. Unlike the two-layer LSTM structure in SCT, our framework employs additional LSTM to process the visual modality sequence to better use the sequence information of image regions.

Moreover, to extract auxiliary information for word selection and inspired by Tree-LSTM and the context gate mentioned above, we design a novel fusion mechanism to couple with the proposed architecture. The Tree-LSTM unit contains one forget gate for each child, which aims to learn syntactic properties

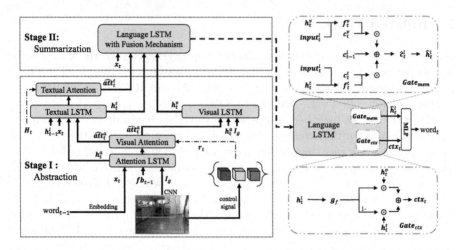

Fig. 1. The framework of our proposed method Shway, which is divided into abstraction stage and summarization stage. h_t^i, c_t^i indicates outputs of the LSTM i at timestep t, and $\hat{att}_t^j$ is the output of attention mechanism j at time step t. fb_{t-1} is the concatenation of previous hidden states h_{t-1}^v, h_{t-1}^l and visual attention att_{t-1}^a. $input_t^l$ is the concatenation of x_t, h_t^v, h_t^l and $\hat{att}_t^t$.

of natural language. We employ similar forget gates to extract generated cross-modal information for language generation.

3 Method

3.1 Overview

Our proposed method models captioning from a cross-modal perspective hierarchically and consists of two stages, as illustrated in Fig. 1.

The abstraction stage is implemented by two layers. In the first layer, attention LSTM $LSTM_{att}$ and visual attention Att_{vis} are employed to obtain the basic context and the visual attention, respectively. And in the second layer, intra-modal information of image or text and outputs from the first layer are fed into visual LSTM $LSTM_{vis}$ and textual LSTM $LSTM_{text}$, respectively. Further more, a textual attention Att_{text} is employed to acquire textual attention.

In the summarization stage, language LSTM $LSTM_{lan}$ is utilized for preliminarily fusing generated information. Then a novel fusion mechanism contains two gate mechanisms is designed to summarize generated contexts. The context gate mechanism $Gate_{ctx}$ is to extract complementary information, and the memory gate mechanism $Gate_{mem}$ is to exploit interactions between decoding units. Finally, word prediction is made with the summarized information.

Given an image I and ground-truth caption $w = [w_1, w_2, ..., w_L]$, $R = [r_1, r_2, ..., r_M]$ is a sequence of a set of extracted region features from the image I, where r_i is switched by the Chunk-shifting gate [6]. Specifically,

$r_i = [r_i^1, r_i^2, ..., r_i^n]$ is a set of region features related to the i-th noun chunk of caption and n is the number of the related regions. Our goal is to generate a sentence $y = [y_1, y_2, ..., y_L]$ which describes the image regions in turn correctly while maintaining the fluency of language, and L is the length of sequence. Following the standard learning paradigm, we learn parameter θ of our model by maximizing the likelihood of the correct caption:

$$\theta^* = \arg\max_{\theta} \sum_{(I,y)} \log p(y|R, I; \theta) \tag{1}$$

$$\log p(y|R, I; \theta) = \prod_{t=1}^{L} \log p(y_t|y_{1:t-1}, r_t, I) \tag{2}$$

where $y_{1:t-1}$ is the slice from 1 to $(t-1)$ elements of y.

3.2 Cross-modal Information Abstraction

At the t-th time step, given the word input w_{t-1}, previous generated contexts and the chosen set of region features r_t, the abstraction stage aims to extract cross-modal information adequately.

First, current word w_{t-1} is embedded into the embedding vector x_t and image descriptor I_g is defined as the average feature of all the image regions as [2]. $LSTM_{att}$ takes the concatenation of previous hidden state h_{t-1}^v from $LSTM_{vis}$, previous hidden state h_{t-1}^l from $LSTM_{lan}$, previous visual attention att_{t-1}^c, image descriptor I_g, as well as the word embedding x_t as input: $input_t^a = [h_{t-1}^v; h_{t-1}^l; att_{t-1}^a; I_g; x_t]$, where [;] indicates concatenation. And we denote the current hidden state of $LSTM_{att}$ as h_t^a.

Following [16], we employ a visual sentinel denoted as s_t that models a component of memory in the visual attention mechanism Att_{vis}. Attention is computed on extracted current regions r_t and the sentinel s_t with query h_t^a:

$$\alpha_t^a = softmax([w^T \tanh(W_{ah} h_t^a + W_{as} s_t); v_t^a]) \tag{3}$$

$$v_t^a = w^T \tanh((W_{ah} h_t^a)\mathbf{1} + W_{ar} r_t), att_t^a = \alpha_{t,1}^a s_t + \sum_{i=2}^{n+1} \alpha_{t,i}^a r_t^{i-1} \tag{4}$$

where α_t^a is the attention weight and att_t^a denotes visual attention result. $\alpha_{t,1}^a$ is the weight of sentinel, and $\alpha_{t,i}^a$, where $i = \{2, 3, ..., n+1\}$, is the attention weight for image regions. W_{ar}, W_{ah} and W_{as} are learnable parameters, and w^T is a row vector, and $\mathbf{1}$ is a vector with all elements set to 1. Furthermore, we model a visual attention context $\hat{att}_t^a$ by simply employing a fully-connected layer whose input is the concatenation of att_{t-1}^a and att_t^a.

Then, to explore information further from vision and language, selective information extraction are realized by setting different inputs for $LSTM_{text}$ and $LSTM_{vis}$: $input_t^t = [h_t^a; h_{t-1}^l; \hat{att}_t^a; x_t]$ and $input_t^v = [h_t^a; \hat{att}_t^a; I_g]$. The hidden states of these two LSTM are denoted as h_t^t and h_t^v, memory cells are denoted as c_t^t and c_t^v. And text attention mechanism $\boldsymbol{Att}_{text}$ is employed after $\boldsymbol{LSTM}_{text}$ to merge generated semantic information:

$$\boldsymbol{u}_t^t = \boldsymbol{w}^T \tanh((\boldsymbol{W}_{th}\boldsymbol{h}_t^t)\boldsymbol{1} + \boldsymbol{W}_{tH}\boldsymbol{H}_t)$$

$$\boldsymbol{\beta}_t^t = \text{softmax}(\boldsymbol{u}_t^t), \boldsymbol{att}_t^t = \sum_{i=1}^{L}\boldsymbol{\beta}_{t,i}^t\boldsymbol{h}_i^l \tag{5}$$

where $\boldsymbol{\beta}_t^t$ is the attention weight and $\boldsymbol{att}_t^t$ denotes visual attention result. $\boldsymbol{H}_t = [\boldsymbol{h}_1^l, \boldsymbol{h}_2^l, ..., \boldsymbol{h}_L^l]$ is a set of hidden states of $\boldsymbol{LSTM}_{lan}$, and its last $L-t+1$ vectors in are set to full of zero elements as we cannot get word information of the future. And $\boldsymbol{W}_{tH}$ and $\boldsymbol{W}_{th}$ are learnable parameters. To learn the relationship between previous and current textual attention results implicitly, we also model a textual attention context $\hat{\boldsymbol{att}}_t^t$ as the visual one by a fully-connected layer.

3.3   Summarizing with Fusion Mechanism

The summarization stage aims to summarize generated contexts for prediction and is implemented with two steps.

First we update $\boldsymbol{LSTM}_{lan}$ with taking inputs $\boldsymbol{input}_t^l = [\boldsymbol{h}_t^v; \boldsymbol{h}_t^t; \hat{\boldsymbol{att}}_t^t; \boldsymbol{x}_t]$ to obtain its outputs,e.g., hidden state $\boldsymbol{h}_t^l$ and memory cell $\boldsymbol{c}_t^l$.

As we have mentioned in Sect. 1, it is crucial for predicting proper words to guarantee the quality of compressed context vectors. At the same time, besides being used as inputs, outputs from the first stage can provide rich auxiliary contexts and suggestions on maintaining or forgetting information. Therefore in the second step, a fusion mechanism which consists of Context Gate Mechanism $\boldsymbol{Gate}_{ctx}$ and Memory Gate Mechanism $\boldsymbol{Gate}_{mem}$, is designed to exploit auxiliary information.

Context Gate Mechanism. To extract complementary information, we revisit information generated before by projecting $\boldsymbol{h}_t^l$ into a context gate, as the bottom right part of Fig. 1 shows.

$$\boldsymbol{g}_l = \sigma(\boldsymbol{W}_{lg}\boldsymbol{h}_t^l), \boldsymbol{ctx}_t = (1 - \boldsymbol{g}_l) \odot \boldsymbol{h}_t^t + \boldsymbol{g}_l \odot \boldsymbol{h}_t^v \tag{6}$$

where σ represents sigmoid function, $\odot$ represents the Hadamard element-wise product and $\boldsymbol{W}_{lg}$ is learnable parameter. As $\boldsymbol{g}_l$ is in the range of $[0, 1]$, information from $\boldsymbol{LSTM}_{text}$ and $\boldsymbol{LSTM}_{vis}$ is balanced adaptively.

Memory Gate Mechanism. Inspired by Tree-LSTM [25], we interact parent $\boldsymbol{LSTM}_{lan}$ with its children $\boldsymbol{LSTM}_{vis}$ and $\boldsymbol{LSTM}_{text}$ by learning two forgetting gates individually, as the top right part of Fig. 1 shows.

$$\boldsymbol{f}_t^t = \sigma(\boldsymbol{W}_f\boldsymbol{input}_t^l + \boldsymbol{U}_f\boldsymbol{h}_t^t)$$

$$\boldsymbol{f}_t^v = \sigma(\boldsymbol{W}_f\boldsymbol{input}_t^l + \boldsymbol{U}_f\boldsymbol{h}_t^v) \tag{7}$$

where $\boldsymbol{W}_f$ and $\boldsymbol{U}_f$ are learnable matrices. Then the memory cell of $\boldsymbol{LSTM}_{lan}$ is updated by:

$$\hat{\boldsymbol{c}}_{t-1}^l = \boldsymbol{c}_{t-1}^l + \boldsymbol{f}_t^t \odot \boldsymbol{c}_t^t + \boldsymbol{f}_t^v \odot \boldsymbol{c}_t^v \tag{8}$$

The new hidden state $\hat{h}_t^l$ will be obtained by updating $\boldsymbol{LSTM_{lan}}$ with refined $\hat{c}_{t-1}^l$. And word probability distribution is computed by a softmax function:

$$p(y_{t+1}|y_t) = softmax(\boldsymbol{W}_{out}[\boldsymbol{ctx}_t; \hat{\boldsymbol{h}}_t^l] + \boldsymbol{b}_{out}) \tag{9}$$

where $\boldsymbol{W}_{out}$ and $\boldsymbol{b}_{out}$ are matrices of learnable weights.

This fusion mechanism applies to binary tree LSTM structure and even more complex tree-structure models. It is beneficial to extract auxiliary information like interactions among units for generating better captions. Experiments show that the proposed fusion mechanism improves model performance significantly.

Additionally, we also utilize the similar chunk-shifting gate to switch regions as [6]. Differently, we represent current visual content by hidden state $\boldsymbol{h}_t^v$ from $\boldsymbol{LSTM_{vis}}$ to compute the attention score, rather than the one from attention LSTM. This procedure is formulated as follows:

$$\boldsymbol{s}_{gate} = \tanh(\boldsymbol{c}_t^v) \odot \sigma(W_{ig}\boldsymbol{input}_t^a + W_{hg}\boldsymbol{h}_t^v) \tag{10}$$

$$gate_{chunk} = \boldsymbol{w}^T \tanh(\boldsymbol{W}_{ga}\boldsymbol{s}_{gate} + \boldsymbol{W}_{ah}\boldsymbol{h}_t^v) \tag{11}$$

$$p(g_t = 1|\boldsymbol{R}) = \frac{\exp gate_{chunk}}{\exp gate_{chunk} + \exp \sum_{i=2}^{n+1} \boldsymbol{\alpha}_{t,i}^a} \tag{12}$$

When $g_t = 1$, the current region set $\boldsymbol{r}_t = \boldsymbol{r}_i$ from $\boldsymbol{R}$ will be shifted into the next one, e.g., $\boldsymbol{r}_{t+1} = \boldsymbol{r}_{i+1}$, and $\boldsymbol{r}_{t+1} = \boldsymbol{r}_i$ otherwise. This gating mechanism forces the model to focus on different visual contents corresponding to different noun chunk in order, which realizes the control over captioning.

3.4 Training and Inference

Given a sequence of the set of image regions $\boldsymbol{R}$, chunk-shifting gate values $g_{1:L}^*$ and ground truth sentence $\boldsymbol{w}$, we utilize cross-entropy loss and CIDEr reinforcement learning to train our model as [6]. For cross-entropy loss which is on word-level and chunk-level, is defined as:

$$
\begin{aligned}
L_{XE}(\theta) = -\sum_{t=1}^{L} \Big(&\log p(w_t|\boldsymbol{w}_{1:t-1}, \boldsymbol{r}_{1:t}) \\
&+ \lambda g_t^* \log p(g_t = 1|\boldsymbol{w}_{1:t-1}, \boldsymbol{r}_{1:t}) \\
&+ (1 - g_t^*)(1 - \log p(g_t^*|\boldsymbol{w}_{1:t-1}, \boldsymbol{r}_{1:t})) \Big)
\end{aligned} \tag{13}
$$

where λ is a trade-off parameter. And for the CIDEr objective function, the negative expectation score is defined as:

$$L_{RL}(\theta) = -E_{w^s \sim p\theta}[r(w^s) + r(g^s)] \tag{14}$$

where r is the CIDEr score function, w^s and g^s are sampled sentence and gate sequence.

In training, the current image region set $\boldsymbol{r}_t$ and word input w_t, are the ground-truth region set and word at timestep t. In testing, the choice of $\boldsymbol{r}_t$ is driven by the chunk-shifting gate, and w_t is sampled from the last prediction by model.

Table 1. Performances on the COCO Entities test split. B4 is short for BLEU-4, M is short for METEOR, R is short for ROUGE-L, C is short for CIDEr, S is short for SPICE. The [†] marker indicates non-controllable methods.

Methods	B4	M	R	C	S	NW
FC-2K[†] [24]	10.4	17.3	36.8	98.3	25.2	0.257
UpDown[†] [2]	12.9	19.3	40.0	119.9	29.3	0.296
NBT[†] [17]	12.9	19.2	40.4	120.2	29.5	0.305
C-LSTM [6]	11.4	18.1	38.5	106.8	27.6	0.275
C-UpDown [6]	17.3	23.0	46.7	161.0	39.1	0.396
SCT [6]	20.9	24.4	52.5	193.0	45.3	0.508
Shway	**21.7**	**25.3**	**53.4**	**201.2**	**46.0**	**0.533**

4   Experiments

4.1   Datasets, Metrics and Experimental Setting

Our experiments are conducted on two image captioning datasets, COCO Entities [6], and Flickr30k Entities [21], which are extracted from MSCOCO and Flickr30k, respectively. MSCOCO has 123,000 images, and Flickr30k has 31,000 images, where each image is paired with five captions. Compared to the original datasets, image regions extracted from the detector are associated with noun chunks, and region sequence is provided for each image-caption pair in Entities datasets. The numbers of train/val/test captions in COCO Entities are 545,202, 7,818 and 7,797. For Flickr30k Entities, those are 144,256, 5,053 and 4,982. Both datasets followed the publicly available splits in [13].

We evaluate our captioning systems simultaneously with several automatic evaluation metrics, namely BLEU-4 from BLEU [20], METEOR [4], CIDEr [27], SPICE [1], and ROUGE [15]. Moreover, we also utilize NW from [6] to test the alignment score of nouns between generated and ground truth sentences.

In our experiments, visual features are extracted by Faster R-CNN [23] with ResNet-101 [12] for image regions, and feature dimension is set to 2048. The dimensions of LSTM layers and attention layers are set to 1000 and 512, respectively. The vocabulary size of COCO Entities is 9,883, and that of Flickr30k Entities is 7,537, and word embedding size is set to 1000.

4.2   Experimental Results and Analysis

Quantitative Analysis. For evaluation of methods on COCO Entities test datasets in Table 1, we compare our model (referred to as **Shway**) with the current controllable methods and conventional methods without any control signals like region sequence. **SCT** [6] employs a two-layer LSTM structure with designed visual sentinel as decoder and shifts regions given a sequence of regions by a gate shift mechanism to control captioning. **Shway** utilizes the same control signal

Table 2. Ablation studies on COCO Entities test split.

Methods	B4	M	R	C	S	NW
v-Shway	20.8	24.7	52.9	194.0	45.5	0.522
t-Shway $w/o\ fm$	20.8	24.5	52.1	191.6	44.8	0.508
t-Shway $w/o\ g_{ctx}$	21.0	24.7	52.7	193.8	45.4	0.511
t-Shway $w/o\ g_{mem}$	21.2	24.6	52.7	194.5	45.1	0.502
t-Shway	21.4	24.9	52.8	196.4	45.6	0.513
Shway $w/o\ fm$	20.9	24.6	52.7	193.6	45.3	0.515
Shway $w/o\ g_{ctx}$	21.2	24.8	52.9	197.3	45.6	0.510
Shway $w/o\ g_{mem}$	21.4	24.8	52.8	198.3	45.7	0.515
Shway	**21.7**	**25.3**	**53.4**	**201.2**	**46.0**	**0.533**

Table 3. Performances on the Flickr30k Entities Karpathy test split.

Methods	Cross-entropy loss						CIDEr optimization					
	B4	M	R	C	S	NW	B4	M	R	C	S	NW
C-LSTM [6]	6.5	12.0	29.6	40.4	15.7	0.078	6.7	12.1	30.0	45.5	15.8	0.079
C-UpDown [6]	10.1	15.2	34.9	69.2	21.6	0.158	10.1	14.8	35.0	69.3	21.2	0.148
SCT [6]	11.3	15.4	**36.9**	74.5	**23.4**	0.152	12.4	16.6	38.8	83.7	23.5	0.221
Shway	**11.5**	**15.9**	**36.9**	**76.3**	22.8	**0.163**	**12.9**	**16.9**	**39.3**	**88.2**	**23.6**	**0.239**

as SCT does, and defines the gate shift mechanism differently with hidden state from $LSTM_{vis}$ as visual content guider rather than $LSTM_{att}$ in SCT. Under cross-entropy loss, Shway overpasses all other works in terms of all metrics and especially improves 8.2% in terms of the CIDEr metric compared to SCT, which shows that our proposed method can capture critical information better.

To testify the effectiveness of exploring cross-modal information with designed two branches, we perform several ablation studies by comparing different variants of Shway in Table 2. We ablate our model by removing $LSTM_{text}$ or $LSTM_{vis}$, and replace their outputs by the ones from $LSTM_{att}$, and name the variants as **v-Shway** and **t-Shway** respectively. The comparisons between experimental results of v-Shway, t-Shway and Shway, show that Shway can achieve better performance on all evaluation metrics and prove that exploring information from cross-modal can achieve better performances. Especially, removing $LSTM_{text}$ decreases the performance of the model significantly, which proves the importance of language information.

To investigate contributions of $Gate_{mem}$ and $Gate_{ctx}$, we perform ablation studies by comparing different variants of t-Shway and Shway in Table 2. Firstly, we denote the model without fusion mechanism as $w/o\ fm$. Then we extend experiments with additionally employing $Gate_{mem}$ and $Gate_{ctx}$ individually and denote the variants as $w/o\ g_{ctx}$ and $w/o\ g_{mem}$ respectively. The results indicate that incorporating both gates can lead to performance improvements, and their effects can be stacked.

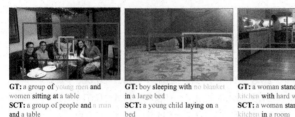

GT: a group of young men and women sitting at a table
SCT: a group of people and a man and a table
Ours: a group of men and women sitting at a table

GT: boy sleeping with no blanket in a large bed
SCT: a young child laying on a bed
Ours: a little boy sleeping on a pillow on a bed

GT: a woman standing in a kitchen with hard wood floors
SCT: a woman standing in a kitchen in a room
Ours: a woman in a kitchen standing on a hardwood floor

GT: a plate with a sandwich and a pickle
SCT: a plate of sandwiches with a pickle
Ours: a white plate topped with sandwiches and a pickle

Fig. 2. Examples of generated captions. Different colors show the associations between regions and noun chunks.

In Table 3, we compare Shway with the current state-of-the-art methods for evaluation on Flickr30k Entities. Under cross-entropy loss, it can be seen that the proposed captioning model achieves better performance in terms of most metrics. To validate the effectiveness of our proposed model further, we train Shway under CIDEr reinforcement learning. Our model outperforms those works in all metrics and significantly improves 4.5% in terms of the CIDEr metric compared with SCT, which approves that Shway is more effective for captioning.

Qualitative Analysis. We visualize some examples of our model compared to the reference and SCT under cross-entropy loss on the COCO Entities test split. As Fig. 2 shows, both models can generate fluent and descriptive sentences of the image. However, our approach has a stronger ability to capture more information in detail and generate higher-quality descriptions.

5   Conclusion

In this paper, we propose the Say in Human-like Way approach for image captioning. Our model is built on a hierarchically recurrent architecture for controllable captioning. It is in a diamond shape and consists of abstraction and summarization stages. The real power of our model lies in its ability to exploit intra- and inter-modal information adequately in vision and language for higher quality captions. The proposed method is shown to improve image captioning performance on COCO and Flickr30k Entities. It will be interesting to apply the interaction method in our model to more cross-modal tasks such as visual question answering.

References

1. Anderson, P., Fernando, B., Johnson, M., Gould, S.: SPICE: semantic propositional image caption evaluation. In: Leibe, B., Matas, J., Sebe, N., Welling, M. (eds.) ECCV 2016. LNCS, vol. 9909, pp. 382–398. Springer, Cham (2016). https://doi.org/10.1007/978-3-319-46454-1_24

2. Anderson, P., et al.: Bottom-up and top-down attention for image captioning and visual question answering. In: Proceedings of the IEEE Conference on Computer Vision and Pattern Recognition, pp. 6077–6086 (2018)

3. Bahdanau, D., Cho, K., Bengio, Y.: Neural machine translation by jointly learning to align and translate. arXiv preprint arXiv:1409.0473 (2014)

4. Banerjee, S., Lavie, A.: METEOR: an automatic metric for MT evaluation with improved correlation with human judgments. In: Proceedings of the ACL Workshop on Intrinsic and Extrinsic Evaluation Measures for Machine Translation and/or Summarization, pp. 65–72 (2005)

5. Chen, S., Jin, Q., Wang, P., Wu, Q.: Say as you wish: fine-grained control of image caption generation with abstract scene graphs. In: Proceedings of the IEEE/CVF Conference on Computer Vision and Pattern Recognition, pp. 9962–9971 (2020)

6. Cornia, M., Baraldi, L., Cucchiara, R.: Show, control and tell: a framework for generating controllable and grounded captions. In: Proceedings of the IEEE/CVF Conference on Computer Vision and Pattern Recognition, pp. 8307–8316 (2019)

7. Deshpande, A., Aneja, J., Wang, L., Schwing, A.G., Forsyth, D.: Fast, diverse and accurate image captioning guided by part-of-speech. In: Proceedings of the IEEE/CVF Conference on Computer Vision and Pattern Recognition, pp. 10695–10704 (2019)

8. Gan, C., Gan, Z., He, X., Gao, J., Deng, L.: StyleNet: generating attractive visual captions with styles. In: Proceedings of the IEEE Conference on Computer Vision and Pattern Recognition, pp. 3137–3146 (2017)

9. Gao, L., Li, X., Song, J., Shen, H.T.: Hierarchical LSTMs with adaptive attention for visual captioning. IEEE Trans. Pattern Anal. Mach. Intell. **42**, 1112–1131 (2019)

10. Ge, H., Yan, Z., Zhang, K., Zhao, M., Sun, L.: Exploring overall contextual information for image captioning in human-like cognitive style. In: Proceedings of the IEEE/CVF International Conference on Computer Vision, pp. 1754–1763 (2019)

11. Gu, J., Cai, J., Wang, G., Chen, T.: Stack-captioning: coarse-to-fine learning for image captioning. In: Proceedings of the AAAI Conference on Artificial Intelligence, vol. 32 (2018)

12. He, K., Zhang, X., Ren, S., Sun, J.: Deep residual learning for image recognition. In: Proceedings of the IEEE Conference on Computer Vision and Pattern Recognition, pp. 770–778 (2016)

13. Karpathy, A., Fei-Fei, L.: Deep visual-semantic alignments for generating image descriptions. In: Proceedings of the IEEE Conference on Computer Vision and Pattern Recognition, pp. 3128–3137 (2015)

14. Kim, D.J., Choi, J., Oh, T.H., Kweon, I.S.: Dense relational captioning: triple-stream networks for relationship-based captioning. In: Proceedings of the IEEE/CVF Conference on Computer Vision and Pattern Recognition, pp. 6271–6280 (2019)

15. Lin, C.Y.: ROUGE: a package for automatic evaluation of summaries. In: Text Summarization Branches Out, pp. 74–81 (2004)

16. Lu, J., Xiong, C., Parikh, D., Socher, R.: Knowing when to look: adaptive attention via a visual sentinel for image captioning. In: Proceedings of the IEEE Conference on Computer Vision and Pattern Recognition, pp. 375–383 (2017)

17. Lu, J., Yang, J., Batra, D., Parikh, D.: Neural baby talk. In: Proceedings of the IEEE Conference on Computer Vision and Pattern Recognition, pp. 7219–7228 (2018)

18. Mathews, A., Xie, L., He, X.: SentiCap: generating image descriptions with sentiments. In: Proceedings of the AAAI Conference on Artificial Intelligence, vol. 30 (2016)

19. Mathews, A., Xie, L., He, X.: SemStyle: learning to generate stylised image captions using unaligned text. In: Proceedings of the IEEE Conference on Computer Vision and Pattern Recognition, pp. 8591–8600 (2018)

20. Papineni, K., Roukos, S., Ward, T., Zhu, W.J.: BLEU: a method for automatic evaluation of machine translation. In: Proceedings of the 40th Annual Meeting of the Association for Computational Linguistics, pp. 311–318 (2002)

21. Plummer, B.A., Wang, L., Cervantes, C.M., Caicedo, J.C., Hockenmaier, J., Lazebnik, S.: Flickr30k Entities: collecting region-to-phrase correspondences for richer image-to-sentence models. In: Proceedings of the IEEE International Conference on Computer Vision, pp. 2641–2649 (2015)

22. Qin, Y., Du, J., Zhang, Y., Lu, H.: Look back and predict forward in image captioning. In: Proceedings of the IEEE/CVF Conference on Computer Vision and Pattern Recognition, pp. 8367–8375 (2019)

23. Ren, S., He, K., Girshick, R., Sun, J.: Faster R-CNN: towards real-time object detection with region proposal networks. arXiv preprint arXiv:1506.01497 (2015)

24. Rennie, S.J., Marcheret, E., Mroueh, Y., Ross, J., Goel, V.: Self-critical sequence training for image captioning. In: Proceedings of the IEEE Conference on Computer Vision and Pattern Recognition, pp. 7008–7024 (2017)

25. Tai, K.S., Socher, R., Manning, C.D.: Improved semantic representations from tree-structured long short-term memory networks. arXiv preprint arXiv:1503.00075 (2015)

26. Vaswani, A., et al.: Attention is all you need. In: Guyon, I., et al. (eds.) Advances in Neural Information Processing Systems, vol. 30. Curran Associates, Inc. (2017)

27. Vedantam, R., Lawrence Zitnick, C., Parikh, D.: CIDEr: consensus-based image description evaluation. In: Proceedings of the IEEE Conference on Computer Vision and Pattern Recognition, pp. 4566–4575 (2015)

28. Vinyals, O., Toshev, A., Bengio, S., Erhan, D.: Show and tell: a neural image caption generator. In: Proceedings of the IEEE Conference on Computer Vision and Pattern Recognition, pp. 3156–3164 (2015)

29. Wang, H., Wang, H., Xu, K.: Swell-and-shrink: decomposing image captioning by transformation and summarization. In: IJCAI, pp. 5226–5232 (2019)

30. Wang, W., Chen, Z., Hu, H.: Hierarchical attention network for image captioning. In: Proceedings of the AAAI Conference on Artificial Intelligence, vol. 33, pp. 8957–8964 (2019)

31. Xiao, H., Shi, J.: Video captioning with text-based dynamic attention and step-by-step learning. Pattern Recogn. Lett. **133**, 305–312 (2020)

32. Xu, K., et al.: Show, attend and tell: neural image caption generation with visual attention. In: International Conference on Machine Learning, pp. 2048–2057. PMLR (2015)

33. Yang, L., Tang, K., Yang, J., Li, L.J.: Dense captioning with joint inference and visual context. In: Proceedings of the IEEE Conference on Computer Vision and Pattern Recognition, pp. 2193–2202 (2017)

DAEMA: Denoising Autoencoder with Mask Attention

Simon Tihon⬤, Muhammad Usama Javaid$^{(\boxtimes)}$⬤, Damien Fourure⬤,
Nicolas Posocco⬤, and Thomas Peel⬤

EURA NOVA, Mont-St-Guibert, Belgium
{simon.tihon,muhammad.javaid,damien.fourure,nicolas.posocco,
thomas.peel}@euranova.eu

Abstract. Missing data is a recurrent and challenging problem, especially when using machine learning algorithms for real-world applications. For this reason, missing data imputation has become an active research area, in which recent deep learning approaches have achieved state-of-the-art results. We propose DAEMA (*Denoising Autoencoder with Mask Attention*), an algorithm based on a denoising autoencoder architecture with an attention mechanism. While most imputation algorithms use incomplete inputs as they would use complete data - up to basic preprocessing (e.g. mean imputation) - DAEMA leverages a mask-based attention mechanism to focus on the observed values of its inputs. We evaluate DAEMA both in terms of reconstruction capabilities and downstream prediction and show that it achieves superior performance to state-of-the-art algorithms on several publicly available real-world datasets under various missingness settings.

1 Introduction

Machine learning researchers and practitioners frequently encounter the problem of missing data. Data can be missing for many reasons. These include system failures, loss of data, or the fact that data was never known, measured or recorded. Missing data can introduce bias and alter the statistical properties of a dataset. This can impact the performance of models learnt from this data, both in obvious (e.g. poor performance due to lack of data) or subtle (e.g. a bias is learnt) ways. Simple approaches consist in discarding samples with missing data, removing an entire feature if it is too often missing or imputing the mean/median value per feature. In practice, these provide a satisfying solution when a small proportion of the data is missing. Otherwise, it is likely to significantly alter the empirical data distribution.

Missing data imputation has received a lot of attention and many approaches have been proposed recently [9,12,21]. The literature can be divided into two

---

S. Tihon and M. U. Javaid—Equal contribution.

I. Farkaš et al. (Eds.): ICANN 2021, LNCS 12891, pp. 229–240, 2021.
https://doi.org/10.1007/978-3-030-86362-3_19

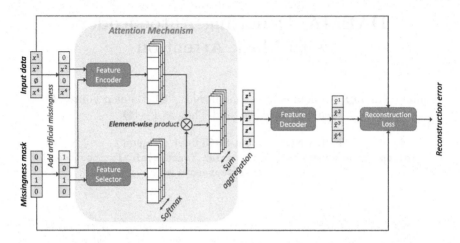

Fig. 1. The goal of DAEMA is to produce a representation of the input which is robust to missingness, so that a *Feature Decoder* can impute the missing data from it. To do so, a *Feature Encoder* produces multiple values for each latent feature. These are then weighted by a *Feature Selector* based on the missingness mask. This mask enables the attention mechanism to focus on the values that are produced using only observed inputs.

categories: discriminative and generative approaches. Discriminative approaches model the conditional probability of each feature given the others. That is, they use all features but one to impute the remaining feature, and iterate over all features to produce a complete dataset. On the other hand, generative approaches model the joint distribution of all features to impute missing data all at once.

Generative approaches for missing data imputation generally involve some form of denoising autoencoder [19]. A denoising autoencoder deals with noise, taking noisy samples as input and learning to reconstruct the cleaned samples. As missing data is a special case of noisy data, a denoising autoencoder can be used to reconstruct the missing parts.

Attention is a very popular technique in the fields of natural language processing and computer vision. Introduced in [18], attention mechanisms can be summed up as paying attention to parts of the input which are relevant to generate an output. Attention enables a model to understand the underlying structure of data better, resulting in better generalisation [21].

To leverage this promising technique, we propose DAEMA (*Denoising Autoencoder with Mask Attention*). It improves on a simple yet efficient denoising autoencoder architecture by adding an attention mechanism based on the missingness mask. Its architecture can be seen in Fig. 1. Thanks to a mask-based attention module, the latent representation produced by DAEMA is a missingness-robust embedding of the original sample. This approach achieves good performance with both randomly and systematically missing data, beating previous state-of-the-art techniques.

2   Related Work

Early approaches have modelled the task of missing data imputation as a predictive task. These are referred to as discriminative approaches. Some of them are based on k-nearest neighbours [17] and support vector techniques [20], using models whose capacity is often insufficient for the task. Others are iterative, such as MissForest [16] and Multiple Imputation using Chained Equation (MICE) [1], which respectively use random forests and linear regressors to predict missing values for one feature at a time. Both approaches impute a same dataset several times, using the previous result to compute the next one more precisely. Since they produce multiple imputation of said dataset, these are referred to as multiple-imputation methods. Having multiple-imputed datasets can be an advantage as it helps to account for the uncertainty in the imputation process. However, these iterative methods are meant to impute whole datasets at once. This can be a drawback in real-world situations, where new data comes everyday.

Due to recent advances in deep learning and more particularly in generative deep-learning, more recent works have modelled the task of missing data imputation as a generative task. The resulting methods are referred to as generative approaches. One such method is called Multiple Imputation using Denoising Autoencoders (MIDA) [4]. It applies the denoising autoencoder approach to missing data imputation. Another method, called Generative Adversarial Imputation Nets (GAIN) [22], leverages a conditional GAN [5] to learn the real distribution of data through adversarial training. However, GANs are known to be hard to train, suffering from non-convergence and mode collapse. WGAN-GP [6] refines GANs to overcome these problems and ensure better training. Other methods, such as VAE [8] and HI-VAE [10], use a variational autoencoder architecture. More recently, MCFlow [12] leverages normalising flows and Monte Carlo sampling for imputation. Finally, GINN [15] exploits graph convolutional networks to take advantage of the information contained in the nearest neighbours at imputation time instead of using only the information contained in each sample being imputed.

A recent deep-learning discriminative method, AimNet [21], achieves state-of-the-art results with a dot-product attention mechanism applied to the individual embedding of each feature. Its attention weights depend only on which feature is being imputed.

Finally, some variants of existing methods have been proposed. In [2], embeddings for categorical input features and gumbel-softmax activation layers for categorical output features are successfully applied to GAIN and to a VAE architecture. In [9], the optimal transport distance between two batches is proposed to be used as a training loss for missing data imputation models. These approaches are complementary to our method.

We propose DAEMA, a generative method based on a denoising autoencoder and an attention mechanism. In contrast to AimNet, our attention mechanism is input-oriented: the attention weights of DAEMA depend on which feature values are missing instead of depending on which feature we want to impute. Therefore, the model can focus on non-missing values and distinguish them from placeholder values. To our knowledge, DAEMA is the first method to use an input-oriented attention mechanism for the imputation problem.

3   Problem Statement

A dataset is defined as $D = \{\mathbf{X}, C, N\}$. $\mathbf{X} \in \mathbb{R}^{n \times d}$ is a matrix of data composed of n samples of d features $\mathbf{x}_i = (x_i^1, \ldots, x_i^d) \in \mathbb{R}^d$. C (resp. N) is the set of indices of categorical (resp. numerical) features, that is, features taking discrete (resp. continuous) values. In this work, in order to keep the loss and metrics simple, we focus on datasets containing only numerical features, i.e. $C = \emptyset$.

For the missing data imputation task, a dataset with missing values in $\mathbf{X}$ is given. We define the missingness-mask matrix $\mathbf{M} \in \{0, 1\}^{n \times d}$ such that x_i^j is missing if and only if $m_i^j = 1$. We denote $D^* = \{\mathbf{X}^*, C, N\}$ the ground truth dataset without missing data. Missing data are generally classified into three different categories [13, 14]:

- Missing completely at random (MCAR) means the probability that a value is missing does not depend on any value in the dataset.
- Missing at random (MAR) means the probability that a value is missing depends only on the observed (non-missing) values.
- Missing not at random (MNAR) means the probability that a value is missing depends on unobserved values or latent variables.

We are interested in learning an imputation function $f : \mathbb{R}^d \times \{0, 1\}^d \rightarrow \mathbb{R}^d; (\mathbf{x}, \mathbf{m}) \mapsto f(\mathbf{x}, \mathbf{m})$. Using the dataset D and the corresponding missingness-mask matrix $\mathbf{M}$, the goal is to find the best function $f^\dagger$ minimizing a reconstruction metric and a metric based on a downstream machine-learning task as described in Sect. 6.2.

4   Our Approach

Figure 1 shows the architecture of DAEMA, which is based on a standard denoising autoencoder. At its core is a mask-based attention mechanism, designed to help the network efficiently use the available data to produce robust latent representations. This in turn makes imputation possible by decoding these very representations.

4.1   Denoising Autoencoder

As a denoising autoencoder, DAEMA takes a noisy input sample $\mathbf{x}$ and produces a clean version $\hat{\mathbf{x}}$ of it. In our case, noise is defined as missingness of data, meaning that ground truth values of the missing data are unknown. It is trained using additional *artificial missingness* in each batch, as the values of the missing features are needed to train the network. As it is impossible for the model to distinguish between originally missing values and artificially missing values, the model reconstructs both. Let $\mathbf{m}$ be the original missingness mask of the input sample $\mathbf{x}$, $\bar{\mathbf{m}}$ the one including artificial missingness and $\bar{\mathbf{x}} = \mathbf{x} \cdot (1 - \bar{\mathbf{m}})$ the sample with artificially missing values.

Because the originally missing values are unknown, the reconstruction loss has to take into account the missingness mask $\mathbf{m}$, as done in GAIN [22] and MCFlow [12]. The masked reconstruction loss used is defined as follows:

$$\ell(\hat{\mathbf{x}}_i, \mathbf{x}_i, \mathbf{m}_i) = \sum_j (1 - m_i^j) \cdot (x_i^j - \hat{x}_i^j)^2 \tag{1}$$

Minimising the loss implies correctly imputing artificially missing data as well as correctly reconstructing observed values. However, the minimisation of the loss is not impacted by originally missing data.

4.2 Mask-Based Attention Mechanism

To help the model focus on non-missing values, we add an attention mechanism into the encoder part of the network. The intuition is that, for different missingness patterns, the model has to focus on different non-missing values to reconstruct the missing ones. By adding an attention mechanism based on the missingness mask, the model can choose the values it has to focus on. As shown in Fig. 1, the attention mechanism is based on three elements: the *Feature Encoder*, the *Feature Selector* and a *Sum aggregation*.

The *Feature Encoder* f_e is a function that takes as input a sample with artificial missingness $\bar{\mathbf{x}}$ and its corresponding missingness mask $\bar{\mathbf{m}}$ and produces d_z feature vectors of dimension d':

$$f_e(\bar{\mathbf{x}}, \bar{\mathbf{m}}) = (\mathbf{f}^1, \dots, \mathbf{f}^{d_z}) \text{ with } \mathbf{f}^j \in \mathbb{R}^{d'} \tag{2}$$

In practice, the *Feature Encoder* is implemented as a multilayer perceptron producing an output of size $d' \cdot d_z$. This output is then reshaped into a two-dimensional feature map of size (d', d_z).

The *Feature Selector* f_s is a function that takes the artificial missingness mask $\bar{\mathbf{m}}$ as input and produces d_z selection vectors of dimension d':

$$f_s(\bar{\mathbf{m}}) = (\mathbf{s}^1, \dots, \mathbf{s}^{d_z}) \text{ with } \mathbf{s}^j \in \mathbb{R}^{d'} \tag{3}$$

It is also implemented using a multi-layer perceptron which produces an output of size $d' \cdot d_z$. This output is then reshaped into a two-dimensional feature map of size (d', d_z).

The objective of the *Feature Encoder* is to create multiple estimation values for each latent feature (i.e. one feature vector $\mathbf{f}^j$ per latent feature $z^j \in \mathbf{z}$) while the goal of the *Feature Selector* is to give more attention to the most meaningful values from each vector $\mathbf{f}^j$ according to the artificial missingness mask $\bar{\mathbf{m}}$.

The *Attention Mechanism* combines feature vectors and selection vectors. To do so, the selection vectors $\mathbf{s}^j$ are normalized with a *softmax* function σ. Then, an element-wise product is used to combine each feature vector $\mathbf{f}^j$ with its selection vector $\mathbf{s}^j$. Finally, a summation aggregates each resulting vector to get the final latent representation $\mathbf{z}$. Mathematically:

$$\mathbf{z} = (\sigma(\mathbf{s}^1)^\mathsf{T} \cdot \mathbf{f}^1, \ldots, \sigma(\mathbf{s}^{d_z})^\mathsf{T} \cdot \mathbf{f}^{d_z}) = (z^1, \ldots, z^{d_z}). \tag{4}$$

5   Technical Implementation

In order to ensure the reproducibility of our results, the architecture and implementation details are thoroughly defined in this section. The full training and testing code of DAEMA is available[1].

5.1   Preprocessing Steps

To evaluate the imputation performance of DAEMA, complete datasets (i.e. without missing values) are needed. To train the model, we create real-world-like datasets D (with missing values) from ground truth datasets D^*. The preparation of all datasets follows these steps:

- We separate the downstream target label from the other features. In real-world applications, the target is unknown during the imputation process as it is predicted by the downstream model afterwards.
- For a few datasets, we remove some samples, such as samples containing naturally missing data or extreme outliers, as detailed in Sect. 6.1.
- We introduce missing values in the ground truth datasets. We use the two *uniform* mechanisms described in the MIDA paper [4] to create both MCAR and MNAR data. For the MCAR setting, each single value has 20% chance to be removed, possibly removing none or all the values of a sample. For the MNAR setting, we randomly choose two features and select the samples for which a) the first feature has a value smaller or equal to the median of that first feature or b) the second feature has a value bigger or equal to the median of that second feature. Then, each single value of the selected samples has 20% chance to be removed.
- We randomly split each dataset into a train set and a test set. We use a 70-30 ratio for all experiments.
- We apply a z-normalisation on the non-missing values by subtracting the mean and dividing by the variance of the training set.

5.2   Detailed Architecture

Inspired by AimNet [21] and GAIN [22], DAEMA has been kept as shallow as possible. The *Feature Encoder* is a multilayer perceptron with two layers both

---

[1] https://github.com/euranova/DAEMA.

using the hyperbolic tangent as activation. The input size is $2d$ ($\bar{\mathbf{x}}$ concatenated with $\bar{\mathbf{m}}$). Both hidden and output layers are of size $d' \cdot d_z$. The output of the *Feature Encoder* is reshaped into a (d', d_z) feature map. The *Feature Selector* is a single fully-connected layer without activation going from dimension d to dimension $d' \cdot d_z$. The output vector is reshaped into a two dimensional matrix of size (d', d_z). The *Feature Decoder* is a single fully-connected layer of dimension d without activation. For our experiments, d' and d_z are set to $2d$.

During the training, the artificial missingness mask $\bar{\mathbf{m}}$ and its corresponding sample $\bar{\mathbf{x}}$ are built on the fly by randomly removing features with a 0.2 probability. Besides, we use the masked reconstruction loss defined in Eq. 1. The model is trained by gradient descent using the Adam optimizer [7] with a learning rate of 0.001 and a batch-size of 64. The training is stopped after 40,000 batch-steps.

All hyperparameters are chosen based on early experiments. Fine-tuning these hyperparameters could probably improve the performance of the algorithm. However, this is out of the scope of this paper and is left for future work.

6   Experimentation

To validate our approach, we compare it to state-of-the-art algorithms on different datasets and with different missingness proportions.

6.1   Datasets

We use seven publicly available real-life datasets, six from the UCI repository [3] and one from the `sklearn.datasets` module [11]: EEG Eye State (14,976 samples, 14 features, 2 classes), Glass (214 samples, 9 features, 6 classes), Breast Cancer (683 samples, 9 features, 2 classes), Ionosphere (351 samples, 34 features, 2 classes), Shuttle (58,000 samples, 9 features, 7 classes), Boston Housing (506 samples, 13 features, regression) and CASP (45,730 samples, 9 features, regression). These datasets have different sizes and different dimensions to perform comprehensive experimentation. Note that the Breast Cancer dataset has samples with *NA* values and the EEG dataset has four extreme outliers in its sixth feature. We remove these samples from the datasets. Boston, Glass, Breast Cancer, Ionosphere and Shuttle datasets are used for experimentation in MIDA [4]. EEG and CASP datasets are used for experimentation in AimNet [21]. As these two models are state-of-the-art and direct competitors to our model, it is more relevant to perform comparison on these datasets.

6.2   Metrics

We use two metrics to compare the algorithms, namely a reconstruction metric and a downstream metric. The reconstruction metric is the normalised root mean square error (*NRMS*) over the missing values of the test set, as in [21]. The normalisation is done using all the ground truth values of the test set. Although NRMS is a direct metric to assess the performance of the models, it favours predicting the mean of multi-modal distributions rather than one of the possible modes. To assess better the ability of the models to capture the structure of the data, we also use a complementary downstream metric. This metric is more relevant regarding real-world situations as missing data imputation is often used as a preprocessing step to train a model. However, this metric is indirect and results in a less precise evaluation.

As downstream models, we use random forests trained and tested respectively on the imputed train set and the imputed test set. The performance of a random forest is measured by the NRMS in the case of a regression and the accuracy in the case of a classification. Because of the randomness of the random forest algorithm, we define the metric as the mean performance of ten random forests trained with different seeds. We use random forests with 100 estimators and at most 1000 leaf nodes per estimator for computational reasons.

To obtain more stable results from each run, the metrics are averaged on five of the last training steps (see Sect. 6.3 for details). To account for the randomness of the dataset preprocessing and the one of the models initialisation and training procedure, each experiment is run ten times, using ten different seeds. All compared algorithms are run on the same ten preprocessed datasets to obtain more significant results. The mean of the ten metric measurements obtained is reported in order to compare the algorithms with each other. The sample variance of the ten values obtained is reported for better reproducibility.

6.3   Compared Algorithms

To validate our approach, we have selected and implemented three state-of-the-art algorithms for comparison: AimNet [21], MIDA [4] and MissForest [16]. We have also implemented a custom denoising autoencoder, which we will refer to as DAE. For DAEMA, we evaluate the model after 39200, 39400, 39600, 39800 and 40000 batch-steps. For AimNet, we use the hyperparameters described in the paper [21]. We evaluate the model after 18, 19, 20, 21 and 22 epochs. For MIDA, we have not found any indication on the batch size. Therefore, we use the whole train set at each training step. Moreover, we use the Adam optimiser with a learning rate of 0.0001 instead of the recommended one as we found it achieves better results. We evaluate the model after 492, 494, 496, 498 and 500 epochs.

We also compare DAEMA with MissForest. However, MissForest targets a fix dataset, as it reconstructs the whole dataset at once. Thus it can be seen as a one shot process only, with a computational burden that makes it difficult to apply on a data stream. To have a fair comparison we had to adapt the algorithm. During the training procedure, we save all predictors produced by each iteration. At test time, each predictor is applied one by one to unseen data. We use random forests of 100 estimators each without any leaf-node limit. The maximum number of iterations is set to 10. For this approach, as the number of steps is dynamically chosen, we evaluate the model only once, i.e. after convergence or after the maximum number of iterations has been reached.

Table 1. State-of-the-art comparison under the MCAR setting. NRMS is reported in the top table and the performance of a downstream random forest using the imputed datasets is reported in bottom one (accuracy for classification and NRMS for regression).

	EEG	Glass	Breast	Ionosphere	Shuttle	Boston	CASP
DAEMA	**0.392** ±.005	**0.714** ±.093	0.678 ±.041	**0.745** ±.035	**0.546** ±.123	**0.635** ±.047	**0.422** ±.069
DAE	0.467 ±.005	0.754 ±.092	**0.645** ±.037	0.799 ±.034	0.597 ±.111	0.645 ±.057	0.460 ±.066
AimNet	0.440 ±.005	0.926 ±.108	0.681 ±.029	0.846 ±.036	0.568 ±.123	0.704 ±.063	0.431 ±.070
MIDA	0.925 ±.015	0.954 ±.108	0.797 ±.020	0.901 ±.020	1.470 ±.401	0.845 ±.064	0.861 ±.051
MissForest	**0.364** ±.006	0.741 ±.076	0.677 ±.050	0.756 ±.040	0.673 ±.182	**0.601** ±.052	**0.379** ±.077
Mean	0.998 ±.013	1.003 ±.112	0.993 ±.035	1.018 ±.023	0.969 ±.077	0.998 ±.048	1.004 ±.030

	Accuracy (higher is better)					NRMS (lower is better)	
	EEG	Glass	Breast	Ionosphere	Shuttle	Boston	CASP
DAEMA	**0.861** ±.004	**0.684** ±.043	**0.973** ±.011	0.932 ±.022	**0.996** ±.001	**0.481** ±.047	**0.708** ±.004
DAE	0.849 ±.003	0.678 ±.034	0.971 ±.011	**0.933** ±.019	0.995 ±.001	0.492 ±.049	0.720 ±.005
AimNet	0.851 ±.004	0.669 ±.043	0.970 ±.011	0.930 ±.022	0.996 ±.001	0.506 ±.053	0.712 ±.006
MIDA	0.823 ±.005	0.665 ±.026	0.973 ±.011	0.930 ±.024	0.994 ±.000	0.505 ±.038	0.761 ±.004
MissForest	**0.869** ±.006	0.675 ±.041	0.971 ±.013	0.931 ±.016	**0.997** ±.000	0.492 ±.045	**0.683** ±.005
Mean	0.824 ±.005	0.669 ±.044	0.968 ±.013	0.927 ±.024	0.996 ±.000	0.495 ±.033	0.752 ±.004
Real	0.925 ±.005	0.750 ±.040	0.973 ±.009	0.940 ±.020	1.000 ±.000	0.372 ±.051	0.615 ±.006

Finally, we also compare DAEMA against a classical denoising autoencoder (DAE). The training procedure of the DAE is similar to the one of DAEMA. The autoencoder is composed of three fully-connected layers, respectively of size $2d$, $2d$ and d, followed by an hyperbolic tangent activation function for the first two layers and no activation function for the last one. We evaluate the model after 39200, 39400, 39600, 39800 and 40000 batch-steps.

6.4 Comparison with State-of-the-Art Algorithms

We compare DAEMA with the other algorithms on seven publicly available datasets both in MCAR and MNAR settings (see Sect. 5.1 for dataset preprocessing). The performance of a simple mean imputation *Mean* and a perfect reconstruction *Real* are also reported as indicative lower and upper bounds.

As shown in Table 1, DAEMA achieves good results in the MCAR setting both in terms of data reconstruction (top table) and downstream task (bottom table) compared to DAE, AimNet and MIDA. It obtains the best performance for six of the seven datasets, sometimes by a huge margin. DAEMA also performs well in the more challenging MNAR setting as shown in Table 2, which can be explained by the kind of patterns an attention mechanism can learn.

We also compare DAEMA with MissForest. We can see DAEMA is very competitive for both missingness settings. The MNAR setting gives a slight advantage to MissForest though. We hypothesise it is because the local nature of MissForest makes it less sensitive to the introduced bias than DAEMA, which models the data distribution on a global scale. However, the scope of MissForest is limited, as it is meant to reconstruct a fix dataset, while DAEMA can process new data, making DAEMA more suitable for real-world applications.

Table 2. State-of-the-art comparison under the MNAR setting. NRMS is reported in the top table and the performance of a downstream random forest using the imputed datasets is reported in bottom one (accuracy for classification and NRMS for regression).

	EEG	Glass	Breast	Ionosphere	Shuttle	Boston	CASP
DAEMA	**0.390** $\pm$.006	0.731 $\pm$.123	0.703 $\pm$.046	**0.765** $\pm$.080	**0.611** $\pm$.253	**0.634** $\pm$.051	**0.429** $\pm$.052
DAE	0.467 $\pm$.006	**0.725** $\pm$.129	**0.656** $\pm$.047	0.807 $\pm$.078	0.683 $\pm$.217	0.644 $\pm$.045	0.465 $\pm$.044
AimNet	0.440 $\pm$.008	0.822 $\pm$.128	0.687 $\pm$.056	0.853 $\pm$.072	0.642 $\pm$.247	0.683 $\pm$.041	0.435 $\pm$.053
MIDA	0.962 $\pm$.023	0.897 $\pm$.119	0.820 $\pm$.069	0.884 $\pm$.060	1.481 $\pm$.244	0.842 $\pm$.033	0.862 $\pm$.032
MissForest	**0.363** $\pm$.006	0.786 $\pm$.231	0.688 $\pm$.051	0.768 $\pm$.085	0.653 $\pm$.178	**0.591** $\pm$.059	**0.386** $\pm$.058
Mean	1.041 $\pm$.024	0.957 $\pm$.119	1.018 $\pm$.041	0.994 $\pm$.057	1.027 $\pm$.148	1.003 $\pm$.046	1.013 $\pm$.030

	Accuracy (higher is better)					NRMS (lower is better)	
	EEG	Glass	Breast	Ionosphere	Shuttle	Boston	CASP
DAEMA	**0.870** $\pm$.004	**0.710** $\pm$.037	0.968 $\pm$.011	0.935 $\pm$.018	**0.997** $\pm$.001	0.469 $\pm$.045	**0.696** $\pm$.011
DAE	0.859 $\pm$.006	0.693 $\pm$.060	**0.969** $\pm$.013	**0.938** $\pm$.016	0.996 $\pm$.001	0.479 $\pm$.048	0.706 $\pm$.013
AimNet	0.862 $\pm$.006	0.681 $\pm$.048	0.966 $\pm$.012	0.932 $\pm$.019	0.997 $\pm$.001	0.482 $\pm$.053	0.698 $\pm$.012
MIDA	0.837 $\pm$.009	0.668 $\pm$.056	0.968 $\pm$.008	0.932 $\pm$.020	0.995 $\pm$.001	0.505 $\pm$.038	0.739 $\pm$.018
MissForest	**0.876** $\pm$.005	0.695 $\pm$.057	0.967 $\pm$.011	0.930 $\pm$.021	**0.997** $\pm$.000	**0.462** $\pm$.053	**0.674** $\pm$.009
Mean	0.837 $\pm$.010	0.672 $\pm$.034	0.963 $\pm$.012	0.932 $\pm$.019	0.997 $\pm$.001	0.509 $\pm$.053	0.732 $\pm$.017
Real	0.924 $\pm$.003	0.748 $\pm$.039	0.969 $\pm$.013	0.940 $\pm$.017	1.000 $\pm$.000	0.392 $\pm$.058	0.618 $\pm$.004

6.5 Missingness Sensitivity

Figure 2 shows the sensitivity of the algorithms with respect to the missingness percentage. Mean imputation provides a lower baseline for imputation. We can see that *AimNet*, *MissForest* and *DAEMA* achieve significantly better performance than mean imputation for EEG and Boston datasets. However, their superiority is limited for the Glass dataset. It can be explained by the fact that the Glass dataset has only a few samples (214 samples), showing that *AimNet*, *MissForest* and *DAEMA* need a sufficient amount of data to model the data distribution. This hypothesis is confirmed by the fact that they also seem to be more impacted by the amount of missing data.

Compared to *MissForest*, we can see that *DAEMA* achieves very competitive performance. *DAEMA* seems to be less impacted by the amount of missingness, giving it an advantage for high missingness rates. Furthermore, as explained in Sect. 6.3, the scope of *DAEMA* is less limited than the one of *MissForest* making it more adapted to real-world applications.

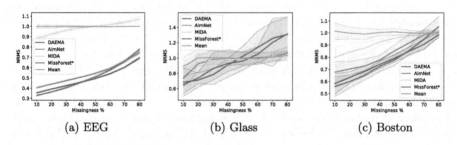

(a) EEG   (b) Glass   (c) Boston

Fig. 2. NRMS reconstruction metric on (a) EEG, (b) Glass and (c) Boston datasets for varying missingness proportions.

7   Conclusion

In this work, we propose a novel algorithm, DAEMA, a denoising autoencoder with an attention mechanism. Unlike state-of-the-art algorithms that learn from the entire input including placeholder values (mean-imputed or zero-imputed), DAEMA focuses on observed values thanks to its specifically designed attention mechanism. We show that, even when applied to a simple denoising autoencoder without hyperparameter tuning, this new attention mechanism outperforms state-of-the-art approaches on several instances of missing data under *missing completely at random* (MCAR) and *missing not at random* (MNAR) settings. These results also propagate nicely to improve the performance on downstream tasks.

References

1. van Buuren, S., Groothuis-Oudshoorn, K.: mice: multivariate imputation by chained equations in R. J. Stat. Softw. **45**(3), 1–68 (2010)
2. Camino, R.D., Hammerschmidt, C.A., State, R.: Improving missing data imputation with deep generative models. arXiv preprint arXiv:1902.10666 (2019)
3. Dua, D., Graff, C.: UCI machine learning repository (2017). http://archive.ics.uci.edu/ml
4. Gondara, L., Wang, K.: MIDA: multiple imputation using denoising autoencoders. In: Phung, D., Tseng, V.S., Webb, G.I., Ho, B., Ganji, M., Rashidi, L. (eds.) PAKDD 2018. LNCS (LNAI), vol. 10939, pp. 260–272. Springer, Cham (2018). https://doi.org/10.1007/978-3-319-93040-4_21
5. Goodfellow, I.J., et al.: Generative adversarial nets. In: NIPS, pp. 2672–2680 (2014). http://papers.nips.cc/paper/5423-generative-adversarial-nets
6. Gulrajani, I., Ahmed, F., Arjovsky, M., Dumoulin, V., Courville, A.C.: Improved training of wasserstein GANs. In: NIPS, pp. 5769–5779 (2017). http://papers.nips.cc/paper/7159-improved-training-of-wasserstein-gans
7. Kingma, D.P., Ba, J.: Adam: a method for stochastic optimization. In: ICLR (Poster) (2015)
8. McCoy, J.T., Kroon, S., Auret, L.: Variational autoencoders for missing data imputation with application to a simulated milling circuit. IFAC-PapersOnLine **51**(21), 141–146 (2018)
9. Muzellec, B., Josse, J., Boyer, C., Cuturi, M.: Missing data imputation using optimal transport. In: International Conference on Machine Learning, pp. 7130–7140. PMLR (2020)
10. Nazabal, A., Olmos, P.M., Ghahramani, Z., Valera, I.: Handling incomplete heterogeneous data using VAEs. Pattern Recogn. **107**, 107501 (2020)
11. Pedregosa, F., et al.: Scikit-learn: machine learning in Python. J. Mach. Learn. Res. **12**, 2825–2830 (2011)
12. Richardson, T.W., Wu, W., Lin, L., Xu, B., Bernal, E.A.: McFlow: Monte Carlo flow models for data imputation. In: Proceedings of the IEEE/CVF Conference on Computer Vision and Pattern Recognition, pp. 14205–14214 (2020)
13. Rubin, D.B.: Inference and missing data. Biometrika **63**(3), 581–592 (1976)
14. Seaman, S., Galati, J., Jackson, D., Carlin, J.D.: What is meant by "missing at random"? Stat. Sci. **28**, 257–268 (2013)

15. Spinelli, I., Scardapane, S., Uncini, A.: Missing data imputation with adversarially-trained graph convolutional networks. Neural Netw. **129**, 249–260 (2020)
16. Stekhoven, D.J., Bühlmann, P.: MissForest—non-parametric missing value imputation for mixed-type data. Bioinformatics **28**(1), 112–118 (2012)
17. Troyanskaya, O., et al.: Missing value estimation methods for DNA microarrays. Bioinformatics **17**(6), 520–525 (2001)
18. Vaswani, A., et al.: Attention is all you need. In: NIPS, pp. 6000–6010 (2017). http://papers.nips.cc/paper/7181-attention-is-all-you-need
19. Vincent, P., Larochelle, H., Bengio, Y., Manzagol, P.A.: Extracting and composing robust features with denoising autoencoders. In: Proceedings of the 25th International Conference on Machine Learning, pp. 1096–1103 (2008)
20. Wang, X., Li, A., Jiang, Z., Feng, H.: Missing value estimation for DNA microarray gene expression data by Support Vector Regression imputation and orthogonal coding scheme. BMC Bioinform. **7**(1), 1–10 (2006). https://doi.org/10.1186/1471-2105-7-32
21. Wu, R., Zhang, A., Ilyas, I., Rekatsinas, T.: Attention-based learning for missing data imputation in HoloClean. In: Proceedings of Machine Learning and Systems, vol. 2, pp. 307–325 (2020)
22. Yoon, J., Jordon, J., Schaar, M.: GAIN: missing data imputation using generative adversarial nets. In: International Conference on Machine Learning, pp. 5689–5698. PMLR (2018)

Spatial-Temporal Traffic Data Imputation via Graph Attention Convolutional Network

Yongchao Ye[1], Shiyao Zhang[2], and James J. Q. Yu[1(✉)]

[1] Guangdong Provincial Key Laboratory of Brain-Inspired Intelligent Computation, Department of Computer Science and Engineering, Southern University of Science and Technology, Shenzhen 518055, China
12032868@mail.sustech.edu.cn, yujq3@sustech.edu.cn
[2] Academy for Advanced Interdisciplinary Studies, Southern University of Science and Technology, Shenzhen 518055, China
syzhang@ieee.org

Abstract. High-quality traffic data is crucial for intelligent transportation system and its data-driven applications. However, data missing is common in collecting real-world traffic datasets due to various factors. Thus, imputing missing values by extracting traffic characteristics becomes an essential task. By using conventional convolutional neural network layers or focusing on standalone road sections, existing imputation methods cannot model the non-Euclidean spatial correlations of complex traffic networks. To address this challenge, we propose a graph attention convolutional network (GACN), a novel model for traffic data imputation. Specifically, the model follows an encoder-decoder structure and incorporates graph attention mechanism to learn spatial correlation of the traffic data collected by adjacent sensors on traffic graph. Temporal convolutional layers are stacked to extract relations in time-series after graph attention layers. Through comprehensive case studies on the dataset from the Caltrans performance measurement system (PeMS), we demonstrate that the proposed GACN consistently outperforms other baselines and has steady performance in extreme missing rate scenarios.

Keywords: Graph attention · Temporal convolution · Data imputation

1 Introduction

In recent years, many data-driven approaches have been proposed with the development of intelligent transportation system (ITS), such as traffic speed

This work is supported by the Stable Support Plan Program of Shenzhen Natural Science Fund No. 20200925155105002, by the General Program of Guangdong Basic and Applied Basic Research Foundation No. 2019A1515011032, and by the Guangdong Provincial Key Laboratory (Grant No. 2020B121201001).

© Springer Nature Switzerland AG 2021
I. Farkaš et al. (Eds.): ICANN 2021, LNCS 12891, pp. 241–252, 2021.
https://doi.org/10.1007/978-3-030-86362-3_20

prediction, traffic signal control, and origin-destination prediction [22]. These data-driven approaches heavily rely on high-quality spatial-temporal traffic data. However, due to various natural and human factors, traffic data collected in practice are often incomplete or corrupted, e.g., about 10% traffic data is missing in Beijing. Some extreme missing scenarios are reported in Alberta, Canada [12]. The average missing rate of traffic data in 7 years was 50%, and the short-term missing rate can reach up to 90%. It is reported that missing data is unfavorable to data-driven models, such as traffic flow prediction [8]. Thus, imputing the missing values by analyzing spatial-temporal traffic features is an urgent issue.

Traditional imputation methods are based on universal interpolation methods such as k-Nearest Neighbor (k-NN) and support vector regression [10]. These methods are inefficient when there are massive missing points. Compared with traditional methods, methods based on deep learning have improved estimation accuracy by capturing temporal or spatial dependency. Denoising stacked autoencoder (DSAE) [5], which combines denoising and stacked autoencoders, is a typical deep model applied to impute traffic data. Subsequent work improved imputation accuracy by using DSAE as a generator and designing a discriminator [4]. However, these methods only focus on isolated road segments and show their limitations in modeling spatial correlation. Further research reconstructed traffic trajectories into a two-dimensional matrix and applied a convolutional neural network (CNN) for encoding and decoding [1].

There is a research gap in the aforementioned imputation methods, especially when they are employed to impute the traffic data in a large region. With a complex network topology, the real-world traffic data is with a non-Euclidean structure. These traditional learning models (such as CNN, etc.) are efficient for data with Euclidean structures, but they are relatively insufficient in modeling non-Euclidean spatial correlation. With a graph structure for relational reasoning, graph neural network (GNN) is a framework that can learn the correlation in topological space [21]. In ITS, GNN and its variants have been applied to traffic forecasting tasks. See [16] for an example. Utilizing graph convolutional layers in a GAN framework, graph convolutional generative autoencoder (GCGA) achieved significant performance in real-time traffic seed estimation [19]. Guo et al. proposed ASTGCN, which captured spatial-temporal correlations by attention mechanism and convolution module [6]. GNN has shown its advantages in modeling topological relationships of the traffic network. However, to the best of our knowledge, traffic data imputation method using GNN-based approaches has not been assessed in the literature.

To bridge the research gap, we propose a novel imputation model, namely, graph attention convolutional network (GACN). The primary efforts of this work are summarized as follows.

1. We design a spatial-temporal block with a graph attention layer and a convolutional layer. Compared with the previous work, the graph attention mechanism can better capture non-Euclidean spatial correlations in traffic networks. As far as we are concerned, this is the first time to apply graph attention network (GAT) [13] in traffic data imputation.

2. We propose an end-to-end traffic data imputation model that follows the encoder-decoder structure. Specifically, both the encoder and the decoder consist of two spatial-temporal blocks for spatial-temporal modeling, which are concatenated to obtain an embedding of the input.
3. We conduct comprehensive case studies on real-world traffic datasets. In addition, we investigate a wide missing rate range from 10% to 90% to evaluate all kinds of practical scenarios. The experimental results demonstrate that the proposed model achieves accurate imputation and maintains steady performance under extreme missing scenarios.

The remainder of this paper is structured as follows. Section 2 briefly reviews the development of traffic data imputation methods and attention mechanism. Section 3 presents the problem formulation and introduces the proposed imputation method. Section 4 represents and analyzes experimental results. Finally, the paper is concluded in Sect. 5.

2 Related Work

2.1 Traffic Data Imputation

Traditional Imputation Approaches. In the early traffic data imputation literature, traditional methods can be summarized into three groups, i.e., prediction, interpolation, and statistical learning [10]. Autoregressive integrated moving average (ARIMA) and its variants are typical prediction examples. One distinct shortcoming of the prediction model is that it only uses the foregoing temporal information of the missing points. Commonly used interpolation methods, e.g., k-NN interpolates missing points by averaging neighboring observed points. However, these methods show their limits by mainly focusing on a single traffic sensor or a road section. On the other hand, statistical learning is another line of traffic data imputation research, such as Probabilistic principal component analysis (PPCA) [9]. More advanced method utilized low-rank tensor structures to represent the traffic data and recover missing points [3].

Deep Learning Based Approaches. In the era of big data, many deep learning based approaches have been proposed for time-series data imputation, but not necessarily traffic data imputation. Generative adversarial networks (GAN), which learn the distribution of training samples, have been applied to create data imputation models. Yoon *et al.* proposed generative adversarial imputation nets (GAIN) [17]. In GAIN, the discriminator was fed with a hint vector which provided auxiliary information about the missing position. Luo *et al.* proposed an end-to-end GAN (E^{2}GAN) framework for multivariate time-series imputation [11]. These universal imputation models usually concentrate on temporal modeling rather than the correlations between different time-series. There are also methods that capture spatial correlations with CNN layers [1,15]. For example, Yang *et al.* designed a GAN model with CNN layers and bidirectional attention [15]. However, these methods neglect the network topology, which is crucial to spatial correlations modeling.

2.2 Graph Attention in ITS

The attention mechanism is first emerged as a method to improve recurrent neural networks' performance on sequence-to-sequence learning tasks. The idea of the attention mechanism is to select features that have a relatively larger impact on the task. In real-world traffic networks, the graph is large-scale and combined with noise. Extracting features from these graphs is difficult and may lead to massive computational cost. A practical solution is to incorporate the attention mechanism on graphs, namely graph attention networks (GAT) [13]. Graph attention mechanism allows a model to focus more on relevant parts of the graph. In ITS-related applications, especially traffic speed prediction, many methods based on graph attention mechanism have been proposed [6,20]. In the reported results, these methods outperform graph convolution networks (GCN) in many scenarios.

Inspired by the above literature and making use of its outstanding capability in modeling complex and dynamic traffic networks, we employ graph attention mechanism in our model to learn the spatial correlations for traffic data imputation.

3 Methodology

The proposed GACN estimates missing values by capturing spatial-temporal correlations from the observations. In this section, we first introduce our data pre-processing techniques, including traffic network representation and traffic data imputation formulation. Then, we present the structure of the proposed GACN. Finally, we give a detailed description of the spatial graph attention and temporal convolutional layers respectively.

3.1 Data Preprocessing

In this paper, we define a traffic network as an undirected graph $G = (V, E, \boldsymbol{A})$, where V is the set of vertexes, i.e., the set of sensors in a specific region $|V| = N$. Edges $e(v_i, v_j) \in E$ represent the spatial correlations between sensors. The adjacent matrix of graph G is represented by $\boldsymbol{A} \in \mathbb{R}^{N \times N}$, in which $a_{ij} = 1$ indicates sensor i and sensor j are adjacent and $a_{ij} = 0$ otherwise. Similar to [20], we generate the adjacent matrix by thresholded Gaussian kernel,

$$a_{ij} = \begin{cases} 1, \exp\left(-\frac{\text{dist}(v_i, v_j)^2}{\sigma^2}\right) \geq \varepsilon \text{ or } i = j \\ 0, \text{ otherwise} \end{cases}, \tag{1}$$

where σ^2 and ε are the thresholds that decide the sparsity of $\boldsymbol{A}$. $\text{dist}(v_i, v_j)$ is the Euclidean distance between sensors i and j, which can be derived from their respective locations.

Suppose a sensor records T observations in a day. We denote the ground truth traffic speed in a day as $\boldsymbol{S} = \{s_i^t\} \in \mathbb{R}^{N \times T}$, where s_i^t is the observation from sensor i at time t. Figure 1 depicts a diagram of traffic data imputation problem.

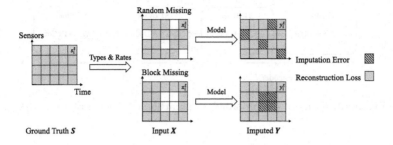

Fig. 1. Diagram of traffic data imputation problem.

We first randomly drop points on a complete observation S as input. A missing mask $M = \{m_i^t\} \in \mathbb{R}^{N \times T}$ that records the missing positions is defined as,

$$m_i^t = \begin{cases} 1, \text{ if } x_i^t \text{ is observed} \\ 0, \text{ if } x_i^t \text{ is missing} \end{cases}. \tag{2}$$

Then the input $X = \{x_i^t\} \in \mathbb{R}^{N \times T}$ can be represented by,

$$X = S \odot M, \tag{3}$$

where $\odot$ is the element-wise multiplication. $x_i^t = 0$ indicates a missing value and $x_i^t = s_i^t$ indicates an observation. Missing rate is defined as the ratio of missing values to the observations. The output of the model is denoted as $Y = \{y_i^t\} \in \mathbb{R}^N \times T$. The imputation error $E(S, Y)$, which is calculated on missing points, is defined as follows,

$$E(S, Y) = \sum_{i,t} m_i^t \|s_i^t - y_i^t\|^2, \tag{4}$$

Take Fig. 1 as an example. The model takes random missing points as input. Then, the imputation error is only calculated on those blocks with diagonal shadow (the missing points).

According to the previous studies, we investigate two traffic data missing types in this study, i.e., random missing (RM) and block missing (BM) [8]. BM is the same as not missing at random (NMR) in [8]. Figure 1 gives an illustration of two missing types, where the blank blocks are the missing points, and the blocks with dark shadows are observations. In RM, which is typically caused by transmission failure, all the missing points are randomly scattered. BM is more commonly caused by data center errors or power failure. The BM missing points are gregarious in the spatial and temporal dimensions.

3.2 Graph Attention Convolutional Network for Imputation

We proposed a graph attention convolutional network (GACN) for traffic data imputation in this paper. As shown in Fig. 2, GACN has an encoder-decoder structure, where the encoder extracts the traffic characteristics, and the decoder

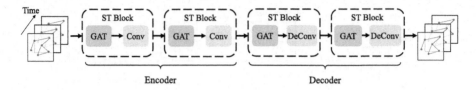

Fig. 2. Structure of the proposed graph attention convolution network.

recovers the input sequence. Both the encoder and the decoder are composed of two spatial-temporal blocks (ST block). In each block, there is a graph attention layer for feature extraction in the spatial dimension and a standard convolutional layer for time-series modeling along the temporal dimension. Specifically, blocks in the encoder apply convolution layers, which perform merging and learn temporal characteristics. Blocks in the decoder apply deconvolution layers, which recover the internal features to their original size.

As illustrated in Fig. 2, the input X of GACN is the observation from a specific region embedded on a graph. Each node has the observation from a sensor in a day, which is denoted as $x_i = \{x_i^1, x_i^2, ..., x_i^T\}$. The red points are missing points which are set to zero in X. And the output of GACN is a graph that has the identical size of the input. The missing positions may change on different timestamps (i.e., in Fig. 2, the red points are on different nodes in different timestamps). We define the reconstruction loss $L(S, Y)$ of GACN as the mean squared error between input and output feature maps. Let the network parameters be θ, the objective of the training is to minimize the reconstruction loss as follow,

$$\arg\min_{\theta} L(S, Y) = \arg\min_{\theta} \sum_{i,t} \|s_i^j - y_i^j\|^2. \tag{5}$$

Note that this reconstruction loss is different from the imputation error mentioned in Eq. 4. As shown in Fig. 1, reconstruction loss is calculated on the entire output with dark shadow while imputation error is only calculated on the missing points. The reason is that missing positions may change on different days. In the training stage, instead of only focusing on the missing points, we pay more attention to learn the correlation and distribution from the entire observation. The network parameter can be optimized by gradient descent algorithms.

3.3 Spatial Graph Attention

The traffic condition of a road section is changing over time. In addition, it is affected by adjacent road sections. Such highly dynamic influence poses challenges in spatial modeling. To address this issue, we apply the graph attention network (GAT) [13] to learn the spatial correlations. GAT captures dynamic spatial correlations by applying a self-attention strategy and calculating dynamic weights between vertexes.

The input of a graph attention layer can be denoted as $H = \{h_1, h_2, ..., h_N\}$, where N is the number of vertexes, $h_i \in \mathbb{R}^F$ represents each vertex that has

F-dimension features. As mentioned in the above section, each sensor has T observed values in a day, i.e., T-dimension features. Thus, the input of the first graph attention layer in GACN is $\boldsymbol{X} \in \mathbb{R}^{N \times T}$, which is with missing points. Since the temporal features are captured by convolutional layers, we set the output dimension the same as the input dimension for all graph attention layers in GACN. With a weight matrix $\boldsymbol{W} \in \mathbb{R}^{F \times F}$, the graph attention layer can transform the input to the output feature space. Consequently, the attention coefficient e_{ij} is calculated by a self-attention mechanism $a : \mathbb{R}^T \times \mathbb{R}^T \to \mathbb{R}$,

$$e_{ij} = a(\boldsymbol{W} h_i, \boldsymbol{W} h_j). \tag{6}$$

The coefficient represents the influence of vertex j on vertex i. Generally, every vertex in the graph affects each other. However, calculating coefficients in the entire graph can be expensive. Thus, considering the graph topology, we only compute the coefficients between adjacent vertexes. The hypothesis is that the adjacent vertexes have more significant influence than non-adjacent vertexes. The output h_i' is only affected by the input from adjacent nodes. Then, with LeakyReLU [14] as the activation function, attention coefficients from neighbors are normalized by softmax,

$$\alpha_{ij} = \frac{\exp(\text{LeakyReLU}(e_{ij}))}{\sum_{k \in \mathcal{N}_i} \exp(\text{LeakyReLU}(e_{ik}))}, \tag{7}$$

where $\mathcal{N}_i$ is a set of adjacent vertexes of i. To prevent overfitting, we randomly dropout normalized attention coefficients in the training stage. Finally, the output features of vertex i are updated by the attention coefficient and the input, which is calculated by,

$$h_i' = \sigma \left(\sum_{j \in \mathcal{N}_i} \alpha_{ij} \boldsymbol{W} h_j \right), \tag{8}$$

where $\sigma(\cdot)$ is a non-linear activation function. We apply exponential linear unit (ELU) here, which is the same as in [13].

3.4   Temporal Convolution and Deconvolution

After the graph attention layer capturing the spatial information from adjacent sensors, a canonical convolutional operation is performed on the temporal dimension. The convolutional layers are with vector-like convolutional kernels which aggregate neighboring values in time-series. After the convolutional layers in the encoder part transform the input into the internal feature maps, the decoder restores the feature maps back to the original size. Besides convolution layers, deconvolution layers perform reversed convolutions that restore the input. We use LeakyReLU which is relatively simple in gradient calculation as the activation function [14]. Both the convolution and deconvolution layers are carefully designed to ensure that the input and output time-series share the same size. The specific hyperparameters of convolution and deconvolution layers are listed in Table 1.

Table 1. Settings of convolution and deconvolution layers

Layer	Kernel	Stride	Padding	Out dimension
Conv1	4	2	1	$T/2$
Conv2	4	2	1	$T/4$
DeConv1	4	2	1	$T/2$
DeConv2	2	2	-	T

4 Case Studites

In this section, we evaluate the performance of the proposed model by case studies. First, we introduce the dataset and detailed experiment settings. Then, we conduct simulations with different missing scenarios and compare the proposed model with other baselines.

4.1 Dataset

PeMSD7[1] is collected from District 7 in California Performance Measurement System (PeMS). PeMS provides real-time and historical 5-min average traffic speed data, which is applied in this study. There are in total over one thousand sensors on the arterial roads of District 7. Similar to [18], we selected 231 sensors from the central area, which have a more complicated spatial distribution. The locations of 231 sensors are shown in Fig. 3a, which are in the downtown of Los Angeles. The investigated time ranges from May 1, 2012, to June 30, 2012, excluding weekends. No missing points are found in this period.

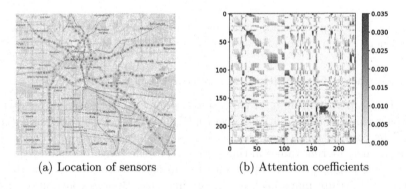

(a) Location of sensors   (b) Attention coefficients

Fig. 3. Sensor distribution of PeMSD7 and results of spatial attention mechanism.

---

[1] http://pems.dot.ca.gov/.

4.2 Experiment Configurations

We investigate two missing data types as mentioned in Sect. 3.1 in this study, i.e., random missing (RM) and block missing (BM). To investigate the proposed model in typical missing scenarios as well as in extreme cases, we select a wide missing rate range from 10% to 90% with 10% interval. For each sample, the missing points are randomly erased according to the missing rate and missing type. Then, the missing points together with the observations are fed into the network. For cross-validation, we sequentially group 80% of the data for training, 10% for validation, and 10% for testing. For samples in both the training and testing stage, the missing points are randomly erased ten times, i.e., the number of input samples is enlarged ten times compared to the original dataset. Similarly, the experiment is repeated ten times to reduce the impact of randomness when evaluating the baselines.

The proposed network is trained by Adam optimizer [7]. The learning rate starts at 0.0005 and is subsequently adjusted with a decay rate of 0.5. The negative slope of LeakyReLU is set to 0.1. And the dropout layer in GAT is with a dropout rate of 0.2. During the training stage, the batch size is set to 8. Same as [18], the thresholds σ^2, ε in Eq. 1 are set to 10 and 0.5, respectively. The model is iterated for 150 epochs. All experiments are implemented with PyTorch and conducted on an NVIDIA GeForce RTX 2080Ti GPU.

The imputation accuracy is evaluated by Mean Absolute Percentage Error (MAPE), which is defined as follows:

$$\text{MAPE} = \frac{1}{n} \sum_{i=1}^{n} \left| \frac{\widehat{x}_i - x_i}{x_i} \right| \times 100\%, \tag{9}$$

where $\widehat{x}_i$ is the imputed traffic speed at i, and x_i is the ground truth observation.

4.3 Baselines

We select the following imputation methods as a comparison of the proposed model:

- **Historical Average (HA)**: In this paper, we average the previous 5 days to estimate the missing values.
- **k-Nearest Neighborhood (k-NN)**: k-NN is a typical example of interpolation-based methods. The imputation is performed by calculating the average value of neighboring points [10]. In this paper, we set $k = 4$.
- **Support Vector Regression (SVR)**: We select SVR as a representative of regression-based imputation methods [2].
- **Denoising Stacked Autoencoder (DSAE)**: We choose DSAE as an example of imputation methods based on deep learning. In this paper, we use the DSAE with the same hyperparameters in [4].
- **Bayesian Gaussian CP decomposition (BGCP)**: Based on probabilistic matrix factorization, BGCP utilized variational Bayes and achieved better performance compared to other tensor-based imputation methods [3].

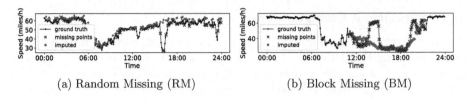

(a) Random Missing (RM)   (b) Block Missing (BM)

Fig. 4. Imputation results of the proposed GACN (30% missing rate).

4.4   Experimental Results

Imputation Results. The attention coefficients matrix is shown in Fig. 3b, where the i-th row presents the spatial correlation between sensor i and each other. As we constructed an undirected graph, the matrix is approximately symmetric. Since the graph attention is calculated on the adjacent nodes, the attention matrix is sparse. To see the detailed imputation results, we randomly select one sensor and visualize the imputation results using the proposed GACN in Fig. 4. The black dot-dashed line is the ground truth observations, and the red dotted line is the output of GACN. The missing points are marked as blue crosses. In Fig. 4a where a random missing scenario is demonstrated, though some sharp fluctuations are smoothed, the proposed model can accurately recover the missing points as well as other observations. Compared to random missing, block missing in Fig. 4b is more difficult. Although the imputed output has the same overall trend as the ground truth, relatively large fluctuation with continuous missing points is not restored well.

Performance Comparison. Figure 5 presents the performance comparison of the proposed GACN and other baselines. In the comparison, we can have the following observations. First of all, GACN achieves the best imputation accuracy in most scenarios and has similar results to other methods at low missing rates (e.g., 10%). Secondly, for the same missing types, while other baselines' performance drops as the missing rate increases, the proposed GACN maintains its outstanding recovery accuracy. The reason is that the proposed GACN learns the overall traffic distribution by reconstruction loss. Methods like KNN and SVR, which only focus on the missing points, can be effective when only a few points are missing. Thirdly, all the methods have better performance in RM than BM, which is in accordance with the results shown in Fig. 4. The proposed GACN has relatively steady MAPE while other methods degenerate rapidly. This observation indicates that spatial correlations of adjacent sensors may provide auxiliary information when missing points are continuously distributed.

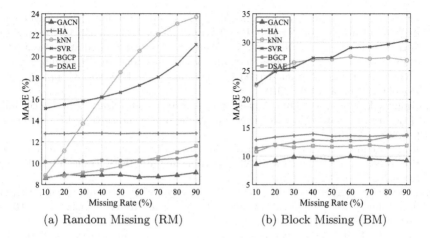

Fig. 5. Imputation MAPE (%) of different methods for different missing types.

5   Conclusion

In this paper, we propose a novel GACN for traffic data imputation. An undirected graph is first utilized to represent the traffic network. Then, data imputation is implemented by a graph attention convolutional network that follows an encoder-decoder structure. Both the encoder and the decoder consist of two stacked spatial-temporal blocks. In each block, a graph attention layer extracts spatial correlations, and a convolution/deconvolution layer models temporal relations of the traffic data. Comprehensive case studies are conducted to evaluate the imputation accuracy of the proposed model. Specifically, we consider two missing types and a wide missing rate range from 10% to 90%. Experimental results show that the proposed method outperforms other imputation baselines and maintains steady performance in extreme missing scenarios. In future studies, we plan to further improve the imputation accuracy by employing the missing mask in the training stage.

References

1. Benkraouda, O., Thodi, B.T., Yeo, H., Menendez, M., Jabari, S.E.: Traffic data imputation using deep convolutional neural networks. IEEE Access **8**, 104740–104752 (2020)
2. Castro-Neto, M., Jeong, Y.S., Jeong, M.K., Han, L.D.: Online-SVR for short-term traffic flow prediction under typical and atypical traffic conditions. Expert Syst. Appl. **36**, 6164–6173 (2009)
3. Chen, X., He, Z., Sun, L.: A Bayesian tensor decomposition approach for spatiotemporal traffic data imputation. Transp. Res. Part C Emerg. Technol. **98**, 73–84 (2019)
4. Chen, Y., Lv, Y., Wang, F.Y.: Traffic flow imputation using parallel data and generative adversarial networks. IEEE Trans. Intell. Transp. Syst. **21**(4), 1624–1630 (2020)

5. Duan, Y., Lv, Y., Liu, Y.L., Wang, F.Y.: An efficient realization of deep learning for traffic data imputation. Transp. Res. Part C Emerg. Technol. **72**, 168–181 (2016)
6. Guo, S., Lin, Y., Feng, N., Song, C., Wan, H.: Attention based spatial-temporal graph convolutional networks for traffic flow forecasting. In: Proceedings of the 33rd AAAI Conference on Artificial Intelligence, AAAI-19. vol. 33, pp. 922–929. Honolulu, Hawaii, USA (2019)
7. Kingma, D.P., Ba, J.: Adam: A method for stochastic optimization. In: Proceedings of the 3rd International Conference on Learning Representations, ICLR. San Diego, CA, USA (2015)
8. Li, L., Zhang, J., Wang, Y., Ran, B.: Missing value imputation for traffic-related time series data based on a multi-view learning method. IEEE Trans. Intell. Transp. Syst. **20**(8), 2933–2943 (2019)
9. Li, Q., Jianming, H., Li, L., Yi, Z.: PPCA-based missing data imputation for traffic flow volume: a systematical approach. IEEE Trans. Intell. Transp. Syst. **10**(3), 512–522 (2009)
10. Li, Y., Li, L., Li, Z.: Missing traffic data: comparison of imputation methods. IET Intell. Transp. Syst. **8**(1), 51–57 (2014)
11. Luo, Y., Zhang, Y., Cai, X., Yuan, X.: E2GAN: end-to-end generative adversarial network for multivariate time series imputation. In: Proceedings of 28th International Joint Conference on Artificial Intelligence, IJCAI-19, pp. 3094–3100. Macao, SAR, China (2019)
12. Tan, H., Feng, G., Feng, J., Wang, W., Zhang, Y.J., Li, F.: A tensor-based method for missing traffic data completion. Transp. Res. Part C Emerg. Technol. **28**, 15–27 (2013)
13. Veličković, P., Cucurull, G., Casanova, A., Romero, A., Lio, P., Bengio, Y.: Graph attention networks. arXiv preprint arXiv:1710.10903 (2017)
14. Xu, B., Wang, N., Chen, T., Li, M.: Empirical evaluation of rectified activations in convolutional network. arXiv preprint arXiv:1505.00853 (2015)
15. Yang, B., Kang, Y., Yuan, Y., Huang, X., Li, H.: ST-LBAGAN: spatio-temporal learnable bidirectional attention generative adversarial networks for missing traffic data imputation. Knowl. Based Syst. **215**, 106705 (2021)
16. Ye, J., Zhao, J., Ye, K., Xu, C.: How to build a graph-based deep learning architecture in traffic domain: a survey. IEEE Trans. Intell. Transp. Syst. **20**, 1–21 (2020)
17. Yoon, J., Jordon, J., van der Schaar, M.: GAIN: missing data imputation using generative adversarial nets. In: Proceedings of the 35th International Conference on Machine Learning, ICML-18, pp. 5689–5698. Stockholm, Sweden (2018)
18. Yu, B., Yin, H., Zhu, Z.: Spatio-temporal graph convolutional networks: a deep learning framework for traffic forecasting. In: Proceedings of the 27th International Joint Conference on Artificial Intelligence, IJCAI-18, pp. 3634–3640. Stockholm, Sweden (2018)
19. Yu, J.J.Q., Gu, J.: Real-time traffic speed estimation with graph convolutional generative autoencoder. IEEE Trans. Intell. Transp. Syst. **20**(10), 3940–3951 (2019)
20. Zhang, C., Yu, J.J.Q., Liu, Y.: Spatial-temporal graph attention networks: a deep learning approach for traffic forecasting. IEEE Access **7**, 166246–166256 (2019)
21. Zhou, J., et al.: Graph neural networks: a review of methods and applications. AI Open **1**, 57–81 (2020)
22. Zhu, L., Yu, F.R., Wang, Y., Ning, B., Tang, T.: Big data analytics in intelligent transportation systems: a survey. IEEE Trans. Intell. Transp. Syst. **20**(1), 383–398 (2019)

EGAT: Edge-Featured Graph Attention Network

Ziming Wang, Jun Chen, and Haopeng Chen$^{(\boxtimes)}$

Shanghai Jiao Tong University, Shanghai, China
{wangziming1022,thunderboy,chen-hp}@sjtu.edu.cn

Abstract. Most state-of-the-art Graph Neural Networks focus on node features in the learning process but ignore edge features. However, edge features also contain essential information in real-world, such as financial graphs. Node-centric approaches are suboptimal in edge-sensitive graphs since edge features are not adequately utilized. To address this problem, we present the Edge-Featured Graph Attention Network (EGAT) to leverage edge features in the graph feature representation. Our model is based on the edge-integrated attention mechanism, where both node and edge features are included in the calculation of the message and attention weights. In addition, the importance of edge information suggests that the edge features should be updated to learn high-level representation. So we perform edge updating with the integration of the features of connected nodes. In contrast to edge-node switching, our model acquires the adjacent edge features with the node-transit strategy, avoiding significant lift of computational complexity. Then we employ a multi-scale merge strategy, which concatenates features of every layer to construct hierarchical representation. Moreover, our model can be adapted to domain-specific graph neural networks, which further extends the application scenarios. Experiments show that our model achieves or matches the state-of-the-art on both node-sensitive and edge-sensitive datasets.

Keywords: Graph neural network · Edge feature · Attention

1 Introduction

Graphs are a popular way to model data in real-world applications, where nodes represent entities and edges represent relationships between entities. In recent years, several works [1,2] have applied neural networks to graph data. Kipf and Welling [3] propose graph convolutional networks (GCN) based on spectral graph theory. Velickovic *et al.* [4] present graph attention networks (GAT) with non-spectral graph methods, which introduce self-attention mechanisms [5] into graph neural networks. These methods focus on node features and achieve good results on node classification tasks, but they do not consider edge features.

However, edge features may play an equal or even more essential role to node features in some data. For example, in a financial transaction graph, nodes contain account information and edges contain transaction data. In an anti-money

© Springer Nature Switzerland AG 2021
I. Farkaš et al. (Eds.): ICANN 2021, LNCS 12891, pp. 253–264, 2021.
https://doi.org/10.1007/978-3-030-86362-3_21

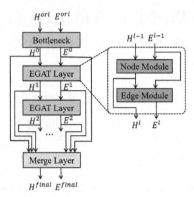

Fig. 1. The architecture of EGAT. H and E represent node features and edge features, respectively. The outputs of each EGAT layer, H^l and E^l, are fed to the merge layer to generate the final representation H^{final} and E^{final}.

laundering task, we often make the judgment based on the pattern of transactions rather than the characteristics of the account itself. In other words, edge data plays a more significant role than node data on this task, which we call *edge-sensitive*. The current node-centric approach cannot handle these tasks properly because they cannot exploit edge features effectively. Additionally, since the edge features are continuous vectors, the heterogeneous graph-based methods, which deal with discrete labels, are also suboptimal to these tasks.

In this paper, we propose the Edge-Feature Graph Attention Network (EGAT) to address this problem. We apply both edge data and node data to the graph attention mechanism, which we call *edge-integrated attention mechanism*. Specifically, both edge data and node data are essential factors for message generation and attentional weight computation. Similarly, the edge features are updated with the adjacent node features to generate high-level representations. In an EGAT layer, we update node features and edge features iteratively so that both node and edge can learn from each other. The final representations of nodes and edges are generated with the concatenation of the outputs of each layer to combine features from multi-scales. Moreover, EGAT is also a general framework that we can integrate custom message functions to adapt to specific areas.

Our main contributions are as follows.

1. To the best of our knowledge, we are the first to propose the introduction of edge features into the graph attention mechanism, making edge features play the same important role as node features. Therefore, our model can deal with the graphs with high dimensional continuous edge features.
2. Our model can handle graphs with different feature preferences, including both node-sensitive and edge-sensitive. Experimental results show that our model exceeds or matches the state-of-the-art on both node-sensitive (Cora, Citeseer, PubMed [6]) and edge-sensitive (AMLSim [7]) datasets.
3. We apply EGAT to specialized graph networks and obtain improved accuracy, showing the compatibility with other message-passing-based methods.

2   Related Work

2.1   Attention Mechanism

Attention mechanism was proposed by Vaswani *et al.* [5] and is popular in natural language processing and computer vision areas. It assigns various weights to related entities, rather than acquiring their features evenly. Velickovic *et al.* [4] proposes graph attention networks (GAT), which introduces the attention mechanism to graph neural networks. GAT computes the attention weights of neighboring nodes, thus focusing on important nodes rather than being affected equally. Additionally, GAT mitigates the over-smoothing problem, which makes it possible to stack more layers. Our work will follow these approaches and extend the application of the attention mechanism in graph neural networks.

2.2   Edge-Featured Approaches

In graph data, edges may contain different types of information. In some graphs, edges have discrete labels, such as the relationship types in knowledge graphs. Several methods for handling heterogeneous graphs can deal with these graphs effectively, such as HAN [8] and R-GCN [9]. On the other hand, edges carry continuous feature vectors in some other graphs. For example, the edges of trading graphs contain the transaction information. Gong and Cheng [10] propose EGNN to exploit these edge features, which uses the edge features to compute the weight matrix to assist propagation node features. This method is still node-centric since the edge features are only used as weights rather than the embedding of the edges. CensNet [11] uses the Edge-Node Switch strategy to update the edge features on the corresponding line graph. This approach treats nodes and edges as equally important entities and produces both node and edge embeddings. However, it suffers performance overhead on dense graphs. In quantum chemistry, several methods [12,13] introduce edge data into the computation of messages during message passing. These methods exploit of edge features adequately and work well on quantum chemistry datasets. However, this specially designed approach may not be suitable for other areas.

3   Method

3.1   Preliminary

Firstly, we present the notation for node and edge features. Given a graph G with N nodes and M edges, we use $H = \{\vec{h}_1, \vec{h}_2, ...\vec{h}_N\}$ to represent node features, where $\vec{h}_i \in \mathbb{R}^{F_H}$. Similarly, we use $E = \{\vec{e}_{i_1 j_1}, \vec{e}_{i_2 j_2}, ...\vec{e}_{i_M j_M}\}$ to represent edge features, where $\vec{e}_{ij} \in \mathbb{R}^{F_E}$ represents the edge between the ith and j^{th} nodes. Superscripts are used to distinguish the stages of node features and edge features. We use E^{ori} and H^{ori} for the input edge and node features, E^l and H^l for the output of the lth EGAT layer, and E^{final} and H^{final} for the final edge and node representations. We may omit the superscript if there is no ambiguity.

Then, we present the definition of the task. The input is a graph G with node features H^{ori} and edge features E^{ori}, and the supervised learning task $\mathcal{T}$ with the corresponding label $\mathcal{L}$ (e.g., edge classification with edge labels). Our model aims to generate the node embedding H^{final} and edge embedding E^{final} that achieve the highest possible performance in the supervised learning task $\mathcal{T}$.

It should be emphasized that there are several related but different tasks. The first one is the heterogeneous graph, where the node and edge features are discrete types (e.g., knowledge graphs). A typical solution is to define different weight matrices for each type, which is unable to apply to our task, where the edge features are continuous. Another related task is the weighted graph. In that case, edge features are used as the weight during the aggregation. However, this approach can only deal with low-dimensional edge features and cannot produce meaningful edge embeddings.

3.2 Architecture Overview

We will start by giving an overview of the whole EGAT network. The EGAT network consists of three types of layers, including the *bottleneck layer*, *EGAT layer*, and *merge layer*. Figure 1 gives the illustration of architecture.

The input node and edge features are firstly fed into the *bottleneck layer* to perform a linear transform. Then, the EGAT layers are sequentially applied to the node and edge features to generate higher-level representations. Inside the EGAT layer, the *node module* is applied before the *edge module*, which meets the property of the edge module (introduced below).

Inspired by [14,15], we adopt *multi-scale strategy* by adding a *merge layer* to build hierarchical features. In the merge layer, we collect the output of the bottleneck layer and each EGAT layer, and aggregate them by concatenation. The final node features H^{final} and edge features E^{final} can be expressed as:

$$\vec{h}_i^{final} = \overset{L}{\underset{l=0}{\|}} \vec{h}_i^{l,out}, \quad \vec{e}_{ij}^{final} = \overset{L}{\underset{l=0}{\|}} \vec{e}_{ij}^{l,out} \tag{1}$$

where L is the number of EGAT layers and $\|$ represents the concatenate operator.

The final node and edge embeddings are used to perform the subsequent task $\mathcal{T}$. With the guide of supervised task $\mathcal{T}$ and label $\mathcal{L}$, the EGAT model could be optimized via backpropagation and refine the node and edge embedding.

3.3 Node Module

The node module accepts node features H and edge features E, then process the *edge-integrated attention mechanism* to update node features according to the adjacent edges and nodes, and finally generates higher-level node features H'.

Firstly, we map the node and edge features to higher-level features with the linear transformation to improve the expression ability. Specifically, weight matrices $\mathbf{W_h} \in \mathbb{R}^{F_H' \times F_H}$ and $\mathbf{W_e} \in \mathbb{R}^{F_E' \times F_E}$ are applied to every node and edge, respectively. Then, an edge-integrated attention mechanism $a:$ $(\mathbb{R}^{F'_H}, \mathbb{R}^{F'_H}, \mathbb{R}^{F'_E}) \rightarrow \mathbb{R}$, which generates the attention weights as follows, are performed on each node:

$$w_{ij} = a(\mathbf{W_h}\vec{h}_i, \mathbf{W_h}\vec{h}_j, \mathbf{W_e}\vec{e}_{ij}) \qquad (2)$$

where w_{ij} indicates the importance of node j and edge ij to node i. Similar to the GAT model [4], normalization will be performed on these weights across all choices of node j, where $h_j \in \mathcal{N}_i$, with a softmax function:

$$\alpha_{ij} = \text{softmax}_j(w_{ij}) = \frac{\exp(w_{ij})}{\sum_{k \in \mathcal{N}_i} \exp(w_{ik})} \qquad (3)$$

where $\mathcal{N}_i$ represents the neighboring nodes of node i.

In our work, the edge-integrated attention mechanism a is a single-layer feed-forward neural network, which can be parameterized as a one-dimensional weight vector $\vec{a} \in \mathbb{R}^{2F'_H + F'_E}$, and applying LeakyReLU [16] as the activation function. The whole process can be formulated as follows:

$$\alpha_{ij} = \frac{\exp(\text{LeakyReLU}(\vec{a}^T[\mathbf{W_h}\vec{h}_i \| \mathbf{W_h}\vec{h}_j \| \mathbf{W_e}\vec{e}_{ij}]))}{\sum_{k \in \mathcal{N}_i} \exp(\text{LeakyReLU}(\vec{a}^T[\mathbf{W_h}\vec{h}_i \| \mathbf{W_h}\vec{h}_k \| \mathbf{W_e}\vec{e}_{ik}]))} \qquad (4)$$

where $\cdot^T$ is the transpose operation and $\|$ represents the concatenation operation.

After acquiring the normalized attention weights, we can perform a weighted sum on these neighboring node features. In addition, a non-linearity σ will be applied to these summation results. The final result can be expressed as:

$$\vec{h}'_i = \sigma\left(\sum_{j \in \mathcal{N}_i} \alpha_{ij}[\mathbf{W_h}\vec{h}_j \| \mathbf{W_e}\vec{e}_{ij}]\right) \qquad (5)$$

The aggregation process is also illustrated in Fig. 2(a).

Note that the new node features $\vec{h}'_i$ consist of neighbor node features and edge features, which allows the representation of the node to integrate the edge information. However, in practice, we often want the input and output node features to keep the same dimension (i.e., $F'_H + F'_E = F_H$). Therefore, we introduce $\lambda \in [0, 1]$ to control the contribution ratio of node features to edge features:

$$F'_H = \lfloor \lambda F_H \rfloor, \quad F'_E = \lceil (1 - \lambda)F_H \rceil \qquad (6)$$

where F'_H and F'_E denote the dimension of node and edge features after linear transformation, respectively. Moreover, we can tune λ according to the feature preferences of specific dataset. For example, we can decrease the λ to integrate more edge features to nodes on edge-sensitive datasets, and vice versa. The detailed impact of λ is introduced in the experiments.

3.4   Edge Module

Similarly, the edge module accepts node features H and edge features E, updates edge features with its adjacent nodes and edges, and finally generates higher-level edge features E'.

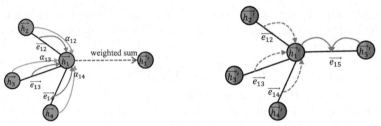

(a) The updating process of Node Module. (b) The updating process of Edge Module.

Fig. 2. The updating process of node module and edge module. Orange and blue represent the node and edge features, respectively. (Color figure online)

An ideal approach to update edge features may include all the adjacent edge and node features. However, the number of adjacent edge pairs could be large in dense graphs, which may increase the computational complexity. As a result, we use the *node-transit* strategy, which uses nodes as transit ports of edge features. Firstly, we aggregate the adjacent edge features to the node with the edge-integrated attention mechanism:

$$\beta_{ij} = \mathrm{softmax}_j(\mathrm{LeakyReLU}(\vec{b}^T[\mathbf{W_h}\vec{h}_i\|\mathbf{W_h}\vec{h}_j\|\mathbf{W_e}\vec{e}_{ij}])) \tag{7}$$

$$\vec{e}_i' = \sum_{j\in\mathcal{N}_i}(\beta_{ij}\mathbf{W_e}\vec{e}_{ij}) \tag{8}$$

where $\vec{e}_i'$ is the aggregated edge features on node i. Note that $\mathbf{W_h}$ and $\mathbf{W_e}$ are not shared among node modules.

Next, we use the aggregated edge features and node features to generate the higher-level edge features with the multilayer perceptron (MLP):

$$\vec{e_{ij}}' = \mathrm{MLP}(\vec{h}_i, \vec{h}_j, \vec{e}_i', \vec{e}_j', \vec{e}_{ij}) \tag{9}$$

3.5 EGAT with Custom Message Function

So far we have introduced the specific node and edge updating method. EGAT is also a framework that can integrate with message-passing-based approaches [12]. Suppose we have such a message passing neural network (MPNN) that:

$$\vec{e_{ij}}' = \mathcal{E}(\vec{h}_i, \vec{h}_j, \vec{e}_{ij}), \quad \vec{m}_{ij}' = \mathcal{M}(\vec{h}_i, \vec{h}_j, \vec{e}_{ij}) \tag{10}$$

where $\mathcal{E}$ means the edge updating function, $\vec{m}_{ij}$ means the message vector and $\mathcal{M}$ is the message function.

We use the *symmetric strategy* to generate the attention weights w_{ij} with the edge-integrated attention mechanism:

$$\begin{aligned} w_{ij} &= a(\vec{h}_i, \vec{h}_j, \vec{e}_{ij}) \\ &= \mathrm{LeakyReLU}(\vec{a}^T[\mathcal{M}(\vec{h}_i, \vec{h}_i, \vec{e}_{ij})\|\mathcal{M}(\vec{h}_i, \vec{h}_j, \vec{e}_{ij})]) \end{aligned} \tag{11}$$

There are three reasons to apply the message function $\mathcal{M}$ to both node i and node j. Firstly, it reuses the calculated message vector $\vec{m}'_{ij}$, thus reduces the performance overhead and the overfitting risk. Secondly, the custom message function $\mathcal{M}$ contains the domain-specific inductive bias, so it is more suitable for specific areas. Thirdly, $\vec{m}'_{ii}$ and $\vec{m}'_{ij}$ are mapped into the same feature space, making the attention vector $\vec{a}$ easier to assess the importance.

Then, we calculate the normalized attention weights α_{ij} with Eq. 3, and finally aggregate messages:

$$\vec{h}'_i = \sigma\left(\sum_{j \in \mathcal{N}_i} \alpha_{ij} \mathcal{M}(\vec{h}_i, \vec{h}_j, \vec{e}_{ij})\right) \tag{12}$$

As for the edge module, we use the custom edge function $\mathcal{E}$ to update edge features. If $\mathcal{E}$ is not specified, we will use the default Edge Module to instead.

4   Experiments

4.1   Dataset and Preprocessing

To show the adaptability on both edge-sensitive and node-sensitive scenarios, we evaluate our models on two categories of datasets, including edge-sensitive AMLSim and node-sensitive citation networks (Cora, Citeseer and PubMed [6]).

AMLSim. AMLSim [7] is a simulated dataset for anti-money laundering, where nodes represent accounts and edge represent the transaction of accounts. Each node has 2 features about account property, and each edge has 4 transaction-related features. Among them, money laundering is primarily related to transaction patterns rather than account properties, so the edge features are more essential than node. In other words, AMLSim is an *edge-sensitive* dataset.

The task of AMLSim is to classify nodes into the eight types, including normal accounts and seven patterns of money laundering. Since nearly 80% of nodes are normal accounts, we use the F_1 score as the metric.

We generate the dataset with the default configuration, except that we enable all money laundering patterns. 100 graphs are generated with different random seeds, and split into 5/5/90 for training, evaluating and testing, respectively.

The dataset is preprocessed as follows. Firstly, we aggregate the multiple transactions between two accounts into one edge. The aggregated edge features contain the number of transactions and the statistic of original features, including the *minimum, maximum, average,* and *standard deviation.* Then, we encode directed edges following the method of [10].

Citation Networks. Cora, Citeseer, and PubMed [6] are three widely used node classification datasets, where nodes and edges represent papers and citation relationships, respectively. We create two edge features following [11], including the cosine similarity of node features and the one-hot encoded edge direction.

To perform a fair comparison with CensNet [11], we follow the same split strategy. Specifically, we evaluate our models with 3% nodes as the training set on Cora, 1% on Citeseer, and 0.1% on PubMed. Additionally, 50% of nodes are used as the validation set, and the rest is the testing set. Since the exact split is not published, we use the GCN [3] as the calibration to minimize the unfairness caused by different partitions. In detail, we split the dataset with several random seeds, among which we select the random seed with the closest accuracy to [11]. In this way, the difficulty of the dataset partition is similar.

4.2 Baselines

We compare our models with both node-centric and edge-featured approaches. The former aggregates edge features to nodes and then applying node-centric methods, while the latter processes edge features directly.

Node-Centric Methods. One approach to processing edge-sensitive graph is aggregating edge features to nodes and then use node-centric methods. Following this approach, we use three baseline methods:

1. **GAT**. We neglect edge features and predict with only node features.
2. **GAT$_{handpick}$**. We attach the statistic of adjacent edge features to nodes, including the *minimum, maximum, average,* and *standard deviation.*
3. **GAT$_{EGAT}$**. We replace the first layer with EGAT. The main difference between GAT$_{handpick}$ is that the aggregation method of GAT$_{EGAT}$ is learnable.

Edge-Featured Methods. We select three typical edge-features methods as the baseline: NNConv [12], MGCN [13], and CensNet [11]. In the experiments, NNConv and MGCN are evaluated on the AMLSim dataset while CensNet is evaluated on the citation networks because the Edge-Node Switching [11] operation of CensNet is too heavy on the AMLSim dataset. Moreover, to evaluate the compatibility of EGAT, we integrate it with NNConv and MGCN, providing two EGAT variants: EGAT$_{NNConv}$ and EGAT$_{MGCN}$.

4.3 Experimental Setup

For all experiments, Batch Normalization [17] is used before the activation function of each layer. We use Adam optimizer [18] with learning rate 0.005. Early stopping strategy is adopted with the patience of 100 epochs. For all the following GAT and EGAT models, we use $K = 8$ attention heads and ELU [19] nonlinearity. The dataset-specific settings are described as follows.

AMLSim. For AMLSim, we apply the EGAT model with 6 layers. The bottleneck layer is a one-layer MLP. We use two-layer MLP as the predicting layer for classification. The outputs of the merge layer are used to process the classification. We use 128 for both node feature and edge feature. The node feature ratio λ is set to 0.25. Dropout [20] with $p = 0.3$ is applied to the output of all layers except for the predicting layer. Besides, we apply L_2 regularization with 0.001.

Table 1. Results on AMLSim dataset. We report the F_1 scores of seven patterns and the classification accuracy. The star labeled methods are ours.

Method	F_1 score								Acc.
	Bipartite	Cycle	Fan-in	Fan-out	Gather-scatter	Scatter-gather	Stack	Avg.	
GAT	0.000	0.000	0.000	0.000	0.086	0.105	0.000	0.027	79.1%
GAT$_{handpick}$	0.769	0.896	0.839	0.878	0.888	0.986	0.574	0.833	97.1%
GAT$_{EGAT}$	0.767	0.902	0.904	0.939	0.936	0.988	0.575	0.859	97.6%
MGCN	0.819	0.942	0.939	0.965	0.972	0.997	0.676	0.901	98.3%
NNConv	0.812	0.924	0.945	0.974	0.975	0.995	0.672	0.900	98.3%
EGAT$_{MGCN}$*	0.808	0.979	0.954	0.981	0.981	0.998	0.695	0.914	98.6%
EGAT$_{NNConv}$*	0.826	0.944	0.950	0.977	0.978	0.998	0.705	0.911	98.5%
EGAT*	**0.856**	**0.991**	**0.965**	**0.986**	**0.987**	**0.999**	**0.774**	**0.937**	**98.9%**

Citation Networks. Since the overfitting is severe in these datasets, we simplify the network structure. The bottleneck layer and the MLP-based predicting layer are removed. Instead, we use GAT to produce the prediction. In all, we use only 2 layers of EGAT. As for hyperparameters, we tried the F_H from $\{32, 64, 128\}$, the F_E from $\{8, 16, 32\}$, the L_2 regulation from $\{0.0002, 0.0005, 0.001\}$, and the dropout from $\{0.6, 0.65, 0.7, 0.75\}$. The node feature ratio λ is set to 0.875. We report the best result from the above combinations.

4.4 Results and Discussions

AMLSim. We compare our model with baselines mentioned above. In Table 1, we report the F_1 scores of all patterns and the classification accuracy.

The results of GAT-based methods show that the F_1 scores drop to a low level if the edge features are neglected. This result is consistent with our analysis in dataset description that the AMLSim is an edge-sensitive dataset. Additionally, the GAT$_{EGAT}$ model outperforms the GAT$_{handpick}$ model, which shows that the learnable aggregation is better than naive handpicked features. However, these methods underperform all the edge-featured methods, because these methods do not take full advantage of edge features.

On the other hand, all the edge-featured methods outperform the GAT-based methods, which shows the superiority of edge feature updating. In particular, the EGAT model gives a higher F_1 score than quantum-chemistry-oriented methods and their EGAT variants. The probable reason is that these models are specially designed, whose inductive bias is not suitable for the AMLSim.

The EGAT model obtains the best F_1 scores for all patterns as well as the highest classification accuracy. Moreover, integrating with EGAT can effectively improve the accuracy of quantum-chemistry-oriented methods. It shows that domain-specific message functions are compatible with EGAT model well, which indicates the potential to apply EGAT model in specific areas.

Table 2. Classification accuracy on citation networks. The data of star labeled methods are provided by [11].

Method	Cora (3%)	Citeseer (1%)	PubMed (0.1%)
GCN* [3]	74.0 ± 2.8%	58.3 ± 4.0%	73.0 ± 5.5%
LNet* [21]	76.3 ± 2.3%	61.3 ± 3.9%	73.4 ± 5.1%
AdaLNet* [21]	77.7 ± 2.4%	**63.3** ± 1.8%	72.8 ± 4.6%
CensNet* [11]	**79.4** ± 1.0%	62.5 ± 1.5%	69.9 ± 2.1%
GCN [3]	74.2 ± 0.4%	58.3 ± 0.7%	73.0 ± 0.9%
GAT	77.5 ± 0.4%	60.2 ± 1.1%	73.2 ± 1.0%
$GAT_{handpick}$	78.2 ± 0.6%	61.0 ± 0.8%	73.9 ± 1.1%
GAT_{EGAT}	78.5 ± 0.4%	59.0 ± 0.5%	73.6 ± 0.5%
EGAT (ours)	79.3 ± 0.7%	59.8 ± 0.5%	**74.7** ± 0.7%

Citation Networks. We compare our model with another edge processing approach, CensNet, on the citation network. The results are shown in Table 2. As mentioned above, we use GCN as the calibration of dataset partition. The result shows that our model obtains the best accuracy on PubMed, and is competitive on Cora. Although, our models do not perform as well on CiteSeer. In conclusion, EGAT model is competitive with state-of-the-art methods.

Summary. The experiment result shows that EGAT achieves the highest F_1 score in edge-sensitive AMLSim dataset and obtain a competitive accuracy node-sensitive citation networks. Moreover, EGAT is compatible to specialized message functions and effectively improves accuracy. Additionally, the complexity of the edge module is $O(|E|(F_E + 2F_H)F_E)$, which is much smaller than Edge-Node Switching operation, so EGAT is more scalable on large and dense graphs.

4.5   Ablation Study

Impact of Layer Number L and Merge Layer. To study the impact of different layer numbers L and the effectiveness of merge layer, we test EGAT on different L, both with and without the merge layer.

Figure 3(a) shows the results. The *EGAT with merge layer* achieves the highest F_1 score at $L = 6$. Despite the multi-scale merge strategy, the accuracy slightly decreases with the increment of depth. The most likely reason is that the dimension of the final features is increased with depth, which causes the overfitting problem of the classification task. On the other hand, in general, the accuracy of *EGAT w/o merge layer* is lower. In practice, the optimum layer number is related to the property of datasets.

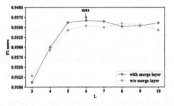
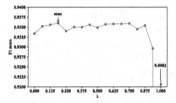

(a) Impact of layers L and merge layer.   (b) Impact of node feature ratio λ

Fig. 3. Impact of hyperparameters, including (a) layer number and (b) node feature ratio. The average F_1 scores are reported (the higher the better).

Impact of Node Feature Ratio λ. We also test different node feature ratio of EGAT model, and Fig. 3(b) shows the result. The selection of λ is a trade-off, where a high λ reduces the information loss of the previously learned node features, but it also restrains the utility of edge features. As the result indicates, λ has little effect on the F_1 score when $\lambda \leq 0.875$, while the F_1 score drops significantly when $\lambda > 0.875$. In practice, the optimum λ is highly related to the preference of datasets. Specifically, higher λ is suitable for node-sensitive datasets, while lower λ is appropriate for edge-sensitive datasets.

5   Conclusion

We propose a new framework EGAT to handle both node and edge features, which extends the scenarios of application of graph neural networks. EGAT exceeds or matches the state-of-the-art on both node-sensitive and edge-sensitive datasets, and can also be combined with domain-specific methods. In the future, we will explore how to apply EGAT to multigraphs and time-related graphs.

References

1. Zhou, J., et al.: Graph neural networks: a review of methods and applications. arXiv e-prints arXiv:1812.08434, December 2018
2. Zhang, Z., Cui, P., Zhu, W.: Deep learning on graphs: a survey. arXiv e-prints arXiv:1812.04202, December 2018
3. Kipf, T.N., Welling, M.: Semi-supervised classification with graph convolutional networks. arXiv e-prints arXiv:1609.02907, September 2016
4. Veličković, P., Cucurull, G., Casanova, A., Romero, A., Liò, P., Bengio, Y.: Graph attention networks. In: International Conference on Learning Representations (2018). https://openreview.net/forum?id=rJXMpikCZ, accepted as poster
5. Vaswani, A., et al.: Attention is all you need. In: Guyon, I., et al. (eds.) Advances in Neural Information Processing Systems, vol. 30, pp. 5998–6008. Curran Associates, Inc. (2017). http://papers.nips.cc/paper/7181-attention-is-all-you-need.pdf

6. Yang, Z., Cohen, W.W., Salakhutdinov, R.: Revisiting semi-supervised learning with graph embeddings. In: Balcan, M., Weinberger, K.Q. (eds.) Proceedings of the 33nd International Conference on Machine Learning, ICML 2016, New York City, NY, USA, 19–24 June 2016. JMLR Workshop and Conference Proceedings, vol. 48, pp. 40–48. JMLR.org (2016). http://proceedings.mlr.press/v48/yanga16.html
7. Weber, M., et al.: Scalable graph learning for anti-money laundering: a first look. arXiv e-prints arXiv:1812.00076, November 2018
8. Xiao, W., et al.: Heterogeneous graph attention network. WWW (2019)
9. Schlichtkrull, M., Kipf, T.N., Bloem, P., Berg, R.v.d., Titov, I., Welling, M.: Modeling relational data with graph convolutional networks. arXiv preprint arXiv:1703.06103 (2017)
10. Gong, L., Cheng, Q.: Exploiting edge features in graph neural networks. arXiv e-prints arXiv:1809.02709, September 2018
11. Jiang, X., Ji, P., Li, S.: CensNet: convolution with edge-node switching in graph neural networks. In: Proceedings of the Twenty-Eighth International Joint Conference on Artificial Intelligence, IJCAI 2019, pp. 2656–2662. International Joint Conferences on Artificial Intelligence Organization, July 2019. https://doi.org/10.24963/ijcai.2019/369
12. Gilmer, J., Schoenholz, S.S., Riley, P.F., Vinyals, O., Dahl, G.E.: Neural message passing for quantum chemistry. arXiv e-prints arXiv:1704.01212, April 2017
13. Lu, C., Liu, Q., Wang, C., Huang, Z., Lin, P., He, L.: Molecular property prediction: a multilevel quantum interactions modeling perspective. arXiv e-prints arXiv:1906.11081, June 2019
14. Shervashidze, N., Schweitzer, P., van Leeuwen, E.J., Mehlhorn, K., Borgwardt, K.M.: Weisfeiler-Lehman graph kernels. J. Machine Learn. Res. **12**(77), 2539–2561 (2011). http://jmlr.org/papers/v12/shervashidze11a.html
15. Xu, K., Li, C., Tian, Y., Sonobe, T., Kawarabayashi, K.i., Jegelka, S.: Representation learning on graphs with jumping knowledge networks. arXiv e-prints arXiv:1806.03536, June 2018
16. Maas, A.L.: Rectifier nonlinearities improve neural network acoustic models (2013)
17. Ioffe, S., Szegedy, C.: Batch normalization: accelerating deep network training by reducing internal covariate shift. arXiv e-prints arXiv:1502.03167, February 2015
18. Kingma, D.P., Ba, J.: Adam: a method for stochastic optimization. arXiv e-prints arXiv:1412.6980, December 2014
19. Clevert, D.A., Unterthiner, T., Hochreiter, S.: Fast and accurate deep network learning by exponential linear units (ELUs). arXiv e-prints arXiv:1511.07289, November 2015
20. Srivastava, N., Hinton, G., Krizhevsky, A., Sutskever, I., Salakhutdinov, R.: Dropout: a simple way to prevent neural networks from overfitting. J. Mach. Learn. Res. **15**(1), 1929–1958 (2014)
21. Liao, R., Zhao, Z., Urtasun, R., Zemel, R.: LanczosNet: multi-scale deep graph convolutional networks. In: ICLR (2019)

Attention and Transformers II

Knowledge Graph Enhanced Transformer for Generative Question Answering Tasks

Chaojie Liang[1,2], Jingying Yang[2], and Xianghua Fu[1(✉)]

[1] Shenzhen Technology University, Shenzhen, China
fuxianghua@sztu.edu.cn
[2] Shenzhen University, Shenzhen, China

Abstract. Generative question answering tasks usually suffer from the challenge of the lack of external knowledge. The generative question answering model cannot understand the intention of questions effectively because the questions asked by users are short and the amount of information is insufficient. Therefore, it needs to be supplemented by external knowledge. In this paper, we propose a generative question answering model combined with knowledge graph (KG-Transformer), which can solve the problem of inaccurate generation caused by the above challenge. The advantage of KG-Transformer is that it designs a knowledge retrieval module which can obtain external knowledge from the knowledge graph as a supplement to the intention of question. Besides, compared with the traditional sentence similarity method and hard fusion, it uses a soft switching mechanism, which can switch between the knowledge vector and the question vector, effectively extracting knowledge information and questions information and then fusion. Experiments on a benchmark dataset demonstrate that our model has robust superiority over compared methods in generating informative and accurate answer.

Keywords: Knowledge graph · Transformer · Question answering

1 Introduction

Building a generative question answering model that is capable of providing informative responses is a long-term goal of artificial intelligence. The current generative question answering models based on Seq2Seq [1–4] and Transformer [5] are faced with the problem of lack of external knowledge. As the question contains little valid information in the generative question answering tasks, it is difficult to extract valid information if model based on Seq2Seq [1–4] or Transformer [5] only encodes a single question without external knowledge or human intervention. Without enough valid information, the model cannot understand the intention of the question well and thus cannot generate accurate answers.

In order to enhance the understanding of the intention of the question, some scholars have begun to study the knowledge graph as supplementary information of questions. He [6] used the information copied from the question and the relevant knowledge retrieved from the trigram of knowledge graph to integrate the

© Springer Nature Switzerland AG 2021
I. Farkaš et al. (Eds.): ICANN 2021, LNCS 12891, pp. 267–280, 2021.
https://doi.org/10.1007/978-3-030-86362-3_22

attention mechanism into the question representation to improve the understanding of the intention of the question. Annervaz [7] proposed a convolution-based knowledge graph entity and relation cluster representation learning model, using attention mechanism to extract fact-supporting knowledge from the task-based knowledge graph. Madotto [8] used memory networks to store knowledge graph, and then used pointer network [9] to switch between the original text and the vocabulary to select words to improve the generative network generation effect. Yang [10] studied the use of a marked attention mechanism to adaptively decide whether to pay attention to background knowledge and decide which part of the knowledge base information to add to improve machine reading. Although these methods have improved in performance, most models except vocabulary distribution combine copy distribution and retrieval distribution, and accurate modeling the dependencies between multiple distributions is quite complex and difficult, which leads to the not comprehensive knowledge obtained from the knowledge graph. An [11] and Tu [12] both proposed a knowledge unit with a key-value structure to integrate knowledge graph triple information into the answer generation model. This method can avoid the modeling of the dependencies of the above distributions and obtain the external knowledge while reducing the complexity. Although the method is feasible, the approach of knowledge fusion does not fully consider the semantic relationship between knowledge information and question information.

Aiming at the problem of lack of external knowledge in traditional generative models, we propose a new generative question answering model that combines knowledge graphs (KG-Transformer) which consists of KGT encoder and KGT decoder. We directly use the Transformer decoding module [5] as the KGT decoder and design a knowledge fusion module composed of a retrieval module that retrieves knowledge graph information and a dual Transformer encoder [5] that encodes knowledge information and question information separately as the KGT encoder. In addition, the soft switching mechanism is used in the knowledge fusion module to flexibly switch between the knowledge vector and the question vector, effectively extract and merge knowledge information and question information, which can improve the accuracy of answer generation and enrich the content of generated answers.

The main contributions of this work are as follows:

- In order to solve the problem of lack of external knowledge, we propose a novel module of knowledge retrieval, which retrieves relevant facts information from knowledge graph and extracts its knowledge information using the Transformer encoder [5].
- Since the knowledge information may contain some lengthy and useless information, we propose a knowledge fusion module, which applies a deep neural network to further extract features and finally fuse the knowledge information with the question information.
- We conduct extensive experiments to demonstrate the superiority of our proposed model for improving generative answers performance in terms of the BLUE [13], topic similarity [14] and human evaluation [15].

2   Related Work

Generative question answering aims at generating meaningful and coherent answer given input question. Various techniques have been proposed to improve the quality of generated answers from different perspectives, including the following aspects:

2.1   Generative Question Answering

Bahdanau [2] combined the Seq2Seq model with the attention mechanism to generate the answer, but the model did not encode the entire input as a fixed-length vector. Serban [16] proposed the hierarchical Seq2Seq model, which modeled the context by adding additional session-level encoders to reduce information loss and produced more accurate answers. Li [17] proposed a dialogue generation model combined with reinforcement learning to explore the possible space of maximizing the expected reward by simulating the dialogue between two virtual machines. Some scholars are also engaged in the research of memory-based Seq2Seq model. The memory network proposed by Sukhbaatar [18] contains a large external memory, and the model can read the external memory storage many times and finally produce an output. Different from the above methods, this paper is a question and answer system mainly based on knowledge graph and Transformer.

2.2   Knowledge Acquisition Method

He [6] first identified the subject entity of the question, and retrieved relevant facts from the knowledge base using the constructed retrieval mechanism based on the subject entity. Madotto [8] stored all relevant information in the memory network, and directly copied the relevant information through the copy mechanism. However, these methods all have to deal with the dependence of multiple distributions including vocabulary distribution, copy distribution and retrieval distribution, which caused the acquired knowledge may not be guaranteed and the model is difficult to train. An [11] and Tu [12] calculated the degree of correlation between the question (or context information), the state of the encoding stage and the key part of the triple, weighted and summed the value part to obtain knowledge. Although the method capture knowledge information to a certain extent, the extracted effective knowledge information is limited. Therefore, we directly use the traditional retrieval-based question answering model to retrieve relevant facts from the knowledge graph and extract knowledge using the Transformer encoder [5], which avoids the dependency of multiple distributions while ensuring access to comprehensive knowledge information.

2.3   Knowledge Fusion Method

He [6] used the retrieval distribution to fuse the facts in the knowledge base into the generation process. Madotto [8] merged the copied historical information into the generation. An [11] directly added knowledge to the question expressions. Tu [12] linearly transformed the knowledge, questions, words predicted at the last moment and the decoded hidden layer state, and applies *softmax* function to calculate the knowledge fusion. However, the knowledge fusion methods of these scholar do not fully consider the degree of semantic matching between question information and knowledge information. Therefore, we first encodes the retrieved knowledge to extract useful features, calculates the degree of correlation with the encoded question, and uses it as a soft switching mechanism to weight the knowledge vector and the question vector separately and then sum them. This fusion method can more effectively extract the semantic features of the question.

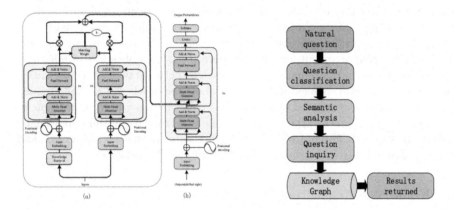

Fig. 1. KG-Transformer structure   **Fig. 2.** Knowledge retrieval module

3   Model

As shown in Fig. 1, KG-Transformer (referred to as KGT) consists of two parts: KGT encoder (Fig. 1(a)) and KGT decoder (Fig. 1(b)). The KGT encoder is a retrieval module and a knowledge fusion module, where the knowledge fusion module is mainly composed of two Transformer encoder modules [5]. In addition, the KGT decoder directly uses the Transformer decoder module [5].

3.1   KGT Encoder

The KGT encoder is composed of a knowledge retrieval module and a knowledge fusion module.

Knowledge Retrieval Module. Knowledge retrieval module (the knowledge retrieval module in Fig. 1(a)) is actually a question answering system based on the knowledge graph. The basic principle is to semantically analyze the question, and then query from knowledge graph and infer to obtain the knowledge information. We use the method of semantic analysis [19] retrieve answers from the knowledge graph, no need to redesign the retrieval distribution and deal with the complex dependencies of multiple distributions, meanwhile it can ensure the accuracy of the retrieved answers.

As shown in Fig. 2, after receiving the question in natural language form, the question answering system based on the knowledge graph first analyzes the question, classifies the question by matching the pre-defined category keyword list, and obtains the question list of categories, at the same time using AC automaton [20] to extract the subject words and keywords in the question to construct an entity dictionary, through question analysis to convert question category information and keyword information into a structured cypher query sentence list. The structured query statement list is queried in the graph database neo4j, and the related answer list is returned. Finally, we performed further processing to obtain answers in the form of natural sentences, which are returned to the user.

Knowledge Fusion Module. The knowledge fusion module (other components than the knowledge retrieval module in Fig. 1(a)) is composed of two parts: Knowledge Encoding Module and Question Encoding Module.

Knowledge Encoding Module is a Transformer encoder [5] (the left half of Fig. 1(a)). We use AC automaton [20] to retrieve the original knowledge information related to the question from the knowledge graph, and then vectorize the knowledge information and input it into the Transformer encoder [5] to obtain the knowledge vector r_k. r_k contains the semantic information of the knowledge retrieved from the knowledge retrieval module.

Question Encoding Module is also a Transformer encoder [5] (the right half of Fig. 1(a)), through using the same calculation method as the knowledge encoding module can obtain question vector r_a. r_a contains all the semantic information of the question, and we can directly decode the question expression. However, in order to enable the generative model to obtain richer semantic information related to the question in the decoding stage, we perform knowledge fusion before decoding. First, we calculate a function of r_a and r_k:

$$f(r_a, r_k) = W_k^1 * r_a * r_k + b_k^1 \tag{1}$$

Where W_k^1 is the weight adjustment matrix and b_k^1 is the offset term. The values of W_k^1 and b_k^1 can be obtained through training.

Then, according to matching degree weight α:

$$\alpha = sigmoid(W_k^2 f(r_a, r_k) + b_k^2) \tag{2}$$

Where W_k^2 is the weight adjustment matrix and b_k^2 is the offset term. The values of W_k^2 and b_k^2 can be obtained through training.

$\alpha \in \mathbb{R}^n$, n is the size of the knowledge unit, which indicates that each piece of knowledge information corresponds to the weight of the question expression. In addition, *sigmoid* is an activation function. The degree of relevance α plays a soft switching role, extracting the information from knowledge representation with the probability of α, and extracting the information from the question representation with the probability of $1 - \alpha$:

$$r_k' = \alpha * r_k \tag{3}$$

$$r_a' = (1 - \alpha) * r_a \tag{4}$$

The soft switching mechanism dynamically adjusts the probability α of knowledge information r_k be 0 and the probability 1-α of question information r_a to 1 if the retrieval system cannot give the answers to the questions without relevant question types in the knowledge base. On the contrary, if there is invalid information in the question, the soft switching mechanism will adjust the probability α of extracting knowledge information r_k to 1 and the probability $1 - \alpha$ of question information r_a to 0. The soft switching mechanism is more flexible than simply adding the weighted knowledge representation and the question representation directly. We prove the validity of the soft switching mechanism through experiments. Finally, the knowledge representation r_k' and the question representation r_a' are fused to generate a new question representation R_a that combines knowledge information:

$$R_a = r_k' + r_a' \tag{5}$$

We use this new semantic representation R_a as the final output of the encoding model for subsequent decoding task.

3.2   KGT Decoder

We use the Transformer decoder as the KGT decoder. In the decoding stage, the model is autoregressive that uses the predicted words as the input of the current step. At the same time, considering the output from the KGT encoder, we select the word with the highest probability from the vocabulary as the output at the current time. Meanwhile, we input the encoding result R_a into the decoder. The decoder outputs y through the Transformer [5] decoder, and y generates a lexical distribution P_{kg} after passing through a linear layer and a softmax layer:

$$P_{kg} = softmax(Vy + b) \tag{6}$$

Where V and b are learnable parameters. P_{kg} is the probability distribution of all vocabularies in the dataset and knowledge graph, from which we can know the probability of predicting vocabulary y:

$$P(y) = P_{kg}(y) \tag{7}$$

In the training phase, the loss function of the time step t is as follows:

$$loss_t = -logP(y_t) \tag{8}$$

The objective function of the model that the total loss of the entire sequence is:

$$Loss = \frac{1}{T} \sum_{t=0}^{T} loss_t \tag{9}$$

4 Experiment

4.1 Datasets

Medical Question Answering Dataset (Referred to as **Medical**): This dataset is provided by [23]. We make some small changes to the original dataset. The processed **Medical** contains 1,000K, 5K, and 5K pairs for training, validation, and testing, respectively.

4.2 Knowledge Graph

The knowledge graph (referred to as **MKG**) we use is a vertical website as a data source and a medical knowledge graph centered on disease[1]. The **MKG** contains 44,000 knowledge entities of 7 entity types, 300,000 relationship magnitude of 10 entity relationship types, 8 attribute types and 18 question types.

It can query information about 8807 kinds of diseases, and the **Medical** contains 901 kinds of diseases. Therefore, we can basically find relevant information in the **MKG**.

4.3 Evaluation

We apply BLEU [13], topic similarity [14] and human evaluation [15] to evaluate the experimental results.

---

[1] https://github.com/liuhuanyong/QASystemOnMedicalKG.

4.4   Baselines

We compare the proposed KG-Transformer with the following baseline models:

ACNM: The first neural dialogue model to apply RNN-based Seq2Seq framework to dialogue generation tasks [1].

RNNsearch: Model combining attention mechanism with Bi-LSTM-based Seq2Seq framework [2].

DIAL-LV: Combining latent variables with standard Gaussian priors and decoders in the Seq2Seq model based on Bi-RNN [3].

Adver-REGS: An adversarial reinforcement learning model consisting of a generator and a discriminator [4]. An RNN-based discriminator is used to evaluate the sequence, and the learning of the generator based on the Seq2Seq model is guided by reinforcement learning to generate answers.

Transformer: Encoding-decoding structure based entirely on attention mechanism [5].

4.5   Implementation Details

In the experiment, the maximum length of the questions and the answers in the **Medical** are both 100, and the size of the vocabulary is 8189. We set the batch size to 32, the number of encoder/decoder layers and hidden layer dimensions to 6 and 256 respectively. The hidden layer dimension of the feedforward network layer is 1024, the learning rate is 0.0001, the number of epochs is 8 and dropout rate is 0.1.

4.6   Experimental Results

We score the proposed method in the light of several metrics that can reflect the accuracy. The details are summarized in Table 1, Table 2 and Table 3, Table 4.

Table 1. Performance of KG-Transformer and five baselines on medical question answering task.

Model	BLEU-1 (%)	BLEU-2 (%)	BLEU-3 (%)	BLEU-4 (%)
ANCM	14.43	24.32	26.33	25.19
RNNsearch	16.37	25.93	27.41	27.01
DIAL-LV	17.27	27.42	28.86	27.20
Adver-REGS	17.64	25.92	26.73	25.00
Transformer	20.22	29.64	30.36	28.26
KGT	**22.10**	**32.51**	**33.04**	**31.78**

Table 2. Greedy Matching (Greedy), Embedding Average (Average), and Vector Extrema (Extrema). Unlike the BLEU, which measure the token-level match, these embedding-based metrics map answers to a vector space and compute the cosine similarity with golden answers, which can to a large extent measure the sentence-level semantic similarity.

Model	Greedy (%)	Average (%)	Extrema (%)
ACNM	94.390	99.565	97.701
RNNsearch	94.438	99.534	97.891
DIAL-LV	95.160	99.674	98.237
Adver-REGS	94.613	99.204	96.537
Transformer	95.188	99.726	98.083
KGT	**95.552**	**99.752**	**98.433**

Automatic Evaluation. Table 1 reports BLEU scores [13] of different models. It can be seen from the Table 1 that in the Seq2Seq model, the BLEU scores [13] of DIAL-LV and Adver-REGS are higher than those of ANCM and RNNsearch, but the effect is not much improved. The BLEU scores [13] of DIAL-LV are relatively higher, because it can directly capture the possible response of a given input. Compared to all Seq2seq models, Transformer has higher BLEU scores [13] due to its self-attention mechanism, which can effectively solve the problem of long distance dependence within a sentence. Compared with Transformer, KG-Transformer has improved by 9%, 10%, 9%, and 12% on the BLEU-1, BLEU-2, BLEU-3, and BLEU-4 [13], respectively. It shows that it is effective to fuse knowledge information of knowledge graph in the generation model.

Table 2 reports the results of embedding-based topic similarity of the different models. As can be seen from the Table 2, compared with the Transformer model with the highest score in the baseline, KG-Transformer model has improved on three evaluation metrics, which further verifies the effectiveness of the knowledge information of the fusion knowledge graph.

Human Evaluation. In order to assist the automatic evaluation, we apply the artificial evaluation proposed by [15] to further evaluate the model. We randomly selected 300 questions from the test set and applied the baseline model and our model KG-Transformer to generate answers. We invited 10 scholars with backgrounds in related fields to let them evaluate the generated answers in terms of fluency, accuracy, and diversity. Results are as Table 3 shows.

From the perspective of fluency analysis, ACNM has the lowest fluency, followed by RNNsearch and DIAL-LV, because they cannot solve the problem of out-of-vocabulary words [24] and the problem of repeated generation [9]. Other models can basically guarantee fluency. In terms of accuracy, the fluency of the Adver-REGS model is higher than that of ACNM, RNNsearch, DIAL-LV, and Transformer, but the accuracy is only 15%, indicating that the discriminator of the Adver-REGS model does not guide the generator well to generate answers

Table 3. Artificial evaluation of the KG-Transformer and five baselines on medical question answering task.

Model	Fluency (%)	Accuracy (%)	Diversity (%)
ACNM	32	34	28.5
RNNsearch	47	35.5	31.5
DIAL-LV	48	21	44.5
Adver-REGS	69.5	15	19
Transformer	66	54	51.5
KGT	**79**	**58**	**70**

Table 4. BLEU score of three models with different knowledge fusion structures.

Model	BLEU-1 (%)	BLEU-2 (%)	BLEU-3 (%)	BLEU-4 (%)
Transformer	20.22	29.64	30.36	28.26
KGT-hard	21.81	30.97	31.34	28.98
KGT-soft	**22.10**	**32.51**	**33.04**	**31.78**

that meet the requirements. Transformer is more accurate than RNN-based models (ACNM, RNNsearch, DIAL-LV, Adver-REGS). In addition, KG-Transformer has the highest score, indicating that combining medical knowledge graph can alleviate the lack of knowledge, and the model can better understand the intent of the question. In terms of diversity, KG-Transformer model is relatively highest because it introduces external knowledge and contains many words that are not found in the vocabulary, which enriches the content generated by the model to a certain extent.

As can be seen from Table 3, on the **Medical**, manual scoring further illustrates that fusion of knowledge graphs can improve the fluency, accuracy and diversity of the model.

Effectiveness Analysis of Knowledge Fusion Structure. In order to verify the superiority of the soft switching mechanism in the knowledge fusion structure, we have designed an ablation experiment, including a generation model without the knowledge fusion structure and two generation models with different knowledge fusion structures.

The Transformer Model does not have a knowledge retrieval module and a knowledge fusion module, so it does not take information from the knowledge graph. It only takes information from the input to generation the answer.

The KG-Transformer-hard Model (KGT-hard) applies the L1 paradigm to calculate the degree of relevance of knowledge and questions, and adds the weighted knowledge to the question to obtain the question representation of the fusion knowledge.

Table 5. Answers generated by different models in **Medical** (The text in blue indicates the generative repeated words, while the text in red shows that KG-Transformer generate the same answer as reference answer.)

Questin:
My baby is 10 days after birth, he felt a little short of breath, nasal congestion, sputum, a little milk spitting, choking, but in a good mental state, whats going on with my baby, please?
Reference answer1:
Hello, you baby maybe have a cold, if cold usually cough, expectoration, fever. Guidance: You can use pediatric aminophenol huangnamin granules to treat, drink plenty of water, pay attention to keep warm is very important, if necessary, use infusion for treatment.
Reference answer2:
Hello, this situation considers upper respiratory tract infections, upper respiratory tract infections generally have nasal congestion, children are relatively small, there may be poor breathing, spitting milk and other symptoms.
ANCM:
Hello, according to your description, the baby's situation is caused by a cold, you can give the baby to take children's cold particles, children's cold particles, children's cold particles, children's cold particles, children's cold particles, drink more water, eat more fruit, drink water and eat more fruits. <unk>
RNNsearch:
Hello hello, according to your description, consider the baby baby's snoring, you can still pay attention to when you can give your baby. Baby babies are recommended <unk>.
DIAL-LV:
Your situation is normal, don't worry, don't worry about advice: hello, I suggest you go to the hospital to do a test, see if there is inflammation, if it is inflammation, can be treated with antibiotics.
Adver-REGS:
Hello, your situation is a certain risk, I suggest you go to the hospital to check. Suggestion: Hello, I suggest you go to the hospital for a comprehensive check to see if there is a problem. If it is calcium deficiency, you can take calcium treatment.
Transformer:
The child has the above symptoms and is considered to be caused by respiratory infections. He can take pediatric aminophenol huangnamin granules and ribavirin granules.
KG-Transformer:
If the baby has the above symptoms, consider the cause of acute upper respiratory tract infection. You can take pediatric aminophenol huangnamin granules and amoxicillin for treatment.

The KG-Transformer-soft Model (KGT-soft) applies a deep neural network to learn a soft switching mechanism, and switches back and forth between knowledge and questions to obtain the question representation of the fusion knowledge.

We compare the BLEU scores of three models on the **Medical**. It can be seen from the data in Table 4 that the BLEU scores of the Transformer are lower than those of the other models with the knowledge fusion module, proving that knowledge graph mitigates the lack of external knowledge to some extent. In addition, we also can clearly see that the BLEU scores of the KG-Transformer-soft are higher than KG-Transformer-hard, indicating that the soft switching mechanism can improve the performance of the model.

Analysis of Generated Samples. Table 5 shows the answers generated by a question on each model. It can be seen from Table 5 that RNN-based models (ACNM, RNNsearch, DIAL-LV, Adver-REGS) all have repetitive generation problems, and the generated sentences have <unk> characters, which cannot solve the problem of out-of-vocabulary words. All models have the ability to generate new words, such as RNNsearch's "snoring", DIAL-LV's "antibiotics", Adver-REGS's "calcium". Compared with the reference answers, these new words are not accurate, indicating that the above three models cannot understand the meaning of the question well. Compared with the reference answers, it was found that the diagnosis of the disease "upper respiratory tract infection" generated by KG-Transformer and the recommended drug "pediatric aminophenol huangnamin granules" are accurate, indicating that KG-Transformer is effective in introducing knowledge information. The generated new word "amoxicillin" was found to be used to treat typhoid fever and other Salmonella infections after reviewing the data. Children can also take it, indicating that KG-Transformer can enrich the generated content.

From the above experimental results, it is shown that KG-Transformer model can generate correct, coherent and natural answers more effectively than existing methods.

5   Conclusion

In response to the problem of lack of external knowledge in the generative question answering model, we propose KG-Transformer. The model is composed of a KGT encoder and a KGT decoder. By using the soft switching mechanism in the knowledge fusion structure, it is possible to flexibly switch between the knowledge vector and the question vector, and effectively extract and integrate knowledge information and question information. We also verified through experiments that KG-Transformer with soft switching mechanism can alleviate the lack of external knowledge, improve the accuracy of answer generation and enrich the content of generated answers.

Acknowledgements. This research is supported by the Scientific Research Platforms and Projects in Universities in Guangdong Province under Grants 2019KTSCX204 and the Stable Support Projects for Shenzhen Higher Education Institutions under Grants SZWD2021011.

References

1. Vinyals, O., Le, Q.: A neural conversational model. arXiv preprint arXiv:1506.05869 (2015)
2. Bahdanau, D., Cho, K., Bengio, Y.: Neural machine translation by jointly learning to align and translate. arXiv preprint arXiv:1409.0473 (2014)
3. Cao, K., Clark, S.: Latent variable dialogue models and their diversity. arXiv preprint arXiv:1702.05962 (2017)
4. Li, J., Monroe, W., Shi, T., Jean, S., Ritter, A., Jurafsky, D.: Adversarial learning for neural dialogue generation. arXiv preprint arXiv:1701.06547 (2017)
5. Vaswani, A., et al.: Attention is all you need. In: Advances in Neural Information Processing Systems, pp. 5998–6008 (2017)
6. He, S., Liu, C., Liu, K., Zhao, J.: Generating natural answers by incorporating copying and retrieving mechanisms in sequence-to-sequence learning. In: Proceedings of the 55th Annual Meeting of the Association for Computational Linguistics (Volume 1: Long Papers), pp. 199–208 (2017)
7. Annervaz, K., Chowdhury, S.B.R., Dukkipati, A.: Learning beyond datasets: knowledge graph augmented neural networks for natural language processing. arXiv preprint arXiv:1802.05930 (2018)
8. Madotto, A., Wu, C.-S., Fung, P.: Mem2Seq: effectively incorporating knowledge bases into end-to-end task-oriented dialog systems. arXiv preprint arXiv:1804.08217 (2018)
9. See, A., Liu, P.J., Manning, C.D.: Get to the point: summarization with pointer-generator networks. arXiv preprint arXiv:1704.04368 (2017)
10. Yang, B., Mitchell, T.: Leveraging knowledge bases in LSTMs for improving machine reading. arXiv preprint arXiv:1902.09091 (2019)
11. An, W., Chen, Q., Yang, Y., He, L.: Knowledge memory based LSTM model for answer selection. In: Liu, D., Xie, S., Li, Y., Zhao, D., El-Alfy, E.S. (eds.) Neural Information Processing. International Conference on Neural Information Processing, pp. 34–42. Springer, Cham (2017). https://doi.org/10.1007/978-3-319-70096-0_4
12. Tu, Z., Jiang, Y., Liu, X., Shu, L., Shi, S.: Generative stock question answering. arXiv preprint arXiv:1804.07942 (2018)
13. Papineni, K., Roukos, S., Ward, T., Zhu, W.-J.: BLEU: a method for automatic evaluation of machine translation. In: Proceedings of the 40th Annual Meeting of the Association for Computational Linguistics, pp. 311–318 (2002)
14. Liu, C.-W., Lowe, R., Serban, I.V., Noseworthy, M., Charlin, L., Pineau, J.: How not to evaluate your dialogue system: an empirical study of unsupervised evaluation metrics for dialogue response generation. arXiv preprint arXiv:1603.08023 (2016)
15. Shen, X., Su, H., Niu, S., Demberg, V.: Improving variational encoder-decoders in dialogue generation. arXiv preprint arXiv:1802.02032 (2018)
16. Serban, I., et al.: A hierarchical latent variable encoder-decoder model for generating dialogues. In: Proceedings of the AAAI Conference on Artificial Intelligence, vol. 31 (2017)

17. Li, J., Monroe, W., Ritter, A., Galley, M., Gao, J., Jurafsky, D.: Deep reinforcement learning for dialogue generation. arXiv preprint arXiv:1606.01541 (2016)
18. Sukhbaatar, S., Szlam, A., Weston, J., Fergus, R.: End-to-end memory networks. arXiv preprint arXiv:1503.08895 (2015)
19. Berant, J., Liang, P.: Semantic parsing via paraphrasing. In: Proceedings of the 52nd Annual Meeting of the Association for Computational Linguistics (Volume 1: Long Papers), pp. 1415–1425 (2014)
20. Aho, A.V., Corasick, M.J.: Efficient string matching: an aid to bibliographic search. Commun. ACM **18**(6), 333–340 (1975)
21. He, K., Zhang, X., Ren, S., Sun, J.: Deep residual learning for image recognition. In: Proceedings of the IEEE Conference on Computer Vision and Pattern Recognition, pp. 770–778 (2016)
22. Ba, J.L., Kiros, J.R., Hinton, G.E.: Layer normalization. arXiv preprint arXiv:1607.06450 (2016)
23. Yan, G., Li, J.: Mobile medical question and answer system with improved char-level based convolution neural network and sparse auto encoder. In: Proceedings of the 2019 Asia Pacific Information Technology Conference, pp. 20–24 (2019)
24. Luong, M.-T., Sutskever, I., Le, Q.V., Vinyals, O., Zaremba, W.: Addressing the rare word problem in neural machine translation. arXiv preprint arXiv:1410.8206 (2014)

GAttANet: Global Attention Agreement for Convolutional Neural Networks

Rufin VanRullen[1,2]([☒]) and Andrea Alamia[1]

[1] CerCo, CNRS, 31052 Toulouse, France
{rufin.vanrullen,andrea.alamia}@cnrs.fr
[2] ANITI, Université de Toulouse, 31062 Toulouse, France

Abstract. Transformer attention architectures, similar to those developed for natural language processing, have recently proved efficient also in vision, either in conjunction with or as a replacement for convolutional layers. Typically, visual attention is inserted in the network architecture as a (series of) feedforward self-attention module(s), with mutual key-query agreement as the main selection and routing operation. However efficient, this strategy is only vaguely compatible with the way that attention is implemented in biological brains: as a separate and unified network of attentional selection regions, receiving inputs from and exerting modulatory influence on the entire hierarchy of visual regions. Here, we report experiments with a simple such attention system that can improve the performance of standard convolutional networks, with relatively few additional parameters. Each spatial position in each layer of the network produces a key-query vector pair; all queries are then pooled into a global attention query. On the next iteration, the match between each key and the global attention query modulates the network's activations— emphasizing or silencing the locations that agree or disagree (respectively) with the global attention system. We demonstrate the usefulness of this brain-inspired Global Attention Agreement network (GAttANet) for various convolutional backbones (from a simple 5-layer toy model to a standard ResNet50 architecture) and datasets (CIFAR10, CIFAR100, Imagenet-1k). Each time, our global attention system improves accuracy over the corresponding baseline.

Keywords: Transformer · Convolution · Global attention · Image classification

1 Introduction

Transformer Attention Networks - Modern Natural Language Processing (NLP) strongly relies on attention mechanisms to handle long-distance relations between elements in a sequence of text. In particular, the Transformer architecture, which uses key-query vector agreement to determine information routing

Supported by ANITI ANR grant ANR-19-PI3A-0004, AI-REPS ANR grant ANR-18-CE37-0007-01 and OSCI-DEEP ANR grant ANR-19-NEUC-0004.

I. Farkaš et al. (Eds.): ICANN 2021, LNCS 12891, pp. 281–293, 2021.
https://doi.org/10.1007/978-3-030-86362-3_23

in feed-forward attention modules, has become an important component of most state-of-the-art language models [24].

More recently, the same Transformer attention strategy has been successfully integrated in state-of-the-art vision architectures. Some studies have proposed to insert separate attention modules within standard convolutional backbones [2,25], while others have suggested to do away with convolutions entirely, and instead rely solely on Transformer operations [2,16,27]. Indeed, it can be demonstrated that convolutions are actually a subset of all operations permitted by Transformer modules [5]—so attention is strictly more expressive than convolution, although it may be less computationally efficient, depending on implementation.

On the one hand, the latest vision Transformer architectures often surpass the performance of convolutional networks on image classification [7,22]. On the other hand, performance need not be the *only* standard by which we should evaluate vision models. For instance, biological plausibility of the resulting architecture also matters: if a computational solution was selected by evolution, it probably deserves attention (no pun intended). Of course, this selection may just be the result of biophysical (e.g. metabolic) constraints that are not relevant to computer vision. But conversely, it could well be that brain-inspired solutions represent a true functional optimum towards machine intelligence; and that the dominant strategy in the field, of iteratively optimizing deep learning architectures with SOTA accuracy as the sole objective, could be driving us towards a local minimum in the space of functional architectures. Here, we look to the brain for inspiration on alternative attention architectures for computer vision.

Visual Attention in the Brain - How is attention implemented in the brain, and how does it differ from current deep learning models in computer vision?

The first thing to note is that deep convolutional networks are, to a first approximation, fairly representative of the computations taking place in the first feedforward sweep of information through the hierarchy of visual brain regions [9,17]. As neural information propagates from the retina through the thalamus, the primary "striate" visual cortex, and subsequent "extra-striate" visual areas, towards temporal cortex regions where object recognition and categorization take place [14], the pattern of synaptic connections between neurons undergoes a systematic increase of receptive field sizes, spatial invariance, and complexity of the neuron's optimal features (from small oriented edges in V1, to full objects or scene classes in infero-temporal cortex). This pattern is compatible with what one would expect from a series of convolutional kernels in deep learning models.

This apparent match between deep convolutional networks and the feedforward sweep of neural activity in the brain [13,26] does not mean that attention plays no role in vision—only that attention typically comes into play *after* this initial feed-forward sweep. In this sense, attention in the brain is thus very different from the way that it has been recently inserted into deep convolutional networks [2,25] or implemented by vision transformers [7,16,22,27], as a direct component of the main feed-forward pass.

The brain comprises a separate and unified attention network (the so-called "fronto-parietal" network) that receives sensory inputs from the various brain regions, and on the basis of this information determines where and how to pay attention [4,12,21]. Subsequently, attention signals from the fronto-parietal network are sent back to the visual stream to modulate neural activations according to attentional priorities [6,11,18]. This is of course a very coarse description that leaves aside important nuances, but in short, attention in the brain is computed outside of the visual cortical hierarchy, based on its initial feedforward activation, and modulating it in an iterative fashion at subsequent steps. Could a similar architecture also benefit deep convolutional networks?

2   Proposed Architecture

Here we present a series of simple experiments to begin addressing this question. Our base architecture is a deep convolutional network pre-trained for image classification, which we augment with a separate attention system, and an iterative attention modulation mechanism implementing a form of "routing by agreement". Attention priority is computed as a matching (or agreement) score between keys and queries, as in Transformer architectures. Here, for simplicity, the queries are pooled across the entire network, effectively implementing a form of Global Attention Agreement (hence the name: GAttANet). While this greatly simplifies the computational demands of the attention network (compared to a full self-attention strategy), this simple first implementation proved sufficient to improve classification accuracy across a variety of backbones and datasets.

Convolutional Network Backbones - Our first backbone was a "toy model" with three convolutional layers followed by two dense (fully-connected) layers, the latter of which served as the classification layer. This was meant as a computationally inexpensive architecture to explore our proposed augmentation with global attention, its individual components and its functional properties. Specifically, we used (3×3) convolutional kernels at each stage, ReLU activation functions, followed by (2×2) max pooling operations to decrease spatial resolution, and 0.2 drop-out as regularization. The input RGB image corresponded to 3 input channels, and the three subsequent convolutional layers comprised respectively 32, 64 and 128 channels. After flattening the output of the last convolutional layer, it was projected onto a dense layer with 256 units (with ReLU activation), then onto a final dense layer for classification, ending with a softmax operation (the number of classes in the dataset, 10 for CIFAR10 and 100 for CIFAR100, dictating the corresponding number of units). The resulting networks, counting around 620,000 to 640,000 parameters (depending on the dataset), were pretrained on CIFAR10 or CIFAR100. We used data augmentation (0–20° rotation, 0–20% shift in width and height, and random horizontal flips), with a batch size of 128, the Adam optimizer (with default parameters) and early-stopping (patience = 50 epochs) until convergence, which typically took less than 500 epochs. The resulting baseline networks reached an accuracy of 83.28% on CIFAR10 and 52.54% on CIFAR100 (see Table 1). These baseline architectures were then augmented with our global attention agreement mechanism, as described in the next section.

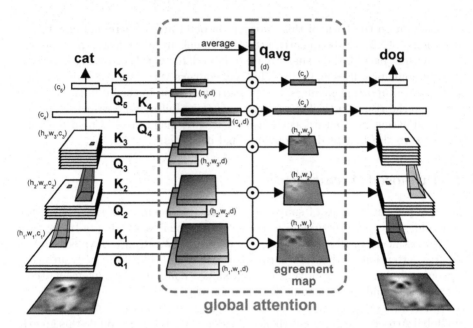

Fig. 1. Proposed GAttANet architecture. A standard convolutional network (here our "toy model" with 3 convolutional layers and 2 dense layers) can be augmented with the global attention agreement system. Each layer's activations are multiplied by Q and K matrices to produce corresponding Query and Key maps. Queries are averaged across all layers and spatial positions, resulting in a unique q_{avg} global query vector. The dot product of this global query with each layer's key determines the layers global attention agreement map, that directly modulates the layer's activations on the next time step. Features that were more or less compatible with the rest of the network are up- or down-regulated (respectively; compare red and blue pixels in the initial vs. final states), and the network's classification can be improved. (Color figure online)

To determine the usefulness of our proposed scheme in more general situations, we also explored standard modern convolutional architectures as backbones, namely ResNet18 and ResNet50, pretrained on ImageNet-1k. These networks comprised respectively 11.7M and 25.6M parameters. The baseline top-1 accuracy was 68.43% for ResNet18 and 74.94% for ResNet50 (see Table 1).

Global Attention Agreement - The general architecture of our proposed Global Attention Agreement system (GAttANet) is illustrated in Fig. 1. Just like in the brain, attention is envisioned here as a separate system from the convolutional visual backbone, that receives information from it (in the form of attention keys and queries) and influences its processing in return (based on the global attention agreement score at each location in the network).

More specifically, the activation in each layer i is turned into a pair of (Key, Query) attention maps (k^i, q^i), via learned linear projection matrices K_i and Q_i. This is done slightly differently for convolutional and dense layers. For a convolutional layer $Conv^i$ of spatial dimensions (h_i, w_i) and c_i channels, the attention matrices are $K_i, Q_i \in \mathbb{R}^{c_i \times d}$ where d is the chosen attention dimension (in our experiments, we varied d between 4 and 64). The attention projection is given by the dot product:

$$
k^i(x, y, m) = \sum_{c=1}^{c_i} (Conv^i(x, y, c) * K_i(c, m))
$$

$$
q^i(x, y, m) = \sum_{c=1}^{c_i} (Conv^i(x, y, c) * Q_i(c, m))
$$

(1)

where $(x, y) \in [1, w_i] \times [1, h_i]$ is a unit's spatial position, and $m \in [1, d]$.

For a dense layer $Dense^j$ of c_j units, the learned attention matrices are $K_j, Q_j \in \mathbb{R}^{c_j \times d}$, and the attention projection is given by the scalar product:

$$
k^j(c, m) = Dense^j(c) * K_j(c, m)
$$

$$
q^j(c, m) = Dense^j(c) * Q_j(c, m)
$$

(2)

where $c \in [1, c_j]$ is a unit's index, and $m \in [1, d]$.

All queries inside the network (across all layers and spatial positions) are then collected and averaged into a single global query q_{avg}, as follows:

$$
q_{avg}(m) = \frac{1}{n_c + n_d} \left(\sum_{i \in \mathbb{C}} \sum_{x=1}^{w_i} \sum_{y=1}^{h_i} \frac{q^i(x, y, m)}{w_i * h_i} + \sum_{j \in \mathbb{D}} \sum_{c=1}^{c_j} \frac{q^j(c, m)}{c_j} \right)
$$

(3)

where $m \in [1, d]$, and $\mathbb{C}$ and $\mathbb{D}$ are the index sets of convolutional layers and dense layers, respectively, of cardinals n_c and n_d.

Next, the q_{avg} global query is compared against each key across the entire network by means of a simple dot product, resulting in the "Global Attention Agreement" score:

$$
gatta^i(x, y) = k^i(x, y, .) \cdot q_{avg}
$$

$$
gatta^j(c) = k^j(c, .) \cdot q_{avg}
$$

(4)

for convolutional and dense layers, respectively.

On the next pass through the network, each unit's computation is modulated (via multiplicative scaling) according to the global attention agreement score assigned to it, i.e.:

$$
Conv^i(x, y, c) := Conv^i(x, y, c) * (1 + \alpha_i * gatta^i(x, y))
$$

$$
Dense^j(c) := Dense^j(c) * (1 + \alpha_j * gatta^j(c))
$$

(5)

where α_i is a learned parameter controlling the strength of attentional modulation for each layer i.

ResNet models are augmented in a slightly different way compared to the toy model. To limit computational demands, only a subset of layers are connected to the global attention system. Specifically, four convolutional layers are chosen to span the model's hierarchy (typically the output layer of a ResNet block), plus two dense layers: the average-pooling layer and the final classification layer (pre-softmax). These chosen layers, and only these, convey keys and queries to the global attention system, and receive attentional modulation in return, as described in Eqs. (1–5).

Training Details - We trained the global attention system on the original datasets (CIFAR10 or CIFAR100 for the toy model, ImageNet-1k for the ResNet models), with the pretrained weights of the convolutional backbone entirely frozen. Thus, the only trained parameters were the key/query matrices K_i and Q_i across the entire network, and the attentional modulation factor α_i for each layer. The number of trained parameters was very small in comparison to the number of weights in the backbone models (see Table 1): with $d = 16$, there were about 20,000 parameters to train for the toy model, 100,000 for the ResNet18 backbone and 200,000 for the ResNet50 (compared to about 600,000, 12M and 25M weights, respectively). During training we applied 0.25 drop-out to keys and queries for regularization in all models; for the toy models, we also used 0.00001 L_2 regularization; for ResNet models, we applied batch-normalization for keys and queries, and layer normalization for the *gatta* attention scores. We used a batch size of 128 for the toy models and 8 for the ResNets; the Adam optimizer with learning rate set to 0.001 (the default) for the toy models and 0.0003 for the ResNets; and early-stopping (patience = 500 epochs for toy models and 1 epoch for ResNets) until convergence, which typically took less than 1000 epochs for toy models and less than 10 epochs for ResNets.

Table 1. Accuracy across models and datasets. The base parameters are pre-trained and fixed (corresponding accuracy listed under 'base acc.'), and we only train the additional attentional parameters ('att. params'). The final accuracy is listed under 'acc. (ours)', in bold for the best accuracy over a given backbone/dataset combination.

Backbone	Dataset	Base params.	Base acc.	Att. dim.	Att. params.	Acc. (ours)
Toy model	CIFAR10	620.4K	83.28%	$d = 16$	15.8K	**85.34%**
Toy model	CIFAR100	643.5K	52.54%	$d = 16$	18.7K	55.54%
				$d = 32$	37.4K	55.86%
				$d = 64$	74.9K	**56.03%**
ResNet18	ImageNet-1k	11.70M	68.43%	$d = 8$	68.9K	68.72%
				$d = 16$	101.4K	68.83%
				$d = 32$	166.5K	**68.84%**
ResNet50	ImageNet-1k	25.64M	74.94%	$d = 4$	78.7K	**75.23%**
				$d = 8$	118.0K	75.21%
				$d = 16$	196.7K	75.18%
				$d = 32$	353.9K	75.20%
				$d = 64$	668.4K	75.18%

3   Results

Accuracy - Table 1 summarizes test set accuracy for the different models and datasets. The proposed GAttANet architecture yields accuracy improvements over the toy models on the order of 2% for CIFAR10 and up to 3.5% for CIFAR100. Given the relatively small increase in parameters, this improvement is noticeable (informal tests with feedforward toy models using comparable parameter numbers, obtained by augmenting the number of convolution channels, did not yield any significant improvement).

For ResNets, performance improvements were robust but more modest: about 0.3–0.4% on ImageNet top-1 accuracy. Obviously, it may be more difficult to optimize a ResNet—a pretty solid model already—compared to our simple toy model. Still, these improvements are not negligible, especially considering the small number of additional parameters. If we use as a reference the slope of the function relating parameters to accuracy between a ResNet18 and a ResNet50, the measured accuracy improvement for a standard ResNet architecture would have required 0.9M additional parameters (8.5 times more than our proposed architecture with $d = 16$). Similarly, using the ResNet50-ResNet101 slope as a reference, it would take a standard ResNet architecture with 3.8M additional parameters to match our augmented version of ResNet50 (which is 48 times more than our proposed architecture with $d = 4$). Therefore, our approach appears viable not just in simple scenarios, but also in state-of-the-art models.

Nonetheless, to limit computational demands, the following explorations of the global attention system were performed with the (more flexible) toy models.

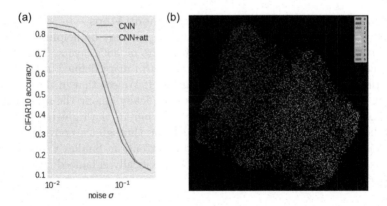

Fig. 2. Results on CIFAR10. (a) Comparison between the baseline model and the attention-augmented model ($d = 16$). Accuracy is plotted as a function of the amount of Gaussian noise (log-scale) added to each image. (b) 2-D UMAP visualization of the learned attention space of the global average query q_{avg}. Points are colored by image category (in alphabetical order). Animal classes (bird, cat, deer, dog, frog, horse) correspond to labels 2–7 and project in a separate region compared to vehicle classes (airplane, automobile, ship, truck) with labels 0–1 and 8–9.

Noise Robustness - To assess the generalization abilities of our proposed strategy with respect to out-of-distribution examples, we exposed the trained models to various levels of additive Gaussian noise on input images. For both CIFAR10 (Fig. 2a) and CIFAR100 (Fig. 4a and b), the performance improvements from our global attention strategy on clean images remained consistently visible across several levels of noise, even increasing for moderate noise (up to 8% point improvements on CIFAR100 with noise $\sigma = 0.03$ to 0.04), and only vanishing when the baseline model (without attention) approached chance level (noise $\sigma = 0.1$ to 0.25).

Properties of the Global Attention Query Space - Figure 2b shows a 2-D embedding of the learned 16-D space of the global attention query q_{avg} across images of the CIFAR10 dataset. It is noteworthy that the 10 classes appear to be separated, in particular along a main direction reflecting the 'animals vs. vehicles' distinction. Although such a separation may already exist in the representation layers of the convolutional backbone, the fact that it is also visible in the global attention system indicates that it has learned (through the key and query matrices) a meaningful representation of image properties. We believe that this could make the system useful not only in a bottom-up attention scenario as here (where the input fully determines the attentional modulation), but also in a top-down attention scenario, where the model's behavior could be controlled by the user in a class-specific way, e.g. when there is a strong prior for a given class (like 'airplane'), or for a given semantic property (like 'vehicle vs. animal'). We plan to explore this avenue in follow-up work.

Visualization of Global Attention Agreement Maps - In addition to the learned space of the global attention query q_{avg}, it may be helpful to visualize global attention agreement maps for each of the model's layers. The resulting map visualizations in Fig. 3 correspond to the *gatta* maps defined in Eq. (4), and schematically illustrated in purple color in Fig. 1. We see that in the final layer, the logit corresponding to the target class is typically among the units with the highest global attention agreement score (red bar in the right-most column). This indicates that on the next feed-forward pass through the convolutional network, this unit's activity will be increased by attention. Similarly, many spatial locations in the 2D agreement maps will be specifically enhanced (red colors) or decreased (blue colors) by attention.

Effect of Attention Dimension d - Table 1 as well as Fig. 4b provide a mixed interpretation for the effects of increasing the dimension d of the key/query attention space. On the one hand, going from $d = 16$ to $d = 64$ proved beneficial for the toy model on CIFAR100, and even more so at moderate levels of added Gaussian noise (Fig. 4b). On the other hand, for ResNet models on ImageNet there was not much effect of increasing d, at least in the range explored. Our global attention strategy was only marginally better for a ResNet18 with $d = 16$

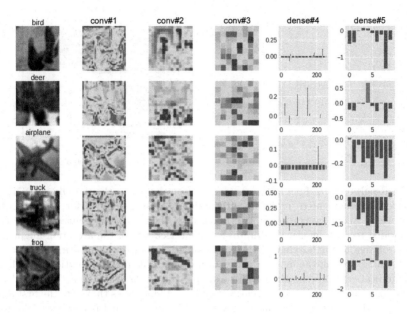

Fig. 3. Visualization of attention agreement scores. For the three convolutional layers, the score is represented as a spatial map, for the two dense layers as a bar plot (neurons along the x-axis). The last dense layer reflects the agreement of the global query q_{avg} with the key from each possible class of CIFAR10. The correct class, highlighted in red, is often the one with highest agreement.

or 32 compared to $d = 8$, and was equally (or more) beneficial for a ResNet50 with $d = 4$ as with $d = 64$. This may be because ResNet backbones are already close to optimal, and there is little room for improvement.

Lesion Experiments - Finally, we asked if attentional modulation of specific convolutional or dense layers in our toy model was critical to the observed attentional improvements. Figure 4c reports CIFAR100 accuracy of the baseline toy model (denoted by '.....' in the figure, i.e. no layer receiving attentional modulation); the full attention-augmented version ('cccdd', all 3 convolutional layers and 2 dense layers receiving attentional modulation); and several ablations of the latter. First, when a single layer's modulation was ablated (marked by a '.' in the figure), effects on the model performance varied from inexistant ('cccd.') to catastrophic ('.ccdd'). However, when only a single layer was modulated at a time (all other modulations ablated), no performance improvements were visible. This indicates that, while some layers may be more important than others, the global attention agreement strategy requires pooling signals across the entire model's hierarchy.

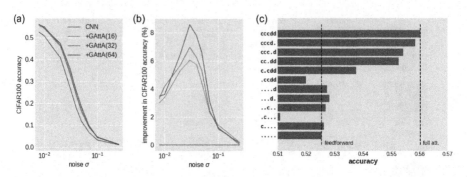

Fig. 4. Results on CIFAR100. (a) Comparison between the baseline CNN and our attention-augmented models (with different dimensions d for the attention key/queries). Accuracy is plotted as a function of the amount of Gaussian noise (log-scale) added to each image. (b) Improvement in accuracy of the attention-augmented models relative to the baseline CNN (c) Lesion studies of the trained model ($d = 16$). After training, we ran the model with certain layers receiving no attention modulation (layers indicated by a '.' on the left; for example, 'c.cdd' indicates that the second convolutional layer did not receive attention, while '...d.' indicates that only the first dense layer received attention). No single layer was sufficient to yield performance improvements in isolation; but some layers impaired the model more than others when they were lesioned (e.g., compare '.ccdd' to 'cccd.').

4 Discussion

We described an attention architecture with a global key/query matching system that pools queries across the entire hierarchy of layers in a convolutional network, and in return modulates each layer's activations based on their global attention agreement score. This proposal is similar to—and in large part also inspired by—the many "vision transformer" architectures in the recent literature [7,16, 22,27], especially those that employ transformer modules *in addition to* (not *instead of*) convolutional layers [2,25]. However, a fundamental difference is that our transformer/attention system is entirely separate from the convolutional backbone—just like the frontoparietal attention system in the brain is separate from the visual regions that it modulates [4,6,11,18,21].

Our system improved classification accuracy compared to each convolutional backbone across multiple datasets, at a minimal cost in terms of additional parameters. Augmenting the feedforward convolutional backbones with a similar parameter budget (i.e. with additional convolutional channels or ResNet blocks) would not produce significant performance improvements (we explicitly tested this for the toy models). It is possible that stand-alone transformer vision models would be more parameter-efficient [7,22], but we view this as an orthogonal question: even if a vision transformer could match or surpass our attention model, it remains a biologically implausible architecture.

Does our global attention system relate to the "Global Workspace" framework for cognition and awareness, advocated by several authors in cognitive science [1,19], neuroscience [15], and more recently also in machine learning [3,23]? As initially proposed, the Global Workspace is a shared multimodal representation used to collect relevant information across multiple independent neural systems, and to broadcast its contents to the rest of the brain. Our model is a unimodal attention system and as such, does not really fit this description. On the other hand, we note that our proposed architecture is highly similar in implementation to the "Shared Global Workspace" recently described by Goyal and colleagues [10]. In their model, each stage of a hierarchical visual Transformer architecture sends and receives information from a separate "workspace" module via a key-query attention mechanism, essentially similar to our global attention system (except for our use of convolutional layers instead of transformer modules). Thus, while we view our proposed attention model as independent from the Global Workspace theory, it may serve as a building block for a future large-scale Global Workspace system.

Several possibilities come to mind for improving our system in the future. For instance, rather than relying on a pretrained network with frozen weights, the convolutional backbone could be trained (or at least fine-tuned) jointly with the global attention system. In addition, could we further increase performance by iterating the global attention agreement mechanism across multiple time steps? For the present model trained on a single iteration, our explorations revealed that this was actually detrimental. A model *trained* for two or more iterations could still outperform ours, but our initial attempts in this direction encountered difficulties in terms of computational demands and numerical stability, so we leave this question open for future work.

Could we use a full self-attention mechanism rather than relying on our global query q_{avg}? That is, compute the entire pairwise map of attention agreement scores between all network locations? Theoretically yes, though this would also require a separate scheme for combining activation values across distinct layers having potentially different channel numbers. This could be achieved, for example, by relying on *value* matrices V_i, as in standard Transformers. In practice, however, this could prove prohibitively costly, as the computational cost of full self-attention grows with $O(N^2)$, instead of $O(N)$ for our pooled global attention (where N is the number of spatial locations in the network). Yet this is definitely one avenue to explore in the future.

Finally, could we also benefit from using *multi-head* attention—or an equivalent strategy allowing attention to simultaneously query multiple input properties? The potential functional advantage in the context of global attention agreement could be an ability for the network to simultaneously "agree" on multiple objects or interpretations. This may be particularly helpful in ambiguous situations, or for images with numerous targets. Such a scheme, unfortunately, appears incompatible with our current system where the final output is a scalar attention modulation score for each location. In ongoing work, we are exploring the possibility of employing complex-valued units, whose phase angles can be controlled by pairwise mutual attention agreement, to achieve a similar purpose. Our hope is that convolutional networks augmented in this way may develop a form of "binding-by-synchrony", whereby clusters of complex phase values delimit distinct objects in the scene, as observed in several neuroscience experiments [8,20].

References

1. Baars, B.J.: Global workspace theory of consciousness: toward a cognitive neuroscience of human experience. Prog. Brain Res. **150**, 45–53 (2005)
2. Bello, I., Zoph, B., Vaswani, A., Shlens, J., Le, Q.V.: Attention augmented convolutional networks. In: ICCV, pp. 3286–3295 (2019)
3. Bengio, Y.: The consciousness prior. arXiv preprint arXiv:1709.08568 (2017)
4. Corbetta, M., Shulman, G.L.: Control of goal-directed and stimulus-driven attention in the brain. Natu. Rev. Neurosci. **3**(3), 201–215 (2002)
5. Cordonnier, J.B., Loukas, A., Jaggi, M.: On the relationship between self-attention and convolutional layers. In: ICLR (2020)
6. Desimone, R., Duncan, J.: Neural mechanisms of selective visual attention. Ann. Rev. Neurosci. **18**(1), 193–222 (1995)
7. Dosovitskiy, A., et al.: An image is worth 16x16 words: transformers for image recognition at scale. arXiv:2010.11929 (2020)
8. Fries, P.: Rhythms for cognition: communication through coherence. Neuron **88**(1), 220–235 (2015)
9. Fukushima, K.: Neocognitron: a hierarchical neural network capable of visual pattern recognition. Neural Netw. **1**(2), 119–130 (1988)
10. Goyal, A.: Coordination among neural modules through a shared global workspace. arXiv:2103.01197 (2021)
11. Hamker, F.H.: The reentry hypothesis: the putative interaction of the frontal eye field, ventrolateral prefrontal cortex, and areas V4, it for attention and eye movement. Cereb. Cortex **15**(4), 431–447 (2005)
12. Itti, L., Koch, C.: Computational modelling of visual attention. Nat. Rev. Neurosci. **2**(3), 194–203 (2001)
13. Kriegeskorte, N.: Deep neural networks: a new framework for modeling biological vision and brain information processing. Ann. Rev. Vis. Sci. **1**, 417–446 (2015)
14. Logothetis, N.K., Pauls, J., Poggio, T.: Shape representation in the inferior temporal cortex of monkeys. Curr. Biol. **5**(5), 552–563 (1995)
15. Mashour, G.A., Roelfsema, P., Changeux, J.P., Dehaene, S.: Conscious processing and the global neuronal workspace hypothesis. Neuron **105**(5), 776–798 (2020)
16. Ramachandran, P., Parmar, N., Vaswani, A., Bello, I., Levskaya, A., Shlens, J.: Stand-alone self-attention in vision models. In: NeurIPS, pp. 68–80 (2019)
17. Riesenhuber, M., Poggio, T.: Hierarchical models of object recognition in cortex. Nat. Neurosci. **2**(11), 1019–1025 (1999)
18. Schafer, R.J., Moore, T.: Selective attention from voluntary control of neurons in prefrontal cortex. Science **332**(6037), 1568–1571 (2011)
19. Shanahan, M.: A cognitive architecture that combines internal simulation with a global workspace. Conscious. Cogn. **15**(2), 433–449 (2006)
20. Singer, W.: Consciousness and the binding problem. Ann. N. Y. Acad. Sci. **929**(1), 123–146 (2001)

21. Szczepanski, S.M., Pinsk, M.A., Douglas, M.M., Kastner, S., Saalmann, Y.B.: Functional and structural architecture of the human dorsal frontoparietal attention network. Proc. Nat. Acad. Sci. **110**(39), 15806–15811 (2013)
22. Touvron, H., Cord, M., Douze, M., Massa, F., Sablayrolles, A., Jégou, H.: Training data-efficient image transformers & distillation through attention. arXiv:2012.12877 (2020)
23. VanRullen, R., Kanai, R.: Deep learning and the global workspace theory. arXiv:2012.10390 (2020)
24. Vaswani, A., et al.: Attention is all you need. In: NeurIPS, pp. 5998–6008 (2017)
25. Wang, F., et al.: Residual attention network for image classification. In: CVPR, pp. 3156–3164 (2017)
26. Yamins, D.L., DiCarlo, J.J.: Using goal-driven deep learning models to understand sensory cortex. Nat. Neurosci. **19**(3), 356–365 (2016)
27. Zhao, H., Jia, J., Koltun, V.: Exploring self-attention for image recognition. In: CVPR, pp. 10076–10085 (2020)

Classification Models for Partially Ordered Sequences

Stephanie Ger[1]([✉]) [ID], Diego Klabjan[1] [ID], and Jean Utke[2] [ID]

[1] Northwestern University, Evanston, IL 60208, USA
`stephanieger@u.northwestern.edu`, `d-klabjan@northwestern.edu`
[2] Allstate Insurance Company, Northbrook, IL 60062, USA
`jutke@allstate.com`

Abstract. Many models such as Long Short Term Memory (LSTMs), Gated Recurrent Units (GRUs) and transformers have been developed to classify time series data with the assumption that events in a sequence are ordered. On the other hand, fewer models have been developed for set based inputs, where order does not matter. There are several use cases where data is given as partially-ordered sequences because of the granularity or uncertainty of time stamps. We introduce a novel transformer based model for such prediction tasks, and benchmark against extensions of existing order invariant models. We also discuss how transition probabilities between events in a sequence can be used to improve model performance. We show that the transformer-based equal-time model outperforms extensions of existing set models on three data sets.

Keywords: Timeseries · Transformers · Recurrent Neural Networks

1 Introduction

With the development of Recurrent Neural Networks (RNNs), many model architectures such as LSTMs and GRUs have been used to classify time series data [3,5]. Extensions such as the attention mechanism have improved classification accuracy dramatically [2]. Attention seeks to improve model performance by learning a trainable weighting for the relative importance of model inputs. Other improvements include architectures such as sequence-to-sequence or sequence-to-one which can be used for video captioning or sentiment analysis, respectively. In addition, attention based models such as transformers have been developed for sequence classification [12].

However, fewer models have been built for set, or order-invariant, inputs. Examples of order-invariant data sets include estimating the red shift of a cluster of galaxies [16]. Existing set-based classification models seek to classify sets by building an order-invariant layer. These models do so by either summing a representation of the inputs or by using attention to determine an order-invariant representation [13,16].

© Springer Nature Switzerland AG 2021
I. Farkaš et al. (Eds.): ICANN 2021, LNCS 12891, pp. 294–305, 2021.
https://doi.org/10.1007/978-3-030-86362-3_24

With the advent of Internet of Things (IoT) and sensor data, it is possible to have inputs from multiple sensors where the order of the inputs is unknown. That is, the time granularity may not be fine enough, leading to multiple inputs, or events, at the same time step. The naïve approach is to average all equal-time events, or time steps with multiple events, and then apply standard sequence models to the output. This is problematic as information is lost through averaging. We propose models that first generate a single representation for equal-time events and then use that representation along with the remaining events in the sequence as the input to a classifier such as a transformer or LSTM. We also propose a model that uses the transition matrix, computed using the subset of ordered events in the training set, as an input to the equal-time layer to determine a single representation that attempts to better capture the true ordering of the data. We propose novel transformer-based methods with and without the transition matrix input and benchmark against extensions of existing set-based models. The set-based transformer models significantly improve on the existing models by 7.4% to 10.1% depending on the data set. Furthermore, we observe an 8.71% improvement over the set-based transformer model when the transition matrix input is used. The main contributions are as follows:

1. a novel transformer-based model for representing equal-time events for partially ordered time series data so that standard sequence classification models can be applied;
2. a novel model that uses a transition matrix to order equal-time events that improves model performance;
3. a computational benchmarking study of existing set models on the partially-ordered data sets.

In the next section, we discuss relevant literature. Section 3 discusses all of the models, while the computational results are presented in Sect. 4.

2   Literature Review

Recently, some models have been developed to deal with unordered set data. These include models that build order-invariant neural networks as well as models that aim to order a set of data. The order-invariant models can be used for tasks such as adding a set of numbers together or sorting a set. Models for set ordering have been developed primarily for ordering a bag of words into a semantically correct sentence.

In [16], a definition of order invariant functions on a set is provided, and it is shown that it is possible to build a neural network architecture that is order-invariant. The Deep Sets model achieves order invariance by applying the same dense layer to each input and summing the outputs. It is suited for tasks such as summing a set of numbers together. Another method defines a way to use an attention mechanism to build a recurrent model that is order-invariant [13]. With recurrent models that are invariant to an input set order, one can build set-to-set, set-to-sequence and sequence-to-set models. In particular, set-to-sequence models can be used to impose an order on an input set.

Many models have been developed that take a set of words as input and produce a semantically correct sentence as output, for example, n-gram language models and Statistical Machine Translation [1,14]. In [10], the model orders a bag of words by using an LSTM hidden state to estimate the probability that a word occurs next in the sentence. These probabilities are then used in adaptive beam search to determine the highest probability ordering of words. Thus, the loss function takes into account both the conditional probability the current word is next given the words that have already been ordered as well as an estimate of the yet-to-be-ordered words.

However, these models are designed for data that is entirely unordered, not partially ordered sequence data. With partially ordered sequence data, it is possible to determine transition probabilities between events from the ordered events, and to use that to order the unordered events in the data assuming said data has an unknown inherent ordering. The idea of using a transition matrix for unordered events borrows from Hidden Markov Models which can learn the most likely sequence of events by considering transition probabilities [11].

Transformers are an attention based model architecture that have been used for encoder-decoder sequence models. Instead of an LSTM cell, the attention mechanism is used to determine the output of the encoder and decoder, by considering the interaction between an event in a sequence and all other events in the sequence. As the attention is computed between each event and the remaining events in the sequence, it seems reasonable that attention used in transformer-based models can also be applied to ordering sequential data where the order is unknown [12]. The difference between the problem that we consider and the set-based models is that we want to determine a representation for the unordered data for use within the context of a sequence model, while set-based models aim at order invariance. Therefore, as transformer models are built on the basis of examining the relative importance of each event in the sequence, it makes sense to base partially-ordered sequence models on transformers.

Transformers have been used in language models such as BERT and XLNet [4,15]. In particular, the XLNet model has an argument in the transformer self-attention, where a relative segment encoding for elements in the sequence is used to compute the attention. The segment encoding value varies based on elements being from the same or a different segment. We borrow this concept to capture a transition matrix input in an equal-time model.

3   Approaches

We consider a partially-ordered sequence $x = (x_1, x_2, \ldots, x_T) \in \mathcal{X}$ where each element x_i of the sequence consists of up to N unordered events, each represented by a vector of dimension M; we have $x_i = \{e_1, e_2, \ldots, e_n\}$ where $e_j \in R^M$ and $n \leq N$. Sequence length T can vary by sequence. In this section, we discuss equal-time models for determining a representation $\tilde{x}_i \in R^M$ for all equal-time events in the sequence. Note that whenever $n = 1$, we set $\tilde{x}_i = x_i$. Each of these set representation models is then incorporated in either an LSTM or a transformer model on the sequence $\tilde{x} = (\tilde{x}_1, \ldots, \tilde{x}_i, \ldots, \tilde{x}_T)$.

3.1   Deep Sets

For the deep set model, the same dense layer is applied to the n unordered events and then the outputs are summed to get

$$\tilde{x}_i = \frac{1}{n} \sum_{i \in n} \mathbf{W} e_i$$

where W are trainable weights. As discussed in [16], this model is invariant to the order of inputs as the parameters are shared and by applying a dense layer we expect the model to learn relevant features for each of the unordered events.

3.2   LSTM Set

We consider the LSTM and attention mechanism technique for order invariant models to compute a single representation for unordered equal-time events [13]. To generate a representation for the equal-time events $x_i = \{e_1, e_2, \ldots, e_n\}$, we apply attention and the LSTM equations N times and use the final output of the LSTM equation as the representation $\tilde{x}_i$ for the unordered events. By applying the attention repeatedly, we compute a representation that encodes the relative importance of each equal-time event. The cell and hidden state (q_0 and r_0) are both initialized as a constant vector and the same attention and LSTM weights are applied at each of the N iterations. We apply the following equations for each of the N iterations and use the final q_t^* as the representation for x_i where q_t^* is determined by concatenating q_t and r_t.

$$
\begin{aligned}
q_t &= LSTM(q_{t-1}^*) \\
d_{i,t} &= V \cdot \tanh(W \cdot [e_i, q_t]) \\
a_{i,t} &= \frac{\exp(d_{i,t})}{\sum_j \exp(d_{j,t})} \\
r_t &= A \cdot a_{i,t} + b \\
q_t^* &= [q_t, r_t]
\end{aligned}
\tag{1}
$$

3.3   Transformers for Equal-Time Events

As in the standard transformer model, we use the set of equal-time events $\{e_1, e_2, \ldots, e_n\}$ and consider weights W_K, W_V and K_Q to compute the value, key and query vectors to compute self-attention. For each attention head, we compute self-attention to get the output of the attention vectors. As the transformer output is the same length as the transformer input, we use attention to output a single representation for each equal-time event. The number of attention heads is a tunable hyperparameter. The difference with standard transformers is that we do not employ positional encoding.

Transition Matrix Input for Transformers. For a dataset where we have inherently ordered data, we can use the ordered events in the training data to compute a transition matrix T. Each entry in this matrix, T_{ij}, is the transition probability from event e_i to event e_j for $e_i, e_j \in x_i$ where x_i is an equal-time event. No additional transformations or filters are applied to the matrix T. Instead of using the transition matrix, which represents only probabilities, to order the unordered equal-time events we alter the model such that the transition matrix can be used in the attention computation of the transformer. Furthermore, the transition matrix might not imply a total order. For example, with a text based data set, one could compute transition probabilities between different parts-of-speech or between different words, though the latter transition matrix is not likely to be useful for computing a total order. Given T and the transformer model discussed earlier, we alter the computation for each attention head so that given the query, value and key vector denoted by q_i, k_i and v_i respectively, instead of the standard transformer attention equation

$$x_j = \sum_i \text{softmax}(q_j k_i) v_i,$$

we consider the transformer attention equation

$$x_j = \sum_i \left[\text{softmax}(q_j k_i) + (q_j + b)^T T_{ij} \right] v_i.$$

where b is a trainable bias.

4   Computational Study

We consider four sequential datasets[1]. Each of these datasets consists of multi-feature sequence data where a subset of time steps in the sequence contains a set of unordered events. The first dataset is sensor data from environmental sensors placed around the city of Chicago where we predict if the sensor reading values exceed a threshold in the next $12\,\text{h}$[2]. The second dataset consists of power readings from household sensors where we predict if five appliances are turned on or off based on power usage[3] [8]. The third dataset considers a meeting transcript dataset where we have multiple speakers who may be speaking at the same time[4] [6]. The goal here is to predict the next word that is spoken in the meeting. As the input is text, we can apply the transformer with transition matrix model on this dataset where we compute the transition probabilities between parts-of-speech (POS). Lastly, a business use case on a large, proprietary data set is discussed.

---

[1] Code and data are available at https://github.com/stephanieger/equal-time/. Three datasets are provided.

[2] https://aot-file-browser.plenar.io/.

[3] https://dataverse.harvard.edu/dataset.xhtml?persistentId=doi:10.7910/DVN/FIE0 S4.

[4] http://groups.inf.ed.ac.uk/ami/download/.

To consider equal time events with $n < N$, we apply different masking strategies for each of the equal time models. In order to apply the LSTM Set model only to time steps with multiple events, (1) is implemented in a recurrent layer with a switch function. The cell and hidden states are both initialized as a constant vector and the same attention and LSTM weights are applied at each of the n iterations. For this transformer model, we mask the attention for any missing events because it is possible to have fewer than N co-occurring events at a given time step. When we implement the additional transition matrix, we compute the transition probability between POS on the training set using only the ordered events and apply these probabilities to the rest of the data.

We compare the classification accuracy across the equal-time models and a baseline model on each dataset. The baseline that we compare against is the averaging model where equal-time events are averaged, such that $\tilde{x}_i = \frac{1}{N}\sum_{i \in N} e_i$, and then processed by LSTM. For the transformer equal-time model, we consider both an LSTM model and a transformer model after the equal-time model has been applied to the data. For all other models, we use LSTM for sequence classification. We write each model as U-V where $U \in \{ds, LSTM, trans, avg\}$ with "ds = deep set," "trans = transformer," and "avg = averaging" represents the underlying equal-time model, and $V \in \{trans, LSTM\}$ encodes the model used on $\tilde{x}$. For example, ds-LSTM represents the model with deep set used for equal time and then the resulting ordered sequence is treated by LSTM.

The transformer equal-time models are compared against the existing models: ds-LSTM, LSTM-LSTM and avg-LSTM. We also consider the trans-trans model as it is an extension of the trans-LSTM model. In each dataset, we have samples of varying length. Instead of padding the data to a maximum sequence length, we instead group samples by sequence length and train on batches of equal length sequences. On both of the sensor datasets, we merge adjacent sensor readings to create equal-time event sets. As the equal-time events on these datasets are synthetically created, we compare the classification results between the datasets with and without equal-time events. All models are implemented in Keras and trained on a single GPU card. For the business use case and sensor datasets, we report the F1-score as they are classification tasks. For the next word prediction task on the meeting transcript data we report perplexity.

4.1 Environmental Sensors

This data set consists of a series of contiguous readings of environmental factors from sensors located around the city of Chicago. The sensor readings include humidity, precipitation, sound in decibels and the amount of light detected. We predict if each of the 52 sensor values will be "large" 12 h in the future. A sensor value is determined to be large if it is at least one standard deviation over the mean. The data consists of partially ordered sequences with up to 80 co-occurring events and at most 60 time steps in the sequence. The distribution of the number of co-occurring events is shown in Fig. 1. As the majority of the time steps have fewer than 10 co-occurring events, the distributions are plotted separately for samples with more than 10 equal time events and samples with fewer than 10 equal time events. The time between sequential readings is computed and if the elapsed time is under a certain threshold, the readings are binned. In this way, multiple sequential readings may be binned together. There are 31 thousand samples in the data set, 70% of which comprise the training set.

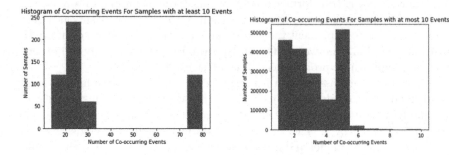

Fig. 1. Histogram of co-occurring events

We observe in Table 1 that the trans-trans model outperforms all pre-existing, or non-transformer, models. The trans-trans model yields an 11.2% improvement over the avg-LSTM model and a 10.1% improvement over the LSTM-LSTM model which is the best existing model for unordered events on this dataset. The improvement over the LSTM-LSTM model is significant with p-value = 1.18×10^{-6}.

Table 1. Environmental sensor performance metrics (F1 score)

Model	Average	Std Dev
avg-LSTM	0.883	0.006
ds-LSTM	0.892	0.006
LSTM-LSTM	0.899	0.006
trans-LSTM	0.908	0.004
trans-trans	**0.983**	**0.001**

As this data is ordered and synthetic equal-time events are created by binning, we can train an LSTM model and a transformer model on the ordered data. On this dataset, the LSTM model returns a test F1-score of 0.930 and the transformer model returns a test F1-score of 0.993. The models trained on the ordered data outperform the models trained on the partially ordered data. This is consistent with our expectations as information is lost when equal-time events are created. It is noteworthy that the trans-trans equal-time model (on the partially ordered data) outperforms the LSTM model on the totally ordered data.

4.2   Household Power

This dataset consists of a sequence of utility readings from a residential household over a two year period. These measurements include water, natural gas and power readings. We use 11 power-related measurements on the household level as features and consider sequences with at most 60 time steps. As with the environmental sensor dataset, readings are binned if the elapsed time between sequential readings is under a set threshold. At a given time step, there are at most 11 co-occurring events as shown in Fig. 2b. We use these household power measurements to determine if five appliances are turned on or off (it is a 5-class problem). These appliances are the furnace, heat pump, wall oven, clothes washer and clothes dryer and we threshold the power usage for each appliance in order to label each appliance as on or off. An appliance is classified as on if the power usage is over one standard deviation above the mean. For each sequence, a prediction is made for each appliance and the F1-scores for each class are averaged. There are 20 thousand samples in the data set 70% of which comprises the training set.

We observe in Table 2a that the trans-trans model outperforms all pre-existing, or non-transformer, models. The trans-trans model yields a 21.7% improvement over the avg-LSTM model and a 7.4% improvement over the ds-LSTM model which is the best pre-existing model for unordered events on this dataset. The improvement over the ds-LSTM model is significant with p-value = 0.02. It is interesting that while the trans-trans model consistently outperforms all pre-existing models on both sensor datasets, the best performing non-transformer model varies between the datasets. This suggests that the non-transformer equal-time models lack consistency.

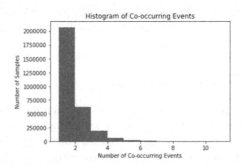

(a) Household Power Performance Metrics (F1)

Model	Average	Std Dev
avg-LSTM	0.533	0.025
ds-LSTM	0.604	0.021
LSTM-LSTM	0.472	0.037
trans-LSTM	0.591	**0.011**
trans-trans	**0.649**	0.027

(b) Histogram of Number of Equal Time Events

Fig. 2. (a) Household power performance metrics (F1) (b) Histogram of number of equal time events

As the utilities readings are ordered and equal-time events are created by binning, we can compare the F1-scores for the equal-time models against the F1-scores for a standard LSTM model and a transformer model on the ordered dataset. On the ordered dataset, the LSTM model returns a test F1-score of 0.653 and the transformer model returns a test F1-score of 0.665. The models trained on the ordered datasets outperform the equal-time models as expected. As we observed on the sensor dataset, the trans-trans model performance is the most similar to the model performance on the ordered data.

Table 2. Power dataset with more equal-time events

Model	Average	Std Dev
avg-LSTM	0.550	**0.017**
ds-LSTM	0.515	0.034
LSTM-LSTM	0.503	0.034
trans-LSTM	0.522	**0.045**
trans-trans	**0.557**	**0.017**

Table 3. Power dataset with fewer equal time events

Model	Average	Std Dev
avg-LSTM	0.573	0.026
ds-LSTM	0.591	0.025
LSTM-LSTM	0.534	**0.013**
trans-LSTM	0.554	0.026
trans-trans	**0.656**	0.019

To examine the effect of the number of equal-time events on model performance, we consider a dataset with more equal-time events and a dataset with fewer equal-time events. These datasets have at most 24 co-occurring events and 5 co-occurring events, respectively. We observe in Table 2 that when there are more equal-time events, the scores for equal-time models are on the whole lower which is expected. The trans-trans model returns the highest average F1-score in all datasets. In addition, the differences in F1-score for the power dataset with more events between the best performing existing model, avg-LSTM, and the trans-trans model are not statistically significant. The trans-trans model outperforms the best performing existing model, ds-LSTM, and the difference is significant with p-value = 0.002 in Table 3. Therefore, we observe that the trans-trans model outperforms the best pre-existing model across different levels of equal-time events.

4.3   Meeting Transcripts

This dataset consists of transcriptions of audio meeting recordings with four speakers in the room from the Augmented Multi-party Interaction (AMI) dataset. These recordings contain both scripted and unscripted meetings. Of the words that are uttered in the recording, 20.2% of words occur on co-occurring events, which make up 7.4% of all timestamps. At a given timestamp, we have at most 9 co-occurring words as shown in Fig. 3b. As this is a language dataset, we consider the next word prediction task. There are 3,586 words in the vocabulary, sequences are on average 35 time steps long and there are 17 thousand samples with 70% in the training set. Words are embedded using a pretrained BERT model [4]. For the transformer model with transition matrix, we use the default NLTK part-of-speech tagger to compute the part-of-speech for each word in the transcript [7]. We report test perplexity for each of the models.

As a baseline comparison, we compare the trans-trans with transition matrix model against both the trans-trans model and a pre-trained GPT-2 model. In order to apply the GPT-2 model, we randomly order equal-time events and then use the XL pre-trained GPT-2 weights to infer the next word [9]. This model returns a test perplexity of 2,226.63. We observe in Table 3a that both transformer models significantly outperform the GPT-2 model. We only benchmark the transition matrix model against the trans-trans model as we want to determine if the transition matrix input improves on the transformer equal-time representation. Furthermore, when we consider the average test perplexity across five runs with different initial seeds, we observe that the transformer model with transition matrix input results in an 8.21% decrease in test perplexity over the trans-trans model.

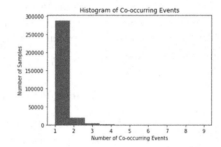

(a) Meeting Transcript Performance Metrics

Model	Average	Std. Dev
trans-trans	1036.40	114.93
trans-trans with transition matrix	**951.47**	**40.12**

(b) Histogram of Number of Equal Time Events

Fig. 3. (a) Meeting transcript performance metrics (b) Histogram of number of equal time events

Therefore, we observe that for the dataset which is inherently unordered, when a random ordering is chosen for equal-time events, it results in a higher perplexity than when an equal-time model is applied. This is the opposite of what is observed in the two sensor datasets, which makes sense as those datasets are inherently ordered and synthetic equal-time events were generated through binning. We also show that the transition matrix input to the self-attention calculation improves model performance. However, the transition matrix input can be considered only for datasets such as this one where the ordering of different event types is known and is meaningful.

4.4   Business Use Case

This dataset consists of a prediction task on a partially ordered sequence dataset. Sequences are at most 100 time steps long and at a given time step we have at most 20 co-occurring events. There are on the order of 1 million samples, with about 70% in the training set. Comparing the results of each of the proposed models against the baseline averaging model in Table 4, we observe that the avg-LSTM model outperforms the proposed equal-time models. When we ensemble across all of the proposed models, we report a test F1-score of 0.22, which outperforms the avg-LSTM model. We do not observe the same improvement in behavior when we ensemble across multiple runs of the averaging models. On this dataset, a non-deep learning model with hand selected features returns an F1-score of 0.22. While these deep learning equal-time models do not outperform a non-deep learning model, we achieve the same F1-score without feature selection. The co-occurrence of events in a superficial sense is arising from the coarse granularity of the time stamps. The transformer approaches not being able to realize gains similar to the ones observed in the other use cases triggered a closer examination of the data. The conclusion was that time stamps for a significant subset of the events represent merely start or end points of longer time periods during which the event in question actually occurred. This is a major difference to the other three use cases. Treating these time stamp as actual event occurrence introduces misleading information. We suspect this to contribute to the performance gap seen in the tranformer models. Consequently, in future work, we will need to consider co-occurence of such events across multiple time steps in a probabilistic sense.

Table 4. Performance metrics

Model	Validation F1	Test F1
avg-LSTM	0.245	0.217
ds-LSTM	0.227	0.207
LSTM-LSTM	0.224	0.207
trans-LSTM	0.229	0.212
trans-trans	0.219	0.204
Ensemble	0.237	0.220

5 Conclusion

We have presented several techniques for classification of partially ordered sequence data. Models were evaluated on four data sets, where it was observed that the transformer model for equal-time events outperforms models that incorporate existing order-invariant techniques. On data sets where the data is inherently ordered and synthetic events are generated by binning, models trained on the ordered sequences outperform the equal-time models. On a language dataset with unordered data, the equal-time models outperform a language model with randomly ordered equal-time events. Finally, we provide evidence on the meeting transcript data that transition probabilities between events can be used to further improve model performance.

References

1. Brown, P.F., Desouza, P.V., Mercer, R.L., Pietra, V.J.D., Lai, J.C.: Class-based N-gram models of natural language. Comput. Linguist. **18**(4), 467–479 (1992)
2. Chorowski, J.K., Bahdanau, D., Serdyuk, D., Cho, K., Bengio, Y.: Attention-based models for speech recognition. In: Advances in Neural Information Processing Systems, pp. 577–585 (2015)
3. Chung, J., Gulcehre, C., Cho, K., Bengio, Y.: Empirical evaluation of gated recurrent neural networks on sequence modeling (2014). arXiv preprint arXiv:1412.3555
4. Devlin, J., Chang, M.W., Lee, K., Toutanova, K.: BERT pre-training of deep bidirectional transformers for language understanding (2018). arXiv preprint arXiv:1810.04805
5. Hochreiter, S., Schmidhuber, J.: Long short-term memory. Neural Comput. **9**(8), 1735–1780 (1997)
6. Kraaij, W., Hain, T., Lincoln, M., Post, W.: The AMI meeting corpus (2005). http://groups.inf.ed.ac.uk/ami/corpus/
7. Loper, E., Bird, S.: NLTK: the natural language toolkit (2002). arXiv preprint cs/0205028
8. Makonin, S., Ellert, B., Bajić, I.V., Popowich, F.: Electricity, water, and natural gas consumption of a residential house in Canada from 2012 to 2014. Sci. Data **3**, 160037 (2016)
9. Radford, A., Wu, J., Child, R., Luan, D., Amodei, D., Sutskever, I.: Language models are unsupervised multitask learners (2019). https://github.com/openai/gpt-2
10. Schmaltz, A., Rush, A.M., Shieber, S.M.: Word ordering without syntax (2016). arXiv preprint arXiv:1604.08633
11. Schuster-Böckler, B., Bateman, A.: An introduction to hidden Markov models. Curr. Protocol. Bioinform. **18**(1), A-3A (2007)
12. Vaswani, A., et al.: Attention is all you need. In: Advances in Neural Information Processing Systems, pp. 5998–6008 (2017)
13. Vinyals, O., Bengio, S., Kudlur, M.: Order matters: sequence to sequence for sets (2015). arXiv preprint arXiv:1511.06391
14. Vogel, S.: SMT decoder dissected: Word reordering. In: International Conference on Natural Language Processing and Knowledge Engineering, pp. 561–566. IEEE (2003)
15. Yang, Z., Dai, Z., Yang, Y., Carbonell, J., Salakhutdinov, R.R., Le, Q.V.: XLNet: generalized autoregressive pretraining for language understanding. In: Advances in Neural Information Processing Systems, pp. 5753–5763 (2019)
16. Zaheer, M., Kottur, S., Ravanbakhsh, S., Poczos, B., Salakhutdinov, R.R., Smola, A.J.: Deep sets. In: Advances in Neural Information Processing Systems, pp. 3394–3404 (2017)

TINet: Multi-dimensional Traffic Data Imputation via Transformer Network

Xiaozhuang Song, Yongchao Ye, and James J. Q. Yu[✉]

Guangdong Provincial Key Laboratory of Brain-inspired Intelligent Computation,
Department of Computer Science and Engineering, Southern University of Science
and Technology, Shenzhen 518055, China
11930376@mail.sustech.edu.cn

Abstract. Missing traffic data problem has a significant negative impact for data-driven applications in Intelligent Transportation Systems (ITS). However, existing models mainly focus on the imputation results under Missing Completely At Random (MCAR) task, and there is a considerable difference between MCAR with the situation encountered in real life. Furthermore, some existing state-of-the-art models can be vulnerable when dealing with other imputation tasks like block miss imputation. In this paper, we propose a novel deep learning model TINet for missing traffic data imputation problems. TINet uses the self-attention mechanism to dynamically adjust the weight for each entries in the input data. This architecture effectively avoids the limitation of the Fully Connected Network (FCN). Furthermore, TINet uses multi-dimensional embedding for representing data's spatial-temporal positional information, which alleviates the computation and memory requirements of attention-based model for multi-dimentional data. We evaluate TINet with other baselines on two real-world datasets. Different from the previous work that only employs MCAR for testing, our experiment also tested the performance of models on the Block Miss At Random (BMAR) tasks. The results show that TINet outperforms baseline imputation models for both MCAR and BMAR tasks with different missing rates.

Keywords: Data mining · Attention network · Data imputation

1 Introduction

In recent years, models based on deep neural networks have been proposed and applied to solve traffic data-related problems, such as traffic prediction, traffic planning, and traffic simulation [18]. These deep learning methods are mostly built on sufficient and reliable historical traffic data, which is the fundamental

This work is supported by the Stable Support Plan Program of Shenzhen Natural Science Fund No. 20200925155105002, by the General Program of Guangdong Basic and Applied Basic Research Foundation No. 2019A1515011032, and by the Guangdong Provincial Key Laboratory (Grant No. 2020B121201001).

I. Farkaš et al. (Eds.): ICANN 2021, LNCS 12891, pp. 306–317, 2021.
https://doi.org/10.1007/978-3-030-86362-3_25

basis of the modern Intelligent Transportation Systems (ITS). However, it is found that the traffic data collection process suffers from information loss or anomaly collection by various factors, and a large amount of data might be missing due to device failure in severe cases [1]. Rather than a high-quality dataset with available data, researchers obtain partially missing data or even sparse data most time. For instance, [14] found that nearly 50% of traffic data was missing in the past seven years at Alberta in Canada. Texas Transportation Institute (TTI) pointed out that their traffic management system had 16%–93% incomplete data [11]. This makes deep learning models trained on ideal traffic data fragile in the practical application, as deep learning models may experience severe performance degradation when the data is corrupted [9]. Thus, building a robust and reliable traffic data imputation method is of great importance for the data-driven models [18].

In the past decades, a number of methods have been proposed to tackle the missing traffic data problem. Two of the most outstanding models among them are Bayesian Gaussian CANDECOMP/PARAFA factorization (BGCP) [2] and Stacked Autoencoder (SAE) [15]. BGCP considers the data imputation problem from the low-rank matrix approximation perspective. However, as it relies heavily on dimensional information, it meets a critical performance decline when the misses appear in random blocks or it needs to impute data with high missing rate. SAE learns to impute from the historical data, which makes it effective in solving the problems encountered by BGCP. However, the design of SAE's fully connected structure is not sufficiently flexible. Fixed-weight layers learn data blindly and require deeper network layers and more parameters to learn about the all the possible missing scenarios.

To tackle the problems listed above, in this work, we propose TINet, a novel missing traffic data imputation framework based on the Transformer structure [12]. The main contribution of our work can be listed as follows:

1. To the best of our knowledge, this is the first work that adopts a Transformer-based deep learning framework to study the problem of missing traffic data imputation. The results show that our model outperforms other baselines.
2. We propose a multi-dimensional embedding representation for the discrete attributes for traffic data, with the spatial embedding learned from a random walk-based graph embedding and the temporal embedding learned from embedding layers.
3. We conduct comprehensive experiments on two real-world datasets to compare TINet with baseline models and give a detailed analysis of experimental results.

2   Related Work

Missing traffic data imputation methods have been researched for decades. The mainstream of traffic data imputation methods can be divided into two categories: (1) Tensor completion models, (2) Data-driven models. Tensor completion models is proposed base on the low-rank property of traffic data, and models built based on the CANDECOMP/PARAFA (CP) decomposition method is among the most representative models for its imputation performance. [2] introduces the idea of tensor completion into traffic data with a Bayesian Gaussian CANDECOMP/PARAFA (BGCP) model, while [3] proposes a Bayesian Probabilistic Matrix Factorization (BPMF) method for traffic data imputation and traffic forecasting. Both these two models perform well under the Missing Completely At Random (MCAR) imputation task. However, it shows a significant performance drop when handling the block missing task. We will discuss this in detail in Sect. 5.

Data-driven approaches largely tackle the above problems for their scalable learning process and use more parameters to capture the data correlation. Stacked Autoencoder (SAE) [15] builds a deep autoencoder structure with a fully connected Network. GAIN [16] uses a generative adversarial training style to generate missing data with the available data. However, GAIN has poor generalizing ability as it trains and tests its model on the same dataset, which causes a severe overfitting problem. Transformer [12] is the current state-of-the-art model for dealing with sequence data in the field of natural language processing. Transformer and its conceptual progeny have topped many benchmark leaderboards in sequence data learning tasks [12]. A Transformer network uses self-attention mechanism to dynamically adjust the weight of input data, and it uses residual connections, layer normalization for better performance [12]. One of the most outstanding Transformer-based work is BERT [5]. It pre-trains the model with massive existing data and two subtasks, Masked Language Model and Next Sentence Prediction, which requires the model to predict the words it masks and the next sentence, respectively. The success of Transformer, especially BERT, shows the great potential of self-attention-based structure in sequence data. In this work, we will introduce how to apply the Transformer structure network to traffic data.

3   Preliminaries

In this section, we elaborate on the preliminaries to the missing traffic data problems. The problem formulation and introductions to the investigated missing types are presented as follows.

3.1   Problem Formulation

In this work, we treat traffic data as a sequence data $D = \{x_1, x_2, \cdots, x_n\}$, with each value in the sequence representing its traffic speed value. Two adjacent data in the sequence have a fixed interval of s minutes, and t_i represents the time of x_i. Each sequence has a corresponding day of week wd_D and a corresponding traffic node v_j. We denote the sequence with missing data with $\widehat{D}$, and value in D, $\widehat{D}$ with x_i, $\widehat{x}_i$, respectively. To simulate the missing data, we introduce a mask tensor $M = \{m_1, m_2, \cdots, m_n\}$ with its value $m_i \in \{0, 1\}$. Therefore, we can get the sequence $\widehat{D}$ with $\widehat{x}_i = x_i \times m_i$. Given D and $\widehat{D}$, we aim to find a model f to learn the objective:

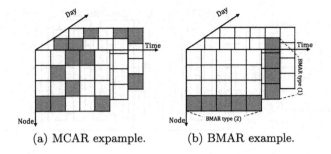

(a) MCAR expample.   (b) BMAR example.

Fig. 1. Visualization example for different missing types. Gray cells refer to missing values, while the white ones are available. For MCAR, missing values appear randomly. For BMAR, missing values appear in block as introduced in Sect. 3.2

$$\min_{\theta} \sum_{i} \left(x_i - f(\widehat{x}_i | \theta) \right)^2 \tag{1}$$

where θ is the parameters of f.

3.2 Missing Types

Missing data have different types. In our study, we mainly study the following two missing types: **MCAR**: The data is missing completely at random; **BMAR**: The data is missing completely at random and appears as blocks. In our experiments, the block missing appears randomly as one of the following types: (1) One or multiple nodes lost their data at arbitrary time. (2) All day data are lost for particular nodes. The visualization examples of MCAR and BMAR can be seen from Fig. 1.

4   TINet

In this section we describe the architecture of our proposed model TINet. Figure 2 depicts the overall architecture.

4.1 Model Architecture

TINet is mainly composed of Transformer modules, where a Transformer module comprises two sub-layers: a Multi-Head Attention sublayer and a position-wise Fully Connected sublayer. A residual connection is incorporated around each of the two-sublayers with layer normalization. According to [12], to promote the Transformer-based model's performance, we set all Transformer layers to produce outputs of dimension d_o. The final Transformer module's output feeds to a fully connected network with size $[d_o, 1]$. Then we can get the final output imputation $\widehat{D}$.

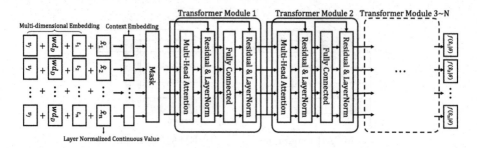

Fig. 2. Overview of TINet.

4.2 Context Embedding

TINet computes a context embedding from its normalized continuous value and discrete attributes for each input value x_i.

Layer Normalized Continuous Value: For continuous value x_i, we normalize it with z-score layer normalization:

$$\bar{x} = \frac{x - \mu}{\sigma} \qquad (2)$$

where μ and σ are the mean and variance of corresponding layer input.

Multi-dimensional Embedding: For a point x_i in the traffic sequence D, TINet selects the day of week wd_D, its daytime t_i, node id v_j as its discrete attributes. For wd_D and t_j, we use two projection layers with l_1 and l_2 dimensions, respectively. For node id v_j, we compute its embedding by applying the Deep Walk method [8]: Firstly, node sequences are generated based on random walk. The transition probability of random walk is defined as

$$P(v_j \mid v_i) = \begin{cases} \frac{W_{ij}}{\sum_{j \in \mathcal{N}(v_i)} W_{ij}}, & v_j \in \mathcal{N}(v_i) \\ 0, & otherwise \end{cases} \qquad (3)$$

where $\mathcal{N}(v_i)$ represents the neighbour nodes of v_i, e_{ij} represents the edge from v_i to v_j, W_{ij} is the historical travel data statistics from v_i to v_j[1], respectively. After finishing the random walk, we apply Skip-Gram algorithm [7] to learn the embedding of node. Assume a walking sequence $Walk = \{v'_1, v'_2, \cdots, v'_n\}$, the learning process of Deep Walk can be summarized by the following formula:

$$\max_{\vartheta} \log \mathrm{P}\left(\left\{(v'_{i-w}), \cdots, (v'_{i+w})\right\} \mid \vartheta(v'_i)\right) \qquad (4)$$

For a given node v'_i in the walking sequence $Walk$, $(v'_i) \in \mathbb{R}^N$ represents its one-hot encoding vector. We feed (v'_i) to a network ϑ. The objective is to maximize the output probability of the nodes near v'_i in $Walk$ with window size w.

---

[1] For PeMS dataset which will be introduced in Sect. 5, we represent W_{ij} by the distance between v_i and v_j as there is no historical travel data statistics.

The intuition of this idea is that the nodes with a closer distance in the walking sequence have similar representation on latent space [8]. ϑ commonly adopts a two-layer fully connected encoder-decoder structure. The first and second fully connected layers are of size $[N, L_v]$ and $[L_v, N]$, where N is the number of node and L_v is hidden size. Typically, the first layer is used to extract embedding vectors of input nodes, the second layer is used to transform them into nodes' one-hot encoding vector close in the walk sequences.

After the embedding of wd_D, t_i and v_j is learned, we concatenate them with normalized continuous value as the context embedding and feed them into the first Transformer module.

4.3   Multi-head Attention Computaion

The context embedding is firstly associated with three learnable weight parameters W_Q, W_K, and W_V, each with size $[L_{em}, k]$ where L_{em} is the length of context embedding, and k is the latent dimension. This process is reflected by

$$
\begin{aligned}
Q &= X \cdot W_Q \\
K &= X \cdot W_K \\
V &= X \cdot W_V
\end{aligned}
\tag{5}
$$

where Q, K, V represents the *query* vector, *key* vector and *value* vector in the self-attention mechanism [12]. $\{\cdot\}$ represents the matrix multiplication operator. We can see that the self-attention mechanism builds the dynamic weights between input data with learnable parameters, and a detailed explanation for attention can refer to the previous work [13]. The final layer output of self-attention layer is:

$$
\mathrm{Att}(Q, K, V) = \mathrm{softmax}(\frac{QK^T}{\sqrt{d_k}})V
\tag{6}
$$

where the resulting output is a context vector of dimension k. $\sqrt{d_k}$ represents the square root of *key* vector, and it leads to more stable gradients. Furthermore, we use a n-head attention mechanism [12], which aims to mine n different attention scores by setting n W_Q, W_K and W_V. [4] shows that a proper number of attention heads can better mine the information in data and enhance the model performance.

5   Case Studies

In this section, we introduce the settings of our experiment. We conduct experiments on two real-world datasets and compare TINet with other baseline models.

5.1   Experimental Settings

Experimental Environment. All experiments are performed on a Linux Server (CPU: Intel(R) Xeon(R) CPU E5-2620v4, GPU: GeForce RTX2080Ti, System: Ubuntu 18.04). All models are conducted with Python 3.7.

Hyperparameter Settings. The number of Transformer modules is 4, and the attention heads are 2. The dimensions l_1, l_2 of projection layers are both set to 8. The self-attention layer's hidden size is set to 16, while the hidden size of the Fully Connected sublayer and the final output dimension d_o are both set to 32. The hidden size L_{em} of Deep Walk is set to 16. The proportions for the training set, validation set, and test set are 70%, 10%, and 20%, respectively. For both TINet and baseline models, we run 20 times and take the results' average as the final comparison. We use Adam optimizer [6] to optimize model parameters. During training, the learning rate is 10^{-3}, and the batch size used in training is 16. We choose the max training epoch 500 for all data-driven models. All the parameters above are set from a empirical grid-search finetuning results. Data-driven models all use an early stopping strategy to avoid the overfitting problem where the validation loss no longer decreases for three consecutive epochs.

Dataset Description. We conduct our experiments on two open datasets:

1. PeMS Dataset[2]: This dataset collects real-time traffic data from nearly 40,000 individual detectors across all major districts in California. Followed by previous work [2,15], we choose the District 5 data ranging from January 1, 2013 to December 31, 2013. All the collected data is preprocessed into 144 road sections, and their information is aggregated every five minutes, which means the data of one day is embedded in a matrix of 288×144.
2. Shenzhen Dataset[3]: This dataset collects raw GPS trajectories in Shenzhen from October 8, 2019 to October 14, 2019. We select the area centered on Futian District area as it only has few missing data. Therefore, we can make intentional data missing simulation expediently. This dataset involves 802 areas. We use the map-matching algorithm to process the raw data and aggregate their traffic information every 5 min.

For missing rate selection, we consider the following two aspects: (1) The performance gap of the models under low missing rate is not significant. (2) The design of TINet method is more inclined to address the imputation tasks with high missing rates. Since that, the missing rates selected in our experiment is 0.1, 0.5, 0.8, 0.9. Before training, we generate datasets with different missing rates. For MCAR, we mask the value in dataset randomly. For BMAR, we randomly select one of the two BMAR types as we introduce in Sect. 3.2. For instance, if type (1) of BMAR is selected, we randomly select an arbitrary time in a day, and mask all data at that time with a high probability of 95%[4]. We repeat this process until the proportion of missing data in the dataset meets the requirements.

5.2 Baselines and Evaluation Metrics

We compare TINet with two categories of methods: matrix completion and data-driven methods. In the former class, we select BPMF [3] and BGCP [2] as the baselines. On the other hand, for data-driven models, we adopt HA [11], SAE [15], and GAIN [16] as the baselines. Besides, we introduce TINet_w, which is a variant of TINet without multi-dimensional embedding, to evaluate the effectiveness of such embedding. We also choose three performance metrics to compute the difference between ground truth Y_i and masked data $\widehat{Y}_i$, including:

1. Mean Absolute Error (MAE):

$$\text{MAE} = \frac{1}{m} \sum_{i=1}^{m} \|(Y_i - \widehat{Y}_i)\| \tag{7}$$

2. Root Mean Squared Error (RMSE):

$$\text{RMSE} = \sqrt{\frac{1}{m} \sum_{i=1}^{m} (Y_i - \widehat{Y}_i)^2} \tag{8}$$

3. Mean absolute percentage error (MAPE):

$$\text{MAPE} = \frac{\|Y - \widehat{Y}\|}{\|Y\|} \times 100\% \tag{9}$$

MAE and RMSE measures the average prediction error of the model. MAPE measures the percentage gap between predicted value and target value (Table 2).

5.3 Experimental Results

Table 1 shows the experimental results, which corresponds to the model's performance for imputing two missing data types on the two datasets. Notably, for GAIN, we can see a significant error in our experiment. We attribute this performance to GAIN's training strategy. GAIN trains and tests its imputation ability on the data without splitting into training, validation, and testing sets. However, we consider this not meeting the practical scenarios. In our experiment, we train models on separate training and validation sets. Under this experimental settings, the obtained results of GAIN are not satisfactory. Furthermore, we can see that TINet_w has an apparent performance degradation compared to TINet, which shows the effectiveness of multidimensional embedding. In the rest of this section, we discuss the experiment results from multiple perspectives:

Matrix Completion Models v.s. Data driven Models. From Table 1 we can see that the data-driven models have a robust performance under high missing rate scenarios. Take the performance of MCAR task on PeMS dataset with 0.9 missing rate as an example, the MAPE of TINet and SAE is 3.05% and 3.63%, while BGCP and BPMF's MAPE reach 14.12% and 15.38%, which are

Table 1. Experimental Results for MCAR task

Performance on MCAR task for PeMS dataset (MAE/RMSE/MAPE(%))			
Missing rate	0.1	0.5	0.8	0.9
HA	3.87/4.29/7.70	3.89/4.88/8.03	3.60/4.26/7.52	3.86/4.84/8.01
BPMF	1.88/2.88/3.60	3.21/5.38/6.86	5.00/7.47/10.31	7.78/10.41/15.38
BGCP	**1.34/1.78/2.55**	1.86/2.49/3.11	4.05/5.21/7.77	7.38/9.96/14.12
SAE	2.17/2.86/3.75	2.03/2.70/3.52	2.17/2.94/3.74	1.92/2.81/3.63
GAIN	38.62/42.42/76.20	40.42/43.50/79.03	42.01/44.25/82.06	46.78/47.81/91.31
TINet$_w$	1.84/2.60/3.32	1.57/1.63/2.54	1.84/2.50/3.35	1.85/2.64/3.38
TINet	1.69/2.41/2.90	**0.97/1.33/1.64**	**1.76/2.34/3.01**	**1.76/2.42/3.05**

Performance on MCAR task for Shenzhen dataset (MAE/RMSE/MAPE(%))			
Missing rate	0.1	0.5	0.8	0.9
HA	10.65/11.93/26.77	10.71/12.74/27.44	10.69/12.97/26.81	10.50/12.81/26.83
BPMF	3.94/5.67/9.43	4.66/6.59/10.79	5.49/7.67/12.91	6.61/8.76/15.61
BGCP	3.51/4.56/8.27	4.25/5.36/10.46	4.89/5.87/11.54	5.73/6.92/13.50
SAE	2.56/3.37/6.02	2.23/2.98/5.25	2.38/2.75/5.60	2.63/3.47/6.19
GAIN	30.04/33.54/77.48	32.54/35.70/81.99	35.11/37.21/88.09	36.08/37.98/90.10
TINet$_w$	1.44/1.61/3.27	1.96/2.33/4.61	2.24/2.70/5.27	2.55/3.14/6.00
TINet	**1.07/1.33/2.52**	**1.26/1.41/3.36**	**1.73/2.11/4.57**	**2.15/2.47/5.20**

Table 2. Experimental Results for BMAR task

Performance on BMAR task for PeMS dataset (MAE/RMSE/MAPE(%))			
Missing rate	0.1	0.5	0.8	0.9
HA	4.13/4.55/8.85	4.55/5.42/8.56	4.28/5.10/8.32	4.22/5.43/8.21
BPMF	10.74/13.69/23.92	13.93/14.40/26.37	19.40/29.42/34.81	19.65/20.01/37.41
BGCP	12.38/14.87/24.50	15.97/20.56/37.18	21.40/27.68/42.89	28.72/36.64/53.11
SAE	2.20/2.90/3.78	4.95/6.69/9.60	5.32/7.04/10.58	5.54/7.25/10.70
GAIN	42.64/45.78/83.08	41.85/44.86/82.21	44.22/45.42/86.60	41.93/45.05/81.96
TINet$_w$	2.48/3.46/4.09	3.13/4.68/4.83	4.43/6.13/8.63	5.05/6.43/10.46
TINet	**1.94/2.46/2.95**	**1.64/2.72/2.98**	**1.82/2.44/3.03**	**1.77/2.48/3.05**

Performance on BMAR task for Shenzhen dataset (MAE/RMSE/MAPE(%))			
Missing rate	0.1	0.5	0.8	0.9
HA	11.24/12.74/28.19	10.94/12.39/27.73	10.91/12.25/27.37	10.82/12.23/27.45
BPMF	8.56/10.62/21.68	9.87/12.47/24.62	8.91/11.37/22.36	20.19/26.10/51.38
BGCP	12.50/16.98/32.08	13.25/17.98/35.23	18.62/24.38/45.64	21.20/27.33/55.30
SAE	3.06/3.51/7.32	5.10/6.65/12.74	5.28/6.81/13.06	5.46/7.09/13.39
GAIN	36.97/39.72/91.21	32.13/35.52/79.87	34.18/36.95/86.23	35.40/37.26/88.43
TINet$_w$	1.47/1.83/3.46	4.07/5.51/11.16	4.83/6.94/12.70	5.40/7.16/13.21
TINet	**1.12/1.35/2.59**	**2.78/4.19/7.41**	**3.43/4.87/9.45**	**3.99/5.72/10.47**

nearly four times higher than the former two. The high missing rate makes the numerical information of each dimension of the matrix or tensor largely lost. Nonetheless, the matrix and tensor factorization techniques rely on this information for inferring the posterior numerical distribution of values on specified positions. Therefore, a high missing rate brings a significant performance drop on

BGCP and BPMF. Besides, the performance of data-driven models is relatively stable under both tasks. We attribute this stability to the scalable parameter learning scheme for deep learning models, as they can continuously learn new data and update network parameters. However, BGCP and BPMF methods both perform low rank approximation to the structure of the input data itself, and do not have such scalability. Meanwhile, BGCP and BPMF are underperforming on BMAR. This can also be attributed to its dependency on dimensional numerical information, and the blocks of missing data can hardly provide such information. There is another interesting observation in the comparison, i.e., BGCP and BPMF do not perform well for MCAR task on Shenzhen dataset. We can see the MAPE of BGCP and BPMF of MCAR task on Shenzhen dataset with 0.1 missing reach 8.27% and 9.43%, respectively. CP decomposition enforces a strict structure assumption by modeling hidden parameters for each dimension, which makes it suitable for highly structured data. However, this also undermines the generalization capability of CP decomposition method for the scenarios that the correlation among data is relatively trivial [10].

Comparison Between TINet and SAE. From Table 1 we can obtain a direct comparison among data-driven models. As GAIN performs poorly during our test due to the overfitting problem, we mainly discuss the difference between SAE and TINet in this comparison. It can be seen that TINet has a slight performance advantage over SAE in all tasks. Moreover, TINet's performance advantage on the Shenzhen dataset is even more significant. In particular, under 0.1 missing rate, TINet got 2.52% MAPE for MCAR task and 2.59% MAPE for BMAR task, while SAE's MAPE reach 6.02% and 7.32%, respectively. We attribute this to the difference in the model architecture. As SAE mainly uses a naïve, fully connected layer as the basic module, this fixed-weight connection makes it difficult for the model to impute data with misses appear in random positions. Furthermore, it needs a larger amount of parameters and a deeper network to learn the parameters suitable for all missing cases for this fixed weight structure. However, this is somehow difficult and computationally expensive. On the other hand, The self-attention mechanism applied in TINet can dynamically adjusts the weights of networks according to the input data, making the model more robust and effective.

Impact of Missing Types. The main difference between MCAR and BMAR is that BMAR causes a complete loss of dimensional information, impacting both BPMF and BGCP. Besides, data-driven models also suffer from a slight performance drop. TINet has the smallest performance gap between the two tasks. We attribute this robust performance to the self-attention mechanism and the multi-dimensional embedding used in TINet, as it models the spatial-temporal relationship among traffic data in a more reasonable way. Additionally, TINet without a self-attention layer is a special case of SAE, and their difference in metrics can reveal the effectiveness of the self-attention layer directly.

5.4 Limitations of Applying Self-attention Mechanism on Long Sequence Data

Applying self-attention mechanism on traffic data has computational and memory requirements which are quadratic with the input sequence length. With contemporary computing hardware and model sizes, this typically limits the input sequence [17]. However, this does not meet the needs of traffic sequence data, as the multi-dimensional traffic data requires a huge attention matrix, which is impractical. Thus, a natural question arises: can we achieve the empirical performance of quadratic full self-attention performance with a network with fewer parameters? In this work, TINet computes time embedding and graph embedding of node to avoid calculating attention of multi-dimensional data. This method is simple and practical to improve the performance of the model. Nevertheless, how to effectively solve the calculation and memory requirements of the self-attention mechanism on long-sequence multi-dimensional traffic data is still a problem worthy of research.

6   Conclusions

In this paper, we study the multi-dimensional traffic data imputation problem with two missing patterns. We design TINet, an effective Transformer-based model to impute data with random data missing and block data missing scenarios. The self-attention-based Transformer Module makes TINet circumventing the limitations of Fully Connected Network. Furthermore, the multi-dimensional embedding not also improves the performance of TINet, but also avoids the excessive calculation of attention on multi-dimensional data. We evaluate TINet and compare the results with other baselines. The result shows that TINet develops superior imputation performance under most scenarios. We also discuss the limitations of applying self-attention mechanism on long sequence traffic data. To overcome these existing drawbacks, we will further extend current work into designing effective and efficient Transformer models for multi-dimensional traffic data in the future.

References

1. Chen, H., Grant-Muller, S., Mussone, L., Montgomery, F.: A study of hybrid neural network approaches and the effects of missing data on traffic forecasting. Neural Comput. Appl. **10**(3), 277–286 (2001)
2. Chen, X., He, Z., Sun, L.: A Bayesian tensor decomposition approach for spatiotemporal traffic data imputation. Transp. Res. Part C Emerg. Technol. **98**, 73–84 (2019)
3. Chen, X., Sun, L.: Bayesian temporal factorization for multidimensional time series prediction. IEEE Trans. Pattern Anal. Mach. Intell. (2021)
4. Correia, G.M., Niculae, V., Martins, A.F.: Adaptively sparse transformers. In: Proceedings of the 2019 Conference on Empirical Methods in Natural Language Processing and the 9th International Joint Conference on Natural Language Processing, pp. 2174–2184 (2019)

5. Devlin, J., Chang, M.W., Lee, K., Toutanova, K.: BERT: pre-training of deep bidirectional transformers for language understanding. In: North American Chapter of the Association for Computational Linguistics: Human Language Technologies, Volume 1 (Long and Short Papers), pp. 4171–4186 (2019)

6. Kingma, D.P., Ba, J.: Adam: a method for stochastic optimization. In: International Conference on Learning Representations, San Diego, CA, USA, 7–9 May (2015)

7. Mikolov, T., Chen, K., Corrado, G., Dean, J.: Efficient estimation of word representations in vector space. arXiv preprint arXiv:1301.3781 (2013)

8. Perozzi, B., Al-Rfou, R., Skiena, S.: DeepWalk: online learning of social representations. In: ACM SIGKDD International Conference on Knowledge Discovery and Data Mining, pp. 701–710 (2014)

9. Redman, T.C.: If your data is bad, your machine learning tools are useless. Harvard Bus. Rev. **2** (2018)

10. Sidiropoulos, N.D., De Lathauwer, L., Fu, X., Huang, K., Papalexakis, E.E., Faloutsos, C.: Tensor decomposition for signal processing and machine learning. IEEE Trans. Sig. Process. **65**(13), 3551–3582 (2017)

11. Smith, B.L., Scherer, W.T., Conklin, J.H.: Exploring imputation techniques for missing data in transportation management systems. Transp. Res. Rec. **1836**(1), 132–142 (2003)

12. Vaswani, A., et al.: Attention is all you need. arXiv preprint arXiv:1706.03762 (2017)

13. Vig, J., Belinkov, Y.: Analyzing the structure of attention in a transformer language model. In: Proceedings of the 2019 ACL Workshop BlackboxNLP: Analyzing and Interpreting Neural Networks for NLP, pp. 63–76 (2019)

14. Xu, J.R., Li, X.Y., Shi, H.J.: Short-term traffic flow forecasting model under missing data. J. Comput. Appl. **30**(4), 1117–1120 (2010)

15. Duan, Y., Lv, Y., Kang, W., Zhao, Y.: A deep learning based approach for traffic data imputation. In: IEEE Conference on Intelligent Transportation Systems, pp. 912–917 (2014)

16. Yoon, J., Jordon, J., Schaar, M.: Gain: missing data imputation using generative adversarial nets. In: International Conference on Machine Learning, pp. 5689–5698. PMLR (2018)

17. Zaheer, M., et al.: Big bird: transformers for longer sequences. Adv. Neural Inf. Process. Syst. **33**, 17283–17297 (2020)

18. Zhu, L., Yu, F.R., Wang, Y., Ning, B., Tang, T.: Big data analytics in intelligent transportation systems: a survey. IEEE Trans. Intell. Transp. Syst. **20**(1), 383–398 (2018)

Sequential Self-Attentive Model for Knowledge Tracing

Xuelong Zhang⑩, Juntao Zhang⑩, Nanzhou Lin, and Xiandi Yang(✉)

School of Computer Science, Wuhan University, Wuhan, China
{2015301500363,juntaozhang,linnzh,xiandiy}@whu.edu.cn

Abstract. With the ongoing development of online education platforms, knowledge tracing (KT) has become a critical task that can help online education platforms provide personalized education. KT aims to find out students' knowledge states and predict whether students can correctly answer the question according to their exercise history. However, existing works fail to incorporate question information and ignore some useful contextual information. In this paper, we propose a novel Sequential Self-Attentive model for Knowledge Tracing (SSAKT). SSAKT utilizes question information based on Multidimensional Item Response Theory (MIRT) which can capture the relations between questions and skills. Then SSAKT uses a self-attention layer to capture the relations between questions. Unlike traditional self-attention networks, the self-attention layer in SSAKT uses Long Short-Term Memory networks (LSTM) to perform positional encoding. Moreover, a context module is designed to capture the contextual information. Experiments on four real-world datasets show that SSAKT outperforms existing KT models. We also conduct a case study that shows our model can effectively capture the relations between questions and skills.

Keywords: Knowledge Tracing · Recurrent Neural Networks · Educational data mining · Attention networks

1 Introduction

Online education platforms, such as massive open online courses and intelligent tutoring systems have attracted great attention due to their convenience. Students can acquire knowledge by solving problems offered by the platforms. For such platforms, a method to get the knowledge states of students is necessary. Knowledge Tracing (KT) is considered to be an effective method to track the knowledge states of the students. The goal of KT is to discover the knowledge states of students based on their past exercise records. The probability that students can correctly answer a problem depends on their knowledge states, which represents how well students have mastered the underlying knowledge concepts behind the problems [19]. If the student has mastered the knowledge concept well, the probability that he or she would correctly answer the problem would be high.

ⓒ Springer Nature Switzerland AG 2021
I. Farkaš et al. (Eds.): ICANN 2021, LNCS 12891, pp. 318–330, 2021.
https://doi.org/10.1007/978-3-030-86362-3_26

Effectively modeling the knowledge states of students is of great significance, however, using numerical simulations to model human learning in real-life is inherently difficult. Early attempts [13,18] for the KT task are mostly based on Recurrent Neural Networks (RNNs). Inspired by the prevalence of Transformer [16], recently Self-Attentive Knowledge Tracing (SAKT) model was proposed by [11], which uses the self-attention mechanism to discover the relevance between past interactions and target exercises. Context-aware Attentive Knowledge Tracing (AKT) [4] also incorporated transformer-like architecture and designed an elaborate attention scoring function for the knowledge tracing task, which has achieved better performance. However, unlike RNN-based models, transformer-like knowledge tracing models lack the ability to effectively capture sequential characteristics and ignore useful contextual information. Besides, question information hasn't been effectively utilized in previous works.

In this paper, we propose a novel KT model which is called Sequential Self-Attentive Knowledge Tracing (SSAKT). Different from existing methods which only use LSTM or transformer, our model combines transformer and LSTM in an effective way. We use a transformer layer to encode the question and the response and use LSTM to encode sequential features and contextual information. The main contributions of our work are summarized as follows:

1. We design a new positional encoding method that uses LSTM instead of the traditional positional encoding method to encode sequential features.
2. We develop a question embedding method that can appropriately capture the relations between questions and skills, which significantly improves the prediction performance.
3. We introduce a context module to capture the contextual information which is ignored by the self-attention mechanism and incorporate the context module into the self-attention layer.
4. We conduct extensive experiments on several benchmark datasets and the results show that our model outperforms the state-of-the-art baselines.

2   Related Works

With the development of deep learning in recent years, neural networks have been successfully applied to many tasks, which inspired researchers to apply deep learning techniques to KT tasks. Deep Knowledge Tracing (DKT) [13] first applied LSTM to KT tasks and achieved substantial improvement in student performance prediction. Yeung et al. found DKT could not reconstruct the input and hidden knowledge state was not smooth across the time, thus proposed DKT+ [18] to address the two problems. Inspired by MANN, Zhang et al. proposed Dynamic Key-Value Memory Networks (DKVMN) [19] which utilizes external matrices to store key-value pairs, the key matrix stores the question representation, and the value matrix stores the mastery of students. Abdelrahman et al. proposed Sequential Key-Value Memory Network (SKVMN) [1] based on DKVMN, which uses a modified LSTM with hops to capture the long-term dependencies between questions. SAKT [11] is the first model that uses the self-attention mechanism in the context of KT. SAKT uses a vanilla transformer decoder to predict the performance of the students. Relation-Aware Self-Attention model (RKT) [12] extends SAKT by introducing an exercise-relation coefficient matrix, which is calculated according to the correct rate of each question. AKT [4] uses modified self-attention called monotonic attention to model the forget behavior of students and uses Item Response Theory (IRT) to model question difficulties, which has achieved great improvement over previous models.

There are some other models that attempt to take other information into account. Prerequisite-driven Deep Knowledge Tracing (PDKT) [2] improves DKT by incorporating prerequisite relations between knowledge concepts. Exercise-aware Knowledge Tracing (EKT) [7] encodes the question using the question text so that question embeddings can contain more information. Nagatani et al. augmented DKT by explicitly adding the time features to the question embeddings [10].

3   Problem Formulation

The goal of knowledge tracing is to track down the learner's knowledge state through a sequence of his or her past learning activities. In this paper, we formulate knowledge tracing as a sequence prediction problem, which requires us to predict whether a learner will correctly answer the question at time step t given his or her exercise history record $X = \{x_1, x_2, ..., x_{t-1}\}$. Each interaction x_i in the sequence X is a tuple (q_i, c_i, r_i), where $q_i \in \{1, ..., Q\}$ is the question ID, $c_i \in \{1, ..., C\}$ is the ID of the skill which the question contains, and $r_i \in \{0, 1\}$ is the learner's response. Under this notation, knowledge tracing can be formalized as follows:

Given a learner's history exercise sequence $X = \{x_1, x_2, ..., x_{t-1}\}$, the goal of knowledge tracing is to predict the probability of correctly answering the question q_t at time step t, i.e. $P_t(r_t = 1|q_t, c_t, X)$.

4   Proposed Method

In this section, we introduce our model Sequential Self-Attentive model for Knowledge Tracing, Fig. 1 shows the overall framework of our model. We first use the embedding layer to encode questions, skills and responses based on the IRT model, and LSTM is used to encode the sequential information into the question-response embedding. To capture the relations between questions and question-response pairs, we use a transformer layer to calculate the attention weights. Finally, the interaction layer is used to produce the final prediction.

4.1   Embedding Layer

Following previous work [19], our model uses embeddings to represent questions and question-response pairs, the questions embeddings are used for querying

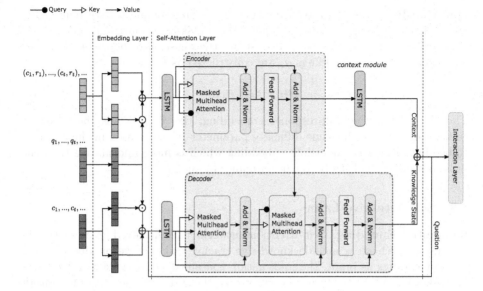

Fig. 1. The overall architecture of SSAKT, where $\odot$ denotes point-wise production operation and $\oplus$ denotes concatenation operation.

the latent knowledge state at the corresponding time step, and the question-response pairs are used to update the knowledge state. In most datasets, the question number is much larger than the skill number. To avoid data sparsity and overparameterization, most of the previous works use the skills covered by the question to represent the question. In this paper, we propose a method to utilize question information to improve the prediction performance.

Question Embedding. Due to limited exercise records and massive questions in the dataset, learning informative question representation is a big challenge. It is useful to learn question representations because whether a student will correctly answer a question depends on not only the related skills of the question and the skill mastery of the students but also the question characteristics (e.g. question difficulty and question discrimination).

Inspired by the MIRT [15], a classic and interpretable method used in psychometrics, we propose a novel method to encode questions and question-response pairs. MIRT uses multidimensional vectors to characterize the problem and the student. In our model, we construct the question embeddings $\boldsymbol{q}_t$ at time step t as follows:

$$\boldsymbol{q}_t = \boldsymbol{c}_t + \boldsymbol{\mu}_t \cdot \boldsymbol{d}_t \tag{1}$$

The $\boldsymbol{c}_t \in \mathbb{R}^d$ is the embedding of the skill covered by question q_t at time step t, which reflect the inherent representation of the skill. $\boldsymbol{\mu}_t \in \mathbb{R}^d$ is the difficulty vector of question q_t, and $\boldsymbol{d}_t \in \mathbb{R}^d$ is the vector which summarizes the variations of questions that cover the skill [4].

Question-Response Embedding. The embeddings of question-response pairs are similar to the question embeddings. We use skill-response embeddings and question difficulty embeddings to construct the question-response embeddings. Question-response embeddings $\boldsymbol{a}_t$ are constructed as follows:

$$\boldsymbol{a}_t = \boldsymbol{s}_t + \boldsymbol{\mu}_t \cdot \boldsymbol{f}_t \tag{2}$$

The $\boldsymbol{s}_t \in \mathbb{R}^d$ is the skill-response embedding, the $\boldsymbol{f}_t \in \mathbb{R}^d$ is the variation embedding. We use the same difficulty parameter $\boldsymbol{\mu}_t$ as we used in the question embedding. Using the question embedding which is more informative than the skill embedding leads to better performance of our model.

4.2   Self-Attentive Layer

Sequential Encoding. Self-attention networks have achieved great success in various research areas include knowledge tracing tasks. However, due to using raw embeddings as input, the information contained in query, key and value is limited. Unlike RNNs which inherently take the order of question into consideration, self-attentive networks don't have a sense of position for each question without positional encoding. To address the problems above, we use LSTM as a positional encoding method to encode the sequential features before inputting the embedding into the self-attention module. The raw embeddings are encoded as follows:

$$\boldsymbol{X} = LSTM(\boldsymbol{I}) \tag{3}$$

where $\boldsymbol{I}$ denotes the raw question or question-response embedding sequence. LSTM can encode positional features into embeddings due to its recurrent structure. Compared to existing positional encoding techniques which model the forget behavior implicitly e.g. sinusoidal positional encoding, LSTM is more effective in modeling forget behavior owing to its gating mechanism, and the weight of distant past exercises is reduced.

Self-Attention Module. To calculate the correlation between current exercise and exercises practiced before, a self-attention module is used in our model. The module consists of an encoder and a decoder, both the encoder and the decoder use the scaled dot-product attention mechanism. The encoder is used to encode the question-response sequence, the decoder encodes the question sequence and calculates the relation between exercises at different time steps. Under this framework, both encoder and decoder have key, query and value matrices $\boldsymbol{W}^K \in \mathbb{R}^{d \times d_k}$, $\boldsymbol{W}^Q \in \mathbb{R}^{d \times d_q}$ and $\boldsymbol{W}^V \in \mathbb{R}^{d \times d_v}$, which can project the input $\boldsymbol{X} \in \mathbb{R}^{N \times d}$ to keys $\boldsymbol{K} \in \mathbb{R}^{N \times d_k}$, queries $\boldsymbol{Q} \in \mathbb{R}^{N \times d_q}$ and values $\boldsymbol{V} \in \mathbb{R}^{N \times d_v}$ as follows:

$$\boldsymbol{Q} = \boldsymbol{X}\boldsymbol{W}^Q, \boldsymbol{K} = \boldsymbol{X}\boldsymbol{W}^K, \boldsymbol{V} = \boldsymbol{X}\boldsymbol{W}^V \tag{4}$$

d_q, d_k and d_v is the dimension of query, key and value vectors respectively and $d_q = d_k$. Let $\boldsymbol{\alpha}$ be the attention weights, $\boldsymbol{\alpha}$ is calculated as follows:

$$\boldsymbol{\alpha} = Softmax(\frac{\boldsymbol{QK}^T}{\sqrt{d_k}}) \tag{5}$$

where n is the number of time steps. To prevent the information leakage from future time steps, we use a triangular matrix to mask the attention weights. We incorporate multi-head attention into our models to capture the relevance between current question and past questions so that different heads can attend to different parts of past exercises. We use H attention heads and concatenate the output of different heads into one vector, then use a fully connected network to project the vector into $\boldsymbol{h}_t^{out} \in \mathbb{R}^d$. The final output of the multi-head attention module is

$$Attn_i = Softmax(Mask(\frac{\boldsymbol{Q}_i\boldsymbol{K}_i^T}{\sqrt{d_k}}))\boldsymbol{V}_i \tag{6}$$

$$\boldsymbol{H}^{out} = [Attn_1, ..., Attn_H]\boldsymbol{W}^{out} \tag{7}$$

where the [,] denotes the concatenation operation, $\boldsymbol{H}^{out}$ is the representation of the entire sequence, we use $\boldsymbol{h}_t^{out}$ to represent the output of multi-head attention module at time step t.

Pointwise FeedForward Network. We apply the Point-wise Feed-Forward Network (FFN) to the output $\boldsymbol{h}^{out}$. FFN adds the non-linearity to the self-attention layer. It contains two linear transformations and a ReLU activation function between, then the final output of self-attention module is as follows:

$$\boldsymbol{h}_t = \boldsymbol{W}^{(1)}(ReLU(\boldsymbol{W}^{(2)}\boldsymbol{h}^{out} + \boldsymbol{b}^{(2)})) + \boldsymbol{b}^{(1)} \tag{8}$$

Residual Connetion and Layernormalization. Following [16], we use layer normalization after masked multi-head attention networks and FFN, and we use residual connection [5] to propagate low-level features.

Context Module. The self-attentive layer is used to capture the dependencies between exercises. However, the self-attentive layer only focuses on the exercises related to the current question, which ignores some useful contextual information. To utilize the contextual information, we need to encode the context into a vector. Inspired by the global context in [17] and the context representation in [6], we use LSTM to encode the contextual information. The LSTM takes the sequential encoded question-response sequence $\hat{\boldsymbol{X}}$ as input and outputs a context sequence.

$$\boldsymbol{C} = LSTM(\hat{\boldsymbol{X}}) \tag{9}$$

4.3   Interaction Layer

Finally, we use an interaction layer to predict the learner's response to the current question q_t. We first add the context vector C_{t-1} at time step $t-1$ to the output of self attention layer h_{t-1} to get the context-aware knowledge state $\tilde{h}$. Then we concatenate raw question embedding q_t and $\tilde{h}_{t-1}$ which reflects the knowledge state of the learner. Finally, the concatenated vector is passed to a fully connected layer ending with Sigmoid activation to output the probability of the correct response.

$$\tilde{h}_t = C_{t-1} + h_{t-1} \tag{10}$$

$$p = \sigma(W^{(4)}(ReLU(W^{(3)}[q_t, \tilde{h}_t] + b^{(3)})) + b^{(4)}) \tag{11}$$

All learnable parameters in our model are trained in an end-to-end fashion by minimizing the binary cross-entropy between the prediction outputs and ground-truth labels.

$$l = -\sum_{i \in T}(r_i log(p_i) + (1 - r_i)log(1 - p_i)) \tag{12}$$

where T denotes all the exercise records in the training set.

5   Experiments

In this section, we conduct extensive experiments on several real-world datasets to evaluate the performance of our model[1]. Then we perform ablation studies on components of our model to validate if these modules are effective. Finally, we visualize the embeddings to further explain the effectiveness of our model.

Table 1. Dataset statistics

	ASSIST2009	ASSIST2017	EdNet	Junyi
#students	4,029	1,709	10,000	7,101
#questions	16,891	3,162	12,098	24,916
#skills	110	102	1,792	1,326
#responses	321,486	941,107	1,173,020	1,577,903
responses per student	79.79	550.67	117.30	222.20
responses per skills	2922.60	854.99	654.58	1189.97
responses per question	19.03	297.63	96.95	63.32

5.1   Datasets

We conduct experiments on four datasets widely used in KT tasks and all of these datasets have question and skill information. The statistics of the datasets are listed in Table 1. We use the area under the curve (AUC) as the evaluation metrics to evaluate the performance on each dataset.

---

[1] Source code will be available at https://github.com/zxlzxlzxlzxlzxl/SSAKT.

- ASSISTment2009 (ASSIST2009)[2] was collected in the school year 2009–2010 on the online tutoring platform ASSISTment.
- ASSISTment2017 (ASSIST2017)[3] is the dataset used in ASSISTment 2017 competition, which spans from middle school to the students' eventual choice of career. It was collected from the same platform as ASSISTment2009.
- EdNet[4] was collected by [3]. Because the entire dataset is too large which makes the training process time-consuming, we randomly sample the exercise sequences of 10,000 students and conduct our experiments on this subset.
- JunyiAcademy[5] was collected from JunyiAcademy, an online platform providing education resources, over the course of a year [14].

Following [19], we remove the records without named skills for ASSIST2009 and ASSIST2017. We also truncate the input sequence whose length is over 200 following [13,19] for efficiency. If the length of an input sequence is over 200, we split it into several sequences whose length is less than 200.

5.2 Baselines

To evaluate the effectiveness of our model, we compare our model against the following models:

- DKT [13] is the first deep KT model using a single-layer LSTM to model the knowledge states of students.
- DKVMN [19] is a Memory Augmented Neural Network based KT model with dynamic key and value matrices where the key matrix stores the latent exercise representations and the value matrix stores the knowledge states.
- DKT-Q is a variant of DKT, which uses questions instead of skills as input.
- DKVMN-Q is similar to DKT-Q, which uses questions instead of skills as input.
- SAKT [11] uses the self-attention mechanism to identify the relevant exercises practiced before and make predictions based on relevant past exercises.
- AKT [4] is a transformer-like KT model with an encoder and a decoder, which uses monotonic self-attention to model forget behavior and uses Rasch model [9] to generate question embeddings.

5.3 Implementation Details

We perform k-fold cross-validation on datasets with $k = 5$. 60% of the dataset are used for training, 20% are the validation set, and the rest are used for testing. The embedding dimensions of questions, skills and question-response pairs

---

[2] https://sites.google.com/site/assistmentsdata/home/assistment-2009-2010-data/skill-builder-data-2009-2010.

[3] https://sites.google.com/view/assistmentsdatamining/.

[4] https://github.com/riiid/ednet.

[5] https://www.kaggle.com/junyiacademy/learning-activity-public-dataset-by-junyi-academy.

are the same and fixed to 256. The dimensions of hidden states in all LSTM are set to 256, the number of attention heads is set to 8. The dropout rate is set to 0.2 to avoid overfitting and a mini-batch size is set to 32. We use the normalized xavier initialization method to initialize the embedding matrices and linear transformation matrices, and all trainable parameters are optimized by Adam optimizer with the learning rate of 0.0001.

5.4   Performance Prediction

We conduct our experiments on the four datasets mentioned above and the results are shown in Table 2, which are the averages of the five-fold cross-validation experiments. From the table, we can notice that SSAKT outperforms other baselines on all datasets. To be specific, our model outperforms other models by at least 0.5%, which demonstrates the effectiveness of our model. It's noticeable that our model SSAKT significantly outperforms other models on the ASSISTment2017 dataset, which shows an increase of at least 2%. The reason can be that ASSISTment2017 has the largest responses per student, which demonstrates that our model is good at capture long-distance dependencies in sequence. In general, AKT and SSAKT significantly outperform other models, which can attribute to the effective utilization of the question information and related skills. Compared to AKT, SSAKT uses more informative question representations and models the forget behavior using LSTM, which helps SSAKT achieve better performance.

Table 2. The performance comparison of all models on four datasets.

Dataset	ASSIST2009	ASSIST2017	EdNet	Junyi
DKT	0.8080	0.7252	0.6928	0.7488
DKVMN	0.8123	0.7121	0.6937	0.7514
SAKT	0.8005	0.6609	0.6919	0.7478
DKT-Q	0.7574	0.7733	0.7325	0.7692
DKVMN-Q	0.7250	0.7492	0.7380	0.7784
AKT	0.8367	0.7640	0.7454	0.7883
SSAKT	**0.8432**	**0.7935**	**0.7510**	**0.7949**

SAKT performs worst in all datasets among all deep models. The possible reason can be that SAKT uses learnable positional embeddings and doesn't model the forget behavior explicitly, thus isn't able to learn effective position representations in these datasets.

We also find that using question embeddings instead of skill embeddings as input may improve the performance. DKT-Q and DKVMN-Q outperform DKT and DKVMN on all datasets except for ASSISTment2009, the reason can be that ASSISTment2009 has the lowest responses per question thus suffers from data sparsity problem. On the contrary, DKT-Q outperforms DKT by 4.8% on ASSISTment2017, which has the largest responses per question.

5.5   Ablation Study

To investigate the effectiveness of different parts in our model, we perform several ablation studies. We compare our model with several variants:

- SSAKT-RQE (Remove Question Embeddings) doesn't use question information, only uses skill embeddings as input.
- SSAKT-RQR (Replace Question embeddings with Rasch model based embeddings) replaces the question embedding mentioned in this paper with the Rasch model-based embeddings [4] used in AKT.
- SSAKT-RSE (Remove Sequential Encoding) removes the sequential encoding layer, which directly takes question embeddings as the input of the encoder and the decoder.
- SSAKT-RSS (Replace Sequence encoding with Sinusoidal encoding) removes the sequential encoding and uses sinusoidal encoding to encode the exercise embeddings instead.
- SSAKT-RC (Remove Context layer) removes the context layer, which only uses the output of the self-attention layer for prediction.

Table 3. Ablation studies

Dataset	ASSIST2009	ASSIST2017	EdNet	Junyi
SSAKT-RQE	0.8191	0.7288	0.6970	0.7518
SSAKT-RQR	0.8338	0.7721	0.7500	0.7930
SSAKT-RSE	0.8367	0.7864	0.7458	0.7905
SSAKT-RSS	0.8307	0.7896	0.7477	0.7935
SSAKT-RC	0.8355	0.7790	0.7482	0.7920
SSAKT	**0.8432**	**0.7935**	**0.7510**	**0.7949**

We don't modify other parts of the model except for the changes mentioned above. The results of ablation studies are shown in Table 3. From the table, we can find that our model SSAKT achieves the best performance among all variants, which demonstrates the effectiveness of different parts of our model. We find that SSAKT-RQE performs worst among all variants of SSAKT, but still outperforms the deep models which only use skills as input, i.e. DKT, DKVMN and SAKT. This fact shows that question information is of great significance, which can greatly improve the performance of our model. Our model SSAKT outperforms SSAKT-RQR on all datasets, especially on ASSIST2009 and ASSIST2017, which reflects that the question embedding method is more effective than the Rasch model-based question embedding used in AKT. SSAKT-RSS outperforms

SSAKT-RSE on most datasets which shows the necessity of position information but is still slightly inferior to our model especially on ASSIST2009, which shows the effectiveness of the sequential encoding layer in our model. From the SSAKT-RC, we can see that some contextual information is ignored by the self-attention layer which leads to a decrease in performance, thus showing the effectiveness of the context layer.

5.6   Visualization of Question Embeddings

We use t-SNE [8] to visualize the question embeddings learned by our model. Figure 2 shows the visualization of question embeddings of two datasets ASSIST2009 and EdNet, where ASSIST2009 is a small dataset while EdNet is significantly larger. The questions covering the same skills are labeled in the same color. We can see that the question embeddings in ASSIST2009 are well-clustered, questions with different skills are separated and questions with the same skills are close to each other. We can also find some well-clustered question embeddings in EdNet, but there are also many question embeddings scattered across the space. The possible reason is that the skill number is large in EdNet, while the question number is close to ASSIST2009, thus the relations between questions and skills are not well learned by the model.

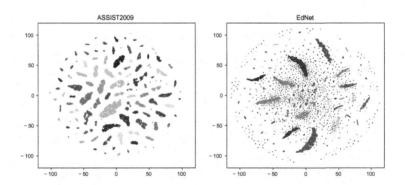

Fig. 2. The visualization of question embeddings. The questions covering the same skills have the same color.

6   Conclusion and Future Work

In this paper, we propose a new KT model SSAKT that combines LSTM and self-attention. Our model first incorporates the question information into question embeddings based on MIRT. Then we design a self-attention layer to capture the relations between exercises. To model the forget behavior, we use LSTM instead of the positional encoding to encode the sequential features. To capture the contextual information ignored by the self-attention module, we design a context module to capture the contextual information. Finally, we use an interaction layer to get the prediction. Experiments on the real-world datasets show that SSAKT outperforms the existing deep KT models. Future work includes i) incorporating question text into our model to improve our question embedding method and ii) incorporating cognitive diagnosis methods to improve the interpretability of our model.

Acknowledgements. This work is partially supported by National Natural Science Foundation of China Nos. U1811263, 62072349, National Key Research and Development Project of China No. 2020YFC1522602.

References

1. Abdelrahman, G., Wang, Q.: Knowledge tracing with sequential key-value memory networks. In: Proceedings of the 42nd International ACM SIGIR Conference on Research and Development in Information Retrieval, pp. 175–184 (2019)
2. Chen, P., Lu, Y., Zheng, V.W., Pian, Y.: Prerequisite-driven deep knowledge tracing. In: 2018 IEEE International Conference on Data Mining (ICDM), pp. 39–48. IEEE (2018)
3. Choi, Y., et al.: EdNet: a large-scale hierarchical dataset in education. In: Bittencourt, I.I., Cukurova, M., Muldner, K., Luckin, R., Millán, E. (eds.) AIED 2020. LNCS (LNAI), vol. 12164, pp. 69–73. Springer, Cham (2020). https://doi.org/10.1007/978-3-030-52240-7_13
4. Ghosh, A., Heffernan, N., Lan, A.S.: Context-aware attentive knowledge tracing. In: Proceedings of the 26th ACM SIGKDD International Conference on Knowledge Discovery and Data Mining, pp. 2330–2339 (2020)
5. He, K., Zhang, X., Ren, S., Sun, J.: Deep residual learning for image recognition. In: Proceedings of the IEEE Conference on Computer Vision and Pattern Recognition, pp. 770–778 (2016)
6. Li, H., Min, M.R., Ge, Y., Kadav, A.: A context-aware attention network for interactive question answering. In: Proceedings of the 23rd ACM SIGKDD International Conference on Knowledge Discovery and Data Mining, pp. 927–935 (2017)
7. Liu, Q., et al.: EKT: exercise-aware knowledge tracing for student performance prediction. IEEE Trans. Knowl. Data Eng. **33**(1), 100–115 (2019)
8. Van der Maaten, L., Hinton, G.: Visualizing data using t-SNE. J. Mach. Learn. Res. **9**(11), 79 (2008)
9. Martínez-Plumed, F., Prudêncio, R.B., Martínez-Usó, A., Hernández-Orallo, J.: Making sense of item response theory in machine learning. In: Proceedings of the Twenty-second European Conference on Artificial Intelligence, pp. 1140–1148 (2016)
10. Nagatani, K., Zhang, Q., Sato, M., Chen, Y.Y., Chen, F., Ohkuma, T.: Augmenting knowledge tracing by considering forgetting behavior. In: The World Wide Web Conference, pp. 3101–3107 (2019)
11. Pandey, S., Karypis, G.: A self-attentive model for knowledge tracing. arXiv preprint arXiv:1907.06837 (2019)
12. Pandey, S., Srivastava, J.: RKT: relation-aware self-attention for knowledge tracing. In: Proceedings of the 29th ACM International Conference on Information and Knowledge Management, pp. 1205–1214 (2020)
13. Piech, C., et al.: Deep knowledge tracing. arXiv preprint arXiv:1506.05908 (2015)

14. Pojen, C., Mingen, H., Tzuyang, T.: Junyi academy online learning activity dataset: a large-scale public online learning activity dataset from elementary to senior high school students (2020). Dataset available from https://www.kaggle.com/junyiacademy/learning-activity-public-dataset-by-junyi-academy
15. Reckase, M.D.: The past and future of multidimensional item response theory. Appl. Psychol. Meas. **21**(1), 25–36 (1997)
16. Vaswani, A., et al.: Attention is all you need. arXiv preprint arXiv:1706.03762 (2017)
17. Yang, B., Li, J., Wong, D.F., Chao, L.S., Wang, X., Tu, Z.: Context-aware self-attention networks. In: Proceedings of the AAAI Conference on Artificial Intelligence, vol. 33, pp. 387–394 (2019)
18. Yeung, C.K., Yeung, D.Y.: Addressing two problems in deep knowledge tracing via prediction-consistent regularization. In: Proceedings of the Fifth Annual ACM Conference on Learning at Scale, pp. 1–10 (2018)
19. Zhang, J., Shi, X., King, I., Yeung, D.Y.: Dynamic key-value memory networks for knowledge tracing. In: Proceedings of the 26th International Conference on World Wide Web, pp. 765–774 (2017)

Multi-object Tracking Based on Nearest Optimal Template Library

Ran Tian, Xiang Zhang$^{(\boxtimes)}$, Donghang Chen, and Yujie Hu

Yangtze Delta Region Institute (Quzhou), University of Electronic Science
and Technology of China, Quzhou 324000, Zhejiang, China
{Tianrr,chendh,huyujie}@std.uestc.edu.cn, uestchero@uestc.edu.cn

Abstract. Noisy detection and similar appearance lead to deteriorated mis-identification and id-switch in Multi-Object Tracking (MOT). To address these problems, we propose a novel Nearest Optimal Template Library (NOTL) associated with two tailor-made methods based on the NOTL. Here, the NOTL is a historical sample set of the tracked objects, and the elements in the NOTL are closest to the complete object at the current instant. It provides reliable appearance information of the object. Then, we use the single object tracker (SOT) for position prediction, and spatio-temporal network for appearance modeling. They can alleviate mis-identification and id-switch problems, respectively. Besides, the triplet loss is used to train our spatio-temporal network further improves the performance. The proposed algorithm achieves 55.3% and 55.1% in MOTA on challenging MOT16 and MOT17 benchmark datasets respectively. These results show our method is competitive with the previous state-of-the-art approaches.

Keywords: Multi-object tracking · Template library · Single object tracker · Spatio-temporal network

1 Introduction

Multiple object tracking (MOT) is a classical research field in computer vision, which focuses on locating and associating the same object in continuous video frames. Tracking-by-detection paradigm is widely used in the MOT approach. This method performs a cross-frame correlation for the given detection results. However, the unreliable detection and high similarity between targets bring problems such as the mis-identification and id-switch for MOT tasks.

In order to reduce mis-identification, the useful method is to predict the position of the tracked object to recover the missed detection. Some methods use linear position prediction to recover the missed objects. But the accuracy of the linear predictor could decrease if it is not updated by detection over a long time. Others utilize nonlinear methods such as the SOT tracker to solve this problem. But the SOT tracker [14,15] is based on template matching which is manually masked in the first frame, while MOT can not provide an accurate template for

© Springer Nature Switzerland AG 2021
I. Farkaš et al. (Eds.): ICANN 2021, LNCS 12891, pp. 331–342, 2021.
https://doi.org/10.1007/978-3-030-86362-3_27

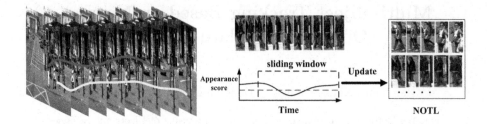

Fig. 1. Nearest Optimal Template Library (NOTL). It selects the targets from the tracklet as the templates according to the appearance score. We get the score of each target and update the library according to the strategy.

the SOT tracker. For the similar appearance, many methods [6,23] based on the CNN network aim at building a robust appearance model to distinguish different targets. But occlusion or interaction could disturb the appearance features and we can not make a judgment when it happens. Therefore, obtaining complete and reliable appearance information of the target is the key to solving the problem.

For this purpose, we propose a novelty online MOT method which includes a Nearest Optimal Template Library (NOTL) and two optimization methods to improve the accuracy of the tracker. The building procedure of the proposed NOTL can be summarized in two steps, shown in Fig. 1. Firstly, we utilize a sliding window to maintain and update the historical appearance information of these objects which have been tracked. We move the sliding window over time and update templates with appearance scores higher than the threshold so that the trajectory in the library is the latest and optimal. Based on the NOTL, we propose two methods to predict the position and distinguish different objects respectively, thereby alleviating these problems in MOT. We use a SOT tracker combines with the NOTL for position prediction. The comprehensive and accurate appearance in the library makes our methods more effective than others. And we combine the constraints of spatio-temporal information with the NOTL to build a network, and train the network with triplet loss [19]. It can make our network learn adaptive features in the library to distinguish different targets in the same frame. Notably, combining spatio-temporal information and triplet loss is the first attempt in MOT task. We tested our algorithm in the datasets of MOT16 and MOT17, and verified that our algorithm is effective.

2   Related Work

Tracking-by-Detection paradigm is a popular framework in recent years. Numerous approaches [4,7,9] combine the detections in a period of time and these use future information when processing the current frame, which is called the offline MOT method. Corresponding to these, the online MOT method [22,26] does not use future information. The effect of the offline method is better than the online method, but real-time performance is the opposite. Majority of MOT methods

[11,12] focused on improving the association by finding a more robust appearance model or combining multi-models. And the tracking result was closely related to the detection.

Position prediction is a very important task in MOT. There are many noisy detections in the public dataset, which greatly affect the performance of the tracker. Generally speaking, position prediction is to establish a model for the target that has been tracked and predict the new position in the new frame through the historical trajectory. Since significant progress has been made on SOT in recent years. Some previous works [6,29] tried to adopt SOT trackers into MOT problem. In SOT, the template is manually in the first frame and they focus on distinguishing the foreground from the object effectively. But in MOT, there is frequent interaction between the targets, taking the detection results as the template is also ambiguous. So the SOT tracker will produce serious id-switch or missed target when occlusion happens.

The objects of MOT are pedestrians, and the difference between classes in the same category is very small, so how to distinguish different people well is a challenging task. In order to solve the problems of similarity. Some methods [20,27] tried to build a discriminative model based on CNN. Recently, RNN had been proposed to learn the temporal information of the object in MOT and established a spatio-temporal attention mechanism [6,29] to solve objects of similar appearance. They all established a spatio-temporal attention mechanism to assign weights to objects in different time and space. Du et al. [8] proposed an adaptive network using LSTM to learn the appearance variation in visual object tracking. Sadeghian et al. [18] successfully joined the appearance, motion, and interaction cues with independent LSTM, combining the learned feature to distinguish different objects. Kim et al. [13] utilized Bilinear LSTM (Bi-LSTM) to improve the learning of long-term appearance models combine with motion, and achieved state-of-the-art performance.

In this work, we mainly use the SOT tracker and spatio-temporal network based on the NOTL to create a new multi-object tracking framework. And certified the improvement of this algorithm.

3 Proposed Method

Our algorithm framework is shown in Fig. 2. First of all, we build the NOTL for the tracked objects according to the strategy we proposed. Based on this template library, we propose a single object tracker (SOT) and spatio-temporal attention network to predict the position and to model the appearance of the tracked objects. Specifically, we train our network by the triplet loss to improve the discernment of the network.

3.1 Build the Nearest Optimal Template Library

The inaccurate detection results provided by the detector make the appearance incomplete and unreliable. The appearance of the object directly affects the effect

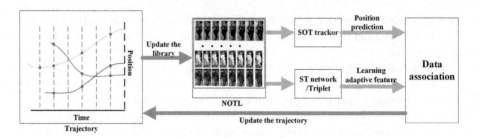

Fig. 2. The overall framework of our approach. Firstly, we build the Nearest Optimal Template Library (NOTL) based on the tracking trajectory we have obtained. Then, we propose to use a single object tracker (SOT tracker) to predict the position and spatio-temporal information to build the appearance model (ST network) based on the NOTL. Finally complete the task of MOT and update our library.

of the appearance-based method. So we need to develop a system to measure appearance and to get reliable appearance information as much as possible. The ideal appearance of the target is the closest to the current moment and is not blocked by the background or other targets. Based on these, we choose to use a sliding window method to build our template. We set a sliding window and make the window progress with time, removing the target farthest from the current moment when the library updated. And it also can ensure the temporal information in the template not be destroyed.

The warehousing standard is important because the occlusion may exist. The occlusion in MOT is divided into two types: background occlusion and mutual occlusion between targets. For the first type of occlusion, the boxes will become farther from the class of 'people', so a pre-trained classifier can be used to score the box. The classification score c_i^t is proportional to the degree of occlusion, Here, c_i^t means the classification score of candidate i in time t. For the second, the maximum Intersection over Union (IOU) at the current time t can be used to measure the mutual occlusion between objects.

$$o_i^t = \underset{i \neq j}{argmax}(\frac{d_i \cap d_j}{d_i \cup d_j}) \quad i \neq j, j = 0, \cdots \tag{1}$$

where the o_i^t is the maximum IOU of the candidate i in time t, d_i and d_j is the coordinate of candidate and other detections. If the maximum value of the IOU calculated by the candidate object i and other detections are less than a certain threshold, it can be considered that the possibility of mutual occlusion between the object and other objects is relatively low.

From these situations, we filter out those samples with bad appearance when select templates, so our template library is more referential. For a candidate b_i^t in time t, the classification score denoted as c_i^t and the maximum IOU in the same time t denoted as o_i^t. We define the update score as:

$$s_i^t = \alpha \cdot c_i^t + \beta \cdot (1 - o_i^t) \tag{2}$$

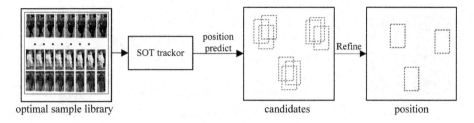

optimal sample library   candidates   position

Fig. 3. Single object tracker based on template library. We successively use the template in NOTL as the template of the SOT tracker. After obtaining several candidates, we refine these to get the final prediction result.

Where the α, β is hyperparameter set according to experience. The template library of the target i updated when the score s_i^t is over the threshold we set.

3.2 Position Predictor

In MOT task, there are many lost situations caused by unreliable detection, which have seriously affected the tracking results in many published methods. Therefore, an accurate position prediction method is essential. The position of the object can be obtained in consecutive frames with SOT, so we use SOT to do position prediction. But SOT trackers are based on template matching and the template is manually marked in the first frame. However, MOT is based on detection and the inaccuracy of the detection results makes it hard to provide a good template for the SOT tracker. We solve this problem by the NOTL.

The NOTL can provide reliable appearance information. We use the historical appearance information of the same object in the template library as the template, and use the SOT tracker to search in the area where the target appears. In this work, the SiameseFC [21] used as our baseline. The model is shown in Fig. 3. We denote the tracked objects as $T = \{T_1, T_2, \ldots, T_i\}$. Each target i has its own template library, which contains history information $T_i = \{A_i^1, \ldots, A_i^N\}$, here N is the length of the slide windows. The feature of object i at the NOTL x_n^i taken as a template and the original image z_{t+1} at time $t + 1$ taken as the search area. We denote the $f_p\left(x_n^i\right)$ are extracted from the library and $f_p\left(z_{t+1}\right)$ is extracted from the image of $t + 1$. The position of the object predicted in the new frame and get the predicted result $x_{t+1}^n, y_{t+1}^n, w_{t+1}^n, h_{t+1}^n$ refer to [21].

We can get M new candidates after predicted by the SOT tracker, then use a classifier and regressor to classify these boxes and fine-tuning. Finally, the most suitable box selected through the non-maximum suppression (NMS).

$$x_{t+1}^i, y_{t+1}^i, w_{t+1}^i, h_{t+1}^i = \text{NMS}(s_{cls}^1, \cdots, s_{cls}^M) \tag{3}$$

where $x_{t+1}^i, y_{t+1}^i, w_{t+1}^i, h_{t+1}^i$ mean the predicted candidates coordinates which contain the horizontal and vertical coordinates of the upper left corner, the width and height of the object i. s_{cls}^n is the score calculated by the classifier

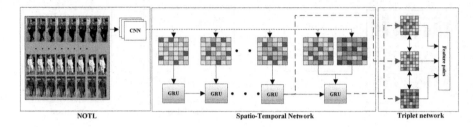

Fig. 4. We extract the appearance features of each target in the NOTL by a pre-trained CNN network, which will be sent into GRU network in turn. Then, we utilize the intermediate feature of GRU as anchor in triplet network (blue dotted line). In the last layers, we take object that is the same to the target as positive sample and another object in the same frame as negative sample (blue and red features), taking them as the last layer's input of the GRU network. And we use these two outputs (red dotted line) as the positive and negative examples of triplet to calculate the final loss. (Color figure online)

of the bounding box predicted by the template n. In addition, we also use the regression network to refine the candidates.

3.3 Appearance Model

In MOT task, the appearance of the targets is similar, which brings great challenges to the association. How to build an efficient appearance is important in MOT tasks. A good appearance model must have strong discrimination and be adaptable because there will be new targets in the video sequence. In addition, the video sequence contains inter-frame and intra-frame information. The position and appearance of a target are continuous between sequence frames. We want to learn these information and use it to distinguish different objects.

Our NOTL library contains the information, and we want to learn through the network. For these purposes, we utilize a spatio-temporal network to learn this information, which is shown in Fig. 4. We extract the appearance of each target in the template library by a CNN network, and use the Gate Recurrent Unit (GRU) network to learn temporal information of the appearance which belongs to the same target. In order to make our network more discriminative, the triplet loss method adopted to train the network.

Spatio-Temporal Network. It is not enough to make accurate judgment rely on appearance characteristics, because the appearance of pedestrians is similar. So we need to combine the spatial position and the appearance of objects in historical. The templates in the NOTL are arranged in chronological order, and for the target i the appearance x_n in the template library has temporal information. And different objects in different spatial positions in the same frame. Generally speaking, the position of the object will not change suddenly, so there is continuity in the spatial position. We use the GRU network to learn this information. Denoting $v_i^1, \cdots, v_i^N$ as the features extracted from the template library of object i by a CNN network. We treat these as the input of the GRU. Then to distinguish different objects by the output of the network. it can be expressed as follows.

$$O_{n-1} = GRU\left(v_i^1, \cdots, v_i^N\right) \tag{4}$$

where O_{n-1} is the feature extracted by GRU, i is the object identification, N is the length of the template.

Triplet Loss and Training Algorithm. Triplet loss is proposed to solve these problems that we need the network has strong ability to distinguish the same and the different. Similarly, the tracker also needs to have this ability, so we use it to train our network.

Triple loss consists of three features. Two of these come from the object i and one from the other object j. We generate a set of triplets S from a tracklet and two images patch, one patch x_i belongs to this tracklet and the other x_j belongs to another tracklet in the same frame. For our spatio-temporal network, we extract the appearance of target i in the NOTL, and put it into the GRU network. The output of the GRU network O_{n-1} is employed as the anchor in the triplet network, as Fig. 4 showed. We respectively take the x_i^N and x_j^N as the input of the last layer of GRU. Then, two different features $O_{positive}$ and $O_{negative}$ are output by GRU. We take these as the positive and negative samples in triplet loss respectively. Here x_i and x_j represent the appearance features of target i extracted in a new frame and different target j in the same frame as x_i.

We aim to ensure that the distance of the positive pair $(O_{n-1}, O_{positive})$ is closer than the negative pair $(O_{n-1}, O_{negative})$ by a distance margin $margin$. The triplet loss is of the form:

$$L_t = max(d(O_{n-1}, O_{positive}) - d(O_{n-1}, O_{negative}) + margin, 0) \tag{5}$$

where the d is the euclidean distance represents the similarity between features. $margin$ is a distance threshold set to 0.5 in our work. We utilize the training dataset of MOT16 to train the network.

Table 1. The results of the ablation study.

Baseline	MOTA	FN	IDS
B1	36.4	68920	1178
B2	52.0	51959	527
B3	53.6	49783	549
B4	54.4	49032	357
B5	55.1	48171	320

4   Experiments

4.1   Dataset and Evaluation Metrics

We utilize MOT16 and MOT17 [16] to evaluate our method. These datasets contain 14 sequences and are split into train and test. MOT16 is provided with one public detections and MOT17 contains three separate tracking benchmarks detected by DPM [10], Faster R-CNN [17], SDP [25]. And we evaluate our results by the MOT benchmark as the metric [3], which includes the following indicators: Multiple Object Tracking Accuracy(MOTA), Multiple Object Tracking Precision (MOTP), False Positives (FP), False Negatives (FN), ID Switches (IDs), the number of Fragment Error (Frag), ID F1 Score (IDF1), Recall, Precision.

4.2   Ablation Study

To demonstrate the contribution of each module in our algorithm, we build different combinations and test on MOT16. A total of five sets of comparative experiments are established. Each approach is described as follows:

B1: We use the classifier and regression to filter the detection results, and associate them with IOU and Hungarian algorithm.

B2: We add the SOT tracker to predict the position based on B1.

B3: In order to certify the improvement of our NOTL to SOT, we build the NOTL for the tracked object, and make prediction based on NOTL.

B4: We use the CNN network to extract the features, and calculate the affinity matrix based on the features to complete the data association.

B5: We use our proposed spatio-temporal network to combine the NOTL for feature matching, and follow the method described to complete the MOT task. Moreover, this result is submitted to the mot challenge website.

4.3   Analysis of the Results

Our results are shown in Table 1. We choose some indicators that can prove the effectiveness of our method. The FN of B3 is lower than the FN of B2, which proves that our NOTL greatly improves the performance of the SOT tracker. We select several scenes from three different sequences for comparison, shown in Fig. 5. The first line is the result obtained by using SOT for position prediction. The second line is the SOT combined with the NOTL for position prediction. It can be seen that more targets have been tracked in the second row. This proves that the library has achieved our purpose.

The IDS of B5 is lower than that of B4, which proves that our spatio-temporal network is more effective than the general appearance model. In order to validate the effectiveness of our appearance model intuitively, we selected a trajectory in the test sequence and compared it with the detection results in the same frame. Prove the effectiveness of our model by comparing the similarity scores given by the network. As shown in Fig. 6, our trajectory and candidates are given on the left, while output scores of the two networks for different targets are shown on the right. Our model has a greater difference in the output-score for the targets, which proves that our model is more discriminative.

Fig. 5. Position prediction results of different predictors. The first row is the results predicted by Siamesefc, and the second row is the results combining with the NOTL. The blue box is the target, the green number is the ID. Each column of images comes from the same frame of the same video (Color figure online)

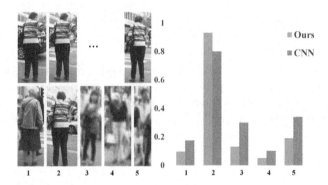

Fig. 6. Scores calculated by different appearance models for different objects. The left is the trajectory and candidates, and the right is the score output by different network. The green and blue bars represent the scores value of our network and the general CNN network, respectively. (Color figure online)

4.4 Benchmark Evaluation

We evaluate our approach on MOT16 and MOT17 benchmark against other methods, including online and offline methods. Table 2 and 3 present the performance on the datasets.

Our novel method is comprehensively compared with some selected methods [6,23,29] based on the spatial-temporal mechanism. These validate the effectiveness of our library and training method. Also, we choose the method [2] using the detector to reclassification. Our algorithm is tested on the public detection

Table 2. Tracking performance on the test set of the MOT16 Benchmark with public detections. We bold the best indicators of the listed methods.

Tracker	Mode	MOTA	MOTP	FP	FN	IDs	Frag	IDF1	Recall	Precision
STAM16 [6]	Online	46.0	74.9	6895	91117	**473**	1422	50.0	50.0	93.0
MOTDT [5]	Online	47.6	74.8	9253	85431	792	1858	50.9	53.1	91.3
Tracktor++ [2]	Online	54.4	78.2	3280	79149	682	1480	52.5	56.6	96.9
TrctrD16 [24]	Online	54.8	77.5	**2955**	78765	645	1515	53.4	56.8	**97.2**
NOTL (ours)	Online	**55.3**	78.2	3385	**77407**	630	1327	52.6	**57.5**	96.9
STRN-MOT16 [23]	Offline	48.5	73.7	9038	84178	747	2919	**53.9**	53.8	91.6
HDTR [1]	Offline	53.6	**80.8**	4714	79353	618	**833**	46.6	56.5	95.6

Table 3. We have selected some indicators of the algorithm on the MOT17 dataset. We bold the best indicators of the listed online and offline methods.

Tracker	Mode	MOTA	MOTP	FP	FN	IDs	Frag	IDF1	Recall	Precision
DMAN [29]	Online	48.2	75.7	26218	263608	2194	5378	55.7	53.3	92.0
Tracktor++ [2]	Online	53.5	78.0	12201	248047	2072	4611	52.3	56.0	96.3
LSST17O [11]	Online	52.7	76.2	22512	241936	2167	7443	57.9	57.1	93.5
TrctrD17 [24]	Online	53.7	77.2	**11731**	247447	1947	4792	53.8	56.1	96.4
NOTL (ours)	Online	**55.1**	78.0	11944	239128	2001	4269	53.2	57.6	**96.5**
LSST17 [11]	Offline	54.7	75.9	26091	**228434**	1242	3726	62.3	**59.5**	92.8
TT17 [28]	Offline	54.9	**78.1**	20236	233295	**1088**	**2392**	**63.1**	58.7	94.2

set. In contrast to other MOT methods, our methods achieve the highest MOTA score by preserving the good performance of other metrics. It also improved in various aspects compared to some offline methods. Table 3 shows the comparison of some new methods on the MOT17 dataset, our method still works well.

5   Conclusion

In this paper, we have proposed a novel online MOT framework based on the Nearest Optimal Template Library (NOTL) assisted by two optimization methods. Our NOTL can build the appearance model of the target effectively, and improve the effect of the methods we proposed. At the same time, our method also combines a variety of information to alleviate the two major challenges in multi-target tracking: position-prediction and appearance modeling. Our method outperforms previous works on the MOT16 and MOT17 benchmarks using public detection. But there is a limitation of our work. Our method cannot achieve the real-time requirements in the actual application. In our future work, we will try to exploit how to improve our method to achieve real-time requirements without deteriorating accuracy.

Acknowledgements. This work was supported by the Project of Quzhou Municipal Government (2020D011), and National Science Foundation of China (U19A2052).

References

1. Babaee, M., Athar, A., Rigoll, G.: Multiple people tracking using hierarchical deep tracklet re-identification. CoRR (2018)
2. Bergmann, P., Meinhardt, T., Leal-Taixé, L.: Tracking without bells and whistles. In: 2019 IEEE/CVF International Conference on Computer Vision, ICCV 2019, Seoul, Korea (South), 27 October–2 November, 2019 (2019)
3. Bernardin, K., Stiefelhagen, R.: Evaluating multiple object tracking performance: the CLEAR MOT metrics. EURASIP J. Image Video Process. **2008**, 1–10 (2008)
4. Chen, J., Sheng, H., Zhang, Y., Xiong, Z.: Enhancing detection model for multiple hypothesis tracking. In: 2017 IEEE Conference on Computer Vision and Pattern Recognition Workshops, CVPR Workshops 2017, Honolulu, HI, USA, 21–26 July, 2017 (2017)
5. Chen, L., Ai, H., Zhuang, Z., Shang, C.: Real-time multiple people tracking with deeply learned candidate selection and person re-identification. In: 2018 IEEE International Conference on Multimedia and Expo, ICME 2018, San Diego, CA, USA, 23–27 July, 2018 (2018)
6. Chu, Q., Ouyang, W., Li, H., Wang, X., Liu, B., Yu, N.: Online multi-object tracking using CNN-based single object tracker with spatial-temporal attention mechanism. In: IEEE International Conference on Computer Vision, ICCV 2017, Venice, Italy, 22–29 October, 2017 (2017)
7. Dehghan, A., Assari, S.M., Shah, M.: GMMCP tracker: globally optimal generalized maximum multi clique problem for multiple object tracking. In: IEEE Conference on Computer Vision and Pattern Recognition, CVPR 2015, Boston, MA, USA, 7–12 June, 2015 (2015)
8. Du, Y., Yan, Y., Chen, S., Hua, Y., Wang, H.: Object-adaptive LSTM network for visual tracking. In: 24th International Conference on Pattern Recognition, ICPR 2018, Beijing, China, 20–24 August, 2018 (2018)
9. Fagot-Bouquet, L., Audigier, R., Dhome, Y., Lerasle, F.: Improving multi-frame data association with sparse representations for robust near-online multi-object tracking. In: Computer Vision - ECCV 2016–14th European Conference, Amsterdam, The Netherlands, 11–14 October, 2016, Proceedings, Part VIII (2016)
10. Felzenszwalb, P.F., Girshick, R.B., McAllester, D.A., Ramanan, D.: Object detection with discriminatively trained part-based models. IEEE Trans. Pattern Anal. Mach. Intell. **32**(9), 1627–1645 (2010)
11. Feng, W., Hu, Z., Wu, W., Yan, J., Ouyang, W.: Multi-object tracking with multiple cues and switcher-aware classification. CoRR (2019)
12. Henschel, R., Zou, Y., Rosenhahn, B.: Multiple people tracking using body and joint detections. In: IEEE Conference on Computer Vision and Pattern Recognition Workshops, CVPR Workshops, Long Beach, CA, USA, 16–20 June, 2019 (2019)
13. Kim, C., Li, F., Rehg, J.M.: Multi-object tracking with neural gating using bilinear LSTM. In: Computer Vision - ECCV 2018–15th European Conference, Munich, Germany, 8–14 September, 2018, Proceedings, Part VIII (2018)
14. Li, B., Wu, W., Wang, Q., Zhang, F., Xing, J., Yan, J.: SiamRPN++: evolution of Siamese visual tracking with very deep networks. In: IEEE Conference on Computer Vision and Pattern Recognition, CVPR 2019, Long Beach, CA, USA, 16–20 June, 2019 (2019)
15. Li, B., Yan, J., Wu, W., Zhu, Z., Hu, X.: High performance visual tracking with Siamese region proposal network. In: 2018 IEEE Conference on Computer Vision and Pattern Recognition, CVPR 2018, Salt Lake City, UT, USA, 18–22 June, 2018 (2018)

16. Milan, A., Leal-Taixé, L., Reid, I.D., Roth, S., Schindler, K.: MOT16: a benchmark for multi-object tracking. CoRR (2016)
17. Ren, S., He, K., Girshick, R.B., Sun, J.: Faster R-CNN: towards real-time object detection with region proposal networks. IEEE Trans. Pattern Anal. Mach. Intell. **39**(6), 1137–1149 (2017)
18. Sadeghian, A., Alahi, A., Savarese, S.: Tracking the untrackable: learning to track multiple cues with long-term dependencies. In: IEEE International Conference on Computer Vision, ICCV 2017, Venice, Italy, 22–29 October, 2017 (2017)
19. Schroff, F., Kalenichenko, D., Philbin, J.: FaceNet: a unified embedding for face recognition and clustering (2015)
20. Tang, S., Andres, B., Andriluka, M., Schiele, B.: Multi-person tracking by multicut and deep matching. In: Computer Vision - ECCV 2016 Workshops - Amsterdam, The Netherlands, 8–10 and 15–16 October, 2016, Proceedings, Part II (2016)
21. Valmadre, J., Bertinetto, L., Henriques, J., Vedaldi, A., Torr, P.H.S.: End-to-end representation learning for correlation filter based tracking. In: The IEEE Conference on Computer Vision and Pattern Recognition (CVPR) (2017)
22. Xiang, Y., Alahi, A., Savarese, S.: Learning to track: online multi-object tracking by decision making. In: 2015 IEEE International Conference on Computer Vision, ICCV 2015, Santiago, Chile, 7–13 December, 2015 (2015)
23. Xu, J., Cao, Y., Zhang, Z., Hu, H.: Spatial-temporal relation networks for multi-object tracking. In: 2019 IEEE/CVF International Conference on Computer Vision, ICCV 2019, Seoul, Korea (South), 27 October–2November, 2019 (2019)
24. Xu, Y., Osep, A., Ban, Y., Horaud, R., Leal-Taixé, L., Alameda-Pineda, X.: How to train your deep multi-object tracker. In: Computer Vision and Pattern Recognition. Seattle, United States (2020)
25. Yang, F., Choi, W., Lin, Y.: Exploit all the layers: fast and accurate CNN object detector with scale dependent pooling and cascaded rejection classifiers. In: 2016 IEEE Conference on Computer Vision and Pattern Recognition, CVPR 2016, Las Vegas, NV, USA, 27–30 June, 2016. IEEE Computer Society (2016)
26. Yang, M., Wu, Y., Jia, Y.: A hybrid data association framework for robust online multi-object tracking. IEEE Trans. Image Process. **26**(12), 5667–5679 (2017)
27. Yoon, Y., Boragule, A., Song, Y., Yoon, K., Jeon, M.: Online multi-object tracking with historical appearance matching and scene adaptive detection filtering. In: 15th IEEE International Conference on Advanced Video and Signal Based Surveillance, AVSS 2018, Auckland, New Zealand, 27–30 November, 2018 (2018)
28. Zhang, Y., Sheng, H., Wu, Y., Wang, S., Lyu, W., Ke, W., Xiong, Z.: Long-term tracking with deep tracklet association. IEEE Trans. Image Process. **29**, 6694 (2020)
29. Zhu, J., Yang, H., Liu, N., Kim, M., Zhang, W., Yang, M.: Online multi-object tracking with dual matching attention networks. In: Computer Vision - ECCV 2018–15th European Conference, Munich, Germany, 8–14 September, 2018, Proceedings, Part V (2018)

TSTNet: A Sequence to Sequence Transformer Network for Spatial-Temporal Traffic Prediction

Xiaozhuang Song[1,2(✉)], Ying Wu[1,2,3], and Chenhan Zhang[1,2,4]

[1] Southern University of Science and Technology, Shenzhen, China
`11930376@mail.sustech.edu.cn`
[2] Guangdong Provincial Key Laboratory of Brain-inspired Intelligent Computation,
Shenzhen, China
[3] University of Leeds, Leeds, UK
[4] University of Technology Sydney, Sydney, Australia

Abstract. Making accurate traffic forecasting is of great importance in smart city-related researches. However, as the traffic features like traffic speed have a complex spatial-temporal characteristics, how to build an accurate traffic prediction model is still an open challenge. In this work, we propose TSTNet, a Sequence to Sequence (Seq2Seq) spatial-temporal traffic prediction model. TSTNet adopts Graph Attention Network (GAT), which can learn the spatial feature aggregation, to build spatial dependency. For temporal dependency, TSTNet applies a Seq2Seq Transformer structure to establish temporal dependency. As a GAT layer's operation only aggregate the attribute information for neighbor nodes, it does not involve any spatial positional information. Similarly, if we apply the Transformer model on sequence learning tasks, the Transformer model also does not involve any temporal positional information as it does not know the exact time slot of different inputs. To solve the above problems, TSTNet implements a spatial-temporal embedding method to obtain the spatial-temporal positional representation for each input data. We evaluate TSTNet on traffic speed prediction tasks with other baselines upon two real-world datasets, the results show that TSTNet outperforms all the baseline models.

Keywords: Sequence to sequence model · Spatial-temporal forecasting · Time series data

1 Introduction and Background

Intelligent Transportation Systems (ITS) have emerged as a popular research subject due to their potential to provide road users with more comfortable and convenient travel experiences and encourage more efficient and reliable traffic systems. Accurate and reliable traffic forecasting is vital for ITS, especially in traffic management, traffic demand prediction, urban planning [4, 8, 20].

© Springer Nature Switzerland AG 2021
I. Farkaš et al. (Eds.): ICANN 2021, LNCS 12891, pp. 343–354, 2021.
https://doi.org/10.1007/978-3-030-86362-3_28

With advances in computing power and the advancement of data acquisition technologies, data-driven approaches to developing accurate traffic forecasting systems have recently gained widespread attention [1,18,19].

Traffic forecasting is difficult due to dynamic intra-dependencies (i.e., temporal connections across one traffic sequence), inter-information (i.e., spatial associations through multiplexed links in traffic networks), multi-source data (i.e., different loop detectors/sensors), and extra-disturbing factors (i.e., weather and accidents). Traditional methods depend solely on the periodicity of time series, e.g., Historical Average (HA) and Autoregressive Integrated Average (ARIMA) [9], which cannot provide a reliable prediction for long-term traffic forecasting on a large scale. To improve the accuracy of long-term forecasting, researchers shift to design new neural network architectures to model temporal correlation by recurrent neural networks (e.g., Long Short-term Memory [3] (LSTM) cells and Gated Recurrent Unit [2] (GRU) cells). However, such RNN variants only capture temporal information in traffic sequences, they neglect the importance of spatial dependency for accurate prediction. To narrow that gap, models derived from Graph Neural Networks (GNN) like DCRNN [5], FC-LSTM [10], Graph-WaveNet [14], STGCN [17] are proposed as a structure that uses graph network to extract finer-grained spatial knowledge. Despite the fact that GNN offers a solution for spatial dependency modeling, they still have issues when combining with Seq2Seq model. When dealing with a long input sequence task, the latent information at the early input order is easily lost in the context vector. Furthermore, due to the order limitations of sequence tasks, those models are unable to perform parallel calculations, resulting in a decline in training efficiency.

Recently, the breaking progress in the field of Natural Language Processing (NLP) arises a heated research interest on Transformer-based model [11]. Transformer is a model based on self-attention mechanism, positional encoding, residual link and layer normalization. It solves the distance problems of Seq2Seq models effectively by directly calculating the attention value of sequence data at all positions. STTN adopts a spatial-Temporal Transformer Network network for traffic flow forecasting. This model explicitly measures the attention of traffic data from spatial and temporal perspective. Then STTN concatenates them as the overall spatial-temporal features. In spite of the promising performance of STTN, this approach is costly in terms of computation and storage, and it is prone to overfitting due to the large number of parameters. We will talk about this in detail in Sect. 4.1.

To overcome the above models' drawbacks, we propose TSTNet, a novel spatial-temporal traffic forecasting model based on graph attention mechanism, and Seq2Seq-based Transformer structure. The main contribution of this is as follows:

1. To the best of our knowledge, we are the first to build a Seq2Seq model with graph attention network and transformer network for traffic forecasting. The results show the effectiveness of our model.
2. We apply a novel spatial-temporal embedding learning algorithm based on random walk for traffic node's spatial representation. This spatial embedding

is concatenated with time embedding, which is learned from a projection layer as the spatial-temporal positional embedding of traffic data.

3. We evaluate our model on two real-world collected GPS datasets. The results show that our model achieves state-of-the-art performance compared to other baselines. Besides, we also give a detailed analysis of experimental results.

2 Methodology

In this section, we first provide the definition of the problem we study. Then, we elaborate on the main structure of TSTNet. Figure 1 depicts the overall structure of TSTNet.

2.1 Problem Definition

Definition 1: Road Network. The topological structure of a city is a directed graph $G = (V, E)$ formed by intertwined roads. $V = \{v_1, v_2, \cdots, v_{N_v}\}$ is the set of road nodes, and $E = \{e_1, e_2, \cdots, e_{N_e}\}$ is the set of edges. We use adjacent matrix as the data structure to store this graph. Let the adjacent matrix be $M \in \mathcal{R}^{N_v \times N_v}$. If there is an edge from node v_i to node v_j, $M_{ij} = 1$. Otherwise $M_{ij} = 0$.

Definition 2: Spatial-temporal Series. The time of a day is divided evenly into T time steps. The spatial-temporal series are represented as

$$S = \{X_i \mid i \in T\} \tag{1}$$

where i represents time step, $X_i \in \mathbb{R}^{N_v \times F}$ represents the F types of traffic features (e.g., traffic speed, traffic demand) for N_v nodes at time step i. The traffic features for node $v_j \in N_v$ in X_i is represented as $x_j \in \mathbb{R}^F$

Definition 3: Traffic Prediction Task. Given the traffic features X_0 (speed, traffic flow volume, etc.) at time step 0, the objective is to predict the traffic features in the next L time steps for road network G as

$$[X_1, \cdots, X_T] = f_\theta \left((X_{-n}, \cdots, X_0) \right) \tag{2}$$

where θ are the parameters of TSTNet. In this work, we focus on the traffic speed prediction task, and X represents the traffic speed.

2.2 TSTNet

In this section, firstly, we introduce how TSTNet uses GAT to establish the spatial dependency of the traffic network. We then introduce Traffic Graph Context Embedding (TGCE), a spatial-temporal hybrid embedding composed of random walk-based graph spatial embedding and temporal embedding learned from the projection layer. TSTNet concatenates obtained traffic spatial dependency with Traffic Graph Context Embedding, and feeds them into the Temporal Transformer Network network. We provide a detailed description of the Temporal Transformer Network network of TSTNet in the last part of this section.

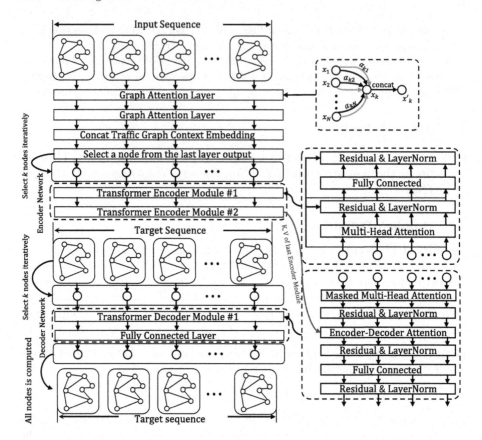

Fig. 1. Overview of TSTNet. Notably, this figure shows the training phase of TST-Net and its Decoder Network is working in a parallel computing. However, in actual prediction tasks, we cannot directly obtain the target sequence. Therefore, in actual prediction tasks with no ground truth, TSTNet obtains its prediction sequence within a classical Seq2Seq prediction style.

Spatial Dependency Modeling. TSTNet adopts GAT to establish spatial dependency for its ability to capture dynamic local spatial features. For each time step t, GAT computes an attention coefficients between v_i and v_j as

$$e_{ij} = a\left(\text{Concat}\left[\mathbf{W}x_i, \mathbf{W}x_j\right]\right) \tag{3}$$

where x_i, x_j is the features of v_i and v_j, respectively. $\mathbf{W} \in \mathbb{R}^{F' \times F}$ is a learnable weight matrix applied to every node for features extraction. e_{ij} indicates the importance of v_j's features to v_i. Typically, we compute the attention coefficients e_{ij} by concatenating $\mathbf{W}x_i$ and $\mathbf{W}x_j$, and feed the combined vector into a fully connected network $\mathbf{a} \in \mathbb{R}^{2F'}$ [11]. Next, the attention score is computed by

$$\alpha_{ij} = \text{softmax}\left(e_{ij}\right) = \frac{\exp\left(e_{ij}\right)}{\sum_{k \in \mathcal{N}_i} \exp\left(e_{ik}\right)} \tag{4}$$

we apply the LeakyReLU activation function for attention coefficients computation. In this form, the graph attention computation can be expressed as:

$$\alpha_{ij} = \frac{\exp\left(\text{LeakyReLU}\left(\mathbf{a}^T \text{Concat}\left[\mathbf{W}x_i, \mathbf{W}x_j\right]\right)\right)}{\sum_{k \in \mathcal{N}_i} \exp\left(\text{LeakyReLU}\left(\mathbf{a}^T \text{Concat}\left[\mathbf{W}x_i, \mathbf{W}x_k\right]\right)\right)} \tag{5}$$

After obtaining the attention value, we use it to compute a linear combination for the features from each node's neighbour. The final output is served as:

$$x_i' = \sigma\left(\sum_{j \in \mathcal{N}_i} \alpha_{ij} x_j \mathbf{W}\right) \tag{6}$$

where $\mathcal{N}_i$ represents the neighbour nodes of v_i. Finally we obtain spatial dependency representation $x_i' \in \mathbb{R}^{F'}$ produced by GAT.

Traffic Graph Context Embedding. As novel graph deep learning methods for traffic-related data-driven models only involve the spatial dependency on nodes' features [11,12]. Most of them ignore the spatial positional information of graph nodes. For example, v_i and v_j have a very close distance in Euclidean space but may not be linked within several hops in Semantic Space. On the words, the hot traffic regions covering central business districts (CBDs) or other important blocks can share semantic relational characteristics but lack a direct or clear Euclidean space connection. Existing graph deep learning methods rarely make use of this knowledge. To capture the spatial information, here we introduce the idea of traffic graph context embedding (TGCE), which is inspired by [7]. The process of TGCE is as follows:

1. Firstly, TGCE adopts a biased walking to obtain the walking sequence of nodes. The biased transition probability from v_i to v_j is defined as $P_{ij} = \frac{I_{ij}}{\sum_{j \in \mathcal{N}(v_i)} I_{ij}}$, where I_{ij} is the historical travel statistics from v_i to v_j.
2. After the walking sequences are obtained, TGCE applies Skip-Gram [6] algorithm to learn the embedding from walking sequences of traffic nodes with a two-layer fully connected network structure with hidden size F^s.

Since the walking sequence generated by TGCE mainly focuses on the neighbors of each start nodes, this methods can effectively compute a graph spatial embedding with highly spatial correlation. We further show this effectiveness in Sect. 4.1. Typically, the TGCE of x_i is represented as $x_i'' \in F^s$.

Temporal Dependency Modeling. After obtaining the graph spatial dependency at each time-step, TSTNet selects K nodes in order from these graph data sequences as a trade-off between time and space, as opposed to STTN, which feeds the sequence data of all graph nodes into the Temporal Transformer Network all at once. The insights of this design are that it can have fewer number of parameters while minimizing the negative effects of over-fitting, and reducing the demand for computing resources. As the computation of K node's temporal sequence is actually independent of each other, we introduce the temporal dependency modeling with a single node v_a first. TSTNet builds a transformer-based Seq2Seq network to learn the temporal dependency of the input sequence. We introduce this from two aspects: Encoder Network and Decoder Network. As the input data of Transformer network does not contain temporal positional information, TSTNet uses an embedding layer for encoding the discrete time information of each input data. The time embedding of x_i can be represented as $x_i''' \in F^t$, where F^t is the hidden size of embedding layer. Time embedding will further be concatenated to each input data before feeding into the Temporal Transformer network. Notably, the data representation of x_i before it's fed into Temporal Transformer Network can be represented as $x^* = \text{Concat}[x', x'', x'''] \in \mathbb{R}^{F^*}$, where $F^* = F' + F^s + F^t$.

TSTNet's structure adopts two transformer encoder modules[1]. Each transformer encoder module is built with a self-attention sublayer and a fully connected sublayer. A residual link is used around each of the two-sublayers with layer normalization. The self-attention computation is composed of three linear transform layer $Q \in \mathbb{R}^{F^* \times d}$, $K \in \mathbb{R}^{F^* \times d}$, $V \in \mathbb{R}^{F^* \times d}$. F^* represents the feature length at each time slot. d represents the hidden size of the Temporal Transformer Network. Q, K, V are also known as *Query*, *Key* and *Value*, as explained further in [11]. They are used to compute the temporal attention for an input data sequence as

$$A(Q, K, V) = softmax(\frac{QK^T}{\sqrt{d_k}})V \tag{7}$$

where $\sqrt{d_k}$ represents the square root of K, and it uses as a normalization for more stable gradients. We can see that these computations can build a dynamic weights adjustment with different input data, rather than a linear layer with fixed weights. The self-attention layer's output is further fed to a fully connected layer for a better feature extraction [11].

For Decoder Network, we use the target sequence of v_a as its input. Assume the target sequence is of length T, for parallel computation, the input sequence of a single node is of size $T \times T \times F$, which is a vector obtained by stacking the target sequence T times. Next we explain the reason of this design: Since our goal is to predict the target sequence with size $T \times F$ and the traffic forecasting in real scenarios can not perceive the ground truth or future data. The input data is then processed a masked-attention layer for masking the unavailable time with a lower triangular matrix for each traffic feature. Next, TSTNet computes the self-attention for masked target sequence, above process is also called the Masked Attention. After masked attention computed, we come key difference between the Transformer-based Seq2Seq model with the RNN-based Seq2Seq models: Rather than representing the input sequence information with a context vector, the Transformer model uses K and V from the last encoder module and involves it into the Decoder Network's Encoder-Decoder Attention layer. This

---

[1] The number of encoder modules and decoder modules are chosen according to the best experimental results.

layer computes attention with K and V from Encoder Network and Q from its previous layer's output with layer normalization and residual link. This method effectively computes the correlation between output sequence and input sequence [11]. The Decoder Network output is of size $T \times T \times d$, TSTNet further flatten it into size $T \times (T*d)$ connected to a fully connected layer with size $[T*d, F]$. Thus, we obtain the final output decoding sequence with a parallel Seq2Seq learning scheme.

Multi-head Attention. To stabilize the learning process of graph attention and the self-attention in the Temporal Transformer Network network, we employ the Multi-head Attention mechanism for its benefits on feature extraction ability [11,12]. We apply k_1 independent attention heads for graph attention and k_2 heads for temporal self-attention computation. Specially, as the attention matrix can be quadratic and resource-consuming with a long time sequence data or large graph data, it is no longer sensible to concatenate them directly. Thus, inspired by [12], we employ an averaging computation for graph attention or temporal self-attention heads in the corresponding computation stage and delay applying the final non-linearity function, it finally can be formulated as

$$A = \sigma \left(\frac{1}{K} \sum_{k=1}^{K} A_k \right) \tag{8}$$

where A_k represents the attention matrix in corresponding computation stage.

Loss Function. TSTNet uses Mean Square Error (MSE) as the objective loss function, it can be expressed as:

$$\min_{\theta} \mathcal{L} \left(f_{\theta} \left(X_i \right), Y_i \right) = \left| f \left(X_i \right) - Y_i \right|^2 \tag{9}$$

3   Experiments

In this section, we evaluate the performance of TSTNet on two real-world city open datasets. Besides, For a better understanding of TSTNet, we provide a ablation study on TSTNet.

3.1   Dataset Description

Chengdu Dataset. This dataset[2] collects GPS data of Didi car-hailing trajectories in the northeastern part of Chengdu city during November 1, 2016 and November 31, 2016. This area has 3223 nodes and 8265 edges.

Xi'an Dataset. This dataset collects GPS data of Didi car-hailing trajectories in the northeastern part of Xi'an city during November 1, 2016 to November 30, 2016. This area has 2656 nodes and 6308 edges.

---

[2] The use of these two datasets needs a permission request. All two datasets can be found at https://outreach.didichuxing.com/app-vue/personal?id=1.

3.2   Data Preprocessing

Since the above datasets contain only raw GPS points, they need to be processed into traffic speed values before training. As we focus on the task of speed prediction, the speed can be intuitively calculated as follows:

$$\Delta t_j = t_{j+1} - t_j \tag{10}$$
$$\text{RD}_j = Vincenty\,(lat_j, lon_j, lat_{j+1}, lon_{j+1}) \tag{11}$$
$$Speed_j = \text{RD}_j / \Delta t_j \tag{12}$$

where t_i represents the timestamp of node i, lat_i and lon_i represent the latitude and longitude of GPS point i. $Vincenty(\cdot)$ represents the Vincenty formula [13], which is used to calculate the distance between two points on the surface of a spheroid. After the speed is calculated, we use the mapmatching approach proposed in [16] to match the GPS points to corresponding edges. The nodes' speed values are the average of GPS points' speed on the connecting edges, and the distance from GPS points to the node is empirically set to less than 300 m.

3.3   Baseline Models and Evaluation Metric

We compare TSTNet on traffic speed forecasting task with some most novel and competitive traffic forecasting models: FC-LSTM [10], STGCN [17], DCRNN [5], Graph WaveNet [14], and STTN [15]. To evaluate the speed forecasting performance of models, we use three metrics to compute the difference between ground truth Y_i and the prediction $\hat{Y}_i$, including:

1. Mean Absolute Error (MAE):

$$\text{MAE} = \frac{1}{m} \sum_{i=1}^{m} \left| (Y_i - \hat{Y}_i) \right| \tag{13}$$

2. Root Mean Squared Error (RMSE):

$$\text{RMSE} = \sqrt{\frac{1}{m} \sum_{i=1}^{m} (Y_i - \hat{Y}_i)^2} \tag{14}$$

3. Accuracy (ACC):

$$\text{ACC} = 1 - \frac{\left| Y - \hat{Y} \right|}{|Y|} \tag{15}$$

MAE, RMSE measures the average prediction error of the model. ACC measures how close the average speed prediction is to the real speed.

3.4   Experimental Settings

Experiment Environment. All experiments are performed on a Linux server (CPU: Intel(R) Xeon(R) CPU E5-2620 v4, GPU: GeForce RTX 2080 Ti, System: Ubuntu 18.04). All experiments are conducted with Pytorch 1.6.0.

Hyperparameter Settings. The total number of time steps in one day is set to 288, which means that the average speed of each road is computed every 5 min. For the traffic graph context embedding algorithm, the random walk step size is 10, and each node walks 10 times. The hidden size of GAT i.e., W and the hidden size of Temporal Transformer Network i.e., d are 16. Attention heads k_1 and k_2 are both set to 2. F^s is set to 8 and F^t is set to 4. We choose the Adam optimizer to optimize network parameters. The learning rate τ during training is 10^{-3}. The batch size used in training is 32, while the number of training epochs is 1000. TSTNet uses an early stopping strategy to avoid overfitting problem when the validation loss no longer increases for three consecutive epochs. The proportions for the training set, validation set, and test set are 70%, 10%, and 20%, respectively. For both TSTNet and baseline models, we run 20 times and take the results' average as the final comparison. All the selection of hyperparameters are based on their performance empirically.

4   Results

Table 1 show the results of TSTNet and other baseline models in forecasting the speed of the city road network in the next 15 min (15 min), 30 min (30 min), and 60 min (60 min) on different datasets. In the following section, we provide reasonable discussions about performance on different models.

4.1   Case Study

From Table 1 we can see that TSTNet outperforms all other models on both datasets. Though STTN adopts a resource-consuming computation by applying spatial and temporal Transformer network on traffic forecasting tasks, TST-Net still has a significant performance advantage over STTN. This reason is attributed to its massive model architecture of STTN, which includes a large number of redundant paramaters. As a result, STTN easily causes an over-fitting problem without regularization. Graph WaveNet and STGCN both use temporal convolutional layers on temporal dependency. However, this design has an obvious drawback as it hardly captures a long-distance temporal relation. DCRNN and FC-LSTM adopt a classical Sequence to Sequence (Seq2Seq) model architecture, but its context vector can fail to capture the information with previous input, which has a long distance. To further understand the advantages of TST-Net, we conduct an ablation study in the next section.

4.2   Ablation Study

We conduct an ablation study by removing one of its components iteratively. These ablations are defined as follows:

1. **TSTNet$_{NGCE}$**: TSTNet without graph context embedding.
2. **TSTNet$_{NTE}$**: TSTNet without temporal embedding.

Table 1. Experiment results.

Model	Chengdu dataset (15 min/30 min/60 min)		
	MAE	ACC (%)	RMSE
FC-LSTM	4.75/4.82/4.92	89.9/89.8/89.8	7.02/7.14/7.19
STGCN	4.57/4.61/4.85	90.2/90.1/89.9	6.73/6.75/7.05
DCRNN	4.38/4.40/4.45	90.6/90.6/90.5	6.59/6.51/6.56
Graph WaveNet	4.34/4.35/4.39	90.7/90.7/90.6	6.41/6.50/6.43
STTN	4.01/4.06/4.09	91.4/91.3/91.2	6.29/6.32/6.37
TSTNet	**3.49/3.52/3.54**	**92.5/92.4/92.4**	**5.86/5.87/5.89**
	Xi'an Dataset (15 min/30 min/60 min)		
	MAE	ACC (%)	RMSE
FC-LSTM	7.77/7.51/7.46	76.8/77.6/77.8	12.62/12.48/12.39
STGCN	6.80/7.06/7.23	79.8/78.9/78.3	11.92/11.84/11.99
DCRNN	6.73/7.00/7.21	79.9/79.1/78.4	10.85/11.95/12.03
Graph WaveNet	6.39/6.46/6.51	80.9/80.8/80.8	10.62/10.78/10.80
STTN	6.00/6.01/6.03	82.1/82.1/82.0	10.48/10.50/10.51
TSTNet	**5.54/5.58/5.56**	**83.4/83.5/83.5**	**10.12/10.17/10.15**

3. **TSTNet$_{TT}$**: TSTNet without GAT. For the traffic features x of one node v in input data sequence at time t. It feeds the Temporal Transformer Network with $x_{TT}^* = [x, x'', x''']$, where x'' is the TGCE of v, and x''' is the embedding of t.
4. **TSTNet$_{ST}$**: TSTNet without temporal Seq2Seq transformer network. It uses the spatial features obtained from GAT and traffic graph context embedding to forecast the target sequence with a fully connected network directly.

The results of our ablation study are shown in Table 2. The performance advantage of TSTNet over TSTNet$_{NGCE}$ and TSTNet$_{NTE}$ reflects the benefits of graph context embedding and temporal embedding. Furthermore, TSTNet$_{NGCE}$ has a minor performance advantage compared to TSTNet$_{NTE}$, which indicates that a proper spatial dependency is relatively more important than the temporal dependency of the spatial-temporal traffic forecasting model. Furthermore, as the TSTNet$_{ST}$ shows a more significant performance degradation compared to TSTNet$_{TT}$, this indicates that there should be a higher priority for temporal dependency modeling in the construction of spatial-temporal traffic forecasting models.

Table 2. Ablation study results.

Model	Chengdu dataset (15 min/30 min/60 min)		
	MAE	ACC (%)	RMSE
TSTNet$_{NGCE}$	3.85/3.88/3.90	91.8/91.7/91.7	6.17/6.21/6.22
TSTNet$_{NTE}$	3.59/3.61/3.62	92.3/92.3/92.2	5.90/5.92/5.93
TSTNet$_{TT}$	4.62/4.65/4.71	90.1/90.1/90.0	6.73/6.80/6.90
TSTNet$_{ST}$	5.12/5.22/5.28	89.0/88.8/88.7	8.13/8.28/8.35
TSTNet	**3.49/3.52/3.54**	**92.5/92.4/92.1**	**5.86/5.87/5.89**
	Xi'an dataset (15 min/30 min/60 min)		
	MAE	ACC (%)	RMSE
TSTNet$_{NGCE}$	5.88/5.92/5.95	82.4/82.3/82.3	10.41/10.44/10.45
TSTNet$_{NTE}$	5.70/5.72/5.73	83.0/82.9/82.9	10.22/10.28/10.20
TSTNet$_{TT}$	7.15/7.32/7.40	78.6/78.1/77.9	11.99/12.15/12.26
TSTNet$_{ST}$	8.19/8.33/8.65	75.5/75.1/74.1	13.11/13.63/14.35
TSTNet	**5.54/5.58/5.56**	**83.4/83.5/83.5**	**10.12/10.17/10.15**

5 Conclusion

In this work, we propose TSTNet, a novel spatial-temporal traffic forecasting model built on a Seq2Seq learning scheme. We use Graph Attention Net to build the spatial dependency of traffic data, and Transformer to build the temporal dependency. The experiment results show TSTNet's superiority over two real-world datasets comparing with the state-of-the-art traffic forecasting approaches. Besides, to further understand TSTNet, we conduct an ablation study and test the efforts of each modules in TSTNet.

In future work, we will expand on current existing work into two main aspects: (1) Minimizing the model's time complexity and space complexity. (2) Further study the interpretability of TSTNet.

References

1. Avila, A., Mezić, I.: Data-driven analysis and forecasting of highway traffic dynamics. Nat. Commun. **11**(1), 1–16 (2020)
2. Chung, J., Gulcehre, C., Cho, K., Bengio, Y.: Empirical evaluation of gated recurrent neural networks on sequence modeling. In: Advances in Neural Information Processing Systems 2014 Workshop on Deep Learning (2014)
3. Hochreiter, S., Schmidhuber, J.: Long short-term memory. Neural Comput. **9**(8), 1735–1780 (1997)
4. Lana, I., Del Ser, J., Velez, M., Vlahogianni, E.I.: Road traffic forecasting: recent advances and new challenges. IEEE Intell. Transp. Syst. Mag. **10**(2), 93–109 (2018)
5. Li, Y., Yu, R., Shahabi, C., Liu, Y.: Diffusion convolutional recurrent neural network: data-driven traffic forecasting. In: International Conference on Learning Representations (2018)

6. Mikolov, T., Chen, K., Corrado, G., Dean, J.: Efficient estimation of word representations in vector space. arXiv preprint arXiv:1301.3781 (2013)
7. Perozzi, B., Al-Rfou, R., Skiena, S.: DeepWalk: online learning of social representations. In: Proceedings of the 20th ACM SIGKDD International Conference on Knowledge Discovery and Data Mining, pp. 701–710 (2014)
8. Silva, B.N., Khan, M., Han, K.: Towards sustainable smart cities: a review of trends, architectures, components, and open challenges in smart cities. Sustain. Urban Areas **38**, 697–713 (2018)
9. Smith, B.L., Demetsky, M.J.: Traffic flow forecasting: comparison of modeling approaches. J. Transp. Eng. **123**(4), 261–266 (1997)
10. Sutskever, I., Vinyals, O., Le, Q.V.: Sequence to sequence learning with neural networks. Adv. Neural. Inf. Process. Syst. **27**, 3104–3112 (2014)
11. Vaswani, A., et al.: Attention is all you need. In: Advances in Neural Information Processing Systems, vol. 30 (2017)
12. Veličković, P., Cucurull, G., Casanova, A., Romero, A., Liò, P., Bengio, Y.: Graph attention networks. In: International Conference on Learning Representations (2018)
13. Vincenty, T.: Direct and inverse solutions of geodesics on the ellipsoid with application of nested equations. Surv. Rev. **23**(176), 88–93 (1975)
14. Wu, Z., Pan, S., Long, G., Jiang, J., Zhang, C.: Graph WaveNet for deep spatial-temporal graph modeling. In: Proceedings of the Twenty-Eighth International Joint Conference on Artificial Intelligence, pp. 1907–1913, July 2019
15. Xu, M., et al.: Spatial-temporal transformer networks for traffic flow forecasting. arXiv preprint arXiv:2001.02908 (2020)
16. Yang, C., Gidofalvi, G.: Fast map matching, an algorithm integrating hidden Markov model with precomputation. Int. J. Geogr. Inf. Sci. **32**(3), 547–570 (2018)
17. Yu, B., Yin, H., Zhu, Z.: Spatio-temporal graph convolutional networks: a deep learning framework for traffic forecasting. In: Proceedings of the 27th International Joint Conference on Artificial Intelligence, pp. 3634–3640 (2018)
18. Yu, B., Lee, Y., Sohn, K.: Forecasting road traffic speeds by considering area-wide spatio-temporal dependencies based on a graph convolutional neural network (GCN). Transp. Res. Part C Emerg. Technol. **114**, 189–204 (2020)
19. Yu, J.J.: Citywide traffic speed prediction: a geometric deep learning approach. Knowl.-Based Syst. **212**, 106592 (2021)
20. Zhao, L., et al.: T-GCN: a temporal graph convolutional network for traffic prediction. IEEE Trans. Intell. Transp. Syst. (2019)

Audio and Multimodal Applications

A Multimode Two-Stream Network for Egocentric Action Recognition

Ying Li[(✉)], Jie Shen, Xin Xiong, Wei He, Peng Li, and Wenjie Yan

University of Electronic Science and Technology of China, Chengdu, China
201821080824@std.uestc.edu.cn, sjie@uestc.edu.cn

Abstract. Video-based egocentric activity recognition involves spatio-temporal and human-object interaction. With the great success of deep learning technology in image recognition, human activity recognition in videos has got increasing attention in multimedia understanding. Comprehensive visual understanding requires the detection and modeling of individual visual features and the interactions between them. The current popular human action recognition approaches based on the visual features extracted from 2-D images, and therefore often lead to unreliable salient visual feature detection and inaccurate modeling of the interaction context between individual features. In this paper, we show that these problems can be addressed by combining data from images and skeletons. First, we propose a pose-based two-stream network for action recognition that effectively fuses information from both skeleton and image at multiple levels of the video processing pipeline. In our network, one stream models the temporal dynamics of the action-related objects from video frames, and the other stream models the temporal dynamics of the targeted 2D human pose sequences which are extracted from raw video. Moreover, we demonstrate that a ConvNet trained on RGB data is able to achieve good performance in spite of limited training data. Our architecture is trained and evaluated on the standard video actions benchmarks of UCF101-24 and JHMDB, where it is competitive with the state of the art. Among them, we have got the best results currently on the JHMDB, the mAP reached 90.6%.

Keywords: Action recognition · Multimodal fusion · Self-attention · Two-stream network

1 Introduction

Understanding human activities from video has always been one of the most popular problem in computer vision. However, there are difficulties in accurately detecting objects and events using 2D convolutional network. The latest advent of wearable devices has led to a growing interest in understanding egocentric actions. Compared with the current convolutional research on third-person activities, egocentric activities usually involve more complex fine-grained human-object interactions in spatial and temporal dimensions. The performance of a

© Springer Nature Switzerland AG 2021
I. Farkaš et al. (Eds.): ICANN 2021, LNCS 12891, pp. 357–368, 2021.
https://doi.org/10.1007/978-3-030-86362-3_29

recognition method depends largely on whether the relevant fine-grained spatio-temporal patterns can be extracted and utilized. However, due to many factors, like frequent egocentric movements, capturing such information is a challenging task.

Although great efforts have been made in action recognition in videos [23,32], the existing action recognition methods are not suitable for dealing with egocentric human-object interaction problems. Most of the recent researches employ a two-branch deep learning architecture for the recognition of egocentric activities [1,22]. However, the traditional optical-flow estimation approaches are computationally expensive and storage demanding [18].

In this paper, we have conducted an extensive evaluation of the features of objects and egocentric actions, and proposed an end-to-end trainable instance-centered attention module that learns to highlight information regions using the appearance of humans or objects instance. We investigate a different architecture based on two separate recognition streams (RGB and skeleton), which are then combined by late fusion. The RGB stream performs action recognition from stacked video frames, while the skeleton stream is trained to recognize action from skeleton-based motion information. Both streams are implemented as ConvNets. Our framework can effectively integrate skeleton motion information with the conventional image at different levels of the processing pipeline including: 1) individual feature extraction; 2) contextual information encoding; and 3) global scene representation.

2   Related Work

Recently, many studies have considered human action recognition. According to the complexity of human action, it can be divided into the following four types of action semantics: primitive action, single-person action recognition, interaction recognition and group action recognition. The earliest method of human behavior recognition was mainly developed by Bobick [3], who proposed the motion energy image (MEI) and motion history image (MHI) for representing actions. Klser extended the histogram of gradients (HOG) feature of the image to the space-time dimension, and proposed the 3DHOG feature to describe the human action in the video [12].

The application of deep learning in computer vision has received considerable attention [9,19,20,29]. In the field of human action recognition, many deep learning-based behavior representation methods have been proposed [16,21,26]. According to the structure of deep learning network, the main representation works can be summarized as methods based on 3D convolutional networks, methods based on two-stream convolutional networks, and those based on long short-term memory (LSTM). Tran [26] proposed to use a 3D convolutional network to learn spatiotemporal features on large-scale video datasets, and connect multiple adjacent consecutive frames so that action information can be captured effectively. However, 3D convolutional improves the recognition performance at the expense of GPU memory. When the memory is constant, the depth of the feature map is limited. Tran [27] proposed decomposition techniques and hybrid architectures, which combine 3D and 2D operations at different levels of the network. Kozlov [13] proposed the method of sequence modeling, which can achieve better results on many tasks while addressing the significant shortcomings of RNNs such as sequential computing or gradient vanishing.

Human posture is used as a high-level clue for action recognition. Jhuang [11] find that high-level pose features greatly outperform low-mid level features, in particular, pose over time is critical. Farrajota combined the information of human skeleton to assist motion recognition to process low-level motions [7]. Baradel [2] proposed a two-stream network to classify activity sequences by extracting features from human poses and RGB frame. Song [14] proposed a separate and temporal attention network for action recognition from pose.

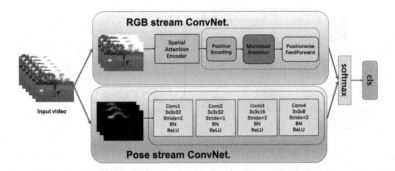

Fig. 1. The proposed pose-based two-stream network. In RGB frame, we sample frames at intervals in the original video as input. These frames first obtain actor-centered visual features through a spatial attention mechanism. Then model the motion in the frame sequence through a self-made decoder containing self-attention mechanism. In pose stream, we first calculate PoTion for video clips [5], and then classify PoTion features through a classification network. Finally, the model merges features of these two streams by point-wise addition before the softmax layer, and then classifies the video through a fully connected layer with softmax.

3   Method

3.1   Network Architecture

In this section, we will explain the proposed pose-based two-stream network in details. Figure 1 shows the architecture of the multimode two-stream network, it includes a RGB stream based on the spatial-temporal attention mechanism and a pose stream based on skeletal motion information. Our method is based on multi-modal data fusion, where pose information can be used to improve action recognition.

RGB Stream ConvNet. RGB stream ConvNet operates on video frames, effectively performing action recognition from images. The static appearance by itself is a useful clue, since some actions are strongly associated with particular objects. In the Spatial Attention Encoder module, images pass through a multi-branch network to model the spatial relationship of objects. Specifically, the visual branch extracts visual features from people, objects and the surrounding environment; the spatial attention branch is used to explore the spatial relationship between people and objects. This module is dedicated to learning the spatial interaction mode between people and objects. Its main function is to generate attention features and enhance visual features by enlarging pairs with high spatial correlation. The model architecture is shown in Fig. 2.

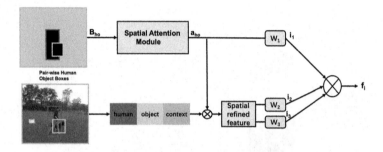

Fig. 2. The detail of Spatial Attention Encoder module. It consists of two branches. Visual branch extracts human, object features. Spatial Attention branch refines the visual features by utilizing the spatial configuration of human-object pair. These operations are repeated for every human-object pair.

For a given human bounding box X_h and object bounding box X_o, two binary maps are generated. For each of the two maps respectively, the pixel values are set to zero except the positions defined by human and object box coordinates X_h and X_o. It will generate a 2-channel binary spatial configuration map B_{ho}. Similar to [4,6], we use a Spatial Attention Module to analyze the spatial position relationship of objects. It first analyze the binary spatial configuration map through a 2-layer convolution. Then through the global average pooling operation and the fully connected layer to generate the spatial attention feature a_{ho}. Since objects and humans are defined in different channels, the convolution on the binary spatial configuration map B_{ho} allows the model to learn the possible spatial relationships between humans and objects. The attention vector a_{ho} encodes the spatial configuration and is set to the same size as the visual feature vector, which allows us to multiply these two vectors to refine the visual features through the spatial configuration.

Finally, we model video frames through a self-attention mechanism module. This module is mainly used to integrate time information within frames. For the acquire frame features of size d, frame embedding is performed, and then the multi-head attention block and the convolution block are repeatedly applied to transform them. In multi-head attention block, the attention mechanism is used to model the temporal relationship between frames by informing each frame with the representation of other frames. It consists of several sequential operations. First, different affine transformations are used to map the vectors of frame representations to multiple key, value, and query spaces. We compute the dot products of the query with all keys, and divide each of them by d_k. Finally the Softmax function is applied to obtain the weights on the values, as shown in Eq. 1. Similar to [13], we cascade the output of each head and pass it to the convolution block. Then, the obtained frame representation is refined by applying the same process for multiple times (Fig. 3).

$$head_i = softmax(\frac{QK^T}{\sqrt{d_k}})V \tag{1}$$

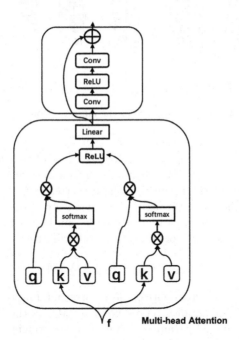

Fig. 3. The architecture of multi-head attention module. Each head uses three trainable transformations to independently transformer the frame embedding features into its query, key and value triples, and apply the self-attention operations.

Pose Stream ConvNet. In this section, we describe how to use pose information to improve the model's action recognition ability. First, the movement of semantic key points is encoded through skeleton-based pose representation introduced by Choutas [5]. Human joints are used as these points to obtain posture motion representation feature, termed is as Potion. The algorithm first obtains the human skeleton information through the human pose estimator, then extracts the heatmap of the key points of the human body in the frame, and obtains the feature representation of the motion by aggregating these probability maps on the time series. The representation of features is achieved by "coloring" each frame according to the relative time of the frame in the video clip and summing it. This focuses on the movement of the relevant key points of the entire video segment, in which the modeling of the movement of the key points is in contrast to the processing of optical flow. Finally, we classify the features through a classification convolutional network as shown in the Fig. 4.

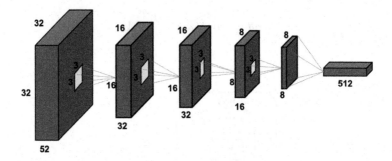

Fig. 4. The architecture of the classification network.

Finally, the motion features from RGB stream and the skeletal information stream are fused before the final softmax layer in a post-fusion manner. Specifically, the model merges the features of the two streams by point-wise addition, and then classifies the video through a fully connected layer with softmax.

Considering that both two-stream networks can be used to perform recognition task. We supervise our model with the following total loss:

$$L_{total} = L_{pos} + L_{rgb} + \lambda_\theta ||\theta||_2 \tag{2}$$

where L_{pos}, L_{rgb} are two cross-entropy loss corresponding to pose position representation and rgb appearance representation. $||\theta||_2$ is the weight decay regularization for all the model parameters, and λ_θ is the weight decaying coefficient which is set to 0.00004 in the experiments.

Due to the similar form of two cross-entry losses, we take L_{rgb} as an example:

$$L_{pos} = -\sum_{m=1}^{M}\sum_{c=1}^{C} y_{m,c} log \widehat{y}_{m,c}^{pos} \tag{3}$$

Where M is action videos and C is the number of classes of human actions, $y_{m,c}$ is the groundtruth label while $\widehat{y}_{m,c}^{pos}$ is the prediction when using pose positions.

4   Experiment

In this section, we first introduce the experimental datasets and implementation details. Then, we compare the proposal two-stream network with several state-of-the-art methods. Finally, we perform model analysis by evaluating the key model components and analyzing the classification result on dataset.

4.1   Dataset

We evaluate our pose-based two-stream network on two benchmarks in action recognition, i.e., JHMDB and UCF101-24. These two datasets are very challenging due to the richer variation in terms of appearance and dynamics. It should be noted that the full body human joints are annotated for the video in JHMDB, but not in UCF101-24.

JHMDB. The JHMDB dataset comes from the HMDB dataset, and is a subset of the HMDB dataset with fewer categories, which excludes categories that mainly include facial expressions (such as smiling faces), interaction with others (such as shaking hands), and actions that can only be done in a specific way (such as a cart). The result contains 21 categories, involving people in a single event. The dataset has removed clips in which the actor is not obvious. For the remaining clips, crop them in time such that the first and last frame roughly correspond to the beginning and end of an actor. This selection-and-cleaning process results in 36–55 clips per action class with each clip containing 15–40 frames. Finally, there are 31838 annotated frames in total.

Fig. 5. Pose estimation examples of UCF101-24 dataset on OpenPose.

UCF101-24. UCF101-24 is a subset of the UCF101 dataset, which consists of 3207 temporally untrimmed videos from 24 sports classes. There is no pose information in UCF101-24 and our work not aim to propose a new pose estimation method, we choose the approach presented in [4] to estimate the person poses of action videos in UCF101-24, which is called PAF. It proposes a part affinity field to associate body parts in a bottom-up way to achieve real-time performance while maintaining high precision. The detection results in UCF101-24 are shown in Fig. 5.

4.2   Implementation Details

We perform our network on the two datasets with the same implement details. The sampled video frame is cropped and resized to 224 × 224 for the ResNet to extract spatial feature maps, and the potion of the corresponding video clip is pre-calculated, which is introduced in [4]. During both training and testing stages, we select 5 frames in every 1 s video clip for action analysis in RGB stream. We implement our network by PyTorch.

Network Training. The layer configuration of our RGB and Pose ConvNets is schematically shown in Fig. 1. The training process of the network can be regarded as the modeling of video sequence frames. The network weights are learnt using the Adam optimizer. For a better convergence, we vary the learning rate in a similar way to the warmup strategy introduced in [28].

For RGB stream, in the training process, we split the video sequence into 1 s clips. For shorter videos, we loop the video as needed to meet the input of the model. Considering that there are many similar frames in a continuous video sequences, the video sequence is sampled once every 6 frames to get the sampled video frame. In each iteration, 5 consecutive sampled frames and the corresponding bounding box coordinates are selected from the above sampled video frames as model input, and the intermediate frame is used as the key frame. The bounding box coordinates of the input frame are all the coordinates of the key frame bounding box, and the bounding box coordinates of the key frame are obtained through the cascade-rcnn detection network.

In pose stream, for each second of the video clip, the pose key points of each frames are obtained. Then calculate the PoTion and use it as the input of the model. Among them, the relevant pose information is provided in the JHMDB dataset and can be used directly. However, there is no pose information in UCF101-24, which needs to be obtained through the OpenPose.

The model in the RGB stream uses ImageNet pretrained ResNet as base network. The classification network in the pose stream is trained from scratch. For all architectures we follow each convolutional layer by a batch normalization layer and a ReLU activation function, except for the last convolutional layers which produce the class scores for each network.

4.3   Experiment Result

To evaluate the performance of the proposed two-stream network, we compare our results with the recent state-of-the-art approaches in action recognition on JHMDB and UCF101-24. Our method recognizes the action category by modeling multiple frames in the video clip, so we utilize video-mAP to evaluate detection accuracy. Our model completes action recognition by analyzing 1 s video clips. In JHMDB, the video clips are shorter, and we can almost completely model and predict each video clip. In UCF101-24, for each clip, we set 0.5 as the threshold for identification, and compare the experimental results with IOU of 0.5.

Table 1. The result on JHMDB

Method	Optical flow	Pre-trained	Backbone	Video-mAP (%)
Two-stream RCNN] [17]	√		VGG	58.5
T-CNN [10]			C3D	61.3
ACT [10]	√		VGG	65.7
AVA baseline [8]	√	Kinetics-400	I3D	73.3
ACRN [24]	√	Kinetics-400	S3D	80.1
Context-Aware RCNN [30]		Kinetics-400	R50-NL	79.2
Dance with flow [31]	√	ImageNet	SSD	74.74
MOC [15]		ImageNet	DLA34	80.5
Ours		**ImageNet**	**resNet34**	**90.6**

Table 2. The result on UCF101-24

Method	Optical flow	Pre-trained	Backbone	Video-mAP (%)
MOC [15]		ImageNet	DLA34	53.8
AVA baseline [8]	√	Kinetics-400	I3D	59.9
Dance with flow [31]	√	ImageNet	SSD	50.3
AIA [25]		Kinetics-400	ResNet50-C2D	75.5
Action detection [1]		Kinetics-400	I3D	77.9
Ours		**ImageNet**	**ResNet34**	**74.9**

The experimental results on dataset JHMDB is shown in Table 1, and the experimental results on dataset UCF101-24 is shown in Table 2. Our results outperformed many methods on both the JHMDB dataset and the UCF101-24 dataset, which indicates the importance of the attention mechanism and demonstrates the effectiveness of the pose information. Generally, the performance of the 3D CNN-based methods were higher than those of the 2D CNN-based methods for action recognition. We can see that our two-stream network based on 2D backbone but achieves the comparable results with other approaches. It should be noted that in our method, we simply insert our attention mechanism module into 2D CNN without too much additional computation, the FLOPS of our model is 4.5×10^9 and the recognition performance could be significantly improved.

Our model can distinguish spatio-temporal feature representations, highlight spatial regions related to action categories, and focus on frames related to action categories through a temporal attention mechanism. Besides, it also outperformed the latest two-stream networks on both datasets, such as Dance with flow [31], AVA baseline [8]. They perform action recognition based on optical flow, which is more expensive to obtain than pose information. We observed that the method appears to work better for JHMDB than UCF101-24. The reason is because the JHMDB provides more detailed pose information. In the JHMDB dataset, there will be fewer frames that are not related to a certain action in the video, and there will be less background noise.

In order to further verify the performance, we verified the improvement of the pose information to the model. As shown in Fig. 6, the recognition result of the two-stream network based on skeletal information is significantly better than the model based on RGB appearance feature alone, such as "sit", "stand", "throw". Compared with the original model, the performance has been significantly improved. This means that our model can effectively focus on the spatial region related to the action category in the frame, and capture the key frame containing information that is relevant to the action class. Figure 6 compares the improvement of the original model after fusing the pose information, and compares it with the groundtruth in the test set. For most of the action categories, our model can perform correct recognition, especially for "run", "stand" and other categories that are difficult to distinguish based on RGB appearance features. These actions can be accurately recognized after adding pose information, which indicates that our model can exploit the discriminative information at frame level and improve the recognition performance of the network through more powerful spatiotemporal feature learning.

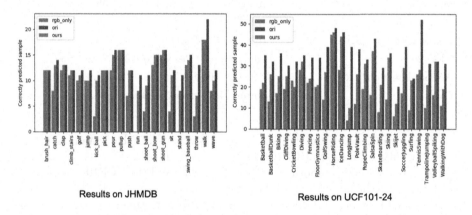

Fig. 6. Results of the classification in each category. The red column is the result on the single-modal. The green column is the result on our pose-based two-stream network. The blue column is the groundtruth on the dataset. The left shows the result on JHMDB, and the right is the result on UCF101-24. (Color figure online)

Furthermore, we discussed the impact of the number of model input frames and the amount of sampling frame intervals. We compared the sampling frame interval of 2, 4, 6, 8 and 10 and get the best result when the interval is 4, the mAP achieved 91.8%. Moreover, we compared the experimental results of modeling frames 3,5 and 7 when the interval sampling is set to 4. The best result is obtained when the number of frames is 5.

5   Conclusion

In this paper, we propose a new problem, using cues from the content of image, and then combined with human-object interaction feature to help recognize human action in the video. Moreover, wo propose to improve the action recognition ability of the model through a method based on multi-modal fusion. Compared with other methods, our method achieves the best performance on two challenging datasets.

While plenty of work studies human action recognition, predicting interactive objects in an action-independent manner is both challenging and practical for various applications, the proposed method shows promising results to tackle this challenge. We demonstrate its advantages over multiple informative baselines. Our action recognition method provides a framework to detect a large number of human actions in a visual scene by using global and local visual cues. The proposed method can recognize actions in indoor environment with stable backgrounds. In future work, we will explore more methods to get better results.

References

1. Attention is all we need: Nailing down object-centric attention for egocentric activity recognition (2018)
2. Baradel, F., Wolf, C., Mille, J.: Pose-conditioned spatio-temporal attention for human action recognition (2017)
3. Bobick, A.F., Davis, J.W.: The Recognition of Human Movement Using Temporal Templates. The Recognition of Human Movement Using Temporal Templates (2001)
4. Cao, Z., Simon, T., Wei, S.E., Sheikh, Y.: Realtime multi-person 2d pose estimation using part affinity fields. arXiv e-prints (2016)
5. Choutas, V., Weinzaepfel, P., Revaud, J., Schmid, C.: Potion: pose motion representation for action recognition. In: 2018 IEEE/CVF Conference on Computer Vision and Pattern Recognition (CVPR) (2018)
6. Du, W., Wang, Y., Yu, Q.: RPAN: an end-to-end recurrent pose-attention network for action recognition in videos (2017)
7. Farrajota, M., Rodrigues, J., Buf, J.: Human action recognition in videos with articulated pose information by deep networks. Pattern Anal. Appl. 22(4), 1307–1318 (2019)
8. Gu, C., et al.: AVA: a video dataset of spatio-temporally localized atomic visual actions (2017)
9. Hahner, S., Iza-Teran, R., Garcke, J.: Analysis and prediction of deforming 3D shapes using oriented bounding boxes and LSTM autoencoders. In: Farkaš, I., Masulli, P., Wermter, S. (eds.) ICANN 2020. LNCS, vol. 12396, pp. 284–296. Springer, Cham (2020). https://doi.org/10.1007/978-3-030-61609-0_23
10. Hou, R., Chen, C., Shah, M.: Tube convolutional neural network (T-CNN) for action detection in videos, pp. 5823–5832. IEEE Computer Society (2017)
11. Jhuang, H., Gall, J., Zuffi, S., Schmid, C., Black, M.J.: Towards understanding action recognition. In: IEEE International Conference on Computer Vision (2014)
12. Klser, A., Marszalek, M., Schmid, C.: A spatio-temporal descriptor based on 3d-gradients. In: British Machine Vision Conference (2010)
13. Kozlov, A., Andronov, V., Gritsenko, Y.: Lightweight network architecture for real-time action recognition (2020)
14. Laha, A., Raykar, V.: An empirical evaluation of various deep learning architectures for bi-sequence classification tasks (2016)

15. Li, Y., Wang, Z., Wang, L., Wu, G.: Actions as moving points. Neurocomputing **395**, 138–149 (2020)
16. Liu, J., Shahroudy, A., Xu, D., Wang, G.: Spatio-temporal LSTM with trust gates for 3D human action recognition. In: Leibe, B., Matas, J., Sebe, N., Welling, M. (eds.) ECCV 2016. LNCS, vol. 9907, pp. 816–833. Springer, Cham (2016). https://doi.org/10.1007/978-3-319-46487-9_50
17. Peng, X., Schmid, C.: Multi-region two-stream R-CNN for action detection. In: Leibe, B., Matas, J., Sebe, N., Welling, M. (eds.) ECCV 2016. LNCS, vol. 9908, pp. 744–759. Springer, Cham (2016). https://doi.org/10.1007/978-3-319-46493-0_45
18. Piergiovanni, A.J., Ryoo, M.S.: Representation flow for action recognition. In: 2019 IEEE/CVF Conference on Computer Vision and Pattern Recognition (CVPR) (2020)
19. Shen, J., Xiong, X., Li, Y., He, W., Li, P., Zheng, X.: Detecting safety helmet wearing on construction sites with bounding-box regression and deep transfer learning. Comput. Aided Civil Infrastruc. Eng. **36**(2), 180–196 (2021)
20. Shen, J., Xiong, X., Xue, Z., Bian, Y.: A convolutional neural-network-based pedestrian counting model for various crowded scenes. Comput. Aided Civil Infrastruc. Eng. **34**(10), 897–914 (2019)
21. Simonyan, K., Zisserman, A.: Two-stream convolutional networks for action recognition in videos. In: Advances in Neural Information Processing Systems 1 (2014)
22. Sudhakaran, S., Escalera, S., Lanz, O.: LSTA: long short-term attention for egocentric action recognition. In: 2019 IEEE/CVF Conference on Computer Vision and Pattern Recognition (CVPR) (2019)
23. Sun, B., Liu, M., Zheng, R., Zhang, S.: Attention-based LSTM network for wearable human activity recognition. In: 2019 Chinese Control Conference (CCC) (2019)
24. Sun, C., Shrivastava, A., Vondrick, C., Murphy, K., Sukthankar, R., Schmid, C.: Actor-Centric Relation Network. Springer, Cham (2018)
25. Tang, J., Xia, J., Mu, X., Pang, B., Lu, C.: Asynchronous interaction aggregation for action detection (2020)
26. Tran, D., Bourdev, L., Fergus, R., Torresani, L., Paluri, M.: Learning spatiotemporal features with 3d convolutional networks. IEEE (2015)
27. Tran, D., Wang, H., Torresani, L., Ray, J., LeCun, Y., Paluri, M.: A closer look at spatiotemporal convolutions for action recognition. In: Proceedings of the IEEE Conference on Computer Vision and Pattern Recognition, pp. 6450–6459 (2018)
28. Vaswani, A., et al.: Attention is all you need. arXiv preprint arXiv:1706.03762 (2017)
29. Véges, M., Lőrincz, A.: Multi-person absolute 3D human pose estimation with weak depth supervision. In: Farkaš, I., Masulli, P., Wermter, S. (eds.) ICANN 2020. LNCS, vol. 12396, pp. 258–270. Springer, Cham (2020). https://doi.org/10.1007/978-3-030-61609-0_21
30. Wu, J., Kuang, Z., Wang, L., Zhang, W., Wu, G.: Context-aware RCNN: a baseline for action detection in videos (2020)
31. Zhao, J., Snoek, C.: Dance with flow: two-in-one stream action detection. In: 2019 IEEE/CVF Conference on Computer Vision and Pattern Recognition (CVPR) (2020)
32. Zheng, Z., Shi, L., Wang, C., Sun, L., Pan, G.: LSTM with uniqueness attention for human activity recognition. In: Tetko, I.V., Kůrková, V., Karpov, P., Theis, F. (eds.) ICANN 2019. LNCS, vol. 11729, pp. 498–509. Springer, Cham (2019). https://doi.org/10.1007/978-3-030-30508-6_40

Behavior of Keyword Spotting Networks Under Noisy Conditions

Anwesh Mohanty[1]([⊠])[iD], Adrian Frischknecht[2][iD], Christoph Gerum[2][iD], and Oliver Bringmann[2][iD]

[1] Indian Institute Technology Bombay, Mumbai 400076, India
[2] University of Tübingen, 72074 Tübingen, Germany

Abstract. Keyword spotting (KWS) is becoming a ubiquitous need with the advancement in artificial intelligence and smart devices. Recent work in this field have focused on several different architectures to achieve good results on datasets with low to moderate noise. However, the performance of these models deteriorates under high noise conditions as shown by our experiments. In our paper, we present an extensive comparison between state-of-the-art KWS networks under various noisy conditions. We also suggest adaptive batch normalization as a technique to improve the performance of the networks when the noise files are unknown during the training phase. The results of such high noise characterization enable future work in developing models that perform better in the aforementioned conditions.

Keywords: Keyword spotting · High noise conditions · Adaptive batch normalization · Sinc convolution network · Temporal convolution ResNet

1 Introduction

Automatic speech recognition is one of the fastest developing fields in artificial intelligence and machine learning. With the advent of smart assistants (e.g. Google assistant, Siri, Cortana) in most of the latest devices, the ability of speech recognition software to recognize certain wake words (e.g. "Ok Google", "Hey Siri") from continuous speech filled with varying levels of background noise becomes paramount in enhancing the user experience.

The networks used for KWS have evolved significantly from the initial Gaussian Mixture Model-Universal Background Models (GMM-UBMs) and Hidden Markov Models (HMMs) to Deep Neural Networks (DNNs) to the current use of different variations of Convolutional Neural Networks (CNNs) [1,3,7,15]. Due to their inherent properties, CNNs can discover robust and invariant representations of the input waveforms provided to them, and have obtained state-of-the-art

---

This work has been partly funded by the European Union (EU) and the German Federal Ministry of Education and Research (BMBF) in the project OCEAN12 (reference number: 16ESE0270).

I. Farkaš et al. (Eds.): ICANN 2021, LNCS 12891, pp. 369–378, 2021.
https://doi.org/10.1007/978-3-030-86362-3_30

performance on several speech recognition tasks carried out under moderate noise conditions.

KWS networks have undergone several transformations in their architectures and currently CNNs provide the best performance under moderate noise conditions. Despite their impressive performance, as demonstrated in Fig. 1, the test accuracy falls at a steep rate once the signal-to-noise ratio (SNR) in the dataset crosses a certain threshold. Considering day-to-day situations like heavy traffic, construction sites etc., the places where there is very high background noise, the current architectures won't give the same performance as they will give in a lower noise environment. This calls for an architecture which can perform the task of KWS under such noisy conditions with a competitive accuracy.

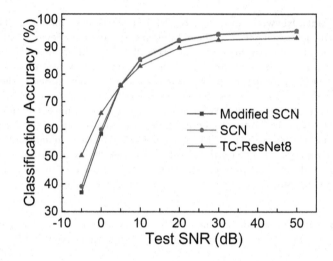

Fig. 1. Performance of networks under varying noise (trained on clean dataset). Classification accuracy of all networks decreases significantly as the level of noise increases beyond a certain threshold.

For our experiments, we use three models for comparison. The first one is the TC-ResNet8 (TC: temporal convolutions) which uses pre-processed MFCC features as inputs for classification. The second one is the SincConv Network (SCN) which classifies on raw audio data and finally the last model is our variation of the SCN but with optimal parameter tuning to reduce the memory footprint and total computation cost without reducing the classification accuracy. We subject the models to different noise conditions to obtain a detailed characterization of the models' performances.

The remainder of the paper is organized as follows. Section 2 gives a brief description of other relevant work going on in this field. Section 3 discusses the basic features of all the architectures used during evaluation. Section 4 outlines the experimental setup and the results respectively. Here we also propose the use of batch normalization (BatchNorm) as a method to adapt the network to unknown noise conditions. Finally, Sect. 5 discusses our conclusions and scope for future work.

2   Related Works

Significant research has been done in the field of KWS in recent times, with a focus on developing compact and accurate models that can be implemented in hardware without consuming too much power. Zhang et al. [18] provides a comparison of performance and hardware requirement (memory and operation count) of Deep Neural Network (DNN), CNN, Long short-term memory (LSTM), and depthwise separable (DS) CNN models on MFCC feature data as input, where the DS-CNN provides the best result. Choi et al. [4] proposed the TC-ResNet which provides state-of-the-art 96.6% accuracy on MFCC input data, as well as a speedup of 385× compared to previous architectures on the Google Speech Commands Dataset [17]. Since pre-processed data like MFCC features won't be always available, few CNN architectures have been developed to work on raw audio data as input. One of the notable ones is the SCN architecture proposed by Mittermaier et al. [11], which uses SincNet [14] and DS convolutions [5] to achieve comparable accuracy to the state-of-the-art TC-ResNet models.

There is very little documentation about the performance of popular KWS networks under high noise, or in situations where the noise present during the inference stage is much different from that during training. Liu et al. [10] have provided a brief noise characterization of the performance of their binary weight network using different types of noise like white, pink and miscellaneous noise in daily-life activities. Huang et al. [9], Raju et al. [13] and Pervaiz et al. [12] have provided detailed studies on the performance of their systems for the task of KWS under noise, but the datasets and the metrics used in these works are all different and cannot be used to draw a comparison with current state-of-the-art models. To the best of our knowledge, we are the first to provide a detailed characterization of popular KWS networks on a standard dataset under varying high noise conditions and provide a simple and efficient solution to improve the accuracy by quite a significant margin in the aforementioned conditions.

3   Model Architectures

In this paper we consider three representative neural networks. Table 1 summarizes the multiply accumulate operations (MACs) and total weights in the considered models and Fig. 2 shows the respective architectures.

Table 1. Summary of models

Model	MACs	Parameters
TC-ResNet8	1.5M	66k
SCN	18M	60k
Modified SCN	7.5M	34.5k

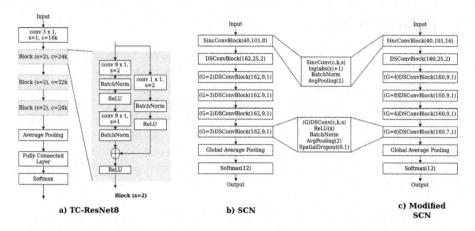

Fig. 2. Architectures of the models. The hyperparameters c, k and s represent the number of output channels, kernel size and stride respectively for all the models. Architectures of TC-ResNet8 and SCN adopted from [4] and [11] respectively.

3.1   TC-ResNet8 Architecture

TC-ResNet8 (Fig. 2) [4] is a CNN architecture which utilizes temporal convolutions, 1-D convolutions along the temporal dimension, for KWS and classifies on the MFCC data (pre-processed from raw audio signals) as input. This model adopts ResNet [6], one of the most popular CNN architectures, but uses $m \times 1$ kernels (m = 3 for the first layer and m = 9 for the other layers) in its layers. By switching to temporal convolutions instead of 2D convolutions, there is a decrease in the output feature map of each layer which leads to a huge reduction in the computational burden and memory footprint of the subsequent layers.

TC-ResNet8 model has shown good performance for KWS with only 66k parameters. There is no bias in the convolution and fully connected layers. Each batch normalization layer has trainable parameters for scaling and shifting. The TC-ResNet8 model has 3 residual blocks and {16, 24, 36, 48} channels for each layer including the first convolution layer.

3.2   SCN Architecture

SCN network (Fig. 2) [11] uses rectangular band-pass filters (in the frequency domains) in the first convolutional layer to classify on the input raw audio waveform. This is equivalent to convolving the input signal with parametrized sinc functions ($\text{sinc}(x) = \frac{\sin(x)}{x}$) in the time domain. The filters can be represented as:

$$H[f, f_1, f_2] = \text{rect}(\frac{f}{f_2}) - \text{rect}(\frac{f}{f_1}) \tag{1}$$

$$h[n, f_1, f_2] = 2f_2\text{sinc}(2\pi f_2 n) - 2f_1\text{sinc}(2\pi f_1 n) \tag{2}$$

From (1), the frequency domain expression of the filters, we can see that a single filter extracts only the information lying between the two frequency levels, f_1 and f_2. This extracted data acts as a feature set for the consequent CNN layers. Since only two parameters, the upper and lower cut-off frequencies, are required to define any sinc filter, this leads to a smaller memory footprint. As suggested in [11], a log-compression activation ($y = \log(\text{abs}(x) + 1)$) is used after the sinc convolutions.

In the subsequent layers we have five grouped DS convolutional blocks. DS convolutions [5] are a great alternative to standard convolutions as they reduce the computation power by a significant value without reducing the effectiveness much. Grouping [8] is introduced to reduce the number of parameters introduced by the pointwise convolutions after each depthwise convolution. Each convolution block is followed by layers for batch normalization, spatial dropout for regularization and an average pooling block. After these 5 blocks we have a global average pooling block followed by a softmax layer to obtain the class posteriors to classify into 12 classes.

3.3 Modified SCN Architecture

As can be seen from Table 1, though there is a decrease in the parameter count when we go from the TC-ResNet8 to the SCN model as well as the added benefit of not spending resources on pre-processing to obtain the MFCC data, the number of MACs inside the latter model is almost 12 times more than the former model (excluding the MACs in pre-processing of raw audio in TC-ResNet8). This huge level of disparity in the computation costs of the two models certainly raises questions over the viability of the SCN network over the TC-ResNet8 while considering a hardware implementation.

Following several experiments, study of the properties of the SCN model and extensive fine-tuning of the hyperparameters, we present the modified SCN model (Fig. 2) which gives comparable accuracy to the original model but reduces the computation cost and memory footprint by almost a factor of two. The subtle changes can be seen in Fig. 2 and Table 1. We change the grouping in CNN layers from alternate (2, 3) grouping to alternate (4, 8) grouping. This impacts primarily the total number of parameters used in the model as can be seen in Table 1. Almost 50% of the computations are carried out in the very first sinc convolution layer. To tackle this issue we double the stride in the sinc convolution layers which leads to decrease in the MACs in the subsequent layers as well.

The primary motivation of the modified SCN architecture is to obtain the best possible optimized version of the SCN architecture without sacrificing any of the advantage the SCN network has over the TC-ResNet8 architecture. The difference in performance due to the architecture changes in Fig. 2 won't be noticeable when running the networks on a modern GPU, but on moving the networks to smaller embedded systems for a more practical setup, there will be a significant change in the latency and power consumption due to the discrepancy in the number of MACs and parameters compared to the SCN network. Based on the optimizations that we have incorporated into the SCN architecture, the modified SCN is able to compete with both the SCN and TC-ResNet8 networks in terms of accuracy and efficiency respectively.

3.4   Batch Normalization Method

In standard neural networks problems, the statistics of batches during training are learned in the BatchNorm layers and used without changing during the test and validation phases. This works well in most cases because the test statistics resemble closely to the training statistics. But when the test statistics vary significantly from the training statistics due to environmental noise, this assumption fails and the model won't perform well. In this case, a better training dataset should be found, but that is not always possible. To tackle this fall in performance and not having to resort to finding a new training set, we adapt a simple modification from Schneider et al. [16] - we do not switch off the BatchNorm layers during the validation and test phases when the noise during test is unknown. This way the network will learn and use the batch norm statistics during inference rather than the training statistics which might vary significantly from the inference statistics, and provide us with better results as seen in Fig. 5 without a significant computation overhead.

4   Experimental Evaluation

The networks mentioned in Sect. 3 have been trained and evaluated on the Google's Speech Commands dataset [17]. The dataset consists of 105,829 one-second (or less) long utterances of 35 different keywords spoken by 2,618 different speakers. We choose the following 10 keywords: "yes", "no", "up","down", "left", "right", "on", "off", "stop", "go", along with classes for unknown and silence. The remaining 25 words are labeled as unknown. The utterances are then randomly divided into training, validation and test sets in the ratio of 80:10:10 respectively.

For noise injection, one-second chunks are chosen randomly from three types of noise present: white, pink and miscellaneous (consisting of samples from real life activities like traffic noises, conversation, flowing water etc.). For the training phase, these chunks are sampled randomly between the SNR range of [−5 dB, +10 dB] and added to the clean dataset. For the validation and test phase, the SNR value is kept fixed at one of the following values: −5 dB, 0 dB, +5 dB, +10 dB. To ensure that the final signal after mixing the noise with the dataset does not get clipped at any instant, we introduce a small gain block to scale the signals so that the SNR remains constant and no clipping takes place.

For the first experiment, all the noise files are available for the training, validation and test phases. For the second experiment, white and pink noise is injected into the training dataset and miscellaneous noise is added to validation and test dataset. Our model is trained for 150 epochs with the Stochastic Gradient Descent (SGD) optimizer with an initial learning rate of 0.1 and learning rate decay of 0.75 after 10 epochs. The model with highest validation accuracy after 150 epochs is saved to evaluate the accuracy on the test set.

4.1   Network Performance When Noise Conditions Are Known

In this case, the noise files in miscellaneous category are available during training, validation and test phase i.e. we can train the model to learn the nature of the noise distribution used and give close to state-of-the-art performance. Random chunks from the noise files are added to the keyword signals at a SNR value chosen randomly between [−5 dB, +10 dB]. The classification accuracies of the different networks are plotted against the noise spectrum in Fig. 3.

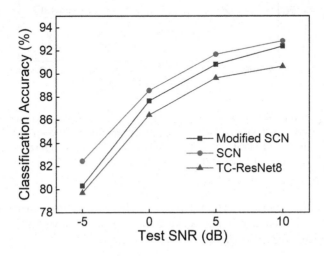

Fig. 3. Performance of networks under known test noise conditions. The network accuracy steadily decreases as the amount of noise in the samples is increased.

As observed from the results of Fig. 3, even the state-of-the-art KWS networks are susceptible to high noise, evident from the ∼10% fall in accuracy as test noise level increases to −5 dB.

4.2   Network Performance When Noise Conditions Are Unknown

In this case, the miscellaneous noise files are only available in the validation and test phases i.e. while training the noise distribution used in the inference stage is unknown. Hence to train the models under noisy conditions, we inject the training dataset with a random mixture of white and pink noise sampled randomly between [−5 dB, +10 dB].

The contrast in the performance of the networks for the two different conditions can be seen in Fig. 4. Though the networks perform satisfactorily under moderate noise (∼10 dB range), the performance deteriorates catastrophically under severe noise conditions. To mitigate this, we enable the networks to learn the batch normalized statistics of the validation and test datasets during the

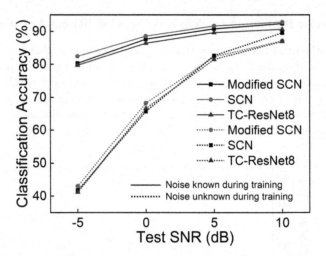

Fig. 4. Comparison of performance when noise conditions are known (solid) and unknown (dotted). At 10 dB there is a small discrepancy between the performance in the two conditions, but at −5 dB there is almost a 40% difference between the network performance in the two different conditions.

corresponding phases rather than depend on the parameters learned during the training phase. The change in the performances of the networks after implementing this is encapsulated in Fig. 5.

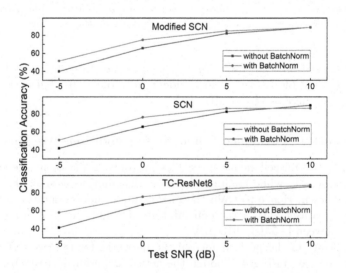

Fig. 5. Comparison of accuracy before and after implementing BatchNorm technique. The BatchNorm method is able to significantly boost the performance of all the models under high unknown test noise conditions.

In Fig. 5, though the performance remains almost similar in moderate noise, there is a steady improvement in the final accuracy as we move towards the higher end of the noise spectrum. The SCN models record an improvement of ~10% and the TC-ResNet model shows a massive rise in accuracy of ~20% at −5 dB test SNR.

5 Conclusions and Future Work

We provide an extensive characterization of the performance of popular KWS networks under heavy noise, and our results show how the existing architectures fail to deliver satisfactory results under non-ideal conditions. We also observe that if the noise in the test phase is not known, training the network by injecting white/pink noise in the training phase performs satisfactorily under moderate noise but fails catastrophically under severe noise conditions. To create networks that perform better under such situations, new models may need to be created.

One solution might be to increase the number of weights and/or layers in the networks and train them on much larger and varied datasets, which also contain an appreciable amount of noise injection. But then this will be contrary to our motive of building networks with small memory footprints. And even though we train the networks using noisy signals, the performance is still sub-par at best. Hence, to create networks that perform better under such situations, new models and algorithms may need to be created. Our BatchNorm algorithm takes one step in that direction by achieving significant enhancement in classification at noisy conditions.

Further improvements to the BatchNorm technique and hardware support for UltraTrail [2] of the aforementioned techniques and networks is left as future work.

References

1. Abdel-Hamid, O., Mohamed, A.R., Jiang, H., Deng, L., Penn, G., Yu, D.: Convolutional neural networks for speech recognition. IEEE/ACM Trans. Audio Speech Lang. Process. **22**(10), 1533–1545 (2014)
2. Bernardo, P.P., Gerum, C., Frischknecht, A., Lübeck, K., Bringmann, O.: UltraTrail: a configurable ultralow-power TC-ResNet AI accelerator for efficient keyword spotting. IEEE Trans. Comput. Aided Des. Integrated Circuits Syst. **39**(11), 4240–4251 (2020)
3. Chen, G., Parada, C., Heigold, G.: Small-footprint keyword spotting using deep neural networks. In: 2014 IEEE International Conference on Acoustics, Speech and Signal Processing (ICASSP), pp. 4087–4091. IEEE (2014)
4. Choi, S., et al.: Temporal convolution for real-time keyword spotting on mobile devices. In: Proceedings of INTERSPEECH 2019, pp. 3372–3376 (2019). https://arxiv.org/abs/1904.03814
5. Chollet, F.: Xception: Deep learning with depthwise separable convolutions. In: Proceedings of the IEEE Conference on Computer Vision and Pattern Recognition (CVPR), pp. 1251–1258 (2017)

6. He, K., Zhang, X., Ren, S., Sun, J.: Deep residual learning for image recognition. In: Proceedings of the IEEE Conference on Computer Vision and Pattern Recognition 2016, pp. 770–778 (2016). https://arxiv.org/abs/1512.03385

7. Hinton, G., et al.: Deep neural networks for acoustic modeling in speech recognition: the shared views of four research groups. IEEE Signal Process. Mag. **29**(6), 82–97 (2012)

8. Huang, G., Liu, S., van der Maaten, L., Weinberger, K.: Condensenet: an efficient densenet using learned group convolutions. In: Proceedings of the IEEE Conference on Computer Vision and Pattern Recognition 2018, pp. 2752–2761 (2018). https://arxiv.org/abs/1711.09224, version 2

9. Huang, Y., Hughes, T., Shabestary, T.Z., Applebaum, T.: Supervised noise reduction for multichannel keyword spotting. In: 2018 IEEE International Conference on Acoustics, Speech and Signal Processing (ICASSP), pp. 5474–5478 (2018). https://doi.org/10.1109/ICASSP.2018.8462346

10. Liu, B., et al.: An ultra-low power always-on keyword spotting accelerator using quantized convolutional neural network and voltage-domain analog switching network-based approximate computing. IEEE Access **7**, 186456–186469 (2019). https://ieeexplore.ieee.org/document/8936893

11. Mittermaier, S., Kürzinger, L., Waschneck, B., Rigoll, G.: Small-footprint keyword spotting on raw audio data with sinc-convolutions arXiv:1911.02086 (2019). https://arxiv.org/abs/1911.02086, version 2

12. Pervaiz, A., et al.: Incorporating noise robustness in speech command recognition by noise augmentation of training data. Sensors **20**, 2326 (2020). https://www.mdpi.com/1424-8220/20/8/2326

13. Raju, A., Panchapagesan, S., Liu, X., Mandal, A., Strom, N.: Data augmentation for robust keyword spotting under playback interference (2018). http://arxiv.org/abs/1808.00563

14. Ravanelli, M., Bengio, Y.: Speaker recognition from raw waveform with Sincnet. In: Proceedings of IEEE Spoken Language Technology Workshop (SLT), pp. 1021–1028, December 2018. https://arxiv.org/abs/2006.16971

15. Sainath, T.N., Parada, C.: Convolutional neural networks for small-footprint keyword spotting. In: Sixteenth Annual Conference of the International Speech Communication Association (2015)

16. Schneider, S., Rusak, E., Eck, L., Oliver Bringmann, W.B., Bethge, M.: Improving robustness against common corruptions by covariate shift adaptation arXiv:2006.16971 (2020). https://arxiv.org/abs/2006.16971

17. Warden, P.: Speech commands: a dataset for limited-vocabulary speech recognition arXiv:1804.03209 (2018). https://arxiv.org/abs/1804.03209

18. Zhang, Y., Suda, N., Lai, L., Chandra, V.: Hello edge: keyword spotting on microcontrollers arXiv:1711.07128 (2017). https://arxiv.org/abs/1711.07128, version 3

Robust Stroke Recognition via Vision and IMU in Robotic Table Tennis

Yapeng Gao[(✉)], Jonas Tebbe, and Andreas Zell

Cognitive Systems, Eberhard Karls University Tübingen, Tübingen, Germany
{yapeng.gao,jonas.tebbe,andreas.zell}@uni-tuebingen.de
http://www.cogsys.cs.uni-tuebingen.de/

Abstract. Stroke recognition in table tennis is a challenging task, due to the variety of the movements. Many different sensors have been adopted in robotic table tennis, with the goal of detecting the players' movements. In this paper, we propose a two-stage approach to directly recognize the table tennis racket's movement. A bounding box around the racket can be extracted from an RGB image in the first stage. An efficient and lightweight CNN architecture is then developed to regress the racket 3D position by fusion of the cropped image and the 3D rotation data from an IMU in the second stage. Together with the rotation data, a robust 6D racket pose is available at a frame rate 100 Hz. In the experiments, two datasets are collected from our KUKA table tennis robot for evaluation and comparisons, which show a position error of 4.7 cm at a range of 6 m. One behavior cloning experiment is performed in order to reveal the potential of this work.

Keywords: Racket pose estimation · Sensor fusion · Table tennis robot

1 Introduction

Human activity detection has spawned a large amount of research in many applications, such as gesture recognition, video surveillance, health care and sports performance analysis. Typically, it includes two steps: feature extraction and action classification. In recent years, a variety of sensors have been applied to obtain the human pose, thereby resulting in different kinds of techniques.

Vision-based methods extract the 2D human joints [6], hand keypoints [18] or 3D human pose [16] as features from RGB cameras. To get more accurate information, the depth maps from RGB-D sensors are included to derive the full 3D human pose [29]. Motion sensor based methods adopt low-cost accelerometers, gyroscopes, and sometimes magnetometers to detect the human's linear acceleration and angular velocity [28] as features. With the fusion of multiple inertial measurement units (IMUs) and a single camera, one can recover accurate 3D human pose in the wild [14].

Supported by the Vector Stiftung and KUKA.

I. Farkaš et al. (Eds.): ICANN 2021, LNCS 12891, pp. 379–390, 2021.
https://doi.org/10.1007/978-3-030-86362-3_31

Fig. 1. Playing with our KUKA table tennis robot. A wearable IMU is mounted at the bottom of the player's racket handle. The quaternion value q_{IMU} streamed from it, is defined as the racket orientation in the IMU frame. One of the stationary cameras fixed on the ceiling is used to capture the human player movements from above (Fig. 2 left). By fusing the images with IMU signals, we can take them as inputs and regress the 3D racket position robustly with the proposed approach. The camera and the IMU are synchronized with a software trigger.

To understand the performance of the players and provide them with a guide to tactics and skills, some systems with different sensors have been designed for sports. An AI Coach system for athletic training [23] is built with a single camera. They design a binary player detector to extract a single player as bounding box in the first frame. To accelerate the detection step, a tracking model based on the detected bounding box is used from the second frame to the last frame. After knowing each player's tubelet, the player 2D pose can be regressed by a pose estimation model. In order to estimate and track player's 3D pose, Bridgeman et al. [5] calculate the correspondences between 2D poses in different camera views. The 2D pose associations can be used to generate the player 3D skeletons.

In robotic table tennis we face many challenges, especially due to the movement of the human opponent, also including some deceptive actions. Each movement creates different types of spin and speed. Therefore, instead of recognizing the human 2D or 3D pose, the main focus in this paper is the table tennis racket pose estimation. This gives our table tennis robot (shown in Fig. 1) the ability to recognize the human stroke pose and consequently mimic the human motion with imitation learning. To achieve this we use a single camera fused with an IMU and develop a novel approach for robustly recognizing human strokes. The main contributions of this paper are as follows:

- We propose a novel two-stage position estimation network for table tennis rackets via vision and IMU. Together with the 3D rotation data retrieved from the IMU, a robust 6D racket pose is available at a frame rate 100 Hz without any special markers.

- The training dataset is created based on simulated views of a racket CAD model. The evaluation dataset is collected from our KUKA robot, which can be annotated automatically with the pre-calibrated transformation matrix between the robot and the camera. Therefore, manually labeling is not needed in our work.
- The experiment shows that our approach achieves the best performance with a position error of 4.7 cm at a range of 6 m. To reveal the goal of this work, we perform an experiment to operate the robot in a human-like way, which is a clone of the human movements.

2 Related Work

Image-based 6D object pose estimation is one of the trendiest topics in computer vision. Recent state-of-the-art methods have shown huge success in detecting the 6D pose of objects in close range to the camera. PoseCNN [26] directly estimates the 6D object pose with an end-to-end network from a single image. Sundermeyer et al. [20] present an implicit method for 3D orientation estimation based on Augmented Autoencoders (AAEs), which is trained on synthetic images. The 3D translation is then computed according to the pinhole camera model. A pixel-wise voting network (PVNet) [17] localizes 2D keypoints on the object using RANSAC and aligns them with 3D keypoints to obtain the 6D pose. The Coordinates-based Disentangled Pose Network (CDPN) [11] uses a Dynamic Zoom In (DZI) technique to compensate the 2D object detection error, which achieves accurate and robust results. However, if the object is too small in the camera or, like the racket, has a texture-less surface and very thin paddle, it is prone to failure using these methods, because of insufficient features.

By labeling special markers on the racket, Zhang et al. [27] could use color thresholding to extract them from two cameras, and the initial racket pose is then computed by the perspective-n-point (PnP) method. To generate a robust pose, they employed an IMU sensor and fused all of the data by means of an extended Kalman filter (EKF), which lead to a 1.1° rotation error. They don't test the position error since there is no dataset available. Gao et al. [8] employ a markerless method by segmenting the racket red side contours from stereo cameras. A stereo matching method is used to align the points on the contours. The final position error is 7.8 mm and the rotation error is 7.2°. Omron [10] puts 9 small and round markers on each racket side for their Forpheus robot, which can accurately predict the moving direction of the racket based on a high-speed camera. However, these methods are neither convenient nor robust, since they are sensitive to the color and brightness and need to be manually adjusted to find the better color thresholding values.

Inspired by the aforementioned methods, we decompose the 6D pose into position and rotation components. A wireless IMU mounted at the bottom of the racket handle is continuously streaming rotation data. By deeply fusing the IMU information and the camera images, a novel CNN-based method is proposed. The output is the racket 3D position and it is trained fully based on a synthetic dataset.

3   Methodology

3.1   Overview

IMUs are widely used in wearable devices to measure human activity in real-time and with high accuracy. In this paper, we mount a MetaMotionR (MMR) IMU [15] at the bottom of the racket handle, as shown in Fig. 2. With Bosch sensor fusion technology [4], the MMR sensor can provide robust linear acceleration and quaternion values via Bluetooth 4.0 at 100 Hz. Kristen Beange [3] has assessed the MMR sensors, which have a robust performance at 1° error in all axes when considering the absolute angle orientation. They compare the IMU with an optical motion capture equipment (Vicon Motion Systems) during controlled, repetitive sinusoidal motion at frequencies of 20 cpm and 40 cpm (i.e., 0.33 Hz and 0.67 Hz, respectively). Therefore, we mainly focus on the 3D racket position estimation by fusing the IMU and camera in this part.

To estimate the racket position of the human player, we propose a novel approach, as shown in Fig. 2. Compared to the single-stage object pose estimation, two-stage methods usually comprise one step for object detection and another for pose regression, which leads to a very fast inference time and is well suited for the real-time operation in sports. The first stage can be easily replaced with any state-of-art method along the development of the 2D object detection in the future.

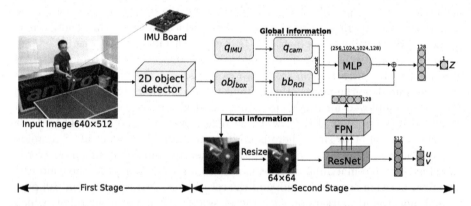

Fig. 2. CNN architecture for the racket position estimation during testing in our scenario. The rotation q_{IMU} is read from a wireless IMU as a 4D quaternion in the IMU frame. It is transformed to the camera frame as q_{cam}. The images with 640×512 pixels are first fed into a pre-trained 2D object detector in order to find the racket bounding box obj_{box} and its position $[x_c, y_c, h, w]$ in pixels. A new region of interest bb_{ROI}, $[x'_{min}, y'_{min}, h', w']$, is computed to compensate the 2D object detection error by Eq. (2). Then quaternions and bb_{ROI} together with the image crops are fed into different network layers in order to extract the global and local features, respectively. The last fully-connected layers output the racket depth Z and the 2D projection point $[u, v]$ of the racket 3D centroid. Finally, X and Y positions can be reconstructed with Eq. (1).

The outputs of our architecture are the depth component Z and the local 2D projection point $[u, v]$ of the racket 3D centroid. Then we can indirectly derive the entire 3D position $[X, Y, Z]$ with the equation below:

$$X = \frac{(x'_{min} + u - c_x) Z}{f_x}, \quad Y = \frac{(y'_{min} + v - c_x) Z}{f_y} \tag{1}$$

where x'_{min}, y'_{min} are the left upper corner in bb_{ROI}. f_x, f_y are the focal lengths in pixels, $[c_x, c_y]$ is a principal point. Here $[u, v]$ is different from $[x_c, y_c]$ which is provided from the object detector, since the later one is not the exact centroid but the center of the detected bounding box. This will affect the $[X, Y]$ a lot when having a large depth Z (from 2.6 m to 5.3 m in our case). Therefore, the position regression problem is decomposed into the following two sub-tasks.

3.2 Racket Centroid Extraction

In order to detect the racket in images, we employ a self-pretrained YOLOv4 [2] model, which is a very fast and accurate one-stage object detector. It can generate a 4-D vector obj_{box} localizing the racket as a 2D bounding box. The obj_{box} is composed of the rectangle center x_c, y_c, height h and width w in image coordinates. To tolerate detection errors and make the subsequent estimation more robust and accurate, we dynamically adjust the obj_{box} to a new region of interest $bb_{ROI} = [x'_{min}, y'_{min}, h', w']$ during training. The bb_{ROI} is computed by the following equations:

$$\begin{cases} s = max(h, w) \\ N = randint(-\alpha s, \alpha s) \\ (h', w') = (\beta s + s, h') \\ (x'_c, y'_c) = (x_c, y_c) + N \\ (x'_{min}, y'_{min}) = (x'_c, y'_c) - 0.5(h', w') \end{cases} \tag{2}$$

where s is the maximum value in h and w. α and β are coefficients to control the center noise N and corner offsets, which are equal to 0.2 and 1.5, respectively. N is a 2D vector of integers, randomly chosen from $-\alpha s$ to αs during training and evaluation, while is set to zero during testing. The resulting obj_{box} has a square size and keeps the same aspect ratio as before.

Finally, it is scaled to the size of 64×64 as the input for the ResNet (see Fig. 2). This *Dynamic Resize* technique is based on the Dynamic Zoom In (DZI) in [11]. In contrast to the DZI that enlarges the crops, here we simply shrink them, since the texture-less surfaces on the racket contain many similar features and it has little influence to the centroid regression. An example with a synthetic image for training is shown in Fig. 3. Then a ResNet18 [9] is deployed to extract the deep features, followed by two dense layers with 512 and 2 units, respectively as shown at the bottom of Fig. 2.

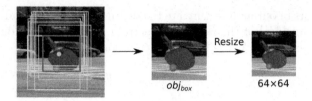

Fig. 3. An example for *Dynamic Resize* during training. **Left**: The detected bounding box (red) from YOLOv4 and the dynamically computed *ROI* candidates (cyan). The bounding box center $[x_c, y_c]$ and the racket centroid $[u, v]$ are marked as blue and green circle, respectively **Middle**: the randomly selected bb_{ROI} for training. **Right**: the final resized crop. (Color figure online)

3.3   Depth Regression

Next, we propose a novel deep fusion approach for the depth Z regression. Intuitively, if we know the bounding box positions in images, the racket 3D position could be estimated by the given camera intrinsics $[f_x, f_y, c_x, c_y]$. However, these positions will change with different orientations and especially if there are occlusions or truncations. To avoid these problems, [25] runs a RetinaNet [12] on the input images and concatenates the generated RoIAlign features and bounding box information as joint features, which are used for translation regression. RoIAlign features are only for predicting rotation. It is a one-stage vehicle pose method, and not sufficiently fast and accurate for sports.

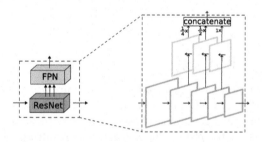

Fig. 4. ResNet-FPN (Feature Pyramid Network).

Inspired from it, we consider the combination of the rotation value q_{cam} and bb_{ROI} as the global features, which are fed into a 4-layer MLP network with 256, 1024, 1024, 128 units separately. The local features indicating the racket local pixel position, size and occlusions, are concatenated with the global network (via $\oplus$ in Fig. 2). A Resnet-FPN network (in Fig. 4) is used for extracting local features, since it includes multi-scale features and can recover the scale ratio information when resizing the *ROI* crops to 64×64. Finally, the depth Z is retrieved as output of a 128-D dense layer.

To train the whole networks, we design a joint position loss function $\mathcal{L}_{\mathrm{pos}}$ to optimize the centroid detection and depth regression as follows:

$$\mathcal{L}_{\mathrm{pos}} = \gamma_1 \cdot |Z - \hat{Z}| + \gamma_2 \cdot \left\| C_{pos} - \hat{C}_{pos} \right\|_1 \tag{3}$$

where Z and $\hat{Z}$ are representing the estimated and ground-truth depth. C_{pos} and $\hat{C}_{pos}$ are the estimated and true centroid pixel positions. γ_1 and γ_2 are used to balance the different errors.

4 Experiments

4.1 Dataset

To train the proposed model, we create a synthetic dataset which can be labeled automatically. A racket CAD model is first reconstructed from a real racket with the free, open-source reconstruction software Meshroom [24], based on the structure from motion (SfM) technique. This results in a reconstructed 3D mesh in Fig. 5 left. Then post-processing is used to remove the background, fill the holes, smooth the surface, blend vertex color, scale the model size, and change the coordinates in Meshlab [7]. The final high-quality 3D model is shown in Fig. 5 right.

Fig. 5. Left: Reconstructed mesh with background from multiple views using Meshroom software. **Right**: the final CAD model with its coordinates.

By using domain randomization (DR) [22], we can generate a set of synthetic images as well as their 6D pose. The racket CAD model is placed in a simulated scene at random positions and rotations. Then, each one is projected into the image plane as the foreground, with a known bounding box. The images from the Pascal VOC dataset are embedded as the background. Each synthetic image is rendered with a random light source position and diffuse reflection. Other techniques, like Gaussian noise, motion blur, ping pong ball and occlusions, are included to reduce the "reality gap". A few examples are presented in Fig. 6(a). Meanwhile, the annotations, including the bounding box positions, racket centroids in pixels and the racket 6D pose, are collected from the simulated 3D scene as the ground truth tags, which are then used to train the object detector and the position regression model, respectively. 50,000 training patterns are collected finally. The resulting range of the depth Z is $[2.6\,\mathrm{m}, 5.3\,\mathrm{m}]$.

For evaluation dataset collection, a usual way that we tried was mounting multiple reflection markers on the racket and then capturing the human player motions with an OptiTrack systems. However, the markers must be placed at the surface in a critical requirement, which would result in many occlusions in images. Therefore, one convenient method is to make use of our KUKA robot that has a racket at the end-effector. This racket differs slightly from the rendered CAD model such that this can also test the robustness against multiple rackets. Another stationary camera opposite to the robot is used to take the images. By moving the robot to given positions and rotations, we collect an evaluation dataset of 208 images (Fig. 6(b)). To obtain the correct pose with respect to the camera coordinate frame, we first calculated the transformation matrix between the robot and the camera by the hand-eye calibration method [21]. The resulting range of the depth Z is from 2.8 m to 5.2 m. To simulate a fast moving racket, we manually apply motion blur (Fig. 6(c)) with a 7×7 kernel on each image for the following comparisons. Due to the high frame rates and fast shutter speed of the cameras, motion blur is actually imperceptible in our case.

(a) Training dataset from synthetic images

(b) Evaluation dataset using another racket in our KUKA robot

(c) Applying motion blur with a 7×7 kernel

Fig. 6. Cropped examples for training and evaluation of the racket position estimation.

4.2   Training and Inference

As shown in Fig. 2, we need to train two separate models one by one for the different stages. To make the first stage (Yolov4) faster, we resize the network input to 512×512 and change the trained model from darknet [2] to the tkDNN [13] framework. The activation function used in the second stage is ReLU [1]. The last two 128-D dense layers for depth Z regression are activated by leaky ReLU, with a negative slope 0.02. The outputs Z and $[u, v]$ are activated by the logistic sigmoid function. All the inputs are normalized for better performance.

To avoid overfitting, we freeze the parameters in the first 4 residual blocks of the ResNet during the beginning 40 epochs. The other hyperparameters are given in the table below (Table 1):

Table 1. Hyperparameters separately for different models.

	Optimizer	Epochs	Batch size	Learning rate
2D object detector	Adam	100	16	3e−3
Position regression	RAdam	100	4	1e−4

The training is processed by a host computer with an NVIDIA RTX 2080Ti GPU, a 3.0 GHz Intel i7-97000 CPU and 32 GB RAM. Each bounding box is extracted by Yolov4 in 7.8 ms, then the depth Z and the centroid $[u, v]$ can be regressed in 1.7 ms. The overall inference rate is around 100 Hz.

4.3   Evaluation

The mAP (mean Average Precision) by Yolov4 is 86.9% for an IoU threshold of 0.5 in the evaluation dataset. To evaluate the position estimation accuracy, we use two metrics: position error E_{trans}, and ≤5 cm. In the ≤5 cm metric, a pose is considered correct if the position error is within 5 cm. Due to some other approaches having large position errors, we extend ≤5 cm to a third metric: ≤10 cm.

Table 2. Evaluation for racket position estimation.

	Sensors	E_{trans}	≤5 cm	≤10 cm
Zhang et al. [27]	Camera, IMU, marker	-	-	-
Gao* et al. [8]	Stereo cameras	2.8 cm	91.8%	100.0%
AAEs [20]	Single camera	39.1 cm	6.7%	17.3.0%
CDPN [11]	Single camera	36.6 cm	7.5%	21.8%
R. Staszak [19]	Single camera	23.5 cm	10.6%	25.0%
OUR (no FPN)	Single camera, IMU	6.8 cm	48.6%	85.1%
OUR (with motion blur)		5.2 cm	60.1%	93.2%
OUR		**4.7 cm**	**65.0%**	**95.5%**

In Table 2, we compare our method with current research in which different sensors are used. Zhang et al. [27] did not show the position error, since they did not have a dataset for evaluation and their method is not compatible with our dataset. The remaining methods are trained and evaluated in our dataset. In order to use stereo cameras in Gao et al. [8], we expand the evaluation dataset by the second well-calibrated camera. Instead of using the color thresholding method to detect the red surface, we extract the racket center either on the red side or on the black side by our centroid regression model. The * indicates it is used with modifications. The resulting performance is the best one. However, it will take twice as much time as ours' and can not extract the rotation value robustly and accurately. Moreover, it needs more effort to pre-calculate the transformation matrix between these two cameras. To get a fair comparison, we replace the rotation head with the true value and only use the translation head in [11, 19, 20]. Among them, [20] and [11] obtain the 3D position under two assumptions: the bounding box size is linearly affected only with respect to the depth Z, and is therefore never changed when having the same Z. These assumptions lead to a large position error when the object is far away from the camera (6 m distance in our case). Although [19] has a bit better results, they still did not take the global pixel positions of the bounding box into consideration. In comparison, our method achieves a more robust performance with the second best accuracy.

Furthermore, two additional experiments, with motion blur (in Fig. 6(c)) and without FPN layers, are performed to simulate a moving racket and do an ablation study, respectively. Figure 7 shows four examples with different movements. To demonstrate this work, we apply the human movements to our KUKA robot with coordinate transformation. The robot uses the penhold grip while playing since it is more flexible and controllable than the shakehand style in our scenario, as shown in the video https://youtu.be/U2YPh_ZwQxQ.

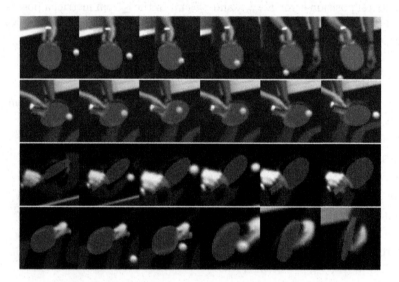

Fig. 7. Four stroke movements for the racket pose estimation.

5   Conclusion

In this paper, we proposed a novel approach for stroke recognition via a camera and IMU. We generated several datasets for training and evaluation. The experiment has shown the proposed method gives a robust performance. With the main goal of improving the capabilities of our table tennis robot in mind, we are planning to apply our approaches to human stroke examples and make the table tennis robot hit the ball by imitating the human movements. In addition, we could also predict the ball's flying trajectory by analyzing the racket pose, since our approach can be run 100 Hz.

However, our approach is going to fail if the detected bounding box is wrong in the first stage. For example, the player's left hand could also be recognized as a racket if there are some circle patterns in the background, as shown in the demo video. In this case, we could utilize the tracking method to identify the coherent relations between frames.

References

1. Agarap, A.F.: Deep learning using rectified linear units (ReLu). CoRR abs/1803.08375 (2018). http://arxiv.org/abs/1803.08375
2. Bochkovskiy, A., Wang, C.-Y., Liao, H.Y.M.: Yolov4: optimal speed and accuracy of object detection. arXiv (2020)
3. Beange, K.: Validation of Wearable Sensor Performance and Placement for the Evaluation of Spine Movement Quality. Ph.D. thesis, University of Ottawa (2019)
4. Bosch : Bosch. https://www.bosch-sensortec.com/
5. Bridgeman, L., Volino, M., Guillemaut, J., Hilton, A.: Multi-person 3D pose estimation and tracking in sports. In: 2019 IEEE/CVF Conference on Computer Vision and Pattern Recognition Workshops (CVPRW), pp. 2487–2496 (2019)
6. Cao, Z., Hidalgo, G., Simon, T., Wei, S.E., Sheikh, Y.: OpenPose: realtime multi-person 2D pose estimation using Part Affinity Fields. arXiv preprint arXiv:1812.08008 (2018)
7. Cignoni, P., Callieri, M., Corsini, M., Dellepiane, M., Ganovelli, F., Ranzuglia, G.: MeshLab: an open-source mesh processing tool. In: Eurographics Italian Chapter Conference, vol. 2008, pp. 129–136 (2008)
8. Gao, Y., Tebbe, J., Krismer, J., Zell, A.: Markerless racket pose detection and stroke classification based on stereo vision for table tennis robots. In: 2019 Third IEEE International Conference on Robotic Computing (IRC), pp. 189–196, February 2019. https://doi.org/10.1109/IRC.2019.00036
9. He, K., Zhang, X., Ren, S., Sun, J.: Deep residual learning for image recognition. In: 2016 IEEE Conference on Computer Vision and Pattern Recognition (CVPR), pp. 770–778 (2016)
10. Kawakami, S., Ikumo, M., Oya, T.: Omron table tennis robot forpheus. https://www.omron.com/innovation/forpheus.html
11. Li, Z., Wang, G., Ji, X.: CDPN: Coordinates-based disentangled pose network for real-time RGB-based 6-DoF object pose estimation. In: Proceedings of the IEEE/CVF International Conference on Computer Vision (ICCV), October 2019
12. Lin, T., Goyal, P., Girshick, R., He, K., Dollár, P.: Focal loss for dense object detection. In: 2017 IEEE International Conference on Computer Vision (ICCV), pp. 2999–3007 (2017)
13. Verucchi, M., Bartoli, L., Bagni, F., Gatti, F., Burgio, P., Bertogna, M.: Real-time clustering and lidar-camera fusion on embedded platforms for self-driving cars. In: 2020 Fourth IEEE International Conference on Robotic Computing (IRC) (2020)

14. von Marcard, T., Henschel, R., Black, M.J., Rosenhahn, B., Pons-Moll, G.: Recovering accurate 3D Human pose in the wild using IMUs and a moving camera. In: Ferrari, V., Hebert, M., Sminchisescu, C., Weiss, Y. (eds.) ECCV 2018. LNCS, vol. 11214, pp. 614–631. Springer, Cham (2018). https://doi.org/10.1007/978-3-030-01249-6_37

15. mbientlab: mbientlab. https://mbientlab.com/

16. Pavllo, D., Feichtenhofer, C., Grangier, D., Auli, M.: 3D human pose estimation in video with temporal convolutions and semi-supervised training. In: Conference on Computer Vision and Pattern Recognition (CVPR) (2019)

17. Peng, S., Liu, Y., Huang, Q., Zhou, X., Bao, H.: PvNet: pixel-wise voting network for 6dof pose estimation. In: IEEE Conference on Computer Vision and Pattern Recognition, CVPR 2019, Long Beach, CA, USA, 16–20 June 2019, pp. 4561–4570 (2019). https://doi.org/10.1109/CVPR.2019.00469

18. Simon, T., Joo, H., Matthews, I., Sheikh, Y.: Hand keypoint detection in single images using multiview bootstrapping. In: CVPR (2017)

19. Staszak, R., Belter, D.: Hybrid 6D object pose estimation from the RGB image. In: ICINCO (2019)

20. Sundermeyer, M., Marton, Z.-C., Durner, M., Brucker, M., Triebel, R.: Implicit 3D Orientation Learning for 6D Object Detection from RGB Images. In: Ferrari, V., Hebert, M., Sminchisescu, C., Weiss, Y. (eds.) ECCV 2018. LNCS, vol. 11210, pp. 699–715. Springer, Cham (2018). https://doi.org/10.1007/978-3-030-01231-1_43

21. Tebbe, J., Gao, Y., Sastre-Rienietz, M., Zell, A.: A table tennis robot system using an industrial KUKA robot arm. In: Brox, T., Bruhn, A., Fritz, M. (eds.) GCPR 2018. LNCS, vol. 11269, pp. 33–45. Springer, Cham (2019). https://doi.org/10.1007/978-3-030-12939-2_3

22. Tobin, J., Fong, R., Ray, A., Schneider, J., Zaremba, W., Abbeel, P.: Domain randomization for transferring deep neural networks from simulation to the real world. In: 2017 IEEE/RSJ International Conference on Intelligent Robots and Systems (IROS), pp. 23–30. IEEE (2017)

23. Wang, J., Qiu, K., Peng, H., Fu, J., Zhu, J.: Ai coach: Deep human pose estimation and analysis for personalized athletic training assistance, pp. 374–382, October 2019. https://doi.org/10.1145/3343031.3350910

24. Wang, Z., Li, J.Z.: Text-enhanced representation learning for knowledge graph. In: IJCAI, pp. 1293–1299 (2016)

25. Wu, D., Zhuang, Z., Xiang, C., Zou, W., Li, X.: 6D-VNet: End-to-end 6DoF vehicle pose estimation from monocular RGB images. In: 2019 IEEE/CVF Conference on Computer Vision and Pattern Recognition Workshops (CVPRW), pp. 1238–1247 (2019)

26. Xiang, Y., Schmidt, T., Narayanan, V., Fox, D.: PoseCNN: a convolutional neural network for 6D object pose estimation in cluttered scenes (2018)

27. Zhang, K., Fang, Z., Liu, J., Wu, Z., Tan, M.: Fusion of vision and IMU to track the racket trajectory in real time. In: 2017 IEEE International Conference on Mechatronics and Automation (ICMA), pp. 1769–1774, August 2017. https://doi.org/10.1109/ICMA.2017.8016085

28. Zhao, Y., Yang, R., Chevalier, G., Gong, M.: Deep residual BIDIR-LSTM for human activity recognition using wearable sensors. CoRR abs/1708.08989 (2017). http://arxiv.org/abs/1708.08989

29. Zimmermann, C., Welschehold, T., Dornhege, C., Burgard, W., Brox, T.: 3D human pose estimation in RGBD images for robotic task learning. In: 2018 IEEE International Conference on Robotics and Automation (ICRA), pp. 1986–1992 (2018)

AMVAE: Asymmetric Multimodal Variational Autoencoder for Multi-view Representation

Wen Youpeng[1], Lin Hongxiang[1], Guo Yiju[1], and Zhao Liang[1,2(✉)]

[1] Dalian University of Technology, Dalian, China
liangzhao@dlut.edu.cn

[2] Key Laboratory for Ubiquitous Network and Service Software of Liaoning Province, Dalian, China

Abstract. Real-world data are typically described using multiple modalities or multiple types of descriptors that are considered as multiple views. The data from different modalities locate in different subspaces, therefore the representations associated with similar semantics would be different. To solve this problem, many approaches have been proposed for fusion representation using data from multiple views. Although effectiveness achieved, most existing models lack precision for gradient diffusion. We proposed Asymmetric Multimodal Variational Autoencoder (AMVAE) to reduce the effect. The proposed model has two key components: multiple autoencoders and multimodal variational autoencoder. Multiple autoencoders are responsible for encoding view-specific data, while the multimodal variational autoencoder guides the generation of fusion representation. The proposed model effectively solves the problem of low precision. The experimental results show that our method is state of the art on several benchmark datasets for both clustering and classification tasks.

Keywords: Multi-view representation · Variational autoencoder · Deep learning

1 Introduction

Real-world data are typically described using multiple modalities or multiple types of descriptors that are considered multiple views. For example, an object may be described as its three views (elevation view, side view, top view). In multimedia content understanding, a multimedia fragment can be described by both its video and audio signals. Another example, in content-based network image retrieval, an object is described by both the visual features of the image and the text around the image. Since the feature data from different modalities locate in different subspaces, the representations associated with similar semantics would be different. Here, this phenomenon is referred to as the heterogeneity gap. Especially in today's world, these multi-view data collected by diverse sensors are highly heterogeneous. The gap between multiple data would hinder the multimodal data from being comprehensively utilized by the subsequent machine learning modules. To solve this problem, many approaches have been proposed for federated representation using data from multiple views [5, 16].

© Springer Nature Switzerland AG 2021
I. Farkaš et al. (Eds.): ICANN 2021, LNCS 12891, pp. 391–402, 2021.
https://doi.org/10.1007/978-3-030-86362-3_32

Most of the current multi-view learning frameworks focus on specific tasks (e.g., fake news detection [6], cluster [28]). These tasks usually have two integral parts, one to extract representations from the multiple data and the other to perform specific tasks with the representations. The two parts are coupled together for the specific task. But it is significant to use the only part for extracting representation. Because we can unify the multi-view data into a low-dimensional representation which is convenient for downstream task algorithms (e.g., K-means, classification algorithms).

There are a complex correlation and a high degree of heterogeneity between the different views, so exploring multiple views representation is a long-term challenge. Canonical Correlation Analysis (CCA) [8] is a classical method to find relationships between multiple views of data. This method reduces the dimensionality of data from multiple views to obtain two representations that have the max linear correlation. Moreover, Deep Canonical Correlation Analysis (DCCA) [1] combines a deep neural network with CCA to learn nonlinear mappings from high dimensional data to low dimensional representations. Deep Matrix Factorization (DMF-MVC) [28] proposed a solution based on deep matrix factorization, which uses semi-non-negative matrix factorization to get the hierarchical semantics of multiple data. Another type of method is mainly based on the framework of autoencoder (e.g., AE^2 − Nets [27], MVAE [6]). Autoencoder [2] is widely used for unsupervised learning on single-view via reducing the dimensionality of input data. AE^2 − Nets [27] proposed taking advantages of AE-net to get a lower-dimensional representation of each view, which is used in degra-net to get a fusion representation. MVAE [6] concatenates encoding which is encoded by the encoder of each view and uses Variational Autoencoder (VAE) [10] to get a representation.

Although current algorithms have achieved effectiveness on multi-view learning, there are still some problems. For the family of CCA [1,8,23] and DMF-MVC [28], they all assume sufficient correlations between different views. Because different views are highly heterogeneous, independence between different views makes these algorithms not work. For the family of AE [6,27], they solve the correlation problem. They extract features from each view individually and use some clever methods (e.g., degrad [27], variational bayes [6]) to get a representation. But because of the gradient diffusion, these networks often have few layers so that it cannot integrate multimodal information fully. Therefore, we proposed a novel algorithm to fully use the information of multi-view for representation learning.

We proposed Asymmetric Multimodal Variational Autoencoder (AMVAE) for multi-view representation learning. The proposed model has two key components, multiple autoencoders and multimodal variational autoencoder. Multiple autoencoders are responsible for encoding view-specific data, while the multimodal variational autoencoder guides the generation of fusion representation. The main contributions of our work are summarized as follows:

- We proposed a novel multi-view representation model - Asymmetric Multimodal Variational Autoencoder (AMVAE) for multi-view representation learning.
- Our proposed model is able to find correlations between different views and therefore leading to a better multimodal shared representation.

- We extensively evaluate the performance of the proposed AMVAE on several datasets for clustering and classification tasks, the results show that our model is state of the art.

The rest of the paper is organized as follows. In Sect. 2, we review the multi-view representation learning briefly. In Sect. 3, we present our proposed model in detail. In Sect. 4, we describe the implementation details of the novel model. Conclusions and future work are presented in Sect. 5.

2   Related Work

The representation learning based on multi-modal data is to complete the learning task by using the relation between different views. Meanwhile, the data of multi-modal is complementary to make up for the shortage of single modal, which has attracted great attention in recent years. For multi-view supervised learning, MVAE [6] proposed a multi-mode variational auto-encoder to capture the shared representation of text and image and was trained for the task of classifying fake news in Twitter. There are methods [18,25] that aggregate decisions from multiple classifiers, where each classifier is based on single modal learning. Under certain assumptions, the results illustrate the advantages of aggregating multi-view classifiers for subsequent tasks. For clustering tasks, algorithms based on joint training [11] and collaborative regularization [12] keep the clustering assumptions consistent for different views. Other multi-view clustering methods mainly focus on the purpose of dimension reduction [26], which take advantage of the complementarity of multiple views and the similarity among the data points for reducing the multi-view dimension.

Unsupervised multi-view representation tasks are challenging because there is no category information to guide the learning process. In the process of solving this challenge, many novel and effective methods have emerged, which are mainly divided into two categories: one is the traditional machine learning method, represented by Canonical Correlation Analysis (CCA) [8], and the other is the deep learning method which takes autoencoder as the prototype. CCA searches the hidden space to maximize the potential relevance between multiple views. Due to its ability to deal with nonlinear correlations, Kernel Canonical Correlation Analysis (KCCA) [23] has been widely applied to the integration or dimension reduction of multi-view features. Deep Canonical Correlation Analysis (DCCA) [1] combines the advantages of deep learning that can effectively extract multi-view features, aiming at learning two deep neural networks (DNN) to maximize the typical correlation between two views.

The other kind of method is mainly the framework of the autoencoder. Under the deep learning framework, the model based on the autoencoder [17] learns a compact representation of the optimal reconstructed input. MVAE [6] adds a variational structure on the basis of the auto-encoder and can learn the probabilistic potential variable model by optimizing the boundary of the marginal likelihood value of the observed multi-view data. $AE^2 - Nets$ [27] proposed inner AE networks to encode the features of each view, while degradation networks reduce dimensions and integrate hidden vectors from multiple views to get multi-view representation. $AE^2 - Nets$ is a relatively new result of multi-view representation learning.

There are some other interesting methods. I. Gallo et al. [4] fused pictures and text together to form a new picture which is classified by CNNs. N. Punn et al. [19] proposed a novel 3D deep neural network components based on inception U-Net architecture [21] for brain tumor segmentation.

3   Asymmetric Multimodal Variational Autoencoder

In this section, we present AMVAE for learning multi-view representation. In this paper, $X = \{X^{(1)}, ..., X^{(V)}\}$ is used to represent multi-view data, where $X^{(v)} \in \mathbb{R}^{d_v \times n}$ is the feature matrix of the vth view in the whole V views, d_v and n being dimensionality of feature space and the number of samples for the vth view respectively. The purpose of multi-view representation learning is to obtain a fused representation. For the goal, we use multiple autoencoders to learn latent vectors from multiple views. Then the multimodal variational autoencoder ensures the representation to be learned.

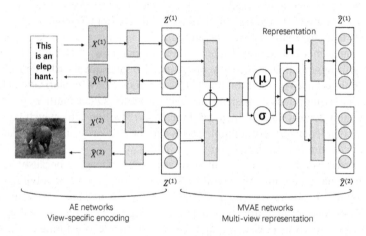

Fig. 1. Overview of Asymmetric Multimodal Variational Autoencoder (AMVAE). The whole net has two main components. The part of the autoencoder networks is to generate view-specific latent features, while the multimodal variational autoencoder fuses the latent code and generates gaussian distribution as representation. The proposed model can be viewed as Asymmetric Multimodal Variational Autoencoder which has a complex encoder.

3.1   Multiple Autoencoders

In order to obtain complete information from every single view, we use Autoencoder networks. The reasons are as follows: 1. Autoencoder is widely used in unsupervised learning, which is exactly consistent with the fact that we have no supervisory information such as category information. 2. Autoencoder can effectively extract the features of high-dimensional data in a single view and reduce noise.

First, the encoder for the vth view is defined as

$$Z^{(v)} = f_e^{(v)}(X^{(v)}, \lambda_e^{(v)}),$$

(1)

where $Z^{(v)} \in \mathbb{R}^{h_v \times n}$ is the latent features of the vth view, h_v is the dimension of latent features. $\lambda_e^{(L,v)} = \{W_e^{(l,v)}, b_e^{(l,v)}\}^L, l \in (0, L)$ is the parameter set, where L is the number of layers of encoder network and $W_e^{(l,v)}, b_e^{(l,v)}$ is the weight and bias between layer l and layer $l + 1$ respectively.

Second, we define the vth view's decoder as follows

$$\hat{X}^{(v)} = f_d^{(v)}(Z^{(v)}, \lambda_d^{(v)}), \tag{2}$$

where $\hat{X}^{(v)} \in \mathbb{R}^{d_v \times n}$ is the matrix reconstructed from $Z^{(v)}$ by decoder. Similar to the encoder, $\lambda_d^{(L,v)} = \{W_d^{(l,v)}, b_d^{(l,v)}\}^L, l \in (0, L)$ is the parameter set of the vth decoder.

In order to obtain the latent features $Z^{(v)}$ of the vth view, we should minimize the end-to-end reconstruction loss, which is defined as follows

$$Loss_{ae-rec} = \frac{1}{2}\sum_{v=1}^{V}\|X^{(v)} - \hat{X}^{(v)}\|. \tag{3}$$

3.2 Multimodal Variational Autoencoder

In Subsect. 3.1, we obtain the latent features for each view, then, we fuse these highly heterogeneous latent features. In this section, we use the structure of MVAE. The encoder of MVAE encodes the latent features of different views into a hidden vector, and the decoder reconstructs the original multi-view feature information from the hidden vector.

The encoder of MVAE fuses the multi-view latent features into a hidden vector, we define it as

$$M^{(v)} = f_{mvae\_e}^{(v)}(Z^{(v)}, \phi_e), \tag{4}$$

$$H_{in} = \phi(W_v \bigoplus_{v=i}^{V} M^{(v)} + b_v), \tag{5}$$

In the Eq. (4), the vth view's latent features $Z^{(v)}$ is nonlinear mapped to $M^{(v)}$ by several fully-connected layers. Then, $M^{(v)}$ are concatenated (operator $\bigoplus$ is used to concatenate vectors) and passed through a fully-connected layer to generate the shared representation H_{in}. In the Eq. (5), W_b and b_v are weight and bias of the fully-connected layer respectively, and ϕ is the activation function. From the shared representation H_{in} we get the mean μ and the variance σ that can be thought of as representing the distribution. Subsequently, we sample a random variable ϵ from the prior Gaussian distribution. The final representation is denoted as

$$H = \mu + \sigma \circ \epsilon, \tag{6}$$

The MVAE decoder is similar in structure to the encoder but upside down, whose goal is to generate reconstruction $\hat{Z}^{(v)} \in \mathbb{R}^{h_v \times n}$ vector from sampled mutimodal representation

$$\hat{Z}^{(v)} = f_{mvae_d}^{(v)}(H, \phi_d). \tag{7}$$

In Fig. 1, the structure of our model is shown clearly. Intuitively, the model is a Multimodal Variational Autoencoder having a more complex encoder. So we called it Asymmetric Multimodal Variational Autoencoder.

MVAE is trained by optimizing reconstruction loss and Kullback - Leibler Divergence. We define the reconstruction loss for the latent feature of each view.

$$Loss_{mvae-rec} = \frac{1}{2} \sum_{v=1}^{V} \| Z^{(v)} - \hat{Z}^{(v)} \|, \tag{8}$$

KL Divergence is used to measure the similarity between two distributions, here we define the KL divergence of the shared representation distribution relative to the target distribution (normal distribution)

$$Loss_{kl} = \frac{1}{2} \sum_{k=1}^{d_h} (\mu_k^2 + \sigma_k^2 - log(\sigma_k) - 1), \tag{9}$$

In the end, our goal is to optimize the sum of all losses.

$$\min_{\{\lambda, \phi\}} (Loss_{ae-rec} + Loss_{mvae-rec} + Loss_{kl}). \tag{10}$$

Finally, we train the whole network until convergence to obtain the shared representation.

4   Experiments

In this section, we compare the proposed model in five benchmark datasets with several state-of-the-art multi-view representation learning models.

Table 1. Clustering performance comparison for different algorithms

Method	Handwritten		ORL		CUB-200		COIL-20		Caltech101-7	
	NMI	ACC	NMI	ACC	NMI	ACC	NMI	ACC	NMI	ACC
FeatConcate	76.40	75.32	78.97	62.41	71.30	73.79	78.21	71.64	56.33	47.22
CCA	69.57	66.81	76.10	57.15	48.51	46.10	69.33	58.69	50.59	46.41
DCCA	75.21	72.49	77.84	62.21	52.57	55.10	76.10	64.12	60.64	58.25
DMF-MVC	72.73	71.98	78.22	66.52	40.50	39.38	72.44	59.61	46.91	57.85
AE^2 − Nets	71.50	82.27	86.73	68.90	**77.82**	77.94	83.37	74.10	**61.66**	**65.28**
MVAE	76.22	78.38	85.40	69.14	68.59	64.20	79.52	68.44	58.27	62.44
Ours	**80.93**	**86.77**	**87.54**	**76.07**	77.17	**78.43**	**84.01**	**75.94**	54.17	56.22

Table 2. Classification performance comparison for different algorithms

Method	Handwritten	ORL	CUB-200	COIL-20	Caltech101-7
FeatConcate	89.70	78.26	82.55	78.50	87.98
CCA	94.45	77.34	64.21	91.23	92.74
DCCA	95.23	84.92	66.76	90.41	92.80
DMF-MVC	94.66	93.13	59.37	95.49	89.43
$AE^2 - $ Nets	96.89	97.90	84.78	96.15	**93.92**
MVAE	95.47	95.29	83.52	95.87	91.25
Ours	**97.25**	**98.11**	**86.19**	**96.77**	92.68

4.1   Experiments Settings

Datasets. To show that our model is working well with diverse datasets, we choose the following datasets.

- **handwritten** [3]: A dataset containing 2000 images consists of 10 handwritten numeral classes from number 0 to 9. We use pix (240 pixel averages in 2×3 windows) and fac (216 profile correlations) as two views.
- **ORL**[1]: it contains 40 subjects and each set of 10 different images.
- **Caltech-UCSD Birds (CUB-200)** [22]: An image dataset of 200 bird species. We use 1024-dimensional features extracted by GoogLeNet and 300-dimensional features based on text.
- **COIL-20** [15]: it contains 1440 images of 20 object categories. Each category has 72 photos of the same object taken from different views. For COIL-2o and ORL, we use Gabor descriptors and gray levels as two views.
- **Caltech101-7** [13]: it contains a subset of 1474 images in 7 categories selected from Caltech101. We use the HOG and GIST descriptors as two views.

Comparison Methods. To verify the validity of our model, we selected six baseline models.

- **FeatConcate:** This method only concatenates different multi-view features.
- **CCA:** Canonical Correlation Analysis (CCA) [8] maximizes the linear correlation of different views to obtain two representations and combine them together.
- **DCCA:** Deep Canonical Correlation Analysis (DCCA) [1] is based on CCA but adds deep neural network to obtain more detailed low-dimensional representation.
- **DMF-MVC:** Deep Semi-nonnegative Matrix Factorization for Multi-View Clustering (DMF-MVC) [28] combines semi-nonnegative matrix factorization with deep neural network to find shared representation of different views, which is used for clustering tasks. Here, we use it for representation learning.
- $AE^2 - $ **Nets:** Autoencoder in Autoencoder Networks ($AE^2 - $ Nets) [27] uses inner autoencoder networks to obtain detailed information of each view, and utilizes degradation networks to get a shared representation.

---

[1] https://www.cl.cam.ac.uk/research/dtg/attarchive/facedatabase.html.

- **MVAE:** Multimodal Variational Autoencoder for Fake News Detection (MVAE) [6] utilizes multiple variational autoencoder to learn probabilistic latent representation and optimizes it by minimizing the Kullback-Leibler Divergence of the shared representation distribution relative to the normal distribution.

Because the dimensions of the input data are different, we set different network structures to different datasets. Our detailed settings are shown in Table 3. We train the model for 300 epochs with an early stopping. The learning rate is 0.001. We set the weight penalty to 0.2. We employ $f(x) = sigmoid(x)$ as the activation function. l_2-norm is used as regularization for initializing the variables. We use Adam [9] as the optimizer. We make the code publicly available[2].

Table 3. Description the structure of our model

Datasets	View	Encoder/decoder of AE networks	Encoder/decoder of MVAE networks	H
Handwritten	view1	(input_shape, 200)	(200, 150, 32)	64
	view2	(input_shape, 200)	(200, 150, 32)	
ORL	view1	(input_shape, 512, 256)	(256, 128, 64)	128
	view2	(input_shape, 512, 256)	(256, 128, 64)	
CUB-200	view1	(input_shape, 512, 256)	(256, 128, 64)	128
	view2	(input_shape, 256, 128)	(128, 128, 64)	
COIL-20	view1	(input_shape, 512, 256)	(256, 128, 64)	128
	view2	(input_shape, 512, 256)	(256, 128, 64)	
Caltech101-7	view1	(input_shape, 1024, 512, 256)	(256, 256)	320
	view2	(input_shape, 256, 128)	(128, 128, 64)	

4.2   Evaluation

We evaluate the effects of the clustering task and the classification task respectively. For the clustering task, we apply k-means algorithm to the shared representation H which is represented by our method. We use k-means because this algorithm is simple and can reflect the quality of representation by Euclidean distance.

We use Accuracy (ACC) [24], Normalized Mutual Information, to evaluate clustering performance. ACC is defined as

$$ACC = \frac{\sum_{i=1}^{n} \delta(y_i, map(l_i))}{n},$$

where n is the number of samples, y_i and l_i are the ground truth label and the resolved label respectively. $map(l_i)$ is used to map the cluster label l_i to the ground truth label. The best mapping can be obtained by the Kuhn-Munkres algorithm [20]. $\delta(x, y)$ equals

---

[2] https://github.com/jirufengyu/AMVAE.

1 when $x = y$, otherwise $\delta(x, y) = 0$. NMI is a standard measure to calculate the similarity between two labels of the same data. It is defined as

$$NMI = \frac{I(y, l)}{max H(y), H(l)}.$$

where $I(y, l)$ is the mutual information between ground truth label y and cluster label l, and function H calculates their entropy.

Details of the performance of the different algorithms are shown in Table 1. Our model works better in four data sets except for the Caltech101-7 data set. As expected, the completely neural network-based method (MVAE, $AE^2 - Nets$) performs better than other methods (DCCAE, DMF-MVC) that combined traditional algorithm and neural network. Since CCA only pursues linear correlation, it does not perform well. $AE^2 - Nets$ performs better than MVAE except for the handwritten dataset. One possible reason is that the handwritten dataset is relatively small, and the degradation networks are overoptimized, resulting in overfitting. Our model not only combines MVAE to effectively integrate multimodal data but also combines multiple AEs of $AE^2 - Nets$ to effectively obtain latent features, so it performs better than the above two methods.

For the classification task, we employ k-nearest neighbours (kNN) algorithm. Similar to the clustering task, we use this method because it is simple and fair for all methods. We use standard accuracy as the metric. We split data into 80% training sets and 20% test sets. Table 2 shows the detailed results of the experiment. The proposed method still performs well on the four data sets. Our method performs poorly on Caltech101-7 for both classification task and clustering task, probably because the information we extract is incomplete by GoogLeNet. Compared with MVAE, our model results are better and show that deeping the depth of the autoencoder network could improve feature extraction.

We conduct ablation studies on five datasets. We evaluate four approaches: 1. multiple AEs represent multi-view data and concatenate them together. 2. MVAE 3. AMVAE 4. AMVAE with mutual information [7] (AMVAE + MI). We use these four methods to get the shared representation and then use clustering algorithm to evaluate the validity of our model. Table 4 shows the performance of the four approaches. AMVAE performs better than both AEs and MVAE. It demonstrates that our model improves the accuracy of clustering effectively. MVAE contributes more to the effective improvement of AMVAE. We also experiment with the method of adding mutual information (MI) [7]. AMVAE + MI performs slightly worse than AMVAE on the first four datasets. One possible cause is overfitting.

Table 4. Ablation studies on five datasets.

Method	Handwritten		ORL		CUB-200		COIL-20		Caltech101-7	
	NMI	ACC	NMI	ACC	NMI	ACC	NMI	ACC	NMI	ACC
AEs	71.45	69.52	72.86	62.39	47.13	54.64	70.08	60.11	52.18	49.76
MVAE	76.22	78.38	85.40	69.14	68.59	64.20	79.52	68.44	58.27	**62.44**
AMVAE	**80.93**	**86.77**	**87.54**	**76.07**	77.17	**78.43**	**84.01**	**75.94**	54.17	56.22
AMVAE + MI	78.65	85.61	84.91	73.43	**78.26**	78.17	82.97	73.23	**59.38**	58.75

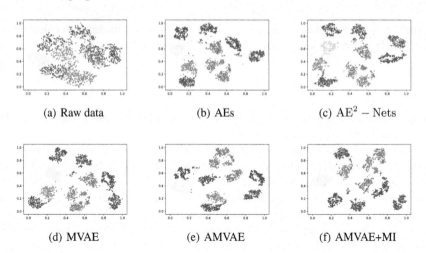

Fig. 2. Visualization of the shared representation using handwritten dataset

As shown in Fig. 2, We visualize our learned shared representation with t-SNE [14] comparing with other methods using handwritten dataset. Figure 2(a) represents the space of concatenating raw data, Fig. 2(b) is the result of AEs, Fig. 2(c) and (d) show the shared representation of $AE^2 -$ Nets and MVAE respectively, and the rest are our proposed model with different strategies. The results demonstrate the shared representations obtained by our method have a more clear distribution structure.

5   Conclusion

This paper introduces a novel model for multi-view representation learning. Our model innovatively uses multiple autoencoders to obtain latent codes and then uses multimodal variational autoencoder to get hidden representations. The experiments show that AMVAE outperforms the comparison state-of-the-art algorithms on most of the data. In the future, we probably extend the current AMVAE. For example, because of the experimental results (superposition autoencoder can better extract features.), we will consider the design of residual multi-view autoencoder networks to obtain a better intact representation.

Acknowledgement. This work is supported by the National Natural Science Foundation of China (61906030), the Science and the Fundamental Research Funds for the Central Universities (DUT20RC(4)009) and Natural Science Foundation of Liaoning Province (2020-BS-063).

References

1. Andrew, G., Arora, R., Bilmes, J., Livescu, K.: Deep canonical correlation analysis. In: International Conference on International Conference on Machine Learning (2013)
2. Cun, Y.L.: Modles connexionnistes de l'apprentissage. Intellectica **2**(1), 114–143 (1987)
3. Dua, D., Graff, C.: UCI machine learning repository (2017). http://archive.ics.uci.edu/ml
4. Gallo, I., Calefati, A., Nawaz, S., Janjua, M.K.: Image and encoded text fusion for multimodal classification. In: 2018 Digital Image Computing: Techniques and Applications (DICTA), pp. 1–7. IEEE (2018)
5. Guo, W., Wang, J., Wanga, S.: Deep multimodal representation learning: a survey. IEEE Access **7**(99), 63373–63394 (2019)
6. Gupta, S., Thirukovalluru, R., Sinha, M., Mannarswamy, S.: MVAE: multimodal variational autoencoder for fake news detection. In: The World Wide Web Conference, pp. 2915–2921 (2019)
7. Hjelm, R.D., et al.: Learning deep representations by mutual information estimation and maximization. arXiv preprint arXiv:1808.06670 (2018)
8. Hotelling, H.: Relations between two sets of variates. Biometrika, 321–377 (1936)
9. Kingma, D.P., Ba, J.: Adam: a method for stochastic optimization. arXiv preprint arXiv:1412.6980 (2014)
10. Kingma, D.P., Welling, M.: Auto-encoding variational bayes. In: ICLR (2014)
11. Kumar, A., Iii, H.D.: A co-training approach for multi-view spectral clustering Abhishek Kumar. In: Proceedings of the 28th International Conference on Machine Learning, ICML 2011, Bellevue, Washington, USA, June 28–July 2 2011 (2011)
12. Kumar, A., Rai, P., Daumé, H.: Co-regularized multi-view spectral clustering. Adv. Neural Inf. Process. Syst. **24**, 1413–1421 (2011)
13. Li, F.F., Fergus, R., Perona, P.: Learning generative visual models from few training examples: an incremental Bayesian approach tested on 101 object categories. In: 2004 Conference on Computer Vision and Pattern Recognition Workshop (2004)
14. Van der Maaten, L., Hinton, G.: Visualizing data using t-SNE. J. Mach. Learn. Res. **9**(11), 2579–2605 (2008)
15. Nene, S.A.: Columbia object image library (COIL-20). Technical report 5 (1996)
16. Ngiam, J., Khosla, A., Kim, M., Nam, J., Lee, H., Ng, A.Y.: Multimodal deep learning. In: ICML, pp. 689–696 (2011). https://icml.cc/2011/papers/399_icmlpaper.pdf
17. Ngiam, J., Khosla, A., Kim, M., Nam, J., Lee, H., Ng, A.Y.: Multimodal deep learning. In: ICML (2011)
18. Oza, N.C., Tumer, K.: Classifier ensembles: select real-world applications. Inf. Fusion **9**(1), 4–20 (2008)
19. Punn, N.S., Agarwal, S.: Multi-modality encoded fusion with 3d inception U-Net and decoder model for brain tumor segmentation. Multimedia Tools Appl., 1–16 (2020)
20. Richardson, R.G.: American mathematical society. A.I.E.E. J. **47**(1506), 100 (1918)
21. Ronneberger, O., Fischer, P., Brox, T.: U-Net: convolutional networks for biomedical image segmentation. In: Navab, N., Hornegger, J., Wells, W.M., Frangi, A.F. (eds.) MICCAI 2015. LNCS, vol. 9351, pp. 234–241. Springer, Cham (2015). https://doi.org/10.1007/978-3-319-24574-4_28
22. Welinder, P., et al.: Caltech-UCSD Birds 200. Technical report. CNS-TR-2010-001, California Institute of Technology (2010)
23. Welling, M.: Kernel canonical correlation analysis. Department of Computer Science University of Toronto, Canada (2005)
24. Xu, W., Liu, X., Gong, Y.: Document clustering based on non-negative matrix factorization. In: Proceedings of ACM SIGIR, pp. 267–273 (2003)

25. Yang, P., Zhou, X., Wang, D.Z., Patwa, I., Gong, D., Fang, C.V.: Multimodal ensemble fusion for disambiguation and retrieval. IEEE Multimedia **23**(2), 42–52 (2016)
26. Zhang, C., Fu, H., Hu, Q., Zhu, P., Cao, X.: Flexible multi-view dimensionality co-reduction. IEEE Trans. Image Process. **26**, 648–659 (2016)
27. Zhang, C., Liu, Y., Fu, H.: AE2-Nets: autoencoder in autoencoder networks. In: 2019 IEEE/CVF Conference on Computer Vision and Pattern Recognition (CVPR) (2019)
28. Zhao, H., Ding, Z., Fu, Y.: Multi-view clustering via deep matrix factorization. In: Proceedings of the Thirty-First AAAI Conference on Artificial Intelligence, AAAI 2017, pp. 2921–2927. AAAI Press (2017)

Enhancing Separate Encoding with Multi-layer Feature Alignment for Image-Text Matching

Keyu Wen[1], Linyang Li[2], and Xiaodong Gu[1(✉)] [iD]

[1] Department of Electronic Engineering, School of Information Science
and Technology, Fudan University, Shanghai 200438, China
{kywen19,xdgu}@fudan.edu.cn
[2] Shanghai Key Laboratory of Intelligent Information Processing,
School of Computer Science, Fudan University, Shanghai 200438, China
lyli19@fudan.edu.cn

Abstract. There is a surge of interest in cross-modal representation
learning, concerning mainly images and texts. Image-Text Matching task
is one major challenge in cross-modal tasks. Traditional methods use
multi-paths to encode features across modalities separately and project
them into a shared latent space. Recently, the development of pre-trained
models inspires people to learn cross-modal features jointly and boost
performances through large-scale data. However, traditional methods are
less effective when both modalities use pre-trained uni-modal encoders.
Methods that encode features jointly would face an unacceptable calculation cost during inference, thus less valuable for real-time applications.
In this paper, we first explore the pros and cons of these methods, then
we propose an enhanced separate encoding framework, using an extra
encoding process to project multi-layer features of pre-trained encoders
into a similar latent space. Experiments show that our framework outperforms current methods that do not use large-scale image-text pairs in
both Flickr30K and MS-COCO datasets while maintaining minimal cost
during inference.

Keywords: Image-text matching · Separate encoding · Cross modal

1 Introduction

With the development of deep learning, neural networks achieve great progress
in computer vision and natural language processing. Cross-modal tasks, mainly
between images and texts, are gaining more and more attention [5]. In this work,
we focus on one major task in cross-modal learning: image-text matching.

The goal of the image-text matching task is to find the most matching pairs
through a large number of given images and texts. Thus, in real-time applications, it is vital to find the best matches of the given images/texts efficiently.

K. Wen and L. Li—Equal contribution.

© Springer Nature Switzerland AG 2021
I. Farkaš et al. (Eds.): ICANN 2021, LNCS 12891, pp. 403–414, 2021.
https://doi.org/10.1007/978-3-030-86362-3_33

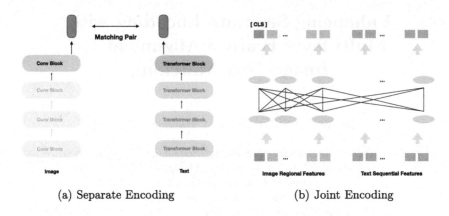

(a) Separate Encoding   (b) Joint Encoding

Fig. 1. Different encoding methods

Traditional solutions in deep learning are to find a shared latent space [25] by encoding image and text features separately. Normally, convolution-based [11] networks are used to encode images while RNN-based [8] networks such as LSTM [12] are applied for text encoding. Then the distance measurements like cosine similarity are used to calculate the similarity of the pooled vectors from different modalities. A triplet ranking loss [25] is then applied to train the neural network for finding the most similar pairs across modalities. These architectures can be illustrated by Fig. 1(a). As shown, features across modalities are isolated since they are separately encoded.

Recently, there has been much progress achieved with the development of pre-trained models in different modalities. These improvements make it possible to joint-encode the features across modalities to learn a joint representation of vision and language.

Pre-trained models push the state-of-the-art performances of many tasks to a new level. In the CV field, the pre-trained models, such as VGG [24] and ResNet [11], have been regarded as the backbone models to extract the visual features for the downstream tasks. In the NLP field, the pre-trained models, exemplified by ELMo [19], GPT [21] and BERT [6], use fine-tuning method to achieve new state-of-the-art performances in downstream tasks like natural language inference [2].

The arise of pre-trained encoders allows separate encoding to encode single modal features with higher representation quality. However, the distribution of pre-trained encoders are different across modalities, thus the traditional usage of bottom-up structures (Fig. 1(a)) would make it difficult to project cross-modality features into a shared latent space.

Later in the cross-modal field, following the idea of applying large-scale data to create pre-trained models, joint encoding methods are based on large-scale image-text paired data [15]. This architecture, shown in Fig. 1(b), combines texts and images together through an attention-based structure [27] encoder to learn joint representations across two modalities. These models, exemplified by Unicoder-VL [15], UNITER [4], achieve new state-of-the-art results on many cross-modal tasks like VQA [1], image-captioning [3] as well as image-text matching [25]. In image captioning and VQA tasks, the goal is to generate corresponding captions or to find answer spans, which requires images and texts to entangle with each other. Joint-encoding models boost these tasks to a whole new level.

However, in the image-text matching task, the goal is to find the most matching pair from a large number of images and texts.

Since joint encoding methods combine the texts and images as inputs to the model, during inference, these models require the pre-trained structure to iterate all possible pairs which take massive calculation consumption. We name such unacceptable cost *Inference Disaster*. Such a problem constrains these models in real-time usage despite its outstanding performance.

As illustrated above, in the image-text matching task, traditional methods are relatively weak in representation encoding compared with joint-encoding methods based on pre-training with large-scale image-text pairs. Meanwhile, the joint-encoding methods suffer from the inference disaster.

In this work, in order to maintain the retrieval efficiency as well as promoting the performance of the model, we propose an **Enhanced Separate Encoding Framework** to modify the separate encoding framework, focusing on excavating multi-layer features of separate pre-trained visual and textual encoders and projecting them to the common subspace.

Our proposed framework is constructed based on separate encoding models, thus is very efficient during inference compared with the joint-encoding methods.

We attach extra encoding modules to align and project features across modalities. These extra modules extract features from the entire pre-trained encoder in different modalities and project them in a shared latent space, thus the representations across modalities are less distant compared with separate pre-trained features.

Experiments show that our proposed framework achieves competitive performances against joint-encoding methods without using large-scale image-text pairs for pre-training and outperforms all previous traditional separate-encoding methods in Flickr30K and MS-COCO dataset.

To summarize our Contributions:

(a) We analyze the traditional separate-encoding methods as well as recent joint-encoding methods, pointing out the importance of both performances and efficiency in the image-text matching task.
(b) We propose a framework to break the limit of separate encoding methods. The framework outperforms all previous separate encoding methods and achieves competitive performances against joint-encoding methods, meanwhile, it does not use large-scale image-text pairs.

2   Related Work

2.1   Traditional Methods in Image-Text Matching

Encoding features from different modalities separately is the major method used before. The goal is to find a better shared latent space of image features and text features. Triplet ranking loss is introduced by [25] and used to narrow down the distance between matching pairs. [9] incorporated a hard negative method to focus on maximum violating negative pairs, which is widely applied by later works. More recently, [14, 28] introduced faster-RCNN network to use regional semantic features to enhance the image encoding quality. Other approaches such as incorporating knowledge graphs [23], using graph networks [16, 29] are explored to further boost the performances. Most of these methods encode image features with pre-trained models such as ResNet and faster-RCNN, while encoding text features with RNNs. Thus, when incorporating pre-trained text encoders, it is more difficult to learn a shared latent space in two different distributions from pre-trained encoders across modalities.

2.2   Pre-trained Models and Joint-Encoding

In computer vision field, ResNet [11] and VGG [24] are widely used as backbones in vision models. These convolution-based structure models are trained using image classification data such as ImageNet. Models like Fast RCNN [10], Faster RCNN [22] are built based on these backbone models and aim for detection and segmentation tasks.

Recent arise of pre-trained models in natural language processing started with ELMo [19], using unsupervised data to train language models. GPT [21] and BERT [6] introduce the attention-based structure called transformer [27], take the NLP research into a new era of pre-training. These successes of pre-trained models motivate researchers to construct cross-modal pre-trained models using large-scale cross-modal datasets. These models use pre-calculated regional features combined with text sequences to create joint-encoded features, exemplified by UNITER [4], Unicoder-VL [15] and LXMERT [26]. These models achieve great performances in cross-modal tasks such as VQA, image captioning; yet in the image-text matching task, the inference efficiency is limited by its joint-encoding nature.

3   Limits of Previous Encoding Methods

3.1   Different Distribution in Separate Encoding

When both modalities are equipped with pre-trained encoders, exemplified by ResNet in images and BERT in texts, the distribution is different inherently, making previous methods difficult to project different modalities into a shared latent space.

3.2   Inference Disaster in Joint Encoding

Joint-Encoding models use large-scale image-text paired data to pre-train the joint-encoding models [4,15,17,26,30].

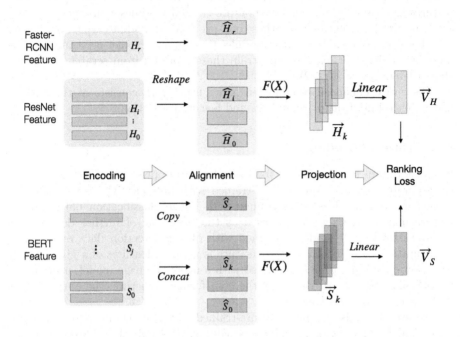

Fig. 2. Structure of enhanced separate encoding framework

Most of these methods firstly encode input image region features that are extracted from an RCNN model trained with [13]. These regional features from original images play roles as tokens in a sequence.

Despite the excellent performances in downstream tasks, such structures would face a massive calculation consume problem during inference in the matching task: Suppose N sequences(captions) and M images are to be examined, which are total $M \times N$ entangled pairs. Suppose the inference time for each pair is T, with a batch-size B. The model needs to went through $M \times N$ times inference, resulting in a time cost $\frac{M \times N \times T}{B}$, which has an $O(n^2)$ time complexity. While inference with separately encoded features only need to run a cosine similarity between pairs, which has an $O(n)$ time complexity.

4   Framework Construction

Separate encoding methods would be less effective in applying pre-trained encoders in both modalities, considering that features in two modalities are under different distribution; meanwhile, joint encoding methods, though encoding jointly, would suffer from a less efficient inference process. Leveraging advantages and disadvantages, we propose an enhanced separate encoding method, aiming to narrow down the distance between features from two different pre-trained encoders. The core motivation is that allowing separately pre-trained features to be further encoded by non-pre-trained modules, thus these features are more similar in nature since these non-pre-trained modules are more aligned.

Therefore, we construct extra modules to align and extract pre-trained cross-modality multi-layer features and train these modules from scratch to learn a shared latent space (Fig. 2).

The entire enhanced separate encoding framework consists of three steps: feature encoding, feature alignment, and feature projection.

4.1 Feature Encoding

First, we obtain the multi-layer features of separate pre-trained encoders.

Separate encoding features are trained with different types of corpora. In image pre-training, ResNet is trained with image classification data and the feature map of ResNet can be used as the backbone of further downstream tasks. Faster-RCNN model is trained with object detection data or semantic segmentation data and the output feature is regional features of a given image. In text pre-training, BERT is trained with a mask language model, using large-scale Wikipedia corpus. Based on the transformer structure, the output is the multi-layer token-level feature.

We use all levels of separately pre-trained features combined to find better cross-modal representations: In image encoding, we denote the ith layer of feature map from ResNet as $H_i \in \mathbb{R}^{W_i \times H_i \times D_i}$; W_i, H_i are the width and height size of the convolution output. We denote the regional feature from faster-RCNN as $H_r \in \mathbb{R}^{N^r \times D_r}$ and N^r is the region number. In text encoding, we denote the jth layer of transformer block output from BERT as $S_j \in \mathbb{R}^{L \times D_j}$, L is the sequence length.

These obtained features are encoded separately from pre-trained models, thus are quite different across modalities.

4.2 Feature Alignment

In text encoding, the output feature is token-level, which is sub-word level feature in BERT specifically. In image encoding, the output features are feature-maps extracted from ResNet features and regional features extracted from RCNN network features. Therefore, it is difficult to directly project these features with different layers and different dimensions into a shared latent space. We manage to convert different layers of features into aligned regional features across modalities by reshaping them via feature concatenation and average pooling.

4.3   Feature Projection

After feature alignment, we have multi-level regional image features and multi-level sub-word textual features. The feature projection is a two-phase process:

Region/Token-Wise Projection. First we project both region features in encoding images and token features in encoding texts into a similar latent space. The token-region matching can be better encoded with attention-based modules as explored by [6,14,15], thus we construct a self-attention based encoder to encode these aligned features.

The encoder $F(X)$ follows a standard transformer structure [27].

$$A = \text{Softmax}(\frac{W_q X W_k^T X}{\sqrt{d}})(W_v X) \tag{1}$$

$$F(X) = \text{LayerNorm}(X + A + \text{FFN}(A)) \tag{2}$$

We feed the aligned feature $\widehat{H}_i$, $\widehat{H}_r$ from image encoder and $\widehat{S}_i$ from text encoder into corresponding transformer blocks to get token/region level features. Considering that we have both ResNet features and faster-RCNN features combined, we duplicate the last layer of $\widehat{S}_k$ to create $\widehat{S}_r$ to match the corresponding $\widehat{H}_r$. We then apply average pooling over the region/token level representations to obtain vectors of the given image and text.

$$\vec{H}_i = AvgPool(F_i(\widehat{H}_i)), \vec{H}_r = AvgPool(F_r(\widehat{H}_r)), \vec{S}_k = AvgPool(F_k(\widehat{S}_k)) \tag{3}$$

Layer-Wise Projection. As mentioned in feature alignment, we use layer concatenation to align multi-level features, which is rigid in nature. We are unaware which level of features across modalities might be encoded more similar, thus we fully connect these vectors, allowing different level of features to match their potential similar features across modalities.

$$\vec{V_H} = Linear(Concat([\vec{H}_0, \cdots, \vec{H}_i, \cdots], \vec{H}_r)) \tag{4}$$

$$\vec{V_S} = Linear(Concat([\vec{S}_0, \cdots, \vec{S}_k, \cdots), \vec{S}_r) \tag{5}$$

These two steps of feature projection encode the features that are inherently different into a similar latent space. Since joint-encoding the concatenated token and region features are not feasible in separate encoding, we decompose the separate encoding features into token-wise and layer-wise, and align them to be encoded into a more similar latent space.

After acquiring the separate encoded vectors $\vec{V_H}$ and $\vec{V_S}$ from two modalities, we use triplet ranking loss to train the entire model.

5   Experiment

5.1   Datasets

We use Flickr30K [20] dataset and MS-COCO [18] to test our enhance separate encoding framework.

In Flickr30K, there are 31,783 images with 5 captions each, and MS-COCO 2014 contains 123,287 images with 5 cations per image. We follow [9] for the train-valid-test split, which is 1k test for Flickr30K, 1k, and 5k for MS-COCO. which results in 113287 training, 5000 validation, and 5000 testing images for MS-COCO. Flickr30K dataset is split into 29783 training, 1000 validation, and 1000 testing images. Our results average over 5 folds of 1k test images and use the full 5000 test images for MS-COCO testing. We use recall by K (R@K) defined as the fraction of queries for which the correct item is retrieved in the closest K points to the query.

5.2   Implementation Details

For both Flickr30K and COCO dataset, we use ResNet152 and Faster-RCNN with ResNet101 as image encoding models. The Faster-RCNN features are extracted following [30], with region number 100 and hidden size 2048. The dimension of 4 layers of feature maps in ResNet152 are [56, 56, 256], [28, 28, 512], [14, 14, 1024] and [7, 7, 2048]. We apply average pooling with pooling window [8, 8], [4, 4], [2, 2] and [1, 1]. After merging and linear transformation, the output features of 4 feature maps are [49, 256], [49, 256], [49, 512], [49, 1024]. The region feature is [100, 1024]. And we use BERT-base as a text encoding model, which contains 12 layers with hidden dimension size 768. We set max sequence length to 32. During feature alignment, we concatenate every 3 layers of BERT output and use linear transformation to obtain 4 layers of features with dimension size [32, 256], [32, 256], [32, 512] and [32, 1024]. We duplicate the last layer to align with region features from faster-RCNN. The transformer block is a 1-layer transformer with 8 heads and an intermediate size 1024.

During training, we use NVIDIA 1080Ti GPUs to train the entire model, with learning rate set to 2e−5, batch-size 128 for Flickr30K, and 320 for MS-COCO dataset. We also ensemble two single models to create an ensemble model of an enhanced separate encoding framework to boost the performances.

5.3   Experiment Setup

We establish baselines testing the matching results as well as inference cost. We implement joint-encoding approaches based on two different joint-encoding structures. In the Unicoder-VL structure, we follow the implementation in [15]. In the LXMERT structure, the core idea is encoding features across modalities jointly only in the higher layers. Thus, we use the first 8 layers of BERT-base structure for text encoding and region-features from Faster-RCNN for image encoding. Then we concatenate the image and text features and feed them into the last 4 layers of BERT-base structure and use the special [CLS] token for similarity score learning.

The inference cost is tested on a single NVIDIA 1080Ti GPU. We set batch-size 128 evaluating our enhanced separate encoding framework. When evaluating joint-encoding methods on 1k test of Flickr30K dataset, we use batch-size 5000 which is the caption number; we iterate each image to calculate the similarity score of the matching pairs.

Table 1. Performances on Flickr30K dataset Unicoder-VL* is further pre-trained with large-scale image-text pairs.

Methods	Image-to-text			Text-to-image			Inference cost	
	R@1	R@5	R@10	R@1	R@5	R@10	Time cost	GPU cost
Joint-encoding methods								
Unicoder-VL [15]	73.0	89.0	94.1	57.8	82.2	88.9	8800 (s)	8X
LXMERT [26]	73.3	92.5	96.5	53.6	81.4	89.0	5807 (s)	6X
Unicoder-VL*	86.2	96.3	99.0	71.5	90.9	94.9	–	–
Separate-encoding methods								
VSE++ [9]	52.9	80.5	87.2	39.6	70.1	79.5	–	–
SCAN [14]	67.4	90.3	95.8	48.6	77.7	85.2	–	–
SCG [23]	71.8	90.8	94.8	49.3	76.4	85.6	–	–
VSRN [16]	71.3	90.6	96.0	54.7	81.8	88.2	–	–
SGRAF [7]	77.8	94.1	97.4	58.5	83.0	88.8	–	–
Ours	79.4	94.9	97.5	63.3	88.0	92.3	61.5 (s)	1X
Ours [ensemble]	**80.9**	**95.5**	**97.9**	**66.0**	**88.8**	**93.1**	63.1 (s)	2X

5.4 Experiment Result

As seen in Table 1 and 2, our enhanced separate encoding framework outperforms previous separate encoding approaches by a large margin, while outperforming joint encoding methods that are trained without image-text pair pre-training.

The calculation cost during inference, as seen in Table 1, is enormous in joint-encoding methods. We use 8 GPUs to run inference in joint-encoding with very large batch-size, still the time cost is unbearable. Meanwhile, without pre-training, the performance of joint-encoding is not superior to separate encoding methods.

Joint-encoding model further pre-trained with large-scale image-text pairs has great performances while it has less competitive performances when only trained with image-text pairs in the given task. This indicates that joint-encoding method relies on using large-scale image-text pairs to enhance the model while joint- Therefore, we believe that separate encoding with our enhanced framework is both effective and efficient.

Table 2. Results on MS-COCO dataset.

Methods	Image-to-text			Text-to-image			Image-to-text			Text-to-image		
	1K test images						5K test images					
	R@1	R@5	R@10	R@1	R@5	R@10	R@1	R@5	R@10	R@1	R@5	R@10
Joint-encoding methods												
Unicoder-VL	75.1	94.3	97.8	63.9	91.6	96.5	–	–	–	–	–	–
Unicoder-VL*	84.3	97.3	99.3	69.7	93.5	97.2	62.3	87.1	92.8	46.7	76.0	85.3
Separate-encoding methods												
VSE++	64.6	90.0	95.7	52.0	84.3	92.0	41.3	71.1	81.2	30.3	59.4	72.4
SCAN	72.7	94.8	98.4	58.8	88.4	94.8	50.4	82.2	90.0	38.6	69.3	80.4
SCG	76.6	96.3	**99.2**	61.4	88.9	95.1	56.6	84.5	92.0	39.2	68.0	81.3
VSRN	76.2	94.8	98.2	62.8	89.7	95.1	53.0	81.1	89.4	40.5	70.6	81.1
SGRAF	79.6	96.2	98.5	63.2	90.7	**96.1**	57.8	–	91.6	41.9	-	81.3
Ours	79.7	96.7	98.7	64.7	90.0	95.1	57.2	84.5	91.4	41.5	72.1	82.0
Ours [ensemble]	**80.4**	**97.0**	98.8	**65.5**	**90.8**	95.7	**58.6**	**85.6**	92.2	42.7	**73.4**	**83.2**

Table 3. Projection study on Flickr30K dataset; R/T-P is region/token-wise projection; L-P is layer-wise projection.

Projection		Image-to-text			Text-to-image		
R/T-P	L-P	R@1	R@5	R@10	R@1	R@5	R@10
		73.9	93.6	96.0	58.0	85.4	90.8
✓		76.1	93.4	96.4	61.4	86.4	91.8
	✓	75.5	93.1	96.4	59.5	85.7	91.3
✓	✓	79.4	94.9	97.5	63.3	88.0	92.3

6   Ablation Studies

6.1   Effectiveness of Feature Projection

The motivation of our enhanced separate encoding framework is to project separately pre-trained features into a similar latent space. Therefore, we construct ablations studies proving that feature projection modules play vital roles in our framework.

We establish baselines on both Flickr30K and COCO dataset. We concatenate the pooled $\widehat{H}$ and $\widehat{S}$ without using $F(X)$ region/token-wise projection or layer-wise linear transformation projection. That is we run baselines without feature projection, we simply use concatenated outputs features from feature align process.

As seen in Table 3, $F(X)$ projection (R/T-P) and linear transformation (L-P) are important in projecting features to be more similar, indicating that though the pre-trained features possess abundant information, they are different inherently across modalities. Therefore, though both projection methods are easy to construct, the idea of allowing separately-pre-trained features to be aligned and further encoded is extremely effective.

7   Conclusions and Future Work

In this paper, we focus on the image-text matching task. Firstly, we analyze the traditional separate encoding methods as well as recent joint-encoding methods based on pre-training with large-scale image-text pairs. We discuss the problems that constrain these methods, then we propose a framework to leverage the advantages and disadvantages of these methods, achieving competitive results while maintaining a minimal inference cost.

In the future, following our analysis, we are hoping to apply large-scale image-text pairs to train the projection modules to take performances of the image-text matching task to a higher level as well as try different languages.

Acknowledgement. This work was supported in part by National Natural Science Foundation of China under grants 61771145.

References

1. Antol, S., et al.: VQA: visual question answering. In: Proceedings of the IEEE International Conference on Computer Vision, pp. 2425–2433 (2015)
2. Bowman, S.R., Angeli, G., Potts, C., Manning, C.D.: A large annotated corpus for learning natural language inference. In: Proceedings of the 2015 Conference on Empirical Methods in Natural Language Processing (EMNLP). Association for Computational Linguistics (2015)
3. Chen, X., et al.: Microsoft coco captions: data collection and evaluation server. arXiv preprint arXiv:1504.00325 (2015)
4. Chen, Y.C., et al.: UNITER: learning universal image-text representations. arXiv preprint arXiv:1909.11740 (2019)
5. Cheng, Q., Gu, X.: Bridging multimedia heterogeneity gap via graph representation learning for cross-modal retrieval. Neural Netw. **134**, 143–162 (2021)
6. Devlin, J., Chang, M., Lee, K., Toutanova, K.: BERT: pre-training of deep bidirectional transformers for language understanding. CoRR abs/1810.04805 (2018). http://arxiv.org/abs/1810.04805
7. Diao, H., Zhang, Y., Ma, L., Lu, H.: Similarity reasoning and filtration for image-text matching. arXiv preprint arXiv:2101.01368 (2021)
8. Elman, J.L.: Finding structure in time. Cogn. Sci. **14**(2), 179–211 (1990)
9. Faghri, F., Fleet, D.J., Kiros, J.R., Fidler, S.: VSE++: improved visual-semantic embeddings. CoRR abs/1707.05612 (2017). http://arxiv.org/abs/1707.05612
10. Girshick, R.: Fast R-CNN. In: Proceedings of the IEEE International Conference on Computer Vision, pp. 1440–1448 (2015)
11. He, K., Zhang, X., Ren, S., Sun, J.: Deep residual learning for image recognition. CoRR abs/1512.03385 (2015). http://arxiv.org/abs/1512.03385
12. Hochreiter, S., Schmidhuber, J.: Long short-term memory. Neural Comput. **9**(8), 1735–1780 (1997)
13. Krishna, R., et al.: Visual genome: connecting language and vision using crowdsourced dense image annotations. CoRR abs/1602.07332 (2016). http://arxiv.org/abs/1602.07332
14. Lee, K., Chen, X., Hua, G., Hu, H., He, X.: Stacked cross attention for image-text matching. CoRR abs/1803.08024 (2018). http://arxiv.org/abs/1803.08024

15. Li, G., Duan, N., Fang, Y., Jiang, D., Zhou, M.: Unicoder-VL: a universal encoder for vision and language by cross-modal pre-training. arXiv preprint arXiv:1908.06066 (2019)

16. Li, K., Zhang, Y., Li, K., Li, Y., Fu, Y.: Visual semantic reasoning for image-text matching. In: ICCV (2019)

17. Li, L.H., Yatskar, M., Yin, D., Hsieh, C.J., Chang, K.W.: VisualBERT: a simple and performant baseline for vision and language. arXiv preprint arXiv:1908.03557 (2019)

18. Lin, T., et al.: Microsoft COCO: common objects in context. CoRR abs/1405.0312 (2014). http://arxiv.org/abs/1405.0312

19. Peters, M.E., et al.: Deep contextualized word representations. CoRR abs/1802.05365 (2018). http://arxiv.org/abs/1802.05365

20. Plummer, B.A., Wang, L., Cervantes, C.M., Caicedo, J.C., Hockenmaier, J., Lazebnik, S.: Flickr30k entities: collecting region-to-phrase correspondences for richer image-to-sentence models. IJCV **123**(1), 74–93 (2017)

21. Radford, A., Narasimhan, K., Salimans, T., Sutskever, I.: Improving language understanding by generative pre-training (2018). https://s3-us-west-2.amazonaws.com/openai-assets/research-covers/languageunsupervised/languageunderstandingpaper.pdf

22. Ren, S., He, K., Girshick, R.B., Sun, J.: Faster R-CNN: towards real-time object detection with region proposal networks. CoRR abs/1506.01497 (2015). http://arxiv.org/abs/1506.01497

23. Shi, B., Ji, L., Lu, P., Niu, Z., Duan, N.: Knowledge aware semantic concept expansion for image-text matching. In: Proceedings of the Twenty-Eighth International Joint Conference on Artificial Intelligence, IJCAI 2019, pp. 5182–5189. International Joint Conferences on Artificial Intelligence Organization, July 2019. https://doi.org/10.24963/ijcai.2019/720

24. Simonyan, K., Zisserman, A.: Very deep convolutional networks for large-scale image recognition. arXiv 1409.1556 (09 2014)

25. Socher, R., Karpathy, A., Le, Q.V., Manning, C.D., Ng, A.Y.: Grounded compositional semantics for finding and describing images with sentences. Trans. Assoc. Comput. Linguist. **2**, 207–218 (2014)

26. Tan, H., Bansal, M.: LXMERT: learning cross-modality encoder representations from transformers. arXiv preprint arXiv:1908.07490 (2019)

27. Vaswani, A., et al.: Attention is all you need. CoRR abs/1706.03762 (2017). http://arxiv.org/abs/1706.03762

28. Wang, Y., et al.: Position focused attention network for image-text matching. CoRR abs/1907.09748 (2019). http://arxiv.org/abs/1907.09748

29. Wen, K., Gu, X., Cheng, Q.: Learning dual semantic relations with graph attention for image-text matching. IEEE Trans. Circuits Syst. Video Technol. (2020)

30. Zhou, L., Palangi, H., Zhang, L., Hu, H., Corso, J.J., Gao, J.: Unified vision-language pre-training for image captioning and VQA. arXiv preprint arXiv:1909.11059 (2019)

Bird Audio Diarization with Faster R-CNN

Roman Shrestha[1](✉)[iD], Cornelius Glackin[1](✉)[iD], Julie Wall[2](✉)[iD],
and Nigel Cannings[1](✉)

[1] Intelligent Voice Ltd., London, UK
{roman.shrestha,neil.glackin,nigel.cannings}@intelligentvoice.com
[2] University of East London, London, UK
j.wall@uel.ac.uk

Abstract. Birds embody particular phonic and visual traits that distinguish them from 10,000 distinct bird species worldwide. Birds are also perceived to be indicators of biodiversity due to their propensity for responding to changes in their environment. An effective, automatic wildlife monitoring system based on bird bioacoustics, which can support manual classification, can be pivotal for the protection of the environment and endangered species. In modern machine learning, real-life bird audio classification is still considered as an esoteric challenge owing to the convoluted patterns present in bird song, and the complications that arise when numerous bird species are present in a common setting. Existing avian bioacoustic monitoring systems struggle when multiple bird species are present in an audio segment. To overcome these challenges, we propose a novel Faster Region-Based Convolutional Neural Network bird audio diarization system that incorporates object detection in the spectral domain and performs diarization of 50 bird species to effectively tackle the 'which bird spoke when?' problem. Benchmark results are presented using the Bird Songs from Europe dataset achieving a Diarization Error Rate of 21.81, Jaccard Error Rate of 20.94 and F1, precision and recall values of 0.85, 0.83 and 0.87 respectively.

Keywords: Deep neural networks · Audio classification · Diarization · Automatic wildlife monitoring

1 Introduction

Bioacoustics, a blend of biology and acoustics, has facilitated several pioneering biodiversity monitoring systems resulting in major advances towards the conservation of species prone to extinction [1,2]. Most of these systems are based on monitoring avian phonetics since bird songs are acknowledged to be the most prominent, reliable, and consistent indicators of biodiversity, capable of providing invaluable insights on the state of the ecology [2]. Unfortunately, tracking birds manually can be an onerous task [3].

© Springer Nature Switzerland AG 2021
I. Farkaš et al. (Eds.): ICANN 2021, LNCS 12891, pp. 415–426, 2021.
https://doi.org/10.1007/978-3-030-86362-3_34

Recent advances in machine and deep learning have made possible the automation of biodiversity monitoring systems. However, the precision of these systems has been severely undermined due to the presence of numerous bird species vocalising in an environment, which can also be further occluded by other environmental sounds [4]. Consequently, this research aims to improve upon traditional bird audio classification approaches by adopting an object detection approach to bird audio diarization, in which objects are in the form of bird audio vocalisations in the spectral domain. This will group an input audio stream into homogeneous segments based on a bird species identity, hence revealing 'which bird sang when' along with the number of distinct bird species singing within a specified time-frame in an ecosystem [5].

This research uses the Bird Songs from Europe corpus, a subset of the Xeno-canto database containing intrinsic audio recordings of the 50 most common bird species in Europe [6]. A Faster Region-Based Convolutional Neural Network (R-CNN) model with a pre-trained ResNet50 Feature Pyramid Network (FPN) backbone was trained with spectrograms and their corresponding annotations obtained from pre-processed bird audio segments. The Faster R-CNN classifier [7] performs object detection based on features extracted to locate bird specific spectral patterns for effective bird species recognition. The rest of this paper is structured into four sections. Section 2 examines the background of this research and details existing approaches in bird audio-based wildlife monitoring, followed by the methodology, experiments and results in Sect. 3. Discussions are provided in Sect. 4 and Sect. 5 provides conclusions and future work.

2   Literature Review

Global concern of ecological deterioration has led to much research on automated bioacoustics monitoring. Accordingly, several annual challenges, such as Conference and Labs of the Evaluation Forum (CLEF), Detection and Classification of Acoustic Scenes and Events (DCASE), Neural Information Processing Scaled for Bioacoustics (NIPS4B), and Machine Learning for Signal Processing (MLSP) have led to the development of some ground-breaking architectures for acoustic wildlife monitoring [1,3]. Even though, modern systems can identify the majority of the species present in a natural setting, a highly accurate automatic bird audio-based wildlife monitoring system capable of identifying all the vocalising species is still missing [3].

The majority of approaches, which contemplate passive wildlife monitoring centred on avian phonetics, share three identical pre-processing measures: a) Noise Filtering, b) Bird audio detection, and c) Feature extraction. Initially, the audio segments are filtered from environmental noise followed by bird audio detection on the filtered chunks that enables the system to identify segments with bird audio, which leads to the extraction of the features relevant for bird species recognition [1]. Early systems of passive bioacoustic monitoring used traditional speech recognition-based techniques, such as template-matching (Dynamic Time Warping) and Hidden Markov Models (HMMs), as they were the most effective audio processing systems of the time [8]. Algorithms that demonstrated success with speech recognition struggled when it came to bird species recognition, as avian phonetics are composed of complex patterns unlike those found in the human voice [8]. Substantial approaches have been developed since this early work, among these systems employing Support Vector Machines (SVMs), Machine Learning and CNN based approaches, have demonstrated gradual progress comparatively [1,2].

Initially, SVMs were not able to achieve much success with bird audio classification, while classifiers utilising decision trees as a base demonstrated better results [9]. Later, it was discovered that SVMs based on syllable segmentation algorithms outperformed the avian phonetics classification models of that time when feature selection computed from combined Mel Frequency Cepstral Coefficients (MFCCs) [10]. The segmentation algorithm was successfully able to filter environmental noise and extract bird audio syllables through the application of a pre-emphasis filter, which focused on high frequencies that were most likely to represent avian phonetics [11]. SVMs also achieved success with multi-class bird audio classification, demonstrating an average accuracy of 98.7% while categorizing 7 distinct bird species from the Xeno-canto database [12] using a Gaussian radial basis function kernel [10].

Further work described how the traditional SVM model was extended to classify 11 species extracted from the Xeno-canto database [12] with 92.8% accuracy [13]. The approach was centred on MFCC-based feature extraction from an acoustic event-based-sifting approach combined with a Gaussian Mixture Model (GMM)-based frame selection for distinguishing specific spectral patterns from the songs of the 11 bird species [13]. In 2018 [14], a two-windows method was adapted to minimise processing time by 24% and node-level space requirements by 43% as a speed boost for the SVM classifier. This approach was evaluated on 214 wildlife recordings from the Xeno-canto database [12], based on 5 species, and achieved a maximum accuracy of 93.85% [14]. Despite this strong performance of the SVM with fewer bird species, the accuracy of the system decreased rapidly as more bird species were included in the classification [14].

In recent years, machine learning-based classifiers have exhibited major improvements for recognising bird species from audio recordings and dominated the leader boards in major competitions [2]. It was found that machine learning classifiers worked relatively well with spectrograms for bioacoustic monitoring. The second-place team for MLSP 2013 employed Extremely Randomized Trees and obtained an area under the curve (AUC) score of 95.05% while categorizing 19 bird species [11]. This work, updated with randomized decision trees [15], proved to be the winning system for the NIPS4B 2013 competition with an AUC score of 91.7% while classifying 87 bird species [15].

Artificial Neural Network-based approaches to bird audio classification began in 1997 when a neural network trained with back propagation on manually collected open source wildlife recordings was evaluated against 6 audio clips corresponding to 1 recording per species and demonstrated 82% accuracy for the task [16]. Deep Neural Networks (DNN), Recurrent Neural Networks (RNN) and CNNs have shown improvements with their ability to extract features and classify images with higher accuracy [16]. Currently, CNNs are mostly preferred for effective feature extraction for spectrogram-based approaches [17].

In BirdCLEF 2016, the winning solution incorporated a simple CNN architecture with five convolutions and one dense layer for the classification of 999 bird species, achieving an official mean Average Precision (mAP) of 0.686 and 0.555 for the foreground species and foreground species mixed with background species, respectively [18]. However, when this system was evaluated for a soundscape with arbitrary bird species singing in the background, it obtained a mAP score of 0.078 [18].

In BirdCLEF 2019 [19,20], the Inception v3 model provided better classification results for biodiversity monitoring, possibly due to the increased number of parameters, which allowed the model to represent the mappings more accurately [19]. The classification mAP (cmAP) is the standard evaluation metric considered for this challenge [20]. The Inception v3 model winning submission [20] was trained with sophisticated data augmentation techniques, such as filtering audio chunks with random transfer functions and applying local time stretching and pitch shifting in time domain identification, along with the use of validation data for fine-tuning the pre-trained network [20]. This result surpassed state-of-the-art model performances by 20%, achieving a cmAP score of 35.6% while classifying 659 bird species from intrinsic recordings belonging to the BirdCLEF 2019 evaluation set [20].

The winning submission of BirdCLEF 2020 [21] achieved a cmAP score of 13.1% while classifying 960 species. Even though the system outperformed other competing systems, most of the species that were present in the test recordings could not be recognised [21]. In this approach, a 1D convolution/Gabor wavelet transformation first layer accepts augmented spectrograms and the remaining layers of the network were determined by performing a Neural Architecture Search (NAS).

The CNN has also performed well with a simultaneous segmentation and classification approach using a five-layer encoder-decoder model [4]. The encoder layers in the network encode high-dimensional features from the spectrograms and the decoder layers decode the encoded features and their location in the spectrogram, allowing the network to execute segmentation and classification simultaneously [4]. The network was able to predict the classes for 19 species with a True Positive Rate (TPR) of 98% on the MLSP 2013 dataset.

Existing systems and architectures are still struggling to perform highly accurate classification of bird species in the wild [21]. The concept of speaker diarization could be applied to perform diarization on bird audio to identify the birds present in an environment and recognise which bird sang when [22]. In the only diarisation-based research on bird audio, an accuracy of 53% was achieved while identifying 10 bird species from the H.J. Andrews Long-Term Experimental Research Forest (HJA) dataset [22]. The performance of the model was satisfactory compared to the standard deep learning-based bird audio classification approaches [11,15] undertaken at that time. Research involving a bird activity detector [22], which detected segments voiced by birds followed by a change point detector, detected a change in speaker/bird turns through the application of Bayesian Information Criterion (BIC) with Agglomerative Clustering.

Our proposed Faster R-CNN model approaches bird audio diarization by performing object detection in the spectral domain and shows significant refinement to the diarization based bio-acoustic monitoring approach.

3 Methodology

3.1 Data Acquisition and Pre-processing

The acquisition of real-life bird audio datasets with sufficient recordings per bird species extracted from a naturally occurring habitat is challenging. Several datasets such as BirdCLEF and RefSys have insufficient recording samples per bird species [23]. Thus, the balanced, medium-sized subset Bird Songs from Europe, consisting of 50 discrete European bird species with 43 high-quality natural recordings per species [6] was used in this work. Pre-processing of the raw input audio consisted of downsampling, conversion to the wav file format, segmentation, overlapping, bird audio detection, merging of audio segments, generation of spectrograms, accurate data annotation and data partitioning for training, validation, and evaluation. Firstly, the 16 kHz audio was downsampled to 8 kHz and converted from mp3 to wav. The wav files were then segmented into uniform 1-s chunks with 50% overlap as depicted in Fig. 1, which played a significant role in increasing the volume of training data.

A Pydub-based [24] bird audio detector operates as the filtering layer that processes the incoming audio stream and combines 1-s segments with bird songs from a certain species with a random 1-s segment representing a different bird species to simulate a complex natural audio recording with multiple bird species in an audio segment, see Fig. 2. Spectrograms facilitate the visualisation of the magnitude of the raw frequencies and signals in an audio chunk as a spectrum of sound over contrasting time-frames [17]. Subsequently, a Short-time Fourier Transfer (STFT)-based spectrogram of size 256×256 pixels was generated using Librosa [25].

Timings for the ground-truth labels were provided by the bird audio detection algorithm, which calculates the bird audio start and end time parameters

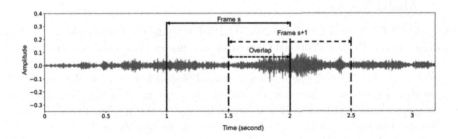

Fig. 1. 50% overlap for each 1-s audio segment

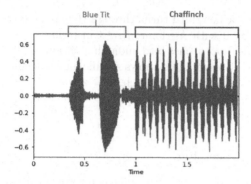
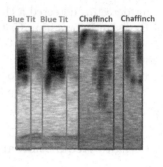

Fig. 2. New waveform (left) and spectrogram (right) generated after merging 1-s audio segments from two random species

for the corresponding chunks associated with the bird species. These parameters in turn specify the start and end coordinates of the bounding boxes along the x-axis, which display 2 s of audio across a visual stretch of 256 × 256 pixels containing the bounding boxes, see Fig. 2. To represent a time frame of 2 s, 1 unit along the axis of the spectrogram should correspond to 0.128 ms as the ratio between 256 and 2,000 yields 1:0.128. Hence, the time frame can be represented in pixels by multiplying the time with 0.128 i.e. $bbox = time(ms) \times 0.128$ where $bbox$ represents the corresponding bounding box co-ordinate for specific time represented as $time(ms)$. However, the coordinates along the y-axis for the bounding box remain as the default, i.e. the minimum value is set to '0' and the maximum value is set to '256'.

The final step in the pre-processing phase deals with accurate annotation in the Pascal Visual Object Classes (VOC) format, which stores bounding box coordinates along with essential information for object detection [7]. Figure 2 depicts a spectrogram sample and visualises the bounding box and labels based on the Pascal VOC format. A total of 297,075 spectrograms were obtained from 91.71 h of intrinsic audio recordings, out of which 247,479 (80%) of the data was used for training, 24,798 (10%) for validation, and the evaluation (test) set was comprised of the remaining 24,798 (10%) spectrogram images.

3.2 Model Training

A Faster R-CNN model with ResNet50 FPN backbone pre-trained on the COCO dataset with a Region Proposal Generator was used to train the model. Figure 3 shows the Faster R-CNN object detection model's functionality pipeline. When a spectrogram is inputted, the Region Proposal Network acts as a selective search layer that generates anchor boxes for all the spectrogram regions. Based on feature maps generated by the ResNet50 architecture, the Region Proposal Layer computes the Region of Interest (ROI) proposals for specific regions in the spectrogram and selects the anchor box and segments that correspond with the extracted features [7]. An Intersection over Union (IoU) score between '0' and

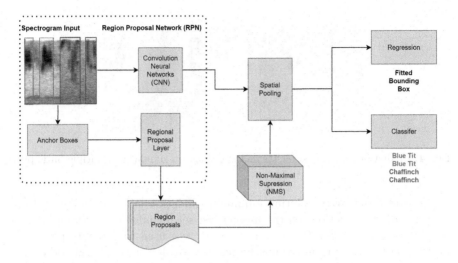

Fig. 3. Faster R-CNN object detection pipeline

'1' is used to compute the magnitude of intersection between the generated proposals and the ground truth labels where an IoU score closer to '1' represents a stronger intersection with the ground truth boxes for the spectrograms. Hence, the proposal regions would undergo a procedure known as Non-Maximal Suppression (NMS) that suppresses all the proposals with an IoU score less than 0.3, such that only boxes with a strong association with the ground truth would be used for training. Spatial pooling is used to select only the most important features from the feature map extracted by the FPN. Finally, bounding box co-ordinates are made more precise by performing regression and the Faster R-CNN classifier predicts the labels for the corresponding bounding boxes based on features extracted from that specific region [7].

To ensure that the model is optimally trained, the Fastai library [26] has been implemented utilising functionalities from the IceVision package [27]. To ensure optimal model training, Smith [28] suggests performing a cycle with two steps of equal length where the model is trained by cycling the learning rate (LR) between the maximum LR and the minimum LR, computed as one-tenth of the maximum LR. In the end, the LR can be reduced lower than the minimum LR i.e. to one-hundredth of the minimum LR, which has been deemed crucial for optimal model training [28].

For transfer learning, the latest version of Fastai makes use of several fit one cycle iterations to fine-tune modules with pre-trained weights more efficiently. Fine-tuning in Fastai allows the model to freeze the backbone by stopping gradient calculations and train only the head accompanied by randomly initialized parameters for the first few epochs [28]. Then, the model can be unfrozen and trained with all the layers, allowing gradient calculations for the parameters to be adjusted until the model is optimally trained. Weights & Biases (W&B) callbacks were used for visualising and tracking the model training [29]. The weights

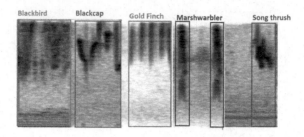

Fig. 4. Predictions generated for test set spectrogram simulating multiple bird species

of the model instance exhibiting minimum validation loss were saved and used for generating predictions on the unseen test set for inference. During inferencing, this trained Faster R-CNN classifier [7] was used to generate predictions for the spectrograms from the unseen test set which also contained additional 5 spectrograms obtained after combining audio-segments from more than two bird species to test if the system could cope with the presence of multiple birds in a common setting as shown in Fig. 4.

Using an NVIDIA GeForce GTX 1080 Ti GPU, the total time to train the model was 8 days and 12 h, with an average training time of 3 h and 13 min per epoch. The model was trained for a total of 60 epochs, during the first 5 epochs the backbone was frozen and only the model head was trained. This was followed by the remaining 55 epochs to train all the layers and adjust the parameters accordingly. For the first 5 epochs, the minimum validation loss achieved was 6.89 with a minimum training loss of 4.09. During the remaining 55 epochs, the validation loss of the model started gradually decreasing from 0.793 to 0.478 until the loss plateaued in the 52nd epoch. Hence, the parameters of the model at the 52nd epoch were saved for inferencing.

3.3   Model Testing

The trained model was evaluated with the 24,798 test set spectrograms, Fig. 5 outlines the Faster R-CNN Inference Pipeline. This model generates predictions on the test set, and a confidence score between '0' and '1' is provided for each prediction where a detection threshold of 0.5 is defined such that predictions with confidence score less than 0.5 are discarded. The predicted outputs were compared with the ground truth reference labels and Diarization Error Rate (DER), Jaccard Error Rate (JER), F1, recall and precision were calculated as evaluation metrics. A sample of predictions for the evaluation set can be seen in Fig. 6, which simulates vocalisation of multiple bird species in a single audio segment obtained by merging the audio segments from random species. The proposed Faster R-CNN model is able to perform bird audio diarization with minimal DER and JER of 21.81 and 20.94, respectively, even under the complex circumstances simulated by combining multiple species in a single audio segment. The model achieved an F1 score of 0.85, with 0.83 precision and 0.87 recall value.

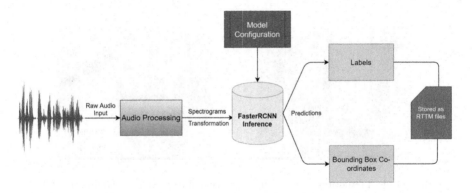

Fig. 5. Faster R-CNN inferencing pipeline

4   Discussion

From the obtained evaluation metrics it is evident that bird audio diarization implemented using the Faster R-CNN model and centered on object detection in the spectral domain is an improvement over previous diarization approaches [22]. This approach has also been shown to cope with the separation of 50 bird species from intrinsic audio recordings compared to the pioneering work with diarization on the HJA dataset that considered only 10 classes. There has been numerous research in the literature focused on bird audio classification, which have used the Xeno-canto database or one of its subsets, such as BirdCLEF, NIPS4B and DCASE. We have chosen three of these models, which have used a similar number of species, in order to compare and validate the performance of our model. Silla Jr. and Kaestner [30] approached acoustic bird species classification with 48 classes extracted from a different subset of the Xeno-canto database, using the Global Model Naive Bayes (GMNB) algorithm. This approach was able to yield an F1 score of 0.50, which outperformed other heirarchial-based classification approaches. Incze et al. [31] used a pre-trained MobileNet-based CNN architecture to classify bird species from another subset of the Xeno-canto database [12]. This approach initially showed promising results for audio classification of two bird species with an accuracy of over 80%, which reduced to below 40% when the number of classes was increased to 10. Finally, the model demonstrated an accuracy of 20% when trying to classify 50 bird species. The authors discussed the need for a deeper network being employed in future. It was observed that transfer learning on the pre-trained VGG16 CNN architecture achieved a bird audio classification accuracy of 73.5% on the evaluation set, on the same Bird Songs From Europe dataset consisting of 50 classes [23]. This demonstrated an improved accuracy on the existing systems for bird species classification, with this number of classes. Table 1 outlines the performance of these three approaches against the performance achieved in this work, based on an evaluation of bird species obtained from the Xeno-canto database.

Blbird Njar   RoFch GrFch   GrWb LowlBowl Ckoo

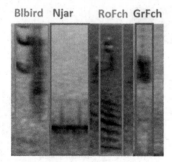 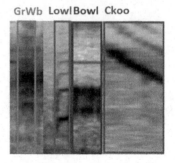

Fig. 6. Sample prediction (left), Blbird = Blackbird; Njar = NightJar; RoFch = RoseFinch; GrFch = GreenFinch, Sample prediction (right), GrWb = Great Warbler; Lowl = Little Owl; Bowl = Boreal Owl; Ckoo = Cuckoo

Table 1 clearly shows that our proposed Faster R-CNN model outperforms standard classification approaches and has the potential to cope with the challenges associated with automated biodiversity monitoring. It was seen that segmentation of bird audio with 50% overlap plays a vital role in increasing the training data. Spectrograms generate distinct patterns based on the energies possessed by avian vocalisation and these patterns differ for every bird species. Functionalities from the Fastai library [26] support model training [28] to achieve minimal validation loss. This work, in performing object detection in the spectral domain for effective spectral pattern recognition could provide a breakthrough for biodiversity monitoring systems through diarization.

Table 1. Model performances

Model	Number of species	Metrics
GMNB [30]	48	0.50 (F1)
MobileNet [31]	50	20% (accuracy)
VGG16 [23]	50	73.5% (accuracy)
Faster R-CNN	50	**0.85 (F1)**

5   Conclusions

A huge amount of research has been invested to build a fully functional automated non-invasive biodiversity monitoring system. However, this research area has lacked an exploration of diarization-based techniques. In this research, we approached bird audio diarization through a Faster R-CNN model, performing object detection in the spectral domain. The results achieved with this novel approach to this challenging problem show promise. It was observed that the augmentation techniques used, such as segmentation with 50% overlap, was crucial for improving the model performance by increasing the training data by 50%.

The functionalities adopted from the Fastai library [26] were also extremely useful for ensuring optimal model training. The inferencing pipeline presented in this approach can be used directly with the pre-trained model weights to generate predictions in a real life-scenario.

Bird audio diarization is able to separate intrinsic avian vocalisations into separate homogeneous segments according to their species, and determine the length of their songs alongside identifying the number of species vocalising in an ecosystem [5]. We believe that this system and its spectral object detection approach can play an important role in the monitoring of population dynamics of bird species within an ecosystem. Our research demonstrates promising results for the diarization of 50 bird species from a subset of the Xeno-canto database. In future work, we aim to tackle larger and more challenging bird audio classification problems presented by challenges such as BirdCLEF, MLSP and DCASE, which would enable us to test and enhance our system further in this domain.

References

1. Dong, X., Jia, J.: Advances in automatic bird species recognition from environmental audio. In: Journal of Physics: Conference Series, vol. 1544, p. 012110 (2020)
2. Kahl, S., Clapp, M., et al.: Overview of BirdCLEF 2020: bird sound recognition in complex acoustic environments. In: Conference and Labs of the Evaluation Forum (CLEF) Task Overview (2020)
3. Kahl, S., Wilhelm-Stein, T., et al.: Large scale bird sound classification using convolutional neural networks. In: Working Notes of Conference and Labs of the Evaluation Forum (CLEF) (2017)
4. Narasimhan, R., Fern, X., Raich, R.: Simultaneous segmentation and classification of bird song using CNN. In: IEEE International Conference on Acoustics, Speech and Signal Processing (ICASSP) (2017)
5. Huang, Z., Watanabe, S., et al.: Speaker diarization with region proposal network. In: IEEE International Conference on Acoustics, Speech and Signal Processing (ICASSP) (2020)
6. Lima, F.: Bird songs from Europe (Xeno-canto) (2020). https://doi.org/10.34740/kaggle/dsv/1029985
7. Ren, S., He, K., et al.: Faster R-CNN: towards real-time object detection with region proposal networks. In: Advances in Neural Information Processing Systems (NeurIPS) (2015)
8. Anderson, S., Dave, A., Margoliash, D.: Template-based automatic recognition of birdsong syllables from continuous recordings. J. Acoust. Soc. Am. **100**(2), 1209–1219 (1996)
9. Mporas, I., Ganchev, T., et al.: Automated acoustic classification of bird species from real-field recordings. In: IEEE International Conference on Tools with Artificial Intelligence (2012)
10. Fagerlund, S.: Bird species recognition using support vector machines. EURASIP J. Adv. Sig. Process. **1**, 64 (2007). https://doi.org/10.1155/2007/38637
11. Ng, H.W., Nguyen, T.N.T.: The 9th annual MLSP competition: second place. In: IEEE International Workshop on Machine Learning for Signal Process (MLSP), pp. 1–2 (2013)

12. Vellinga, W.: Xeno-canto - bird sounds from around the world. Xeno-Canto Foundation for Nature Sounds. https://doi.org/10.15468/qv0ksn
13. Zhao, Z., Zhang, S., et al.: Automated bird acoustic event detection and robust species classification. Ecol. Inform. **39**, 99–108 (2017)
14. Weerasena, H., Jayawardhana, M., et al.: Continuous automatic bioacoustics monitoring of bird calls with local processing on node level. In: IEEE Region 10 Conference (TENCON), pp. 235–239 (2018)
15. Lassek, M.: Bird song classification in field recordings: winning solution for NIPS4B 2013 competition. In: Neural Information Process Scaled for Bioacoustics (NIP4B): From Neurons to Big Data, pp. 176–181 (2013)
16. McIlraith, A.L., Card, H.C.: Bird song identification using artificial neural networks and statistical analysis. In: IEEE Canadian Conference on Electrical Computer Engineering, Engineering Innovation: Voyage of Discovery, vol. 1, pp. 63–66 (1997)
17. Schuller, B.: Intelligent Audio Analysis. Signals and Communication Technology, pp. 99–124. Springer, Heidelberg (2013). https://doi.org/10.1007/978-3-642-36806-6
18. Sprengel, E., Jaggi, M., et al.: Audio based bird species identification using deep learning techniques. In: Working Notes of Conference and Labs of the Evaluation Forum (CLEF) (2016)
19. Koh, C.Y., Chang, J.Y., et al.: Bird sound classification using convolutional neural networks. In: Working Notes of Conference and Labs of the Evaluation Forum (CLEF) (2019)
20. Lassek, M.: Bird species identification in soundscapes. In: Working Notes of Conference and Labs of the Evaluation Forum (CLEF) (2019)
21. Muhling, M., Franz, J., et al.: Bird species recognition via neural architecture search. In: Working Notes of Conference and Labs of the Evaluation Forum (CLEF) (2020)
22. Maina, C.: Audio diarization for biodiversity monitoring. In: IEEE AFRICON International Conference on Green Innovation for African Renaissance, pp. 1–5 (2015)
23. Lima, F.: Audio classification in R. poissonisfish (2020). https://poissonisfish.com/2020/04/05/audio-classification-in-r/
24. Robert, J., Webbie, M., et al.: Pydub. Github (2018). http://pydub.com/
25. McFee, B., Lostanlen, V., et al.: Librosa/librosa: 0.8.0. Zenodo (2020)
26. Howard, J., Gugger, S.: Fastai: a layered API for deep learning. Information **11**(2), 108 (2020)
27. Vazquez, L., Hassainia, F.: IceVision: an agnostic object detection framework. Github (2020). https://github.com/airctic/icevision
28. Smith, L.N.: Cyclical learning rates for training neural networks. In: IEEE Conference on Applications of Computer Vision (WACV), pp. 464–472 (2017)
29. Biewald, L.: Experiment tracking with weights and biases. Weights and Biases (2020). https://www.wandb.com/
30. Silla Jr., C.N., Kaestner, C.A.A.: Hierarchical classification of bird species using their audio recorded songs. In: IEEE International Conference on Systems, Man, and Cybernetics (2013)
31. Incze, A., Jancso, H., et al.: Bird sound recognition using a convolutional neural network. In: IEEE International Symposium on Intelligent Systems and Informatics (SISY) (2018)

Multi-modal Chorus Recognition
for Improving Song Search

Jiaan Wang[1], Zhixu Li[1(✉)], Binbin Gu[4], Tingyi Zhang[1], Qingsheng Liu[5],
and Zhigang Chen[2,3]

[1] School of Computer Science and Technology, Soochow University, Suzhou, China
jawang1@stu.suda.edu.cn, zhixuli@suda.edu.cn
[2] iFLYTEK Research, Suzhou, China
[3] State Key Laboratory of Cognitive Intelligence, iFLYTEK, Hefei, China
[4] University of California, Irvine, USA
[5] Anhui Toycloud Technology, Hefei, China

Abstract. We discuss a novel task, Chorus Recognition, which could potentially benefit downstream tasks such as song search and music summarization. Different from the existing tasks such as music summarization or lyrics summarization relying on single-modal information, this paper models chorus recognition as a multi-modal one by utilizing both the lyrics and the tune information of songs. We propose a multi-modal Chorus Recognition model that considers diverse features. Besides, we also create and publish the first Chorus Recognition dataset containing 627 songs for public use. Our empirical study performed on the dataset demonstrates that our approach outperforms several baselines in chorus recognition. In addition, our approach also helps to improve the accuracy of its downstream task - song search by more than 10.6%.

Keywords: Chorus recognition · Song search · Multi-modal data

1   Introduction

Nowadays, music streaming services have become mainstream ways for people to enjoy music. As a key function of music streaming services, song search aims to search for target songs by a segment of lyrics or tune. Despite its importance, the song search capabilities offered by the existing applications are still unsatisfactory.

According to our study, the song search in popular music applications (e.g., Youtube Music, QQ Music and Netease Cloud Music) often flawed in two ways. On the one hand, when the searching lyrics segment or tune segment is short, plenty of irrelevant songs might be returned by the song search. On the other hand, when searching with a long lyrics or tune segment towards a large song library, the searching speed would be greatly slowed down. The major reason for the above defects is that the existing song searches take fine-grained keywords or fragments of tunes as the basic searching unit, which are often shared by many

© Springer Nature Switzerland AG 2021
I. Farkaš et al. (Eds.): ICANN 2021, LNCS 12891, pp. 427–438, 2021.
https://doi.org/10.1007/978-3-030-86362-3_35

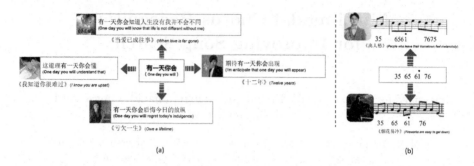

Fig. 1. (a) Song search by lyrics keywords. (b) Song search by tune fragments.

songs such as the example shown in Fig. 1, resulting in too many matching targets, thus reducing the efficiency and accuracy of song searches.

In this paper, we propose to improve the song search experience by identifying the most impressive part of a song, namely the chorus of the song. This allows the song search to primarily focus on lyrics or tunes belonging to chorus. Therefore, the length of the songs' searchable part could be greatly shortened, and the overlaps between the lyrics or tunes of different songs could be significantly reduced. As a result, both the accuracy and efficiency of the song search are expected to be enhanced.

Given the motivation above, we discuss a novel task called **Chorus Recognition**, aiming at identifying the chorus of a given song. In order for better song search experience, we model Chorus Recognition as a multi-modal task where both lyrics and tune of songs would be taken into account. There are some other music-relevant tasks like music summarization and lyrics summarization. Music summarization utilizes the tune of music to identify the most representative parts, lyrics summarization focuses on extracting or generating a short summary of the lyrics of songs. Either task only considers single-modal information. Thus, their approaches could not be directly adopted in Chorus Recognition.

Unfortunately, there is no publicly available dataset for the Chorus Recognition task. Some existing related datasets cannot meet the needs of this task. For example, the RWC music dataset [10] which has been widely used in the music summarization task, only has manual annotation of the start and end times of each chorus section in each song, and do not provide the lyrics information.

In this work, we first build a CHOrus Recognition Dataset (CHORD) which contains 27k lyrics lines from 627 songs, each of which has been labeled with a boolean value to indicate whether it belongs to the chorus. Then, based on this dataset, we propose the first multi-modal Chorus Recognition model which utilizes both the lyrics and tune information. Our contributions are summarized as follows:

– In order for better song search experience, we propose a novel upstream task called Chorus Recognition, aiming at identifying the chorus of a given song.

Futhermore, we construct the first CHOrus Recognition Dataset (CHORD) and release it for further research[1].

- We propose a novel multi-modal Chorus Recognition model, where multi-modal features are employed.
- Our empirical study not only shows the effectiveness of our model in chorus recognition, but also demonstrates its effectiveness in improving the performance of song search with human evaluation.

2 Related Work

Existing researches on song search explore how to search target songs through various given information [4,5,12,20]. Wang et al. [20] study how to use multi-granularity tags to query songs. Buccoli et al. [4] explore how to search songs through a text description. Leu et al. [12] and Chen et al. [5] make use of the tune segment to search target songs. But there are few influential works on lyrics-based song search. The lyrics search mechanism in the existing music apps basically borrows from general search engine. However, different from the ordinary texts, lyrics are the carrier of melody. The fact that the lyrics lines and their corresponding melodies can be divided into intro, verse and chorus has never been recognized by the existing work.

There are some other music tasks related to Chorus Recognition like music summarization and lyrics summarization. Music summarization, also named as music thumbnailing, works on extracting a short piece of music to represent the whole piece. Previous works typically assume that the repeated melody pattern can represent the whole music. They use Self-Similarity Matrix (SSM) or Hidden Markov Model (HMM) methods to divide the song into several segments and then extracted the most frequent ones as the result [2,6]. Nevertheless, many songs do not follow this assumption. To solve this problem, Bittner et al. [3] propose to do peak detection near the location where the user often pulls the progress bar to, because users usually prefer the representative part of a song. Also, Huang et al. [11] consider that the most emotional part of a song usually corresponds to the highlight, so they use music emotion classification as a surrogate task for music summarization. Lyrics summarization aims to preserve key information and the overall meaning of lyrics. As a special kind of text summarization task, Fell et al. [9] propose to employ the generic text summarization models over lyrics.

3 The Chorus Recognition Task and Dataset

3.1 Task Overview

The chorus of music is usually the most representative and impressive part of the music, which consists of one or several segments from the music. Given music $M = \{(S_1, A_1), (S_2, A_2), \cdots , (S_k, A_k)\}$, where S_i denotes the i-th lyrics line, A_i

---

[1] https://github.com/krystalan/MMCR.

denotes its corresponding audio piece in M and k represents the number of lyrics lines in M. The goal of Chorus Recognition is to decide whether (S_i, A_i) $(1 \leq i \leq k)$ belongs to the chorus part of M.

3.2 Dataset Collection

Music Collection. We collected different types of Chinese songs from the popular song lists on QQ music[2]. Due to the copyright reasons, we only reserved the songs available for free download. We randomly selected 1000 songs as the basic data for building CHOrus Recognition Dataset (CHORD). These songs cover many genres, such as rock, pop, classical, and so on. After a song is downloaded, two related files are available: MP3 file and LRC file. The MP3 file stores all the audio information of the song. The LRC file records each lyrics line and its corresponding timeline information.

Ground-Truth Chorus Annotation. In order to annotate the data more efficiently, we developed a strict annotation standard for the chorus to guide data annotation. Based on its corresponding audio piece, each lyrics line is marked as "0" or "1". "0" represents that the lyrics line is not in the chorus part, and "1" represents the opposite. We have 22 out of 25 annotators pass our annotation qualification test. All these annotators are undergraduate students in the music school of our university. During the process of annotation, each song will be assigned to three different annotators separately. If three annotating results are consistent, the annotation will be passed directly. Otherwise, the final annotation will be confirmed by the data specialists. In the end, all the data specialists will recheck the annotating results, and the questionable data will be re-annotated until the annotation meets all its requirements.

Statistics. After the data annotation process, we only keep 627 songs because some song files are invalid or some of their lengths are too short (e.g., less than 60 s). Finally, CHORD contains 27k lyrics lines and each song contains an average of 43.17 lyrics lines. In our experiments, we divide CHORD into train, validation and testing sets with a rough ratio of 80/10/10.

4   Model

Our proposed model MMCR (**M**ulti-**M**odal **C**horus **R**ecognition) consists of three parts. Given a lyrics line S_i and its corresponding audio piece A_i from music M. Firstly, the information of A_i (i.e., tune information) is represented by the Mel Frequency Cepstrum Coefficient (MFCC) feature and chord feature. Secondly, the information of S_i (i.e., lyrics information) is obtained through a Pre-trained Language Model and Graph Attention Networks [18]. Lastly, upon getting the final feature F_i of (S_i, A_i) based on its corresponding tune information and lyrics information, a classifier is used to predict whether the (S_i, A_i) belongs to the chorus.

---

[2] https://y.qq.com/.

4.1   Tune Information

Audio piece A_i is represented by MFCC feature and chord feature. MFCC feature has been widely used as the basic feature of audio in the field of speech recognition, speaker recognition, etc. [1]. The MFCC feature of audio piece A_i is denoted by M_i. Note that although each type of audio has the MFCC feature, only music audio has chord sequence which represents its melody. Chord sequence in music is just like word sequence in natural language. Thanks to skip-gram model [14], we can obtain pre-trained chord embedding by training skip-gram model on the LMD MIDI dataset [16] with chord modeling task (given central chord to predict surrounding chords), which is similar to obtain word embedding through language modeling task. For audio piece A_i, its chord sequence is denoted by $\{c_1, c_2, \cdots, c_{l_i}\}$ which extracted by an off-the-shelf script. Then, each chord c_j is converted to chord embedding CE_j based on pre-trained chord embedding. The chord feature of audio piece A_i (denoted by C_i) is obtained by concatenating each chord embedding,

$$C_i = C(A_i) = CE_1 \oplus CE_2 \oplus \cdots \oplus CE_{l_i} \qquad (1)$$

where $\oplus$ means the concatenation operation.

4.2   Lyrics Information

In order to get lyrics information of a given lyrics line S_i. The whole sequence of S_i is input to BERT [8] which calculate the representation of each token through stacked transformer encoders [17]. Then, we use the final representation of token [CLS] (denoted by L_{Bert_i}) as the basic semantic information of S_i, because it aggregates information from the whole lyrics line through BERT. Note that, L_{Bert_i} only contains the semantic information of lyrics line S_i itself. Intuitively, different lyrics lines from the same song can be complementary to each other. For example, if two lyrics lines have similar words or tune, we can use one lyrics line to enrich the representation of another, making the lyrics embedding more meaningful. Inspired by HSG [19], we use Graph Attention Networks [18] to show how we achieve this purpose.

As shown in Fig. 2(a), given music M, we first construct a heterogeneous graph which consists of three types of nodes, i.e., sentence nodes, word nodes, and chord nodes. Each sentence node corresponds to a lyrics line in M. For each word (or chord) in the lyrics (or tune) of M, we create a word (or chord) node for it. We connects each sentence node with the word (or chord) nodes if the sentence (or its corresponding tune) contains the words (or chords). The graph takes the importance of relationships as their edge feature. We denote e_{ij} as the edge feature between word nodes and sentence nodes and e_{ij}^* as the edge feature between chord nodes and sentence nodes. The representation of word nodes and chord nodes are initialized by GloVe embeddings [15] and chord embeddings. For each sentence node, L_{Bert_i} is set to the initial value. Besides, we consider TF-IDF values as the edge weights which indicate the importance between each pair of nodes.

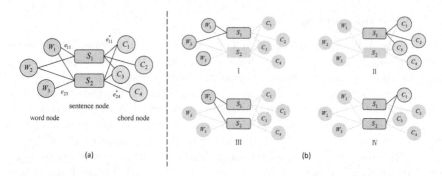

Fig. 2. (a) The heterogeneous graph for a song. (b) The information propagation order in the heterogeneous graph.

After initialization, we use Graph Attention Networks [18] to update the representations of each node in the heterogeneous graph. Formally, given a constructed graph with node features and edge features, the graph attention (GAT) layer is designed as follows:

$$Z_{ij} = LeakyReLU(W_a[W_q h_i; W_k h_j; e_{ij}^{(*)}]) \tag{2}$$

$$\alpha_{ij} = \frac{exp(z_{ij})}{\sum_{l \in N_i} exp(z_{il})} \tag{3}$$

$$u_i = \sum_{j \in N_i} \alpha_{ij}^k W^k h_j \tag{4}$$

h_i is the hidden states of input nodes, W_a, W_q, W_k, W_v are trainable weights. α_{ij} means the attention weight between h_i and h_j. We calculate it based on h_i, h_j and the corresponding edge feature e_{ij}. After that, we use the attention weight to aggregate other nodes' information (i.e., u_i) for the central node. In addition, the multi-head attention can be denoted as:

$$u_i = \|_{k=1}^K \left(\sum_{j \in N_i} \alpha_{ij}^k W^k h_j \right) \tag{5}$$

where $\|_{k=1}^K$ means multi-head attention. After obtaining the additional information (i.e., u_i) for the central node, we update the representation of central node by combining the original representation h_i and the additional information u_i as follows:

$$h_i^{'} = u_i + h_i \tag{6}$$

where $h_i^{'}$ is the updated representation of the central node. Inspired by transformer [17], we leverage a position-wise feed-forward (FFN) layer which consists of two linear transformations after each graph attention layer.

As shown in Fig. 2(b), the information propagation order is built in the heterogeneous graph. Firstly, we use word nodes to enrich the representation of sentence nodes (i). Secondly, the sentence nodes are enriched by chord nodes (ii). Lastly, we enrich the representation of word nodes and chord nodes with the representation of sentence nodes (iii and iv). Through the above process, the representation of the lyrics line S_i is enriched by the global information from the whole song. We denote the contextual representation of lyrics line S_i by L_{HG_i}. Finally, in order to supplement the position information of S_i in the whole lyrics, we add sinusoid positional embeddings [17] to L_{HG_i}. The final lyrics feature is denoted by L_i.

4.3   Multi-modal Fusion for Classification

While three features (i.e., MFCC feature, chord feature and lyrics feature) have been obtained seperately, the final representation of (S_i, A_i) is obtained by concatenating MFCC feature M_i, chord feature C_i and lyrics feature L_i.

$$F_i = L_i \oplus M_i \oplus C_i \tag{7}$$

Then, the final representation F_i is input to a sigmoid classifier to predict whether the (S_i, A_i) belongs to the chorus of the given music M. The cross-entropy loss is used as the training objective for the developed model.

5   Experiments

5.1   Implementation Detail

We set our model parameters based on the preliminary experiments on the validation set. We use the python script[3] to get MFCC feature $M_i \in R^{t_i \times 13}$ for audio piece A_i, where t_i is decided by the length of A_i. Futhermore, the first dimension of MFCC feature is pruned (or padded) to 1280. For pre-trained chord embedding, we empirically limit the size of chord vocabulary to 500, and set the dimension of chord embedding to 64. We leverage the off-the-shelf script[4] to extract chord sequences from the LMD-full dataset [16], and train skip-gram model [14] on those sequences. To build the heterogeneous graph, we limit the size of vocabulary to 50k and only 12 most common chords are used in chord nodes. We initialize word nodes with 300-dimensional GloVe embeddings [15]. To get rid of the noisy common words, we further remove 10% of the vocabulary with low TF-IDF values over the whole dataset. We pre-train the parameters of the graph attention (GAT) layer with next lyrics line prediction task, which is similar to next sentence prediction (NSP) [8]. Then we fix the parameters of the graph attention layer in the chorus recognition task. In MMCR, we do grid search of learning rates [2e−4, 4e−4, 6e−4, 8e−4] and epochs [3–6] and find the model with learning rate 6e−4 and epochs 5 to work best. Besides, training uses the Adam optimizer with batch sizes of 128 and the default momentum.

---

[3] https://github.com/jameslyons/python_speech_features.

[4] https://github.com/yashkhem1/Chord-Extraction-using-Machine-Learning.

5.2 Metrics and Approaches

We compare the developed model with typical baselines and new baselines which proposed in the latest years, in terms of accuracy, precision, recall and F1 score.

- **TextRank** [13]: TextRank is an unsupervised graph-based text summarization method that computes each sentence's importance score based on eigenvector centrality within weighted-graphs.
- **PacSum** [21]: PacSum is also an unsupervised text summarization algorithm. Different from TextRank, PacSum builds graphs with directed edges and employs BERT to better capture sentential meaning.
- **Ext-BERT**: Extractive summarizer with BERT learns the semantic of each lyrics line in a purely data-driven way. The method calculates each lyrics line importance score based on their semantics.
- **RNAM-LF** [11]: Recurrent Neural Attention Modeling by Late Fusion is a supervised music thumbnailing algorithm proposed in recent years, which provides the music highlight span for a given song.

5.3 Results

As shown in Table 1, MMCR significantly improves the performance compared with other approaches. The first part of Table 1 contains two unsupervised text summarization methods. These two methods only calculate the importance scores of lyrics lines and we only keep the most important K lyrics lines as a result. K represents how many lyrics lines belong to the chorus part in each song from the testing set of CHORD (different song has different K value). The second part is the supervised models based on lyrics embedding. Ext-BERT has been explained above, Ext-BERT-wwm-ext is just replace BERT [8] with BERT-wwm-ext [7]. RNAM-LF [11] is a music thumbnailing algorithm. Since it has been trained on tens of thousands of music data on tasks different from ours, we used the pre-trained RNAM-LF directly to get the highlighted span in music. After obtaining the highlight span of music, only if, at least half of a lyrics line is within this span, we then predict that the lyrics line belongs to the chorus part.

5.4 Ablation Study

To evaluate the effectiveness of each feature (MFCC feature, chord feature or lyrics feature), we removed some features respectively from our model in the testing set.

The models shown in Table 2 are explained below:

Chord (Random) only uses randomly initialized chord embedding and update the embedding during the process of training. **Chord (skip-gram, fix)** uses pre-trained chord embedding as a fixed value. **Chord (skip-gram, fine-tune)** uses pre-trained chord embedding and fine tuning it in chorus recognition task. **Ext-BERT** and **Ext-BERT-wwm-ext** are same as the models we introduce above. These two models only use lyrics feature. **MFCC** only considers the

Table 1. Performance comparison of different models on CHORD. Acc.: accuracy, P: precision, R: recall.

Model	Acc.	P	R	F1
TextRank	49.21	48.15	48.15	48.15
PacSum	64.09	63.34	63.34	63.34
Ext-BERT	69.65	68.17	71.35	69.73
Ext-BERT-wwm-ext	70.39	69.16	71.35	70.24
RNAM-LF	67.87	67.21	67.17	67.19
MMCR (BERT)	85.44	**86.56**	83.19	84.84
MMCR (BERT-wwm-ext)	**85.94**	85.52	**85.83**	**85.67**

Table 2. Result of ablation experiment on CHORD. Acc.: accuracy, P: precision, R: recall.

Model	Acc.	P	R	F1
Chord (Random)	54.25	53.03	57.60	55.22
Chord (Skip-gram, fix)	55.89	54.71	57.66	56.14
Chord (Skip-gram, fine-tune)	56.06	54.36	64.11	58.84
Ext-BERT	69.65	68.17	71.35	69.73
Ext-BERT-wwm-ext	70.39	69.16	71.35	70.24
MFCC	81.84	80.54	84.38	82.42
MFCC+Lyrics (BERT)	85.21	84.71	85.17	84.94
MFCC+Lyrics (BERT-wwm-ext)	85.56	84.86	**85.83**	85.34
MMCR (BERT)	85.44	**86.56**	83.19	84.84
MMCR (BERT-wwm-ext)	**85.94**	85.52	**85.83**	**85.67**

MFCC feature to handle the chorus recognition task. **MFCC+Lyrics** approach combines MFCC feature and lyrics feature, the lyrics feature has been extracted from BERT [8] or BERT-wwm-ext [7] respectively.

As can be seen from Table 2, MFCC is the most important feature among these three features, as we find that MFCC achieves much better performance when only one of three features is considered. The results also demonstrate that we can use lyrics feature and chord feature to make the overall representation more meaningful and achieve better performance on chorus recognition task. Besides, the results indicate that BERT-wwm-ext is better than BERT in extracting lyrics feature.

5.5   Evaluation on Song Search

We also demonstrate the effectiveness of our model in the song search task with human evaluation. Our song search experiment uses keywords to search for songs.

We compare our model with several applications and typical baselines:

Table 3. Result of song search task. Hits@n means the proportion of correct song in top n ranks.

Methods	Hits@1	Hits@3
Youtube Music	0.73	0.84
QQ Music	0.75	0.86
Netease Cloud Music	0.69	0.79
TF-IDF	0.55	0.71
MMCR	**0.83**	**0.91**

- **MMCR**: We calculate the chorus probability of each lyrics line by MMCR on our music database which has about 370k popular Chinese songs. Several lyrics lines from different songs may contain the same keyword input. We return the song whose lyrics line has the maximum chorus probability.
- **TF-IDF**: The term frequency (TF) is the number of times w_i occurs in S_j and the inverse document frequency (IDF) is made as the inverse function of the out-degree of w_i [19]. When several lyrics lines from different songs contain the keyword, we compute the average TF-IDF value of keyword in each song and return the song with the highest value.
- **Youtube Music**[5], **QQ Music**[6] and **Netease Cloud Music**[7]: All of the three music applications provide song search services for users. Among them, Youtube Music is extremely popular and serves the worldwide users. QQ Music and Netease Cloud Music are the two most popular music applications in China.

In our human evaluation, we construct candidate keywords set for each song in our music database. Given a song, we first extract chorus lyrics lines by MMCR. Then we collect all three or four consecutive words from each chorus lyrics line. If the consecutive words appear in at least two other songs' non-chorus part, it will be added to the candidate keywords set of the given song. We choose three or four consecutive words as keyword for the following reasons: (1) too few words may be identified as a song title by music apps; (2) too many words leads to the probability of the keyword appearing in other songs dropping significantly.

The specific process of human evaluations is as follows: (a) Choose a song from our music database which has about 370k popular Chinese songs. (b) Choose a keyword from the candidate keywords set of the song. (c) Use the selected keyword to search songs by all applications and methods. (d) We give one point if the target song (i.e., the song selected in the first step) is within the top k (k = 1 or 3 in our evaluation) search results and zero otherwise.

We also make the following restrictions to ensure the fair comparison: (a) the selected keyword needs to be identified as a part of lyrics rather than a song

---

[5] https://music.youtube.com/.

[6] https://y.qq.com/.

[7] https://music.163.com/.

title by all apps. (b) The search result of applications only retains songs which also appear in our music database. (c) All the applications are not logged in, because the search results may be influenced by the users' preference due to the built-in recommendation system. (d) Each song can be selected at most once.

We ask 30 volunteers to do human evaluation for 20 times per person. The result of the song search is shown in Table 3. Each score represents the average result of human evaluation. As we can see, our method achieves better performance in the scenario of song search by keywords. Specifically, TF-IDF only use the lyrics information, which leads to uncompetitive result. Note that the lyrics lines and their corresponding melodies have never been recognized by existing work. So, our approach achieves better performance than these methods. Specifically, our model improves the accuracy of this task by more than 10.6% compared with the second best approaches.

6 Conclusion

In this work, we develop a multi-modal chorus recognition model. Through the improved BERT and graph attention networks, we achieved better lyrics embedding. Also, by leveraging the pre-trained chord embedding we enhanced the performance of the model. We showed the superior performance of our model compared to existing work on CHORD.

Acknowledgement. We would like to thank all anonymous reviews for their constructive comments to improve our paper. Jiaan Wang would like to thank Duo Zheng and Kexin Wang for the helpful discussions. This work was supported by the National Key R&D Program of China (No. 2018AAA0101900), the National Natural Science Foundation of China (Grant No. 62072323, 61632016), Natural Science Foundation of Jiangsu Province (No. BK20191420), the Collaborative Innovation Center of Novel Software Technology and Industrialization, and the Priority Academic Program Development of Jiangsu Higher Education Institutions.

References

1. Alías, F., Socoró, J.C., Sevillano, X.: A review of physical and perceptual feature extraction techniques for speech, music and environmental sounds. Appl. Sci. **6**, 143 (2016)
2. Bartsch, M., Wakefield, G.: Audio thumbnailing of popular music using chroma-based representations. IEEE Trans. Multimedia **7**, 96–104 (2005)
3. Bittner, R.M., et al.: Automatic playlist sequencing and transitions. In: International Society for Music Information Retrieval (2017)
4. Buccoli, M., Zanoni, M., Sarti, A., Tubaro, S.: A music search engine based on semantic text-based query. In: 2013 IEEE 15th International Workshop on Multimedia Signal Processing (MMSP), pp. 254–259 (2013)
5. Chen, X., Kong, X.: An efficient music search method in large audio database. In: 2018 3rd International Conference on Mechanical, Control and Computer Engineering (ICMCCE), pp. 484–487 (2018)

6. Cooper, M., Foote, J.: Summarizing popular music via structural similarity analysis. In: 2003 IEEE Workshop on Applications of Signal Processing to Audio and Acoustics (IEEE Cat. No. 03TH8684), pp. 127–130 (2003)
7. Cui, Y., et al.: Pre-training with whole word masking for Chinese BERT. arXiv preprint arXiv:1906.08101 (2019)
8. Devlin, J., Chang, M.W., Lee, K., Toutanova, K.: BERT: pre-training of deep bidirectional transformers for language understanding. In: NAACL-HLT (2019)
9. Fell, M., Cabrio, E., Gandon, F.L., Giboin, A.: Song lyrics summarization inspired by audio thumbnailing. In: International Conference Recent Advances in Natural Language Processing (2019)
10. Goto, M., Hashiguchi, H., Nishimura, T., Oka, R.: RWC music database: popular, classical and jazz music databases. In: International Society for Music Information Retrieval (2002)
11. Huang, Y., Chou, S.Y., Yang, Y.: Pop music highlighter: marking the emotion keypoints. Trans. Int. Soc. Music. Inf. Retr. **1**, 68–78 (2018)
12. Leu, J., Changfan, C., Su, K.W., Chen, C.: Design and implementation of a fixed-mobile convergent music search engine (FMC-MUSE). Wirel. Pers. Commun. **70**, 1911–1923 (2013)
13. Mihalcea, R., Tarau, P.: Textrank: Bringing order into text. In: EMNLP (2004)
14. Mikolov, T., Chen, K., Corrado, G.S., Dean, J.: Efficient estimation of word representations in vector space. arXiv preprint arXiv:1301.3781 (2013)
15. Pennington, J., Socher, R., Manning, C.D.: Glove: global vectors for word representation. In: EMNLP (2014)
16. Raffel, C.: Learning-based methods for comparing sequences, with applications to audio-to-midi alignment and matching. Ph.D. thesis, Columbia University (2016)
17. Vaswani, A., et al.: Attention is all you need. In: Advances in Neural Information Processing Systems, pp. 5998–6008 (2017)
18. Velickovic, P., Cucurull, G., Casanova, A., Romero, A., Liò, P., Bengio, Y.: Graph attention networks. arXiv preprint arXiv:1710.10903 (2018)
19. Wang, D., Liu, P., Zheng, Y., Qiu, X., Huang, X.: Heterogeneous graph neural networks for extractive document summarization. In: Proceedings of the 58th Annual Meeting of the Association for Computational Linguistics, pp. 6209–6219. Association for Computational Linguistics, Online, July 2020
20. Wang, J.C., Shih, Y.C., Wu, M.S., Wang, H.M., Jeng, S.K.: Colorizing tags in tag cloud: a novel query-by-tag music search system. In: Proceedings of the 19th ACM international conference on Multimedia, pp. 293–302 (2011)
21. Zheng, H., Lapata, M.: Sentence centrality revisited for unsupervised summarization. In: Proceedings of the 57th Annual Meeting of the Association for Computational Linguistics, pp. 6236–6247. Association for Computational Linguistics, Florence, Italy, July 2019

FaVoA: Face-Voice Association Favours Ambiguous Speaker Detection

Hugo Carneiro$^{(\boxtimes)}$, Cornelius Weber, and Stefan Wermter

Department of Informatics, Knowledge Technology, Universität Hamburg,
Vogt-Koelln-Str. 30, 22527 Hamburg, Germany
{hugo.cesar.castro.carneiro,cornelius.weber,
stefan.wermter}@uni-hamburg.de
http://www.informatik.uni-hamburg.de/WTM/

Abstract. The strong relation between face and voice can aid active speaker detection systems when faces are visible, even in difficult settings, when the face of a speaker is not clear or when there are several people in the same scene. By being capable of estimating the frontal facial representation of a person from his/her speech, it becomes easier to determine whether he/she is a potential candidate for being classified as an active speaker, even in challenging cases in which no mouth movement is detected from any person in that same scene. By incorporating a face-voice association neural network into an existing state-of-the-art active speaker detection model, we introduce FaVoA (**Fa**ce-**Vo**ice Association **A**mbiguous Speaker Detector), a neural network model that can correctly classify particularly ambiguous scenarios. FaVoA not only finds positive associations, but helps to rule out non-matching face-voice associations, where a face does not match a voice. Its use of a gated-bimodal-unit architecture for the fusion of those models offers a way to quantitatively determine how much each modality contributes to the classification.

Keywords: Active speaker detection · Face-voice association · Crossmodal · Audiovisual · Deep learning

1 Introduction

The task of active speaker detection (ASD) consists of determining from which individuals in an audiovisual footage a given speaking activity originates. The combined use of auditory and visual modalities is fairly common in multimodal learning, including tasks like speech enhancement [9], speaker diarisation [7], speech reconstruction [14], and active speaker detection [1]. ASD is closely related to other audiovisual multimodal learning tasks, and a high-performing

The authors thank Leyuan Qu for the constructive feedback and suggestions, and acknowledge partial support from the German Research Foundation DFG under project CML (TRR 169).

I. Farkaš et al. (Eds.): ICANN 2021, LNCS 12891, pp. 439–450, 2021.
https://doi.org/10.1007/978-3-030-86362-3_36

ASD model might help in paving the way for better models for those tasks to emerge. Related tasks include speech enhancement [9] and speech separation [7,15].

Recent solutions to the problem of detecting speaking activity in the wild involve the use of 3D convolutions [6,17], information from other individuals in the same scene [1] and the optical flow of facial movements [10]. Although being very powerful, those models still face some difficulties depending on the resolution or the inclination of a person's face [1,10,16]. Most of them also struggle when working with medium- to long-term time spans [6,10,16,17].

In cases where faces are not clear enough, ASD must rely mainly on the auditory modality. However, in scenes where there are two people talking to each other and their faces are not clear enough – due to a low resolution or to a high yaw inclination of their faces –, neither the visual nor the auditory modalities can provide enough information on their own. The existence of a module capable of retrieving a frontal face representation from the speaker's voice might provide information useful for speaker disambiguation in such challenging scenarios. Face-voice association applications show that it is actually possible to retrieve a frontal face representation from a speaker's speech signal [11,13].

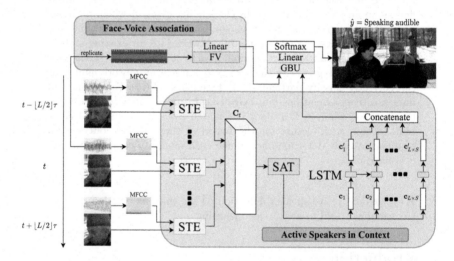

Fig. 1. Active Speakers in Context (ASC) uses feature representations of face crops and audio provided by short-term encoders (STE). Through a pairwise analysis of feature representations of different speakers at distinct time steps made by a self-attention module (SAT) and the subsequent temporal refinement made by a long short-term memory (LSTM), ASC classifies an active speaker. By adding a face-voice association module (FV), FaVoA supports the classification of active speakers in challenging scenarios where the context does not provide enough information. The face-voice association module is combined with the output of ASC via a gated bimodal unit (GBU). Modules and layers in yellow are pretrained and fixed, those in violet are pretrained but are also updated during fine-tuning, and the ones in blue are trained from scratch. (Color figure online)

The retrieved frontal face can be useful in cases in which the voice of the person speaking does not match the face of the person being classified for any of several reasons, e.g., difference in gender, ethnicity, age and so on. Additional information obtained via the crossmodal aspect of face-voice association, where one can relate one speech signal with a person's face, can help determining some clear cases that can be challenging for other models. For instance, if the mouth of the actual speaker in the scene is not seen for some reason, and no mouth movement is detected from any other participant in the scene. A non-speaking person whose face does not match the actual speaker's voice would be classified as not speaking. The actual speaker can also be properly classified if the face of no other scene participant matches the voice.

The contributions of this paper include the creation of FaVoA (**Fa**ce-**Vo**ice **A**ssociation **A**mbiguous Speaker Detector), a model (depicted in Fig. 1) capable of detecting speaking activities in scenarios in which the context does not provide enough information, e.g., several people speaking simultaneously. We furthermore provide a quantitative evaluation on how much face-voice association actually contributes to the detection of speaking activity.

The remainder of the paper is structured as follows. Section 2 presents the approaches that have been proposed to tackle the active speaker detection task, as well as applications of face-voice association. Section 3 introduces the model used in this research to address the task of active speaker detection. The model performance was assessed and compared with state-of-the-art architectures. The details on the experimental setup as well as its results are presented in Sect. 4. That section also offers a discussion on those results, as well as an analysis on how much importance face-voice association plays in ASD. Finally, Sect. 5 summarises the findings of this research and offers possibilities for future works.

2   Related Works

2.1   In-the-Wild Active Speaker Detection

AVA-ActiveSpeaker [16] was the first dataset built for in-the-wild active speaker detection. It was composed of videos in different resolutions with actors speaking in various distinct languages. Labels were provided for some speakers in selected frames of those videos depending on their speaking activity. The labels could be "not speaking", "speaking audible" and "speaking not audible". The dataset was built as part of a task at the 2019 ActivityNet Challenge. The task used mean average precision (mAP) as its evaluation metric and the audibly speaking activity as the positive class for that matter. Two competitors [6,17] achieved a higher mAP than the baseline provided by Roth et al. [16]. Both models depended on a lip synchronisation preprocessing step, and could only achieve a high performance when working with short-term time spans and usually in scenarios in which there was only one person speaking [1,6,17].

To address the shortcoming of previous models, Alcázar et al. [1] propose Active Speakers in Context (ASC), a model whose main intuition is to leverage active speaker context from long-term inter-speaker relations. It differs from previous approaches by using not only the information of the face of the target individual and of the audio input, but also that of the faces of other individuals detected at the same timestamp [1]. The addition of the information from the context in which a speaking activity happens grants ASC an mAP higher than that of Zhang et al. [17], but still lower than that of the ensemble models of Chung [6]. Even though the context aids in some challenging scenarios, it may not prove useful in scenarios in which the mouth of the speaker is not seen due to low resolution or for the speaker not facing the camera, and when there are several people speaking simultaneously.

Dense optical flow is also used for ASD, as a means to strengthen facial motion visual representation and this way avoid confusions that happen to audio-visual fusion-based models due to factors such as non-speaking facial motion, varied lighting and low-resolution footage [10]. The inclusion of the dense optical flow grants the model a performance higher than the baseline model of Roth et al. [16] in two distinct metrics [10], yet no mAP comparison is offered. No comparison with any other architecture is provided either. Similar to other models, the performance of that approach degrades when dealing with faces in low resolution or that are highly tilted.

2.2   Learning of Face-Voice Association

Learning of face-voice relations results from continuous and extensive exposure to audiovisual stimuli [8]. Psychology studies with infants indicate that the ability to make arbitrary face-voice associations emerge in humans between two and four months of age [3]. In the area of active speaker detection, the advantage of matching visual and auditory representations was shown via the use of contrastive loss by some models [10,17]. Those implementations, however, do not explicitly make use of the advantages face-voice associations can provide.

Applications of face-voice association in audiovisual crossmodal representation learning include the assembling of models capable of generating human faces from speech inputs [5,13], as well as of models that can retrieve or match inputs from one modality given inputs of the other modality [11,12]. The performance of active speaker detection models degrades in cases where faces have a very small resolution or a large yaw angle [10]. The ability to retrieve frontal facial embeddings from speech embeddings might provide additional information capable of helping with those challenging cases.

2.3   Gated Bimodal Unit

To determine if face-voice association presents an actual contribution to the task of ASD and in which cases it contributes the most, one should be able to evaluate its contribution quantitatively. Gated multimodal units (GMUs) [2] are modality fusion mechanisms capable of providing quantitative values on the contribution of a given modality to the classification of a dataset entry. The gated bimodal unit (GBU) is a special case of the GMU oriented for the case where there are only two modalities to be fused. GMUs incorporate ideas from feature and decision fusion [2]. The model architecture is based on the flow control of gated neural networks, e.g., gated recurrent units (GRUs) [4]. Given embeddings $\mathbf{e}_1, \mathbf{e}_2 \in \mathbb{R}^d$ from

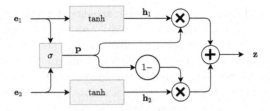

Fig. 2. GBU inner structure

different modalities, the GBU outputs a fused embedding $\mathbf{z} \in \mathbb{R}^d$. As indicated in Fig. 2, the GBU architecture is similar to the update gate of a GRU. In that sense, the GBU fused modality $\mathbf{z}$ is given by

$$\mathbf{z} = \mathbf{p} \odot \mathbf{h}_1 + (\mathbf{1} - \mathbf{p}) \odot \mathbf{h}_2, \tag{1}$$

$$\mathbf{p} = \sigma\left(\mathbf{W}_p\left(\mathbf{e}_1 \parallel \mathbf{e}_2\right) + \mathbf{b}_p\right), \tag{2}$$

$$\mathbf{h}_i = \tanh\left(\mathbf{W}_i \mathbf{h}_i + \mathbf{b}_i\right), \tag{3}$$

where $\odot$ denotes the Hadamard product, σ the sigmoid function, $\parallel$ vector concatenation and $\mathbf{1} \in \mathbb{R}^d$ an all-one vector. It is worth noticing from Eqs. 1 and 2 that $\mathbf{p}$ can be interpreted as a vector of probabilities $p_1, p_2, \ldots, p_d$ that indicate the relevance of each modality in every element $z_i \in \mathbf{z}$. In other words, $z_i \in \mathbf{z}$ is composed of a linear combination of $h_{1,i} \in \mathbf{h}_1$ and $h_{2,i} \in \mathbf{h}_2$. The contribution of $h_{1,i}$ in z_i is given by p_i and that of $h_{2,i}$ is given by the complement of p_i, i.e., $1 - p_i$. Besides the case in which $p_i = 0.5$, one of the modalities will provide a major contribution to z_i while the other will deliver a minor contribution.

3   Model Architecture and Training Method

3.1   Input Data, Active Speakers in Context, and FaceVoice

FaVoA incorporates the context information of Active Speakers in Context (ASC) [1] and the face-voice association provided by FaceVoice [11]. And as such, the proposed model requires input data that can be fed to both models. Figure 1 shows the architecture of the model, how it receives the input data and how it processes it. For the part imported from ASC, given a frame and a person in that frame, the model receives that person's face as a 144×144 image, as well as the audio input from that particular part of the video, which is converted to a MFCC spectrogram. Both inputs are sent to a short-term encoder, denoted as STE in Fig. 1, which outputs a vector $\mathbf{u} \in \mathbb{R}^{1024}$. The STE is composed of two ResNet-18 CNNs [1], one for each modality, which output vectors of 512 dimensions, which are then concatenated to produce $\mathbf{u}$ [1]. The STE was pretrained with the weights provided by Alcázar et al. [1] and kept fixed during training. From FaceVoice, only its voice subnetwork was used, which is denoted as FV in Fig. 1. It requires 10 s of continuous speaking activity as input. However, it is not common for datasets built for active speaker detection to have the same person speaking for such a long time. To work around this restriction, the same audio input sent to STE was replicated until the repeated input had the length of 10 s. This approach was taken because the semantics of what is being said was irrelevant for this task and only the speaking activity was of interest. Given a 10-second audio input, FV then outputs a vector representation $\mathbf{a} \in \mathbb{R}^{128}$. FV was pretrained with the weights provided by Kim et al. [11], but unlike STE its weights were not kept fixed.

In order to make use of the context in which a given speaking activity takes place, the vector representations $\mathbf{u}$ provided by the STE are combined and organised in a tensor $\mathbf{C}$. Tensor $\mathbf{C}$ is built in such a way that it may contain information from the time steps before and after the given speaking activity as well as from other speakers in the same scene. $\mathbf{C}$ has dimensions $L \times S \times 1024$, where L is the number of frames used for the context and S is the number of speakers. Those L frames are defined according to a specific time step t, in which the speaking activity to be classified happens. The frames must be selected in a way that time step t lies at the centre of the frame sequence. A sequence of L frames should contain every frame from time step $t - \lfloor L/2 \rfloor \tau$ to $t + \lfloor L/2 \rfloor \tau$ with hops of τ units of time between each selected frame. It is worth noticing that the sequence of frames does not need to be contiguous. Given the frame of interest at time step t, a set of S speakers in that frame is selected. If there are only $S' < S$ speakers on the frame of interest, then information of some of those S' may be used more than once when working with that frame of interest. In a similar fashion, if some selected speaker appears only in a part of the frame sequence, its foremost activity is replicated all the way until the first frame of the sequence, and analogously its last activity is also replicated all the way until the last frame of the sequence. A more detailed explanation on the selection of frames and speakers can be found in the ASC original paper [1]. Tensor $\mathbf{C}$ is then subjected to a self-attention unit (SAT in Fig. 1) and a single-layer LSTM for the sake of context refinement. The LSTM produces outputs $\mathbf{c}'_i \in \mathbb{R}^{128}, 1 \leq i \leq L \times S$, which are concatenated into a vector representation $\mathbf{s} \in \mathbb{R}^{L \times S \times 128}$. SAT and LSTM were pretrained with the weights provided by Alcázar et al. [1] and were subjected to updates during training.

3.2   Fusing Speaking Context and Face-Voice Association

By combining the embedding $\mathbf{a}$, provided by FaceVoice, with $\mathbf{s}$, provided by ASC, it is expected that the benefits of face-voice association might aid the active speaker detection model even in cases in which the context is not enough, e.g., when there are several people speaking simultaneously, or when the faces of the speakers are either in low resolution or very tilted. The fusion of those embeddings is made by a GBU unit, but since it requires both modality embeddings to have the same dimension, embedding $\mathbf{a}$ is presented to a ReLU and a linear layer, which outputs a vector representation $\mathbf{a}' \in \mathbb{R}^{L \times S \times 128}$. Both $\mathbf{a}'$ and $\mathbf{s}$ are then fused by the GBU unit, which produces a fused vector representation $\mathbf{z} \in \mathbb{R}^{L \times S \times 128}$. The probability $q(\mathbf{x})$ of a given input $\mathbf{x}$ being classified as "speaking audible" is obtained by projection from $\mathbf{z}$ with a linear layer and then the application of a softmax operation over the two classes.

FaVoA was trained on a single NVIDIA GeForce RTX 2080 Ti GPU with 11 GB GDDR6 memory. A single cross-entropy loss $\mathcal{L}$ was used to train it using PyTorch. The loss is given by

$$\mathcal{L} = -y \log(q(\mathbf{x})) - (1 - y) \log(1 - q(\mathbf{x})), \tag{4}$$

where y represents the expected label, which should be 1 if there is audible speaking activity, and 0 otherwise. The model weights were updated through a backpropagation algorithm, by trying to minimise the cumulative loss in every training mini-batch. Data was sent to the model via mini-batches of size 16. Similar to ASC, the model optimisation was done with the ADAM optimiser with an initial learning rate $\gamma = 3 \times 10^{-6}$ and learning rate decay $\eta = 0.1$ every 10 epochs.

4   Experiments

4.1   Dataset

The AVA-ActiveSpeaker dataset is the first dataset intended for the task of active speaker detection that can be considered to be "in the wild". Prior to its publication, datasets crafted for this task were mainly composed of high resolution videos with the speakers facing the camera [16]. AVA-ActiveSpeaker contains videos spoken in very distinct languages, with some of them with low resolution and with video and audio not well synchronised. Speakers may also appear in different video depths, which may cause facial information to be less clear for a learning system, and usually they are not looking at the camera.

The AVA-ActiveSpeaker dataset contains 153 videos, split into 120 for training and 33 for validation. The training dataset is composed of 29,723 speaking/non-speaking streams, ranging from 23 to 304 annotated entries, performed by a total of 10,156 distinct actors, some of them appearing in up to 2,165 dataset entries. The validation dataset has 8,015 streams of speaking/non-speaking activity that range from 14 to 305 dataset annotated entries. Those streams are captured from the performance of 2,515 distinct actors, with some of them having up to 2,143 entries of activity stored in the validation dataset. Table 1 displays the label distribution among those datasets.

Table 1. Label distribution of training and validation splits of the AVA-ActiveSpeaker dataset.

	Not speaking	Speaking audible	Speaking not audible
Training	1,969,134	682,404	24,776
Validation	567,815	192,748	7,744

4.2 Experimental Results

To evaluate FaVoA, its performance was compared with AV-GRU-f2, the baseline model provided by Roth et al. [16], ASC (Active Speaker in Context) [1], Chung's TC-LSTM Ensemble + Wiener smoothing [6] and Zhang et al.'s Multi-Task Learning model [17]. Following the indications on the 2019 ActivityNet challenge, mAP is employed as the metric for this comparison. Table 2 presents the achieved performance of state-of-the-art models and compares them with that of the model described in Sect. 3.

Comparisons were also made with Huang and Koishida's F+O+A VCE-CL (Facial Image, Optical Flow and Audio Signal Visual-Coupled Embedding with Contrastive Loss) [10]. It, however, does not offer performance values using the mAP metric. Because of this, a comparison is here provided using other metrics instead, namely the area under the ROC curve (AUC) and the balanced accuracy. Those metrics were also published for AV-GRU-f2 [16]. Performance results of those models, as well as FaVoA's, are also offered by Table 2. Table 2 shows that not only FaVoA outperformed AV-GRU-f2 in every metric, but it also presents an mAP considerably higher than that of the multi-task learning approach [17], which was the runner-up in the 2019 ActivityNet challenge. Its AUC is also close to that obtained by V+O+A VCE-CL [10].

4.3 Contribution of Face-Voice Association to Active Speaker Detection

Ablation studies are performed to determine whether a given addition to a model makes an actual difference in its performance. However, they do not offer quantitative measures of how much that addition contributes to the classification. For multimodal classification, this is an important issue if one wants to better understand whether some modality contributes more than another to a given task. The use of GBU for crossmodal integration allows to determine if a given classification favours one modality or another. In the case of this study, the interest lies in determining if the classification is mostly due to context information (from ASC) or to face-voice association (from FaceVoice).

Table 2. Comparison with state-of-the-art models on the validation subset.

	mAP ↑	AUC ↑	Balanced accuracy ↑
ASC [1]	0.871	N/A	N/A
TC-LSTM Ensemble + Wiener [6]	0.878	N/A	N/A
Multi-Task Learning [17]	0.840	N/A	N/A
V+O+A VCE-CL [10]	N/A	0.932	0.869
AV-GRU-f2 [16]	0.821	0.910	0.814
FaVoA	0.847	0.928	0.846

In order to quantify the contribution of each modality, one can use the vector **p** produced by the GBU sigmoid unit (see Fig. 2 and Eq. 2). For every entry of the dataset, a vector **p** can be extracted. This vector contains elements p_i, whose values range from 0 to 1. Each element p_i represents a degree of contribution of modality input e_1 (see Fig. 2) to element $z_i \in z$. In turn, the degree of contribution of modality input e_2 to element $z_i \in z$ is $1 - p_i$. By taking the fraction of elements of **p** whose value is greater than 0.5, one can determine the fraction of elements of **z** that favours modality input e_1 rather than e_2. This way, one can get a quantitative measure of the contribution of modality input e_1 to the classification and consequently, the contribution of e_2 is simply one minus the contribution of e_1. In our case modalities e_1 and e_2 correspond to the resulting vector representation of the FaceVoice module and the one of ASC.

The graph of Fig. 3a presents a histogram of the degree of contribution of face-voice association to the detection of speaking activity in entries of the validation set. The horizontal axis of the graph represents the degree of contribution of face-voice association, ranging from 0 to 1. The vertical axis represents the number of entries in the dataset for which the face-voice association had a particular degree of contribution. It can be noticed in the graph that context has a greater contribution to the classification than face-voice association in the entries of the validation set. Nevertheless, context is never favoured by all elements of the GBU output. Besides, face-voice association has a degree of contribution greater than 0.15 for nearly 40% of the entries, and for 303 entries this degree of contribution can get higher than 0.3.

The contribution graph has three modes. The highest peak and its surrounding values correspond mostly to active speakers whose faces are clearly visible, or to silence. The region surrounding the leftmost peak corresponds to dataset

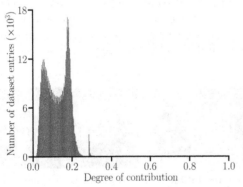

(a) Number of entries per degree of contribution.

(b) Face-voice association has a much higher degree of contribution for the man marked in green than for the other actors.

Fig. 3. Degree of contribution of face-voice association in entries of the validation set.

records where there is some sound activity and the face of the active speaker is not entirely clear or the face being analysed is clearly not from the active speaker. The rightmost part of the graph, with degrees of contribution greater than 0.275, corresponds to entries in which there are very loud sounds. Figure 3b depicts a scene in which the GBU assigns a reasonably higher degree of contribution of face-voice association for the man in the foreground (0.198) than for the other actors (0.098 for the woman in the foreground, and 0.129 and 0.132 for the actors in the background). This happens due to the presence of a male voice in the scene and the higher resolution of the face of the man in the foreground.

4.4   Comparison with Active Speakers in Context

The integration of FaceVoice into FaVoA offers the capability of classifying some instances of speech activity in which ASC failed. Figure 4 presents three cases in which the context information may be ambiguous and face-voice association proves useful. This may happen when actors are facing sideways and a facial feature may be mistaken for an open mouth. In Fig. 4a, ASC wrongly classifies the facial hair for an open mouth, and classifies the man as speaking and the woman as not speaking. Face-voice association prevents this misclassification by recognising the female voice and associating it to the woman.

ASC can also mistakenly classify speaking people as not speaking if the mouth of every person in the scene cannot be clearly seen due to low resolution (Fig. 4b) or if people are speaking simultaneously (Fig. 4c). ASC classifies every person in both figures as not speaking. Face-voice association can aid with correctly classifying the speaker of Fig. 4b due to the age difference. Regarding the scene depicted in Fig. 4c, ASC tends to classify a person as not speaking if someone in the same scene context seems to be already speaking. Thus ASC classifies both speaking women as not speaking, since the speaking activity of one of them triggers ASC to classify the other as not speaking and vice versa. Given the presence of female voices, FaVoA presents a less hesitant behaviour in classifying both women whose faces are not partially hidden as speaking.

(a) Wrong gender.   (b) Low resolution.   (c) Multiple speakers.

Fig. 4. Examples of cases in which the context does not provide enough information and face-voice association is required for a correct active speaker detection. In the subfigures, people who are not speaking are marked with a red bounding box and those speaking with a green bounding box. (Color figure online)

FaVoA presents some difficulties in comparison to ASC in scenes where the person is not speaking, but his/her voice can be heard narrating something. It also makes some mistakes in case there is some chanting and the voice of the person who is chanting somehow resembles that of the person being classified. Finally, ASC tends to more precisely classify some speaking activities (model outputs are mostly either close to 0 or to 1), whereas the outputs of FaVoA vary reasonably in the range between 0 and 1.

5 Conclusion

This paper offers a study on the role of face-voice association in the task of active speaker detection. FaVoA provides a better classification in some challenging scenarios, such as low-resolution faces and several simultaneous speakers. Cross-modal learning models integrate the information from different modalities as a means to better tackle tasks in which one or more of those modalities do not provide enough useful information for some reason. By considering a person's characteristics by his/her voice, FaVoA makes use of the benefits of crossmodality in order to better determine the active speakers in a scene even in cases where the mouth of a speaker cannot be seen. The use of GBU for modality fusion allowed for determining quantitatively the contribution of face-voice association in ASD. By analysing that contribution, some cases of non-speaking activity can be immediately identified, which can help preventing the misclassification of some person as actively speaking. Cases in which there are several speakers can also be identified based on the degree of contribution of face-voice association. In future work, face-voice association may be used to support tackling other cross-modal tasks that involve conversational datasets in which speaker faces may not be clear. Additional directions for improvement in active speaker detection include the addition of other modalities, e.g., gaze and face keypoints.

References

1. Alcázar, J.L., et al.: Active speakers in context. In: IEEE/CVF Conference on Computer Vision and Pattern Recognition (CVPR) (2020)
2. Arevalo, J., Solorio, T., Montes-y-Gómez, M., González, F.A.: Gated multimodal units for information fusion. In: 5th International Conference on Learning Representations, ICLR 2017, Workshop Track Proceedings (2017). OpenReview.net
3. Bahrick, L.E., Hernandez-Reif, M., Flom, R.: The development of infant learning about specific face-voice relations. Dev. Psychol. 41(3), 541–552 (2005)
4. Cho, K., et al.: Learning phrase representations using RNN encoder-decoder for statistical machine translation. In: Proceedings of the 2014 Conference on Empirical Methods in Natural Language Processing (EMNLP), Doha, Qatar, pp. 1724–1734. Association for Computational Linguistics (2014)
5. Choi, H.S., Park, C., Lee, K.: From inference to generation: end-to-end fully self-supervised generation of human face from speech. In: 8th International Conference on Learning Representations, ICLR 2020, Addis Ababa, Ethiopia, 26–30 April 2020 (2020). OpenReview.net

6. Chung, J.S.: Naver at Activitynet Challenge 2019 - Task B Active Speaker Detection (AVA) (2019). https://research.google.com/ava/2019/Naver_Corporation.pdf
7. Chung, J.S., Huh, J., Nagrani, A., Afouras, T., Zisserman, A.: Spot the conversation: speaker diarisation in the wild. In: Interspeech 2020, 21st Annual Conference of the International Speech Communication Association, pp. 299–303. ISCA (2020)
8. Gaver, W.W.: What in the world do we hear? An ecological approach to auditory event perception. Ecol. Psychol. **5**, 1–29 (1993)
9. Hou, J., Wang, S., Lai, Y., Tsao, Y., Chang, H., Wang, H.: Audio-visual speech enhancement using multimodal deep convolutional neural networks. IEEE Trans. Emerging Top. Comput. Intell. **2**(2), 117–128 (2018)
10. Huang, C., Koishida, K.: Improved active speaker detection based on optical flow. In: Proceedings of the IEEE/CVF Conference on Computer Vision and Pattern Recognition (CVPR) Workshops (2020)
11. Kim, C., Shin, H.V., Oh, T.H., Kaspar, A., Elgharib, M., Matusik, W.: On learning associations of faces and voices. In: Proceedings of Asian Conference on Computer Vision (ACCV) (2018)
12. Nagrani, A., Albanie, S., Zisserman, A.: Learnable PINs: cross-modal embeddings for person identity. In: European Conference on Computer Vision (2018)
13. Oh, T., et al.: Speech2Face: learning the face behind a voice. In: 2019 IEEE/CVF Conference on Computer Vision and Pattern Recognition (CVPR), pp. 7531–7540 (2019)
14. Qu, L., Weber, C., Wermter, S.: LipSound: Neural mel-spectrogram reconstruction for lip reading. In: Interspeech 2019, 20th Annual Conference of the International Speech Communication Association, pp. 2768–2772. ISCA (2019)
15. Qu, L., Weber, C., Wermter, S.: Multimodal target speech separation with voice and face references. In: Interspeech 2020, 21st Annual Conference of the International Speech Communication Association, pp. 1416–1420. ISCA (2020)
16. Roth, J., et al.: AVA-ActiveSpeaker: an audio-visual dataset for active speaker detection. In: ICASSP 2020–2020 IEEE International Conference on Acoustics, Speech and Signal Processing (ICASSP), pp. 4492–4496 (2020)
17. Zhang, Y.H., Xiao, J., Yang, S., Shan, S.: Multi-task learning for audio-visual active speaker detection (2019). https://research.google.com/ava/2019/Multi_Task_Learning_for_Audio_Visual_Active_Speaker_Detection.pdf

Bioinformatics and Biosignal Analysis

Identification of Incorrect Karyotypes Using Deep Learning

Jing Peng[1,3], Chengchuang Lin[1,3], Gansen Zhao[1,3(✉)], Aihua Yin[2(✉)],
Hanbiao Chen[2], Li Guo[2], and Shuangyin Li[1,3]

[1] School of Computer Science, South China Normal University, Guangzhou, China
{pengjing,chengchuang.lin,gzhao}@m.scnu.edu.cn
[2] Medical Genetic Centre and Maternal and Children Metabolic-Genetic Key
Laboratory, Guangdong Women and Children Hospital, Guangzhou, China
yinaiwa@vip.126.com
[3] Key Lab on Cloud Security and Assessment Technology of Guangzhou,
Guangzhou, China

Abstract. Karyotyping is a vital cytogenetics technique widely applied
in prenatal diagnosis and genetic screening. Heavily dependent on the
experience of the cytogeneticist and easily affected by the attention, karyotype analysis is a time-consuming and error-prone task, and incorrect
karyotypes may result in misdiagnosis conclusions. This paper proposes
an effective identification framework for incorrect karyotypes based on
deep learning technology. Firstly, a chromosome classifier is trained and
utilized to classify chromosome instances in karyotypes performed manually by cytogeneticists. Afterward, when the categories of chromosome
instances classified by the classifier are not identical to those categories
classified by cytogeneticists, the proposed framework identifies these corresponding karyotypes as unreliable. Finally, the expert team review
these unreliable karyotypes and confirmed their correctness. Extensive
experiments show that the proposed framework achieves 100% *recall*
and 88.89% $F1$ score on incorrect karyotypes, which demonstrates the
advancement and promising effectiveness of the proposed framework to
address the issue of incorrect karyotypes.

Keywords: Incorrect karyotypes identification · Karyotype analysis ·
Chromosome classification · Deep learning

1 Introduction

According to the Birth Defects Report [12] reported by the secretariat of the
World Health Organization, congenital diseases account for 7% of all newborn

Supported by China National Social Science Foundation (No. 19ZDA041), the National
Key-Area Research and Development Program of China (2018YFB1404402), Key-Area
Research and Development Program of Guangdong Province (No. 2019B010137003),
Guangdong Science & Technology Fund (No. 2016B030305006, No. 2018A07071702,
No. 201804010314), Guangzhou Science & Technology Fund (No. 201804010314),
VeChain Foundation (No. SCNU-2018-01).

I. Farkaš et al. (Eds.): ICANN 2021, LNCS 12891, pp. 453–464, 2021.
https://doi.org/10.1007/978-3-030-86362-3_37

deaths. Chromosomal abnormalities are responsible for many congenital genetic diseases, such as *Down syndrome, Patau syndrome, Edward syndrome*, and *Klinefelter syndrome* [1].

In general, a healthy human cell has 23 pairs of chromosomes, including 22 pairs of autosomes and a pair of sex chromosomes (X and Y sex chromosome in a male cell and double X sex chromosome in a female cell) [8]. However, chromosomal abnormalities may occur from some specific hostile environmental factors or errors in cell divisions. To identify various genetic disorders that result from the changes in the number or structure of chromosome instances, the karyotype analysis is the most frequently-used approach in hospital. Figure 1 presents an example of karyotyping where the left sub-figure illustrates a metaphase cell microphotograph G-band chromosome image and the right sub-figure denotes the corresponding karyotype analyzed by an experienced cytogeneticist.

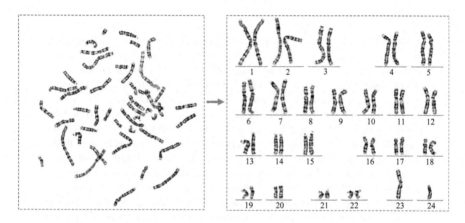

Fig. 1. An example of karyotyping where the left sub-figure illustrates a metaphase cell microphotograph G-band chromosome image and the right sub-figure denotes the corresponding karyotype analyzed by an experienced cytogeneticist.

In the clinical karyotyping practices, the karyotype analysis is a tedious and error-prone task [10]. Incorrect karyotypes occasionally occur due to various objective or subjective reasons, such as similarities among different categories of chromosomes and the experience of cytogeneticist. Accordingly, each analyzed karyotype is required to be reconfirmed by a expert team, which greatly increases the time cost.

Inspired by the existing successes of deep learning, this paper proposes an effective incorrect karyotypes identification framework (Fig. 2) based on deep learning. The contributions and highlights of this paper includes: (1) This paper identifies the challenges of incorrect karyotypes identification and is the first work to address the issue of incorrect karyotypes based on deep learning. (2) The paper introduces a state-of-the-art chromosome classifier and an effective assessment strategy to boost the performance of the proposed framework significantly; (3) Extensive rigorous experiments have been conducted to demonstrate the effectiveness of the proposed identification framework.

The paper is organized as follows. Section 2 reviews the related work on natural image classification and chromosome classification. Section 3 introduces the proposed framework to address the issue of incorrect karyotypes. To verify the efficacy of the proposed framework, Sect. 4 introduces the experimental verification objectives, experimental designs, data, and corresponding experimental results. Finally, Sect. 5 concludes this paper.

2   Related Work

A strong chromosome classifier plays a critical role in the proposed framework, and medical image classification has been widely accepted as a more challenging task compared to natural image classification. According, this section reviews the development of natural image and chromosome classification based on deep learning.

2.1   Image Classification

Recently, many deep learning-based models have been proved more effective for natural image classification tasks than traditional machine learning approaches that heavily relied on hand-crafted feature engineering. Motivated by the ImageNet [2] large-scale visual recognition challenge (*ILSVRC*), the most authoritative annual computer vision competition started in 2010, the accuracies of state-of-the-art models on ILSVRC have been improved significantly from 2010 to 2020. Accompanied by the *ILSVRC* competition, many remarkable images classification deep learning-based models have been proposed, such as AlexNet [5], VGGNets [15], GoogLeNet [16], ResNet [3], and ResNeXt [18]. These successful models are successively applied in medical image recognition tasks, including but not limited to chromosome classification tasks, which has considerably promoted medical artificial intelligence.

2.2   Chromosome Classification

Benefit from the achievements of deep learning-based models for natural image classifications, some chromosome classification methods based on deep learning have been proposed and obtained promising results in various corresponding private datasets. For example, Kusakci et al. [6] presented a two-stage chromosome classification method named Competitive SVM Teams (*CSVMTs*). Their results evaluated on a database consisting of 4,400 samples yielded 91.00% classification accuracy. Xi et al. [4] presented a CNNs (with six convolutional layers, three pooling layers, four dropout layers, and two fully connected layers) for the chromosome classification task. The classifier hit an accuracy score with 93.79% on a database containing 4,184 images. Inspired by the Inception-ResNet

[17] achievement in ImageNet image classification challenge competition, a chromosome classification method named CIR-Net [8] was proposed and obtained 95.98% classification accuracy on a public dataset consisting of 2,990 samples. Qin et al. [13] designed a Varifocal-Net to address the chromosome classification issue whose method includes a global-scale network (*G-Net*) and a local-scale network (*L-Net*). Evaluation results from 1909 karyotypes showed that their proposed Varifocal-Net achieved the highest accuracy per patient case of 99.2% accuracy for both category and polarity tasks.

Different from previous work, this paper pays more attention to identification incorrect karyotypes. To be more specific, we propose a identification framework to check if cytogeneticists misclassified the karyotype. Compared to prior research, we carry the work forward and first notice the issue of incorrect karyotypes. That is to say, our proposed framework can be considered as a valid and reliable tool for the secondary screening of karyotype in clinical practice, rather than to fulfill the reconfirm task totally dependent on manual labour.

3   Proposed Approach

This section first makes a problem statement for the issue of incorrect karyotypes identification and then presents the details of the proposed framework, whose overview is illustrated by Fig. 2. The proposed framework includes the method of data pre-processing, the chromosome classification, and the incorrect karyotypes identification.

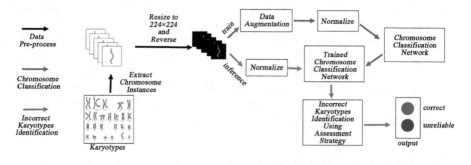

Fig. 2. The overview of the proposed framework for incorrect karyotypes identification.

3.1   Problem Statement

Given a karyotype K_j analyzed by a cytogenetics expert, we let $\Phi(\cdot)$ denote an identifier whose input is a karyotype, and output is Y_j representing the reconfirmed result of the corresponding karyotype. Accordingly, the issue of incorrect karyotypes identification can be regarded as finding a quality-enough identifier

$\Phi(\cdot)$ that has the ability to identify unreliable karyotypes accurately, which can be formalized as Eq. 1.

$$Y_j = \Phi(K_j) \tag{1}$$

This work addresses this issue in the following stages. Firstly, it extracts all chromosome instances $X_j, (< c_j^1, c_j^2, \cdots, c_j^N >)$ and their corresponding label $L_j, (< l_j^1, l_j^2, \cdots, l_j^N >)$ from the given karyotype K_j, where c_j^k denote the kth chromosome instance of K_j and l_j^k represents the kth chromosome category of c_j^k given by an expert. Then, this paper trains a chromosome classifier $\mathcal{F}(\cdot)$ and infers the labels L_j' of X_j, which can be formalized as Eq. 2.

$$L_j' = \mathcal{F}(X_j) \tag{2}$$

Finally, this paper proposes an assessment strategy $\mathcal{A}$ to calculate the consistency of two label vectors L_j and L_j'. When vector L_j and vector L_j' are identical, the value of Y_j is zero, which means that the karyotype is correct; otherwise, the value of Y_j is one, which means that the karyotype is unreliable. Accordingly, the proposed framework can be formalized as Eq. 3.

$$\begin{aligned} Y_j &= \Phi(K_j) \\ &= \mathcal{A}(L_j, L_j') \\ &= \mathcal{A}(L_j, \mathcal{F}(X_j)) \end{aligned} \tag{3}$$

3.2   Date Pre-processing

Given a karyotypes K_j, we first extract chromosome instances into a unified resolution of 300×300 pixels from the karyotypes, then determines the categories of chromosome instances by their category number below the corresponding instances (See right sub-figure of Fig. 1). To get chromosome instances X_j and their corresponding labels L_j, an efficient chromosome extraction algorithm is required.

More specifically, there are four rows of chromosomes in a given karyotypes K_j, and chromosome instances are arranged in a fixed order and relative position. Therefore, the designed algorithm first scans a given karyotypes and determines the start and end cursors for each row. Then, the algorithm resolves how many chromosome instances in each row and records the start and end column cursors of each chromosome instance. Finally, the algorithm extracts each chromosome instance in order and marks the corresponding labels.

3.3   Chromosome Classification

The proposed framework constructs the chromosome classification network $\mathcal{F}(\cdot)$ by transferring the ResNeSt [19]. The ResNeSt model enables attention across feature-map groups and outperforms other networks with similar model complexities. This improvement boosts the performance of downstream tasks like object detection, instance segmentation and semantic segmentation, which is why the proposed framework applies the ResNeSt model to classify chromosomes to ensure its good generalization ability.

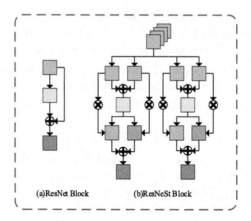

Fig. 3. The difference between the ResNet block and ResNeSt block. The orange squares indicate the input feature maps of the given block, and the output feature maps are marked as brown. The yellow, cyan, blue and green squares are the intermediate feature maps. (Color figure online)

Figure 3 depicts the difference between ResNet Block and ResNeSt Block. ResNet introduces a Residual Connection instead of hoping each few stacked-layer directly to fit a desired underlying mapping to address the gradient degradation problem of deeper neural networks. ResNet architecture has become one of the most popular CNN architecture whose superiority has been proved in various computer vision applications. ResNeSt proposes a ResNeSt Block consisting of Residual Connection, Feature-map Group [18], and Split Attention [7], aiming to improve ResNet through a simple architectural modification. Each block of ResNeSt divides the feature-map into several groups and finer-grained subgroups, where the feature representation of each group is determined via a weighted combination of the representations of its subgroups. ResNeSt model demonstrates its state-of-the-art performances on various benchmarks and can be easily transferred to the downstream task.

The proposed chromosome classifier $\mathcal{F}(\cdot)$ is built by replacing the fully connected layer header of ResNeSt. Additionally, this work adopts label smoothing loss [17] to boost the performance of the proposed classifier.

3.4   Incorrect Karyotypes Identification

In the general natural image classification tasks, the predicted probabilities of predetermined categories are calculated at the end of the fully connected layer in each model. For the chromosome classification task, a probability distribution over predicted 24 classes would be generated by applying the softmax activation function.

However, in a correctly analyzed normal human karyotypes, each chromosome category has two instances. Therefore, the important prior knowledge that a normal karyotypes contains 23 pairs of chromosomes classified into 24 categories can be applied to boost the performance of the chromosome classification network.

To maximize the *precision* of incorrect karyotypes identification, this paper proposes an assessment strategy including three stages. In the first stage, given a karyotypes K_j needed to identify, 46 chromosome instances X_j and corresponding labels L_j are extracted through data pre-processing. Then, the proposed framework loads the trained chromosome classification network to infer the labels of X in the same batch. Therefore, a 46 rows × 24 colums probability distribution matrix P is obtained where P_{ij} denotes the probability of the ith chromosome belonging to the jth category. In the second stage, the assessment strategy $\mathcal{A}_1$ iterates the probability matrix P to figure out categories E that have more than two chromosome instances and excludes redundant chromosome instances into a set M according to the rank of their probabilities. Meanwhile, categories that have less than the required number of instances are recognized as E. In the last stage, the proposed strategy reassigns each chromosome instance of M into the most suitable category in E according to the corresponding probability. It is noteworthy that the sex chromosomes need to be specially handle, because the number of X chromosome and Y chromosome will change with the sex.

4   Experiments and Results

4.1   Dataset and Metric

The clinical chromosome dataset is obtained from the Guangdong Women and Children Hospital. All privacy information of patients has been removed before these karyotypes being collected. This dataset contains 1680 karyotypes, including 1400 karyotypes for training and validating and 280 karyotypes to test the proposed framework. All the extracted chromosome instances are padding into a unified resolution of 300 × 300 and then are resized to 224 × 224 in order to speed up training. Furthermore, the training set is augmented by flipping, elastic transformation, optical distortion and affine transformation. We stochastically exchange labels between two similar chromosomes in a karyotype to simulate incorrect karyotypes in the testing subset.

The issue of incorrect karyotypes identification is a binary classification problem. Accordingly, this work adopts the well-accepted evaluated metrics (*Precision, Accuracy, Recall,* and F_1) for evaluating the proposed framework. Before calculating these evaluated metrics, the following criterion should be clarified.

– True Positive (TP): The number of incorrect karyotypes that are identified as unreliable.

- False Positive (FP): The number of correct karyotypes that are identified as unreliable.
- True Negative (TN): The number of correct karyotypes that are identified as correct.
- False Negative (FN): The number of incorrect karyotypes that are identified as correct.

Based on the above criterion, the evaluated metrics of proposed identification framework *Precision, Recall, Accuracy*, and F_1 can be calculated as Eq. 4, Eq. 6, Eq. 5, and Eq. 7. It should be pointed out that we also separately compared performance of proposed chromosome classifier with previous study, and the metrics were adopted as other researches including precision, recall, accuracy and F1 for multi-class classifier.

$$Precision = \frac{TP}{TP + FP} \tag{4}$$

$$Recall = \frac{TP}{TP + FN} \tag{5}$$

$$Accuracy = \frac{TP + TN}{TP + FP + TN + FN} \tag{6}$$

$$F_1 = \frac{2 \times precision \times recall}{precision + recall} \tag{7}$$

4.2 Implementation Details

To train the chromosome classification network $\mathcal{F}(\cdot)$ and boost the performance of proposed framework, this work uses *Label Smoothing Loss*. As in research [17], the *Label Smoothing Loss* was first applied in natural image classification that allows regularizing the classifier layer by estimating the marginalized effect of label-dropout during training. The *Label Smoothing Loss* is defined as:

$$H(q',p) = (1 - \epsilon)H(q,p) + \epsilon H(u,p) \tag{8}$$

Label Smoothing Loss is a mixture loss combining cross-entropy losses $H(q,p)$ and $H(u,p)$ with weight $1 - \epsilon$ and ϵ, where p is the predicted distribution over labels and u is fixed distribution. Since the blurred distinction between different chromosome categories, we need to encourage the models to be less confident and guarantee the generalization simultaneously.

The proposed framework was implemented with the PyTorch 1.7. The incorrect ratio of karyotypes was set to 0.2 in testing karyotypes. We implemented the Vanilla [20], CNN [4], ChromeNet [14], CIR-Net [8], MixedNet [9] in strict accordance with their origin paper. All implemented chromosome classification network was pre-trained on the ImageNet dataset and optimized using stochastic gradient descent algorithm. All experiments use the same dataset described as above. The initial learning rate was $1e - 2$, and adjusted dynamically using a cosine learning rate schedule with the minimum learning rate with $1e-5$. Training is done for 500 epochs with a weight decay of $1e-4$ and momentum of 0.9, and we use a mini-batch of size 64 at each training iteration. We monitored the loss value and saved the best-trained weight on the validation set. The experiments have been carried out on a server equipped with a 12 GB Nvidia GeForce GTX 2080Ti, Intel Xeon E5-2678 CPU and 256 GB RAM. The source code is available at github.

4.3   Experimental Results and Analyses

A robust incorrect karyotypes identification framework requires a better chromosome classifier. Therefore, this paper has conducted experiments to evaluate the performance of the proposed chromosome classifier and evaluate the incorrect karyotypes identification performance of the proposed framework. The experimental results contain two parts: including chromosome classification results (Table 1) and incorrect karyotypes identification results (Table 2).

Table 1. The chromosome classification performance comparisons between existing state-of-the-art chromosome classification methods.

Chromosome classification methods	Year	*Precision*	*Recall*	*Accuracy*	*F1*
Vanilla [20]	2018	95.40%	94.73%	95.47%	95.01%
CNN [4]	2019	94.33%	93.59%	94.70%	93.88%
ChromeNet [14]	2019	95.06%	94.62%	95.23%	94.81%
CIR-Net [8]	2020	98.57%	98.21%	98.64%	98.38%
MixNet [9]	2020	98.92%	98.71%	98.92%	98.81%
The proposed classification method	/	**99.31%**	**99.27%**	**99.33%**	**99.29%**

Evaluations on the Proposed Chromosome Classification Method. According to the chromosome classification results shown in Table 1, the proposed chromosome classifier has achieved 99.31% precision, 99.27% recall, 99.33% accuracy, 99.29% F1 on the clinical test set, which is better than existing state-of-the-art chromosome classification methods [4,8,9,14,20]. The chromosome classification performance comparison shown in Table 1 demonstrates the outstanding of the proposed chromosome classifier.

Evaluations on the Proposed Kayogram Identification Framework. Based on the proposed advanced chromosome classifier, this paper has evaluated the incorrect karyotypes identification performance of the proposed framework on the condition of with and without the proposed assessment strategy $\mathcal{A}$, respectively. The experimental results have concluded in Table 2.

Table 2. Summarization of the incorrect karyotypes identification performance of the proposed framework.

	Precision	Recall	Accuracy	F1
All karyotypes	78.57%	90.63%	85.00%	81.19%
All karyotypes + $\mathcal{A}$	**90.00%**	**96.88%**	**95.00%**	**92.83%**
Incorrect karyotypes	57.14%	100.00%	/	72.72%
Incorrect karyotypes + $\mathcal{A}$	**80.00%**	**100.00%**	/	**88.89%**

According to the experimental results, without the proposed assessment strategy $\mathcal{A}$, the proposed framework has recalled 100% incorrect karyotypes and achieved 90.63% general *Recall* score. Meanwhile, the proposed framework has achieved an 81.19% identification F_1 score on all test karyotypes and a 72.72% F_1 score on incorrect karyotypes. Furthermore, experimental results have shown that the proposed assessment strategy $\mathcal{A}$ has significantly boosted the incorrect karyotypes identification performance of the proposed framework. Combining with the proposed strategy, the F_1 value on all test karyotypes has been improved 11.64% from 81.19% to 92.83% while the F_1 value on incorrect karyotypes has been improved 16.17% from 72.72% to 88.89%. The *Recall* value has been improved 6.25% from 90.63% to 96.88%. The *Precision* value on all karyotypes has been improved 11.43% from 78.57% to 90.00% while this metric on incorrect karyotypes has been improved 22.86% from 57.14% to 80%. The experimental results have demonstrated the effectiveness of the proposed assessment strategy for the proposed framework to address the issue of incorrect karyotyping identification.

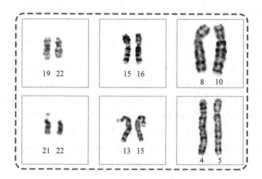

Fig. 4. Examples of misclassification of chromosome pairs. In each misclassified pairs, two chromosome instances are very similar and indistinguishable but belong to different categories.

Explorations of Reasons for Misidentifications. To explore the reasons why false positives still appear, we recorded the misidentified karyotypes and their corresponding mispredicted chromosome instances. In most cases, the reported false positives were misprediction of two chromosome instances. However, this phenomenon is primarily caused by the poor quality of testing karyotypes. To support our observations, Fig. 4 shows a group of misclassified chromosome tuples from six misidentified karyotypes. According to these examples, there are only very slight differences between two misclassified chromosome instances. Moreover, each chromosome instance has very few effective pixels, resulting in extremely limited feature information that the classifier can learn. With the improvement of the quality of chromosome images, we believe that this error rate still has a decline interval.

According to rigorous experiments and corresponding results, the proposed framework has achieved excellent incorrect karyotypes identification performance with a 100% recall score of incorrect karyotypes, which means the proposed framework has identified all incorrect karyotypes analyzed by cytologists manually. These results have demonstrated the promising prospect of the proposed framework for the quality guarantee of karyotypes to avoid the false terminations of healthy babies or the birth of defective babies.

5 Conclusion

In this paper, we proposed a novel and powerful identification framework to address the issue of incorrect karyotypes. More specifically, we introduced a state-of-the-art chromosome classifier, an effective karyotypes assessment strategy and a training methodology of incorrect karyotypes identification. This paper is the first work that realizes the serious consequences of incorrect karyotypes, and the experimental results with a 100% recall score of incorrect karyotypes have demonstrated the preeminent performance of the proposed framework. Besides, the contrast experiment of chromosome classification and incorrect karyotypes identification further proves the reasonability of our proposed framework.

In future works, we plan to investigate additional strategies to further improve the performance of the identification framework, such as confident learning [11]. Deployment of the current method in real-time screening and diagnosis is also to be achieved in the future.

References

1. Campos-Galindo, I.: Cytogenetics techniques. In: Garcia-Velasco, J., Seli, E. (eds.) Human Reproductive Genetics, pp. 33–48. Elsevier, Amsterdam (2020)
2. Deng, J., Dong, W., Socher, R., Li, L.J., Li, K., Fei-Fei, L.: Imagenet: a large-scale hierarchical image database. In: 2009 IEEE Conference on Computer Vision and Pattern Recognition, pp. 248–255. IEEE (2009)
3. He, K., Zhang, X., Ren, S., Sun, J.: Identity mappings in deep residual networks. In: Computer Vision – ECCV 2016, pp. 630–645. Springer, Cham (2016). https://doi.org/10.1007/978-3-319-46493-0_38

4. Hu, X., et al.: Classification of metaphase chromosomes using deep convolutional neural network. Journal of Computational Biology **26**(5), 473–484 (2019)
5. Krizhevsky, A., Sutskever, I., Hinton, G.E.: Imagenet classification with deep convolutional neural networks. Commun. ACM **60**(6), 84–90 (2017)
6. Kusakci, A.O., Ayvaz, B., Karakaya, E.: Towards an autonomous human chromosome classification system using competitive support vector machines teams (csvmt). Exp. Syst. Appl. **86**, 224–234 (2017)
7. Li, X., Wang, W., Hu, X., Yang, J.: Selective kernel networks. In: Proceedings of the IEEE Conference on Computer Vision and Pattern Recognition, pp. 510–519 (2019)
8. Lin, C., et al.: Cir-net: automatic classification of human chromosome based on inception-resnet architecture. In: IEEE/ACM Transactions on Computational Biology and Bioinformatics (2020)
9. Lin, C., Zhao, G., Yin, A., Guo, L., Chen, H., Zhao, L.: Mixnet: a better promising approach for chromosome classification based on aggregated residual architecture. In: 2020 International Conference on Computer Vision, Image and Deep Learning (CVIDL), pp. 313–318. IEEE (2020)
10. Lin, C., et al.: A novel chromosome cluster types identification method using ResNeXt WSL model. Med. Image Anal. **67**, 101943 (2020)
11. Northcutt, C.G., Jiang, L., Chuang, I.L.: Confident learning: estimating uncertainty in dataset labels. arXiv preprint arXiv:1911.00068 (2019)
12. Organization, W.H., et al.: Birth Defects: Report by the Secretariat. Sixty-Third World Health Assembly, Geneva, Switzerland (2010)
13. Qin, Y., et al.: Varifocal-net: a chromosome classification approach using deep convolutional networks. IEEE Trans. Med. Imag. **38**(11), 2569–2581 (2019)
14. Remya, R., Hariharan, S., Vinod, V., Fernandez, D.J.W., Ajmal, N.M., Gopakumar, C.: A comprehensive study on convolutional neural networks for chromosome classification. In: 2020 Advanced Computing and Communication Technologies for High Performance Applications (ACCTHPA), pp. 287–292. IEEE (2020)
15. Simonyan, K., Zisserman, A.: Very deep convolutional networks for large-scale image recognition. arXiv preprint arXiv:1409.1556 (2014)
16. Szegedy, C., et al.: Going deeper with convolutions. In: Proceedings of the IEEE Conference on Computer Vision and Pattern Recognition, pp. 1–9 (2015)
17. Szegedy, C., Vanhoucke, V., Ioffe, S., Shlens, J., Wojna, Z.: Rethinking the inception architecture for computer vision. In: Proceedings of the IEEE Conference on Computer Vision and Pattern Recognition, pp. 2818–2826 (2016)
18. Xie, S., Girshick, R., Dollár, P., Tu, Z., He, K.: Aggregated residual transformations for deep neural networks. In: Proceedings of the IEEE Conference on Computer Vision and Pattern Recognition, pp. 1492–1500 (2017)
19. Zhang, H., et al.: Resnest: split-attention networks. arXiv preprint arXiv:2004.08955 (2020)
20. Zhang, W., et al.: Chromosome classification with convolutional neural network based deep learning. In: 2018 11th International Congress on Image and Signal Processing, BioMedical Engineering and Informatics (CISP-BMEI), pp. 1–5. IEEE (2018)

A Metagraph-Based Model for Predicting Drug-Target Interaction on Heterogeneous Network

Peng Ke[1], Yuqi Wen[2], Zhongnan Zhang[1(✉)], Song He[2(✉)], and Xiaochen Bo[2(✉)]

[1] School of Informatics, Xiamen University, Xiamen 361005, China
zhongnan_zhang@xmu.edu.cn
[2] Beijing Institute of Radiation Medicine, Beijing 100850, China

Abstract. Determining drug-target interactions (DTIs) is an important task in drug discovery and drug relocalization. Currently, different models have been proposed to predict the potential interactions between drugs and targets. However, how to make full use of the information of drugs and targets to improve the prediction performance is still a great challenge. We define the problem of DTI prediction as a link prediction problem in a heterogeneous network and propose a new method, named MGDTI. The heterogeneous network includes known drug-target interactions and drug-drug and target-target similarity relationships. Firstly, we use the frequent subgraph mining algorithm to extract important metagraphs representing the network structure and semantic features without using domain knowledge and experience; then the matrix factorization method based on multiple commuting matrices is used to obtain the embedding representations of drugs and targets from multiple metagraphs; finally link prediction tasks are performed to predict the potential interactions between drugs and targets. We compare MGDTI with four classic heterogeneous network embedding methods and the experimental results show that MGDTI could achieve a better prediction performance.

Keywords: Drug-target interaction · Heterogeneous network · Metagraph · Link prediction

1 Introduction

Drug research and development is a long and expensive process. It is reported that, on average, only one compound in every 10,000 new chemical entities can eventually become a drug, and the whole process takes more than ten years and an investment of more than 800 million US dollars [1]. In recent years, drug development has shifted from traditional experimental methods to computer-aided development [2]. The target of computer-aided drug development is to find drugs that can interact with specific target proteins. The prediction of drug-target interaction (DTIs) refers to the recognition of interactions between drugs and the protein targets in the human body. Therefore, DTI

P. Ke and Y. Wen—Equal contribution.

© Springer Nature Switzerland AG 2021
I. Farkaš et al. (Eds.): ICANN 2021, LNCS 12891, pp. 465–476, 2021.
https://doi.org/10.1007/978-3-030-86362-3_38

prediction is an important task for early evaluation of potential new drugs, and can reduce the cost of capital, time, and resources in the process of drug development.

In recent years, many machine learning-based methods have been proposed for DTI prediction, such as network reasoning [3–5], matrix factorization [6, 7], kernel-based method [8], collaborative filtering [9], clustering [10], and label propagation [11]. However, due to the rapid growth of biomedical data, the relationships among the data entities involved are becoming more and more complex. These existing methods do not make full use of the latent information of these complex relationships. Heterogeneous networks can better express the relationships among different types of entities and are more universal.

In a heterogeneous network, nodes represent different types of entities, such as targets and drugs, and the edges between nodes represent the relationships among these nodes, such as drug-drug similarity, target-target similarity, and drug-target correlation. Each node in the network can be represented by a low-dimensional latent feature embedding. Different downstream tasks can be implemented based on these low-dimensional feature embeddings. The objective of this study is to predict drug-target interactions, which is defined as the link prediction problem on a heterogeneous network. Some scholars have conducted in-depth research on the node embedding of heterogeneous networks and proposed a series of methods, including metapath2vec [12], HIN2vec [13], HeteSpaceyWalk [14], JUST [15], PTE [16], HEER [17], GATNE [18], RHINE [19] and so on. Some of the above methods, such as metapath2vec, HIN2vec, HeteSpaceyWalk and GATNE, are based on random walk, which requires pre-defined metapath templates, or knowledge and experience in related fields when defining metapaths. Moreover, metapath cannot fully capture the complex semantic information of heterogeneous networks. Other methods based on first-order (second-order) proximity, such as PTE and HEER, are mainly used in tasks of node classification, and do not perform well in link prediction tasks.

To address the above issues, in this study, we propose a new drug-target interaction prediction method based on heterogeneous network, named MGDTI.

The core contributions of this study are as follows:

1. A heterogeneous network is constructed based on known drug-target interactions, drug-drug similarity and target-target similarity relationships, which could provide rich potential semantic information among different entities;
2. A frequent subgraph mining algorithm is used to extract important metagraphs that represent network structure and semantic features, and no longer rely on relevant domain knowledge and experience;
3. Multiple metagraphs are used to obtain the embedding representation of drugs and targets, which can capture the complex semantic features and potential association information of heterogeneous network more comprehensively.

2   Data and Definition

2.1   Data Source

In this study, the similarity relationships among 580 drugs from [20] are used to represent the drug-drug similarity matrix $S^D \in R^{580 \times 580}$. And the similarity relationships among 2681 target genes from [21] are used to represent the target-target similarity matrix $S^T \in R^{2681 \times 2681}$. $S_{i,j}^D$ represents the similarity between drugs d_i and d_j, and $S_{i,j}^T$ represents the similarity between targets t_i and t_j. The values in S^D and S^T are real numbers between 0 and 1. In addition, the interaction relationships of 580 drugs and 2681 targets were obtained from the DrugBank [22], which is represented as the matrix $P \in \{0, 1\}^{580 \times 2681}$, including a total of 2187 known drug-target interaction relationships. If $P_{i,j} = 1$, it indicates that drug d_i has been experimentally confirmed to interact with target t_j. Otherwise, the interaction between them is unknown.

2.2   Problem Definition

Generally, a heterogeneous graph is represented as $G = (V, E, \mathcal{A}, \mathcal{R})$, where $V = \{v_1, \cdots, v_m\}$ is the set of nodes and $E = \{e_1, \cdots, e_n\}$ is the set of edges. The topology of the graph is represented as an adjacency matrix $A \in \{0, 1\}^{m \times m}$, where $A_{i,j} = 1$ means there is a link between nodes v_i and v_j, otherwise $A_{i,j} = 0$. $\mathcal{A}$ represents the node type set, $\mathcal{R}$ is the edge type set, and $|\mathcal{A}| + |\mathcal{R}| > 2$. The adjacency matrix A can be divided into $|\mathcal{A}| \times |\mathcal{A}|$ submatrices. $A^{\mathcal{A}_i, \mathcal{A}_j}$ represents the adjacencies between nodes of type $\mathcal{A}_i$ and nodes of type $\mathcal{A}_j$, $A^{\mathcal{A}_i, \mathcal{A}_j}$ is the transpose of $A^{\mathcal{A}_j, \mathcal{A}_i}$, and $A^{\mathcal{A}_i, \mathcal{A}_i}$ represents the adjacencies among nodes of type $\mathcal{A}_i$.

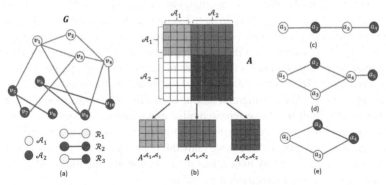

Fig. 1. (a): The topology of the heterogeneous graph G; (b): The adjacency matrix and submatrices of G; (c)–(e): Metagraph examples.

In this study, we define the drug-target interaction prediction problem as the link prediction problem on the heterogeneous network G (Fig. 1(a)), which includes two types of nodes and three types of undirected edges. Therefore, $|\mathcal{A}| = 2$ and $|\mathcal{R}| = 3$. $\mathcal{A}_1$ and $\mathcal{A}_2$ represent the node type of drug and target, respectively. $\mathcal{R}_1, \mathcal{R}_2$ and $\mathcal{R}_3$ represent the edge type of drug-drug association, target-target association, and drug-target interaction, respectively. For each $v_i \in \mathcal{A}_1$ and $v_j \in \mathcal{A}_1$, if $S_{v_i, v_j}^D > \alpha$, $A_{i,j} = 1$. And for each $v_i \in \mathcal{A}_2$ and $v_j \in \mathcal{A}_2$, if $S_{v_i, v_j}^T > \alpha$, $A_{i,j} = 1$. α is a pre-set similarity threshold. Similarly, for each $v_i \in \mathcal{A}_1$ and $v_j \in \mathcal{A}_2$, if $P_{v_i, v_j} = 1$, $A_{i,j} = 1$. $A^{\mathcal{A}_1, \mathcal{A}_2}$ represents the relationships between drug nodes and target nodes, $A^{\mathcal{A}_1, \mathcal{A}_1}$ represents target-target associations, and $A^{\mathcal{A}_2,\mathcal{A}_2}$ represents drug-target associations, as shown in Fig. 1(b).

For the given heterogeneous network G, the goal is to predict unknown edges between drug nodes and target nodes in G.

3 Methods

In this section, we will introduce the MGDTI model in detail. Before introducing the model, we first give the definition of metagraph.

A metagraph is an acyclic graph with a single source node n_s and a single sink node n_t. Given a graph $G = (V, E, \mathcal{A}, \mathcal{R})$, a metagraph can be defined as $M = (\mathcal{A}_M, \mathcal{R}_M, n_s, n_t)$, where $n_s \in \mathcal{A}_M$, $n_t \in \mathcal{A}_M$, $\mathcal{A}_M \subseteq \mathcal{A}$ and $\mathcal{R}_M \subseteq \mathcal{R}$. $\mathcal{A}_M$ and $\mathcal{R}_M$ represent the node set and edge set of M, respectively.

For a path of length p in metagraph M, it can be defined as a sequence of p nodes $(a_1, a_2,...,a_p)$, where $a_i \in \mathcal{A}_M (1 \leq i \leq p)$, $a_1 = n_s$ and $a_p = n_t$. There may exist only one path or multiple paths in a metagraph. Since the objective of this study is to find potential drug-target interactions, the source-sink node pair of an effective metagraph should be a drug-target node pair or a target-drug node pair. Given that G is an undirected graph, the above two cases are symmetric. Therefore, we only consider the case that source node is drug and sink node is target.

In Fig. 1, (c) and (d) denote two metagraphs of G, respectively. There is only one path of length 4 in Fig. 1(c), where a_1 is the source node and a_4 is the target node. In Fig. 1(d), the metagraph includes two paths of length 4, which are (a_1, a_2, a_4, a_5) and (a_1, a_3, a_4, a_5), and a_1 and a_5 are the source node and the target node, respectively.

The prediction model includes three parts: metagraphs discovery, node embedding, and link prediction. The overall framework of the model is shown in Fig. 2.

First, we use the frequent subgraph mining algorithm to obtain a series of subgraphs of G; then a set of non-repetitive representative metagraphs that conform to the above metagraph definition is selected from these subgraphs; next, we calculate the commuting matrix of each metagraph, and the node embeddings of drugs and targets are obtained from the commuting matrix by matrix factorization. Finally, the link prediction task is performed based on the obtained node embeddings.

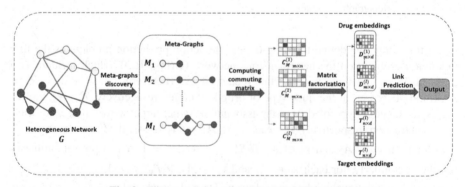

Fig. 2. The overall flowchart of the MGDTI method.

3.1 Metagraph Discovery

The traditional idea of metagraph discovery includes two steps: (1) find out a series of metapaths according to the prior knowledge; (2) simply combine several metapaths to construct a set of metagraphs. In this way, the quality of the metagraph is directly determined by the known prior knowledge. Once the prior knowledge is insufficient or incomplete, the quality of the discovered metagraphs will be poor, which will directly affect the performance of downstream tasks.

In order to avoid the influence of prior knowledge on metagraph discovery, we adopt the method of frequent subgraph mining to obtain metagraphs. The basic idea is that if a subgraph in graph G appears frequently, it is important for graph G and can be used as a metagraph to retain important structure and semantic information in G. The metagraph discovery method is divided into two steps. Firstly, the frequent subgraph mining algorithm is used to find all frequent subgraphs in G according to a given frequent threshold τ. Secondly, a group of representative subgraphs that conform to the given metagraph definition is selected from the frequent subgraphs. The specific algorithm is shown in Algorithm 1.

Algorithm 1: Metagraph discovery
Input: $G = (V, E, \mathcal{A}, \mathcal{R})$; Frequency threshold τ; Source node n_s; Target node n_t
Output: Metagraph set C
1. $\mathcal{F}, C \leftarrow \emptyset$
2. **for each** $e \in E$ **do**
3. $\quad f_{\mathcal{R}_e}{+}{+};$ //$\mathcal{R}_e$ represents the type of edge e
4. $\quad$ **for each** $\mathcal{R}_i \in \mathcal{R}$ **do**
5. $\qquad$ **if** $f_{\mathcal{R}_i} > \tau$
6. $\qquad\quad \mathcal{F} \leftarrow \mathcal{F} \cup \mathcal{R}_i;$ //add edge type $\mathcal{R}_i$ to set $\mathcal{F}$
7. **for each** $e \in E$ **do**
8. $\quad$ **if** $\mathcal{R}_e \in \mathcal{F}$
9. $\qquad C \leftarrow C \cup$ SUBGRAPHEXTENSION $(e, G, \tau, \mathcal{F});$
10. $\qquad E \leftarrow E - e;$
11. **for each** M $\in C$ **do**
12. $\quad$ **if** (M.$source$ <> n_s) **or** (M.$target$ <> n_t)
13. $\qquad C \leftarrow C - M;$ //remove M from set C
14. **Return** C;

First, the algorithm obtains the frequency of all edge types in graph G (Lines 2–3). $f_{\mathcal{R}_i}$ represents the number of times that the edge type $\mathcal{R}_i \in \mathcal{R}$ appears in G. If the frequency $f_{\mathcal{R}_i}$ is not less than the frequent threshold τ, this edge type is frequent and will be added to the set $\mathcal{F}$ (Lines 4–6). For each edge e in G, if $\mathcal{R}_e \in \mathcal{F}$, the SUBGRAPHEXTENSION algorithm [23] will be executed. This algorithm first initializes a subgraph, and then uses the frequent edges in $\mathcal{F}$ to extend the subgraph that conforms to the frequent threshold τ (Lines 7–10). Finally, for each frequent subgraph $M \in C$, if the source node is not n_s or the sink node is not n_t, M is removed (Lines 11–13). At last, the set $C = \{M_l\}_{l=1}^L$ containing all metagraphs can be obtained.

3.2 Node Embedding

In order to obtain the potential embedding representations of all drugs and targets, the commuting matrix $\mathbf{C}_M$ of each metagraph needs to be calculated first. The commuting matrix [24] represents the similarity between the source node and the sink node in metagraph M.

M can be composed of several sub-metagraphs, which are defined as follows:

(1) There is only one path $(a_i, a_{i+1}, \ldots, a_j)$ in the sub-metagraph, such as Fig. 1(c).
(2) The sub-metagraph contains $s > 1$ independent paths that share the same source and sink nodes, such as $\left(a_i, a_{i+1}^{(1)}, \ldots, a_{j-1}^{(1)}, a_j\right)$, $\left(a_i, a_{i+1}^{(2)}, \ldots, a_{j-1}^{(2)}, a_j\right)$, ..., and $\left(a_i, a_{i+1}^{(s)}, \ldots, a_{j-1}^{(s)}, a_j\right)$. In Fig. 1(e), the sub-metagraph has two paths.

For the first type of sub-metagraph, the commuting matrix $\mathbf{C}_{SM}^{i,j}$ is calculated as Eq. (1):

$$\mathbf{C}_{SM}^{i,j} = A^{a_i,a_{i+1}} \cdot A^{a_{i+1},a_{i+2}} \cdot \ldots \cdot A^{a_{j-1},a_j}. \tag{1}$$

For the second type of sub-metagraph, the commuting matrix $\mathbf{C}_{DM}^{i,j}$ is calculated as Eq. (2):

$$\mathbf{C}_{DM}^{i,j} = \odot_{x=1}^{s} (A^{a_i,a_{i+1}^{(x)}} \cdot A^{a_{i+1}(x),a_{i+2}^{(x)}} \cdot \ldots \cdot A^{a_{j-1}(x),a_j}). \tag{2}$$

$\odot$ is the Hadamard product. The commuting matrix of a metagraph M can be obtained by multiplying the commuting matrices of its several sub-metagraphs. For example, in Fig. 1(d), the commuting matrix $\mathbf{C}_M = ((A^{a_1,a_2} \cdot A^{a_2,a_4}) \odot (A^{a_1,a_3} \cdot A^{a_3,a_4})) \cdot A^{a_4,a_5}$. If G has L different metagraphs, we can get L different commuting matrices, denoted by $\left\{\mathbf{C}_M^{(l)}\right\}_{l=1}^{L}$. Then we adopt matrix factorization (MF) [25] to extract the latent features of drugs and targets from the obtained commuting matrices to solve the sparsity problem of the commuting matrices. $\mathbf{C}_M^{(l)}$ can be decomposed into two low-rank matrices, $D^{(l)}$ and $T^{(l)}$, as shown in Eq. (3). They represent the potential features of all drugs and targets obtained from the commuting matrix of the l-th metagraph in low-dimensional vector space.

$$\mathbf{C}_M^{(l)} \approx D^{(l)} \times T^{(l)\top}. \tag{3}$$

The objective function that needs to be optimized in matrix factorization is shown in Eq. (4):

$$\min_{D^{(l)},T^{(l)}} \frac{1}{2} P_\Omega \left(D^{(l)} T^{(l)\top} - \mathbf{C}_M^{(l)}\right)_F^2 + \frac{\lambda_d}{2} \|D^{(l)}\|_F^2 + \frac{\lambda_t}{2} \|T^{(l)}\|_F^2 \tag{4}$$

where if $A_{d_i,t_j} = 1$, $[P_\Omega(\mathbf{X})]_{ij} = \mathbf{X}_{ij}$; otherwise, $[P_\Omega(\mathbf{X})]_{ij} = 0$. λ_d and λ_t are the regularization hyper-parameters that are used to avoid overfitting. For each metagraph, we can obtain two embedding matrices, one for drugs and one for targets. Therefore, we get L embedding matrices for drugs and L embedding matrices for targets, denoted as $\left\{D^{(1)}, \ldots, D^{(L)}; T^{(1)}, \ldots, T^{(L)}\right\}$.

3.3 Link Prediction

In order to perform the task of link prediction of drug-target interactions, we need to obtain a single embedding for each drug or target node separately. Therefore, for each drug node, its embedding is integrated according to Eq. (5); for each target node, its embedding is integrated according to Eq. (6):

$$D_i = \frac{1}{L} \sum_{l=1}^{L} D_i^{(l)}, \tag{5}$$

$$T_j = \frac{1}{L} \sum_{l=1}^{L} T_j^{(l)}, \tag{6}$$

where $D_i^{(l)} \in R^{1 \times d}$ and $T_i^{(l)} \in R^{1 \times d}$ represent the embedding representation of drug i and target j obtained from the l-th metagraph, respectively. Then, the cosine similarity between the drug node embedding and the target node embedding is treated as the probability of the existence of a link between the two nodes. The cosine similarity is defined as Eq. (7):

$$\cos(x, y) = \frac{x \cdot y}{\|x\| \|y\|}. \tag{7}$$

The drug-target pair with cosine similarity greater than β is predicted to have an interaction.

4 Experiments and Analysis

The experiments are designed to answer the following four questions:

1. Do the metagraphs obtained by our method capture the semantic information of a given heterogeneous network more fully than the metagraphs designed based on experiences?
2. How does the frequent threshold τ affect the performance of the model?
3. What is the impact of the embedding dimension on the performance of link prediction?
4. Will our model (MGDTI) outperform other node embedding models based on heterogeneous network?

4.1 Assessment Metrics

The assessment metrics used in this study are F1-score, Precision@k and AUPR.

Area Under the Precision-Recall Curve (AUPR): Recall is the fraction of retrieved instances among all relevant instances. Precision measures the model's accuracy in classifying a sample as positive. These metrics are used to construct a Precision-Recall Curve which illustrates how the increase in recall affects precision. AUPR is the area under the Precision-Recall curve.

Precision@k: Link prediction tasks are usually interested in the quality of highly ranked results. Precision@k is the fraction of correct predictions in top k predictions, which is defined as Eq. (8):

$$\text{Precision@}k = \frac{\left| E_{\text{pred}}\left(1:k\right) \cap E_{obs} \right|}{k}. \tag{8}$$

$E_{\text{pred}}\left(1:k\right)$ is the set of the top k predictions and E_{obs} is the set of hidden edges. This is a link-quality metric.

F1-score is often used to determine the accuracy of the method. It can consider both the precision and the recall, which can reflect the accuracy of the method in a balanced way. It can be defined as Eq. (9):

$$F_1 = 2 \cdot \frac{\text{precision} \cdot \text{recall}}{\text{precision} + \text{recall}}. \tag{9}$$

4.2 Experimental Setup

We first obtain the embedding representation of drugs and targets, and then perform link prediction tasks to evaluate the effectiveness of our proposed method. The link prediction task is to randomly hide a certain percentage of known links from the original network, and the goal is to predict the hidden links. We randomly hide 20% of the drug-target associations in the heterogeneous network as a test set to evaluate the performance of the model, and use the rest of the network as a training set. The parameters used in the experiments and their values are listed in Table 1.

Table 1. The parameters and settings used in the experiments.

Parameter	Setting
Embedding dimension (d)	[10,20,30,50,64,128]
Frequency threshold (τ)	[100,200,300,400,500]
λ_d	0.01
λ_t	0.01
α	0.003
β	0.35

4.3 Results and Analysis

Comparison of Different Metagraph Discovery Methods
We use the node embeddings obtained by our method and the embeddings from metagraphs designed by experiences for comparison. When designing metagraphs based on

Table 2. The impact of different metagraphs discovery methods on prediction performance.

	AUPR	F1-score	Precision@128
MGDTI	**0.893**	**0.882**	**0.992**
Experiences-based	0.879	0.789	0.961

experiences [4], the length of any path in the metagraph is set to be no more than 5, and all possible metagraphs are obtained. Table 2 shows the comparison results.

As can be seen from Table 2, the prediction results obtained by using our method are slightly better than those based on experiences. The subgraphs obtained by MGDTI are more important in the heterogeneous network since they reappear in the network many times. They can reflect important link relationships among nodes, and can better capture the potential semantic information in the heterogeneous network. Therefore, the results of link prediction based on our approach are better than those of the experience-based method.

Influence of the Frequent Threshold τ on the Performance of the Model
In the metagraph discovery algorithm, the frequent threshold τ will have a direct impact on the obtained metagraphs. Figure 3(a) shows the comparison of link prediction performances based on metagraphs obtained with different frequent thresholds.

As can be seen from Fig. 3(a), with the increase of τ, the link prediction performance of the model generally declines. This is because with the increase of frequent threshold, the number of frequent subgraphs satisfying the threshold decreases, and there may be some important structural information in these filtered subgraphs. This will make selected metagraphs unable to completely capture semantics information in the heterogeneous network, resulting in missing some important structural information. If the frequent threshold is set too small, it will lead to many repetitive and useless information in the frequent subgraphs, and will increase the cost of subsequent node embedding. So, we use the frequent threshold $\tau = 100$ as the best parameter.

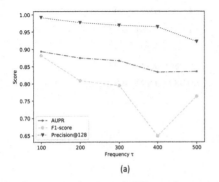
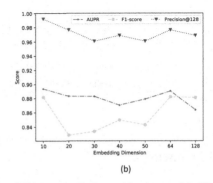

(a)   (b)

Fig. 3. (a): The impact of different frequency thresholds on prediction performance; (b): The impact of different embedding dimensions on prediction performance.

Impact of the Embedding Dimension on Link Prediction

The goal of node embedding is to map the high-dimensional feature vectors to a low-dimensional latent space and capture the implicit features expressed by nodes. The dimensional size of the node embedding has an impact on capturing the hidden feature information expressed by the original high-dimensional drugs and target nodes. Figure 3(b) shows the performances of link prediction task with node embeddings in different dimensions. It can be seen that the overall performance fluctuates but the change is small. This indicates that our node embedding method has been able to fully extract the potential feature information of nodes with a small embedding dimension.

Comparison with Other Methods

We compare our method with four classic methods, including JUST [15], Hin2vec [13], GATNE [18] and FMG [26]. All of them are designed for heterogeneous network embedding representation learning, and have good performances. They all use their original parameter settings in this experiment.

As can be seen from Table 3, the three metapath-based approaches (JUST, Hin2vec and GATNE) have a good performance, which shows that metapath is a good method for network representation learning. However, our method (MGDTI) has significantly better performance in both AUPR and F1-score. This is because in heterogeneous networks, metagraphs can capture the complex semantic features and the potential relationships between nodes more comprehensively than metapaths. FMG is also a metagraph-based method, and MGDTI performs better than FMG, indicating that metagraphs obtained by MGDTI can better capture the complex semantic features than those defined by FMG.

Table 3 also illustrates the comparison results on Precision@k. In the top 128 links, MGDTI made only 1 wrong prediction, while other methods made more than 3 wrong predictions, and the performance of MGDTI is much better in the top 256 links.

Table 3. Comparison different methods on AUPR, F1-score, and Precision@k

	AUPR	F1-score	Precision@k			
			32	64	128	256
JUST	0.846	0.712	1	1	0.97	0.90
Hin2vec	0.854	0.724	1	1	0.984	0.933
GATNE	0.835	0.722	1	1	0.906	0.767
FMG	0.879	0.789	1	0.984	0.961	0.933
MGDTI	**0.893**	**0.882**	1	0.984	**0.992**	**0.949**

5   Conclusions

In this study, we propose a new method, named MGDTI, to predict the unknown interactions between drugs and targets. We use frequent subgraph mining algorithm to extract important metagraphs representing network structure and semantic features, which solves the problem that traditional methods rely on relevant domain knowledge and experience for metagraph discovery. Then the matrix factorization method based on multiple commuting matrices is used to obtain the embedding representations of drugs and targets from multiple metagraphs. Finally, link prediction task is performed to predict potential interactions between drugs and targets. MGDTI can effectively learn the correlation information between drugs and targets, and make full use of the latent feature information in heterogeneous network for prediction. We compare MGDTI with other classic methods and prove its superiority and robustness.

References

1. Hutchins, S., Torphy, T., Muller, C.: Open partnering of integrated drug discovery: continuing evolution of the pharmaceutical model. Drug Discov. Today 7(16), 281–283 (2011)
2. Kapetanovic, I.: Computer-aided drug discovery and development (CADDD): in silico-chemico-biological approach. Chemico Biol. Interactions 171(2), 165–176 (2008)
3. Luo, Y., Zhao, X., Zhou, J., et al.: A network integration approach for drug-target interaction prediction and computational drug repositioning from heterogeneous information. Nat. Commun. 8(1), 1–13 (2017)
4. Thafar, M., Playan, R., Ashoor, H., et al.: DTiGEMS+: drug–target interaction prediction using graph embedding, graph mining, and similarity-based techniques. J. Cheminform. 12(1), 1–17 (2020)
5. Lu, Z., Wang, Y., Zeng, M., et al.: HNEDTI: prediction of drug-target interaction based on heterogeneous network embedding. In: 2019 IEEE International Conference on Bioinformatics and Biomedicine (BIBM). IEEE (2019)
6. Peska, L., Buza, K., Koller, J.: Drug-target interaction prediction: a Bayesian ranking approach. Comput. Methods Programs Biomed. 152, 15–21 (2017)
7. Ye, Y., Wen, Y., Zhang, Z., et al.: Drug-Target Interaction Prediction Based on Adversarial Bayesian Personalized Ranking. BioMed Research International, vol. 2021. Article ID 6690154 (2021)
8. Nascimento, A., Prudêncio, R., Costa, I.: A multiple kernel learning algorithm for drug-target interaction prediction. BMC Bioinform. 17(1), 1–16 (2016)
9. Koohi, A.: Prediction of drug-target interactions using popular Collaborative Filtering methods. In: 2013 IEEE International Workshop on Genomic Signal Processing and Statistics. IEEE (2013)
10. Zhang, X., Li, L., Ng, M.: Drug–target interaction prediction by integrating multiview network data. Comput. Biol. Chem. 69, 185–193 (2017)
11. Zhang, W., Chen, Y., Li, D.: Drug-target interaction prediction through label propagation with linear neighborhood information. Molecules 22(12), 2056 (2017)
12. Dong, Y., Chawla, N., Swami, A.: metapath2vec: scalable representation learning for heterogeneous networks. In: Proceedings of the 23rd ACM SIGKDD International Conference on Knowledge Discovery and Data Mining (2017)
13. Fu, T., Lee, W., Lei, Z.: Hin2vec: explore meta-paths in heterogeneous information networks for representation learning. In: Proceedings of the 2017 ACM on Conference on Information and Knowledge Management (2017)
14. He, Y., Song, Y., Li, J., et al.: Hetespaceywalk: a heterogeneous spacey random walk for heterogeneous information network embedding. In: Proceedings of the 28th ACM International Conference on Information and Knowledge Management (2019)

15. Hussein, R., Yang, D., Cudré-Mauroux, R.: Are meta-paths necessary? Revisiting hetero-geneous graph embeddings. In: Proceedings of the 27th ACM International Conference on Information and Knowledge Management (2018)
16. Tang, J., Qu, M., Mei, Q.: Pte: predictive text embedding through large-scale heteroge-neous text networks. In: Proceedings of the 21th ACM SIGKDD International Conference on Knowledge Discovery and Data Mining (2015)
17. Shi, Y., Zhu, Q., Guo, F., et al.: Easing embedding learning by comprehensive transcription of heterogeneous information networks. In: Proceedings of the 24th ACM SIGKDD International Conference on Knowledge Discovery and Data Mining (2018)
18. Cen, Y., Zou, X., Zhang, J., et al.: Representation learning for attributed multiplex hetero-geneous network. In: Proceedings of the 25th ACM SIGKDD International Conference on Knowledge Discovery and Data Mining (2019)
19. Lu, Y., Shi, C., Hu, L., et al.: Relation structure-aware heterogeneous information network embedding. In: Proceedings of the AAAI Conference on Artificial Intelligence (2019)
20. He, S., Wen, Y., Yang, X., et al.: PIMD: an integrative approach for drug repositioning using multiple characterization fusion. Genom. Proteomics Bioinform. **18**, 565 (2020)
21. Wu, L.-L., Wen, Y.-Q., Yang, X.-X., Yan, B.-W., He, S., Bo, X.-C.: Synthetic lethal interactions prediction based on multiple similarity measures fusion. J. Comput. Sci. Technol. **36**(2), 261–275 (2021). https://doi.org/10.1007/s11390-021-0866-2
22. Law, V., Knox, C., Djoumbou, Y., et al.: DrugBank 4.0: shedding new light on drug metabolism. Nucl. Acids Res. **42**(D1), D1091–D1097 (2014)
23. Elseidy, M., Abdelhamid, E., Skiadopoulos, S., et al.: Grami: frequent subgraph and pattern mining in a single large graph. Proc. VLDB Endowm. **7**(7), 517–528 (2014)
24. Sun, Y., Han, J., Yan, X., et al.: Pathsim: Meta path-based top-k similarity search in heterogeneous information networks. Proc. VLDB Endowm. **4**(11), 992–1003 (2011)
25. Mnih, A., Salakhutdinov, R.: Probabilistic matrix factorization. Adv. Neural Inf. Process. Syst. **20**, 1257–1264 (2007)
26. Zhao, H., Yao, Q., Li, J., et al.: Meta-graph based recommendation fusion over heterogeneous information networks. In: Proceedings of the 23rd ACM SIGKDD International Conference on Knowledge Discovery and Data Mining (2017)

Evaluating Multiple-Concept Biomedical Hypotheses Based on Deep Sets

Juncheng Ding$^{(\boxtimes)}$ and Wei Jin

University of North Texas, Denton, TX 76201, USA
`junchengding@my.unt.edu`, `wei.jin@unt.edu`

Abstract. Given hypotheses that connect two "irrelevant" concepts of interest via one or multiple concepts, Hypothesis Generation (HG) attempts to judge their meaningfulness and compare or rank them accordingly. HG can accelerate scientific research and is becoming increasingly important. The basic idea of prior studies is to conduct a two or higher-order search between the two input concepts for the one-concept and multiple-concept hypotheses to evaluate them. However, these approaches inevitably encounter exponential-growing searching space when addressing multiple-concept hypotheses, making it impractical to tackle such hypotheses. We propose HG Set Net (HSN) that forms a hypothesis with any number of connecting concepts as a set and learns to evaluate the set to address this problem. HSN can evaluate any hypotheses with the same complexity and avoid higher-order search, making it computationally possible to evaluate hypotheses with numerous concepts. Besides, we present a double-margin loss to train HSN to resolve the lack of labeled hypotheses. Experiments show that HSN can not only address hypotheses with efficiency but also outperform previous approaches. The double-margin loss also reveals to boost HSN's performance.

Keywords: Hypothesis Generation · Bioinformatics · Data mining

1 Introduction

Understanding and creating human knowledge is one of artificial intelligence's ultimate goals. Hypotheses Generation (HG), which creates seeds for new knowledge based on understanding existing knowledge, has long been a task of the above kind (Fig. 1). In a typical knowledge discovery process, an investigator generates hypotheses through reviewing relevant publications and then experiments to verify them. However, it often requires significant efforts for sifting through large amounts of documents to find relevant information.

HG becomes challenging due to the vast amount of literature. This problem is especially severe in the biomedical domain. The most recognized biomedical literature search tool PubMed has indexed more than 30 million records, and what is more serious, more than 500,000 records are added to it every year.

© Springer Nature Switzerland AG 2021
I. Farkaš et al. (Eds.): ICANN 2021, LNCS 12891, pp. 477–490, 2021.
https://doi.org/10.1007/978-3-030-86362-3_39

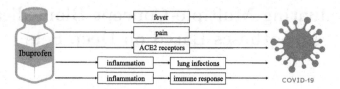

Fig. 1. An example of Hypotheses Generation (HG). There can be different hypotheses connecting "Ibuprofen" and "COVID-19". An HG system aims to evaluate their meaningfulness and rank them where meaningful ones rank high.

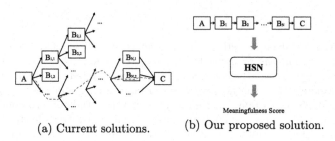

(a) Current solutions.   (b) Our proposed solution.

Fig. 2. A comparison between current HG solutions and our proposed HSN. Current solutions evaluate a hypothesis (as a dashed line connecting the two concepts of interest) via comparing it with all hypotheses of the same N. The process involves a high-order search for multiple-concept hypotheses and will encounter the exponential growth of to-be-explored paths, making it impractical to address multiple-concept hypotheses. HSN evaluates hypotheses of ANY N via directly outputting their meaningfulness scores of the same scale to tackle the above problem.

Although the enormous amount presents the investigators with opportunities for more hypotheses and knowledge, it tremendously challenges them. One can hardly read related publications exhaustively before making hypotheses.

Generally, HG aims to find concepts bridging the previously "irrelevant" ones in a semantically meaningful way according to existing publications. For example, the pioneer Don Swanson [12] found from the literature that "Fish Oil" can alleviate "blood viscosity" and "vasoconstriction", and the two concepts are positively related to "Raynaud Disease". The hypothesis from the above findings is that "Fish Oil" may relieve "Raynaud Disease" via the connecting concepts "blood viscosity" and "vasoconstriction", which are verified by clinical trials later [5]. An HG system should recognize such hypotheses as meaningful ones, i.e., scoring or ranking them high among plausible hypotheses.

The basic idea of current HG approaches is a search between the two input concepts of interest (A and C) [1,3,4,6,8,11,15,17] as in Fig. 2a. The search starts from the concept A. It first finds all relevant B_1 and evaluate $A \rightarrow B_1$'s meaningfulness. Similarly, the process iteratively finds and evaluates $B_1 \rightarrow B_2, B_2 \rightarrow B_3, \cdots, B_{N-1} \rightarrow B_N, B_N \rightarrow C$. The last step aggregates all the possible connections above as different hypotheses $A \rightarrow B_1 \rightarrow B_2 \rightarrow \cdots \rightarrow B_N \rightarrow C$ and evaluates their meaningfulness. The output is a rank of

$A \rightarrow B_1 \rightarrow B_2 \rightarrow \cdots \rightarrow B_N \rightarrow C$ where meaningful hypotheses rank high. These approaches use different metrics to find relevant $B(s)$ and evaluate the meaningfulness between two concepts. To decide the meaningfulness of a hypothesis with N intermediate concepts, they have to exhaustively evaluate all hypotheses of the same N and compare between these hypotheses. While showing great performance on hypotheses with $N = 1$, these approaches will encounter the problem of exponential-growing searching space when N becomes larger. The problem makes it impractical to find hypotheses with numerous concepts even though such hypotheses are also meaningful and of practical value [3,4,15].

This paper solves the above exponential-growing searching space problem in HG. Specifically, the task is to evaluate hypotheses with any number of concepts efficiently. Despite its value and significance, the task is much more challenging than tasks in typical HG settings. The reasons are listed below:

1. *Hypotheses with Large Numbers of Concepts.* Current HG solutions mainly focus on hypotheses with only one connecting concept [6,8], and it becomes impractical to quantitatively evaluate hypotheses with more than one connecting concepts due to the exponential-growing searching space.
2. *Hypotheses with Variable Numbers of Concepts.* Current approaches evaluate hypotheses via comparing them with hypotheses of the same N [6,8,15] and cannot compare hypotheses with different N. However, if an HG approach can evaluate hypotheses with different N, it will avoid high-order searches for multiple-concept hypotheses via comparing them with one-concept hypotheses instead. Therefore, it is necessary to compare hypotheses with different N on their meaningfulness to solve fulfill the task.

To address the above challenges, we propose a novel framework for HG in this paper. We assume any hypotheses to be evaluated as a set of concepts and introduce HG Set Net (HSN) to learn to score the set on its meaningfulness. HSN can evaluate a hypothesis set containing any number of concepts with the same computational complexity, solving the first challenge above. It scores any hypotheses into the same scale to resolve the second challenge. Moreover, we also present a double-margin loss to train HSN using only the existing literature, overcoming the lack of a comprehensive training dataset in HG. We believe this is a transformative direction of HG research, solving the exponential explosion problem caused by high-order search fundamentally.

In the experiments, we show that HSN can evaluate hypotheses with different N effectively and efficiently and outperform baselines significantly. Moreover, experiments also justify the advantage of our proposed double-margin loss.

2   Related Work

Hypotheses Generation (HG) is beneficial to both knowledge discovery and bioinformatics research [14]. The initial works [12,13] discovered novel associations (e.g., Fish Oil $\rightarrow$ Raynaud Disease) via connecting known but disjoint knowledge. While pioneering the HG research, these manual methods are inefficient.

Therefore, later studies focused on automatic HG, and they differ in how to quantify the connections between two concepts, i.e., $B_i \rightarrow B_{i+1}$ even though sharing the same search-based strategy as in Sect. 1.

In automatic HG, primary works [11,17] use co-occurrence between concepts (e.g., term frequency, inverse document frequency) to quantify the connections. [7,17] also employ statistical measurements to evaluate the meaningfulness of connections. The above approaches advanced HG research. However, they cannot assure that the connections are semantically meaningful, i.e., these solutions may present connections that are statistically significant but semantically meaningless, and such connections are useless in HG. To solve such a problem, recently, researchers use neural embeddings [1,8,16] and other neural network-based techniques [6] to capture the latent semantics of concepts in quantifying connections and further advance HG research. Nevertheless, all these approaches that adopt the search strategy to evaluate the connections as introduced in Sect. 1 will encounter the problem of exponential-growing searching space when addressing multiple-concept hypotheses. In this regard, we propose a neural network-based approach to evaluate any hypotheses with the same computational complexity and avoid the searches for multiple-concept hypotheses.

Another line of HG researches [3,4,15] attempted to avoid high-order searches via using external database (e.g., SemMedDB) to filter the connecting concepts B_i. They can significantly reduce the searching space and ensures semantically meaningful connections between concepts. However, these approaches cannot find implicit connections because they rely on pre-defined schema. To circumvent this drawback, we model all concepts in a latent space and are thus able to evaluate any implicit connections.

We take inspirations from Deep Sets [18] which shows superior performance on learning to represent set data. Given the nature of our hypotheses and documents, our proposed framework stems from Deep Sets, and we adapt Deep Sets as a module in our proposed model. We also propose a strategy to train our model based on negative sampling [9].

3   Methodology

We firstly present preliminaries and an overview of our framework. After the overview, we describe our approach in three parts: the HSN model, the double-margin loss to train HSN, and how HSN addresses HG in different settings.

3.1   Preliminaries

In HG, the literature refers to a collection of documents being searched. We choose MEDLINE, the largest bibliographic database in the biomedical domain, as our document collection for generating biomedical hypotheses. It contains more than 30 million documents (articles or conference abstracts) and is freely accessible via PubMed. Each document contains information such as its publication metadata and several Medical Subject Headings (MeSH) terms. MeSH is a human-controlled vocabulary with approximately 26 thousand terms, and each term represents a concept. PubMed indexes each document with several MeSH terms indicating its content. Therefore, we can use a bag of MeSH terms to represent a document [2,8]. Likewise, we can form a hypothesis as a MeSH term set to evaluate it. These sets, as different combinations of MeSH terms, differ in their biomedical meaningfulness, i.e., an existing document is a meaningful set, and HG aims to determine new sets' (hypotheses') meaningfulness.

3.2   Overview

We define our task as scoring hypotheses on their biomedical meaningfulness. The input is a hypothesis as a set containing the two MeSH terms of interest and the connecting MeSH terms. The output is a real-number score indicating its meaningfulness which can be used to rank or compare hypotheses. We propose HSN (HG Set Net) as in Fig. 2b to fulfill this task. HSN scores any hypotheses as sets without high-order searches and into the same scale, solving the two challenges in Sect. 1.

We train HSN using the existing documents. Specifically, we propose a double-margin loss based on negative sampling [9]. The training process samples "better" and "worse" documents from existing ones and updates HSN to better distinguish the three types, i.e., "better", "original", and "worse" documents.

3.3   HSN Structure

HSN encodes a set of L MeSH terms $\{M_1, M_2, \cdots, M_k, \cdots, M_L\}$ into a vector in the latent semantic space whose *norm* indicates the set's meaningfulness. Generally, HSN has an *encoding*, a *message-passing*, and a *readout* module in Fig. 3a *encoding* encodes the input MeSH terms as well as the set into the latent space as the MeSH term vectors and the set global vector. These vectors feed further into *message-passing* which ensures that both the MeSH term vectors and the set global vector contain the context information in the set. *readout* decodes the set global vector as the output vector whose *norm* represents the set's biomedical meaningfulness. We detail each module below.

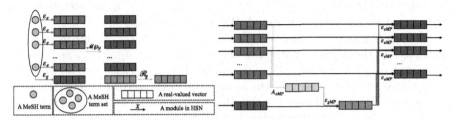

(a) The HSN Structure. It takes in a set of MeSH terms and outputs and a vector whose *norm* indicates the set's meaningfulness.

(b) The HSN's $\mathcal{MP}$ Module. It updates the set global vector and the MeSH term vectors according to each other alternatively.

Fig. 3. The structure of HSN.

MeSH Encoding $\mathcal{E}_e$. This module encodes MeSH terms $(M_i, i = 1, 2, \cdots, L)$ into the latent space as $\vec{v}_{i,enc,}, i = 1, 2, \cdots, L$. It uses an *embedding* layer $(\mathcal{E}_{emb})$ to encode MeSH terms into dense embeddings, and a two-layer Multiple-Layer Perceptron (MLP) as in Eq. 1 after the embedding layer to encode the embeddings into the latent space. We also add *LayerNorm* layers $(\mathcal{E}_{LN})$ after both $\mathcal{E}_{emb}$ and $\mathcal{E}_{MLP}$ to avoid over-fitting. Equation 2 is our detailed implementation of the encoding module. $\mathcal{E}_e$ is identical for all inputs.

$$\mathcal{E}_{MLP}(\vec{v}) = \mathcal{L}_2\left(\mathcal{L}_1(\vec{v})\right), \mathcal{L}_t(\vec{v}) = ReLU(\mathbf{A}_t\vec{v}) \tag{1}$$

$$\vec{v}_{i,enc} = \mathcal{E}_e\left(M_i\right) = \mathcal{E}_{LN}\left(\mathcal{E}_{MLP}\left(\mathcal{E}_{LN}\left(\mathcal{E}_{emb}\left(M_i\right)\right)\right)\right) \tag{2}$$

Global Encoding $\mathcal{E}_g$. HSN generates a default global vector $\vec{v}_{g,init} = [0.5]$ for the input set and uses an MLP as in Eq. 1 to encode the global vector into $\vec{v}_{g,enc}$, in the same latent space as MeSH term vectors, as $\vec{v}_{g,enc} = \mathcal{E}_{MLP}(\vec{v}_{g,init})$. The set global vector will contain the set's context information after updating.

Message-Passing $\mathcal{MP}$. This module ensures the set global vector and the MeSH term vectors contain the set's context information after the two *encoding* modules. Given that each hypothesis or document is a set of MeSH terms, this *message-passing* module exchanges the information between the set global vector and the MeSH terms vectors as in Deep Sets [18]. It has two steps: Set Update (SU) and MeSH Update (MU). SU first updates the set global vector according both to terms' and its previous one. After SU, MU updates each term's vector independently according to its previous one and the updated global vector. $\mathcal{MP}$ runs N times using the identical network, and Eq. 3 and Fig. 3b presents its n_{th} round $\mathcal{MP}_n$.

$$\vec{v}_{g,n+1,mp}, \vec{V}_{n+1,mp} = \mathcal{MP}\left(\vec{v}_{g,n,mp}, \vec{V}_{n,mp}\right), \text{where}$$
$$\vec{v}_{g,n+1,mp} = SU\left(\vec{v}_{g,n,mp}, \vec{V}_{n,mp}\right), \text{and } \vec{V}_{n+1,mp} = MU\left(\vec{v}_{g,n+1,mp}, \vec{V}_{n,mp}\right) \tag{3}$$

where $\vec{V}_{n,mp}$ is the concatenation of MeSH term vectors input to $\mathcal{MP}_n$ as $[\vec{v}_{1,n,mp}; \vec{v}_{2,n,mp}; \cdots; \vec{v}_{L,n,mp}]$, and $\vec{v}_{g,n,mp}$ is the set global vector before $\mathcal{MP}_n$. The input of $\mathcal{MP}_0$ is $\vec{v}_{g,enc}$ and $\vec{V}_{enc} = [\vec{v}_{1,enc}; \vec{v}_{2,enc}; \cdots; \vec{v}_{L,enc}]$, and it outputs $\vec{v}_{g,N,mp}$ and $\vec{V}_{N,mp}$ in the last round. We describe SU and MU below.

SU first aggregates term vectors $\vec{v}_{i,n,mp}, i = 1, 2, \cdots, L$ into one vector $\vec{v}_{aggr,n,mp}$. It then concatenates the aggregated vector $\vec{v}_{aggr,n,mp}$ and the set global vector $\vec{v}_{g,n,mp}$ into $\vec{v}_{concat,g,n,mp}$ and feeds $\vec{v}_{concat,g,n,mp}$ into an MLP for the updated set global vector, which can take in the term's information after such process. Equation 4 presents the SU block in $\mathcal{MP}_n$. MU concatenate each term's vector $\vec{v}_{i,n,mp}$ and the updated global vector $\vec{v}_{g,n+1,mp}$ into $\vec{v}_{concat,i,n,mp}$ and feed it into an MLP for each term's updated vector. Each term will include the set's global information after this step. Equation 5 presents the n_{th} MU step and MU is identical for all MeSH terms.

$$\vec{v}_{aggr,g,n,mp} = AGGR_{SU}\left(\vec{V}_{n,mp}\right) = \sum_{l=1}^{L}\vec{v}_{l,n,mp}$$

$$\vec{v}_{concat,g,n,mp} = CONCAT\left(\vec{v}_{g,n,mp}, \vec{v}_{aggr,g,n,mp}\right)$$ \hfill (4)

$$\vec{v}_{g,n+1,mp} = \mathcal{E}_{MLP}\left(\vec{v}_{concat,g,n,mp}\right)$$

$$\vec{v}_{concat,i,n,mp} = CONCAT\left(\vec{v}_{g,n+1,mp}, \vec{v}_{i,n,mp}\right)$$ \hfill (5)

$$\vec{v}_{i,n+1,mp} = \mathcal{E}_{MLP}\left(\vec{v}_{concat,i,n,mp}\right)$$

Readout $\mathcal{R}_g$. After N rounds of $\mathcal{MP}$, we can get the updated set global vector $\vec{v}_{g,N,mp}$ containing all the set's context information. $\mathcal{R}_g$, as in Fig. 3a, further decodes the set global vector into the output vector $\vec{v}_{g,output}$ indicating the set's meaningfulness, via Eq. 6. The output score is the *norm* of the final output vector as $S_{set} = |\vec{v}_{g,output}|$.

$$\vec{v}_{g,output} = \mathcal{R}_g\left(\vec{v}_{g,N,mp}\right) = \mathcal{E}_{MLP}\left(\vec{v}_{g,N,mp}\right) \tag{6}$$

To conclude, the HSN scores a set on its meaningfulness as Eq. 7. Note that the $\mathcal{E}_{MLP}$ in HSN has the same structure as Eq. 1 but do not share parameters unless specified. We tested the latent size of $[32, 64, 128]$ and chose 64 as a balance of performance and efficiency.

$$S_{set} = HSN(\{M_1, M_2, \cdots, M_L\}) \tag{7}$$

3.4 Double-Margin Loss

We present our training of HSN in this subsection. Recall that we have only existing documents rather than labeled hypotheses, our training process takes the idea of negative sampling that trains a model using existing and randomly sampled instances. We randomly add one concept into an existing document to make it less meaningful ("worse") in the sampling based on the nature of biomedical document sets. For example, "{Fish Oil, Raynaud Disease, Blood Viscosity}" is meaningful, and will be less meaningful if we add "Fracture" as "{Fish Oil, Raynaud Disease, Blood Viscosity, Fracture}". Similar to negative sampling, we can train HSN to distinguish the "worse" and original documents.

Furthermore, we propose a double-margin loss to better train HSN via sampling both less meaningful and more meaningful documents. Specifically, in the sampling process, we also sample more meaningful ("better") documents via randomly removing one concept from an existing one, in contrast to the "worse" document generation. In this regard, we train HSN to distinguish the three types of documents: "worse" documents, original documents, and "better" documents by the double-margin loss. We argue that we can achieve a better set of network parameters via the double-margin loss than the typical negative sampling solution described above. Following negative sampling, the sampling processes are independent in each iteration during the training.

Specifically, in the training process, we generate two documents from an existing one $D_{original} = \{M_1, M_2, \cdots, M_L\}$ as $D_{better} = \{M_1, M_2, \cdots, M_{k-1}, M_{k+1}, \cdots, M_L\}$ by randomly removing a MeSH term and $D_{worse} = \{M_1, M_2, \cdots, M_L, M_{L+1}\}$ by randomly adding a MeSH term. Every choice of random MeSH terms is independent and follows a uniform distribution over the MeSH vocabulary. After sampling, HSN will score them as S_{worse}, $S_{original}$, and S_{better} respectively. We propose a double-margin loss function defined on the three scores as in Eq. 8 and minimize it to train HSN.

$$\mathcal{L} = \sum_{N_{doc}} \left\{ [\tau_1 - S_{better}]_+ + [\tau_2 - S_{original}]_+ + S_{worse} \right\} \tag{8}$$

where τ_1 and τ_2 are the two margins, $[x]_+$ is defined as $[x]_+ = max(x, 0)$, and N_{doc} is the number of original documents. Our proposed loss function ensures same-scaled output scores and a stable and efficient training process. Firstly, the regression-like loss guarantees the scores of any hypotheses are on the same scale and addresses the second challenge in Sect. 1. Secondly, we sample only two documents from an existing one in each epoch independently, ensuring a stable and efficient training process similar to negative sampling-based training.

We employ the *ADAM* optimizer with a default learning rate of 0.001. The margins τ_1 and τ_2 are 6 and 3 chosen from [1–6] because the model converges much faster using these two margins than other combinations on all datasets. The mini-batch size is 3072.

3.5   Applying HSN to HG

After training, HSN can score any hypothesis. It solves an HG problem in three settings. The first one is to rank several hypotheses on their meaningfulness when a researcher already has some and wants to find the best ones. HSN takes them as inputs and outputs their respective scores for ranking. In the second scenario, HG needs to evaluate a single hypothesis. We solve such a problem by randomly generating several hypotheses on the same input concepts of interest, estimating the distribution of scores, and checking the single hypothesis's score relative to the distribution. A hypothesis whose score is above one standard deviation than the mean is regarded meaningful. The last setting is to generate hypotheses without knowing any candidate. We generate candidate hypotheses via enumerating all combinations and use HSN to rank them as the first setting.

4   Experiments

We conduct experiments in three groups: 1) the empirical study and analysis showing that HSN can handle any hypotheses effectively and efficiently; 2) the quantitative analysis justifying the advantage of HSN over baselines;

3) evaluating the double-margin loss. We describe datasets before experiments and results.

4.1   Datasets

In the empirical study, we use the most recognized query "Fish Oil" and "Raynaud Disease" in HG, which has long been a famous case with many verified-to-be-true hypotheses [10]. The quantitative analysis follows the standard method that cuts off the data into two parts according to a cutoff date, generates hypotheses according to the pre-cutoff data, and evaluates whether a hypothesis is a good one using the post-cutoff data [17]. We use five widely accepted "golden datasets" below. HSN's settings are the same on five datasets for uniformity.

1. Fish Oil (FO) & Raynaud Disease (RD) (1985)
2. Magnesium (MG) & Migraine Disorder (MIG) (1988)
3. Somatomedin C (IGF1) & Arginine (ARG) (1994)
4. Indomethacin (INN) & Alzheimer Disease (AD) (1989)
5. Schizophrenia (SZ) & Calcium - Independent Phospholipase A2 (CI-PA2) (1997)

In the preprocessing, we select documents published before the cutoff date and containing either one of the input terms to build the training corpus. The step can significantly ease model training without compromising the performance. To verify that the preprocessing introduces no bias, we add TF-IDF, the standard approach to distinguish between documents, as a comparative approach in our experiments.

4.2   Empirical Study

In this experiment, we examine whether HSN can replicate the one-concept and multiple-concept true hypotheses regarding "Fish Oil" and "Raynaud Disease". After training, we feed several such hypotheses into HSN and see whether HSN can distinguish them from random ones as the second setting in Sect. 3.5.

Specifically, we checked hypotheses listed in Table 1 that are verified to be true by domain experts [4,12]. As for the reference, we generated 10,000 different hypotheses containing 1 to 7 MeSH terms (the choices MeSH terms and the number of MeSH terms are both random) other than "Fish Oil" and "Raynaud Disease". We use HSN to score them as Eq. 7 and calculate the *mean* and *std* of the scores which are 0.017752 and 0.021220 respectively. We consider a hypothesis as meaningful if its score is above one *std* from the *mean*.

Table 1. Scores of true hypotheses By HSN. Bold numbers indicates that HSN scores the respective hypotheses as meaningful. HSN scores all verified true hypotheses, either one-concept or multiple-concept ones, as meaningful and in the same complexity.

Valid hypotheses	Scores
Fish Oil, Blood Viscosity, Raynaud Disease	**0.067301**
Fish Oil, Vasoconstriction, Raynaud Disease	**0.067295**
Fish Oil, Epoprostenol, Raynaud Disease	**0.067286**
Fish Oil, Prostaglandins E, Raynaud Disease	**0.067360**
Fish Oil, Epoprostenol, Platelet Aggregation, Raynaud Disease	**0.067260**
Fish Oil, Epoprostenol, Blood Viscosity, Raynaud Disease	**0.067271**
Fish Oil, Epoprostenol, Vascular Resistance, Raynaud Disease	**0.067260**
Fish Oil, Epoprostenol, Prostaglandins, Platelet Aggregation, Raynaud Disease	**0.067248**
Fish Oil, Epoprostenol, Eicosanoic Acids, Alprostadil, Raynaud Disease	**0.067408***

We list the scores of the true hypotheses as in Table 1. The bold numbers indicate that HSN scores the respective hypotheses as meaningful. We can observe from Table 1 that HSN scores all the true hypotheses, both one-concept and multiple-concept ones, as meaningful. Moreover, HSN's scoring complexity for both one-concept and multiple-concept hypotheses are identical as in Table 2, i.e., addressing the first challenge in Sect. 1. The results show that HSN can find the two types of hypotheses effectively and efficiently.

Table 2. A comparison of (time) complexity between search-based solutions and HSN when evaluating a hypotheses. N is the number of concepts in the hypotheses, and M is the averaged number of possible connections of a MeSH term.

Method	Search-based approaches	HSN
Time Complexity	$\mathcal{O}(M^N)$	$\mathcal{O}(N)$

We can also observe from Table 1 that the one-concept and multiple-concept hypotheses' scores are in the same range, enabling the comparisons across hypotheses with different numbers of MeSH terms, i.e., addressing the second challenge in Sect. 1. That the scores are in the same range also addresses the concern that the varied number of MeSH terms in a document may be a clue for HSN scoring, validating our document sampling strategy.

Interestingly, we can see that even though the hypotheses "Fish Oil, Epoprostenol, Eicosanoic Acids, Alprostadil, Raynaud Disease" has three intermediate concepts, it has the highest scores in Table 1. This score shows that hypotheses with more intermediate concepts can be more meaningful than those with less, verifying the necessity of evaluating multiple-concept hypotheses.

4.3 Quantitative Analysis

We evaluate HSN statistically in this section. Specifically, these experiments rank hypotheses using different approaches and compare the rankings' consistency with the ground truth ranking. We describe our ground truth ranking and base-lines before presenting the results.

Ground Truth Generation. A hypothesis should be more meaningful if more documents discuss it in the future [17]. Therefore, we cut off the data into two parts according to a cutoff date. No publications discuss the hypotheses before cutoff, and we can evaluate a hypothesis by checking the number of documents mentioning it after cutoff. Therefore, the ground truth score is defined as: $gt(B)$ = #(A,B)+#(B,C), where A and C are the two input MeSH terms and B is the intermediate term in a hypothesis, $\#(i,j)$ is the number of documents in the post-cutoff data containing both term i,j. We use the scores to rank the plausible hypotheses as the ground truth ranking in our statistical evaluation.

Comparative Methods. To compare between HSN and current advance-ments, we implement three baselines in our comparison: TF-IDF, Lift, and Word Embedding. The following are the details.

- **TF-IDF:** To evaluate the bias introduced by preprocessing, we compare HSN with TF-IDF. This baseline ranks candidate hypotheses using their interme-diate terms' TF-IDF values in the pre-cutoff data and is a representative of the co-occurrence-based HG solution [11,17].
- **Lift:** We also compare HSN with approaches based on statistical measure-ments. This baseline ranks hypotheses using $lift(A, B) + lift(B, C)$ scores measuring the importance of hypotheses among candidates to represent such researches [7,17].
- **Word Embeddings (Embedding):** Embedding-based approaches have achieved the state-of-the-art performance in HG research [1,8]. To make a fair comparison with such approaches, this baseline uses *word2vec* [9], iden-tical to the *MeSH encoding* module in HSN, to encode each MeSH and rank hypotheses.

Experiment Results. We compare the rankings, by each approach and on each dataset, with the ground truth rankings using the Spearsman's correlation scores at different k. Tables 3, 4, 5, 6, 7 list the scores on the five datasets. Higher scores indicate better rankings, and bold numbers indicate that the respective approach achieves the best performance in the group.

Table 3. Spearman correlation at differ-ent k for FO-RD.

k	500	800	1000	1200
TF-IDF	−0.255	−0.328	−0.344	−0.418
Lift	−0.015	−0.012	0.009	0.115
Embedding	0.282	0.247	0.215	0.184
HSN	**0.349**	**0.355**	**0.329**	**0.304**

Table 4. Spearman correlation at differ-ent k for MIG-MG.

k	500	800	1000	1200
TF-IDF	−0.258	−0.324	−0.374	−0.397
Lift	0.058	0.157	0.225	0.304
Embeddings	0.296	0.316	0.335	0.300
HSN	**0.311**	**0.466**	**0.426**	**0.401**

Table 5. Spearman correlation at different k for INN-AD.

k	500	800	1000	1200
TF-IDF	−0.293	−0.375	−0.399	−0.464
Lift	0.248	0.341	0.365	0.352
Embeddings	0.207	0.137	0.170	0.203
HSN	**0.374**	**0.405**	**0.418**	**0.372**

Table 6. Spearman correlation at different k for IGF1-ARG.

k	500	800	1000	1200
TF-IDF	−0.264	−0.317	−0.359	−0.382
Lift	0.091	0.089	0.190	0.157
Embeddings	0.175	0.215	0.219	0.179
HSN	**0.275**	**0.377**	**0.441**	**0.339**

Table 7. Spearman correlation at different k for SZ-CI, PA2.

k	500	800	1000	1200
TF-IDF	−0.212	−0.280	−0.327	−0.301
Lift	−0.116	−0.104	−0.178	−0.2201
Embeddings	0.155	0.173	0.201	0.199
HSN	**0.497**	**0.436**	**0.402**	**0.441**

Fig. 4. HSN trained with the double-margin loss outperforms HSN trained without it at all ks.

In Tables 3, 4, 5, 6, 7, we can see that the TF-IDF approach's scores are always low. It shows that the preprocessing does not benefit the performance. The statistical measurement-based approach Lift performs better than TF-IDF because it can employ the statistics to evaluate hypotheses. Furthermore, the word embedding-based approach can capture latent semantics and perform even better, consistent with the previous research. Our proposed model achieves higher scores than the embedding-based approaches. The reason is that our unified model structure can ensure optimal embeddings and scoring mechanisms in contrast to embedding-based approaches that learn the embeddings and score hypotheses separately. To conclude, HSN outperforms its counterparts on all five datasets in the statistical evaluation. The results reveal that HSN can not only address the challenges in addressing multiple-concept hypotheses but also improve performance.

4.4   Double-Margin Loss Evaluation

Our proposed double-margin loss training scheme can train HSN without using labeled hypotheses, which is the first solution of such kind in HG. To evaluate its advantage over simple negative sampling-based training scheme, we compare it with "single-margin" loss that only samples "worse" documents and trains HSN using the "worse" documents and the original documents. Similar to the quantitative evaluation, this experiment compares HSN trained with two losses on the five datasets. Figure 4 presents the Spearman's correlation scores at different k on the "Fish Oil - Raynaud Disease" dataset by HSN trained with our proposed double-margin loss and HSN trained without our proposed double-margin loss (with the "single-margin"). The results show that HSN trained with the double-margin loss outperforms HSN trained without it all the time. The results on the other four datasets are similar and we omit them for brevity. These experiments justify that the double-margin loss can improve the performance of HSN.

5 Conclusion

This paper proposes a model HSN for HG. HSN can compare one-concept and multiple-concept hypotheses effectively and efficiently. It is the first HG solution to solving such a problem to the best of our knowledge. Importantly, HSN solves the exponential explosion problem caused by high-order search in traditional approaches fundamentally, and we believe this is a transformative direction of HG research. Moreover, we can train HSN using only the existing documents, overcoming the lack of labeled hypotheses, and propose a double-margin loss to better train the model. We conduct extensive experiments verifying those advantages.

References

1. Akujuobi, U., Spranger, M., Palaniappan, S.K., Zhang, X.: T-PAIR: temporal node-pair embedding for automatic biomedical hypothesis generation. IEEE Trans. Knowl. Data Eng. 1 (2020)
2. Bhattacharya, S., Ha-Thuc, V., Srinivasan, P.: MeSH: a window into full text for document summarization. Bioinformatics **27**(13), i120–i128 (2011)
3. Cameron, D., et al.: A graph-based recovery and decomposition of Swanson's hypothesis using semantic predications. J. Biomed. Inform. **46**(2), 238–251 (2013)
4. Cameron, D., Kavuluru, R., Rindflesch, T.C., Sheth, A.P., Thirunarayan, K., Bodenreider, O.: Context-driven automatic subgraph creation for literature-based discovery. J. Biomed. Inform. **54**, 141–157 (2015)
5. Cohen, A.M., Hersh, W.R.: A survey of current work in biomedical text mining. Brief. Bioinform. **6**(1), 57–71 (2005)
6. Crichton, G., Baker, S., Guo, Y., Korhonen, A.: Neural networks for open and closed literature-based discovery. PLoS ONE **15**(5), e0232891 (2020)
7. Hu, X., Zhang, X., Yoo, I., Wang, X., Feng, J.: Mining hidden connections among biomedical concepts from disjoint biomedical literature sets through semantic-based association rule. Int. J. Intell. Syst. **25**(2), 207–223 (2010)
8. Jha, K., Xun, G., Wang, Y., Zhang, A.: Hypothesis generation from text based on co-evolution of biomedical concepts. In: KDD 2018, pp. 843–851 (2019)
9. Mikolov, T., Sutskever, I., Chen, K., Corrado, G.S., Dean, J.: Distributed representations of words and phrases and their compositionality. In: NeurIPS 2013, pp. 3111–3119 (2013)
10. Smalheiser, N.R.: Rediscovering Don Swanson: the past, present and future of literature-based discovery. J. Data Inf. Sci. **2**(4), 43–64 (2017)
11. Srinivasan, P.: Text mining: generating hypotheses from MEDLINE. J. Assoc. Inf. Sci. Technol. **55**(5), 396–413 (2004)
12. Swanson, D.R.: Fish oil, Raynaud's syndrome, and undiscovered public knowledge. Perspect. Biol. Med. **30**(1), 7–18 (1986)

13. Swanson, D.R., Smalheiser, N.R.: An interactive system for finding complementary literatures: a stimulus to scientific discovery. Artif. Intell. **91**(2), 183–203 (1997)

14. Thilakaratne, M., Falkner, K., Atapattu, T.: A systematic review on literature-based discovery: general overview, methodology, & statistical analysis. ACM Comput. Surv. **52**(6), 1–34 (2019)

15. Wilkowski, B., et al.: Graph-based methods for discovery browsing with semantic predications. In: AMIA 2011, vol. 2011, p. 1514 (2011)

16. Xun, G., Jha, K., Gopalakrishnan, V., Li, Y., Zhang, A.: Generating medical hypotheses based on evolutionary medical concepts. In: ICDM 2017, pp. 535–544 (2017)

17. Yetisgen-Yildiz, M., Pratt, W.: A new evaluation methodology for literature-based discovery systems. J. Biomed. Inform. **42**(4), 633–643 (2009)

18. Zaheer, M., Kottur, S., Ravanbakhsh, S., Poczos, B., Salakhutdinov, R.R., Smola, A.J.: Deep sets. In: NeurIPS 2017, Long Beach, CA, USA, pp. 3391–3401 (2017)

A Network Embedding Based Approach to Drug-Target Interaction Prediction Using Additional Implicit Networks

Han Zhang[1], Chengbin Hou[1,2], David McDonald[1], and Shan He[1(✉)]

[1] School of Computer Science, University of Birmingham, Birmingham, UK
{hxz325,dxm237,s.he}@cs.bham.ac.uk
[2] Department of Computer Science and Engineering,
Southern University of Science and Technology, Shenzhen, China

Abstract. Identifying novel drug-target interactions (DTIs) is a crucial step in drug discovery. Since experimentally determining DTIs is expensive and time-consuming, it becomes popular to employ computational methods for providing promising candidate DTIs. However, in the existing computational methods, the drug implicit network and target implicit network constructed from a DTI network (a bipartite network) have been ignored in the DTI prediction problem, while such implicit networks constructed from a bipartite network have been proven useful in other problems, e.g., the link prediction task in a bipartite network. Motivated by that, we propose a novel DTI prediction method which considers the implicit networks in addition to drug structure similarity network and target sequence similarity network. The experiments over five real-world DTI datasets demonstrate the competitive performance of the proposed method compared to the state-of-the-art methods. The code is available at https://github.com/BrisksHan/NE-DTIP.

Keywords: Drug-Target Interaction Prediction · Network embedding · Implicit networks · Network topology

1 Introduction

Identifying novel drug-target interactions (DTIs) is a crucial step in drug discovery. Since experimentally determining DTIs is expensive and time-consuming [10], it is desirable to develop computational methods to identify promising candidate DTIs to accelerate the speed of drug discovery.

Over the years, many computational methods have been proposed to identify novel DTIs. The existing methods could be categorised into three groups. The first group is the target structure based methods [15]. These methods simulate the docking process of drugs. However, the 3D structures of the proteins are required as the input, yet, the 3D structures of many proteins are unavailable. The second group is the ligand similarity based methods [14]. These methods use the structural similarity between ligands to predict interactions, however,

© Springer Nature Switzerland AG 2021
I. Farkaš et al. (Eds.): ICANN 2021, LNCS 12891, pp. 491–503, 2021.
https://doi.org/10.1007/978-3-030-86362-3_40

the sequence similarities between targets are ignored in predicting DTIs. The third group is the machine learning based methods [2,16,17,19,26,28,33,34,36]. They often take the DTI network, drug structural similarity network (DSSN), and target sequence similarity network (TSSN) as the inputs to train a machine learning model for predicting DTIs. Note that, the machine learning based methods have attracted a lot of research interests in recent years. Most of them focus on identifying novel DTIs from known DTIs, as a drug might bind to more than one target [33], which could lead to successful drug repositioning.

Although many computational methods have been proposed to tackle the DTI prediction problem, the implicit networks constructed from the known DTI network are ignored in existing works. However, it has been shown the implicit networks constructed from a bipartite network can improve the performance of the link prediction task in the bipartite network [29]. Besides, the implicit relations can also improve the performance of recommender systems [35].

Motivated by the success of using implicit networks or relations in other problems, we suggest to also consider the *implicit networks* extracted from the DTI network (a bipartite network) in the DTI prediction problem. The implicit networks, i.e., drug implicit network (DIN) and target implicit network (TIN), are constructed using the second-order proximity in the DTI network. It is worth noticing that, an edge in DIN indicates that two drugs would bind to at least one common target and an edge in TIN indicates that two targets would bind to at least one common drug, while DSSN (or TSSN) represents the structural similarity directly calculated between two drugs (or two targets). The topological structures of DIN and TIN would be different from the topological structures of TSSN and DSSN, as they are computed from different perspectives.

To incorporate the implicit networks, we propose a method termed as Network Embedding based Drug-Target Interaction Prediction (NE-DTIP). Specifically, NE-DTIP is a machine learning based method and it includes two stages: the feature vector construction stage and the DTI classification stage. During feature vector construction stage, DIN and TIN are constructed from the DTI network. After that, drug embeddings and target embeddings are learned from DIN, TIN, DSSN, and TSSN using a network embedding method. *Unlike previous methods, the proposed method additionally considers two homogeneous networks, i.e., TIN and DIN, both of which are generated based on the implicit relations of a given DTI network.* During DTI classification stage, the drug-target pairs in DTI network are regarded as positive samples, while randomly sampled unknown drug-target pairs in the DTI network are regarded as negative samples. The feature vector of each training sample (for a drug-target pair) is constructed via concatenating the corresponding drug embeddings and target embeddings. Finally, all samples are used to train a classifier for DTI predictions.

We employ five real-world DTI datasets to evaluate the performance of NE-DTIP. Comparing against four state-of-the-art methods, NE-DTIP outperforms the existing methods on three out of five datasets. We also conduct a case study to verify the top-20 DTI predictions by NE-DTIP on the latest dataset, and it is interesting to find that six out of twenty novel DTIs (i.e., new DTIs not recorded in the dataset) are supported by recent studies.

2 Related Work

The machine learning based DTI prediction methods can be categorised into three groups. The first group is the distance based methods [16,34,36]. Those methods embed the drugs and targets into a unified space based on the known DTIs and the similarities between drugs and targets. Then, the novel DTI predictions are made based on the distance between the drugs and targets in the unified space. The second group is the bipartite local prediction based methods [2,19,32]. Those methods learn two classifiers. The first classifier predicts targets for a given drug and the second classifier predicts drugs for a given target. Given a drug-target pair, the two classifiers are jointed together to make a prediction. The third group is the feature vector based methods [17,26,28]. Those methods construct feature vectors for drugs and targets. Then, the known DTIs are treated as positive samples and unknown DTIs are treated as negative samples. The feature vectors of drug-target pairs are constructed via concatenating the corresponding drugs and targets. Then, a classifier is employed to predict DTIs.

3 Notation and Problem Definition

Homogeneous Network: All of DIN, DSSN, TIN, and TSSN are homogeneous networks, i.e., all nodes of a network are the same type. Let $G = (V, E)$ be a homogeneous network, where V denotes a set of nodes and $E \subseteq V \times V$ denotes edges. The number of nodes in V is denoted with $|V|$. For any node pair (v_i, v_j), where $i \in [1, ..., |V|]$ and $j \in [1, ..., |V|]$, there is a non-negative edge weight w_{ij} which describes the strength of connection between the two nodes. The weight is 0 if two nodes are not connected in E. All the edge weights are represented in a $|V| \times |V|$ matrix $W = [w_{ij}]$. Note that, there is no self-loop in this work, i.e., $w_{ii} = 0 \ \forall i \in [1, ..., |V|]$ in all homogeneous networks.

DTI Network: DTI network is a bipartite network, i.e., nodes are in two sets and there is no edge between nodes in the same set. Let $B = (V^D, V^T, E^{DTI})$ be a DTI network, where V^D denotes a set of drugs, V^T denotes a set of targets and $E^{DTI} \subseteq V^D \times V^T$ denotes edges, as there is no drug-drug edge or target-target edge in the DTI network. For any node pair (v_i^D, v_j^T), where $i \in [1, ..., |V^D|]$ and $j \in [1, ..., |V^T|]$, w_{ij}^{DTI} is used to describes the strength of interaction, and the weight is 0 if there is no interaction between a drug-target pair. All the edge weights are represented in a $|V^D| \times |V^T|$ matrix $W^{DTI} = [w_{ij}^{DTI}]$.

DTI Prediction Problem: The aim of DTI prediction is to infer a DTI prediction matrix $M \subseteq V^D \times V^T$ for all drug-target pairs, given the inputs, i.e., DTI network, DSSN, and TSSN. Each entry in the outputs M should reflect the possibility of the existence of the interaction between a drug-target pair.

4   Method

The proposed method as shown in Fig. 1 includes two stages. The feature vector construction stage is discussed in Sect. 4.1–4.3. The DTI classification stage is discussed in Sect. 4.4. And the pseudocode is summarised in Algorithm 1.

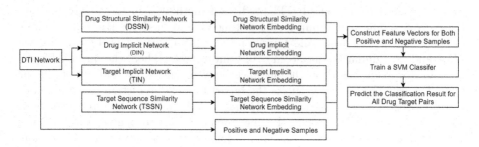

Fig. 1. The framework of the proposed method.

4.1   Network Construction

Construction of Implicit Networks for DIN and TIN. The implicit networks $G^{DIN} = (V^D, E^{DIN})$ and $G^{TIN} = (V^T, E^{TIN})$ are constructed from the DTI network $B = (V^D, V^T, E^{DTI})$. Both of the implicit networks are homogeneous networks, each node represents a drug in G^{DIN} and a target in G^{TIN}, and an edge between two nodes indicates the corresponding nodes share at least one common neighbour in the DTI network. Following the definition in [8], for any node pair in DIN and TIN, the edge weight is defined as:

$$w_{ij}^{DIN} = \sum_{k \in [1,...,|V^T|]} w_{ik}^{DTI} w_{jk}^{DTI} \; \forall i, j \in [1,...,|V^D|] \text{ and } i \neq j \qquad (1)$$

$$w_{ij}^{TIN} = \sum_{k \in [1,...,|V^D|]} w_{ki}^{DTI} w_{kj}^{DTI} \; \forall i, j \in [1,...,|V^T|] \text{ and } i \neq j \qquad (2)$$

where, w_{ij}^{DIN} denotes the edge weight for node pair (v_i^D, v_j^D) in DIN and w_{ij}^{TIN} denotes the edge weight for node pair (v_i^T, v_j^T) in TIN.

Construction for DSSN and TSSN. The edge weight in DSSN is calculated via applying either Tanimoto coefficient [30] or [12] to pairs of drug molecular structures, while the edge weight in TSSN is calculated via applying Smith-Waterman algorithm to pairs of protein sequences [24]. The DSSN and TSSN are fully connected as each node pair would have a positive similarity score as weight. However, many edges are not informative as the corresponding edge weights are very small. By removing edges with small weights, the speed of network embedding process can be significantly improved. Since it is difficult to set cut-off scores for both drug structural similarity score and target sequence similarity score, we introduce an edge density parameter α to remove the non-informative edges, as it has been shown the DSSN shows strong community structures via only keeping the edges with high similarity scores [27]. In both DSSN and TSSN, we rank edges by weights and use the edge density parameter α to denote the proportion of edges to keep, i.e., $\alpha = 0.1$ means only the top 10% of edges are kept.

4.2 Network Embedding

A network embedding method is employed to learn low dimensional node embeddings for constructing feature vectors. The reasons are that the rows and columns of the weight matrix of a network only contain the first-order proximity information, and they are sparse and high dimensional. Those factors made the weight matrix sub-optimal for the downstream machine learning task.

The modified DeepWalk [13,22] is employed to learn the node embeddings, as it has been widely recognised as a simple, efficient, and effective algorithm in the network embedding field [9]. The modified DeepWalk includes three parts: 1) Random walks that capture the topological structure of a network; 2) A sliding window that encodes the node similarity from node sequence into the node pairs D; 3) Skip-gram negative sampling model (SGNS) [20] that learns the node embeddings based on the frequency of node pairs in D and SGNS is employed instead of the original method in DeepWalk to reduce the computational cost.

The modified DeepWalk is applied to DSSN, DIN, TSSN, and TIN to learn drug and target embeddings. The embeddings from the four networks can be denoted as $Z^{DSSN} \in \mathbb{R}^{|V^D| \times d}$, $Z^{DIN} \in \mathbb{R}^{|V^D| \times d}$, $Z^{TSSN} \in \mathbb{R}^{|V^T| \times d}$, and $Z^{TIN} \in \mathbb{R}^{|V^T| \times d}$ respectively, where d is the embedding dimension.

4.3 Feature Vector Construction for Training Samples

The feature vectors of training samples are constructed based on the learned embeddings: Z^{DSSN}, Z^{DIN}, Z^{TSSN}, and Z^{TIN}. The positive samples are the edges from the DTI network. For the $m-th$ drug-target pair $(v_i^D, v_j^T) \in E^{DTI}$, the feature vector of positive samples $Z_m^{positive}$ is constructed by:

$$Z_m^{positive} = Z_i^{DSSN} \oplus Z_i^{DIN} \oplus Z_j^{TSSN} \oplus Z_j^{TIN} \qquad (3)$$

For $m-th$ positive sample, there is a corresponding label $y_m^{positive} = 1$. The negative samples are constructed from the unknown pairs in the DTI network as those pairs have not be experimentally validated, hence, they are unlikely to have interactions. For the $h-th$ randomly sampled drug-target pair $(v_i^D, v_j^T) \notin E^{DTI}$, the feature vector $Z_h^{negative}$ can be constructed by:

$$Z_h^{negative} = Z_i^{DSSN} \oplus Z_i^{DIN} \oplus Z_j^{TSSN} \oplus Z_j^{TIN} \qquad (4)$$

the corresponding label of the negative sample is $y_h^{negative} = -1$. In the training samples, the ratio of positive samples to negative samples is 1:10.

Algorithm 1. NE-DTIP: Network Embedding based DTI Prediction

Input: DTI network; DSSN; TSSN; edge density parameter α; number of walks per node r; walk length l; window size w; number of negative samples q; embedding dimension d; kernel parameter γ for the SVM classifier; tolerance parameter c for training the SVM classifier;

Output: DTI prediction matrix $M \in \mathbb{R}^{|V^D| \times |V^T|}$.

1: Construct DIN and TIN (two implicit networks) from DTI network. The edge weights in DIN and TIN are constructed by Eq (1) and Eq (2) respectively.
2: Keep the top α proportion of edges in DSSN and TSSN.
3: **for** DIN, TIN, DSSN, and TSSN **do**
4:    Apply the modified DeepWalk to learn the node embeddings.
5: **End for**
6: Construct feature vectors for positive samples (from known DTIs) and randomly sampled negative samples (from unknown DTIs) as training samples.
7: Train a SVM classifier using training samples, which yields a trained SVM classifier.
8: Construct feature vectors for all drug-target pairs.
9: Feed all feature vectors (from the last step) into the trained SVM classifier to learn the DTI prediction matrix M.
10: **return** DTI prediction matrix M.

4.4 DTI Prediction

A support vector machine (SVM) with *Platt scaling* [23] classifier is trained to separate positive and negative samples as SVM has been shown to be accurate and robust [1]. For a drug-target pair, the probability of classifying a feature vector as a DTI edge can be written as:

$$p(y = 1|x) = \frac{1}{1 + \exp(-(\sum_{k=1}^{p} y_k a_k K(x, x_k) + b))} \tag{5}$$

where p is the number of training samples, K indicates the kernel function, $a = (a_1, ..., a_p)$ and b are learnable parameter. The kernel function provides the non-linear ability to classify samples without having to project the features of samples into higher dimensional space. In this work, we use Radial basis function kernel [3] to calculate the distance between samples. The parameters in Eq. (5) are *learned* using matrix decomposition via transforming it to a quadratic programming problem [6], in which a tolerance parameter c is introduced.

After all the parameters being learned, we start to *infer* the DTI prediction matrix M. For all drug-target pairs, the feature vectors are constructed as described before. After that, all feature vectors for all drug-target pairs are fed into the trained decision function to infer the DTI prediction matrix M.

Table 1. The statistics of five DTI datasets.

	NR	GPCR	IC	E	DT-IN
# of DTI edges (in a DTI network)	90	635	1476	2926	4978
# of drug nodes (in both DTI and DIN networks)	54	223	210	445	732
# of targets nodes (in both DTI and TIN networks)	26	95	204	664	1915
# of implicit drug-drug edges (in a DIN network)	218	2748	2546	5137	25628
# of implicit target-target edges (in a TIN network)	54	668	8843	15497	46843

5 Experiments

5.1 Datasets

The experiments are conducted on five benchmark datasets. Four of those datasets are published in [34] and they are nuclear receptor (NR), G-protein-coupled receptors (GPCR), ion channel (IC), and enzyme (E). All of those four datasets are obtained from DrugBank [31]. The fifth dataset drug-target inhibition (DT-IN) is published in [17], in which, the DTIs are obtained from multiple sources, and only the DTIs with the binding threshold below 10 μM are kept.

For all the benchmark datasets, DSSNs, and TSSNs are pre-computed. There is a difference in constructing the DSSNs between those datasets. For NR, GPCR, IC, and E, the drug structural similarity scores are constructed using [12], while for DT-IN, the drug structural similarity score is constructed using Tanimoto coefficient. The target sequence similarity scores in all of the five datasets are constructed using Smith-Waterman algorithm [24].

5.2 Baselines

The DTI prediction task can be viewed as classifying an imbalanced datasets. The datasets are imbalanced as there is far more unknown edges than the known edges in the DTI network. Following previous works [17,28], the metric of evaluating the performance of predicting DTI is the area under precision and recall curve (AUPR), as it is more suitable for imbalanced datasets. Other popular metrics such as the area under receiver operating characteristic curve (AUC) would give an optimistic evaluation of the prediction [7].

Five independent ten-fold cross validations are conducted to evaluate the performance of the DTI prediction methods on each dataset. To calculate the AUPR of the testing edges, the randomly sampled unknown edges are treated as negative samples. Following the experimental setting in NeoDTI [28], the ratio of the testing edges to the randomly sampled unknown edges is 1:10.

Table 2. The AUPR scores on five benchmark datasets.

	Netlaprls		BLM-NII		NRLMF		NeoDTI		NE-DTIP	
	AUPR	st.d.	AUPR	st.d.	AUPR	st.d.	AUPR	st.d.	AUPR	st.d..
NR	0.2288	0.0486	**0.3617**	0.0984	0.3336	0.0629	0.2308	0.0835	0.2906	0.0992
GPCR	0.4149	0.0358	0.4578	0.0434	**0.4979**	0.0392	0.4966	0.0624	0.4398	0.0628
IC	0.4704	0.0291	0.4763	0.0276	0.5201	0.0278	0.5841	0.0356	**0.6077**	0.0397
E	0.6930	0.0265	0.7299	0.0285	0.7352	0.0294	0.7844	0.0267	**0.7963**	0.0248
DT-IN	0.7816	0.0230	0.8024	0.0231	0.8484	0.0186	0.8560	0.0161	**0.8610**	0.0145

The best results are in bold. The st.d. is the abbreviation for standard deviation.

5.3 Compared to Other Methods

The compared methods are Netlaprls [32], BLM-NII [19], NRLMF [16], and NeoDTI [28], which have been introduced in related works. Although there are newer methods, those methods take additional networks such as drug-drug interaction and target-target interaction as inputs, yet those additional networks may not available in some datasets. For fairness, the inputs are DTI network, DSSN, and TSSN for all methods. The hyper-parameters of the compared methods are obtained via conducting a grid search on DT-IN using a ten-fold cross validation. The set of hyper-parameters with the highest performance in AUPR is selected to conduct all experiment on all five datasets.

The experiments of our method are conducted using the following hyper-parameters unless otherwise specified. The edge density hyper-parameter α for DSSN and TSSN is set as 0.1. For the hyper-parameters in the modified Deep-Walk, the hyper-parameters for embedding dimension, number of walks, walk length l, window size w, and negative sample number q are set to 128, 10, 80, 10, and 5 respectively, as these parameters have been shown the good performance in most cases according to [13,22]. For the hyper-parameters in SVM, γ and the tolerance hyper-parameter c are set to $1/(11|E^{DTI}|)$ and 1 respectively, both of which are according to [6].

The result is shown in Table 2, from which, we have two observations. First, our method shows very competitive performance comparing to other methods, as our method consistently outperforms other methods over the three largest datasets (see Table 1 for the size). Second, the performance of our method is affected by *implicit relations* between drugs and targets. It can be seen from Table 1, there are far more edges in implicit networks constructed from IC, E, DT-IN than that of the implicit networks constructed from NR and GPCR. Due to the sparseness of implicit networks in NR and GPCR, many nodes are isolated in the corresponding implicit networks. As a result, the embeddings learned from the DIN and TIN with less implicit relations (in NR and GPCR datasets) are less informative, which degrades the performance of our method.

5.4 The Effect of Implicit Networks

To evaluate the performance gain by adding the implicit networks in predicting DTIs, we investigate the DTI prediction performance by using node embeddings

Table 3. The effect of implicit networks.

DSSN + TSSN $d = 128$		DSSN + TSSN $d = 256$		NE-DTIP	
AUPR	st.d.	AUPR	st.d.	AUPR	st.d.
0.8075	0.0171	0.8063	0.0172	0.8610	0.0145

from DSSN and TSSN to construct to feature vectors and this method is named as DSSN+TSSN. The experiments are conducted on DT-IN with five independent ten-fold validations. The embedding dimension d of the DSSN+TSSN is set as 128 and 256, while the embedding dimension d of NE-DTIP is set as 128 as previous. The reason for the additional dimension setting $d = 256$ for DSSN+TSSN is to make the dimensions of feature vectors of DSSN+TSSN and NE-DTIP to be the same. The experimental result is draw in Table 3. From it, we can conclude there is a performance gain by adding implicit networks, as NE-DTIP significantly outperforms DSSN+TSSN in both experimental settings. It demonstrates the effectiveness of the proposed method by additionally incorporating the implicit networks. The reason is that the topological structures of DIN and TIN are different from that of the DSSN and TSSN. As a result, the node embeddings from DIN and TIN could provide additional useful features for the prediction model to improve its performance.

5.5 Parameter Sensitivity

For the proposed method, an important hyper-parameter α is investigated. For the parameter sensitivity analysis, α is set to 0.01, 0.04, 0.1, 0.4, and 1.0 with other parameters fixed. The effect to the DTI prediction is shown in Table 4. It can be seen that the proposed method performs the best with $\alpha = 0.04$ and $\alpha = 0.1$, while there is a performance loss if α is set to a too low or too high value. The reason for the performance loss of setting $\alpha = 0.01$ is that many informative relations are removed. However, the reason for the performance loss of setting $\alpha = 0.4$ and 1.0 is that most uninformative relations are kept. By keeping those uninformative edges, node pairs with very small similarity scores could co-exist in the training node pair set D. As a result, the distance between the node embeddings do not reflect the structure/sequence similarity between the nodes. This is further verified by an additional performance loss in setting $\alpha = 1$ compared to setting $\alpha = 0.4$.

5.6 A Case Study of Novel DTI Prediction

We conduct a case study on DT-IN dataset to find whether the novel DTIs (excluding the known DTIs recorded in the dataset) predicted by our method can be supported by recent studies. In this experiment, all the known DTIs are first used to train our model. The trained model is then used to predict novel DTIs. The top-100 novel DTIs predicted by our method are shown in Fig. 2.

We search for the supporting studies over the top-20 predicted DTIs. It is interesting to find that six of them are supported by recent studies. Sunitinib

inhibits EPHB2 [18], GSK3B [5], and SYK [21]. The treatment of using Sunitinib substantially increases ErbB3 [11]. Bosutinib is an inhibitors to KDR [4].
Haloperidol would down regulate CHRM2 [25].

Table 4. The effect of edge density parameter α.

$\alpha = 0.01$		$\alpha = 0.04$		$\alpha = 0.1$		$\alpha = 0.4$		$\alpha = 1$	
AUPR	st.d.	AUPR	st.d.	AUPR	st.d.	AUPR	st.d.	AUPR	st.d.
0.8547	0.0140	0.8608	0.0153	0.8610	0.0145	0.8536	0.0151	0.8491	0.0159

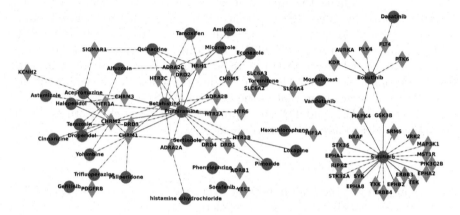

Fig. 2. The top-100 DTIs predicted by the proposed method on DT-IN dataset. Each
circle represents a drug. Each diamond represents a target. The edges between nodes
indicate novel DTI predictions (i.e., new DTIs not recorded in the dataset). The top-20
DTI predictions are in solid lines, while the remaining ones are in dashed lines.

6   Conclusion

In this work, we propose a novel DTI prediction method, namely NE-DTIP, by
additionally considering the implicit networks. Experiments over five benchmark
datasets demonstrate the competitive performance of the proposed method compared to other state-of-the-art methods, especially on the datasets with densely
connected implicit networks. Further experiments suggest that there is a significant performance gain in incorporating the implicit networks, which however,
are ignored in the previous related works. Finally, a case study indicates that
the proposed method is capable of predicting novel DTIs.

The future work can be conducted from the following directions. The first
direction is to increase the robustness of utilising the implicit relations. If the
implicit network is too sparse, the features generated by network embedding
module of NE-DTIP would not be informative. As a result, the performance of

DTI prediction would be degraded. The second direction is to further incorporate other networks such as drug-drug interaction network, target-target interaction network and drug-side-effect network, since these networks with the more information may increase the performance of DTI prediction.

References

1. Archana, S., Elangovan, K.: Survey of classification techniques in data mining. Int. J. Comput. Sci. Mob. Appl. **2**(2), 65–71 (2014)
2. Bleakley, K., Yamanishi, Y.: Supervised prediction of drug-target interactions using bipartite local models. Bioinformatics **25**(18), 2397–2403 (2009)
3. Broomhead, D.S., Lowe, D.: Radial basis functions, multi-variable functional interpolation and adaptive networks. Technical report, Royal Signals and Radar Establishment Malvern, United Kingdom (1988)
4. Brown, S.A., Nhola, L., Herrmann, J.: Cardiovascular toxicities of small molecule tyrosine kinase inhibitors: an opportunity for systems-based approaches. Clin. Pharmacol. Ther. **101**(1), 65–80 (2017)
5. Calero, R., Morchon, E., Johnsen, J.I., Serrano, R.: Sunitinib suppress neuroblastoma growth through degradation of MYCN and inhibition of angiogenesis. PLoS ONE **9**(4), e95628 (2014)
6. Chang, C.C., Lin, C.J.: LIBSVM: a library for support vector machines. ACM Trans. Intell. Syst. Technol. (TIST) **2**(3), 1–27 (2011)
7. Davis, J., Goadrich, M.: The relationship between precision-recall and ROC curves. In: Proceedings of the 23rd ICML, pp. 233–240 (2006)
8. Deng, H., Lyu, M.R., King, I.: A generalized co-hits algorithm and its application to bipartite graphs. In: Proceedings of the 15th ACM SIGKDD, pp. 239–248 (2009)
9. Goyal, P., Ferrara, E.: Graph embedding techniques, applications, and performance: a survey. Knowl. Based Syst. **151**, 78–94 (2018)
10. Haggarty, S.J., Koeller, K.M., Wong, J.C., Butcher, R.A., Schreiber, S.L.: Multidimensional chemical genetic analysis of diversity-oriented synthesis-derived deacetylase inhibitors using cell-based assays. Chemi. Biol. **10**(5), 383–396 (2003)
11. Harvey, P.A., Leinwand, L.A.: Oestrogen enhances cardiotoxicity induced by Sunitinib by regulation of drug transport and metabolism. Cardiovasc. Res. **107**(1), 66–77 (2015)
12. Hattori, M., Okuno, Y., Goto, S., Kanehisa, M.: Development of a chemical structure comparison method for integrated analysis of chemical and genomic information in the metabolic pathways. J. Am. Chem. Soc. **125**(39), 11853–11865 (2003)
13. Hou, C., Zhang, H., He, S., Tang, K.: Glodyne: global topology preserving dynamic network embedding. IEEE Trans. Knowl. Data Eng. (2020)
14. Keiser, M.J., Roth, B.L., Armbruster, B.N., Ernsberger, P., Irwin, J.J., Shoichet, B.K.: Relating protein pharmacology by ligand chemistry. Nat. Biotechnol. **25**(2), 197–206 (2007)
15. Keiser, M.J., et al.: Predicting new molecular targets for known drugs. Nature **462**(7270), 175–181 (2009)
16. Liu, Y., Wu, M., Miao, C., Zhao, P., Li, X.L.: Neighborhood regularized logistic matrix factorization for drug-target interaction prediction. PLoS Comput. Biol. **12**(2), e1004760 (2016)

17. Luo, Y.Y., et al.: A network integration approach for drug-target interaction prediction and computational drug repositioning from heterogeneous information. Nat. Commun. **8**(1), 1–13 (2017)
18. Martinho, O., et al.: In vitro and in vivo analysis of RTK inhibitor efficacy and identification of its novel targets in glioblastomas. Transl. Oncol. **6**(2), 187-IN20 (2013)
19. Mei, J.P., Kwoh, C.K., Yang, P., Li, X.L., Zheng, J.: Drug-target interaction prediction by learning from local information and neighbors. Bioinformatics **29**(2), 238–245 (2013)
20. Mikolov, T., Sutskever, I., Chen, K., Corrado, G.S., Dean, J.: Distributed representations of words and phrases and their compositionality. In: NeurIPS, vol. 26, pp. 3111–3119 (2013)
21. Noé, G., et al.: Clinical and kinomic analysis identifies peripheral blood mononuclear cells as a potential pharmacodynamic biomarker in metastatic renal cell carcinoma patients treated with sunitinib. Oncotarget **7**(41), 67507 (2016)
22. Perozzi, B., Al-Rfou, R., Skiena, S.: DeepWalk: online learning of social representations. In: ACM SIGKDD, pp. 701–710 (2014)
23. Platt, J., et al.: Probabilistic outputs for support vector machines and comparisons to regularized likelihood methods. Adv. Large Margin Classifiers **10**(3), 61–74 (1999)
24. Smith, T.F., Waterman, M.S., et al.: Identification of common molecular subsequences. J. Mol. Biol. **147**(1), 195–197 (1981)
25. Swathy, B., Banerjee, M.: Haloperidol induces pharmacoepigenetic response by modulating miRNA expression, global DNA methylation and expression profiles of methylation maintenance genes and genes involved in neurotransmission in neuronal cells. PLoS ONE **12**(9), e0184209 (2017)
26. Thafar, M.A., et al.: DTiGEMS+: drug-target interaction prediction using graph embedding, graph mining, and similarity-based techniques. J. Cheminformatics **12**(1), 1–17 (2020)
27. Vogt, M., Stumpfe, D., Maggiora, G.M., Bajorath, J.: Lessons learned from the design of chemical space networks and opportunities for new applications. J. Comput. Aided Mol. Des. **30**(3), 191–208 (2016)
28. Wan, F., Hong, L., Xiao, A., Jiang, T., Zeng, J.: NeoDTI: neural integration of neighbor information from a heterogeneous network for discovering new drug-target interactions. Bioinformatics **35**(1), 104–111 (2019)
29. Wang, Y., Jiao, P., Wang, W., Lu, C., Liu, H., Wang, B.: Bipartite network embedding via effective integration of explicit and implicit relations. In: International Conference on Database Systems for Advanced Applications, pp. 435–451 (2019)
30. Willett, P., Barnard, J.M., Downs, G.M.: Chemical similarity searching. J. Chem. Inf. Comput. Sci. **38**(6), 983–996 (1998)
31. Wishart, D.S., et al.: DrugBank: a comprehensive resource for in silico drug discovery and exploration. Nucl. Acids Res. **34**(suppl_1), D668–D672 (2006)
32. Xia, Z., Wu, L.Y., Zhou, X., Wong, S.T.: Semi-supervised drug-protein interaction prediction from heterogeneous biological spaces. BMC Syst. Biol. **4**, S6 (2010). https://doi.org/10.1186/1752-0509-4-S2-S6
33. Xie, L., Xie, L., Kinnings, S.L., Bourne, P.E.: Novel computational approaches to polypharmacology as a means to define responses to individual drugs. Annu. Rev. Pharmacol. Toxicol. **52**, 361–379 (2012)
34. Yamanishi, Y., Araki, M., Gutteridge, A., Honda, W., Kanehisa, M.: Prediction of drug-target interaction networks from the integration of chemical and genomic spaces. Bioinformatics **24**(13), i232–i240 (2008)

35. Yu, L., Zhang, C., Pei, S., Sun, G., Zhang, X.: WalkRanker: a unified pairwise ranking model with multiple relations for item recommendation. In: Proceedings of the AAAI Conference on Artificial Intelligence, vol. 32 (2018)
36. Zong, N., Kim, H., Ngo, V., Harismendy, O.: Deep mining heterogeneous networks of biomedical linked data to predict novel drug-target associations. Bioinformatics **33**(15), 2337–2344 (2017)

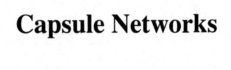

Capsule Networks

CNNapsule: A Lightweight Network with Fusion Features for Monocular Depth Estimation

Yinchu Wang[1], Haijiang Zhu[1(✉)], and Mengze Liu[2]

[1] College of Information Science and Technology, Beijing University of Chemical Technology, Beijing, China
zhuhj@mail.buct.edu.cn
[2] PetroChina Jidong Oilfield Company, Hebei, China

Abstract. Depth estimation from 2D images is a fundamental task for many applications, for example, robotics and 3D reconstruction. Because of the weak ability to perspective transformation, the existing CNN methods have limited generalization performance and large number of parameters. To solve these problems, we propose CNNapsule network for monocular depth estimation. Firstly, we extract CNN and Matrix Capsule features. Next, we propose a Fusion Block to combine the CNN with Matrix Capsule features. Then the skip connections are used to transmit the extracted and fused features. Moreover, we design the loss function with the consideration of long-tailed distribution, gradient and structural similarity. At last, we compare our method with the existing methods on NYU Depth V2 dataset. The experiment shows that our method has higher accuracy than the traditional methods and similar networks without pre-trained. Compared with the state-of-the-art, the trainable parameters of our method decrease by 65%. In the test experiment of images collected in the Internet and real images collected by mobile phone, the generalization performance of our method is further verified.

Keywords: Monocular depth estimation · Matrix capsule · Fusion block

1 Introduction

Depth estimation is a fundamental research in computer vision. It mainly depends on professional equipments and computer vision algorithms. The depth maps of the real-world are useful for many applications including robotics [1], self-driving cars [2], SLAM [3], augmented reality [4], 3D reconstruction [5], and segmentation [6]. Depth estimation methods mainly include structured light,

Supported by the National Natural Science Foundation of China under grant No. 61672084 and the Fundamental Research Funds for the Central Universities under grant No. XK1802-4.

I. Farkaš et al. (Eds.): ICANN 2021, LNCS 12891, pp. 507–518, 2021.
https://doi.org/10.1007/978-3-030-86362-3_41

TOF (Time of Flight), binocular vision and monocular vision. Compared with the other methods, monocular vision has the advantages of simple structure, wide vision and low cost. Therefore, there are many recent studies focusing on monocular depth estimation [7–10].

The early monocular depth estimation methods mainly rely on the computer vision algorithms [11–13]. With the continuous optimization of deep learning and GPU acceleration technology, automatic learning image structural features based on CNN (Convolutional Neural Network) has gradually become an important method for monocular depth estimation [14–16]. In 2014, Eigen et al. [17] first used CNN for monocular depth estimation and proposed multi-scale deep network. Compared with the traditional methods, this method achieved higher accuracy. But, the resolution of output images are low. To solve this problem, Laina et al. [18] proposed a full convolution depth estimation network with Encoder-Decoder. They proposed a new up-sampling method, and first used the inverse Huber loss as the optimization function. Further, they deepen the network and achieved good performance without post-processing. Nevertheless, they did not make full use of multi-scale information, which limits the further improvement of depth estimation. Based on this problem, in 2017, Xu et al. [19] proposed a network with CRF (Conditional Random Field) model. They extracted multi-scale CNN features maps and integrated these maps to achieve better performance. Due to the lack of contextual information, the results were still inadequate. To solve this problem, Hao et al. [20] adopted ResNet-101 as the backbone network based on transfer learning research. They used dilated convolution to extract context information. Meanwhile, they constructed AFB (Attention Fuse Block) and CRB (Channel Reduce Block) to fuse the features in the decoder stage. After that, many scholars used transfer learning method and replaced different backbone network to improve the performance of depth estimation, such as using VGG [20], DenseNet [16,21], etc. However, in order to reduce the impact of perspective transformation, these methods always need complex networks to cover all samples. Meanwhile, these networks have large number of parameters and the generalization performance is limited. To solve these problems, we propose a lightweight CNNapsule network to integrate Matrix Capsule features into CNN with Fusion Block. Moreover, Encoder-Decoder is constructed to realize end-to-end training. In the end, the experiments show that our method achieves better performance.

When humans perceive the depth of the real-world, there are many overlapping areas with similar features. Humans can learn these features and perspective transformation for depth estimation. Based on this, we take advantage of the invariability of perspective with the Matrix Capsule features [22]. Firstly, we extract CNN and Matrix Capsule features in the encoder stage. Next, the perspective invariant pose matrices of Matrix Capsule features are mapped into feature maps. Then the generated feature maps are concatenated with CNN features for decoder module. After that, the skip connections method is used to make full use of multi-scale features. Moreover, we design a loss function with the consideration of depth difference, gradient and structural similarity. In addition, we realize end-to-end training. Finally, the experiments verify the effectiveness of our proposed method. The paper is structured as follows: Sect. 2 describes Matrix Capsule features, Fusion Block and CNNapsule architecture in detail. The experiment results on NYU Depth V2 and real images are presented in Sect. 3. Finally, a conclusion is provided in Sect. 4.

2   Proposed Method

In this section, we first introduce Matrix Capsule features. Then we describe our Fusion Block for feature fusion. After that, we give the complete architecture of our method in detail. In addition, the effective loss function is given. Finally, the data augmentation used in training is explained.

2.1   Matrix Capsule Features

Matrix Capsule features [22] are as shown in Fig. 1. The set of capsules in layer l is denoted as I_l. Every capsule has a pose matrix, $M_{4\times4}$, and an activation probability, $a_{1\times1}$. In between each capsule i in layer l and each capsule j in layer $l+1$ is a 4×4 trainable transformation matrix, W_{ij}. These W_{ij}s (and two learned biases per capsule) are the only stored parameters and they are learned discriminatively. The pose matrix of capsule i is transformed by W_{ij} to cast a vote $V_{ij} = M_i W_{ij}$ for the pose matrix of capsule j. The poses and activations of all the capsules in layer $l+1$ are calculated by using EM algorithm which gets as input V_{ij} and a_i for all $i \in I_l$, $j \in I_{l+1}$ [22]. The combination results of V_{ij}s and a_js are Matrix Capsule Features. In our experiments, the iteration of EM algorithm is set to 3.

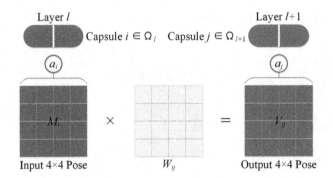

Fig. 1. Matrix Capsule features with pose matrix

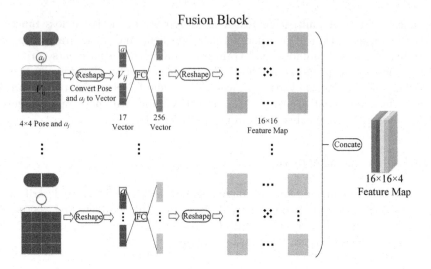

Fig. 2. Convert Matrix Capsule features to feature maps

2.2 Fusion Block

In order to integrate Matrix Capsule features into CNN, we propose a Fusion Block for feature fusion. As shown in Fig. 2, Matrix Capsule features are firstly reshaped into vectors with length n. Next, these vectors are mapped into longer vectors with length n^2 through a fully connected layer. Then the mapped vectors are reshaped into $n \times n$ feature maps. After that, an $n \times n \times m$ feature map is formed through m different $n \times n$ feature maps. Finally, we use three 1×1 convolutional layers to widen the channels to balance the contribution between Matrix Capsule and CNN features. In our experiments, we set the parameter n as 16 and m as 4.

2.3 CNNapsule Architecture

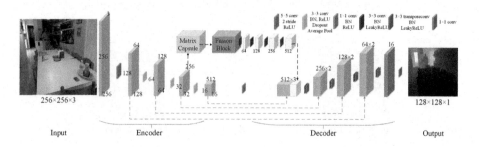

Fig. 3. Overview of our network architecture (Color figure online)

Our CNNapsule architecture is based on Encoder-Decoder and shown in Fig. 3. Firstly, considering the high computational complexity of directly extracting capsule features from input images, we adopt a convolution of 5×5 with the stride of 2 to extract low-level features. Next, we use 4 blocks to extract multi-scale features. Each block contains a convolutional layer, a BN (Batch Normalization) layer, ReLU activation function, a dropout layer (rate = 0.2) and an average pooling layer. Meanwhile, on the basis of the fourth convolutional layer, the Matrix Capsule features were generated for Fusion Block. Then, the fusion features can be obtained from our proposed Fusion Block. After that, in the decoder stage, we concatenate the channels of fusion features (yellow block in Fig. 3), CNN features (orange block in Fig. 3) and decoder features (blue block in Fig. 3). Besides high resolution feature maps were obtained by transposed convolution and leaky ReLU activation function with parameter $\alpha = 0.2$. Finally, the last convolutional layers results in depth map of spatial resolution 128×128 pixels.

2.4 Loss Function

An effective loss function is beneficial to train networks and different consideration regarding the loss function can accelerate the training speed and improve the overall depth estimation performance. There are many variations on the loss function employed for optimizing the network [16,17,23,24]. Jiao et al. [23] found that NYU Depth V2 dataset has a long-tailed distribution. It means that hard samples with large depth pixel values have very limited contribution and it leads the models tend to predict smaller depth values. So we design an adaptive depth loss L_{depth} as:

$$L_{depth} = \frac{1}{N} \sum_p^N y_p^* [f(y_p^*) - f(y_p)] \tag{1}$$

$$f(y) = min(\frac{1}{y}, 1000.0) \tag{2}$$

where N is the number of pixels, y^* is the ground truth depth map and y is the prediction of the depth estimation network. Meanwhile, the pixels of ground truth are normalized to $[0, 1]$.

Then, in order to retain edge information of depth maps, gradient similarity is considered to design gradient loss L_{grad} as:

$$L_{grad} = \frac{1}{N} \sum_p^N |\boldsymbol{g}_x[f(y_p), f(y_p^*)]| + |\boldsymbol{g}_y[f(y_p), f(y_p^*)]| \tag{3}$$

where $\boldsymbol{g}_x$ and $\boldsymbol{g}_y$, respectively, compute the difference in the x and y components for the depth image gradients of $f(y)$ and $f(y^*)$.

At last, we consider the SSIM (Structural Similarity) effectiveness on our model and design the SSIM loss function as follows:

$$L_{SSIM}(y) = 1 - SSIM[f(y_p), f(y_p^*)] \tag{4}$$

Based on these considerations, we design the loss function as:

$$L_{cost} = L_{depth} + L_{grad} + \lambda L_{SSIM} \tag{5}$$

We empirically found and set $\lambda = 0.5$ as a reasonable weight.

2.5   Data Augmentation

In order to improve the generalization performance of our network, we augment the training data with random online transformation:

- *Brightness*: Change the brightness of the input images with a probability of 0.5, and the brightness range is $[0.5, 1.5]$.
- *Contrast*: Change the contrast of the input images with a probability of 0.5, and the contrast range is $[0.5, 1.5]$.
- *Saturation*: Change the saturation of the input images with a probability of 0.5, and the saturation range is $[0.4, 1.2]$.
- *Color*: Exchange R and G channels of the input images with a probability of 0.25.
- *Flip*: Flip the input and target images horizontally with a probability of 0.5.
- *Translation*: Input and target images are randomly cropped to 224×224. To fit the network, the input images are resized to 256×256 and the target images are resized to 128×128.

We change the brightness, contrast and saturation of the input images to simulate the transformation of the lightness in the real scene. Meanwhile, the effectiveness of switched R and B channels has been demonstrated by relevant study [16]. Image translation does not preserve the world-space geometry of the scene. This problem can be corrected in the case of scaling by dividing the depth values by the scale (making the image s times larger effectively moves the camera s times closer) [17]. Flips are geometry-preserving.

3   Experiments

We train our model on NYU Depth V2 [25] with our proposed data augmentation. Moreover, we also download some indoor images outside of the dataset from the Internet and collect some real indoor images with our mobile phone. We use these images for qualitative test. Our network training and test environment is Win10+Tensorflow1.13.0 and the GPU is GTX2060.

3.1   Evaluation

We quantitatively compare our method against existing methods using the standard six metrics used in prior work [17]. These error metrics are defined as:

- average relative error (rel): $\frac{1}{N} \sum_p^N \frac{|y_p - y_p^*|}{y_p^*}$;
- root mean square (rms): $\sqrt{\frac{1}{N} \sum_p^N (y_p - y_p^*)^2}$;
- average error (log_{10}): $\frac{1}{N} \sum_p^N |log_{10}(y_p) - log_{10}(y_p^*)|$;
- threshold accuracy (δ_i): % of y_p^* s.t. $max(\frac{y_p}{y_p^*}, \frac{y_p^*}{y_p}) = \delta < threshold$ for $threshold = 1.25, 1.25^2, 1.25^3$.

3.2   NYU Depth V2

NYU Depth V2 is a dataset which contains 120K training samples and 654 testing samples. It is always used for the indoor depth estimation task. RGB inputs are downsampled from 640×480 to 256×256 and the ground truth images are downsampled to 128×128. In particular, points for which there is no depth value are left unfilled in training. Learning rates are 0.01 for all layers. Momentum is 0.9. Training took 52h and was performed for 0.75M iterations. Due to the limited performance of the GPU, batch size is only set to 4 in our experiments. In order to compare the different methods clearly, we resize all the results to the same resolution in Fig. 4, Fig. 5 and Fig. 6.

Table 1. Comparison on the NYU Depth V2.

Method	rel↓	rms↓	log_{10}↓	δ_1 ↑	δ_2 ↑	δ_3 ↑	Output
Zheng et al. [26]	0.257	0.915	0.305	0.540	0.832	0.948	–
Liu et al. [27]	0.230	0.824	0.095	0.614	0.883	0.971	–
Wang et al. [28]	0.220	**0.745**	0.094	0.605	0.890	0.970	–
Eigen et al. [17]	0.215	0.907	–	0.611	0.887	0.971	80×60
Ours (No Fusion Block, batch size $= 4$, L_{cost})	0.226	0.792	0.092	0.637	0.887	0.970	128×128
Ours (batch size $= 2$, L_{cost})	0.216	0.757	0.088	0.657	0.897	0.973	128×128
Ours (batch size $= 4$, L_{depth})	0.229	0.817	0.094	0.605	0.883	0.971	128×128
Ours (batch size $= 4$, L_{cost})	**0.214**	0.760	**0.087**	**0.663**	**0.900**	**0.973**	$\mathbf{128 \times 128}$

During the test, we use bilinear interpolation to resize the prediction images to 640×480. Then we evaluate the results on the pre-defined center cropping by Eigen et al. [17]. Since our network did not adopt pre-trained and fine-tune strategies, we compare our method with traditional algorithms and the networks without pre-trained. We do pseudo color processing for better visualization. Qualitative results are shown in Fig. 4. In the second row, our method gives a clearer result of the bookshelf. Moreover, in the third row, our result has better texture information in the lamp. Meanwhile, quantitative results are provided in Table 1. As can be seen, compared with traditional algorithms and similar

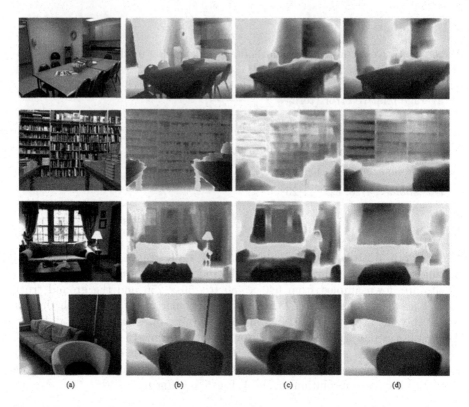

Fig. 4. Depth prediction on NYU Depth V2: (a) input RGB images (b) ground truth (c) results using Eigen et al. [17] (d) our estimated depth maps

networks without pre-trained, our method (batch size = 4, L_{cost}) achieves the best performance on all but one quantitative metrics. In addition, our method has higher output resolution.

The comparison with other methods is shown in Fig. 5. Although we do not use transfer learning and pre-trained, our results also have similar prediction performance with the existing method based on transfer learning. Furthermore, our results even have clearer textures on some samples. In the second row, since we consider the long-tailed distribution, we have a better result on large pixels. In particular, a comparison of network parameters and iterations is shown in Table 2. Compared with the state-of-the-art, the trainable parameters of our method decrease by 65%. Moreover, our method needs fewer iterations to converge.

Table 2. Comparison of network parameters and iterations.

Method	Parameters	Iterations
Fu et al. [15]	110M	3M
Alhashim et al. [16]	42.6M	1M
Ours	**14.9M**	**0.75M**

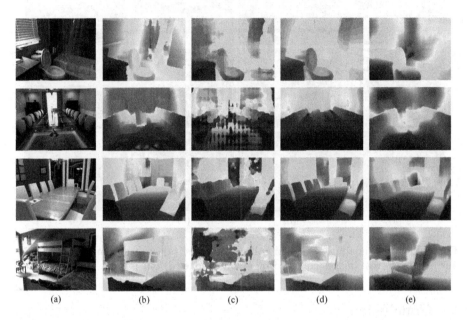

| (a) | (b) | (c) | (d) | (e) |

Fig. 5. Qualitative comparison of NYU Depth V2 between our method and other methods (based on transfer learning): (a) input RGB images (b) ground truth (c) results using Fu et al. [15] (d) results using Alhashim et al. [16] (e) our estimated depth maps

3.3   Internet and Real Collected Images

In order to further verify the generalization performance of our method, we collect some images from the Internet and some real images by mobile phones. We directly predict the depth of these images with our model trained on NYU Depth V2. Some visualization results are shown in Fig. 6. As can be seen, even if the test images are not consistent with the training dataset, the estimation results are still robust to some content.

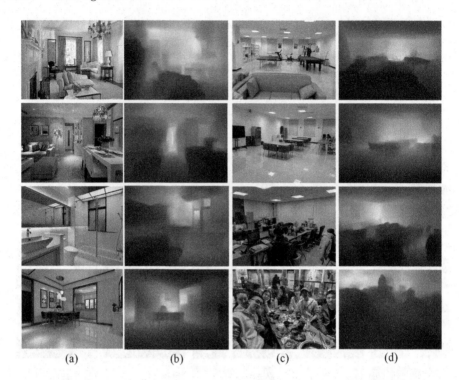

(a)   (b)   (c)   (d)

Fig. 6. Depth estimation results for collected images: (a) images from the Internet (b) our results (c) real images collected by mobile phone (d) our results

4   Conclusion

In this work, we proposed a lightweight CNNapsule network for monocular depth estimation. We have constructed Fusion Block to fuse Matrix Capsule into CNN features. Complete depth estimation network has been established with Encoder-Decoder. Meanwhile, we have considered three influential parts to design loss function for parameter optimization. The experiments have verified the effectiveness of our method. Moreover, compared with the existing state-of-the-art method, our estimation results also have certain advantages in some scenes.

Acknowledgements. This work was supported in part by the National Natural Science Foundation of China under grant No. 61672084 and the Fundamental Research Funds for the Central Universities under grant No. XK1802-4.

References

1. Gao, W., Wang, K., Ding, W., Gao, F., Qin, T., Shen, S.: Autonomous aerial robot using dual-fisheye cameras. J. Robot. Syst. **37**(4), 497–514 (2020)

2. Saleem, N.H., Chien, H.J., Rezaei, M., Klette, R.: Effects of ground manifold modeling on the accuracy of Stixel calculations. IEEE Trans. Intell. Transp. Syst. **20**(10), 3675–3687 (2020)
3. Civera, J., Davison, A.J., Montiel, J.M.M.: Inverse Depth parameterization for monocular SLAM. IEEE Trans. Robot. **24**(5), 932–945 (2008)
4. Ping, J., Thomas, B.J., Baumeister, J., Guo, J., Weng, D., Liu, Y.: Effects of shading model and opacity on depth perception in optical see-through augmented reality. J. Soc. Inform. Display **28**, 892–904 (2020)
5. Yang, X., Zhou, L., Jiang, H., Tang, Z.: Mobile3DRecon: real-time monocular 3D reconstruction on a mobile phone. IEEE Trans. Visual Comput. Graphics **26**, 3446–3456 (2020)
6. Hazirbas, C., Ma, L., Domokos, C., Cremers, D.: FuseNet: incorporating depth into semantic segmentation via fusion-based CNN architecture. In: Lai, S.-H., Lepetit, V., Nishino, K., Sato, Y. (eds.) ACCV 2016. LNCS, vol. 10111, pp. 213–228. Springer, Cham (2017). https://doi.org/10.1007/978-3-319-54181-5_14
7. Atapour-Abarghouei, A.: Real-time monocular depth estimation using synthetic data with domain adaptation. In: IEEE/CVF Conference on Computer Vision & Pattern Recognition (2018)
8. Ji, R.R., et al.: Semi-Supervised adversarial monocular depth estimation. IEEE Trans. Pattern Anal. Mach. Intell. **42**(10), 2410–2422 (2020)
9. Zhang, M.L., Ye, X.C., Xin, F.: Unsupervised detail-preserving network for high quality monocular depth estimation. Neurocomputing **404**, 1–13 (2020)
10. Huang, K., Qu, X., Chen, S., Chen, Z.: Superb monocular depth estimation based on transfer learning and surface normal guidance. Sensors **20**(17), 4856 (2020)
11. Konrad, J., Wang, M., Ishwar, P.: 2D-to-3D image conversion by learning depth from examples. In: Proceedings of Conference on Computer Vision and Pattern Recognition Workshops, pp. 16–22 (2012)
12. Li, N.B., Shen, N.C., Dai, N.Y., Hengel, A.V.D., He, N.M.: Depth and surface normal estimation from monocular images using regression on deep features and hierarchical CRFs. In: Proceedings of Conference on Computer Vision and Pattern Recognition (CVPR), pp. 1119–1127 (2015)
13. Eigen, D., Fergus, R.: Predicting depth, surface normals and semantic labels with a common multi-scale convolutional architecture. In: IEEE International Conference on Computer Vision (2015)
14. Ye, X. C., Chen, S. D., Xu, R.: DPNet: detail-preserving network for high quality monocular depth estimation. Pattern Recogn. **109** (2021)
15. Fu, H., Gong, M., Wang, C., Batmanghelich, N., Tao, D.: Deep ordinal regression network for monocular depth estimation. In: 2018 IEEE/CVF Conference on Computer Vision and Pattern Recognition 2002–2011 (2018)
16. Alhashim, I., Wonka, P.: High quality monocular depth estimation via transfer learning. arXiv: 1812.11941 (2018)
17. Eigen, D., Puhrsch, C., Fergus, R.: Depth map prediction from a single image using a multi-scale deep network. In: NIPS (2014)
18. Laina, I., Rupprecht, C., Belagiannis, V., Tombari, F., Navab, N.: Deeper depth prediction with fully convolutional residual networks. In: 2016 Fourth International Conference on 3D Vision (3DV), pp. 239–248 (2016)
19. Xu, D., Ricci, E., Ouyang, W., Wang, X., Sebe, N.: Multi-scale continuous CRFs as sequential deep networks for monocular depth estimation. In: Proceedings of the IEEE Conference on Computer Vision and Pattern Recognition, pp. 5354–5362 (2017)

20. Hao, Z., Li, Y., You, S., Lu, F.: Detail preserving depth estimation from a single image using attention guided networks. In: 2018 International Conference on 3D Vision (3DV), pp. 304–313 (2018)
21. Yeh, C.H., Huang, Y.P., Lin, C.Y., Chang, C.Y.: Transfer2Depth: dual attention network with transfer learning for monocular depth estimation. IEEE Access **99**, 1–1 (2020)
22. Hinton, G. E., Sabour, S., Frosst, N.: Matrix capsules with EM routing. In: International Conference on Learning Representations (2018)
23. Jiao, J., Cao, Y., Song, Y., Lau, R.: Look deeper into depth: monocular depth estimation with semantic booster and attention-driven loss. In: Ferrari, V., Hebert, M., Sminchisescu, C., Weiss, Y. (eds.) ECCV 2018. LNCS, vol. 11219, pp. 55–71. Springer, Cham (2018). https://doi.org/10.1007/978-3-030-01267-0_4
24. Ummenhofer, B., et al.: DeMoN: depth and motion network for learning monocular stereo. In: 2017 IEEE Conference on Computer Vision and Pattern Recognition (CVPR), pp. 5622–5631 (2017)
25. Silberman, N., Hoiem, D., Kohli, P., Fergus, R.: Indoor segmentation and support inference from RGBD images. In: Fitzgibbon, A., Lazebnik, S., Perona, P., Sato, Y., Schmid, C. (eds.) ECCV 2012. LNCS, vol. 7576, pp. 746–760. Springer, Heidelberg (2012). https://doi.org/10.1007/978-3-642-33715-4_54
26. Zheng, C., Cham, T.J., Cai, J.: T2Net: synthetic-to-realistic translation for solving single-image depth estimation tasks. In: Proceedings of the European Conference on Computer Vision (ECCV), pp. 767–783 (2018)
27. Liu, M., Salzmann, M., He, X.: Discrete-continuous depth estimation from a single image. In: Proceedings of Conference on Computer Vision and Pattern Recognition (CVPR), pp. 716–723 (2014)
28. Wang, P., Shen, X., Lin, Z., Cohen, S., Price, B., Yuille, A.L.: Towards unified depth and semantic prediction from a single image. In: Proceedings of the IEEE Conference on Computer Vision and Pattern Recognition, pp. 2800–2809 (2015)

Learning Optimal Primary Capsules
by Information Bottleneck

Ming-fei Hu[1]([✉]), Jian-wei Liu[1], and Wei-min Li[2]

[1] Department of Automation, College of Information Science and Engineering,
China University of Petroleum, Beijing Campus (CUP), Beijing, China
[2] Shanghai University, Shanghai, China

Abstract. Capsule network provides comparable results on several benchmark datasets with only two convolutional layers. The shortcomings of highly cost in dynamic routing and unsatisfactory performance on complex datasets are mainly caused by primary capsules, they are filled with trivial redundant features mainly because of the lack of feature compression process. We introduce a novel algorithm for exploiting better performance with limited capacity based on the information bottleneck theory, which defines optimal representation of supervised learning that it is to extract minimal sufficient statistics of the input with respect to the output. Optimal primary capsules are solved by injecting constraint variable in the representation instead of variational information bottleneck, this process can be in turn to add a regularization term to loss function. Our algorithm allows more flexible prior distribution, and it is convenient to apply and optimize. Our experiments validate that our method can make Capsule Network achieve better performance with fewer primary capsules and reduce computation complexity significantly.

Keywords: Information bottleneck · Capsule network · Representation learning · Compression

1 Introduction

Convolutional neural networks (CNNs) have played an important role in computer vision tasks, there are still some limitations such as remain invariance and the inability to understand spatial relationships between features caused by pooling layer. To address these limitations, a representational variant named Capsule Network (CapsNet) proposed by [1–3] that shows promising results in some basic datasets. However, there is no effective algorithm to compress primary capsules, the techniques used to prevent overfitting such as dropout and data augmentation cannot eliminate redundant information in the representation. The trivial redundant features in primary capsules lead to highly cost in dynamic routing and unsatisfactory performance on complex datasets.

To solve this, we attend to use information bottleneck theory to compress the primary capsules and reduce computation complexity. In the view of information bottleneck [4, 5], optimal representation of supervised learning is to extract minimal sufficient

© Springer Nature Switzerland AG 2021
I. Farkaš et al. (Eds.): ICANN 2021, LNCS 12891, pp. 519–528, 2021.
https://doi.org/10.1007/978-3-030-86362-3_42

statistics of the input with respect to the output. But this method is difficult to perform because of its definition. Deep VIB [8] is the most common trick to address information bottleneck which parameterizes model by using a neural network, it gets an evidence lower bound by leveraging the variational inference and uses the reparameterization trick for back-propagating the gradient efficiently.

However, the assumption of the posterior distribution in Deep VIB is inflexible for CapsNet, for example, it is unrealistic to assume that the posterior is Gaussian. In this paper, we focus on formalizing the idea for optimal primary capsules with information bottleneck conveniently. We propose a new method to control the information flow from input by adding multiplicative constraint variable instead of VIB. Our method allows arbitrary representation distribution and avoids posterior, it can equivalently be encoded as the constraint variable in primary capsule layer. Then we introduce how to use our method to compress primary capsules and build a loss function about the constraint variable, it is used to encourage the representation to carry out the task with minimal features. As we show in various experiments, our method can reduce the number of the primary capsules with lower computation complexity and achieve better results than baseline CapsNet with binary dropout and data-augmentation.

More specifically, we summarize our main findings:

1) We first construct optimal representation of CapsNet to improve performance, and reduce calculation complexity by information bottleneck theory, which can compress primary capsules effectively.
2) We provide a novel method to approximate information constraint by injecting multiplicative constraint variable in the representation, this method aims at building convenient and flexible assumption by avoiding posterior. Then, we propose a regularization term to limit information flow from input to representation.
3) Using our method to compress primary capsules in CapsNet for optimal representation. We evaluating the performance of our method on several benchmark datasets with different capacities, the results show that our method can achieve better results with fewer primary capsules.

CapsNet: CapsNet comprises only two convolutional layers and a dynamic routing process between two capsule layers, each capsule is a vector encapsulated a group of neurons that represents the instantiation parameters such as an object or a part. Convolutional layers are used to get features from the image without pooling layer, these features are divided into small groups of neurons called primary capsule, all of them compose the representation. Dynamic routing mechanism is a novel algorithm used to cluster primary capsules to classified capsules which are long instantiation vectors if and only if it is present in the input. The classified capsule with the longest length is predicted result, it depends on the separate marginal loss function. Decoder can reconstruct the input from the practical capsule representation predicted by model, the Euclidean distance between the input and the reconstruction is minimized during training as a regularization term.

CapsNet works well in the MNIST dataset, but the performance on complex datasets such as CIFAR10 is not satisfactory compared with the CNNs. Another disadvantage is that the dynamic routing is an extremely computationally expensive procedure due to the redundant primary capsules. When the input is MNIST dataset the primary capsules of the best result contained 1152 primary capsules which are 12 times input dimension, but the accuracy is very close to the best when the number of primary capsules is 288. CapsNet has no feature compression process such as pooling layer, its representation is filled with trivial and redundant features, it is the main reason for poor performance on complex datasets and excessive computation.

Information Bottleneck: It suggests that the representation should be an efficient feature, and its relevant information in the input variable about the target is brief in perspective of information theoretic concepts, its objective has the form:

$$I(z; y) - \beta I(x; z) \tag{1}$$

where $I(\cdot)$ denotes the mutual information which is always difficult, β is a positive constant to tradeoff sufficiency and minimum. Despite being a pivotal across machine learning and data science, mutual information is intractable in the high-dimensional continuous variables of deep learning constitutionally because of the joint probability distribution [6]. The binning algorithm proposed by [7] segments the neuron's output activations into several equal intervals, it can be used to optimize this function only when all random variables are low-dimensional discrete variables. For high-dimensional continuous variables of deep neural networks, an approximation algorithm named variational inference is needed.

2 Proposed Framework

Our purpose is to construct optimal primary capsules which can achieve better performance with fewer features in perspective of information theoretic concepts, therefore we attend to use the information bottleneck to constrain the representation. The first term in Eq. (1) can be replaced by the marginal loss function in CapsNet, since the second term can be seen as a regularization method to limit information flow of capsules in our method.

Mutual information is a fundamental quantity leverage for measuring the relevant information, but it is always difficult to compute directly:

$$I(x; z) = \int \int p(x, z) \log \frac{p(x, z)}{p(x)p(z)} dz dx \tag{2}$$

where $p(x, z)$ is the joint probability distribution, $p(x)$ and $p(z)$ are the marginals. VIB is needed to estimate these distributions which are difficult to address, then Eq. (2) can be rewrite as:

$$\begin{aligned}
I(x; z) &= \int \int p(x, z) \log \frac{p(x,z)}{p(x)p(z)} dz dx \\
&= \int \int p(x) p(z|x) \log \frac{p(z|x)}{p(z)} dz dx \\
&= \mathbb{E}_{x \sim p(x)} \big[\mathrm{KL}(p(z|x) || p(z)) \big]
\end{aligned} \tag{3}$$

where KL denotes the Kullback-Leibler divergence. It is still intractable due to the posterior distribution $p(z|x)$ and the marginal distribution $p(z)$, since we propose a simple way to approximate it inspired by local reparemeterization [9] and information dropout [10].

Local reparemeterization trick suggests that the uncertainty about the posterior can equivalently be encoded as a multiplicative variable in the activation of the representation. According to this trick, a constraint variable ε is a random sample drawn from conditional probability distribution $p(\varepsilon|h)$ that depends on the input, the constraint variable is injected in the representation as noise with multiplicative:

$$t = z \odot \varepsilon, \quad \varepsilon \sim p(\varepsilon|x)$$

where $\odot$ denotes multiplicative, t denotes our optimal representation.

Figure 1 describes the structure of our method: variable h_1 and h_2 are hidden layers in front of z, $\alpha(\cdot)$ denotes a neural network that x is input, $p(\varepsilon)$ is the probability distribution of the output, we can get constraint variable ε through sampling operation from posterior distribution $p(\varepsilon|x)$. Then constraint variable should be rescaled in the allowed range and add a small value for numerical stability. After a multiplication between constraint variable ε and representation z, a restricted variable t is the optimal representation that it is used as input of the decoder for task y.

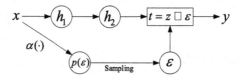

Fig. 1. The architecture of our method to approximate information bottleneck

Now the KL divergence term can be rewrite as:

$$\begin{aligned}
&KL(p(\varepsilon) \| p(z)) \\
&= \int p(\varepsilon) \log \frac{p(\varepsilon)}{p(z)} dz \\
&= -H(p(\varepsilon)) - \int p(\varepsilon) \log p(z) dz
\end{aligned} \tag{4}$$

There are two probability distributions need to fix for computing KL divergence: constraint distribution $p(\varepsilon)$ and prior distribution $p(z)$. To compute efficiently and analysis simply, a natural choice for constraint distribution is the log-normal distribution $\log N(0, \alpha^2(x))$ with mean zero and standard deviation parameterized by $\alpha(x)$. Notice that these neural networks used for information constraints on the representation are additional network, they won't affect the structure of the model.

Prior would be desirable to use a log-uniform $p(\log(z))$ which is a scale invariant prior from a theoretical point of variational dropout. In this setting, we can easy to write Eq. (4) as follow:

$$\begin{aligned}
L_{IB} &= -KL(p(\varepsilon) \| p(t)) \\
&= H(p(\varepsilon)) + \log c \\
&= \log \alpha(x) + c
\end{aligned} \tag{5}$$

This is an information constraint in loss function that penalizes the input related information in the representation, it is easy to optimization and convenient to apply on other models. A standard normal distribution is a good fit for prior, using this prior we can compute the KL divergence easily:

$$
\begin{aligned}
L_{\mathrm{IB}} &= -\mathrm{KL}(p(\varepsilon)\,\|\,p(t)) \\
&= \mathrm{KL}\big(N(0,\alpha^2(x))\,\|\,N(\mu,\sigma^2)\big) \\
&= \tfrac{1}{2\sigma^2}\big(\alpha^2(x)+\mu^2\big) - \log\tfrac{\alpha(x)}{\sigma} - \tfrac{1}{2}
\end{aligned}
\tag{6}
$$

Indeed, it is usually to assume that the prior is a standard normal distribution $N(0, 1)$, in this case the loss function of information constraint is:

$$
L_{\mathrm{IB}} = \frac{1}{2}\alpha^2(x) - \log\alpha(x) - c
$$

3   Optimal Primary Capsules

In this section, we would show how to use our method to get optimal primary capsules and loss function. First, we use a neural network for constraint variable ε, notice that the size of ε should be same as the representation. Second, ε is divided into small groups after scaling and reshaping, these groups can be seen as constraint capsules which should have the same size as the primary capsules. Last, the optimal representation is the product of primary capsules and the random samples from constraint capsules. Figure 2 shows how to compress primary capsules for optimal representation marked by a dotted line.

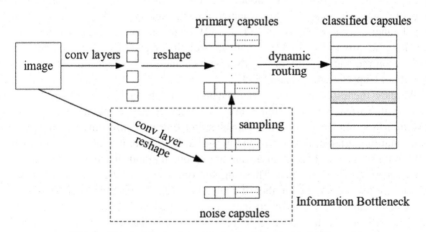

Fig. 2. Constrain primary capsules by information bottleneck

When the activation function of primary capsule layer is not squashing in other models, constraint variable should inject into the weights of representation before non-linear function. For instance, there is such a common network, the prior distribution is uniform $p(z) = \frac{c}{z}$ and the activation function is the rectified linear unit (ReLU) which is unbounded and frequently zero, we can assume the prior $p(z) = c'$ when z is zero, where c' denotes a constant in the interval 0 to 1, the final prior has the form $p(z) = c'\delta(z) + \frac{c}{z}$ where δ is the Dirac delta function. Now we can get the following loss function:

$$L = L_{\text{Caps}} + \beta L_{\text{IB}} \tag{7}$$

4 Experiments

4.1 Datasets and Experimental Settings

We used Keras libraries for all the models. For the training procedure, we used RMSprop with an initial learning rate of 0.001 and an exponential decay rate of 0.9. All the experiments are performed on RTX-2080ti with 16 GB RAM. We test our method with several benchmark datasets, MNIST [11], Fashion-MNIST [12] and CIFAR10 [13]. We present various experimental results comparing the behavior of the standard CapsNet, CapsNet with dropout [14] and data augmentation, the results show that our method is able to compress the representation and improve performance of limited capacity, but other methods can't.

4.2 Classification Results with Different B

Parameter β in loss function is a hyper-parameter to adjust the mutual information between input and representation. To show the effect on classification results with different β, we train some CapsNet models on MNIST dataset with $\beta \in \{0.01, 0, 1, 100\}$, we get back the original CapsNet when $\beta = 0$. In each value of β, we train 9 models with channel $\in \{1, 4, 8, 12, 16, 20, 24, 28, 32\}$, channel can represent increasing model capacity gradually from 1 to 32, we can get back the original CapsNet when channel = 32, for example, the capacity of CapsNet with channel = 4 is four times as large as the capacity of CapsNet with channel = 1.

We show the results in Fig. 3. When the number of channels is from 1 to 32, CapsNet models with different β have similar curve changes. It maybe because that the Squash activation function of the primary capsules and routing can normalize the values of representation variable, the size of the noise hardly affects the information constraint of the representation. This is an advantage of our method that the additional hyper-parameters β needn't to adjust. These three models with different β can achieve best accuracy 99.69% when the number of channels is 12. The results will achieve the next peak when channel = 20, and then show a downward trend. When $\beta = 0$, the original CapsNet will get the first peak at 99.63% when the channel = 8, and then show a downward trend until channel = 24, it will get best result 99.64% when channel is 32, this setting is equal to baseline CapsNet. Our method can get better results than the baseline by using 37.5% capsules. It can suggest that in our method, the primary capsules of the CapsNet can achieve better representation whatever the value of β is.

We compare our method with binary dropout, information dropout and data augmentation as baseline on different network sizes and architectures. Binary dropout is

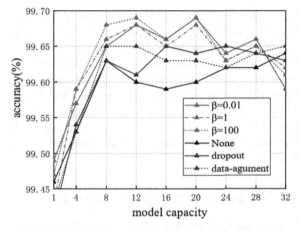

Fig. 3. Classification results on MNIST with different β

set a drop probability of 0.2 on primary capsules and data augmentation is set width shift range = height shift range = 0.5. Information dropout is similar to our method, it can be regarded as a generalization of dropout that is motivated by the Information Bottleneck principle, so it should use multiple times in layer like binary dropout, each information dropout uses a Sigmoid activation function and the noise is come from the previous layer. When regularization term is none, we will get original CapsNet. If this term is dropout, it has the same curve with original CapsNet when channel is from 1 to 12, the best result is 99.66% when channel is 16. Data augmentation has a similar curve to dropout, it gets best result at 99.65% when channel is 8 and 32. Table 1 shows the testing error and the number of primary capsules on MNIST with different β for ours, original CapsNet, binary dropout and data-augmentation.

Table 1. Classification error on MNIST

Method	Error (%)	Primary capsules
CapsNet	0.36	1152
Binary dropout	0.35	864
Data augmentation	0.34	1152
Ours ($\beta = 0.01$)	**0.31**	720
Ours ($\beta = 1$)	0.32	**432**
Ours ($\beta = 100$)	**0.31**	**432**

Neither dropout or data augmentation has no compression and significant performance improvement, it may be because that binary dropout on primary capsules will destroy the integrality of the representation. As a result of the instantiation parameters of a specific type of entity, each primary capsule may contain different levels and types of relevant features such as position, size and orientation, it's not enough to activate parts of primary capsules or neurons in capsules randomly. Dynamic routing is viewed as a kind of attention mechanism that allows each capsule at one level to attend to some capsules and to ignore others at below level, in other word, CapsNet can learn the intrinsic spatial relationship between part and whole and then generalizes to novel viewpoints [15], data augmentation by adding the gathered information from various viewpoints or converting pixel intensities doesn't work as well as it does on CNNs. Information dropout constrains the information flow between one layer and the next, it may have adverse effects on the representation learning.

4.3 Classification Results with Fashion-MNIST and CIFAR10

To see the effect of our method on different network size and other datasets, we train on Fashion-MNIST and CIFAR10 with $\beta = 0.01$ and a variable number of channels, similar to Sect. 4.2, and all the results are the best of three times and run 80 epochs. We show the result on Fashion-MNIST in Fig. 4 (a), the CapsNet with our method can achieve the best accuracy 92.10% with 24 channels which outperforms the best accuracy of the original CapsNet 91.98% with 32 channels.

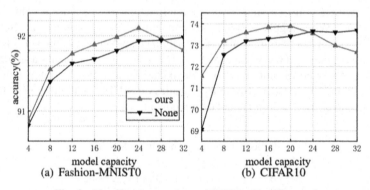

Fig. 4. Classification results on MNIST with different β

In Fig. 4 (b), we plot the accuracy of two CapsNet as the model capacity grows, the accuracy of our method is better than the original CapsNet when the channel is less than 24. The best accuracy 73.89% that our model achieves is comparable to the original CapsNet (73.80%), but only 62.5% of primary capsules are used. CapsNet with our method uses 24 capsule blocks to achieve the best result in gray Fashion-MNIST images, but only 20 in the more complex RGB CIFAR10 images which seems counterintuitive. In fact, the number of primary capsules in each capsule block is different which is related to the input size. In our setting, each capsule block contains 64 primary capsules on Fashion-MNIST images and 36 primary capsules on CIFAR10 images. Table 2 shows the testing error and the number of primary capsules on Fashion-MNIST and CIFAR10.

Table 2. Classification error on MNIST

Dataset	Method	Error (%)	Primary capsules
Fashion-MNIST	CapsNet	8.02	1152
	Ours	7.90	864
CIFAR10	CapsNet	26.20	2048
	Ours	26.11	1280

5   Conclusion

In this paper, we develop a novel method for exploring the information bottleneck in a simple way, and we use this method to compress primary capsules for optimal representation. We show that our approximate algorithm can be optimized by adding a regularization term in loss function which is related to injecting a constraint variable in primary capsules, it allows flexible assumption and can be minimized efficiently. The optimal representation is proven to achieve preferable results with fewer primary capsules and reduce calculation significantly.

We have successfully demonstrated the convenient compression capability of information bottleneck, there are several extensions that we would like to explore in future work. The most notable direction is that optimal representation compressed may have other benefits, such as increased disentanglement to the decoder or robustness to adversarial inputs. The second interesting direction would be considering to extend our algorithm to general neural networks such as CNNs. Lastly, we believe that exploring more precise estimation algorithm instead of ours or a measure easy to calculate instead of mutual information could bridge the gap between the theory and the practice on neural networks.

Acknowledgements. This work was supported by the Science Foundation of China University of Petroleum, Beijing (No. 2462020YXZZ023).

References

1. Kosiorek, A.R., Sabour, S., Teh, Y.W., et al.: Stacked capsule autoencoders. In: NIPS Neural Information Processing Systems, pp. 3856–3866 (2017)
2. Sabour, S., Frosst, N., Hinton, G.: Matrix capsules with EM routing. In: ICLR International Conference on Learning Representations, pp. 1–15 (2019)
3. Kosiorek, A.R., Sabour, S., Teh, Y.W., et al.: Stacked capsule autoencoders. In: NIPS Neural Information Processing Systems, pp. 15486–15496 (2019)
4. Tishby, N., Zaslavsky, N.: Deep learning and the information bottleneck principle. In: IEEE Information Theory Workshop, pp. 1–5 (2015)
5. Shwartz-Ziv, R., Tishby, N.: Opening the black box of deep neural networks via information. arXiv preprint arXiv:1703.00810 (2017)

6. Paninski, L.: Estimation of entropy and mutual information. Neural Comput. **15**(6), 1191–1253 (2003)
7. Tishby, N., Pereira, F.C., Bialek, W.: The information bottleneck method. arXiv preprint physics/0004057 (2000)
8. Alemi, A.A., Fischer, I., Dillon, J.V., et al.: Deep variational information bottleneck. In: ICLR International Conference on Learning Representations, pp. 2575–2583 (2015)
9. Kingma, D.P., Salimans, T., Welling, M.: Variational dropout and the local reparameterization trick. In: NIPS Neural Information Processing Systems, pp. 2575–2583 (2015)
10. Achille, A., Soatto, S.: Information dropout: Learning optimal representations through noisy computation. IEEE Trans. Pattern Anal. Mach. Intell. **40**, 2897–2905 (2018)
11. LeCun, Y., Cortes, C.: MNIST handwritten digit database (2010)
12. Xiao, H., Rasul, K., Vollgraf, R.: Fashion-MNIST: a novel image dataset for benchmarking machine learning algorithms. arXiv preprint arXiv:1708.07747 (2017)
13. Krizhevsky, A., Hinton, G.: Learning multiple layers of features from tiny images (2009)
14. Srivastava, N., Hinton, G., Krizhevsky, A., et al.: Dropout: a simple way to prevent neural networks from overfitting. J. Mach. Learn. Res. **15**(1), 1929–1958 (2014)
15. Hinton, G.E., Krizhevsky, A., Wang, S.D.: Transforming auto-encoders. In: Honkela, T., Duch, W., Girolami, M., Kaski, S. (eds.) ICANN 2011. LNCS, vol. 6791, pp. 44–51. Springer, Heidelberg (2011). https://doi.org/10.1007/978-3-642-21735-7_6

Capsule Networks with Routing Annealing

Riccardo Renzulli$^{(\boxtimes)}$ (iD), Enzo Tartaglione$^{(\boxtimes)}$ (iD), Attilio Fiandrotti$^{(\boxtimes)}$ (iD), and Marco Grangetto$^{(\boxtimes)}$ (iD)

Computer Science Department, University of Turin, 10149 Turin, TO, Italy
{riccardo.renzulli,enzo.tartaglione,attilio.fiandrotti,
marco.grangetto}@unito.it

Abstract. Capsule Networks overcome some shortcomings of convolutional neural networks organizing neurons into groups of *capsules*. Capsule layers are dynamically connected by means of an iterative routing mechanism, which models the connection strengths between capsules from different layers. However, whether routing improves the network performance is still object of debate. This work tackles this issue via Routing Annealing (RA), where the number of routing iterations is annealed at training time. This proposal gives some insights on the effectiveness of the routing for Capsule Networks. Our experiments on different datasets and architectures show that RA yields better performance over a reference setup where the number of routing iterations is fixed (even in the limit case with no routing), especially for architectures with fewer parameters.

Keywords: Capsule networks · Routing · Annealing

1 Introduction

Capsule Networks (CapsNets) [8,9,16], received lots of attention lately as they tackle several shortcomings of Convolutional Neural Networks (CNNs). The human visual system is known to recognize objects (e.g., faces) decomposing them in hierarchy of parts (e.g., mouth and nose) with poses imposing coordinate frames to represent shapes [7]. While CNNs can detect the presence of objects in an image, they cannot however capture the spatial relationships between its parts mainly due to max pooling layers progressively dropping spatial information. CapsNets attempt to preserve and leverage an image representation as a hierarchy of parts with poses introducing two architectural novelties.

First, neurons are organized in groups called *capsules*, where each capsule accounts for a different *visual entity*, e.g. for a different part of an object. Then, neurons inside each capsule account each for a different property or attribute of the object such as pose (position, size, orientation) and properties (color, deformation, etc.) [16]. The output of each capsule is a vector, where the normalized vector length is the probability that the image contains the object the capsule accounts for [16].

© Springer Nature Switzerland AG 2021
I. Farkaš et al. (Eds.): ICANN 2021, LNCS 12891, pp. 529–540, 2021.
https://doi.org/10.1007/978-3-030-86362-3_43

Second, pooling layers are replaced by a *routing algorithm*, which captures the part-objects spatial relationships between one capsule layer and the following. Unlike conventional neural networks, each capsule chooses to which capsules of the next layer to forward its output. Capsules activations are multiplied by learnable weight matrices in order to cast the votes for how the poses of the capsules of the next layer will be. The routing algorithm iteratively computes the *agreement* between the predictions of a capsule layer for the following layer. The routing algorithm outputs both the poses of the following capsule layer and the probabilities with which parts are assigned to objects. Therefore, the information flow across layers is not given by the network topology anymore, rather it is dynamically controlled by the routing algorithm.

Recently, the contribution of the routing algorithm to CapsNets generalization ability and robustness to affine transformations has been questioned [5,14]. Typically, the number of routing iterations r is fixed once and for all during training and inference. Dropping the routing procedure is equivalent to run just one iteration (uniform routing in [14], $r = 1$) so that the coupling coefficients are not updated and they are all initialized equally. In [5,14] it is shown that by simply averaging the predictions instead of finding the coupling coefficients between capsules through the routing algorithm yields better results. To the present date, it is not clear whether the routing algorithm improves the performance of CapsNets and what is the optimal number of iterations.

This work provides new evidence on the benefits of routing proposing *Routing Annealing (RA)*, a novel technique where the number of routing iterations is iteratively found at training time. With RA, the number of iterations of the routing algorithms increases whenever the network performance reaches a loss plateau. We observed that, for the same number of routing iterations, a gradual ramp thereof allows to reach better minima of the loss function. Our experiments over multiple datasets show better performance when using RA, especially when the number of capsules in the network is limited, i.e. where CapsNets performance is weaker. We also found that the number of routing iterations depends on the number of capsules, their dimensions and on the dataset itself.

The rest of this work is organized as follows. In Sect. 2 we first provide the background on CapsNets instrumental to understanding this work, then we discuss recent literature on routing. Next, in Sect. 3 we present *Routing Annealing* (RA), our proposed training procedure for CapsNets. Finally, in Sect. 4 we experiment with RA and a reference routing algorithm over multiple datasets, highlighting the benefits of the former. Section 5 drawn the conclusions and discusses further developments of this work.

2   Background and Related Works

This section first describes those aspects of CapsNet instrumental to the understanding of this work, namely their architecture and the routing algorithm introduced by Sabour et al. [16]. Then, we review the literature especially related to the routing algorithm and we make some considerations on this procedure.

2.1   CapsNet Architecture

Figure 1 shows the CapsNet architecture proposed in [16] for MNIST classification, consisting in one convolutional layer and two *capsule layers*. Due to its relevance for our work and for sake of simplicity, our overview on CapsNets will focus on this specific architecture.

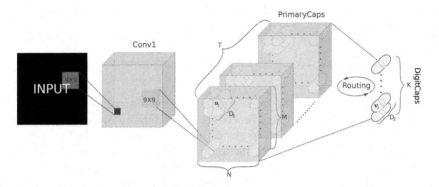

Fig. 1. CapsNet architecture described in [16]. There are one convolution layer (Conv1) and two capsule layers (PrimaryCaps and DigitCaps). The routing algorithm controls the information flow between capsule layers.

The first layer (Conv1) is a convolutional layer that converts pixel intensities to the *activities* that are given in input to the first capsule layer.

The PrimaryCaps layer is implemented as a convolutional layer with a 9×9 filters [16] and $T \times D_1$ channels where T is the number of *primary capsules* types and D_1 is the dimension of a capsule vector. Overall, there are $T \times M \times N$ primary capsules. Let us denote as u_j primary capsules vectors normalized with the squashing function introduced in [16]. Each capsule is composed of a pose vector whose magnitude models the probability that the object that detects is present in the image. The output layer (*DigitCaps*) comprises of K D_2-dimensional *digit capsules* v_j, one for each output class.

The information flow between primary and digit capsules is governed by a routing algorithm which aims to organize these capsules into a part-whole hierarchy. One of the most employed is the one introduced in [16]. This is an iterative procedure that computes both the poses of digit capsules from the poses of primary capsules and the strengths of the connections between the latter two. Each primary capsule predicts a pose for each digit capsule: if there are a lot predictions agreeing with each others, this means that they are in correct spatial-relationship to activate a specific digit capsule. The routing algorithm aims to find *clusters* of these agreements. Let $W_{ij} \in \mathbb{R}^{D_1 \times D_2}$ be the matrix which projects the information flow between the i-th primary capsule and the j-th digit capsule. This can be learned through standard error gradient backpropagation. The *prediction*, or *vote*, of a primary capsule i for the digit capsule j is defined

---

Algorithm 1. Dynamic routing algorithm

1: **procedure** ROUTING($\hat{u}_{j|i}$, r)
2:     for each primary capsule i and digit capsule j: $b_{ij} \leftarrow 0$
3:     **for** r iterations **do**
4:         for each primary capsule i: $c_i \leftarrow$ softmax(b_i)
5:         for each digit capsule j: $s_j \leftarrow \sum_i c_{ij} \hat{u}_{j|i}(b_i)$
6:         for each digit capsule j: $v_j \leftarrow$ squash(s_j)
7:         for each primary capsule i and digit capsule j: $b_{ij} \leftarrow b_{ij} + v_j \cdot \hat{u}_{j|i}$
8:     **end for**
9:     **return** v_j
10: **end procedure**

---

as $\hat{u}_{j|i} = W_{ij} u_i$ which is the input for the routing algorithm described in [16] and shown in Algorithm 1. This procedure shows how to dynamically compute the poses v_j of the digit capsules given the predictions $\hat{u}_{j|i}$. At the beginning of the routing algorithm (line 2) the logits b_{ij} are initialized equally and they are the log prior probabilities that capsule i should be coupled to capsule j. The core of the routing algorithm is depicted in lines 3–8. At every iteration, a "routing softmax" (line 4) is applied to the logits b_{ij} to obtain the corresponding coupling coefficient c_{ij}. Then, the total input s_j of capsule j of the DigitCaps layer is computed as the weighted average of the input predictions (line 5). Each vote $\hat{u}_{j|i}$ is weighted by the corresponding coupling coefficient c_{ij}. v_j is defined as the normalized "squashed" s_j (line 6). Then each b_{ij} is refined by measuring the agreement between the output v_j of a capsule j and the prediction $\hat{u}_{j|i}$ (line 7). Therefore, if there is a strong agreement, the corresponding link strength b_{ij} between capsules i and j is increased, decreased otherwise. Finally, after r iterations of lines 4–7, the routing algorithm output the final pose v_j for each digit capsule.

2.2 Literature Review and Considerations on the Routing Algorithm

Ever since, different routing algorithms and architectures for capsule networks have been proposed and have found applications in various tasks [2,4,11,18]. We refer to routing-based CapsNets as those models that employ a routing algorithm in the architecture of the network. Hinton et al. [9] employ the Expectation-Maximization algorithm for the iterative routing procedure and build a deeper capsule network with convolutional capsule layers. Wang et al. [17] model the routing strategy as an optimization problem that minimizes a clustering-like loss and a KL divergence between the coupling distribution. Li et al. [13] reduce the computational complexity of the routing process using master and aide branches. Hahn et al. [6] describe a *self-routing* method that incorporates mixture-of-experts into capsule network models so as they do not require agreements anymore. De Sousa Ribeiro et al. [3] replace the routing algorithm with variational inference of part-object connections in a probabilistic capsule network, leading to a significant speedup without sacrificing performance. Furthermore, Ahmed et al. [1] exploit attention modules and differentiable binary router to remove the recurrence of the routing algorithm to estimate the coupling coefficients. Lenssen et al. [12] exploit group convolutions to guarantee equivariance of pose vectors as well as invariance of output activations. Rajasegaran et al. [15] propose a deep capsule network architecture which uses a novel 3D convolution based dynamic routing algorithm aiming at improving the performance of CapsNets for more complex image datasets.

Despite of all the contributions mentioned before it is still no clear if CapsNets really need a routing algorithm. Paik et al. [14] highlight that running just one iteration of the routing algorithm (namely assigning the connection strengths uniformly or randomly) leads to better results. This is explained as more iterations of the routing algorithms do not change the classification result but polarize the link strengths [14]. Gu et al. [5] mitigate this problem with a simple but effective solution in which the transformation matrices are shared between all capsule types. However, in contrast with the present work, they do not change the number of iterations during the training process neither the number of capsule types and their dimensions, which as we will see they do have a strong impact on the number of iterations of the routing algorithm.

3   Methodology

This section first describes the standard methodology training algorithm and *Routing Annealing* (RA), the routing training technique we propose in this work, and then discusses its relation with the simulated annealing.

3.1   Training with Fixed Routing

As a reference, Algorithm 2 shows the standard strategy for training a CapsNet. The network parameters are optimized with standard backpropagation of the error gradients for a number of epochs until some stop criterion is met. For each epoch, the forward pass (line 5–11) is computed, followed by error gradients backpropagation and parameter update (line 12). The training procedure ends when the loss computed over a validation set does not decrease for p epochs in a row (p is usually termed as *patience*). The algorithm returns the network (i.e., the learned parameters set) that yields the lowest loss on the validation set. In this procedure, as can be note from line 6 which refers to Algorithm 1, the number of routing iterations r is fixed once for all (usually, $r = 3$), so we refer to this technique as *Fixed Routing* (FR). Notice that when the trained network is deployed for inference, the routing algorithm is executed for r iterations, as well. A standard procedure towards optimising the iterations number would be to optimize r with a grid-search strategy: one runs as many simulations as r values to test, during which r is kept constant. However, we experimentally show that this approach leads to sub-optimal performance, which motivates the design of our routing technique.

Algorithm 2. Training with *Fixed Routing*: learns the network parameters for a fixed number of iterations r.

1: **procedure** FIXED-ROUTING(r, p)
2:    initialize CapsNet
3:    $e \leftarrow 0;\ \ \mathcal{L}^\star \leftarrow 0;\ e^\star \leftarrow 0$.
4:    **while** $e - e^\star < p$ **do**
5:        compute all primary capsules poses $\boldsymbol{u}_i$ and votes $\hat{\boldsymbol{u}}_{j|i}$
6:        compute all digit capsules poses: $\boldsymbol{v}_j \leftarrow$ ROUTING($\hat{\boldsymbol{u}}_{j|i}$, r)
7:        evaluate current loss $\mathcal{L}$ on the validation set
8:        **if** $\mathcal{L} < \mathcal{L}^\star$ **then**
9:            $\mathcal{L}^\star \leftarrow \mathcal{L};\ e^\star \leftarrow e$
10:        **end if**
11:        $e \leftarrow e + 1$
12:        backpropagate error gradients and update parameters
13:    **end while**
14:    **return** CapsNet network of epoch $e^\star$ with the best loss value
15: **end procedure**

3.2   Training with Routing Annealing

In this section we propose *Routing Annealing* (RA), an iterative method to jointly optimize the number of routing iterations $r^\star$ and the network parameters. In a nutshell, RA finds $r^\star$ adaptively during training for a given capsule architecture over a given dataset and is described in pseudo-code as Algorithm 3. The algorithm takes as input: r_0, the initial value of r; r_T, the maximum value for r; s, the schedule used to increase r; the patience p, in number of epochs. Let us denote as r_k the value of r at step k: we say that every time r increases, an *annealing step* is performed. We denote as $\mathcal{L}_k^\star$ and $e_k^\star$ the lowest losses achieved so far and the corresponding epochs for each r_k. The main difference between Algorithm 2 and 3 lies in line 3 where we loop over the possible values of r instead over the number of epochs and in line 8 where the number of routing iterations is increased. In line 5, Algorithm 1 is used as core routing algorithm. At step k, we increase r by s if the validation loss $\mathcal{L}_k^\star$ does not decrease for p epochs (lines 7–8). Every time r is increased, the training does not start from scratch again. Instead it is resumed with the network weights with the best loss achieved with the previous value of r, namely the network at epoch $e_{k-1}^\star$ (line 9). Here we assume that we save the network weights for each epoch. When r reaches the maximum allowed r_T, the training procedure ends and best network obtained during training along with the corresponding number of routing iterations is returned (lines 16–17). To summarize, RA increases the value of r when the validation loss does not decrease for p epochs in a row. As an upper bound for the number of routing iterations, we stop the training when r reaches its maximum value r_T. When r increases, the training restarts with the weights of the network with the best validation loss obtained with its previous value. By comparison, using the standard training procedure mentioned in Sect. 3.1, the weights need to be reinitialize for every simulation with a different value for r.

Algorithm 3. Training with *Routing Annealing*: learns the number of iterations r^* jointly with the network parameters.

1: **procedure** ROUTING-ANNEALING(r_0, r_T, s, p)
2:     r; $r \leftarrow r_0$; $\mathcal{L}_0^* \leftarrow +\infty$; $e_0^* \leftarrow 0$, $e \leftarrow 0$; $k \leftarrow 0$
3:     **while** $r \leq r_T$ **do**
4:         compute all primary capsules poses u_i and votes $\hat{u}_{j|i}$
5:         compute all digit capsules poses: $v_j \leftarrow$ ROUTING($\hat{u}_{j|i}$, r)
6:         evaluate loss $\mathcal{L}$ on the validation set
7:         **if** ($\mathcal{L} \geq \mathcal{L}_k^*$) **and** ($e - e_k^* \geq p$) **then**
8:             $k \leftarrow k + 1$; $r \leftarrow r + s$; $r_k \leftarrow r$; $\mathcal{L}_k^* \leftarrow +\infty$; $e_k^* \leftarrow 0$
9:             load CapsNet network of epoch e_{k-1}^*
10:        **else if** $\mathcal{L} < \mathcal{L}_k^*$ **then**
11:            $\mathcal{L}_k^* \leftarrow \mathcal{L}$; $e_k^* \leftarrow e$
12:        **end if**
13:        $e \leftarrow e + 1$
14:        backpropagate error gradients and update parameters
15:    **end while**
16:    $k^* \leftarrow \arg\min_k \mathcal{L}^*$; $r^* \leftarrow r_{k^*}$
17:    **return** CapsNet network of epoch $e_{k^*}^*$ and r^*
18: **end procedure**

3.3   Rationale

RA takes inspiration from the *simulated annealing* (SA) algorithm, a probabilistic technique used in combinatorial-optimization problems to minimize a cost function. In our approach, we relate the temperature of our system being inversely proportional to the number of routing iterations r: the highest r, the highest the agreement between the capsules and the lowest the noise.

The number of routing iterations relates to the distribution of the coupling coefficients c_{ij}. According to Algorithm 1, when r is low, the agreement is low as well. When $r = 1$, all the coupling coefficients will have the same value, $\frac{1}{K}$. Increasing the routing iterations, a certain number of coupling coefficients becomes dominant over others, since Algorithm 1 looks for capsule's agreement. Considering that c_{ij} are normalized values, we can say that, for the i-th capsule $\sum_{j \in \mathcal{K}_i} c_{ij} \to 1$ and $\sum_{j \in \overline{\mathcal{K}_i}} c_{ij} \to 0$, where $\mathcal{K}_i$ is a subset of the K coupling coefficients for the i-th primary capsule and $\overline{\mathcal{K}_i}$ is its complementary set. When $r = 1$, the cardinality of $\mathcal{J}_i$ is exactly K, but increasing r, its cardinality drops to some optimal value K_i^*: this means that the i-th primary capsule will be coupled to K_i^* digit capsules only, avoiding noisy coupling to the others (which are $K - K_i^*$). A visual representation of this effect is displayed in Fig. 2. As r increases, many coupling coefficients drop to zero, while others converge to higher coupling values. In this way, the routing algorithm learns how to build relationships between primary and digit caps, discarding noisy information, which helps in improving the generalization of the model. In the next section we are going to test on-the-field our RA strategy, observing in particular the generalization capability of the RA models compared to the other state-of-the-art approaches.

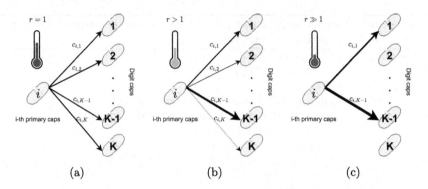

Fig. 2. Routing coupling coefficients between the i-th primary capsule and K digit capsules. The highest the line weight, the highest the corresponding coupling coefficient. When $r = 1$ (a) the coupling coefficients have all the same value, while increasing r (b, c) a portion of the coupling parameters survives, while the others drop to zero. In the case of (c), $K^* = 2$ and $\mathcal{K}_i = \{1, K - 1\}$.

4   Experiments

In this section we compare our proposed Routing Annealing (RA) method in Algorithm 3 against the reference method in Algorithm 2. First we show that, with RA, the network performs better as the number of routing iterations r improves, whereas this is not the case with the reference algorithm. Then, we further validate RA on multiple datasets and settings showing that it delivers best gains especially where the number of parameters the network can afford is low, i.e. where CapsNets performance is weaker.

4.1   Experimental Setup

We experiment with the CapsNet in Fig. 1 at classifying natural images in a fully supervised scenario. We consider the MNIST, Fashion-MNIST and CIFAR10 datasets. For all datasets, 5% of the training set samples are reserved for validation. MNIST and Fashion-MNIST are composed of 28×28 images; concerning CIFAR10, we randomly crop the original 32×32 images into 24×24 patches for training whereas crops from the image center are used for testing as done in [16]. Our experiments consider several flavors of the architecture in Fig. 1 with different types $T \in \{1, 2, 4, 8, 16, 32\}$ and dimensions $(D_1, D_2) \in \{(2, 4), (4, 8), (8, 16)\}$ of capsules. We train the network minimizing a *margin loss* [16] with the Adam optimizer [10] with a constant learning rate equal to 0.001 and a batch size of 128. No weight decay, dropout or other regularization techniques were used.

Concerning the proposed RA method, we train the network with the procedure in Algorithm 3, with the following configuration: $r_0 = 1$, $r_T = 50$, $s = 1$ and $p = 10$. As we discussed in Sect. 3.2, RA can be applied to any iterative routing algorithm but this work use as base routing algorithm the one described in Algorithm 1.

About the reference method, we use FR which employs the procedure in Algorithm 2, i.e. where the number of routing iterations r is fixed (common values in literature are $r = 1$ [5] or $r = 3$ [16]).

4.2   Preliminary Analysis on MNIST

Preliminary, we assess the effect of the number of routing iterations r on MNIST for a minimal capsule network where the PrimaryCaps layer has only $T = 1$ capsule types and vectors have dimension $D_1 = 2$ while the DigitCaps layer vectors have $D_2 = 4$ elements. This network has only 65k parameters, which helps isolating the effect of r, whereas the architecture in [16] has 6M parameters (8.2M with the decoder).

In Fig. 3 we report the learning curves for FR and RA. For FR, we train a new CapsNet from scratch for each and every value of r. In the case of RA, instead, we train one model only, where we gradually increase the number of routing iterations (when the network loss reaches a plateau). We plot the best loss and accuracy values for every r. Figure 3 shows that as r increases, the proposed RA enables decreasing loss that reflects into higher classification accuracy. Conversely, with a fixed routing strategy, the loss function diverges as r increases. We explain the gap between the two loss curves with the following hypothesis. Each iteration of the routing algorithm strengthens or weakens the connections between a capsule of the primary layer and all the capsules of the digit layer. Therefore, imposing high r for all the training epochs leads the CapsNet to be overconfident on its predictions on the link strengths, preventing the network form learning the correct connections between the capsules.

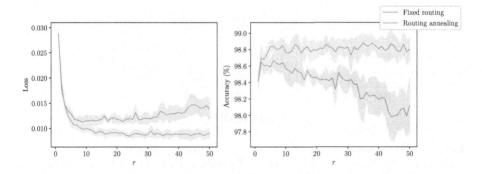

Fig. 3. Loss function (left) and classification accuracy (right) on MNIST test set for a CapsNet with $T = 1$, $D_1 = 2$, $D_2 = 4$ (means and stds of 5 seeds) as a function of the number of routing iterations r.

4.3   Results

Next, we experiment with the more complex datasets Fashion-MNIST and CIFAR10. Figure 3 showed that RA performs better than the fixed routing reference for large r values.

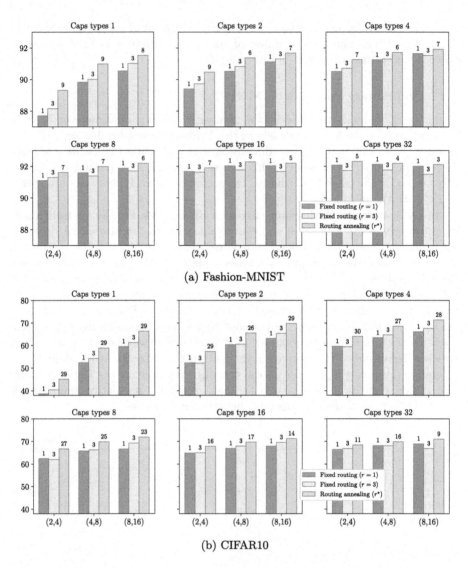

Fig. 4. Classification accuracy (%) on Fashion-MNIST (a) and CIFAR10 (b) test set for different capsule types T and dimensions (D_1, D_2). On top of each bar it is shown the number of iterations r used during training/inference, for RA it is shown the median value of $r^\star$.

For fixed routing experiments we only consider $r = 1$ and $r = 3$, as done in much of the recent literature. Figure 4a and 4b show that RA performs better than fixed routing (both $r = 1$ and $r = 3$) in all the settings. Such experiments brought us to the following observations.

First, coherently with our previous findings on MNIST, RA delivers the most appreciable gains when the network can afford only few learnable parameters. We recall here that for each capsule we have a matrix of weights W_{ij} and these matrices have shapes $D_1 \times D_2$, namely the dimensions of the capsule vectors. This means that the number of capsules types T and their dimensions, along with the convolutional layers, drive the number of parameters of the network. This behaviour can be explained observing that finding agreements between many high-dimensional capsule is not trivial. Running more iterations of the routing algorithm tends to polarize the coupling coefficients, namely the link strengths between capsules, such that it results in a simple route where each primary capsule sends its output to only one digit capsule Therefore, when there are a lot of capsules, introducing some level of uncertainty with a low value of r helps the network to not be overconfident on its predictions and to not overfit on the training data. As a matter of fact, Fig. 4a shows that with 32 capsule types of 8-dimensional primary capsules and 16-dimensional digit capsules, our proposed method RA finds $r^\star = 3$, namely the value used in the original formulation of CapsNets in [16]. Second, in high-dimensional settings the same conclusions about routing as in [5] and in [14] hold for the fixed routing procedure, which achieves higher accuracy with $r = 1$ than $r = 3$. Nevertheless, RA always achieves better performance in all cases, sometime even with fewer routing iterations.

Third, Fig. 4b shows that $r^\star$ for CIFAR10 is not the same as for Fashion-MNIST in Fig. 4a for identical network conditions. This means that despite $r^\star$ differs from dataset to dataset, nevertheless our method can find it.

5   Conclusion

In this work we proposed a novel training technique for routing-based CapsNets where the number of iterations is iteratively found at training time rather than being fixed. This work also shows experiments in settings with a different number of capsule types and their dimensions, namely the network capacity in terms of trainable parameters, and on several datasets. We show that this value depends heavily on the size of the network and on the dataset used. Typically, the smaller the network, the higher the number of iterations the network requires to improve its generalization capability. Given the potentiality of our technique, in future works we plan to apply RA on more complex and sophisticated routing algorithms such as EM routing [9].

References

1. Ahmed, K., Torresani, L.: STAR-caps: capsule networks with straight-through attentive routing. In: Advances in Neural Information Processing Systems, vol. 32, pp. 9101–9110. Curran Associates, Inc. (2019)
2. Algamdi, A.M., Sanchez, V., Li, C.T.: Dronecaps: recognition of human actions in drone videos using capsule networks with binary volume comparisons. In: 2020 IEEE International Conference on Image Processing (ICIP), pp. 3174–3178 (2020)

3. De Sousa Ribeiro, F., Leontidis, G., Kollias, S.: Introducing routing uncertainty in capsule networks. In: Advances in Neural Information Processing Systems, vol. 33, pp. 6490–6502. Curran Associates, Inc. (2020)

4. Duarte, K., Rawat, Y., Shah, M.: Videocapsulenet: a simplified network for action detection. In: Advances in Neural Information Processing Systems, vol. 31, pp. 7610–7619. Curran Associates, Inc. (2018)

5. Gu, J., Tresp, V.: Improving the robustness of capsule networks to image affine transformations. In: Proceedings of the IEEE/CVF Conference on Computer Vision and Pattern Recognition (CVPR), June 2020

6. Hahn, T., Pyeon, M., Kim, G.: Self-routing capsule networks. In: Advances in Neural Information Processing Systems, vol. 32, pp. 7658–7667. Curran Associates, Inc. (2019)

7. Hinton, G.: Some demonstrations of the effects of structural descriptions in mental imagery. Cogn. Sci. **3**, 231–250 (1979)

8. Hinton, G.E., Krizhevsky, A., Wang, S.D.: Transforming auto-encoders. In: Honkela, T., Duch, W., Girolami, M., Kaski, S. (eds.) ICANN 2011. LNCS, vol. 6791, pp. 44–51. Springer, Heidelberg (2011). https://doi.org/10.1007/978-3-642-21735-7_6

9. Hinton, G.E., Sabour, S., Frosst, N.: Matrix capsules with EM routing. In: International Conference on Learning Representations (2018)

10. Kingma, D.P., Ba, J.: Adam: a method for stochastic optimization. In: 3rd International Conference on Learning Representations, ICLR 2015, Conference Track Proceedings, San Diego, CA, USA, 7–9 May 2015 (2015)

11. LaLonde, R., Xu, Z., Irmakci, I., Jain, S., Bagci, U.: Capsules for biomedical image segmentation. Med. Image Anal. **68**, 101889 (2021)

12. Lenssen, J.E., Fey, M., Libuschewski, P.: Group equivariant capsule networks. In: Advances in Neural Information Processing Systems, vol. 31, pp. 8844–8853. Curran Associates, Inc. (2018)

13. Li, H., Guo, X., Dai, B., Ouyang, W., Wang, X.: Neural network encapsulation. In: Ferrari, V., Hebert, M., Sminchisescu, C., Weiss, Y. (eds.) ECCV 2018. LNCS, vol. 11215, pp. 266–282. Springer, Cham (2018). https://doi.org/10.1007/978-3-030-01252-6_16

14. Paik, I., Kwak, T., Kim, I.: Capsule networks need an improved routing algorithm. In: Proceedings of The Eleventh Asian Conference on Machine Learning. Proceedings of Machine Learning Research, PMLR, Nagoya, Japan, vol. 101, pp. 489–502, 17–19 November 2019

15. Rajasegaran, J., Jayasundara, V., Jayasekara, S., Jayasekara, H., Seneviratne, S., Rodrigo, R.: DeepCaps: going deeper with capsule networks. In: 2019 IEEE/CVF Conference on Computer Vision and Pattern Recognition (CVPR), pp. 10717–10725 (2019)

16. Sabour, S., Frosst, N., Hinton, G.E.: Dynamic routing between capsules. In: Advances in Neural Information Processing Systems, vol. 30, pp. 3856–3866. Curran Associates, Inc. (2017)

17. Wang, D., Liu, Q.: An optimization view on dynamic routing between capsules. In: ICLR (2018)

18. Zhao, Y., Birdal, T., Deng, H., Tombari, F.: 3D point capsule networks. In: Proceedings of the IEEE/CVF Conference on Computer Vision and Pattern Recognition (CVPR), June 2019

Training Deep Capsule Networks
with Residual Connections

Josef Gugglberger$^{(\boxtimes)}$, David Peer$^{(\boxtimes)}$ (iD), and Antonio Rodríguez-Sánchez$^{(\boxtimes)}$ (iD)

University of Innsbruck, Innsbruck, Austria
josef.gugglberger@student.uibk.ac.at,
antonio.rodriguez-sanchez@uibk.ac.at

Abstract. Capsule networks are a type of neural network that have recently gained increased popularity. They consist of groups of neurons, called capsules, which encode properties of objects or object parts. The connections between capsules encrypt part-whole relationships between objects through routing algorithms which route the output of capsules from lower level layers to upper level layers. Capsule networks can reach state-of-the-art results on many challenging computer vision tasks, such as MNIST, Fashion-MNIST and Small-NORB. However, most capsule network implementations use two to three capsule layers, which limits their applicability as expressivity grows exponentially with depth [20]. One approach to overcome such limitation would be to train deeper network architectures, as it has been done for convolutional neural networks with much increased success. In this paper we propose a methodology to train deeper capsule networks using residual connections, which is evaluated on four datasets and three different routing algorithms. Our experimental results show that in fact, performance increases when training deeper capsule networks. The source code is available on https://github.com/moejoe95/res-capsnet.

Keywords: Capsule network · Residual capsule network · Deep capsule network

1 Introduction

Capsule Networks were introduced by Sabour et al. [23], although the idea behind *capsules* was earlier introduced by Hinton et al. [6]. A capsule represents a group of neurons, and each neuron in a capsule can be seen as an instantiation parameter of some object in the image. In other words, a capsule is a vector of neurons, where its length would define the capsule's *activation*, representing the presence of an object or object-part in the input. The vector's orientation relates to certain properties of the object. Capsules can also be in matrix form, together with a scalar variable that represents its activation, as it was described by Hinton et al. in [7] as *Matrix Capsules*.

Capsules of a lower layer *vote* for the pose of capsules in the upper layer, by multiplying its own pose with a transformation matrix. Transformation matrices

© Springer Nature Switzerland AG 2021
I. Farkaš et al. (Eds.): ICANN 2021, LNCS 12891, pp. 541–552, 2021.
https://doi.org/10.1007/978-3-030-86362-3_44

are obtained through training and model viewpoint-invariant part-whole relationships, so that the change in viewpoint to an object does not change the agreement between capsules. This makes capsule networks better suited than classical CNNs for 3D viewpoint object recognition [7]. The aforementioned votes are weighted by a coefficient, which is computed dynamically by a *routing* algorithm. This routing algorithm computes the agreement between two capsules, where a high value is given to strongly agreeing capsules. The first dynamic routing algorithm - called routing-by-agreement or RBA - was proposed by Sabour et al. [23]. RBA computes the agreement between capsules by a dot product of the predicted activation of the lower level capsule with the pose of the current capsule. Later, Hinton et al. [7] published an improved routing algorithm based on expectation maximization, called EM routing. Routing capsule networks with RBA [23] improved the state-of-the-art accuracy on MNIST and outperformed previous approaches on an MNIST-like dataset with highly overlapping digits. Through EM routing, Hinton et al. [7] reported new state-of-the-art performances on the Small-NORB dataset, reducing the error rate by 45%.

In order to obtain the best performance results, it is of great importance to design very deep networks as has been shown with classical CNNs [24]. However, most capsule network implementations use two to three capsule layers, which may be the reason behind their low performance on more complex data when compared to CNNs. We believe that the performance of capsule networks can be also greatly increased by designing and training deeper network architectures. CNNs use skip connections [5] to stabilize the training process but have not yet been considered for the training of deep capsule networks. Rajasegaran [21] et al. uses residual connections, but only one routing iteration for all capsule layers except the last one. They claim that a capsule layer with only one routing iteration can be approximated with a classical single 2D convolutional layer and therefore only one capsule layer exists in their architecture[1]. In contrast we show in this paper how skip connections can be used between multiple capsule layers and not only convolutional layers.

In this work, we will show experimentally that the performance of deep capsule networks can be improved by adding residual connections between capsule layers for three different and commonly used routing algorithms: routing-by-agreement (RBA) by Sabour et al. [23], EM routing by Hinton et al. [7], and scaled-distance-agreement (SDA) routing by Peer et al. [16]. The evaluation was performed on four well-known datasets: MNIST, Fashion-MNIST, SVHN and Small-NORB.

2   Related Work

The first capsule network with a dynamic routing mechanism was proposed by Sabour et al. [23]. The authors showcased the potential of capsule networks on MNIST, using an algorithm called *routing-by-agreement*. Later, Hinton et al.

---

[1] https://github.com/brjathu/deepcaps/issues/15.

[7] came up with the more powerful EM routing algorithm. Since then, various different routing algorithms have been presented, every new implementation obtains better results when compared to previous methods. Other routing algorithms worth of mention are *scaled distance agreement routing* [16], *inverted dot-product attention routing* [25] and *routing via variational bayes* [22] just to name a few.

Kosiorek et al. [10] presented a network called *stacked capsule autoencoders*, which is able to reach state-of-the-art results for unsupervised classification on MNIST and SVHN. However, our goal is to train deep capsule networks in a supervised fashion and compare different routing mechanisms to each other.

Capsule networks show state-of-the-art performance on many simple datasets like MNIST as well as on datasets where we want to model viewpoint invariant part-whole relationships, like Small-NORB. However, the design and training of capsule networks for more complex data is still an open question. Capsule networks do not perform at the same level as modern CNN architecture. For example, in CIFAR-10 [11], capsule networks reach an error rate of about 9% [22], compare it to the 3% error rate of CNN approaches [26].

Late implementations have tried to improve capsule networks results on CIFAR-10. Xi et al. [27] were able to improve the baseline model by using a more powerful feature extractor in front of the capsule network, and training the network in an 4-model ensemble. Similarly, Ai et al. [2] presented a capsule network named *ResCaps*, having a residual sub-network in front of the capsule network. Although called ResCaps, the authors do not use skip connections between capsule layers, as opposed to our work. Rajasegaran et al. [21] were able to reach remarkable results on CIFAR-10, Fashion-MNIST and SVHN by stacking up 16 convolutional capsule layers with residual connections. They report an accuracy of 92.74% on CIFAR-10, 97.56% on Fashion-MNIST, and 94.73% on SVHN. Differently to the work presented in this paper, the authors did not use dynamic routing in the network, but only on one layer of a residual connection in the last block. Peer et al. [19] proposed a way to train deeper capsule networks that use routing-by-agreement or EM routing. The authors proved theoretically and showed experimentally, that these two routing algorithms can be improved by adding a bias term to the pre-activations in RBA and adding a bias term to the pose matrix in EM routing.

On the other hand, training very deep convolutional neural networks shows excellent results for a wide range of tasks in computer vision. Simonyan et al. [24] conducted a comprehensive study on how network depth influences the performance of CNNs. In that work, VGG provided an error rate of 23.7% on ImageNet [3], while the older and not so deep AlexNet [12] performed with an error rate of 40%. At some point, simply stacking up a higher number of layers does not improve the accuracy of a network, because of the *vanishing/exploding* gradient problem [8]. Proper weight initialization, as done by Glorot et al. [4], and normalization techniques, such as batch normalization [9] where able to overcome those issues to some extend. Even so, very deep networks still face a *degradation* problem [5], such that when the accuracy gets saturated, it drops fast, resulting in a high training error. The solution to this degradation problem was presented as the *deep residual learning framework*. Additionally, the *conflicting bundles problem* [18] becomes more present using deeper networks, where the floating point precision of GPUs and CPUs can be another reason for this problem. The authors showed in that work that residual connections can help to resolve this problem of underperformance in the case very deep convolutional neural networks.

3   Training Deep Capsule Networks

The depth of a CNN is a very important hyper-parameter because expressivity has been proved to grow exponentially with depth [20]. We will show in this chapter how to train deep capsule networks in order to improve the performance of this type of neural networks. Simply "stacking up" layers is not a proper strategy to follow and leads to failure when using routing algorithms such as routing-by-agreement and EM routing [27]. We hypothesize we can be succeed at training deep capsules through the use of residual connections between capsule layers. In this section we will analyze in detail this hypothesis and provide the details of the network architecture for the different routing procedures.

3.1   Routing Algorithms

Dynamic routing in capsule layers is a much more sophisticated strategy than just the classical pooling operation present in CNNs. We conducted our experiments using the following three routing algorithms, as they are widely used: 1. Routing-by-agreement (RBA) [23], 2. Expectation-maximization (EM) routing [7], and 3. Scaled-distance-agreement (SDA) routing [16].

The goal of a routing algorithm is to compute the agreement between lower level capsules (child capsules) and higher level capsules (parent capsules). This agreement is represented by the length of a vector and acts as a weight, determining the parent capsule(s) to which a child capsule *routes* its output. Routing is typically implemented iteratively, requiring usually just two to five iterations for convergence [7,16,22,23]. We use two routing iterations for all our experiments because this gives a good trade-off between accuracy and training time.

RBA and SDA-routing (Algorithm 1) have a very similar structure. The iterative process starts by calculating the coupling coefficients between child capsules and parent capsules, which sum up to 1 by applying the *softmax* function over the agreements. Each capsule in the higher level layer then calculates a weighted average with the coupling coefficient and the votes from the lower level capsule layer, which are *squashed* to a value between 0 and 1. In RBA, the agreement is computed by a dot product of the current pose and the votes from each child capsule. Finally the agreement tensor is updated and the procedure continues for a fixed amount of routing iterations. On the other hand, SDA calculates the agreement by inverse distances instead of the dot product, as can be seen in line 8 of Algorithm 1. This ensures that active lower level capsules do not

[1] **Input:** v_i, $\hat{u}_{j|i}$, r, l

1 $b_{ij} \leftarrow 0$

2 $\hat{u}_{j|i} \leftarrow min(||v_i||, ||\hat{u}_{j|i}||) \cdot \frac{\hat{u}_{j|i}}{||\hat{u}_{j|i}||}$

3 **for** r *iterations* **do**

4 $\qquad c_{ij} \leftarrow \frac{b_{ij}}{\sum_k exp(b_{ik})}$

5 $\qquad s_j \leftarrow \sum_i c_{ij} \cdot \hat{u}_{j|i}$

6 $\qquad v_j \leftarrow \frac{||s_j||^2}{1+||s_j||^2} \cdot \frac{s_j}{||s_j||}$

7 $\qquad t_i \leftarrow \frac{log(0.9(J-1)) - log(1-0.9)}{-0.5 mean_j (||\hat{u}_{j|i} - v_j||)}$

8 $\qquad b_{ij} \leftarrow ||\hat{u}_{j|i} - v_j|| \cdot t_i$

9 **end**

10 **return** v_j

Algorithm 1: Scaled distance agreement routing algorithm. $\forall$ capsules i of child capsule layer l and J parent capsules on layer $l + 1$, with r routing iterations and predictions $\hat{u}_{j|i}$ from child capsule with activation v_i.

couple with inactive higher level capsules and that the prediction is limited by the activation of the corresponding capsule (line 2). The runtime complexity of both algorithms is linear in the number of routing iterations.

EM routing works by fitting the mixtures of Gaussians parameters through expectation maximization. This Gaussian mixture model clusters datapoints into Gaussian distributions, each described by a mean μ and a standard deviation σ. Starting with random assignments, the expectation maximization (EM) algorithm iteratively assigns the datapoints to Gaussians and recomputes μ and σ. The EM routing algorithms formulates the problem of routing as a clustering problem, assigning lower level capsules to higher level capsules. EM routing was proposed first together with Matrix-Capsules, which uses a matrix and a separate scalar for representing the activation instead of the length of the vector.

3.2   Applying Residual Learning to Capsule Networks

The starting point of residual learning is that a deep network should perform at least as good as a shallower one [5]. In order to make this possible, identity-shortcut connections are inserted, skipping one or more layers and simply adding their output to the output of a deeper layer. Those skip connections do not contain learnable parameters, and as such, layers can be replaced by the identity function. In deep neural networks performance decreasing layers occur with higher probability. It is known that residual connections bypass those layers such that the accuracy of the trained model is increased [18].

We include shortcut connections between capsule layers as explained next. The output of a capsule layer is element-wise added to the capsule layer that is located two layers deeper into the network. We add the shortcut connection after routing has happened, because this approach yielded the best results. We also did experiments on adding skip connections before routing or doing another

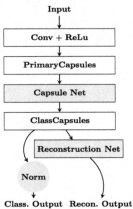

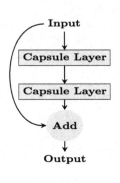

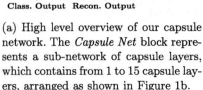

(a) High level overview of our capsule network. The *Capsule Net* block represents a sub-network of capsule layers, which contains from 1 to 15 capsule layers, arranged as shown in Figure 1b.

(b) Skip connections are element-wise added to the output of the two layer above capsule layer.

Fig. 1. Architecture of our capsule network (Fig. 1a) with detailed view of the capsule sub-network (Fig. 1b). Given dimensions apply to the datasets MNIST and Fashion-MNIST.

squashing after the element-wise addition but did not achieve good results. This design is shown in Fig. 1b and is in stark difference to *ResCaps*, presented by Ai et al. [2], where a residual sub-network is located in front of the capsule network. The authors replaced the single convolutional layer that we used before the *PrimaryCapsule* layer by a residual sub-network, to provide better features to the capsule network. The implementation of Rajasegaran [21] et al. uses only one routing iteration for all capsule layers except the last one i.e. all layers are implemented as classical 2d-convolutional layers except the last one, which is also confirmed by the original authors on GitHub[2]. Opposed to that, our network uses more than one routing iteration in every capsule layer. Additionally, we will show in the experimental evaluation, that the performance will not drop as the network depth is increased (also known as the degradation problem), regardless of the used routing algorithm.

4   Experimental Evaluation

In this section we describe the experimental setup. First, we will explain in detail the network architecture and setup. Next, we will we will describe the datasets used to evaluate our model. We will finish this section with the results of our experiments.

---

[2] https://github.com/brjathu/deepcaps/issues/15.

4.1 Setup

The general architecture is shown in Fig. 1a. The input is fed into a normal convolutional layer with a fixed kernel size of $(9, 9)$ and a stride of 1. We then apply another convolution with a $(9, 9)$ kernel and a stride of 2 inside the layer *PrimaryCapsules* and reshape into capsule form. Both convolutions use the ReLu activation function. The first *Capsule* layer has 512 incoming capsules and 32 outgoing capsules with a dimension of 8. Afterwards, we feed into a sub-network containing capsule layers, which contains 1 to 15 fully connected capsule layers, where each capsule is represented by a 12 element vector. The last capsule layer, the *ClassCapsule* layer, has one capsule of dimension 16 for each class contained in the dataset. Dynamic routing between capsule layers is either done by RBA, SDA or EM routing.

Residual connections were added between every second layer in the *Capsule Net* sub-network of Fig. 1a as shown in Fig. 1b. Skip connections do not contain any learnable parameters since the dimensionality of capsule layers do not vary across the inserted connections. Figure 1b shows that the tensors coming from the skip connections are element-wise added to the output of the two layer deeper capsule layer.

The reconstruction network contains three densely connected layers, where layer one and two uses *ReLu*, and the last layer implements a *sigmoid* activation. The reconstruction network is used to compute the *reconstruction loss* [23], used for training the capsule network. The sum of squared differences between the input pixels of the image and the output from the reconstruction network is used in the objective function. The overall loss function used for training is the sum of the *margin* loss [23] and the reconstruction loss, which is weighted by a scalar factor.

Weights of the transformation matrices were initialized randomly from a normal distribution with a standard deviation of 0.2 and a mean of 0. The weights of the bias terms were initialized with a constant value of 0.1. While training, the network receives random crops of 24×24, and on inference center crops are used. We trained with a batch size of 128, and used Adam optimizer with a constant learning rate of 1^{-4}. For networks deeper than 13 layers we used a batch size of 64, because of memory constraints of our GPU. We weighted the reconstruction loss with a factor of 1^{-5}, and trained each model for 30 epochs.

Our implementation[3] of the capsule network uses Tensorflow [1] Version 2.3.

4.2 Datasets and Data Augmentation

We evaluated our model on four different datasets: MNIST [13], Fashion-MNIST [28], Small-NORB [14], and SVHN [15].

MNIST is a dataset of 28×28 greyscale images of handwritten digits, containing 10 classes, representing the digits from 0–9. Fashion-MNIST is a little bit more involved than MNIST, but with a very similar structure. It also contains

---

[3] https://github.com/moejoe95/res-capsnet.

Table 1. Test accuracy for capsule networks using RBA with 3–11 capsule layers, trained with and without skip connections. Results are averaged over at least two runs.

Dataset	Method	3	4	5	6	7	8	9	10	11
MNIST	RBA	0.995	0.992	0.990	0.937	0.114	0.114	0.114	0.114	0.114
	RBA+Skip	0.995	**0.995**	**0.995**	**0.993**	**0.988**	**0.993**	**0.993**	**0.993**	**0.989**
Fashion	RBA	0.890	**0.888**	0.866	0.774	0.100	0.100	0.100	0.100	0.100
MNIST	RBA+Skip	**0.891**	0.887	**0.890**	**0.884**	**0.856**	**0.882**	**0.878**	**0.846**	**0.813**
SVHN	RBA	0.923	0.913	0.865	0.675	0.378	0.196	0.196	0.196	0.196
	RBA+Skip	0.923	**0.927**	**0.920**	**0.911**	**0.82**	**0.898**	**0.895**	**0.731**	**0.783**
Small	RBA	0.886	0.862	0.757	0.527	0.200	0.200	0.200	0.200	0.200
NORB	RBA+Skip	**0.891**	**0.889**	**0.892**	**0.856**	**0.838**	**0.851**	**0.857**	**0.697**	**0.524**

Table 2. Test accuracy for capsule networks using SDA routing with 3–16 capsule layers, trained with and without skip connections.

Dataset	Method	3	4	5	6	7	8	9	10	11	12	13	14	15	16
MNIST	SDA	0.994	0.994	0.994	0.993	0.993	0.992	0.992	0.990	0.989	0.985	0.978	0.491	0.673	0.392
	SDA+Skip	0.994	0.994	0.994	0.993	**0.994**	**0.994**	**0.994**	**0.993**	**0.993**	**0.993**	**0.992**	**0.992**	**0.991**	**0.991**
Fashion	SDA	0.890	0.890	0.887	0.886	0.885	0.881	0.883	0.877	0.871	0.866	0.841	0.798	0.625	0.192
MNIST	SDA+Skip	**0.891**	0.890	**0.891**	**0.890**	**0.890**	**0.887**	**0.885**	**0.884**	**0.886**	**0.884**	**0.886**	**0.883**	**0.884**	**0.882**
SVHN	SDA	**0.919**	0.915	0.911	0.902	0.897	0.892	0.898	0.892	0.873	0.766	0.825	0.671	0.634	0.341
	SDA+Skip	0.918	**0.924**	**0.920**	**0.915**	**0.911**	**0.909**	**0.909**	**0.906**	**0.904**	**0.898**	**0.902**	**0.898**	**0.896**	**0.892**
Small	SDA	0.887	0.881	0.876	0.877	**0.874**	0.863	0.877	0.864	0.860	0.862	0.855	0.840	0.721	0.323
NORB	SDA+Skip	**0.900**	**0.906**	**0.893**	**0.887**	0.885	**0.882**	**0.879**	**0.872**	**0.873**	**0.874**	**0.874**	**0.875**	**0.870**	**0.871**

greyscale images of size 28×28 and there are 10 distinct classes, each representing a type of clothing. Small-NORB is a dataset of greyscale 96×96 images showing objects from different elevations, azimuths and under different lighting conditions. It contains 5 classes of toys. SVHN is a dataset of 32×32 RGB images showing real world pictures of house numbers. As MNIST, it contains 10 classes representing the digits from 0–9.

We applied data augmentation by adding random brightness with intensities $[-0.25, 0.25)$ to the images in Small-NORB and SVHN. On Fashion-MNIST we augmented the data by horizontally flipping pixels of images with a probability of 50%. After data augmentation, we normalized per image to have zero mean and a variance of 1. We scaled down images of Small-NORB to the size 28×28.

4.3   Results

Tables 1 and 2 show the results of training capsule networks using the two similar routing algorithms RBA and SDA, comparing the cases where there were no skip connections with the ones in the presence of skip connections for MNIST, Fashion-MNIST, SVHN and Small-NORB. We can see that both routing algorithms benefit from skip connections. These results also show that SDA is more robust than RBA for routing deeper capsule networks with and without skip connections. In the case of no skip connections, RBA-routing shows a dramatic

Table 3. Test accuracy for capsule networks using EM routing with 3–16 capsule layers, trained with and without skip connections. Results are averaged over at least two runs.

Dataset	Method	3	4	5	6	7	8	9	10	11	12	13	14	15	16
MNIST	EM	0.995	**0.995**	0.995	0.994	0.993	0.992	0.992	0.991	0.990	0.990	0.989	0.988	0.823	0.767
	EM+Skip	0.995	0.994	0.994	0.994	**0.994**	**0.994**	**0.993**	**0.992**	**0.991**	**0.992**	**0.992**	**0.992**	**0.991**	**0.990**
Fashion MNIST	EM	0.890	0.889	**0.890**	0.882	0.881	0.875	0.875	0.876	0.869	0.871	0.866	0.862	0.855	0.856
	EM+Skip	**0.892**	0.889	0.888	**0.885**	**0.882**	**0.882**	**0.879**	**0.878**	**0.882**	**0.877**	**0.880**	**0.872**	**0.879**	**0.874**
SVHN	EM	0.932	0.921	0.906	0.898	0.888	0.887	0.881	0.880	0.878	0.869	**0.869**	0.856	**0.855**	0.789
	EM+Skip	0.932	**0.926**	**0.919**	**0.909**	**0.903**	**0.902**	**0.894**	**0.893**	**0.879**	0.885	0.598	**0.882**	0.418	**0.877**
Small NORB	EM	**0.899**	0.887	0.870	0.875	0.872	0.873	0.867	0.863	**0.869**	0.846	0.855	0.860	0.841	0.832
	EM+Skip	0.893	**0.893**	**0.885**	**0.880**	0.872	**0.882**	**0.872**	**0.873**	0.862	**0.863**	**0.871**	0.862	**0.867**	**0.852**

decrease in performance after 7 layers, while SDA holds up to depths of 13 layers. In some cases, RBA barely performs better than chance after just using 7 layers, such as in MNIST, Fashion-MNIST and Small-NORB. On the other hand, if we use skip connections, RBA performs well up to 11 layers of depth and SDA up to at least 16 layers. Table 3 provides the results for capsule networks using EM-routing for the four used datasets. This routing algorithm exhibits the highest robustness of the three used in this work. While there is also a benefit of using skip connections, the increase of performance when using EM routing is smaller as with RBA and SDA.

We can better analyze the training behavior at different depths in Fig. 2 with skip (blue line) and without skip connections (red line). The top row (2a–d) shows the trend for RBA, the second row (2e–f) for SDA, last row corresponds to EM-routing (2g–j). We show all three routing algorithms for MNIST (first column), Fashion-MNIST (second column), SVHN (fourth column) and Small-NORB (fourth column). From this figure we can extract that in the case of RBA, after 5 to 6 layers the performance of the network drops without using skip connections and above 7 or 8 layers, performance drops to around chance. On the other hand, with skip connections the performance keeps stable and the drop in performance happens much later.

In the case of SDA-routing, the benefits of using residual connections between capsule layers appears later, but after layer 13 − 14 the network with residual connections performs significantly better on every dataset. Finally, for EM-routing, we can observe positive impact of residual connections on MNIST Fashion-MNIST and Small-NORB. However, there were two cases on the SVHN dataset (with 13 and 15 layers) where surprisingly, the network with residual connections performed slightly worse.

The results of our extensive experimental evaluation shows that there is an improvement in the performance of deep capsule networks using residual connections, this improvement was quite significant for the case of RBA. For SDA-routing and EM-routing, our results show that both routing strategies also benefited from skip connections, although to a lesser degree than for RBA.

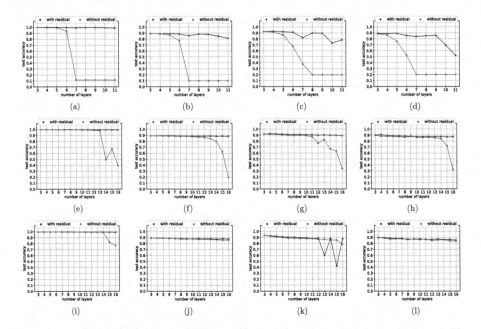

Fig. 2. Results for capsules networks at different depths, trained with (blue curve) and without (red curve) the use of skip connections. Plotted are the accuracies using RBA (first row), SDA-routing (second row) and EM-routing (third row) for MNIST (2a, 2e and 2i respectively), Fashion-MNIST (2b, 2f and 2j respectively), SVNH (2c, 2c and 2k respectively), and Small-NORB (2d, 2h and 2l respectively). (Color figure online)

5   Conclusions and Future Work

In related work residual connections are either used before the capsule layers in the classical convolutional part or only a single capsule layer is used [2,21]. In this paper we have shown that its indeed possible to use residual connections together with multiple capsule layers. More precisely, we showed experimentally that training deep capsule networks greatly benefit from residual connections in terms of performance and stability. We experimented with three different routing algorithms on four datasets, and were able to train deep capsule networks in all cases. Even so, the test accuracy for deeper networks is significant larger when using residuals in almost all configurations. Therefore, we believe that in future work an extension of this work to convolutional capsule layers would further improve the accuracy, reduce the computational complexity and also enable the training on more complex datasets. Additionally, through the use of auto-tuning for deep capsule networks [17], we could remove unused capsule layers from trained residual capsule networks and further improve the performance.

References

1. Abadi, M., et al.: TensorFlow: large-scale machine learning on heterogeneous systems (2015). https://www.tensorflow.org/, software available from tensorflow.org
2. Ai, X., Zhuang, J., Wang, Y., Wan, P., Fu, Y.: ResCaps: an improved capsule network and its application in ultrasonic image classification of thyroid papillary carcinoma. Complex Intell. Syst. **39**, 1–9 (2021)
3. Deng, J., Dong, W., Socher, R., Li, L.J., Li, K., Fei-Fei, L.: ImageNet: a large-scale hierarchical image database. In: 2009 IEEE Conference on Computer Vision and Pattern Recognition, pp. 248–255. IEEE (2009)
4. Glorot, X., Bengio, Y.: Understanding the difficulty of training deep feedforward neural networks. In: Proceedings of the Thirteenth International Conference on Artificial Intelligence and Statistics, pp. 249–256. JMLR Workshop and Conference Proceedings (2010)
5. He, K., Zhang, X., Ren, S., Sun, J.: Deep residual learning for image recognition. In: Proceedings of the IEEE Conference on Computer Vision and Pattern Recognition, pp. 770–778 (2016)
6. Hinton, Geoffrey E.., Krizhevsky, Alex, Wang, Sida D..: Transforming autoencoders. In: Honkela, Timo, Duch, W.łodzisław, Girolami, Mark, Kaski, Samuel (eds.) ICANN 2011. LNCS, vol. 6791, pp. 44–51. Springer, Heidelberg (2011). https://doi.org/10.1007/978-3-642-21735-7_6
7. Hinton, G.E., Sabour, S., Frosst, N.: Matrix capsules with EM routing. In: International Conference on Learning Representations (2018)
8. Hochreiter, S.: Untersuchungen zu dynamischen neuronalen netzen. Diploma, Technische Universität München, vol. 91, no. 1 (1991)
9. Ioffe, S., Szegedy, C.: Batch normalization: accelerating deep network training by reducing internal covariate shift. In: International Conference on Machine Learning, pp. 448–456. PMLR (2015)
10. Kosiorek, A.R., Sabour, S., Teh, Y.W., Hinton, G.E., Stafford-Tolley, M.J.: Stacked capsule autoencoders. In: Advances in Neural Information Processing Systems, vol. 32 (2019)
11. Krizhevsky, A.: Learning multiple layers of features from tiny images. Technical Report. Citeseer (2009)
12. Krizhevsky, A., Sutskever, I., Hinton, G.E.: ImageNet classification with deep convolutional neural networks. Adv. Neural Inf. Process. Syst. **25**, 1097–1105 (2012)
13. LeCun, Y., Cortes, C., Burges, C.J.: MNIST - handwritten digits (2010). http://yann.lecun.com/exdb/mnist/
14. LeCun, Y., Huang, F., Bottou, L.: Learning methods for generic object recognition with invariance to pose and lighting. In: IEEE Computer Society Conference on Computer Vision and Pattern Recognition (2004)
15. Netzer, Y., Wang, T., Coates, A., Bissacco, A., Wu, B., Ng, A.Y.: Learning methods for generic object recognition with invariance to pose and lighting. In: Reading Digits in Natural Images with Unsupervised Feature Learning NIPS Workshop on Deep Learning and Unsupervised Feature Learning (2012)
16. Peer, D., Stabinger, S., Rodríguez-Sánchez, A.: Increasing the adversarial robustness and explainability of capsule networks with gamma-capsules. arXiv preprint arXiv:1812.09707 (2018)
17. Peer, D., Stabinger, S., Rodríguez-Sánchez, A.: Auto-tuning of deep neural networks by conflicting layer removal (2021)

18. Peer, D., Stabinger, S., Rodríguez-Sánchez, A.: Conflicting bundles: adapting architectures towards the improved training of deep neural networks. In: Proceedings of the IEEE/CVF Winter Conference on Applications of Computer Vision, pp. 256–265 (2021)

19. Peer, D., Stabinger, S., Rodríguez-Sánchez, A.: Limitation of capsule networks. Pattern Recogn. Lett. **144**, 68–74 (2021)

20. Raghu, M., Poole, B., Kleinberg, J., Ganguli, S., Sohl-Dickstein, J.: On the expressive power of deep neural networks. In: international conference on machine learning. pp. 2847–2854. PMLR (2017)

21. Rajasegaran, J., Jayasundara, V., Jayasekara, S., Jayasekara, H., Seneviratne, S., Rodrigo, R.: DeepCaps: going deeper with capsule networks. In: Proceedings of the IEEE/CVF Conference on Computer Vision and Pattern Recognition, pp. 10725–10733 (2019)

22. Ribeiro, F.D.S., Leontidis, G., Kollias, S.: Capsule routing via variational Bayes. In: Proceedings of the AAAI Conference on Artificial Intelligence, vol. 34, pp. 3749–3756 (2020)

23. Sabour, S., Frosst, N., Hinton, G.E.: Dynamic routing between capsules. In: Proceedings of the 31st International Conference on Neural Information Processing Systems, pp. 3859–3869 (2017)

24. Simonyan, K., Zisserman, A.: Very deep convolutional networks for large-scale image recognition. arXiv preprint arXiv:1409.1556 (2014)

25. Tsai, Y.H.H., Srivastava, N., Goh, H., Salakhutdinov, R.: Capsules with inverted dot-product attention routing. In: International Conference on Learning Representations (2019)

26. Wistuba, M., Rawat, A., Pedapati, T.: A survey on neural architecture search. arXiv preprint arXiv:1905.01392 (2019)

27. Xi, E., Bing, S., Jin, Y.: Capsule network performance on complex data. arXiv preprint arXiv:1712.03480 (2017)

28. Xiao, H., Rasul, K., Vollgraf, R.: Fashion-Mnist: a novel image dataset for benchmarking machine learning algorithms (2017)

Cognitive Models

Interpretable Visual Understanding with Cognitive Attention Network

Xuejiao Tang[1], Wenbin Zhang[2(✉)], Yi Yu[3], Kea Turner[4],
Tyler Derr[5], Mengyu Wang[6], and Eirini Ntoutsi[7]

[1] Leibniz University of Hannover, Hanover, Germany
`xuejiao.tang@stud.uni-hannover.de`
[2] Carnegie Mellon University, Pittsburgh, USA
`wenbinzhang@cmu.edu`
[3] National Institute of Informatics, Tokyo, Japan
`yiyu@nii.ac.jp`
[4] Moffitt Cancer Center, Tampa, USA
`Kea.Turner@moffitt.org`
[5] Vanderbilt University, Nashville, USA
`tyler.derr@vanderbilt.edu`
[6] Harvard Medical School, Boston, USA
`mengyu_wang@meei.harvard.edu`
[7] Freie Universität Berlin, Berlin, Germany
`eirini.ntoutsi@fu-berlin.de`

Abstract. While image understanding on recognition-level has achieved remarkable advancements, reliable visual scene understanding requires comprehensive image understanding on recognition-level but also cognition-level, which calls for exploiting the multi-source information as well as learning different levels of understanding and extensive commonsense knowledge. In this paper, we propose a novel Cognitive Attention Network (CAN) for visual commonsense reasoning to achieve interpretable visual understanding. Specifically, we first introduce an image-text fusion module to fuse information from images and text collectively. Second, a novel inference module is designed to encode commonsense among image, query and response. Extensive experiments on large-scale Visual Commonsense Reasoning (VCR) benchmark dataset demonstrate the effectiveness of our approach. The implementation is publicly available at https://github.com/tanjatang/CAN.

1 Introduction

Visual understanding is an important research domain with a long history that attracts extensive models such as Mask RCNN [1], ResNet [2] and UNet [3]. They have been successfully employed in a variety of visual understanding tasks such as action recognition, image classification, pose estimation and visual search [4]. Most of them gain high-level understanding by identifying the objects in view based on visual input. However, reliable visual scene understanding requires not

© Springer Nature Switzerland AG 2021
I. Farkaš et al. (Eds.): ICANN 2021, LNCS 12891, pp. 555–568, 2021.
https://doi.org/10.1007/978-3-030-86362-3_45

only recognition-level but also cognition-level visual understanding, and seamless integration of them. More specifically, it is desirable to identify the objects of interest to infer their actions, intents and mental states with an aim of having a comprehensive and reliable understanding of the visual input. While this is a natural task for humans, existing visual understanding systems suffer from a lack of ability for higher-order cognition inference [5].

To improve the cognition-level visual understanding, recent research in visual understanding has shifted inference from recognition-level to cognition-level which contains more complex relationship inferences. This directly leads to four major directions on cognition-level visual understanding research: 1) image generation [6], which aims at generating images from given text description; 2) image caption [7], which focuses on generating text description from given images; 3) visual question answering, which aims at predicting correct answers for given images and questions; 4) visual commonsense reasoning (VCR) [5], which additionally provides rational explanations along with question answering and has gained considerable attention [8]. Research on VCR typically necessitates pretraining on large scale data prior to performing VCR tasks. They usually fit well towards the properties that the pre-training data possessed but their generalization on other tasks are not guaranteed [9]. To remove the necessity of pre-training, another line of research focuses on directly learning the architecture of a system to find straightforward solutions for VCR [10]. However, these methods suffer commonsense information loss where the last hidden layer is taken as output while jointly encoding visual and text information.

In this paper, we focus on the generic problem of visual scene understanding, where the characteristics of multi-source information and different levels of understanding pose great challenges to comprehensive and reliable visual understanding: 1) **Multi-source information.** Visual understanding entails information from different sources. It is difficult for the model to capture and fuse multi-source information and to infer the rationale based on the fusion of collective information and commonsense [11]. 2) **Various levels of understanding.** Cognition requires accumulation of an enormous reservoir of knowledge. Comprehensive cognition from limited datasets is even more challenging, and requires consideration of different levels of understanding [5]. 3) **Difficulty in learning commonsense.** The learning of commonsense from the dataset is a hard problem per se. Unlike humans who can learn an unlimited commonsense library from daily life effortlessly, learning extensive commonsense knowledge for a model is an open problem.

To address the above challenges, we propose a novel Cognitive Attention Network (CAN) for interpretable visual scene understanding. We first design a new multimodal fusion module to fuse image and text information based on guided attention. Then we introduce an co-attention network to encode the commonsense between text sequences and visual information, followed by an attention reduction module for redundant information filtering. The novelty of this research comes from four aspects:

– A new VCR model for comprehensive and reliable visual scene understanding.
– A new multimodal fusion method that jointly infers the multi-source information.
– A new co-attention network to encode commonsense.
– Extensive experiments comparing with state-of-the-art works and ablation studies.

The rest of the paper is organized as follows. Related studies are first discussed in Sect. 2. Section 3 presents the notations and problem formulation. We describe our method in Sect. 4, followed by the experimental results in Sect. 5. Finally, Sect. 6 concludes the paper.

2   Related Work

From individual object level scene understanding [1] which aims at object instance segmentation and image recognition, to visual relationship detection [12] which captures the relationship between any two objects in image or videos, state-of-the-art visual understanding models have achieved remarkable progress [13]. However, that is far from satisfactory for visual understanding as an ideal visual system necessitates the ability to understand the deep-level meaning behind a scene. Recent research on visual understanding has therefore shifted inference from recognition-level to cognition-level which contains more complex relationship inferences. Rowan et al. [5] further formulated Visual Commonsense Reasoning as the VCR task, which is an important step towards reliable visual understanding, and benchmarked the VCR dataset. Specifically, the VCR dataset is sampled from a large sample of movie clips in which most of the scenes refer to logic inferences. For example, "Why isn't Tom sitting next to David?", which requires high-order inference ability about the scene to select the correct answer from available choices. Motivated studies generally fall into one of the following two categories based on the necessity of pre-training dataset.

The first line of research, pre-training approaches, trains the model on a large-scale dataset then fine-tunes the model for downstream tasks. The recent works include ERNIE-ViL-large [8] and UNITER-large [9]. While the former learns semantic relationship understanding for scene graph prediction, the latter is pre-trained to learn joint image-text representations. However, the generalizability of these models relies heavily on the pre-training dataset and therefore is not guaranteed.

Another line of research is independent of large-scale pre-training dataset, and instead studies the architecture of a system to find a straightforward solution for VCR. R2C [5] is a representative example in this line of efforts in which attention based deep model is used for visual inferencing. More recently, a dynamic working memory based memory cells framework is proposed to provide prior knowledge for inference [14]. Our model more closely resembles this method with two distinctions: i) a parallel structure is explicitly designed to relax the dependence on the previous cells, alleviating the drawback of information lose of long dependency memory cell for long sequences, and ii) a newly proposed co-attention network rather than dynamic working memory cell to ease model training but also to enhance the capability of capturing relationship between sentences and semantic information from surrounding words.

3   Notations and Problem Formulation

Given the input query $\mathbf{q} := \{q_1, q_2, ..., q_m\}$ and the objects of the target image $\mathbf{o} := \{o_1, o_2, ..., o_n\}$, the general task of VCR is to sequentially predict one correct response from the responses represented as $\mathbf{r} := \{r_1, r_2, ..., r_i\}$. Figure 1 shows a typical VCR task, where $\mathbf{q}$ is to elicit information for Q ("How is [1] feeling about [0] on the phone?") or both Q and its correct answer A ("She is listening attentively.") depending on the specific sub-task discussed hereafter, $\mathbf{r}$ provides all possible answers or all reasons also depending on the specific sub-task, and $\mathbf{o}$ consists of objects of the image, i.e., person 0–2, tie 3, chair 4–6, clock 7 and vase 8. The three sub-tasks of VCR can then be represented as:

1) Q2A: is to predict the answer for the question. In this task, the inputs include: a) query $\mathbf{q}$: question Q only, b) responses $\mathbf{r}$: all possible answers, c) objects $\mathbf{o}$, and d) given image, i.e., Fig. 1. This sub-task needs to predict A based on the inputs.
2) QA2R: is to reason why the answer is correct. Compared to the previous Q2A task, the query $\mathbf{q}$, in addition to question Q, also includes the correct answer A and the responses $\mathbf{r}$ that are four given reasons. The aim of this sub-task is

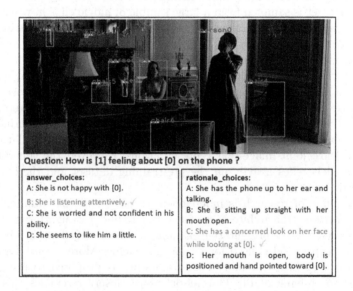

Fig. 1. A VCR example with the correct answer and rationale highlighted in green. (Color figure online)

then to predict the correct reason R ("She has a concerned look on her face while looking at [0]") for its input.

3) Q2AR: is to integrate the results from the previous two tasks as the final result. The correct and wrong results will be shown and recorded for final performance evaluation.

4   The Proposed Framework

The proposed Cognitive Attention Network (CAN) consists of four modules as shown in Fig. 2: a) *feature extraction module* generates feature representations from the given multi-source image and text input, b) *multimodal feature fusion module* integrates the extracted heterogeneous features; c) *co-attention network* encodes the fused features; and d) *attention reduction module* filters redundant information. The following subsections discuss the four modules in details.

4.1   Feature Extraction

Extracting informative features from multi-source information plays an important role in any machine learning application, especially in our context where the feature itself is one of the learning targets. As shown in Fig. 2, for the image feature extraction, the original image information source is the image along with its objects, which is given by means of related bounding boxes serving as a point of reference for objects within the images. The bounding boxes of given image and objects are then fed into the deep nets to obtain sufficient information from original image information source. Concretely, CAN extracts image features by a deep network backbone ResNet50 [15] and fine-tunes the final block of the network after RoiAlign. In addition, the skip connection [2] is adopted to circumvent the gradient vanishing problem when training the deep nets.

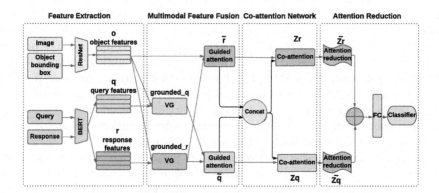

Fig. 2. The architecture of the proposed CAN consists of four modules to achieve interpretable visual understanding.

In term of the text feature extraction, the original text information source includes Query (Q or Q together with A) and Response (given answers or reasons). The text information is then extracted in a dynamic way in which the attention mechanism is employed to encode information from words around them in parallel [16], resulting text features including query features q and response features r.

4.2   Multimodal Feature Fusion

After features from heterogeneous information sources are extracted from the previous module, a multimodal feature fusion module is designed to fuse them, including: 1) a visual grounding unit to learn explicit information by aligning relevant objects with query and response; 2) a guided attention unit to learn implicit information that is omitted during visual grounding.

Visual Grounding (VG). To fuse the previously extracted heterogeneous features, i.e., related object features o along with text features q and r, a visual grounding module is designed to learn joint image-text representations explicitly.

To this end, VG firstly identifies related objects in query and response by using tags contained therein. Taking Fig. 1 as example, object features [person 0] and [person 1] are learned to match tags [0] and [1] in query q and responses r, while object features [person 2], [tie 3], [chair 4], [chair 5], [chair 6], [clock 7] and [vase 8] are omitted due to the lack of corresponding tags in q and r. Next, the aligned representations are fed into a one-layer bidirectional LSTM [17] to learn joint image-text representations. The learned image-query and image-response representations are denoted as $grounded\_q := \{grounded\_q_1, grounded\_q_2, \cdots, grounded\_q_j\}$ and $grounded\_r := \{grounded\_r_1, grounded\_r_2, \cdots, grounded\_r_j\}$, respectively.

Guided Attention (GA). After the VG stage, CAN learned an explicit joint image-text representations. However, the implicit information, which is important for commonsense inference including unidentified objects as well as reference relationship between grounded representations, is omitted. The guided attention module, shown as the two blocks within the purple dashed square in the bottom of Fig. 3, is therefore designed to learn these implicit information, allowing for the attention on the two types of implicit but important correlations. Note that the unit of this guided attention module is also the atomic structure of the following co-attention network (c.f., Sect. 4.3). Specially, right hand side unit captures the implicit information between image-response representations $grounded\_r$ and image objects features o. Back to the running example in Fig. 1, VG focuses on learning explicit information that is relevant to person 0 and person 1, and omits the explicit information associated with other objects, i.e., tie 3, chair 4–6, clock 7 and vase 8. This unit is designed to identify such implicit correlations between $grounded\_r$ and o. On the other hand, the left unit learns the implicit relationship between image-response representations $grounded\_r$ and image-query representations $grounded\_q$. For example in Fig. 1, both "[1]" in the question ("How is [1] feeling about [0] on the phone") and "She" in the answer ("She is listing attentively") refer to identical person 1, but such implicit information is not learnable at VG stage. This unit accounts for such implicit correlations among *grounded_r* and *grounded_q*. Note that attention can also be guided between *grounded_q* and *o*. However, *grounded_q* contains much lesser information than *grounded_r* as query normally entails lesser words and could be inferred from responses. Such an attention is therefore not considered to simplify the model with limited information loss. In the following, we will discuss the details of the proposed guided attention unit.

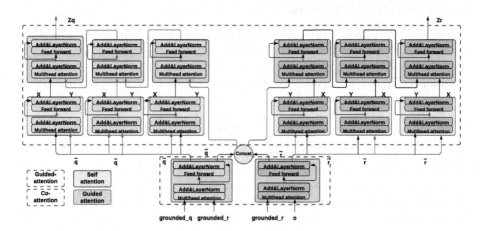

Fig. 3. Attention network of contextualizing feature representations. It consists of self-attention module and guided attention module to encode commonsense among image, query and response representations.

A guided attention unit is composed of a multi-head attention layer and a feed-forward layer. To speed up training, we additionally add LayerNorm for normalization behind both of these two layers. Recall that the aim of GA is to learn the omitted implicit information. To this end, GA first takes o and *grounded_q* or *grounded_r* as the input depending on the focused type of implicit information to guide the attention. Here, we employ the multi-head attention [18] to guide this process. More specifically, multi-head attention consists of h divided attention operations, referred as *heads*, through scaled dot-product attention. Formally put,

$$MultiHead(Q_1, K_1, V_1) = Concat(head_1, ..., head_h)W^O \qquad (1)$$

where Q_1 is *grounded_r*, both K_1 and V_1 are o or *grounded_q*, $W_i^{Q_1}, W_i^{K_1}, W_i^{V_1}, W^O$ are trainable linear transformation parameters, and h is the total number of heads which can be formulated as:

$$head_i = Attention(Q_1 W_i^{Q_1}, K_1 W_i^{K_1}, V_1 W_i^{V_1}) \qquad (2)$$

$$Attention(Q_1, K_1, V_1) = softmax(\frac{Q_1 K_1^T}{\sqrt{d_k}})V_1 \qquad (3)$$

where T is the transpose operation, d_k represents the dimension of input K_1, and i is the ith head of total h heads. In practise, $head_i$ outputs the attention weighted sum of the value vectors V_1 by softmax.

Next, the output of multi-head features are transformed by a feed-forward layer, which consists of two fully-connected layers with ReLU activation and dropout. Finally, GA outputs the fused multimodal representations $\widetilde{q}$ and $\widetilde{r}$ with weight information among o, $grounded\_q$ and $grounded\_r$.

4.3   Co-attention Network

Given the fused image-text representations $\widetilde{q}$ and $\widetilde{r}$, we further propose a co-attention network to encode commonsense between the fused image-text representations for visual commonsense reasoning. The input of the network, in addition to $\widetilde{q}$ and $\widetilde{r}$, therefore further considers their joint representation X defined as:

$$X = \widetilde{q}\|\widetilde{r} \tag{4}$$

where $\|$ is the concatenation operation.

The red dashed square of Fig. 3 shows the structure of the co-attention network, consisting of two co-attention modules for attending query and response commonsense, respectively. In specific, the former is used for encoding commonsense between X and $\widetilde{q}$, thus learning the attended commonsense for query jointly considers response. The latter then focuses on encoding commonsense between X and $\widetilde{r}$, capturing the attended commonsense for response taking query into consideration. These two co-attention modules share the same structure, comprised of two sub-units: i) the self attention units, which are the blocks with yellow background in Fig. 3, aiming at attending weighted information concerning each other within a sentence; ii) the blocks with green background depicted guided attention units to attend weighted information inter-sentence-wise as opposed to intra-sentence-wise attention of the self attention units.

Self Attention. The structure of self attention is similar to guided attention (c.f., Sect. 4.2). The difference comes from self attention takes identical inputs, i.e., query Q_1, key K_1 and value V_1 are identical, for the sake of capturing pairwise relationship in a sequence. In details, pairwise relationship between samples in a sequence is learned by the multi-head attention layer. For input sequence $X = [x_1, x_2, ..., x_m]$, the multi-head attention learns the relationship between $< x_i, x_j >$ and outputs attended representations. Subsequently, the attended representations are transformed by a feed-forward layer which contains two fully-connected layers with ReLU activation and dropout.

Pairwise Guided Attention. In comparison to self attention, pairwise guided attention focuses on inter-sentence-wise attention and can be regarded as guided attention learning weighted information among different sentences. When taking two different sentences representations $X = [x_1, x_2, ..., x_m]$ and $Y = [y_1, y_2, ..., y_m]$ as the inputs, X is the query Q_1 while key K_1 and Value V_1

are Y, guiding the attention learning for X. Specifically, the multi-head layer in a guided attention unit attends the pairwise relationship between the two paired input sequences $< x_i, y_j >$ and outputs the attended representations. A feed-forward layer is then applied to transform the attended representations. The co-attention network finally outputs Z_q and Z_r, which are attention information over both images and texts.

4.4   Attention Reduction

After the previous multilayer data encoding, CAN now contains rich multi-source attention information. Among them, not all of them are necessarily to be innegligible. An attention reduction module is therefore further designed to select information with the most important attention weights. In details, the output of attention network $\underset{l \in \{q,r\}}{Z_l}$ are fed into a multilayer perceptron (MLP) to learn attention weights, outputting $\underset{l \in \{q,r\}}{\widetilde{Z}_l}$:

$$\widetilde{Z}_l = \sum_{i=1}^{m} \alpha_l^i z_l^i, \; \alpha = softmax(MLP(Z_l)) \tag{5}$$

where α is the learned attention weights and i is the position in a sequence.

For better gradient flow through the network, CAN also fuses the features by using LayerNorm on the sum of the final attended representations,

$$c = LayerNorm(W_{x1}^T \widetilde{Z}_q + W_{x2}^T \widetilde{Z}_r) \tag{6}$$

where W_{x1}^T and W_{x2}^T are two trainable linear projection matrices.

The fused feature c is then projected by another FC layer for classification, which is used to find the correct answer and reason from given candidates, e.g., "B. She is listening attentively" and "C. She has a concerned look on her face while looking at [0]" among all other candidate answers and reasons in Fig. 1.

5   Experimental Results

This section evaluates the performance of our model in comparison to state-of-the-art visual understanding models. The experiments were conducted on a 64-bit machine with a 10-core processor (i9, 3.3 GHz), 64 GB memory with GTX 1080Ti GPU.

5.1   Dataset

The VCR dataset [5] consists of 290k multiple-choice questions, 290k correct answers, 290k correct rationales and 110k images. The correct answers and rationales are labeled in the dataset with >90% of human agreements. As shown previously in Fig. 1, each set consists of an image, a question, four available answer choices, and four reasoning choices. The correct answer and rationale are provided in the dataset as ground truth.

5.2   Understanding Visual Scenes

We compare our method with several state-of-the-art visual scene understanding models based on the mean average precision metric for the three Q2A, QA2R and Q2AR tasks, respectively, including: 1) MUTAN [19] proposes a multimodal based visual question answering approach, which parametrizes bi-linear interactions between visual and textual representations using Tucker decomposition; 2) BERT-base [18] is a powerful pre-training based model in natural language field and is adapted for the commonsense reasoning; 3) R2C [5] encodes commonsense between sentences with LSTM; 4) DMVCR [14] trains a dynamic working memory to store the commonsense in training as well as using commonsense as prior knowledge for inference. Among them, BERT-base adopts pre-training method, while MUTAN, R2C and DMVCR are non pre-training methods. The obtained results are summarized in Table 1.

Table 1. Comparison of results between CAN and other methods on VCR dataset with the best performance marked in bold.

Models	Q2A	QA2R	Q2AR
MUTAN [20]	44.4	32.0	14.6
BERT-base [18]	53.9	64.5	35
R2C [5]	61.9	62.8	39.1
DMVCR [14]	62.4	67.5	42.3
CAN	**71.1**	**73.8**	**47.7**

In these results, it is clear that CAN consistently outperforms other methods across all tasks and is the only method capable of handling all tasks properly. Specially, CAN outperforms MUTAN by a significant margin. This is expected as CAN incorporates a reasoning module in its encoder network to enhance commonsense understanding while MUTAN only focuses on visual question answering without reasoning. In addition, to alleviate the lost information when encoding long dependence structure for long sentences of other methods, CAN further encodes commonsense among sentences with attention weights in parallel for a better information maintenance, which also leads to its superior performance over the others.

5.3   Ablation Studies

We also perform ablation studies to evaluate the performance of the proposed guided attention for multimodal fusion and co-attention network encoding. As one can see in Table 2, when taking out guided attention unit, the prediction result decreases 4.2% in Q2A task and 5.7% lower in QA2R task. It indicates guided attention can help the model learn implicit information from images, query and response representations, by attending the object in the images and the corresponding noun in the sentence. In addition, if we replace co-attention encoder network with LSTM encoder, the prediction result decreases 2.5% in Q2A task and 4.6% in QA2R task. Compared to LSTM keeping the memory among sentences, our proposed co-attention encoder network can attend the commonsense among various sentences and words with multi-head attention mechanism, thus capturing rich information from more aspects.

Table 2. Comparison of ablation studies.

Models	Q2A	QA2R
LSTM encoder	68.6	69.2
Without GA	66.9	68.1
CAN	**71.1**	**73.8**

5.4   Qualitative Results

We evaluate the proposed framework with qualitative examples, which are shown in Fig. 5.4. The candidate with green color represents the correct choice along with the check mark by ✓ labeling the prediction by the proposed model. As the qualitative results show, our method works well for most of the visual scenes. For instance, in Fig. 4(a), the query is "Why isn't [person 0] sitting next to [person 1]?", our model predicts the correct answer: "B. They were both looking for something", and the correct rationale "C. Him picking up and then staring at the envelope means it was something he was looking for". By co-attending the commonsense for [person 0] and [person 1] among the textual information in query, response and image representation, our model can select the correct answer and rationale for both Q2A and QA2R tasks.

Moreover, we can gain more insight into how the model understands the scene by co-attending the visual information and text information to predict the correct answer and rationale. For example in Fig. 4(b), the question is "How is [person 0] feeling?", our model predicts the correct answer "B. [person 0] is upset and disgusted", and the correct rationale, "D. Her mouth is open, body is positioned and hand pointed toward [person 0]". This result shows that our model performs well by fusing multimodal features and co-attending the visual and textual information.

Figure 4(c) shows two more challenging scenarios. CAN successfully predicted the correct answer and rationale for Question 1 but provided the incorrect answer with right rationale. Recall that question answering task (Q2A) and answer justification task (QA2R) are two separate tasks, and QA2R task performs on the condition that the correct answer is given. Therefore, the result of QA2R is independent of Q2A, and CAN can still predict the correct rationale in this challenging setting.

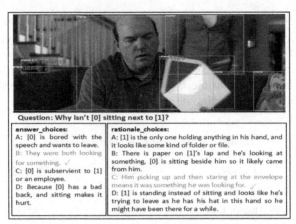

Question: Why isn't [0] sitting next to [1]?

answer_choices:	rationale_choices:
A: [0] is bored with the speech and wants to leave.	A: [1] is the only one holding anything in his hand, and it looks like some kind of folder or file.
B: They were both looking for something. ✓	B: There is paper on [1]'s lap and he's looking at something, [0] is sitting beside him so it likely came from him.
C: [0] is subservient to [1] or an employee.	C: Him picking up and then staring at the envelope means it was something he was looking for. ✓
D: Because [0] has a bad back, and sitting makes it hurt.	D: [1] is standing instead of sitting and looks like he's trying to leave as he has his hat in this hand so he might have been there for a while.

(a) Qualitative example 1. CAN predicts correct answer and rationale.

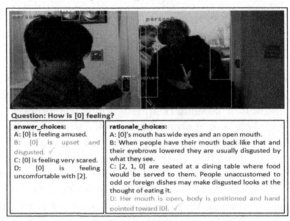

Question: How is [0] feeling?

answer_choices:	rationale_choices:
A: [0] is feeling amused.	A: [0]'s mouth has wide eyes and an open mouth.
B: [0] is upset and disgusted. ✓	B: When people have their mouth back like that and their eyebrows lowered they are usually disgusted by what they see.
C: [0] is feeling very scared.	C: [2, 1, 0] are seated at a dining table where food would be served to them. People unaccustomed to odd or foreign dishes may make disgusted looks at the thought of eating it.
D: [0] is feeling uncomfortable with [2].	D: Her mouth is open, body is positioned and hand pointed toward [0]. ✓

(b) Qualitative example 2. CAN predicts correct answer and rationale.

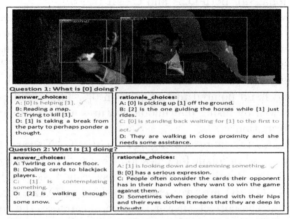

Question 1: What is [0] doing?

answer_choices:	rationale_choices:
A: [0] is helping [1]. ✓	A: [0] is picking up [1] off the ground.
B: Reading a map.	B: [2] is the one guiding the horses while [1] just rides.
C: Trying to kill [1].	C: [0] is standing back waiting for [1] to the first to act. ✓
D: [1] is taking a break from the party to perhaps ponder a thought.	D: They are walking in close proximity and she needs some assistance.

Question 2: What is [1] doing?

answer_choices:	rationale_choices:
A: Twirling on a dance floor.	A: [1] is looking down and examining something. ✓
B: Dealing cards to blackjack players.	B: [0] has a serious expression.
C: [1] is contemplating something.	C: People often consider the cards their opponent has in their hand when they want to win the game against them.
D: [2] is walking through some snow. ✓	D: Sometimes when people stand with their hips and their eyes clothes it means that they are deep in thought.

(c) Qualitative example 3. CAN predicts incorrect answer but correct rational in Question 2.

Fig. 4. Qualitative examples. Prediction from CAN is marked by ✓ while correct results are highlighted in green. (Color figure online)

6 Conclusion

In this paper we propose a novel cognitive attention network for visual commonsense reasoning to achieve interpretable visual understanding. This work advances prior research by developing an image-text fusion module to fuse information between images and text as well as the design of a novel inference module to encode commonsense among image, query and response comprehensively. Extensive experiments on VCR benchmark dataset show the proposed method outperforms state-of-the-art by a wide margin. One promising future direction is to explore visual reasoning with fairness constraints [21].

References

1. Vuola, A., Akram, S., Kannala, J.: Mask-RCNN and U-Net ensembled for nuclei segmentation. In: 16th International Symposium on Biomedical Imaging (ISBI), pp. 208–212 (2019)
2. He, K., Zhang, X., Ren, S., Sun, J.: Deep residual learning for image recognition. In: Proceedings of the IEEE Conference on CVPR, pp. 770–778 (2016)
3. Barkau, R.L.: UNet: one-dimensional unsteady flow through a full network of open channels. user's manual. Technical reports, Hydrologic Engineering Center Davis CA (1996)
4. Papandreou, G., et al.: Towards accurate multi-person pose estimation in the wild. In: CVPR, pp. 4903–4911 (2017)
5. Zellers, R., Bisk, Y., et al.: From recognition to cognition: visual commonsense reasoning. In: CVPR, pp. 6720–6731 (2019)
6. Gregor, K., Danihelka, I., et al.: DRAW: a recurrent neural network for image generation. In: International Conference on Machine Learning, pp. 1462–1471 (2015)
7. Vinyals, O., Toshev, A., Bengio, S., Erhan, D.: Show and tell: a neural image caption generator. In: CVPR, pp. 3156–3164 (2015)
8. Yu, F., Tang, J., Yin, W., et al.: ERNIE-ViL: knowledge enhanced vision-language representations through scene graph. arXiv preprint arXiv:2006.16934 (2020)
9. Chen, Y.-C., et al.: UNITER: learning universal image-text representations (2019)
10. Lin, J., Jain, U., et al.: TAB-VCR: tags and attributes based VCR baselines (2019)
11. Natarajan, P., Wu, S., et al.: Multimodal feature fusion for robust event detection in web videos. In: CVPR, pp. 1298–1305 (2012)
12. Yang, X., Tang, K., et al.: Auto-encoding scene graphs for image captioning. In: CVPR, pp. 10 685–10 694 (2019)
13. Carreira, J., Zisserman, A.: Quo Vadis, action recognition? A new model and the kinetics dataset. CoRR, vol. abs/1705.07750 (2017)
14. Tang, X., et al.: Cognitive visual commonsense reasoning using dynamic working memory. In: International Conference on Big Data Analytics and Knowledge Discovery. Springer (2021)
15. You, Y., Zhang, Z., et al.: ImageNet training in minutes. In: Proceedings of the 47th International Conference on Parallel Processing, pp. 1–10 (2018)
16. Devlin, J., Chang, M.-W., et al.: BERT: pre-training of deep bidirectional transformers for language understanding. arXiv preprint arXiv:1810.04805 (2018)
17. Huang, Z., Xu, W., et al.: Bidirectional LSTM-CRF models for sequence tagging. arXiv preprint arXiv:1508.01991 (2015)

18. Vaswani, A., et al.: Attention is all you need. arXiv preprint arXiv:1706.03762 (2017)
19. Ben-younes, H., Cadéne, R., Cord, M., Thome, N.: MUTAN: multimodal tucker fusion for visual question answering. CoRR (2017)
20. Ben-Younes, H., Cadene, R., Cord, M., Thome, N.: MUTAN: multimodal tucker fusion for visual question answering. In: ICCV, pp. 2612–2620 (2017)
21. Zhang, W., Ntoutsi, E.: FAHT: an adaptive fairness-aware decision tree classifier. In: International Joint Conference on Artificial Intelligence (IJCAI), pp. 1480–1486 (2019)

A Bio-Inspired Mechanism Based on Neural Threshold Regulation to Compensate Variability in Network Connectivity

Jessica López-Hazas[✉] and Francisco B. Rodriguez[✉]

Grupo de Neurocomputación Biológica, Dpto. de Ingeniería Informática Escuela Politécnica Superior, Universidad Autónoma de Madrid, 28049 Madrid, Spain
jessica.lopez-hazas@estudiante.uam.es, f.rodriguez@uam.es

Abstract. In the olfactory system of insects, the synapses between two populations of neurons, the projection neurons (PN) in the antennal lobe and the Kenyon Cells (KC) in the mushroom body, do not show reproducibility between individuals or associative learning. Despite this, the system is still capable of learning and discriminating odorants. This suggests that it must have some mechanism to compensate the effects of the variability in the structure of PN-KC connections. The nature of this mechanism remains unknown. This work explores the hypothesis that the regulation of KCs sensitivity through their neural thresholds makes possible not only the generation of sparse coding, but a more stable representation of patterns that makes the whole system robust to the variations in the connections to PNs. By comparing the behavior of a model of the insect olfactory system that includes the learning of the KCs neural thresholds to other model that does not include this mechanism, it is found that the model with this mechanism has a more stable accuracy and a more robust inner representations of patterns. These results are coherent with the hypothesis proposed and hints that regulation of the sensibility of KCs through their neural thresholds could potentially help the system to adapt and select the most meaningful PN-KC connections in a context of the random variability in them that is found in nature.

Keywords: Neural computation · Pattern recognition · Bio-inspired neural networks · Random connectivity · Olfactory system · Antennal lobe · Projection neurons · Kenyon cells sensitivity

1 Introduction

The olfactory system of insects has been extensively studied and it is an example of how biological neural networks can use very simple but powerful strategies to discriminate hundreds of patterns. Some of these strategies include the use of random connection topologies [3,5,12], fan-out phases [5,23], regulation of neural threshold [19,24] and neural activity control to generate sparse code [5,14,21,25].

© Springer Nature Switzerland AG 2021
I. Farkaš et al. (Eds.): ICANN 2021, LNCS 12891, pp. 569–580, 2021.
https://doi.org/10.1007/978-3-030-86362-3_46

However, there are still unresolved questions about this system, and this work focuses on some aspects of the random connectivity found in some parts of the system. But first, let us briefly consider the functioning of the olfactory system of insects.

The olfactory system of insects is organized in different layers, each one with a certain function. The olfactory receptor neurons (ORNs), placed on the insect antennae, capture the information about the chemical compounds in the air [17]. This information is sent to the antennal lobe (AL). The AL includes the olfactory glomeruli, projection neurons (PN) and local inter-neurons (LN). The glomeruli send their output to both the LNs and PNs. A simple diagram of this system can be observed in Fig. 1 panel (a) and (b).

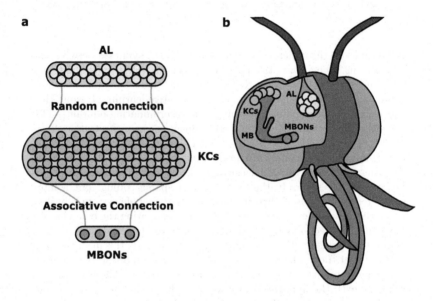

Fig. 1. (a) Structure of the biological olfactory system of insects. The ORNs capture the information about chemical compounds and send it to the PNs in the AL. PNs send this information to the MB through their random connections with KCs. KCs use sparse coding to represent the information. The MBONs are responsible for the final identification of stimuli. (b) Outline of the computational model based on neural networks used to imitate the behavior of the system and explore the relationship between the random connectivity between PNs and KCs and the sensitivity of KCs. The model is a single hidden layer neural network with supervised learning.

A population of Kenyon Cells (KCs) in the mushroom body (MB) receives the information from the antennal lobe through their connections to the PNs, as indicated in 1 Panel (b). One of the key characteristics of KCs is that they show little activity, since each of them only responds to very specific odorants and remains silent the rest of the time. Thus, it is believed that they use sparse coding to represent stimuli [2,23,27]. Apart from that, KCs are much more numerous than PNs (for example, in the locust, the proportion between them is 1 : 50 [23]), which also contributes to the emergence of sparse coding [9,27]. Finally, the association between the representations made by the KCs and the identity of each chemical compound is made by associative learning in the synapses between the KCs and the mushroom body output neurons (MBONs). From there, the information travels to more advanced processing centers.

This work focuses on the connections between PNs and KCs. The pattern of connectivity between these neurons seems not to show reproducibility across individuals and there is no learning process in their synapses either, which remain unaltered [5,11,12]. In [12], it was showed that a stochastic matrix of connections is sufficient to represent the PN-KC connectivity and still have a functional system able to learn. There have been various previous attempts to find the value of some of the parameters in this layer of connections, like the probability of connection between a PN and a KC (p_c). Through computational models and the examination of neuro-physiological records, p_c was given values that range from 0.01 to 0.5, with no consensus [3,5,8,13,15,22,26]. Other studies have tried to determine the topology of the connections, if there is any, and their observations suggest that there are subgroups of KCs depending on the number of PNs they are connected to, being some groups more important to the discrimination task than others [4,8]. Beyond this discussion around PN-KC connections, the truth is that the olfactory system of insects is perfectly capable of learning and discriminate odorants despite the inter-individual variability and randomness in the connections between these two neuronal populations. Finding the best value of p_c may be useful in a computational model, but it is hard to believe that biological systems use fixed values. Hence, the question remains of how the neural networks in the olfactory system of insects compensate for this variability.

This work proposes the hypothesis that KCs are responsible for this robustness towards the variability of their connections to the PNs. Their low activity and different degrees of sensibility towards stimuli [19,20,24], mediated by their firing thresholds, make possible not only the generation of sparse coding, but a more stable representation of patterns that makes the whole system resilient to the variations in the connections from PNs. To test this hypothesis, two models of the insect olfactory system are used. One of them includes the mechanism for regulating the activity of KCs by learning their firing thresholds and the other does not include this mechanism. This allows to examine the behavior of both systems towards variations in the probability of PN-KC connection (p_c) and random changes in the structure of said connections when the system needs to resolve a classification task.

2   Materials and Methods

This section explains the details about the models used to compare the effect of including the regulation mechanism of KC thresholds in the behavior of the system when there is variability in the PC-KC connections. The metrics used to examine said behavior are described as well: accuracy and cosine similarity between the internal representations of the patterns.

2.1   Models of the Insect Olfactory System

The two proposed models are based on a single hidden layer neural network and supervised learning. In them, the input layer (X) corresponds to the PNs, the hidden layer (Y) to the KCs and the output (Z) to the MBONs. A schema of this model is shown in Fig. 1 panel (a). The neural network is trained to resolve a classification problem.

To represent the PN-KC connectivity, both models use the approach of most models of the olfactory system, where every possible connection between a PN and a KC exists with probability p_c [5,11,12,18,19]. The result is a randomly generated matrix of binary values (C). In it, the value 1 indicates the existence of a connection and 0 its absence. This matrix remains unchanged through the learning process. To imitate the variability in these connections observed in nature, the value of p_c can be changed or its structure can be altered by randomly generating it from a different random seed.

Regarding the connections between KCs and MBONs, given that in the biological system there is associative learning in this layer, in the model their weights (W) are adjusted using the gradient descent algorithm [16]. When a pattern is presented to the network, it is assigned the class indicated by the MBON that activates the most, with as many MBONs as there are classes.

The characteristics explained in the previous paragraphs are common to both models. However, one of them includes a mechanism to imitate the behavior of KCs in the biological system, regulating the level of activity of the population of these neurons through the adjustment of their firing thresholds. This mechanism is explained below.

KCs Gain Control: The adjustment of neural thresholds is a very important point in the computational properties of the olfactory system of insects. For example, in [19,20,24], it is demonstrated that a heterogeneous distribution of firing thresholds to generate sparse activity results in a better performance of the neural network. This threshold adjustment mechanism is also used in other contexts, such as recurrent neural networks, to produce sparse activity adapted to the recovery patterns of the network, thus increasing its load capacity [6,7].

In order to introduce this mechanism of threshold adjustment to control the activity of the KCs in the model proposed in this work, a new set of adjustable parameters called θ that represent the firing thresholds of the KCs are added to the model. With the introduction of this new parameters, the activation function of the KCs would be:

$$y_j = \sigma \left(\sum_{i=1}^{N_{PN}} x_i c_{ij} - \theta_j \right) , \tag{1}$$

where x_i is the activation value for the ith PN, c_{ij} takes the values 0 or 1 depending on whether the connection between the PN (x_i) and the KC (y_j) exists according to the p_c selected and θ_j is the firing threshold of the KC (y_j).

The thresholds θ are adjusted using the gradient descent algorithm, adding a new term to the cost function that allows to regulate the activation of KCs neurons until reaching the desired level. This term is called Mushroom Body Gain Control (GC_{MB}) and it is expressed as:

$$GC_{MB}(\mathbf{y}) = \frac{1}{2} \left(\frac{1}{N_{KC}} \sum_{j=1}^{N_{KC}} y_j - s \right)^2 , \tag{2}$$

where N_{KC} is the number of KCs in the hidden layer, $\mathbf{y} = (y_1, ..., y_{N_{hidden}})$ is the vector with the activation of each KC and $s \in [0.0, 1.0]$ is the parameter that allows to control the level of activity in the hidden layer from no activity when $s = 0.0$ up to the maximum activity when $s = 1.0$. For example, for $s = 0.1$ there is an activity in the KC population of 10%, which would be approximately the value observed in the biological system.

Therefore, when comparing the two models against variations in PN-KC connectivity, one of them will include the previous mechanism for adjusting the KC thresholds, while the other will not include said mechanism.

2.2 Separability Measure in KCs

In order to compare the discrimination capacity between the two models, the quality (in terms of degree of discrimination) of the internal representations of the input patterns made by KCs is measured. For each pattern, it is computed how much its representation differs from that of the rest of the patterns belonging to its class (intra-class) and to each of the other classes (inter-class). The metric use for this is cosine similarity [10]. Cosine similarity is a measure that works well with long and sparse vectors, like the internal representations of KCs. Given that the vectors that are going to be compared only contain positive values (the activation of KCs), the range of cosine similarity is between 0.0 and 1.0. The value 0.0 indicates that two representations are completely different and the value 1.0, that they are completely similar. The representations of a class will be better the greater the intra-class distance, since it is desirable that the patterns belonging to the same class are similar to each other, and a small inter-class distance, since it means that the representations of patterns belonging to different classes are less alike.

2.3 Input Patterns

The classification problems used to evaluate the model are two well known ones: MNIST [1], where handwritten numbers must be recognized, and fashion-MNIST [29], similar to MNIST but using images of different types of clothing. In addition, other dataset generated artificially using Gaussian patterns is used. The

Gaussian patterns have 250 points that represent the number of PNs that the olfactory system of insects has approximately. Patterns belonging to different classes are centered in different points. These Gaussian patterns are difficult to distinguish from each other due to the amplitude of their variance and the noise that is added to them, since the Gaussian patterns are more similar the ones the olfactory system would find in nature [19, 28]. Some examples of the patterns in each dataset are displayed in Fig. 2.

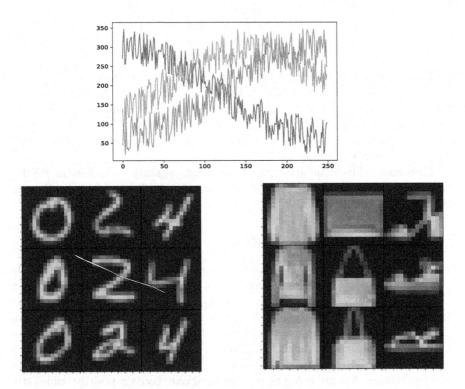

Fig. 2. Examples of some of the input patterns of the three datasets used to study the model. For each one, patterns belonging to the same and different classes are shown to give an idea of the intra and inter-class variability in each of them. The top figure corresponds to three examples of different classes of the Gaussian patterns generated artificially, each centered on a different point. For these patterns, the inter-class separability is controlled through the variance of the Gaussian distribution and, the intra-class separability, by the random noise added to each pattern. The bottom left figure displays three examples belonging to three different classes of the handwritten digits from MNIST. The bottom right shows other three examples belonging to three different classes from the clothing images in fashion-MNIST.

3   Results

This section includes all the results from the comparison between the model with the mechanism to control the activity of KCs and the simple model that does not include said mechanism.

3.1   Accuracy of the Models for Different p_c

To carry out the simulations of the models, all the values of p_c in the interval $[0.1, 0.9]$ with a step of 0.1 are used. For each of the p_c values, 10 instantiations of the system with certain random seeds are made, and 5-fold cross-validation is applied for each simulation. In the case of the model that includes the control of the activity of KCs, the s parameter is set in such a way that the average activity in the layer is 10%, according to the observations on the biological system [23]. Apart from all this, the system is also tested using different ratios between the number of PNs and KCs, to see if this has any influence on the performance. These ratios are $[1 : 0.25, 1 : 0.5, 1 : 1, 1 : 2, 1 : 5, 1 : 10, 1 : 25]$.

The mean accuracy of the model is computed for each one of the combinations of p_c and PN-KC ratio for the 10 random seeds. Results are shown in Fig. 3. In this figure, panel (a) represents the accuracy of the model without the activity control of KCs and panel (b) the accuracy of the model that includes this mechanism, in both cases for different PN-KC ratios. The results for the Gaussian patterns are the ones in the first row, MNIST in the second row and fashion-MNIST in the last row.

The first observation that can be made about these results is that the ratio of PN-KC neurons has a noticeable influence on the accuracy of the model and, in general, the higher the number of KCs per PN, the better the accuracy. This is consistent with what was previously known about the functioning of the olfactory system and the existence of a fan-out phase between PN and KCs that facilitates the generation of sparse coding and discrimination [5].

Secondly, it can be observed that the model without adjustment of thresholds to control the KCs (Fig. 3 panel a), is much more sensitive to changes in the value of p_c than the model that incorporates this mechanism (Fig. 3 panel b), for which the accuracy remains almost stable and without variations regardless of the value that p_c takes. This is an indication that, in the model with thresholds, they could be compensating for the variability caused by the different p_c and increasing the stability of the system.

Finally, regarding the changes in the structure of the connections, it can be observed that in the model without threshold adjustment there is a greater standard deviation in the value of each point for the different instantiations of p_c that were simulated. On the contrary, in the model with the threshold adjustment, the standard deviation of each point is much smaller in comparison, indicating that the system is also more robust when it has to face this type of variability.

These results are coherent with the hypothesis proposed and show how the regulation of the sensibility of KCs through their neural thresholds could

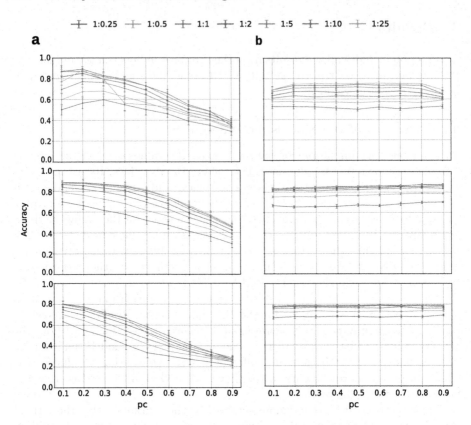

Fig. 3. Comparison of the accuracy of the models without (first column) or with (second column) the adjustment of the thresholds of the KCs for p_c between 0.1 and 0.9, for different ratios between the number of PNs and KCs ($[1 : 0.25, 1 : 0.5, 1 : 1, 1 : 2, 1 : 5, 1 : 10, 1 : 25]$). Every point in the graph corresponds to the mean accuracy for 10 simulations of the model with certain random seeds. The first row of the graph corresponds to the Gaussian patterns, the second to the MNIST and the third to fashion-MNIST. In the case of the model that includes the regulation of KCs thresholds, its accuracy remains stable despite the changes in p_c. Moreover, the standard deviation of the accuracy for the 10 simulations is also lower for this model. This could be caused by the adjustment of the neural thresholds, which could be compensating for these variations and making the system resilient to them.

potentially help the system to adapt and select the most meaningful PN-KC connections in a context of great random variability in them.

3.2   Separability of KCs Inner Representations

In this section, the cosine similarity was measured between patterns belonging to the same class (intra-class distance) and to different classes (inter-class distance), as described in Sect. 2.2. The results are presented in Fig. 4, and were obtained for one of the simulations of the model that includes the mechanism to regulate the activation of KCs (lighter colors) and for the model that does not include it (stronger colors), in order to compare how it influences the intra and inter-class distances. This process is repeated for three different values of p_c, 0.1, 0.5 and 0.9 and a PN-KC ratio of 1 : 25. In Fig. 4, the first column of results corresponds to the Gaussian patterns, the second one to MNIST and the third one to the fashion-MNIST dataset.

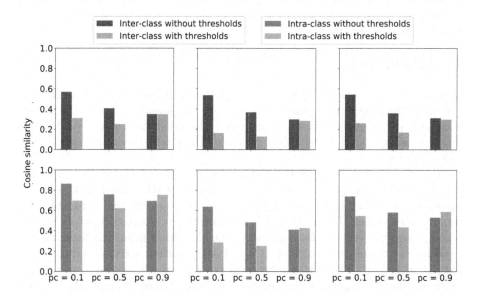

Fig. 4. Comparison between the inter-class cosine similarity (upper row) and intra-class (lower row) achieved by the model with adjustment of the thresholds of KCs and the model without this adjustment. The first column corresponds to the Gaussian patterns, the second to the MNIST and the third to the fashion-MNIST. The results are also obtained for three possible values of p_c, 0.1, 0.5 and 0.9.

In the case of intra-class distance, in the lower row of the figure, it can be observed that the model without the learning of neural thresholds of KCs generally gets a greater intra-class distance than the model with learning of thresholds. However, for the model without thresholds, this intra-class distance becomes smaller the greater the value of p_c, to the point that it is surpassed by the model with thresholds for $p_c = 0.9$. This behavior could explain the degradation of the accuracy of the model without thresholds for greater values of p_c in Fig. 3. On the other hand, for the model with thresholds, it seems that the different sensitivity in KCs absorbs the reduction in the intra-class distance observed in the model without thresholds, since it remains more stable for different p_c or even gets better in the case of $p_c = 0.9$.

For the inter-class distance, in the upper row of the figure, the model with the adjustment of thresholds have a better inter-class distance for all the datasets and cases except for $p_c = 0.9$, where it is equal to the model without them. In this last case, the reason why the model with thresholds achieves a better classification error could have to do with the fact that the intra-class distance is bigger than for the model without them.

So, these results show that the control of the activity of KCs can increase the quality of the internal representation of information in the system. In the case of patterns from different classes, it increases the distance between their representations regardless of p_c, while regarding the representations of the patterns of the same class, it makes the similarity of their representations stable across different p_c.

4   Conclusions

In this work, the connectivity between the PN and KCs neurons in the olfactory system of the insects was examined to answer the question of why the system is capable of processing information despite the great variability found in the connections between PNs and KCs, regarding the probability of connection and in its structure.

The hypothesis to explain this behavior is that the effects of this variability are absorbed by the adjustment of the sensitivity of KCs through their neural thresholds, that helps the system to generate more stable and separable pattern representations. To test this idea, two models of the insect olfactory system based on neural networks were presented. One of them included a learning rule to adjust the neural thresholds of KCs and regulate their activity, and the other did not include it. The performance and the separability of their inner representations were compared using the accuracy and the cosine similarity between representations for three different datasets. Results show that the model that includes the KC thresholds adjustment achieves a stable accuracy, regardless of the value of p_c, and also improves the internal representations.

This work contributes to shed some light on the debate about the PN-KC connectivity in the olfactory system of insects. The results are promising since they show that it is not critical to determine the specific value for the probability of connection between neurons or the structure of connections anymore, since the system, thanks to the regulation of the sensitivity of KCs, is capable of adapting to different parameters and variations and still function properly.

From the results presented in this manuscript, some future work and questions that would be interesting to consider is analyzing further the behavior of the system and answer questions such as how the PN-KC ratio influences the intra/inter-class separability, which values of p_c appear naturally in the system as a consequence of the regulation of the activity of KCs, the impact of noise and the complexity level of inputs patterns or what happens if the PN-KC connections are altered once the system is trained to solve a problem.

Acknowledgments. We acknowledge support from MINECO/FEDER TIN2017-84452-R and PID2020-114867RB-I00 (http://www.mineco.gob.es/). We thank Aaron Montero for his design for Fig. 1.

References

1. MNIST handwritten digit database (1998). http://yann.lecun.com/exdb/mnist/
2. Bazhenov, M., Stopfer, M., Sejnowski, T.J., Laurent, G.: Fast odor learning improves reliability of odor responses in the locust antennal lobe. Neuron **46**(3), 483–492 (2005)
3. Caron, S.J., Ruta, V., Abbott, L.F., Axel, R.: Random convergence of olfactory inputs in the Drosophila mushroom body. Nature **497**(7447), 113–117 (2013)
4. Eichler, K., et al.: The complete connectome of a learning and memory centre in an insect brain. Nature **548**(7666), 175–182 (2017)
5. García-Sanchez, M., Huerta, R.: Design parameters of the fan-out phase of sensory systems. J. Comput. Neurosci. **15**(1), 5–17 (2003)
6. González, M., Dominguez, D., Rodríguez, F.B., Sánchez, Á.: Retrieval of noisy fingerprint patterns using metric attractor networks. Int. J. Neural Syst. **24**(7) (2014)
7. González, M., Sánchez, Á., Dominguez, D., Rodriguez, F.B.: Ensemble of diluted attractor networks with optimized topology for fingerprint retrieval. Neurocomputing **442**, 269–280 (2021)
8. Gruntman, E., Turner, G.C.: Integration of the olfactory code across dendritic claws of single mushroom body neurons. Nat. Neurosci. **16**(12), 1821–1829 (2013)
9. Gupta, N., Stopfer, M.: Olfactory coding: giant inhibitory neuron governs sparse odor codes. Curr. Biol. **21**(13), R504–R506 (2011)
10. Han, J., Kamber, M., Pei, J.: Data Mining: Concepts and Techniques. Elsevier Inc., San Francisco (2012)
11. Huerta, R., Nowotny, T.: Fast and robust learning by reinforcement signals: explorations in the insect brain. Neural Comput. **21**(8), 2123–2151 (2009)
12. Huerta, R., Nowotny, T., García-Sanchez, M., Abarbanel, H.D.I., Rabinovich, M.I.: Learning classification in the olfactory system of insects. Neural Comput. **16**(8), 1601–1640 (2004)
13. Jortner, R.A., Farivar, S.S., Laurent, G.: A simple connectivity scheme for sparse coding in an olfactory system. J. Neurosci. **27**(7), 1659–1669 (2007)
14. Kreiman, G.: Neural coding: computational and biophysical perspectives. Phys. Life Rev. **1**(2), 71–102 (2004)
15. Li, F., et al.: The connectome of the adult Drosophila mushroom body: implications for function. bioRxiv pp. 1–86 (2020)
16. Lopez-Hazas, J., Montero, A., Rodriguez, F.B.: Strategies to enhance pattern recognition in neural networks based on the insect olfactory system. In: Kůrková, V., Manolopoulos, Y., Hammer, B., Iliadis, L., Maglogiannis, I. (eds.) ICANN 2018. LNCS, vol. 11139, pp. 468–475. Springer, Cham (2018). https://doi.org/10.1007/978-3-030-01418-6_46
17. Meyerhof, W., Korsching, S.: Chemosensory Systems in Mammals, Fishes, and Insects., vol. 47. Springer (2009). doi: 10.1007/978-3-540-69919-4
18. Montero, A., Huerta, R., Rodriguez, F.B.: Regulation of specialists and generalists by neural variability improves pattern recognition performance. Neurocomputing **151**(Part 1), 69–77 (2015)
19. Montero, A., Huerta, R., Rodriguez, F.B.: Stimulus space complexity determines the ratio of specialist and generalist neurons during pattern recognition. J. Franklin Inst. **355**(5), 2951–2977 (2018)

20. Montero, A., Lopez-Hazas, J., Rodriguez, F.B.: Input pattern complexity determines specialist and generalist populations in drosophila neural network. In: Kůrková, V., Manolopoulos, Y., Hammer, B., Iliadis, L., Maglogiannis, I. (eds.) ICANN 2018. LNCS, vol. 11140, pp. 296–303. Springer, Cham (2018). https://doi.org/10.1007/978-3-030-01421-6_29

21. Olshausen, B.A., Field, D.J.: Sparse coding of sensory inputs. Curr. Opin. Neurobiol. **14**(4), 481–487 (2004)

22. Pawletta, P., Mamlouk, A.: Modeling odor responses of projection neurons and Kenyon cells in insects. Flavour **3**(Suppl 1), P13 (2014)

23. Perez-Orive, J., Mazor, O., Turner, G.C., Cassenaer, S., Wilson, R.I., Laurent, G.: Oscillations and sparsening of odor representations in the mushroom body. Science **297**(5580), 359–365 (2002)

24. Rodriguez, F.B., Huerta, R.: Techniques for temporal detection of neural sensitivity to external stimulation. Biol. Cybern. **100**, 289–297 (2009)

25. Rodriguez, F.B., Huerta, R., Aylwin, M.L.: Neural sensitivity to odorants in deprived and normal olfactory bulbs. PLoS ONE **8**(4), e60745 (2013)

26. Sanda, P., Kee, T., Gupta, N., Stopfer, M., Bazhenov, M.: Classification of odorants across layers in locust olfactory pathway. J. Neurophysiol. **115**(5), 2303–2316 (2016)

27. Stopfer, M.: Central processing in the mushroom bodies. Curr. Opin. Insect. Sci. **6**, 99–103 (2014)

28. Stopfer, M., Jayaraman, V., Laurent, G.: Intensity versus identity coding in an olfactory system. Neuron **39**(6), 991–1004 (2003)

29. Xiao, H., Rasul, K., Vollgraf, R.: Fashion-mnist: a novel image dataset for benchmarking machine learning algorithms (2017)

A Predictive Coding Account for Chaotic Itinerancy

Louis Annnabi[✉], Alexandre Pitti, and Mathias Quoy

ETIS UMR 8051, CY University, ENSEA, CNRS, Pontoise, France
{louis.annnabi,alexandre.pitti,mathias.quoy}@ensea.fr

Abstract. As a phenomenon in dynamical systems allowing autonomous switching between stable behaviors, chaotic itinerancy has gained interest in neurorobotics research. In this study, we draw a connection between this phenomenon and the predictive coding theory by showing how a recurrent neural network implementing predictive coding can generate neural trajectories similar to chaotic itinerancy in the presence of input noise. We propose two scenarios generating random and past-independent attractor switching trajectories using our model.

Keywords: Predictive coding · Free energy principle · Dynamical systems · Neural networks

1 Introduction

Chaotic Itinerancy (CI) describes the behavior of large non-linear dynamical systems consisting in chaotic transitions between quasi-attractors [7,14]. It was first observed in a model of optical turbulence [4], using globally coupled map in a chaotic system [6] and in high dimensional neural networks [14]. From a neuroscientific point of view, this phenomenon is interesting as such systems exhibit complex behaviors that usually require a hierarchical structure in neural networks. Studying CI could help better understanding the mechanisms responsible for the emergence of structure in large populations of neurons.

In cognitive neuroscience, it is believed that attractors or quasi-attractors could represent perceptual concepts or memories, and that cognitive processes such as memory retrieval or thinking would require neural trajectories transitioning between such attractors. CI is also gaining interest in neurorobotics, as it allows to design agents with the ability to autonomously switch between different behavioral patterns without any external commands. Several studies have tried to model CI with learned attractor patterns. [10,15] propose a method where this functional structure emerges from a multiple-timescale RNN. Behavioral patterns are encoded in a rapidly varying recurrent population while another

This work was funded by the CY Cergy-Paris University Foundation (Facebook grant) and partially by Labex MME-DII, France (ANR11-LBX-0023-01).

© Springer Nature Switzerland AG 2021
I. Farkaš et al. (Eds.): ICANN 2021, LNCS 12891, pp. 581–592, 2021.
https://doi.org/10.1007/978-3-030-86362-3_47

population with a longer time constant controls transitions between these patterns. [5] models CI, using reservoir computing techniques [9], with the interplay between an input RNN and a chaotic RNN where desired patterns have been learned with innate trajectory training [8].

In this work, we try to model the attractor switching behavior of CI with a RNN implementation taking inspiration from the Predictive Coding (PC) theory. We propose a model performing random and past-independent transitions between stable and plastic limit-cycle attractors.

According to PC [2,12], the brain is hierarchically generating top-down predictions about its sensory states, and updating its internal states based on a bottom-up error signal originating from the sensory level. This view can be implemented by having the generative model intertwined with error neurons that propagate the information in a bottom-up manner through the hierarchy. An online computation of the error at each level of the generative model makes it possible to dynamically infer the hidden states, using only local update rules. The proposed model implements PC using the free-energy formulation [3], providing a variational Bayes frame for the inference mechanisms.

We show how an RNN implementation based on PC can be trained to generate a repertoire of limit cycle attractor trajectories, and how adding noise into the neural dynamics causes random transitions between the learned patterns.

2   Methods

In this section, we present the proposed RNN model and the corresponding derivations for the free-energy. We then describe the two hypothesized situations in which our model could exhibit attractor transitions dynamics, that we label mode A and mode B.

2.1   RNN Model

Figure 1 represents our proposed RNN model implementing predictive coding. This implementation takes inspirations from several works on RNN modeling [3,11,13].

RNNs can be introduced as directed graphical models forming temporal sequences of hidden states h_t. RNNs can also include a sequence of input variables, and a sequence of output variables. The model we present here only considers outputs, that we denote $\mathbf{x}_t$. Such RNNs are parameterized by recurrent weights controlling the temporal evolution of $\mathbf{h}_t$, and output weights translating $\mathbf{h}_t$ into outputs $\mathbf{x}_t$.

Taking inspiration from [3], we introduce hidden causes into our generative model. Hidden causes, that we denote $\mathbf{c}_t$, are variables influencing the temporal dynamics of $\mathbf{h}_t$. Contrary to hidden states, this variable is static and doesn't evolve according to recurrent weights. Hidden causes differ from model parameters, as they are a random variable on which we can perform inference. They also differ from inputs, as they are not an observable variable with known value.

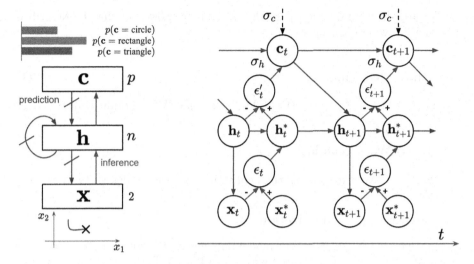

Fig. 1. RNN model. Left: Functional block diagram of the model. The layers of the model interact through top-down connections (blue) and bottom-up connections (green). Right: Temporally unfolded computation graph of the model. (Color figure online)

We still use the subscript t on $\mathbf{c}_t$, since our model will perform inference at each time step, providing new estimates of the hidden causes variable.

To model the influence of the hidden causes variable $\mathbf{c}_t$ onto the temporal dynamics of the hidden states $\mathbf{h}_t$, we use a three-way tensor of shape (n, n, p) where n is the hidden state dimension and p is the hidden causes dimension. The outcome of the dot product of this tensor by the hidden causes $\mathbf{c}_t$ is a matrix of shape (n, n). We can thus see the three-way tensor as a basis of size p in a dimensional space of recurrent weight matrices, and hidden causes as coordinates in this basis used to select particular temporal dynamics. Following this intuition that different hidden causes will lead to different hidden state dynamics, we choose to have one hidden causes vector for each attractor we want to learn with our model. To make sure these attractors don't interfere with each other during the training phase, we enforce one-hot embeddings for the hidden causes, with the activated neuron corresponding to the index of the attractor we want to learn. It ensues that the hidden causes dimension will be equal to the number of attractors we learn with this model.

This three-way tensor comprises a large number of parameters, causing this model to scale poorly if we increase the dimension of the hidden causes (i.e. the number of attractor patterns we learn). To address this issue, [13] proposes to factor the tensor into three matrices such that for all i, j, k, $\mathbf{W}_{\text{rec}}^{ijk} = \sum_{l<d} \mathbf{W}_{\mathbf{p}}^{il} \cdot \mathbf{W}_{\mathbf{f}}^{jl} \cdot \mathbf{W}_{\mathbf{c}}^{kl}$. We introduce a factor dimension d that we can be set arbitrarily to control the number of parameters. In our experiments, we used $d = n/2$.

The top-down, prediction pass through our network can thus be described
with the following equations:

$$\mathbf{h}_t = f(\mathbf{c}_{t-1}, \mathbf{h}_{t-1}^*) \tag{1}$$

$$= (1 - \frac{1}{\tau})\mathbf{h}_{t-1}^* + \frac{1}{\tau}\mathbf{W_f} \cdot ((\mathbf{W_c}^T \cdot \mathbf{c}_{t-1}) \odot (\mathbf{W_p}^T \cdot \tanh(\mathbf{h}_{t-1}^*))) \tag{2}$$

$$\mathbf{x}_t = g(\mathbf{h}_t) \tag{3}$$

$$= \mathbf{W_{out}} \cdot \tanh(\mathbf{h}_t), \tag{4}$$

where we have introduced a time constant τ for the hidden state dynamics.

2.2   Free-Energy Minimization

As explained in introduction, our model implements PC with a bottom-up error
propagation circuitry, represented with green lines in Fig. 1. The error neurons,
denoted ϵ and ϵ', compute the difference between predicted and target values
at each layer. By propagating these errors originating from the output layer,
onto the upper layers, this architecture is able to perform online inference of the
hidden variables (states and causes) of the RNN.

Inference in the proposed model can be formulated as a free-energy min-
imization process. The detailed derivations of our model's equations based on
the free-energy principle are provided in Annex A. We obtain the following equation for the free-energy:

$$\mathcal{E}(\mathbf{h}, \mathbf{c}) = \frac{(\mathbf{x}^* - \mathbf{x})^2}{2\sigma_x^2} + \frac{(\mathbf{h}^* - \mathbf{h})^2}{2\sigma_h^2} - \log p(\mathbf{c}) + C \tag{5}$$

In this equation, $\mathbf{x}$ and $\mathbf{h}$ denote prior predictions while $\mathbf{h}^*$ denotes the
approximate posterior estimation based on bottom-up information. $\mathbf{x}^*$ denotes
the observed value. C is a constant value that does not impact gradient calculations.

The probability $p(\mathbf{c})$ is the prior probability on the hidden causes variable. In
this article, we use a Gaussian mixture prior, defined in the following equation:

$$p(\mathbf{c}) = \sum_{k=1}^{p} \pi_k \mathcal{N}(\mathbf{c}; \mu_\mathbf{k}, \sigma_c^2 \mathbb{I}_p) \tag{6}$$

Note that the number of Gaussians in the mixture model is equal to p, which
is the number of attractors, also equal to the dimension of $\mathbf{c}$.

The temporal dynamics of $\mathbf{h}$ and $\mathbf{c}$ can be found by computing the free-
energy gradients with regard to these variables. The bottom-up, inference pass
through our network is described by the following equations:

$$\epsilon_t = \mathbf{x}_t - \mathbf{x}_t^* \tag{7}$$

$$\mathbf{h}_t^* = \mathbf{h}_t - \frac{1}{\sigma_x^2} \mathbf{W_{out}}^T \cdot \epsilon_t \tag{8}$$

$$\epsilon_t' = \mathbf{h}_t - \mathbf{h}_t^* \tag{9}$$

$$\mathbf{c}_t = \mathbf{c}_{t-1} - \frac{1}{\sigma_h^2} \mathbf{W_c} \cdot ((\mathbf{W_f}^T \cdot \epsilon_t') \odot (\mathbf{W_p}^T \cdot \tanh(\mathbf{h}_{t-1}^*))) + \frac{\partial \log p(\mathbf{c}_{t-1})}{\partial \mathbf{c}_{t-1}} \tag{10}$$

The last term in Eq. 10 will pull $\mathbf{c}$ towards values with high prior probability.

Compared to the RNN proposed in [11], our model comprises hidden causes in the generative model. Additionally, the feedback connections perform gradient descent on the free-energy, instead of being additional parameters to be learned.

2.3 Training

Algorithm 1: RNN Training

Initialize the RNN model;
$\mathbf{h}_{init} \sim \mathcal{N}(0, 1)$;
for $0 \leq i < I$ **do**
    for $0 \leq k < p$ **do**
        $\mathbf{h}_0 \leftarrow \mathbf{h}_{init}$;
        $\mathbf{c}_0 \leftarrow \text{one\_hot}(k)$;
        $(\mathbf{x}_0, \ldots, \mathbf{x}_T) \leftarrow \text{RNN}(\mathbf{h}_0, \mathbf{c}_0)$;
        $\mathcal{L} \leftarrow \text{MSE}((\mathbf{x}_0, \ldots, \mathbf{x}_T), (\mathbf{x}_0^*, \ldots, \mathbf{x}_T^*))$;
        $\text{backprop}(\mathcal{L}, \text{RNN.parameters}())$;
        $\text{update}(\text{RNN.parameters}())$;
    end
end

The model can be trained with gradient descent on the free-energy functional using only local update rules. The output weights $\mathbf{W_{out}}$ can be trained in order to reduce the discrepancy between the observed value $\mathbf{x}_t^*$ and its prediction $\mathbf{x}_t$. Similarly, all the weights $\mathbf{W_p}$, $\mathbf{W_f}$ and $\mathbf{W_c}$, responsible for the temporal dynamics of $\mathbf{h}$, can be trained in order to reduce the error between the posterior estimation $\mathbf{h}_t^*$ and its prior estimation $\mathbf{h}_t$.

However, such learning rules would not consider the delayed influence of the recurrent weight parameters onto the trajectory. In this article, we instead use the backpropagation through time algorithm for the training of the model parameters, using only the forward pass described in Eqs. (2) and (4) for gradient computations (all the bottom-up updates are detached from the computation graph).

For each limit cycle attractor $(\mathbf{x}_{0,k}^*, \mathbf{x}_{1,k}^*, \ldots, \mathbf{x}_{T,k}^*)$ of the p trajectories we want to learn, we initialize the hidden causes to the one-hot encoding of k (all coefficients set to 0 except for the k-th coefficient that is set to 1). All trajectories start from a same random initial hidden state $\mathbf{h}_{init}$. The training method is described in Algorithm 1, where I denotes the number of training iterations and T denotes the length of the target trajectories. During our training, we used the Adam optimizer with a learning rate of 0.01, and a batch size of p corresponding to the inner loop in the previous algorithm.

2.4   Mode A

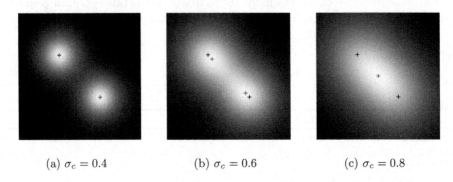

(a) $\sigma_c = 0.4$ (b) $\sigma_c = 0.6$ (c) $\sigma_c = 0.8$

Fig. 2. Gaussian mixture probability distributions with $p = 2$. The Gaussians centers $\mu_0 = (1,0)$ and $\mu_1 = (0,1)$ are represented in black. The red points represent the minima of the distributions. In the general case, the prior means μ_k will correspond to the one-hot vectors activated on the k-th dimension, and the mixture coefficients π_k will be set uniformly : $\pi_k = 1/p$. (Color figure online)

Here we describe one way to simulate attractor switching behavior using the proposed model. This method, that we label mode A, varies the parameters σ_c used to dynamically infer hidden causes during the trajectory.

First, we are in a situation where no target $\mathbf{x}^*$ is provided by the environment, in other words, the RNN performs a closed-loop trajectory generation. In this situation, we replace the error in the bottom level by low amplitude noise. This noise propagates in the RNN with feedback connections and in particular, influences the hidden causes variable.

As represented in Fig. 2, the parameter σ_c determines the shape of the prior distribution on hidden causes. With low values of σ_c, the complexity term in Eq. (10) will pull the hidden causes variable towards one of the prior means μ_k. These values for $\mathbf{c}$ correspond to temporal dynamics that have previously been trained to match each of the desired attractors. With high values of σ_c, the Gaussians merge into a concave function with a global maximum corresponding to the average of all the prior means μ_k. In this situation, the complexity term in Eq. (10) will pull the hidden causes variable towards this average value, for which no training was performed.

The idea of mode A is to periodically vary σ_c in order to alternate between phases where the hidden causes are pulled towards learned attractor dynamics values, and phases where the hidden causes are pulled towards the average of the prior means.

2.5 Mode B

We describe a second method to simulate attractor switching behaviors, that we label mode B. In mode B, the parameter σ_c remains constant and equal to 0.4, instead we vary the parameter σ_h.

We can see from Eq. (10) that this parameter controls the importance of the bottom-up signal in the hidden causes update. In our case, since the error that is propagated up into the model is pure noise, the parameter σ_h can be seen as controlling the noise level that we add to the hidden causes at each time step. For high values of σ_h, the additive noise level will remain too low to pull the hidden causes outside of the basin of attraction created by the last term of Eq. (10) and represented in Fig. 2a. For values of σ_h that are low enough, the additive noise can make the hidden causes $\mathbf{c}$ escape from its basin of attraction.

Similarly to mode A, the idea behind mode B is to periodically vary σ_h in order to alternate between low noise phases where hidden causes remain close to a value corresponding to the learned attractor dynamics, and high noise phases where the hidden causes escape their attraction basin.

3 Results

In this section, we present the results we obtained with the proposed model. We analyze the simulations of our network in mode A and mode B for the generation of attractor switching trajectories.

3.1 Training

We initialize our model with an output dimension of 2, a hidden state dimension of $n = 100$, and a hidden causes dimensions of $p = 3$, equal to the number of attractor trajectories we want to learn. The network has a time constant of $\tau = 5$. Finally, we set $\sigma_o = 1$, $\sigma_h = 10$ and $\sigma_c = 0.1$ during training. Note that the parameters σ_h and σ_c will be varying during the simulations in mode A and B.

The three target trajectories are periodic patterns representing a circle, a square, and a triangle, with a period of 60 time steps, repeated to last for 1000 time steps.

The model was trained during 1000 iterations using the method described in Algorithm 1.

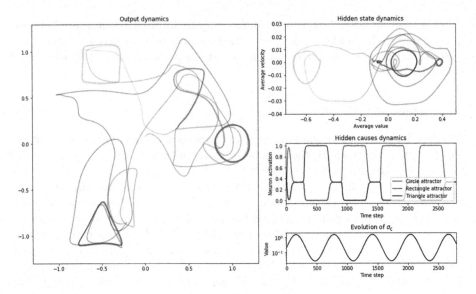

Fig. 3. Simulation in mode A. Left: Output trajectory generated by the model in mode A. The line colors in RGB values correspond to the activations of the three neurons of **c** throughout the trajectory. Top-right: Average velocity of the hidden state according to its average value throughout the trajectory. Middle-right: Evolution of the three hidden causes neuron activations over time. Bottom-right: Evolution of the σ_c coefficient over time.

3.2   Mode A

We now use the trained network in mode A, with the parameters settings $\sigma_o = 10$, $\sigma_h = 0.1$, and σ_c varying according to the function $\sigma_c(t) = 0.2 \cdot \exp\{2\sin(t/100)\}$. The results are recorded in Fig. 3.

We can observe that the RNN switches between the three attractors. When σ_c is high, the hidden causes converge towards the center value. This center value corresponds to the hidden state dynamics and output dynamics depicted in gray. This value of the hidden causes seems to correspond to a point attractor, which was not something directly enforced by the training procedure. Starting from this configuration, when σ_c decreases, the hidden causes falls into one of the three attracting configurations that were trained to correspond to the three limit cycle attractors.

3.3   Mode B

We now use the trained network in mode B, with the parameters settings $\sigma_o = 10$, $\sigma_c = 0.4$ and σ_h varying according to the function $\sigma_h(t) = 0.04 \cdot \exp\{2\sin(t/300)\}$. The results are recorded in Fig. 4.

We can observe that the RNN again switched between the three attractors. When σ_h is high, the hidden causes remain in a stable position corresponding

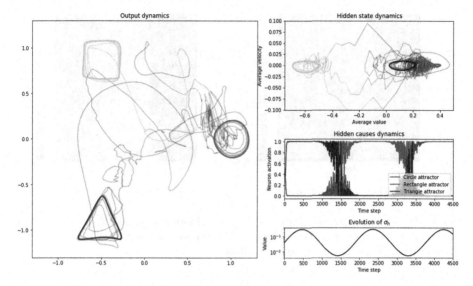

Fig. 4. Simulation in mode B. Left: Output trajectory generated by the model in mode B. The line colors in RGB values correspond to the activations of the three neurons of **c** throughout the trajectory. Top-right: Average velocity of the hidden state according to its average value throughout the trajectory. Middle-right: Evolution of the three hidden causes neuron activations over time. Bottom-right: Evolution of the σ_h coefficient over time.

to the learned limit cycle attractor dynamics. When we decrease σ_h, the noise level applied onto the hidden causes at each time step increases to the point where **c** escapes its basin of attraction, to fall back into one of the three stable configuration once the noise level resettles.

3.4 Transition Matrices

In this section, we want to verify whether the attractor switching behavior follows a uniform probability distribution or if some transitions are more likely to occur than others. We view the RNN as a Markov chain with three configurations. For modes A and B, we record 2000 attractor transitions that we use to build an estimation of the transition matrix of that Markov chain. The results are displayed in Fig. 5.

For mode A, we can see that the probability of switching to a certain state seems independent from the previous state. This result can be explained by the fact that the intermediary, neutral configuration that the networks reaches before switching to a new configuration corresponds to a fixed point. If we let enough time for the hidden state to reach this fixed point, it would no longer hold any memory of the previous configuration. Additionally, the probability distribution is not uniform, as rectangle states happen more often than others.

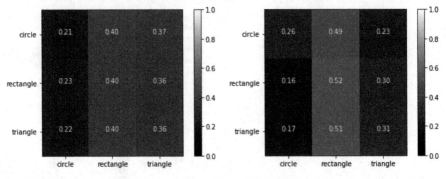

(a) Transition matrix for mode A.   (b) Transition matrix for mode B.

Fig. 5. Transitions matrices for modes A and B. Lines correspond to previous states and columns to next states. For instance, the estimated probability of switching from circle to triangle attractors in mode B is 0.23.

For mode B, this bias is still present but contrary to mode A, the probability to reach a certain state depends on the previous state. The transitions are thus past-dependent.

4   Conclusion

In this study, we have shown how an RNN model implementing PC could exhibit attractor switching behaviors using an input noise signal. Here, we compare our results with other works aiming at modeling this behavior.

The approach described in [15] requires to train a separate RNN for each primitive. In opposition, we have shown that our model can embed different dynamics within one RNN, and as such should scale better to an increased number of primitives. On the other hand, one limitation of the model presented by [5] is that quasi-attractors have a set duration, and the behaviour they yield can't last longer than this trained duration. In contrast, since our model relies on real trained limit-cycle attractors, any periodical behavior can be maintained for as long as desired.

In this article, we have tried to propose mechanisms that will provide random transitions between attractors, regardless of the past attractor state. However, if we were to model cognitive mechanisms such as memory retrieval, it could be interesting to have such a dependency. Following this idea, we could envision a mode C where we would periodically set the parameter σ_c to a very large value. When σ_c is very high, the prior probability over **c** converges to a flat function, thus making the last term of Eq. 10 negligible. In such a setup, **c** would evolve following a Gaussian random walk. When σ_c is reset to its initial value, **c** should converge to the closest mixture mean. Alternating between low values of σ_c and very high values would thus result in a succession of random walk and convergence phases for $\mathbf{c}$, that should maintain information about the previously visited attractor configurations.

A   Free-Energy Derivations

In this section, we provide the derivations for Eq. 5. We start from the following probabilistic graphical model:

$$p(\mathbf{c}) = \sum_{k=1}^{p} \pi_k \mathcal{N}(\mathbf{c}; \mu_k, \sigma_c^2 \mathbb{I}_p) \tag{11}$$

$$p(\mathbf{h}|\mathbf{c}) = \mathcal{N}(\mathbf{h}; f(\mathbf{c}, \mathbf{h}_{t-1}); \sigma_h^2 \mathbb{I}_n) \tag{12}$$

$$p(\mathbf{x}|\mathbf{h}) = \mathcal{N}(\mathbf{x}; g(\mathbf{h}); \sigma_x^2 \mathbb{I}_2) \tag{13}$$

Where f and g correspond to the top-down predictions described respectively in Eq. 2 and 4. Note that here, $\mathbf{c}$, $\mathbf{h}$ and $\mathbf{x}$ denote random variables, and should not be confused with the variables of the computation model presented in the main text. Since free-energy will be used to perform inference on the hidden variables, and that it's not possible to update the past hidden variable $\mathbf{h}_{t-1}$, we consider it as a parameter and not a random variable of the probabilistic model. We only perform inference on $\mathbf{c}$ and $\mathbf{h} = \mathbf{h_t}$.

We introduce approximate posterior density functions $q(\mathbf{h})$ and $q(\mathbf{c})$ that are assumed to be Gaussian distributions of means $\mathbf{m}_h$ and $\mathbf{m}_c$. Given a target for $\mathbf{x}$, denoted $\mathbf{x}^*$, the variational free energy is defined as:

$$\mathcal{E}(\mathbf{x}*, \mathbf{m}_h, \mathbf{m}_c) = \mathrm{KL}(q(\mathbf{c}, \mathbf{h}) \| p(\mathbf{c}, \mathbf{h}, \mathbf{x}^*)) \tag{14}$$

$$= -\mathbb{E}_q[\log p(\mathbf{c}, \mathbf{h}, \mathbf{x}^*)] + \mathbb{E}_q[\log q(\mathbf{c}, \mathbf{h})] \tag{15}$$

The second term of Eq. 15 is the entropy of the approximate posterior distribution, and using the Gaussian assumption, does not depend on $\mathbf{m}_h$ and $\mathbf{m}_c$. As such, this term is of no interest for the derivation of the update rule of $\mathbf{m}_h$ and $\mathbf{m}_c$, and is replaced by the constant C_1 in the remaining of the derivations. Using the Gaussian assumption, we can also find simplified derivations for the first term of Eq. 15, and grouping the terms not depending on $\mathbf{m}_h$ and $\mathbf{m}_c$ under the constant C_2, we have the following result:

$$\mathcal{E}(\mathbf{x}*, \mathbf{m}_h, \mathbf{m}_c) = -\log p(\mathbf{x}^*|\mathbf{h}) - \log p(\mathbf{m}_h|\mathbf{c}) - \log p(\mathbf{m}_c) + C_1 + C_2 \tag{16}$$

$$= \frac{(\mathbf{x}^* - g(\mathbf{h}))^2}{2\sigma_x^2} + \frac{(\mathbf{m}_h - f(\mathbf{c}, \mathbf{h}_{t-1}))^2}{2\sigma_h^2} - \log p(\mathbf{m}_c) + C \tag{17}$$

where $C = C_1 + C_2 + C_3$ and C_3 corresponds to the additional terms obtained when developing $\log p(\mathbf{x}^*|\mathbf{h})$ and $\log p(\mathbf{m}_h|\mathbf{c})$.

[1] provides more detailed derivations and a deeper hindsight on the subject.

B   Linked Videos

Here is the link to a video showing animated example trajectories in modes A and B (https://youtu.be/LRJQr8RmeCY).

References

1. Buckley, C.L., Kim, C.S., McGregor, S., Seth, A.K.: The free energy principle for action and perception: a mathematical review. J. Math. Psychol. **81**, 55–79 (2017). https://doi.org/10.1016/j.jmp.2017.09.004
2. Clark, A.: Whatever next? predictive brains, situated agents, and the future of cognitive science. Behav. Brain Sci. **36**(3), 181–204 (2013). https://doi.org/10.1017/S0140525X12000477
3. Friston, K., Kiebel, S.: Predictive coding under the free-energy principle. Philos. Trans. Roy. Soc. Lond. Ser. B Biol. Sci. **364**, 1211–1221 (2009)
4. Ikeda, K., Otsuka, K., Matsumoto, K.: Maxwell-Bloch turbulence. Prog. Theoret. Phys. Suppl. **99**, 295–324 (1989). https://doi.org/10.1143/PTPS.99.295
5. Inoue, K., Nakajima, K., Kuniyoshi, Y.: Designing spontaneous behavioral switching via chaotic itinerancy. Sci. Adv. **6**(46) (2020). https://doi.org/10.1126/sciadv.abb3989
6. Kaneko, K.: Clustering, coding, switching, hierarchical ordering, and control in a network of chaotic elements. Physica D Nonlinear Phenomena **41**(2), 137–172 (1990). https://doi.org/10.1016/0167-2789(90)90119-A
7. Kaneko, K., Tsuda, I.: Chaotic itinerancy. Chaos Interdisc. J. Nonlinear Sci. **13**(3), 926–936 (2003). https://doi.org/10.1063/1.1607783
8. Laje, R., Buonomano, D.: Robust timing and motor patterns by taming chaos in recurrent neural networks. Nat. Neurosci. **16**(7), 925–935 (2013)
9. Lukoševičius, M., Jaeger, H.: Reservoir computing approaches to recurrent neural network training. Comput. Sci. Rev. **3**(3), 127–149 (2009). https://doi.org/10.1016/j.cosrev.2009.03.005
10. Namikawa, J., Nishimoto, R., Tani, J.: A neurodynamic account of spontaneous behaviour. PLoS Comput. Biol. **7**(10), 1–13 (2011). https://doi.org/10.1371/journal.pcbi.1002221
11. Ororbia, A., Mali, A., Giles, C.L., Kifer, D.: Continual learning of recurrent neural networks by locally aligning distributed representations. IEEE Trans. Neural Netw. Learn. Syst. **31**(10), 4267–4278 (2020)
12. Rao, R., Ballard, D.: Predictive coding in the visual cortex a functional interpretation of some extra-classical receptive-field effects. Nat. Neurosci. **2**, 79–87 (1999)
13. Taylor, G.W., Hinton, G.E.: Factored conditional restricted Boltzmann machines for modeling motion style. In: Proceedings of the 26th Annual International Conference on Machine Learning, ICML 2009, pp. 1025–1032. Association for Computing Machinery, New York (2009)
14. Tsuda, I.: Chaotic itinerancy as a dynamical basis of hermeneutics in brain and mind. World Futures **32**(2–3), 167–184 (1991). https://doi.org/10.1080/02604027.1991.9972257
15. Yamashita, Y., Tani, J.: Emergence of functional hierarchy in a multiple timescale neural network model: a humanoid robot experiment. PLoS Comput. Biol. **4**(11), 1–18 (2008). https://doi.org/10.1371/journal.pcbi.1000220

A Computational Model of the Effect of Short-Term Monocular Deprivation on Binocular Rivalry in the Context of Amblyopia

Norman Seeliger[(✉)] and Jochen Triesch

Frankfurt Institute for Advanced Studies, Frankfurt, Germany

Abstract. Treatments for amblyopia focus on vision therapy and patching of one eye. Predicting the success of these methods remains difficult, however. Recent research has used binocular rivalry to monitor visual cortical plasticity during occlusion therapy, leading to a successful prediction of the recovery rate of the amblyopic eye. The underlying mechanisms and their relation to neural homeostatic plasticity are not known. Here we propose a spiking neural network to explain the effect of short-term monocular deprivation on binocular rivalry. The model reproduces perceptual switches as observed experimentally. When one eye is occluded, inhibitory plasticity changes the balance between the eyes and leads to longer dominance periods for the eye that has been deprived. The model suggests that homeostatic inhibitory plasticity is a critical component of the observed effects and might play an important role in the recovery from amblyopia.

Keywords: Amblyopia · Binocular rivalry · Neural network · Plasticity

1 Introduction

Amblyopia (greek, meaning *dull* or *blunt sight*) is a developmental disorder of the visual system in which the brain and an eye are not working well together. For people suffering from amblyopia one eye—the then called amblyopic eye—shows little visual acuity as well as a decreased contrast and motion sensitivity [9]. Patients typically also suffer from poor stereo vision. Neither can be related to structural abnormalities nor can it be entirely recovered during adulthood. Amblyopia can be caused by, e.g., a muscle imbalance (strabismic amblyopia) as well as by a difference in sharpness of vision between the eyes (anisometropic amblyopia) during the first 3–5 years of life. Different causes lead to different characteristics of amblyopia, e.g., regarding visual acuity and contrast sensitivity [1]. Considering these causes and their consequences, the suppression of the amblyopic eye's neural representation by the fellow eye seems to be the primary cause for a failing contribution of the amblyopic eye to vision. Indeed, it was

© Springer Nature Switzerland AG 2021
I. Farkaš et al. (Eds.): ICANN 2021, LNCS 12891, pp. 593–603, 2021.
https://doi.org/10.1007/978-3-030-86362-3_48

found that for all major forms of amblyopia the degree of interocular, GABAergic suppression correlates with the depth of amblyopia [14,21].

Under normal viewing conditions, the input to both eyes is nearly identical and just differs slightly due to different viewing angles. When both eyes are presented with non-matching input, however, most people report fluctuations between the perceptions of these inputs with the observer perceiving only one eye's image at a time. This phenomenon is called binocular rivalry. The fluctuations in perception during binocular rivalry are stochastic and show a mean duration of about 2 s [4]. They are thought to arise due to a competition between neural populations representing the two different percepts, which is mediated by mutual inhibition. Recent computational models of binocular rivalry focused on addressing this mutual inhibition with alternations in perception being allowed due to adaptation [5,13] and/or noise in the network [20]. Since amblyopia and binocular rivalry both rely on competition between the eyes, they may be related at a mechanistic level.

A recovery from amblyopia can be achieved best during childhood, e.g., by the most common treatment incorporating eye patches during an occlusion therapy. Here, the strong eye is occluded for several hours per day over multiple months. Recently, Lunghi and others combined the patching therapy with a novel measure for neuronal plasticity which incorporates binocular dynamics [15–17]. They first showed that after a short-term monocular deprivation of 150 min, the occluded eye dominates perception under binocular rivalry in healthy adults [15]. The strength of this effect correlated with decreased GABA levels after patching [16], diminished over time, and went back to a normal state after 90 min. In a following study, they found that this effect is also present for the patched fellow eye of amblyopes undergoing standard occlusion therapy [17]. Moreover, the recovery rate from amblyopia could be predicted: the stronger the dynamics are altered after the patching, the more the amblyopic eye could recover after months of treatment. Zhou et al. [27] added to this finding by successfully applying an inverse occlusion therapy in adult amblyopes for which, again, the binocular balance was the key aspect for recovery.

The physiological mechanisms responsible for the observed effects are still unknown, however. Therefore, the current work aims to provide a better understanding of potential mechanisms leading to the effects described above. We hypothesized that inhibitory plasticity may be the central mechanism giving rise to the observed effects. To test the plausibility of this hypothesis, we first created a spiking neural network model that produced alternations in dominance between two competing neuron groups, which were stimulated simultaneously. Second, one of the groups was deprived of its normal input for a certain amount of time. Inhibitory plasticity altered the rivalry dynamics during deprivation and lead to longer dominance durations for the previously deprived population. This effect was accompanied by a temporary reduction in GABA-levels, as observed experimentally. Based on these findings, we conclude that inhibitory plasticity is a plausible explanation for the observed experimental findings.

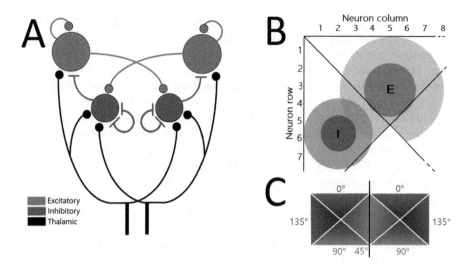

Fig. 1. Model architecture and connectivity. A) Modeled layer IV with exc. (blue) and inh. populations (red) as well as thalamic drive (solid black). Excitatory synapses are displayed as bulbs, inhibitory synapses as lines. **B)** Connectivity within one ocular dominance column following a Gaussian probability function (exc: σ of 3, inh: $\sigma = 2$). Lines separate regions of exc. neurons that respond to the same orientation. The second column is placed adjacent (not shown) and shows the same connectivity. **C)** Pinwheel architecture of the model. Black line separates ocular dominance columns. (Color figure online)

2   Methods

The current model aims to represent a part of layer IV of the primary visual cortex. It incorporates pyramidal neurons (excitatory, regular-spiking) and parvalbumin neurons (inhibitory, fast-spiking) in two interconnected layers. The excitatory neuron layer consists of 200 neurons and the inhibitory layer of 50 neurons to maintain ratios between these two groups as seen in experiments. The general structure of the model is displayed in Fig. 1.

Each layer consists of two ocular dominance columns, which incorporate a pinwheel structure, once clockwise and once counter-clockwise, which indicate neuron populations with a varying orientation preference. For each dominance column, 100 exc. and 25 inh. neurons are divided into 4 groups which then share the same orientation preference (e.g. exc. neurons 1–25: left eye, preference of $0°$).

Neurons in the model are of the standard leaky-integrate-and-fire type. They include a slow hyperpolarizing current to model neuronal spike rate adaptation and white Gaussian membrane noise that is added to the membrane voltage. The general formulation is adapted from [6]. When the membrane potential of a neuron reaches a threshold (mean value -57.3 mV for exc. neurons, -58.0 mV for inhibitory neurons, both with a standard deviation of 0.1 mV), a spike is generated and the neuron's membrane potential is set back to -70.0 mV for excitatory neurons and -60.0 mV for inhibitory neurons.

Synapses are modeled as conductance-based. Upon arrival of a presynaptic spike, the synapse's conductance is increased by the synaptic weight w and then decreases exponentially with a time constant specific to the synapse type ($\tau_{AMPA} = 3$ ms, $\tau_{NMDA} = 80$ ms, $\tau_{GABA_A} = 10$ ms). The different synapse types are used to model external stimulation by the thalamus (AMPA-mediated), recurrent excitation provided by adjacent excitatory neurons and not explicitly modeled layer V/VI neurons alike (AMPA- and NMDA-mediated) as well as inhibition from inhibitory neurons (GABA$_A$-mediated).

The spike rate adaptation mechanism works similarly. Upon each postsynaptic spike, the conductance is increased by a parameter w_{SRA} and then decays exponentially with the time constant $\tau_{SRA} = 996$ ms.

Considering plasticity in the model, STDP was implemented only at inhibitory to excitatory connections for which a symmetric STDP window has been assumed with a pairing of pre- and postsynaptic spikes leading to potentiation independent of the relative order of the events:

$$\Delta W(x) = A_I \exp^{-\frac{|\Delta t|}{\tau_{STDP}}}. \tag{1}$$

Here, Δt denotes the time between pre- and postsynaptic spikes, τ_{STDP} is the time constant for the STDP and A_I is a constant for the maximum possible weight change. An online implementation of a nearest-neighbor STDP rule is used with every spike leading to a trace, which is evaluated once a spike of the corresponding pre- or postsynaptic neuron occurs. For homeostatic purposes, an α-parameter is also introduced which reduces the synaptic weight by a small amount α for every presynaptic spike of an inhibitory neuron and which is independent of spike times of the corresponding postsynaptic excitatory neuron [25].

The global connectivity of the network promotes inhibition between groups in different ocular dominance columns which are driven by different sensory stimuli. This is in line with experimental findings showing that inhibition is prominent from one ocular dominance column towards the other [10]. This inhibition is mediated by long-range excitatory connections from excitatory neurons of one eye's dominance column towards inhibitory neurons of the other eye's dominance column. For the local connectivity within one ocular dominance column, every neuron pair has a chance to become connected that drops of with increasing distance following a Gaussian probability function (exc: σ of 3, inh: $\sigma = 2$; see Fig. 1B). Thus, the longest axons stem from excitatory rather than inhibitory neurons [19]. Connectivity parameters were adapted from Ahmed et al. [2] for the relative contributions of thalamic and cortical projection ratios and from Potjans et al. [23] for cortico-cortical connection ratios. Axonal delays are heterogeneous (exc. to exc. 1.5 ms, inh. to exc. 0.5 ms, exc. to inh. 1.0 ms and inh. to inh. 1.0 ms).

Every neuron is stimulated via 10 spike trains (40 Hz, interocular correlation of 0.08 and intraocular correlation of 0.25). The same input is also provided to the inhibitory populations which target the excitatory populations of both eyes (see Fig. 1). During the simulated patching, the input towards one eye is set 10 Hz and is uncorrelated while the input to the other eye is left unchanged.

For the computation of dominance durations, mean firing rates are calculated for the two groups belonging to the eyes using a rectangular sliding window with a width of 300 ms. The population which is more active than the other population is labeled as *dominant* at this moment. Switches in dominance are indicated when the suppressed population becomes at least twice as active as the formerly active population. Periods with mixed perceptions and transitions between dominance durations of competing groups are not treated differently for the current analysis. For the comparison of distributions of dominance durations, a Kolmogorov-Smirnow test is used for the dominance durations of one eye before and after the patching.

The model is implemented using Brain2 [24]. The program code is available at GitHub under https://bit.ly/38jZQgX and licensed under GNU General Public License v3.0.

3   Results

3.1   General Network Behavior

An example of the network's activity is given in Fig. 2. Here, the excitatory populations representing the left (bottom row) and right (top row) eye compete for dominance when neurons that prefer orthogonal orientations are stimulated simultaneously. These populations show varying dominance durations with a mean slightly above 2 s as seen in experiments [4] (Fig. 3). The inhibitory populations show the inverse activity (data not shown).

3.2   Effect of Patching

We modeled the patching procedure used in experiments. Participants typically watch a movie containing a wide range visual stimuli or are free to perform their normal everyday activities while the patch is applied. The stimulus before and after the patching depends on the particular experiment (e.g. unrestricted input or specific tasks). For the purpose of our model, we provide the rivaling input for the entire time. Dominance durations are calculated for the first and last third, inhibitory weights are recorded for the entire time. To save simulation time, we accelerated the effect of plasticity to reduce the time required to simulate the occlusion to 100 s. Figure 4 shows a representative example of the effect of the simulated patching on the network dynamics. In part (A), the mean of the inhibitory weights targeting the corresponding excitatory populations is shown with the green/red vertical lines indicating the start/end of the occlusion. Before the patch is applied, the inhibitory weights towards both populations slightly diverge since one population is slightly stronger than the other due to random factors in the initialization of the network. As soon as the patching starts, however, the mean inhibitory weight towards the occluded

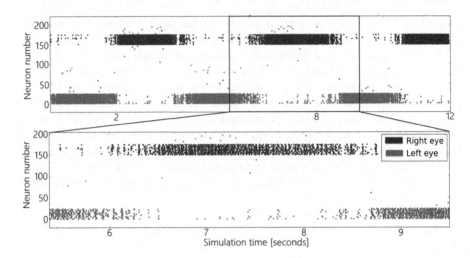

Fig. 2. Rasterplots of network activity Example of the network activity under basal rivaling conditions. The stimulated populations are left eye, 0° (red) and right eye, 90° (blue). Other colors correspond to other eye, orientation combinations. (Color figure online)

eye drops substantially while the mean inhibitory weight towards the open eye shows an increase. When the patching stops, the reverse is visible: the strengths of inhibitory weights towards the formerly occluded eye rise again to the level of the unoccluded eye. The mean inhibitory weight towards the unoccluded eye starts to decrease. Both means seem to approach each other in a time frame comparable to the patching duration.

The impact of these altered weights on rivaling dynamics can be seen in Fig. 4B (data from 18 different simulations). Before the patching, every eye shows average dominance durations of roughly the same length (left: 2069 ms; right: 2164 ms). Afterwards, this behavior is dramatically altered. The formerly occluded population can be active for very long time periods and now possesses a significantly prolonged mean dominance duration of 3212 ms (KS-Test: $p < 0.001$). The eye which stayed open during the patching has its mean dominance duration significantly reduced to 1667 ms (KS-Test: $p < 0.001$). The change in dominance duration length for the occluded eye is stronger than the change for the eye which remained open. Thus, the model reproduces the changes in dominance durations after patching observed experimentally.

4   Discussion

We aimed to create a model that captures and explains the experimental effects observed by Lunghi and others [15–18]. The main focus lied in creating a spiking neural network model with inhibitory plasticity to explain how the dynamics of binocular rivalry are altered in response to monocular deprivation. Our network

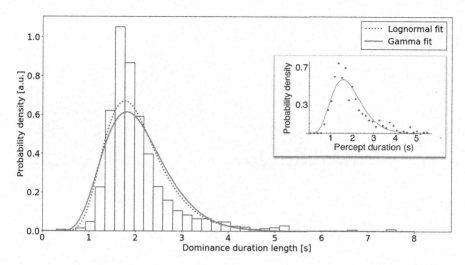

Fig. 3. Dominance duration distribution Distribution of dominance durations for the model together with a gamma fit and a lognormal fit. Inset: Perception duration lengths found in experiments with a fitted gamma distribution (see [4]).

captures these effects and demonstrates how the occlusion of one eye can lead to a temporary relief of the corresponding part of the primary visual cortex from inhibition. This then allows for a re-balancing of the total network undisturbed from a potential suppression by the other eye.

In the model and with the occlusion of one eye, the input towards inhibitory neurons targeting the corresponding excitatory population is only partially decreased due to the drive coming from the eye which remains open. This presynaptic inhibitory activity, however, has little to no postsynaptic excitatory activity with which the spikes could be correlated. Thus, the inhibitory weight of these synapses decreases over time during the occlusion and only starts to regain strength after the patch is lifted. At this third stage, the chance of correlated activity is elevated which leads to a strong potentiation of the targeting inhibitory weight. A similar, but inverted, effect can be seen for the eye which remains open: during the occlusion, the inhibitory neurons for the open eye gain nearly all of their input from the same neurons which drive the excitatory population. Thus, the activity is highly correlated and leads to a potentiation of the average inhibitory weight. Interestingly, we also found a similar impact of the patching in a variant of this network without feed-forward inhibition (data not shown). In this variant, the inhibition towards the open eye remained stable but the occluded eye experiences a decreased inhibition. Both versions of the model lead to the occluded population dominating after the patching under rivaling conditions. This effect is also robust with respect to the condition of the network at the moment of patching—since the strength of the eyes differs in healthy people in general and in amblyopic people in particular, completely balanced conditions would be a rather unrealistic setting. The reaction of the

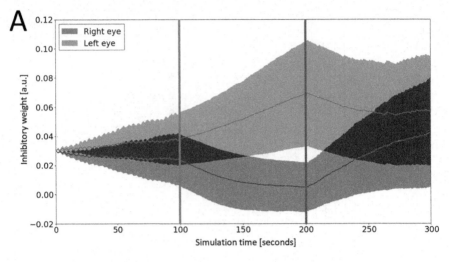

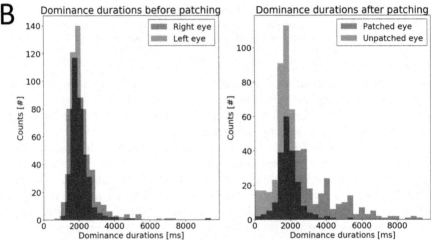

Fig. 4. Effect of patching A) Evolution of the inhibitory weight (mean and standard deviation) targeting excitatory neurons of the open (top) and occluded eye (bottom). Vertical green and red lines indicate, respectively, the start and end of the occlusion. One exemplary weight evolution was chosen. **B)** Dominance durations before (left) and after (right) the patching (combined data from 18 simulations). (Color figure online)

network to the occlusion directly results from the used parameters (e.g. for the STDP) and thus, the ability of the network to show plastic changes due to this treatment could be linked to the overall plasticity of the brain. This could explain why Lunghi et al. could predict the recovery rate from amblyopia based on the impact of short-term occlusion on binocular rivalry.

The network also agrees with details of the results by Lunghi et al. [15]. The increase in dominance duration length of the formerly occluded eye exceeds the decrease for the eye which remained open. Also, the time constants seem to fit: in the experiment, the patching had shown an impact for a duration which is slightly shorter than the time the patching was performed. A similar time frame can be seen in the model.

Also, our model is robust to various design choices. In the network, excitatory neurons only connect to excitatory neurons with a rather similar orientation preference (up to 45°) while avoiding excitatory neurons with opposite preferences. However, an architecture where excitatory neurons only connect to neurons showing the same preference would also be plausible. This approach leads to similar results in the current model. The same is true for a variant of the model where projections crossing the ocular dominance column border are not provided by excitatory neurons towards inhibitory populations, but by inhibitory populations targeting the other eye. This architecture also yielded comparable results.

But what might be the implications of reduced inhibition in the brain? Parvalbumin-positive (PV+) inhibitory neurons play an important role in guiding cortical plasticity, with the maturation of these neurons marking the onset of critical periods, e.g., in the visual cortex. Reopened periods for ocular dominance plasticity later in life are, however, achieved through reduced inhibition. This is shown for example by Kuhlmann et al. [12], who re-enabled juvenile-like plasticity in the visual cortex by artificially inhibiting the activity of PV+-neurons. This then allowed excitatory neurons to become plastic again. Barnesd et al. [3] added the finding that the recovery of neurons responding preferentially to a patched eye depends on the amount of correlated activity, which matches the findings of our model. With regards to amblyopia, there also is recent computational evidence highlighting the importance of cortical plasticity for a potential recovery [8]. There are different possible mechanisms of how PV+ neurons can guide cortical plasticity, one of which is the strong effect of perisomatic inhibition onto backpropagating action potentials and the temporal window in which arriving inputs can sum up and provoke a response of the target neuron. A release of that inhibition together with increased excitability can help these otherwise suppressed neurons to compete, which is important to consider for strongly suppressed populations that represent an amblyopic eye. Another interesting aspect is a possible effect of PV+ neurons on the tPA enzyme (tissue plasminogen activator), which is more active following monocular deprivation and supports pruning mechanisms, which are important for ocular dominance plasticity [22].

Most of these aspects, however, take place in higher layers such as layer II/III. Nevertheless, a key role of parvalbumin-positive neurons and their plasticity was made clear by the studies mentioned above. PV+ neurons also receive potent thalamic input [11], show a specific degree of orientation tuning [26], and change their levels of activity under locomotion [7]. The latter point is consistent with [18] showing increased effects of the patching paradigm when combined with physical exercise. Therefore, inhibitory neurons in general and parvalbumin neurons, in particular, could be a key player in plastic changes also in layer IV during ocular dominance alterations and an important mediator of a possible recovery from amblyopia.

Acknowledgments. This work was supported by an ERA-NET NEURON grant (JTC2015), the German Ministry for Education and Research (BMBF, grant number 01EW1603A). JT acknowledges support from the Johanna Quandt foundation. The authors thank Dr. Florence Kleberg for her input and contributing ideas as well as Samuel Eckmann and Lukas Klimmasch for support and fruitful discussions.

References

1. Abrahamsson, M., Sjöstrand, J.: Contrast sensitivity and acuity relationship in strabismic and anisometropic amblyopia. Br. J. Ophthalmol. **72**, 44–49 (1988). https://doi.org/10.1136/bjo.72.1.44
2. Ahmed, B., Anderson, J.C., Douglas, R.J., Martin, K.A., Nelson, J.C.: Polyneuronal innervation of spiny stellate neurons in cat visual cortex. J. Comp. Neurol. **341**, 39–49 (1994). https://doi.org/10.1002/cne.903410105
3. Barnes, S.J., Sammons, R.P., Jacobsen, R.I., Mackie, J., Keller, G.B., Keck, T.: Subnetwork-specific homeostatic plasticity in mouse visual cortex in vivo. Neuron **86**, 1290–1303 (2015). https://doi.org/10.1016/j.neuron.2015.05.010
4. Brascamp, J.W., van Ee, R., Pestman, W.R., van den Berg, A.V.: Distributions of alternation rates in various forms of bistable perception. J. Vis. **5**, 287–298 (2005). https://doi.org/10.1167/5.4.1
5. Cao, R., Pastukohv, A., Aleshin, S., Mattia, M., Braun, J.: Instability with a purpose: how the visual brain makes decisions in a volatile world. bioRxiv 2020.06.09.142497. https://doi.org/10.1101/2020.06.09.142497
6. Deco, G., Thiele, A.: Cholinergic control of cortical network interactions enables feedback-mediated attentional modulation. Eur. J. Neurosci. **34**, 146–157 (2011). https://doi.org/10.1111/j.1460-9568.2011.07749.x
7. Dipoppa, M., Ranson, A., Krumin, M., Pachitariu, M., Carandini, M., Harris, K.D.: Vision and locomotion shape the interactions between neuron types in mouse visual cortex. Neuron **98**(3), 602–615 (2018). https://doi.org/10.1016/j.neuron.2018.03.037
8. Eckmann, S., Klimmasch, L., Shi, B.E., Triesch, J.: Active efficient coding explains the development of binocular vision and its failure in amblyopia. Proc. Nat. Acad. Sci. U.S.A. **117**, 6156–6162 (2020). https://doi.org/10.1073/pnas.1908100117
9. Hess, R.F., Mansouri, B., Dakin, S.C., Allen, H.A.: Integration of local motion is normal in amblyopia. J. Opt. Soc. Am. A Opt. Image Sci. Vis. **23**, 986–992 (2006). https://doi.org/10.1364/josaa.23.000986
10. Katz, L.C., Gilbert, C.D., Wiesel, T.N.: Local circuits and ocular dominance columns in monkey striate cortex. J. Neurosci. Official J. Soc. Neurosci. **9**, 1389–1399 (1989)
11. Kloc, M., Maffei, A.: Target-specific properties of thalamocortical synapses onto layer 4 of mouse primary visual cortex. J. Neurosci. Official J. Soc. Neurosci. **34**, 15455–15465 (2014). https://doi.org/10.1523/JNEUROSCI.2595-14.2014
12. Kuhlman, S.J., Olivas, N.D., Tring, E., Ikrar, T., Xu, X., Trachtenberg, J.T.: A disinhibitory microcircuit initiates critical-period plasticity in the visual cortex. Nature **501**(7468), 543–546 (2013)
13. Laing, C.R., Chow, C.C.: A spiking neuron model for binocular rivalry. J. Comput. Neurosc. **12**, 39–53 (2002). https://doi.org/10.1023/a:1014942129705
14. Li, J., et al.: The role of suppression in amblyopia. Invest. Ophthalmol. Vis. Sci. **52**, 4169–4176 (2011). https://doi.org/10.1167/iovs.11-7233

15. Lunghi, C., Burr, D.C., Morrone, C.: Brief periods of monocular deprivation disrupt ocular balance in human adult visual cortex. Curr. Biol. CB **21**, R538–R539 (2011). https://doi.org/10.1016/j.cub.2011.06.004

16. Lunghi, C., Emir, U.E., Morrone, M.C., Bridge, H.: Short-term monocular deprivation alters GABA in the adult human visual cortex. Curr. Biol. CB **25**, 1496–1501 (2015). https://doi.org/10.1016/j.cub.2015.04.021

17. Lunghi, C., Morrone, M.C., Secci, J., Caputo, R.: Binocular rivalry measured 2 hours after occlusion therapy predicts the recovery rate of the amblyopic eye in anisometropic children. Invest. Ophthalmol. Vis. Sci. **57**, 1537–1546 (2016). https://doi.org/10.1167/iovs.15-18419

18. Lunghi, C., Sale, A.: A cycling lane for brain rewiring. Curr. Biol. CB **25**, R1122–R1123 (2015). https://doi.org/10.1016/j.cub.2015.10.026

19. McLaughlin, D., Shapley, R., Shelley, M., Wielaard, D.J.: A neuronal network model of macaque primary visual cortex (v1): orientation selectivity and dynamics in the input layer 4Calpha. Proc. Nat. Acad. Sci. U.S.A. **97**, 8087–8092 (2000)

20. Moreno-Bote, R., Rinzel, J., Rubin, N.: Noise-induced alternations in an attractor network model of perceptual bistability. J. Neurophysiol. **98**, 1125–1139 (2007). https://doi.org/10.1152/jn.00116.2007

21. Narasimhan, S., Harrison, E.R., Giaschi, D.E.: Quantitative measurement of interocular suppression in children with amblyopia. Vis. Res. **66**, 1–10 (2012). https://doi.org/10.1016/j.visres.2012.06.007

22. Oray, S., Majewska, A., Sur, M.: Dendritic spine dynamics are regulated by monocular deprivation and extracellular matrix degradation. Neuron **44**, 1021–1030 (2004). https://doi.org/10.1016/j.neuron.2004.12.001

23. Potjans, T.C., Diesmann, M.: The cell-type specific connectivity of the local cortical network explains prominent features of neuronal activity (2011)

24. Stimberg, M., Brette, R., Goodman, D.F.M.: Brian 2, an intuitive and efficient neural simulator. eLife **8**, e47314 (2019). https://doi.org/10.7554/eLife.47314

25. Vogels, T.P., Sprekeler, H., Zenke, F., Clopath, C., Gerstner, W.: Inhibitory plasticity balances excitation and inhibition in sensory pathways and memory networks. Science (New York, N.Y.) **334**, 1569–1573 (2011). https://doi.org/10.1126/science.1211095

26. Wilson, D.E., et al.: Gabaergic neurons in ferret visual cortex participate in functionally specific networks. Neuron **93**, 1058–1065.e4 (2017). https://doi.org/10.1016/j.neuron.2017.02.035

27. Zhou, J., et al.: Inverse occlusion: a binocularly motivated treatment for amblyopia. Neural Plast. **2019**, 5157628 (2019). https://doi.org/10.1155/2019/5157628

Transitions Among Metastable States Underlie Context-Dependent Working Memories in a Multiple Timescale Network

Tomoki Kurikawa[(✉)] [iD]

Department of Physics, Kansai Medical University, Shinmachi 2-5-1, Hirakata, Osaka, Japan
kurikawt@hirakata.kmu.ac.jp

Abstract. Transitions between metastable states are commonly observed in the neural system and underlie various cognitive functions such as working memory. In a previous study, we have developed a neural network model with the slow and fast populations, wherein simple Hebb-type learning enables stable and complex (e.g., non-Markov) transitions between neural states. This model is distinct from a network with asymmetric Hebbian connectivity and a network trained with supervised machine learning methods: the former generates simple Markov sequences. The latter generates complex but vulnerable sequences against perturbation and its learning methods are biologically implausible. By using our model, we propose and demonstrate a novel mechanism underlying stable working memories: sequentially stabilizing and destabilizing task-related states in the fast neural dynamics. The slow dynamics maintain a history of the applied inputs, e.g., context signals, and enable the task-related states to be stabilized in a context-dependent manner. We found that only a single (or a few) state(s) is stabilized in each epoch (i.e., a period in the presence of the context signal and a delayed period) in a working memory task, resulting in a robust performance against noise and change in a task protocol. These results suggest a simple mechanism underlying complex and stable processing in neural systems.

Keywords: Sequence · Multiple timescale · Working memory

1 Introduction

Neural trajectories are commonly observed in neural systems [12] and are involved in temporal information processing, such as working memory [19] decision-making [6]. The organization and processing of task-related information through these trajectories is an essential question in neuroscience.

Two theoretical approaches are proposed to answer the question. In this approach, each pattern in the trajectory is represented as a metastable state,

© Springer Nature Switzerland AG 2021
I. Farkaš et al. (Eds.): ICANN 2021, LNCS 12891, pp. 604–613, 2021.
https://doi.org/10.1007/978-3-030-86362-3_49

wherein synaptic connectivity in a neural network is formed through Hebbian learning. An asymmetric connection from the current to the successive pattern [1,3,4,14,16–18] leads to transitions between patterns. These sequences of metasable states are robust to noise and are widely observed in neural systems [12]. A transition between these states is explicitly embedded into connectivity (i.e., the connectivity composed of correlations between the current and the next patterns), resulting in a next pattern being determined only by the current pattern. Hence, the generation of non-Markov sequences depending on the long history of previous patterns is not possible.

In another approach [2,10,11,20] trained recurrent neural networks (RNNs) were used to generate neural trajectories using machine learning methods. RNNs reproduce neural trajectories observed in neural systems, and how these trajectories encode and process information over time has been investigated. These models allow for generating complex sequences dependent on the history. However, parameters are finely tuned through non-biologically plausible learning, and the parsimonious principle of temporal information processing in neural dynamics is unclear. Thus, a simple and biologically plausible model that generates long-history-dependent sequences is necessary.

To this end, we have studied a neural network model with fast and slow neural dynamics [9], wherein the slow dynamics integrate previous information and regulate fast dynamics. Using this model, in this study, we propose a novel mechanism underlying stable working memories: stabilizing and destabilizing task-related states at an adequate time. We also examine whether our model performs a context-dependent working memory task wherein history-dependent computation is necessary.

2 Model

2.1 Neural Dynamics

Our model is based on a previous study [9] that showed that an RNN with multiple timescales enables the learning of sequential neural patterns including non-Markov sequences. The model has two populations with different timescales connected to each other (Fig. 1A). One population comprises N fast neurons x, and the other comprises N slow neurons y. The fast population receives an external stimulus and generates a target response corresponding to the given input. These neurons evolve according to

$$\tau_x \dot{x}_i = \tanh\left(\beta_x I_i\right) - x_i, \tag{1}$$

$$\tau_y \dot{y}_i = \tanh(\beta_y x_i) - y_i, \tag{2}$$

$$I_i = u_i + \tanh(r_i) + (\eta_\mu^\alpha)_i, \tag{3}$$

$$u_i = \sum_{j \neq i}^{N} J_{ij}^X x_j, \tag{4}$$

$$r_i = \sum_{j \neq i}^{N} J_{ij}^{XY} \tanh(y_j),$$ (5)

where J_{ij}^X is a recurrent connection from the i to j-th neuron in the population of x and $\boldsymbol{J}^{XY}$ is a connection from the i-th neuron in the population of y to the j-th neuron in the population of x. The mean values of J^X and J^{XY} are set to zero with a variance equal to $1/N$. N, β_x, and β_y are set to $100, 2.0$, and 2.0, respectively, while the time scales of x and y, denoted as τ_x and τ_y, are set to 1 and 33, respectively. I_i is the i th element of an input pattern.

2.2 Learning Process

In our model, only J^X is plastic and changes according to

$$\dot{J}_{ij}^X = \epsilon(\xi_i - x_i)(x_j - u_i J_{ij}^X)/N,$$

where ϵ is the learning speed, and it is set to 0.03. ξ_i is the i-th element of a target $\boldsymbol{\xi}$, which is an N-dimensional pattern. In previous studies [5,7,8], we demonstrated that a single population with a single timescale learns mappings between constant input and target patterns using this learning rule. In the current two-population model, there are two inputs for the fast sub-network—one is from an external input and the other is from the slow sub-network that stores previous information. Thus, the synaptic dynamics can modify the connection to generate a target pattern depending not only on the currently applied input but also on the preceding input, as shown in [9]. We, in the present study, demonstrate this model performs a context-dependent task.

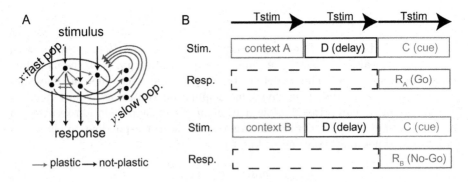

Fig. 1. A: Schematic of our model. B: Context-dependent task. T_{stim} denotes the stimulus duration.

3 Results

3.1 Context-Dependent Task

First, we consider learning a simple context-dependent task that is composed of two context signals, a delayed signal and a cue signal (Fig. 1B). In this task, one of the context signals is applied to fast neurons, followed by the delayed signal. Finally, the cue signal is applied. On applying the cue signal, the network is required to generate "Go" pattern or "No-Go" pattern depending on the context signal. When the applied context signal is A, the network should generate the Go pattern, while it should generate the No-Go pattern when the context signal is B. Here, we denote Go and No-Go patterns as R_A and R_B, respectively. Thus, the network must maintain the context signal to generate an adequate response pattern.

The signal and response patterns are random N-bit binary patterns, each element of which corresponds to a neuron of x, with probabilities $P(X_i = \pm 1) = 1/2$, where X_i is the activity state of the i-th element of patterns $X = A, B, C, R_A$, and R_B. All elements of the delayed signal D are -1. We apply the context, the delayed, and the cue signal sequentially with duration time $T_{stim} = 60$ as an external input η in Eq. 2, as illustrated in Fig. 1B. If the fast dynamics reach R_A (or R_B), namely $\sum R_{Ai} x_i / N > 0.95$, a trial is completed, and the next trial starts. Now, the target patterns are defined only when the cue signal is applied. Therefore, the learning process runs only during the cue signal application; otherwise, only the neural dynamics run.

We show successful trials in the context-dependent task in Fig. 2A. In the presence of the context signal A, fast neural dynamics already show a high overlap with R_A, while they show quite different patterns in the presence of B. The slow dynamics follow the fast dynamics in both cases. The fast dynamics change slightly upon the delayed signal after the context signal A, while they change drastically after B. Although the network receives the same delayed signals, quite different neural dynamics emerge owing to the slow dynamics that reflect the preceding context signals. Finally, the fast dynamics converge to the correct target R_A or R_B depending on the preceding context signals A and B, respectively. We measured the success rate across 20 trials for each context signal, resulting in a 95% success rate (Fig. 2B).

To examine the role of the slow dynamics in this task, we analyzed the neural dynamics with $\tau_y = 1$, i.e., the dynamics of the two populations change with the same timescale. In this case, the neural dynamics y do not store the history of the fast dynamics x over a long time. We plot two trajectories for the context A and B in Fig. 2C. In the present of the context signals, two trajectories show different behaviors depending on the identity of the context signals. After the presentation of the context signal, the difference between the two trajectories rapidly decreased during the delayed epoch and the cue one. Thus, the network generates the same neural patterns (in this case, R_A) in both contexts A and B in the presence of the cue signal. Altogether, these results show that the

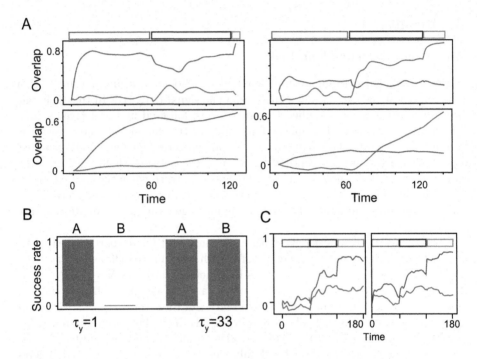

Fig. 2. A: Neural dynamics after being trained in the context-dependent task for the context A and B in the left and right panels, respectively. The neural dynamics of x and y are plotted by computing their overlaps with R_A (red line) and R_B (green line), respectively. The top panels represent the neural dynamics of x, whereas the bottom panels represent the neural dynamics of y. The colored bars above the top panels represent context signals A and B, the delay signal, and the cue signal in red, green, black, and cyan, respectively. B: Success rate of the context-dependent task for $\tau_y = 33$ and 1. For each condition, we plot the success rate of the response to contexts A and B separately. C: Neural dynamics for $\tau_y = 1$ for the context A and B in the left and right panels, respectively. The neural trajectories are plotted in the same manner as in panel A. (Color figure online)

population with the slow timescale enables successful performing the context-dependent task.

3.2   Delayed Match to Sample Task

In the task analyzed above, the network is required to store only the context information irrespective of the cue signals; this is because the correct response is uniquely determined by the context signal. However, the required responses are commonly dependent on cue signals in addition to context signals, as analyzed in [11,19]. Subsequently, we examined whether our model performs such a complex context-dependent task (denoted as a delayed match to the sample task), as shown in Fig. 3A. This task is based on procedure similar to the task analyzed above.

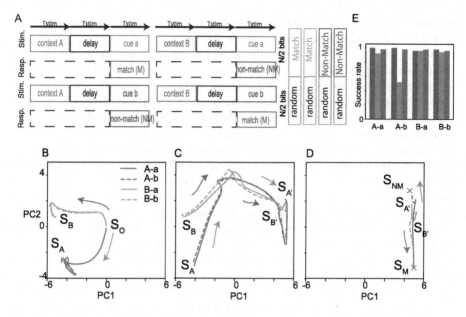

Fig. 3. A: Schematic of the delayed match to sample task. B–D: Fast dynamics are plotted on two principal component spaces (B, C, and D: the dynamics in the presence of the context signal, the delayed one, and the cue one, respectively). The four trajectories represent fast dynamics under different conditions. E: Success rate against noise and perturbation for each condition. The performances for normal, perturbation in initial states, and modified T_{stim} situations are shown in blue, orange, and green, respectively.

There are two context signals, A and B, and two cues, a and b, and the same-name patterns (i.e., A and a, or B and b) belong to the same category. A network is required to "Go" (denoted as matched pattern M) when the context and cue signal in the same category are given, while it is required to "No-Go" (denoted as non-matched pattern NM) when these cues are in a different category. Unlike the previous task, the network should generate two different patterns depending on the cue signals, in addition to the context signals.

The context and cue signals ($A, B, a,$ and b) and response patterns (M and NM) are the random N-bit patterns generated in the same manner as in the previous task. There are two M patterns for $A - a$ and $B - b$ as well as two NM patterns for $A - b$ and $B - b$. When the two M (NM) patterns are the same, the learning performance is poor. Thus, we add random perturbation parts to M and NM, as shown in Fig. 3A. The delay signal and learning procedure are the same as that in the previous task.

First, we present four trajectories corresponding to the four conditions (two contexts by two cues) in Figs. 3B–D. Here, the fast neural dynamics are projected onto the 2D principal component (PC) space after averaging over 20 trajectories for each condition. The projected trajectories for four different conditions are shown by solid and dotted lines in different colors.

In the presence of context signals, neural trajectories are separated into two groups according to the context signals and converge into neural states S_A and S_B. Following the context signals, the delay signals are applied. Two groups of trajectories evolve from S_A and S_B and reach S'_A and S'_B with a decrease in the distance between the two groups. Although the difference decreases, that between neural states in the slow dynamics remains high at the end of the delay epoch, and the information of the preceding context signal is retained in the slow dynamics. Finally, applying the cue to the network separates the four trajectories into the match (S_M) and non-match (S_{NM}) states depending on the contexts and cues. The trajectories diverge into different states in the presence of the same cue owing to the slow dynamics that reflect the context signals. In this manner, the network performs the delayed match to sample task. To precisely evaluate the performance of this model, we measured the success rate for 20 trials for each condition, resulting in more than 90% trials being successful for all conditions.

In a noisy system such as a neural system, information processing should be robust against noise and perturbations. We explore the robustness of our model against perturbations in the initial states and the change in stimulus duration T_{stim}. First, for the modification of T_{stim}, we changed T_{stim} for each epoch (the context signal, the delay signal, and the cue signal) from $T_{stim} = 60$ to $T_{stim} = 66$ in the test process after training the network with $T_{stim} = 60$. We measured the success rate by 20 trials for modified T_{stim} and observe that such perturbations do not reduce the success rate compared to the normal situation, as shown in Fig. 3E.

Next, we analyze the robustness against the perturbations of the initial states, wherein the initial states of the fast and slow dynamics, x and y, in the test process are selected randomly from a larger distribution around the origin in the neural state space than those in the learning process. We set the initial states of x and y in the test process to random N-dimensional states uniformly sampled from a closed interval $[-0.2, 0.2]^N$, whereas in the learning process, the initial states are limited to a smaller closed interval $[-0.01, 0.01]^N$. Therefore, almost all initial states in the test process are novel for the network. By measuring the success rate against 20 trials for the perturbation case, we observed that 90% of all trials were successful for three conditions, while more than 50% of all trials were successful for one condition (context A – cue b). The network successfully performs the delayed match to sample task with highly volatile initial states, except for A – b condition. In total, these results indicate that our learning process generates a network model robust against perturbations of the initial states and signal duration.

Why is such robust information processing possible? To answer this question, we analyzed the stability of neural trajectories in each epoch (i.e., in the presence of context, delayed, and cue signals) in the test process. First, to explore the robustness during the signal epoch, the initial states are randomly generated

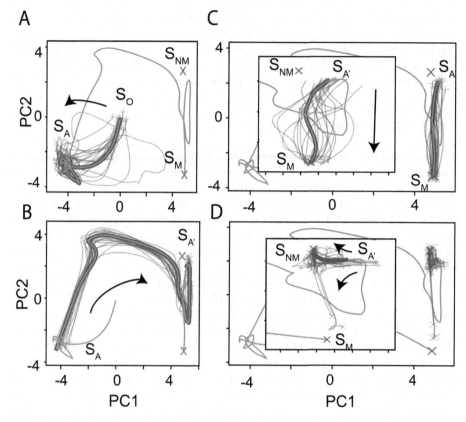

Fig. 4. A–C: Neural trajectories with perturbed initial states projected on 2D PC space for context A–cue a condition. Trajectories during the context signal, the delayed one, and the cue one are plotted on A, B, and C, respectively. D: Neural trajectories during the cue signal for the context A–cue b condition.

around S_O in the same manner as the perturbation case, and the fast and slow dynamics run according to Eqs. 2 and 3. Figure 4A demonstrates these trajectories in the presence of the context A. Neural trajectories from the perturbed initial states converge to and remain around S_A for some time. S_A is stable and attracts trajectories starting from a broad area of the neural state space in the context A epoch. The same analysis in the delayed and cue epochs revealed that S_B, S'_A, S'_B, S_M, and S_{NM} are stable states in the corresponding epochs, as shown in Figs. 4B and C. After changing the signal, each state is destabilized. S'_A and S'_B are stable for the same delay signals depending on the preceding contexts. S_M and S_{NM} are stable dependent on the context and the cue. The slow dynamics store the context information and stabilize the different states through interaction with the cue signal. These results demonstrate that successive stabilization and destabilization of the epoch-specific states underlie the stable performance of the delayed match to the sample task.

In contrast, S_{MN} in the presence of b (i.e., the correct target state for A – b condition) is less stable than the other task-related states, resulting in some trajectories not reaching S_{NM}, but S_M, as shown in Fig. 4D. Thus, the task often fails. These results indicate that our model robustly performs a delayed match to sample task by sequential stabilization of the task-related states.

4   Discussion and Summary

We have proposed and demonstrated that sequential stabilization of task-related states leads to the robust performance of the context-dependent task. During each epoch (i.e., in the presence of the context signal, the delayed one, and the cue one), the epoch-specific states are stabilized and destabilized in the fast dynamics through the regulation of the slow dynamics. The slow dynamics maintain the previous stimulus and enable the neural state in the fast dynamics to transit from one state to another in context-dependent (i.e., non-Markov) manner.

Such transitions of neural states are distinguished from the typical models of the transitions. Although asymmetric Hebbian connection model [1,3,4,14, 16–18] generates transitions between metastable states, the current pattern is determined only by the immediately preceding pattern and, consequently, non-Markov sequences are not allowed. Sophisticated training methods of RNNs [2,10,11,20] generate complex neural trajectories, but how such trajectories are formed is unclear and the stability of these trajectories is poor [10].

Recent theoretical studies revealed relevance of the stable states in neural processing [21,22]. In these studies, several stable states exist in the neural state space and the adequate input drives the neural state from one stable state to another for performing the cognitive tasks, e.g., flip-flop function and generation of muscle activity. Thus, initial states before being applied the input are crucial for performing a task. In contrast, in our model, the input stabilizes a single (or a few) state(s) in the fast dynamics depending on the previous inputs stored in the slow dynamics. Hence, neural states beginning from a broader area converge the adequate state. Our proposed model sheds light on neural processing by the hierarchical timescale structure, which are commonly observed in the neural system [13,15].

Acknowledgments. We thank Kunihiko Kaneko for fruitful discussion for our manuscript. This work was partly support by JSPS KAKENHI (no. 20H00123).

References

1. Amari, S.I.: Learning patterns and pattern sequences by self-organizing nets of threshold elements. IEEE Trans. Comput. **100**(11), 1197–1206 (1972)
2. Chaisangmongkon, W., Swaminathan, S.K., Freedman, D.J., Wang, X.J.J.: Computing by robust transience: how the fronto-parietal network performs sequential. Category Based Decis. Neuron **93**(6), 1504–1517.e4 (2017)

3. Gros, C.: Neural networks with transient state dynamics. New J. Phys. **9**, 109 (2007)
4. Kleinfeld, D.: Sequential state generation by model neural networks. Proc. Nat. Acad. Sci. **83**, 9469–9473 (1986)
5. Kurikawa, T., Barak, O., Kaneko, K.: Repeated sequential learning increases memory capacity via effective decorrelation in a recurrent neural network. Phys. Rev. Res. **2**(2), 023307 (2020)
6. Kurikawa, T., Haga, T., Handa, T., Harukuni, R., Fukai, T.: Neuronal stability in medial frontal cortex sets individual variability in decision-making. Nat. Neurosci. **21**(12), 1764–1773 (2018)
7. Kurikawa, T., Kaneko, K.: Embedding responses in spontaneous neural activity shaped through sequential learning. PLoS Comput. Biol. **9**(3), e1002943 (2013)
8. Kurikawa, T., Kaneko, K.: Dynamic organization of hierarchical memories. Plos One **11**(9), e0162640 (2016)
9. Kurikawa, T., Kaneko, K.: Multiple-timescale Neural Networks: Generation of Context-dependent Sequences and Inference through Autonomous Bifurcations. arXiv preprint, p. 2006.03887 (2020)
10. Laje, R., Buonomano, D.V.: Robust timing and motor patterns by taming chaos in recurrent neural networks. Nature neuroscience **16**(7), 925–933 (2013)
11. Mante, V., Sussillo, D., Shenoy, K.V., Newsome, W.T.: Context-dependent computation by recurrent dynamics in prefrontal cortex. Nature **503**(7474), 78–84 (2013)
12. Miller, P.: Itinerancy between attractor states in neural systems. Curr. Opinion Neurobiol. **40**(5), 14–22 (2016)
13. Murray, J.D., et al.: A hierarchy of intrinsic timescales across primate cortex. Nat. Neurosci. **17**(12), 1661–1663 (2014)
14. Recanatesi, S., Katkov, M., Romani, S., Tsodyks, M.: Neural network model of memory retrieval. Front. Comput. Neurosci. **9**, 1–11 (2015)
15. Runyan, C.A., Piasini, E., Panzeri, S., Harvey, C.D.: Distinct timescales of population coding across cortex. Nature **548**(7665), 92–96 (2017)
16. Russo, E., Treves, A.: Cortical free-association dynamics: distinct phases of a latching network. Phys. Rev. E **85**(5), 1–21 (2012)
17. Seliger, P., Tsimring, L.S., Rabinovich, M.I.: Dynamics-based sequential memory: winnerless competition of patterns. Phys. Rev. E Stat. Phys. Plasmas Fluids Related Interdisciplinary Top. **67**(1), 4 (2003)
18. Sompolinsky, H., Kanter, I.: Temporal association in asymmetric neural networks. Phys. Rev. Lett. **57**(22), 2861–2864 (1986)
19. Stokes, M.G., Kusunoki, M., Sigala, N., Nili, H., Gaffan, D., Duncan, J.: Dynamic coding for cognitive control in prefrontal cortex. Neuron **78**(2), 364–375 (2013)
20. Sussillo, D., Abbott, L.F.: Generating coherent patterns of activity from chaotic neural networks. Neuron **63**(4), 544–557 (2009)
21. Sussillo, D., Barak, O.: Opening the black box: low-dimensional dynamics in high-dimensional recurrent neural networks. Neural Comput. **25**(3), 626–649 (2013)
22. Sussillo, D., Churchland, M.M., Kaufman, M.T., Shenoy, K.V.: A neural network that finds a naturalistic solution for the production of muscle activity. Nat. Neurosci. **18**(7), 1025–1033 (2015)

Author Index